ENCYCLOPAEDIA OF EDUCATIONAL TERMS

(In 5 Vol.)

ENCYCLOPAEDIA OF EDUCATIONAL TERMS

(In 5 Vol.)

Edited & Compiled by:

Ekta Thani, Rohit Sharma, Anoop Jain, Mohit Sharma, Kanika K., C.H. Judd, & L.B. Earhart

Vol. IV

SPORTS PUBLICATION

4264/3, Ansari Road, Darya Ganj, Delhi-2
Ph.: 23290142, 27241050, 27562163 (R)

Published by:

Lokesh Thani

SPORTS PUBLICATIONS

H.O. 4264/3, Ansari Road, Darya Ganj, New Delhi-110002
B.O. WP-474, Ist Floor, Shiv Market, Ashok Vihar, Delhi-52
Phones: 23290142, 27241050,
(R) 27562163, (M) 9868028838
E-mail: sportspublication1@rediffmail.com
Website: *www.sportsbookshouse.com*

I.S.B.N. – 81-87818-68-9

PRINTED IN INDIA 2004

Laser Typeset by:

JAIN MEDIA GRAPHICS

B-4/40-A, Lawrence Road, (Keshav Puram),
New Delhi-110035 Ph.: 27183573, (M) 9811430646

Printed by:

BANDEMATRAM PRESS

Maujpur, Delhi

Price: Rs. 4,200/- (In 5 Vol.)

VOL. IV

PART 5

BIOCHEMISTRY

This unique work exhibits many important terms and its meaning along with instances where necessary.

No area of biological science in recent times has become so prominent as the biochemistry. Biochemistry Terminology has been compiled as a clear immediately accessible reference book. Every aspect of its conception and layout has been planned to help the reader to find information he/she needs with minimum difficulty.

The purpose of this dictionary is to clarify definitions and obscure meanings of technical terms and phrases that form the vast vocabulary. Many of the words defined are common words, which have been given unusual meanings in different countries by different researchers. Some of the words find their roots in the slang in different languages, and have been very well accepted in common usage. Most the terms came from a wide range of disciplines, particularly biological sciences—bacteriology, cell biology, enzymology, genetics, microbiology, pharmacology and toxicology.

Like any other branch of science, Biochemistry have their own language. It is essential to have good command over such a language in order to understand these subjects. Therefore, it is endeavoured to compile a glossary with a wide range of entries representing biochemical processes occurring in plants, living organisms along with specific enzymes, reactions, intermediates, inhibitors and precursors.

The salient features of the present work are:

- A to Z terms that covers many subjects which comes under Biochemistry.
- Vast definitions are explained with instances where necessary.
- Alphabetically arranged terms from A to Z.

This unique book is an effort to keep pace with continuing rapid developments and expanding vocabularies in Biochemistry. Throughout the process of compilation and editing this encyclopaedic dictionary our sincere effort was to prepare the dictionary to serve as a ready reference for the readers.

Efforts has been made carefully to write the entries in a clear and lucid form to provide both straight forward definitions and invaluable background information.

With the rapid unveiling of the aetiological factors and also with the changes in the classification, the field of Biochemistry has undergone a continuous change and refinements which require a dictionary for its completion. Moreover, the definitions of various terms is the backbone of understanding a subject, its research and its communication.

The impetus for writing the present work has come largely from clinical practice and teaching.

The selection of the terms has been made on the reading of the current literature. Even then many well-known but little used terms may not be found. There are omissions, some deliberate, some accidential. Words that could not be found in a standard dictionary are omitted, unless they have a special connotation.

All suggestions, comments from readers on omissions or shortcomings will be always welcomed.

PART 6

PHILOSOPHY

The present study exhibits many important terms and its meaning along with instances where necessary.

The present work has been compiled as a clear immediately accessible reference book. Every aspect of its conception and layout has been planned to help the reader to find information he/she needs with minimum difficulty.

The purpose of this book is to clarify definitions and obscure meanings of technical terms and phrases that form the vast vocabulary. Many of the words defined are common words, which have been given unusual meanings in different countries by different researchers.

Some of the words find their roots in the slang in different languages, and have been very well accepted in common usage. Most the terms came from a wide range of disciplines, particularly philosophy.

The main purpose of this book is to serve the students of philosophy as a reference book. Conceptual clarity is one of the indispensable prerequisites for any proper philosophical enquiry. One who lacks conceptual clarity in his field of interest is like a fish out of water.

In this world of flux, many changes do take place as regards the usage of key concepts of terms in various fields of human investigation. Unless one keeps track of such changes in use, one cannot really read between the lines. Apart from this, many new terms have been introduced into philosophical literature.

The salient features of this book are:

- A to Z terms that covers many subjects which

comes under Philosophy.

- Vast definitions are explained with instances where necessary.
- Alphabetically arranged terms from A to Z.

The reason why this book is created is that most of the students enter college and university departments of philosophy without having any background in the subject. Just as it is impossible to solve the riddles of mathematics without knowing the importance of numerals, it is impossible to do any rigorous philosophical study without knowing the meaning of those key concepts that one comes across in philosophical literature.

The prima facie duty of every student of philosophy is to get acquainted with the technical philosophical terms. The only way to get acquainted with such terminology is to approach a Encyclopaedic Dictionary of Philosophy which provides the student with a brief elucidation of a term or a concept.

In compiling a book of this kind, it is essential to draw upon the work of many authorities and seek the advice of colleagues, to all of whom the author is deeply indebted.

All comments from users on omissions or shortcomings will be most welcome.

PART 5

BIOCHEMISTRY

A 24 protein
the protein complex resulting from the conjugation of ubiquitin to histone H2A. The amount of H2A histone that is in the form of A 24 varies in different cells. Some evidences exist to suggest that chromatin which includes actively transcribed DNA sequences is enriched in 24 protein.

a band
a transverse dark band, consisting of thick and thin filaments.

abietic acid
a diterpene carboxylic acid, and the isomeric neoabietic acid, can easily be interconverted. These two resin acids are the main component of rosin (up to 90%), from which they could be obtained by treatment with heat or acids, possibly as products of the rearrangement of other diterpene carboxylic acids. Amber contains derivatives of A.a.

abiogenesis
the hypothesis that all living organisms have been created from non-living matter by spontaneous generation.

ablastin
an antibody that inhibits the reproduction of Trypanosoma lewisi, a parasite of the rat, and appears to have no other function.

abrin
a protein present in the seeds of Abrus precatorius, that is toxic and has anti-tumour activity. It interferes with the binding of aminoacyl t-RNA to ribosomes.

abscisic acid (ABA)
sesquiterpene, naturally occurring growth inhibitor controlled various phases of growth and development of plant. It shows optical and geometrical isomerization. Natural ABA is 2 cis+ form. Synthetic ABA is racemic mixture of these isomers.

abscission inhibitors
growth regulators i.e., auxins and probably cytokinins which help in keeping abscission zone target cells in a quiescent state. These prevent or reduce abscission.

abscission zone
layer of thin walled parenchymatous cells formed at the base of petiole or pedicel. During abscission senescence of distal tissue triggers the hydrolysis of middle lamellae of these cells and thus organ is separated from the parent plant. Then a protective layer of corky cells is formed to protect the wound.

absolute configuration
determination of real arrangement of atoms (or groups of atoms) around chiral centre. Absolute configuration is described according to R-S nomenclature. It has been established that absolute configuration of enantiomers of glyceraldehyde is in accordance with their arbitrarily adopted configuration.

absolute humidity

amount of water vapour present in the atmosphere. It is expressed as grams of water in a cubic meter of air.

absorption

1. (in physiology). The transfer of substances, especially digested food, from the lumen of the alimentary tract to the blood or lymph. Little is absorbed from the mouth, although some drugs may be. Ethanol and some organic acids are absorbed from the stomach; in ruminants most of the volatile fatty acids produced in the rumen by microbial fermentation are absorbed through the walls of the rumen, reticulum and omasum. In general, water ions, and nutrients are absorbed chiefly through the walls of the small intestine; which is lined with minute finger-like projections that greatly increase its surface area. Water and ions are also absorbed from the large intestine. Absorption may occur by simple diffusion, by facilitated diffusion (involving a carrier mechanism in the cell membrane), or by active transport (including pinocytosis). Fats are absorbed as fatty acids and glycerol separately, to be reconstituted in the mucosal cells and enter the lymphatic vessels as chyle. Proteins are absorbed mainly as amino acids and peptides; intact proteins are absorbed in the newborn receiving colostrum, but to a much lesser extent in adults. Carbohydrates are absorbed as simple sugars (monosaccharides), except in herbivores where fermentation in the large intestine produces volatile fatty acids, which are absorbed through the walls of the caecum and colon. 2. (in pharmacology). The process whereby drugs are transferred from the alimentary tract or site of the injection/ administration to the blood.

absorption band

portion of the electromagnetic spectrum from which a molecule absorbs radiant energy.

absorption cell

in studies on radiation absorption the small vessel containing investigated sample (liquid or gaseous). Distance between the two parallel propagation windows, perpendicular to direction of radiation determines thickness of investigated sample.

absorption spectrum

spectrum arising as a result of propagation of electromagnetic radiation through absorbing medium. When the light from a high temperature source producing a continuous emission spectrum is passed through a medium through a spectroscope, the spectrum reveals dark regions where absorption has taken place (continuous, line, and band types). In general, medium absorbs those wavelengths which it would omit if its temperature were raised high enough. Solids and liquids show broad continuous absorption spectra, while gases give more discontinuous types.

abundance

(i) the ratio of number of atoms of a particular isotope in a mixture of isotopes of an element, to the total number of atoms present. It is expressed as a percentage.

(ii) the number of individuals of a species in an area, population or community.

(iii) the average number of molecules of a specific mRNA type in a given cell. A = NRf/M where N is Avogadro's number, R is the RNA content of the cell in gram, f is the fraction of specific mRNA relative to the total RNA content of the cell, and M is molecular weight of mRNA in daltons.

acceleration globulin

a globulin that acts to accelerate the conversion of prothrombin to thrombin in blood clotting; found in blood plasma in an inactive form.

accelerator

1. a compound added to a photographic developer to increase its chemical activity, e.g., quaternary ammonium compounds and alkaline substance. 2. a compound that greatly reduced the time required for vulcanization of natural and synthetic rubbers at the same time improving the ageing and other physical properties. The major organic accelerators include amines, guanidines, thiazoles, and dithiocarbamates. 3. a substance that greatly reduces the setting time when added to plaster, mortar, concrete, or cement.

acceptor

(i) a protein accepting dissimilar molecule e.g., growth regulatory acceptors. Here the ligand is covalently bonded to the acceptor.

(ii) the atom which receives hydrogen in the formation of a hydrogen bond.

acceptor control ratio

the ratio between oxygen uptake per unit time, in presence of ADP and the rate of oxygen uptake in absence of ADP. It can be measured either in intact cell or in isolated mitochondria.

acceptor end

the trinucleotide CCA at the 3' -end of the t-RNA. The amino acid becomes esterified to the 2' or 3' position of the terminal adenine nucleotides in this sequence.

acceptor site

the site of ribosom at which the incoming aminoacyl t-RNA is bound during protein synthesis.

acetaldehydase

an enzyme that catalyzes the oxidation of acetaldehyde to acetic acid.

acetaldehyde, ethanal
CH_3-CHO_4. The important intermediate in the degradation of carbohydrates. m.p. — 123°C, b.p. 201°C. In its activated form (Thiamine pyrophosphate), it gets involved in a number of reaction (alcoholic fermentation). Two molecules can undergo acyloin condensation to form acetoin.

acetic fermentation
oxidation of alcohol to produce acetic acid by the action of bacteria of the genus Acetobacter.

acetohydroxy acid reductoisomerase
an enzyme which catalyzes the conversion of 2 acetohydroxybutyrate or 2 acetolactate into 2, 3 dihydroxy 3-methylvalerate or 2, 3 dihydroxy isovalerate during isoleucine and valine synthesis respectively.

acetohydroxy and synthetase
an enzyme which catalyzes the conversion of pyruvate to α-acetoacetate which is further utilized for leucine synthesis. It also catalyzes formation of acetohydroxybutyrate from α-ketobutyrate during isoleucine synthesis.

acetoin 3-hydroxy 3-2-butanone, acetyl methyl carbinol CH_3-CO-CHOH-CH_3
a reduction product of diacetyl which arises under certain conditions as a side product of the pyruvate decarboxylase (EC 4.1.1.1) reaction. It is also formed by decarboxylation of acetologetate by acetolactate decarboxylase (EC 4.1.1.5).

acetolactic acid $C_5H_8O_4$
a monocarboxylic acid formed as an intermediate in the synthesis of the amino acid valine.

acetone fermentation
formation of acetone by the metabolic action of certain anaerobic bacteria on various carbohydrates.

acetone powder
a preparation of liquid free, dried plant material that is produced from acetone extract of tissue by removal of the acetone with vacuum filtration. It is used in the course of isolation and purification of insoluble enzymes.

aceto-orcein
dye consisting of a solution of orcein in acetic acid. Squash preparation of chromosomes are often stained with aceto-orcein.

acetylase
any enzyme that catalyzes the formation of acetyl esters.

acetylcholine
the acetic acid ester of the organic base choline; the neurotransmitter released at the synapses of parasympathetic nerves and at neuromuscular junctions. Acetylcholine was the first chemical to be identified and proven as a neurotransmitter. It is synthesized in cholinergic nerve terminals by the enzyme

choline acetyltransferase, which acetylates choline, the acetyl group being transferred from acetyl coenzyme A. After relaying a nerve impulse, acetylcholine is rapidly broken down by the enzyme cholinesterase. Parasymphathetic agents, such as atropine, are anticholinergic i.e., the prevent acetylcholine from functioning as a neurotransmitter. Parasympathomimetic, are cholinergic, i.e. they enhance or mimic the effects of acetylcholine.

acetyl-coenzyme A, acetyl-CoA, active acetate $CH_3Co \sim SCoA$

it is a derivative of acetic acid in which the acetyl residue is bound by a high-energy bond to the free SH-group of coenzyme A. The very reactive thioester has a high potential for transfer of the acetyl group, and is therefore a universal intermediate which provides the C_2 fragment for numerous syntheses.

acetyl ornithinase

an enzyme capable of catalyzing the conversion of N-acetylornithine to ornithine during citrulline synthesis.

acetyl ornithine glutamate acetyl transferase

an enzyme which catalyzes the conversion of glutamate to ornithine.

acetyl phosphate CH_3-$COOPO(OH)_2$

an energy-rich phosphate. It is the product of acetate activation in some organisms: acetate + ATP = Ap. + ADP; the reaction is catalysed by acetate kinase (EC 2.7.2.1). The back reaction can be used for ATP spythesis, for example in the phosphoroclastic cleavage of pyruvate.

acetyluramic acid

disaccharide found in linear polymers in peptidoglycan that occurs in the periplasm between the inner and outer membranes of gramnegative bacteria.

acetyl value

the acetyl value of a fat is the number of milligrams of potassium hydroxide required to neutralize the acetic acid liberated when 1 g of the acetylated fat is saponified. It is a measure of the number of free hydroxyl groups in the fat.

achirality

lack of chirality, identity of configuration of molecule with its mirror image, caused by the presence of plane of symmetry, or centre of symmetry, or four-fold inversion (symmetry) axis in molecule.

achroglobine

a colourless respiratory pigment present in some mollusks and urochordates.

acid

1. a compound of hydrogen in which some or all of the hydrogen atoms may be replaced by an atom or atoms of a metal, and which is capable of forming hydrogen

ions when dissolved in water. The acids are classified as organic if they contain the -COOH, carboxyl group(s), e.g., acetic acid, CH_3CH_2COOH; propionic acid, CH_3COOH; oxalic acid, HOOC-COOH. The aromatic organic acids are further classified as orthometa-, or para-, according to the location of the carboxyl group, -COOH, in relation to another substituent in the cyclic compound.

2. according to Bronsted and Lowry, an acid is a proton donor, and a base is a proton acceptor. An acid becomes a base after proton transfer. This base is called conjugate base of the acid. By the same logic, when a base accepts a proton in a proton transfer reaction, it becomes an acid. This acid is the conjugate acid of the base. Because new acids and bases are created, the proton transfer reaction can reverse itself in order to continue proton transfer, although it may go largely to completion in one direction or the other.

3. a further extension of the acidbase concept was made by Lewis. According to this concept, an acid is a substance that can accept a pair of electrons, while a base is a substance that can donate a pair of electrons. Since Lewis acids seek substances having electrons pairs to which they can become bound, Lewis acids are said to be electrophilic (electron loving) in character and an acid displacement reaction is said to be electrophilic displacement reaction.

4. a useful modification of the Lewis concept is the classification of acids (and bases) as either hard or soft depending on such properties as electronegativity, tendency to polarize, and oxidation state, these in turn relating to the availability of vacant orbitals. Hard acids are in a high oxidation state, and their outer electrons are relatively stable; they tend to associate with hard bases. Soft acids have the opposite properties.

acid growth hypothesis

it explains the mechanism of cell extension under the influence of auxin. Accordingly, protons are extruded into medium, pH of medium is decreased thus cell wall becomes soft by affecting hydrolyzing enzyme activity. New cell wall material supply and deposition on the inner side of the membrane are increased resulting in extension of cells or segments.

acidic amino acids

amino acids that carry a net negative charge at a neutral pH. Glutamic acid and aspartic acid are examples of such amino acids, possessing negatively charged side-chains at normal cellular pH.

acidic dyes
any of a number of dyes (such as acid fuchsin) that specifically stains positively charged material since the dye carries a net negative charge.

acidic protein
protein that possesses a net negative charge at neutral pH because it is rich in acidic amino acids. Most proteins in eukaryotic cells are acidic, notable exceptions being the basic proteins, the histones. Some acidic proteins are believed to have important roles as gene-regulatory molecules.

acidolysis
1. a chemical reaction involving the decomposition of a molecule, with the addition of the elements of an acid to the molecule; the reaction is comparable to hydrolysis or alcoholysis, in which water or alcohol is used in place of acid. Also known as acyl exchange. 2. the metasynthesis between organic compound and acid, latter serving additionally as solvent.

acid phosphatase
an enzyme in blood which catalyzes the release of phosphate from phosphate esters; optimum activity at pH 5.

acid rain
an environmental phenomenon in which SO_2 and nitrous oxide, emitted by industrial combustion react with rain water to form dilute sulphuric and nitric acids. It leads to acidification of stream, lakes etc., and loss of their fish life. Marbel becomes dull. yellow.

acid value
1. the number of milligrams of potassium hydroxide required to neutralize the free acids present in the one gram of oil, fat, or wax. The determination is made by titrating the sample in hot 95% ethyl alcohol using phenolphthalein as indicator. It is therefore, a measure of the degree of hydrolysis of the fat. 2. The acidity of a solution expressed in terms of normality.

aconitase
an enzyme involved in the Krebs citric acid cycle that catalyzes the breakdown of citric acid to cisaconitic and isocitric acids.

aconitate hydratase, aconitase (Ec 4.2.1.3)
a hydratase which catalyses one stage of the tricorboxylic acid cycle, the reversible interconversion of citrate and isocitrate. The reaction proceeds via the enzyme-bound intermediate, cis-aconitate.

aconitic acid
an unsaturated tricarboxylic acid, usually occurring in the cis form, but sometimes in the trans. cis-A.a., m.p. 130°C., trans-A.a., m.p. 194 to 195°C. The anionic form of cis- aconitic acid (protpen-cis-1, 2, 3-trioic acid) is important as an

intermediate in the isomerization of citrate to isocitrate in the Tricarboxylic acid cycle.

aconitum alkaloids

a group of terpene alkaloids, some of them very poisonous, from various aconite (Aconitum) species. The best-known representative has been aconitine.

acrasin

the chemotactic substance thought to be secreted by, and to effect arrgegation of, myxamebas during their fruiting phase.

acridines

class organic molecules with two properties that render them of great biological importance. They act as mutagen, causing additions or deletions of bases in DNA, especially in plasmids, bacteriophage, and mitochondria. Many acridines have the property of intercalating between adjacent base pairs of DNA and so inducing partial unwinding of the helix. Many are also fluorescent in ultraviolet light and form useful fluorescent stains for such cellular organelles as nuclei and nucleoli. Examples of acridines are acridine orange, acriflavine and proflavine. Some have been used as cytotoxic drugs in cancer chemotherapy and bacterial infection.

acridine orange

one of the acridines; produces mutations involving reading frame shifts and other mutation involving deletions or insertion of nucleotides. It is also effective as a fluorescent stain in living cells since, under ultraviolet irradiation, acridine orange binding will give DNA-containing structures a green fluorescence and RNA-containing structures an orange fluorescence. It also interferes with replication of some bacterial plasmids and can be used to eliminate F-factor from F^+-E coli.

acriflavine

the yellow substance used as an antiseptic. It is a mixture of 2, 8-diamino-10-methylacridinium chloride and 2, 8-diaminoacridine dihydrochloride. Acriflavine is also an active mutagen and is particularly effective in the induction of the petite mutant in yeast.

acrosin

a proteolytic enzyme located in the acrosome of a spermatozoon; thought to be involved in penetration of the egg.

actin filament

a thin filament of striated muscle that consists largely of actin and that is linked to thick filaments by means of cross bridges which protrude from them; a myofilament.

actinomycin D

antibiotic that inhibits the synthesis of RNA by intercalating between the bases of DNA, especially in regions that are rich in cytosin and guanine. Synthesis of ribosomal RNA is particularly sensitive to the drug.

activated carboxylic acid
the derivatives of carboxylic acids which are very reactive, and thus capable of reaction which the free acids do not undergo.

activation
(i) conversion to a more active form,
(ii) when activity of an enzyme is increased in presence of a metal ion.
(iii) drying of chromatographic support.
(iv) the conformational changes of a receptor upon the binding of hormone.
(v) the Ist stage in the conversion of a spore to a vegetative cell.

activation energy
a form of energy required for completion of a chemical reaction. Various enzymes lower the activation energy of biochemical reactions by forming activation complex with the substrate.

activator molecule
molecule that specifically activates or induces a biochemical reaction; most frequently applied to molecules that act as gene regulators.

active acetaldehyde
a hydroxyethylthiamine pyrophosphate, abb. HETPP, the activated form of acetaldehyde formed by decarboxylation of active pyruvate. The aldehyde is bound to the C-2 atom of the thiazole ring of thiamine pyrophosphate. HETPP is an intermediate in alcoholic fermentation.

active ingredient
the part of a substance from which the biological activity is obtained.

active one-carbon units abb. c_1 units
C_1 fragments which are activated by binding to tetrahydrofolic acid, or less commonly, to thiamine pyrophosphate. The active ethylenediamine group of tetrahydrofolic acid serves as a carrier for the metabolic transfer of a formyl or methyl or group.

active site
part of an enzyme that specifically binds the substrate(s) and catalyzes product formation. The active site consists of two, often overlapping, regions; the binding site, which recognizes and binds the substrate(s); the catalytic site, which catalyzes the reaction once binding has occurred. The amino acids in each of these regions are not necessarily adjacent in the linear polypeptide, but are brought together by the folding of the protein molecule. The active site, whether occurring on the surface of the enzyme or buried in a cleft, occupies only about 5% of the total

surface of the enzyme molecule. The initial binding of the substrate involves the formation of the non-covalent bonds (e.g., hydrogen bonds, electrostatic bonds, hydrophobic interactions), van der Waal's forces with chemical groups at the active site. These groups may move position slightly in order to accommodate the substrate (the induced fit theory), so the active site resides in a flexible region of the protein and does not usually involve rigid structures. During catalysis covalent bonds may be formed, and then broken, as part of the reaction mechanism. Catalysis generally involves one or more of the following; optimal spatial alignment of the substrate(s) on the enzyme surface; distortion of the bond angles and stretching of bond lengths; transfer of protons or electrons (acid/base catalysis include the chemically reactive side chains of the amino acids histidine, lysine, arginine, serine threonine tyrosine, cysteine, glutamic acid and aspartic acid, and for some enzymes as coenzymes of cofactor.

active sulphate

1. the compound 3'-phosphoadenosine-5'-phosphosulphate that serves as a sulphating agent in esterification of sulphate with the alcoholic and phenolic hydroxyl groups. 2. the compound adenosine-5' phosphosulphate that serves as an intermediate in the synthesis of the 3'-phosphoadenosine-5'-phosphosulphate and can be reduced directly to sulphite in Desulphovibro desulphuricans.

active transport

a process in which solute molecules or ions move across a biomembrane from lower to higher concentration, i.e., against the concentration gradient.

actomyosin

a protein complex consisting of myosin and actin; the major constituent of a contracting muscle fibril.

acyl

a carbonyl group (C=O) attached to an alkyl or aryl group. It may also be described as the group which remain after the removal of an -OH group from an organic acid. Acyl groups occur in several series of organic compounds. Acetyl and benzoyal groups are specific types of acyl groups.

acyl carrier protein

a protein in fatty acid synthesis that picks up acetyl and malonyl groups from acetyl coenzyme- A and malonyl conenzyme A and links them by condensation to form β-keto acidacyl carrier protein, releasing carbon dioxide and the sulphydryl form of acyl carrier protein. It exists at least in two isoform differing in amino acid sequence. These are required for fatty acid synthetase activity.

acyl carrier protein transacylase
a rate limiting enzyme encountered in fatty acids synthetase system. It catalyzes the formation of medium chain fatty acids products by transferring acetyl-CoA to ACP-SH, forming acetyl-S-ACP and CoA.

acyl-CoA synthetase
an enzyme which catalyzes the forming of acyl-CoA from fatty acid using adenosine triphosphate and CoA during fatty acid oxidation in gly-oxysome.

acyl-coenzyme A oxidase
an enzyme which catalyses the formation of acyl CoA from propionyl-CoA during oxidation of odd number C atom containing fatty acids.

acyl-diaminopimelate deacylase
an enzyme which catalyses the formation of L, L-diaminopimelate from N-acyldiaminopimelate during lysine synthesis.

acyl lipids
the lipids forming a major part of plants membrane. These are water insoluble containing long hydrocarbons chains. Mostly glycerol is backbone in their structure. Such acyl lipids are of the two types:
(a) the glycosyliglyceride, and
(b) the glycerophospholipids, which are neutral and polar respectively.

acyl transferase
an enzyme which catalyses the transfer of the palmityl moiety of palmityl-ACP to a suitable acceptor e.g., 1-monoacylglycerol-P during ACP-chain termination.

adamkiewiez reaction
the production of a violet colour upon treatment of a solution containing protein with acetic acid and sulfuric acid.

adaptor hypothesis
a suggestion made by Crick to explain the transition of the genetic code. He proposed that there must be an adaptor between the information-carrying nucleic acid and the protein being synthesized which was able to "recognize" both kinds of molecules. The discovery of tRNA and the corresponding amino acyl-tRNA synthetase confirmed his hypothesis.

additive
when interaction of two or more compounds is equal to the sum of their individual effects.

adenase
an enzyme that catalyzes the hydrolysis of adenine to hypoxanthine and ammonia.

adenine
a purine base, 6-aminopurine, occurring in ribonucleic acid and deoxyribonucleic acid and as a component of adenosinetriphosphate.

adenine phosphoribosyltransferase
an enzyme which catalyzes the reaction between purine and 5-

phosphoribosyl-pyrophosphate to form purine nucleotide and pyrophosphate.

adenosine $C_{10}H_{13}N_5O_4$
a nucleoside composed of adenine and D-ribose.

adenosinediphosphate $C_{10}H_{15}N_5O_{10}P_2$
a coenzyme composed of adenosine and two molecules of phosphoric acid that is important in intermediate cellular metabolism. Abbreviated ADP.

adenosine phosphates, adenine ribonucleotides
important as components of nucleic acids and as the major form in which chemical free energy is stored and transferred. They are also important metabolic regulators for example in glycolysis and the tricarboxylic acid cycle. The biologically significant derivatives, including cyclic adenosine 3', 5-monophosphate, carry the phosphate ester on the C-5 of the ribose.

adenosine phosphate sulphate kinase
an enzyme which is catalyzes the formation of phosphoadenosine phosphate sulphate from adenosine 5'-phosphate sulfate using adenosine triphosphate. This reaction consumes 5 Kcal energy per mole of the sulphate reduction.

adenosine triphosphate ATP
a nucleotide that is of fundamental importance as a carrier of chemical energy in all living organism. It consists of adenine linked to D-ribose (i.e., adenosine); the D-ribose component bears three phosphate groups, linearly linked by covalent bonds, adenosine triphosphate drives most of an organism's energy - requiring reactions by yielding the high free-energy of its phosphate-phosphate (pyrophosphate) bonds. It is formed in the mitochondria of cells under aerobic conditions by the oxidative phosphorylation of the adenosine diphosphate (adenosine disphosphate) and also by transfer of phosphate to adenosine diphosphate from other energy-rich molecules, for example phosphoenol-pyruvate; this latter is the only means of energy generation under anaerobic conditions. Of the three phosphate groups in adenosine triphosphate, two are attached by pyrophosphate bonds, and hydrolysis of these bonds results in a substantial release of free energy. This energy release on hydrolysis of adenosine triphosphate is used widely in biological systems to drive energy-requiring processes, adenosine triphosphate is derived from adenosine diphosphate during photosynthesis, using solar energy, and during oxidative phosphorylation in which energy from carbohydrate catabolism is used.

adenylate kinase
an enzyme which catalyzes the formation of adenosine diphosphate by phosphorylation of adenosine monophosphate with adenosine triphosphate.

adenylate kinase, myokinase (EC 2.7.4.3)
a trimeric enzyme found in the mitochondria of muscles and other tissues. It is resistant to heat and acid. It catalyses the conversion of two molecules of ADP into ATP + AMP, thus making available the energy of the ADP. At equilibrium, the concentrations of the three adenosine phosphates are nearly equal.

adenyl control hypothesis
regulation of cellular metabolism by feed back effects that are function of the relative amount of adenosine monophosphate, adenosine diphosphate, and adenosine triphosphate in the cell.

adenyl cyclase
the enzyme that catalyzes the formation of the cyclic adenosine monophosphate from adenosine triphosphate by the splitting out of the pyrophosphate. This enzyme is involved in many cellular processes and particularly in the action of the polypeptide hormones attach to the plasma membrane of a cell they stimulate adenyl cyclase to produce cyclic adenosine monophosphate. This is the initial step in the second messenger system, which enables these hormones to effect the gene expression of the cells to which they bind.

adenylysulfate reductases
enzymes of sulfur metabolism which reduce either phosphoadenylsulfate (APS reductase) or adenylylsulfate. Adenylylsulfate reductase, (EC 1.8.99.2) has been identical with one component of the sulfate reductase in sulfate assimilation since adenylylsulfate is the donor of the sulfate group.

adhesion
the attractive interaction between a liquid and a solid phase e.g., between water and the walls of a small capillary.

adipocellulose
a type of cellulose found in the cell walls of cork tissue.

adjusted retention time
absolute retention time of a substance which does not interact with stationary phase. It is expressed in mm of chart and denoted with Rt.

adjuvant
a mixture of substances that delays the release of antigen after injection into an animal. The most commonly used is Freund's adjuvant. Incomplete Freund's contains oil and an emulsifier. The complete adjuvant also contains mycobacteria.

adler test for blood
1. on acidulating with acetic acid, an aqueous solution

containing blood, and adding solutions of benzidine and hydrogen peroxide, a blue colour is produced. 2. Blood stains or spots on saturation with a solution of malachite green (leucobase form), and moistening with hydrogen peroxide, develop green colour. Many modifications of these tests have been described.

A DNA

form of double helical DNA which, like the common B forms, is a right-handed double helix of antiparallel strands, but differing slightly in helical pitch and base pair orientation from the B form. Only very localized regions of DNA occur as A-form molecules but the A-form helix is the most stable configuration for double stranded RNA.

adoptive tolerance

the immunological tolerance acquired by an animal organism when it is injected with lymphocytes from another organism.

adrenal corticosteriods, adrenocorticoids, corticosteriods, corticoids, cortins

an important group of steroid hormones, formed in the adrenal cortex in response to adrenocorticotropic hormone. These are structurally related to pregnane; they contain a carboxyl group with a neighbouring α β-unsaturated bond in ring A, a ketol side chain in position 17, and other oxygen functions, particularly in positions 11, 17, 21 and 11. More than 30 steriods have been found in the adrenal cortex.

These are biosynthesized from cholesterol via progesterone; the latter is converted into A.c. by stepwise hydroxylation in positions 17, 21 and 11.

adrenal gland, suprarenal gland, glandula suprarenalis

a heavily vasculated, vertebrate endocrine gland, weighing about 15 g in the adult human. There are two adrenal glands one just above each kidney. The adrenal gland consists of two developmentally and functionally distinct parts; the mesodermal adrenal cortex (AC) and the ectodermal adrenal medulla (AM). The AC, which contains three histologically distinct zones, produces and exports glucocorticoids and mineralocorticoids in response to the action of the pituitary hormones, corticotropin and renin/angiotensi II, respectively. The AC also produces sex steroids.

adrenaline tolerance test

a test used in the diagnosis of glycogen storage disease type I; the test is based on measuring the level of the blood glucose as a function of time following the injection of an individual with adrenaline.

adrenocorticotropic hormone ACTH

a polypeptide hormone of 39 amino acids that stimulates the synthesis and secretion of the adrenal cortical hormones by the adrenal cortex. The adrenocorticotropic hormone is secreted by the anterior lobe of the pituitary gland. The release of ACTH is controlled by ACTH-releasing hormone (ACTHRH or CRH), produced by the hypothalamus; glucocorticoids act on the hypothalamus and pituitary gland to decrease ACTHRH and ACTH production. However, stressors, such as fear, pain, and toxins, can override the negative feedback to cause increased ACTH release and glucocorticoid concentration in the plasma.

adrenodoxin

a non-haeme iron protein that functions as an electron carrier in microsomal, nonphosphorylating electron transport systems.

adsorption chromatography

separation of the solutes is based on an adsorption equilibrium between a stationary solid or liquid and mobile liquid or gas phase.

adsorption isotherm

a plot of the fractional saturation as a function of the ligand concentration at a constant temperature. It is represented by Langmuir model.

aerobic

requiring the presence of air or oxygen to live, grow, and reproduce; the term is applied exclusively to microorganisms of various types, especially those used in the activated sludge process for industrial and municipal waste treatment. Its opposite, anaerobic, refers to an organism that can live without air or oxygen, or to a digestion process from which air is excluded.

affinity chromatography

a chromatographic method, where separation of the solutes is due to an equilibrium between macromolecule and a small molecule for which it has a high biological specificity and hence affinity.

affinity labeling

a method for introducing a label into the active site of an enzyme by relying on the tight binding between the enzyme and its substrate (or cofactors).

aflatoxins

a group of substances produced by the fungus Aspergillus flavus. It is produced when the fungus grows on groundnuts and causes acute liver damage in different species of animals.

after ripening

various physiological and biochemical changes occurring in fruit or seed after separation from the parent plant, e.g., some seeds need after ripening storage under dry conditions for losing dormancy, some fruits require after ripening to become edible.

agar-agar

a polysaccharide plant slime from various red algae. It consists of about 70% polygalactan, which is about 70% agarose and 30% agaropectin.

agglomeration

combination or aggregation of small particles suspended in a liquid into clusters of approximately spherical shape. The food industry uses this term in the sense of increasing the particle size of powdered food products. Because such powders tend to be hydrophobic due to the high surface tension of water, agglomeration causes them to be more readily dispersible in water. The operation is known as instantiating. The agglomerates have varying degrees of voids (open spaces), and have loosely bound, foam-like structures. They are formed by the mechanical means in chamber spray dryers, tubes, or fludized beds, usually in the presence of moisture.

agglutination

clumping of bacterial and other cells that is bought about by an antigen-antibody reaction between the particular antigens on the cell surface and added antibodies.

aggregation

a general term describing the combination of coalescence of particles dispersed in a suspension into clusters or clots, which either precipitate or are removed by filtration. Such particles may be macromolecules of proteins, soaps, and other colloids (aggregates of which called micelles), or larger particles, such as red cells in blood, rubber hydrocarbon in latex, and fat particles in milk. There are several types of aggregation:

(i) agglutination, which is chiefly the cohesion of bacterial cells, as in antigen-antibody reactions;

(ii) coagulation, the irreversible clotting of the proteins, etc., brought about by electrolytes, enzymes, or heat;

(iii) flocculation, the formation of clumps of dispersed colloidal solids such as carbon black in rubber mixes; and

(iv) agglomeration.

airoponics

the method of increasing the growth of plants in an oxygen rich environment, without soil where the plant-root zone is suspended in a growing chamber and intermittently pulsemisted with a nutrient solution.

agglutinin

one of a class of substances found in blood to which certain foreign substances or organisms have been added or admixed. As the name indicates, agglutinins have the characteristic property of causing agglutination, especially of the foreign substances or organisms responsible for their formation.

aglycon
the nonsugar compound resulting from the hydrolysis of glycosides; an example is 3, 5, 7, 3', 4'- pentahydroxyflavylium, or cyanidin.

agmatine $C_5H_{14}N_4$
needle like crystals with a melting point of 231°C; soluble in water; a product of the enzymatic decarboxylation of argenine. Also known as 4-(aminobutyl) guanidine.

agonist
any substance capable of initiating a response in the neuro-effector tissue. Substances which can initiate a response in the tissue but which cannot initiate the maximal response is known as a partial agonist. Substances which prevent an agonist from initiating a response are known as antagonists.

agropine
a rare amino acid derivative which is produced by a certain type of crown gall tumour.

alanine
one of the 20 common amino acids. It carries balanced charges at neutral pHs.

albinism
absence of pigmentation (i.e., melamin) in skin, eyes and hair. It occurs widely among animals, and in man is determined by a recessive autosomal gene. The term is sometimes applied to plants that are white, or at rophyll in leaves and stems.

albizzlin, 2-amino-3-unreidopropionic acid: $H_2NCONHCH_2CH(NH_2)$-COOH
a nonproteogenic amino acid which is occurring primarily in species of the genus Albizzia. It is presumably formed from cabamylphosphate and 2, 3-diaminopropionic acid by transcarbamylation. It is an antagonist of glutamine.

albomycin
an antibiotic which is synthesized by Actinomyces subtropicus. It is a cyclic polypeptide with a pyrimidine base (cytosine). It is effective against both Gram-positive and Gram-negative bacteria, and inhibits the aerobic metabolism of Staphylococcus aureus and Escherichia coli.

albumin
any of a group of plant and animal proteins which are soluble in water, dullute salt solutions, and 50% saturated ammonium sulfate.

albumin-globulin ratio
the ratio of the concentrations of albumin to globulin in blood serum.

albuminoid ammonia
ammonia obtained by decomposition of albuminous material. The quantity present is utilized in water analysis to determine the percentage of organic nitrogen in the sample.

albumose
a protein derivative formed by the action of hydrolytic enzyme,

such as protein.

alcohol dehydrogenase

an enzyme which catalyzes the oxidation of normal and branched-chain aliphatic and aromatic alcohols and carbonyl compounds to their aldehyde derivatives using NAD, NADP or their analogues. It is a metalloenzyme with four atoms of zinc per molecule. It is important in anaerobic glycolysis.

alcoholic fermentation

in this glucose molecule is broken down into two molecules of ethanol and two molecules of CO_2. It occurs in many yeasts. The same enzymatic pathway of glycolysis is followed except two last steps.

alcoholometry

the determination of the proportion of ethanol in spirits and other solutions; usually performed by measuring the relative density of the liquid at a standard temperature by a specially graduated hydrometer.

alcohols

hydrocarbon derivatives carrying one or more hydroxyl (-OH) group. In nature alcohols in the form of esters are important components of the essential oils, fats and waxes. A number of lower A., ethanol for example, are formed by fermentative processes from carbohydrates and proteins.

aldehyde

any of the various organic compounds with the terminal -CHO group and the general formula $C_nH_{2n}O$. They are formed from alcohols by either dehydrogenation or oxidation, and thus occupy an intermediate position between primary alcohols and the acids obtained from them by further oxidation. Aldehydes are quite reactive and participate in oxidation, reduction, addition and polymerization reactions. A wide variety of aldehydes have been found in plants and animals, sometimes in combination with sugars, but more frequently as the free carbonyl compound. Many of these natural substances are important as flavourings and perfume ingredients.

aldehyde lyase

any enzyme that catalyzes the nonhydrolytic cleavage of an aldehyde.

aldolactonase

an enzyme which catalyzes the conversion of L-gluonic acid to L-gluonon-y-lactone during ascorbic acid synthesis.

aldolase

an enzyme in anaerobic glycolysis that catalyzes the cleavage of fructose 1, 6-diphosphate to glyceraldehyde-3-phosphate; used also in the reverse reaction.

aldonic acids

sugar acids where -CHO of aldose sugars are oxidized by some oxidizing agents or by specific enzymes e.g., D-glucose will form D-gluconic acid.

aldose

one of the monosaccharides in which a terminal carbon atom (C-I) is an aldehyde group; e.g., arabinose, ribose. The simplest example is glyceraldehyde (a triose having three carbon atoms) and the most abundant in nature is the hexose glucose. The C-1 aldehyde group in hexoses can react rapidly and reversibly with the C-5 hydroxyl group to form an intramolecular hemiacetal; the ring structure so produced is a pyranose and is the predominant form of these aldoses in solution.

aldoses

the polyhydroxyaldehydes, one of the two main subdivision of monosaccharides. These are characterized by their terminal aldehyde group —CHO, which is always given the number 1 in systematic nomenclature.

aldosterone $C_{21}H_{28}O$

a steroid hormone extracted from the adrenal cortex that functions chiefly in regulating sodium and potassium metabolism.

aleuroneplast

when protein granules or crystals are predominant, the leucoplast is known as aleuroneplast.

algae

a large mixed group of simple plants, largely found in marine or freshwater habitats, although some algae are terrestrial. The term algae has taxonomic significance but is generally used to encompass those plants showing little cell differentiation and no real differentiation of leaves, stems, and roots. Algae can be unicellular (e.g., chlamydomonas), colonial (e.g., vol-vox), filamentous (e.g., spirogyra), or thalloid (e.g., fucus). It also includes the prokaryotic blue-green algae. All algae contain chlorophyll but this may be masked by various accessory pigments, these being one of the major characteristics used to divide the algae into some seven divisions, this number varying with different classifications. Other characters used to classify the algae are the nature of storage products, the types of cell wall, the form and number of flagella, ultrastructural cell details, and reproductive processes.

alizarin

1, 2-dihydroxynthraquinone, a red dye m.p. 290° C. It occurs in the root of the madder plant (Rubia tinctorum L.) and other Rubiaceae in combination with 2 moles glucose, forming the compound ruberythric acid.

alkaline lipase

an enzyme which catalyses the degradation of lipids into free fatty acids and glycerol during seed germination.

alkaline phosphatase

enzyme commonly extracted from E. coli and used in nucleic

acid sequencing and gene manipulation to remove terminal 5' - phosphoryl groups. Alkaline phosphatases are also present in eukaryotes (e.g., in vertebrate intestinal cells).

alkaloids

one of a group of organic compounds found in plants, that are poisonous, insoluble crystalline compounds. They contain nitrogen and usually occur as salts of acids such as citric, malic, and succinic acids. Their function in plants remains obscure, but it is suggested that they may be nitrogenous end-products of metabolism, or they may have a protective function against herbivores. Important examples are quinine, nicotine, atropine, opium, morphine, codeine, and strychnine. They occur mainly in the poppy family, the buttercup family, and the nightshade family of plants. The term is now restricted to basic substances derived from plants and excludes the simpler amino derivatives, as aniline, quinoline, propylamine etc., which were formerly included in this classification. Certain other substances, i.e., the purine bases, such as caffeine, theobromine, etc., although products of vegetable organisms, are not now included among the alkaloids. Alkaloids exhibit a variety of physical and chemical properties. All of them possess carbon, hydrogen and nitrogen and in most cases oxygen as elements. Like basic compounds they form their crystalline salts with acids like hydrocholic acid, sulphuric acid, citric acid, and tartaric acid. The free alkaloids are insoluble or slightly soluble in water but their salts are freely soluble. However, they are soluble in non-polar solvents such as ether or chloroform. Therefore, alkaloids are separated from non-polar compounds by salt formation, extracting the lipid soluble-portion and basifying the solution with an alkali carbonate or ammonia. Most of the alkaloids are crystalline solids with definite melting points, some of them are amorphous and few (coniine, nicotine) are liquid. They are generally colourless compounds but few are coloured substances. e.g., berberine (yellow), betaine (red), tylophorine (dull yellow), and cones-sine (pale yellow). They are generally bitter in taste and are optically active. On treatment with phosphotungstic acid, phosphomolybdic acid, picric acid, potassium mercuric-iodide and tannic acid they yield insoluble precipitates (double salts).

Alkaloids have been reported in various plant parts such as in whole aerial plant (Lobelia, Tylophora, Ephedra), in leaves

(Datura, Belladonna, Coca), in bark (Kurchi, Cinchona) in stem (Withanina), in rhizomes and roots (Ipecac, Rauwolfia, Aconite); in flowering buds (Hyoscymus) and in seeds (Nux vomica, Physostigma, Colchicum). Several alkaloids have been found in cultures of microorganisms, e.g., in bacteria, fungi (Ergot) and algae. Amphibian alkaloids such as toad venous (bufotoxin) and salamander alkaloids (salamandarine) are of animal origin. Alkaloids with complicated chemical structures (strychnine) are less widespread in nature than simple compounds (nicotine).

Alkaloids are capable of exhibiting extensive and well-marked pharmacological activities like analgesic (cocaine, morphine, codeine), antiamoebic and emetic (emetin), anticholinergic (atropine, hyoscyamine, scopolamine) antihypertensive (reserpine, deserpine), antimalarial (quinine, cinchonine), antitumor (vinblastine, vincristine), antitussive (codeine, noscapine), cardiac depressant (quinidine), central stimulant (caffeine, strychnine, brucine), diuretic (theobromine, theophylline), oxytocic (ergometrine, ergotamine), ophthalmic and cholinergic (physostigmine, pilocarpine), skeletal muscle relaxant (tubocurarine), and smooth muscle relaxnt (papaverine, theophylline).

The following classification of alkaloids is widely accepted:

Derivatives of aryl-substituted amines; e.g., adrenaline, benzedrine, ephedrine, neocynephrine, tyramine.

Derivatives of imidazole; e.g., pilocarpine.

Derivatives of pyridine and piperidine; e.g., anabasine, coniine, ricinine.

Derivatives of pyrrole; e.g., carpaine, hygrine, nicotine.

The complex alkaloids containing condensed fused ring system are classified as:

Aporphine alkaloids; e.g., apomorphine, isothebaine, corydine.

Alkaloids containing pyrrole rings fused with other rings; e.g., gelsemine, physostigmine, vasicine, yohimbine.

Tropine alkaloids; e.g., atropine, cocaine, ecgonine, scopolamine, tropine.

Alkaloids containing fusion of two piperidine rings are classified as:

Berberine alkaloids; e.g., cinochonine, quinine, quinidine.

Lupine alkaloids; e.g., lupanine, sparteine.

Cryptopine alkaloids; e.g., dictamine, galipoline, lycorine.

Isoquinoline alkaloids; e.g., peliotine, sarsoline, anhalidine.

Papaverine alkaloids; e.g., codamine, homolaudanosine,

papaverine.

Bis-benzylisoquinoline alkaloids; e.g., bebeverine, trilobine.

Morphine and related alkaloids; e.g., morphine, codeine, and thebaine.

Phthalide isoquinoline alkaloidsnarcotine alkaloids; e.g., hydrastine, narcotine, narceine.

Other alkaloids; e.g., hydrastine, narcotine, narceine, brucine, colaoidine, strychuine.

alkaloidal reagent

a substance or mixture of substances used to separate or detect alkaloids, either by precipitating them, or by giving characteristic colour reactions with them, etc. Representative alkaloidal reagents are solutions of phosphomolybdic acid, potassium mercuric iodide, tannic acid, and chloroplatinic acid.

alkane group

saturated hydrocarbon group with general formula C_nH_{2n+2} e.g., methane, ethane. These are comparatively less active and end with ane.

alkylating agent

compound that causes the substitution of an alkyl group for an active hydrogen atom in organic compounds. Many alkylating agents are chemical mutagens (e.g., busulfan and nitrogen mustard).

allantoate amino hydrolase

an enzyme which catalyses the hydrolysis of allantoate to urea and ureidoglycollate.

allantoic acid $C_4H_8N_4O_4$

a crystalline acid obtained by hydrolysis of allantoin; intermediate product in nucleic acid metabolism.

allantoin $C_4H_6N_4O_3$

a crystalline oxidation product of uric acid found in allantoic and amniotic fluids and in fetal urine.

allatum hormone

an insect hormone that affects differentiation after molting and that is required for vitellogenesis in the adult female.

allergen

antigen or hapten that induces an allergic reaction, particularly through the production of antibodies of immunoglobulin IgE. The allergen and antibody combine to form a histamine-like substance, which in turn weakens the blood vessels sufficiently to release fluids. This causes the commonly experienced edema, sneezing and swelling well-known to hay fever sufferers. Only those who are predisposed to certain allergens are capable of forming such anti-bodies. Severe allergens can cause extremely serious conditions (anaphylaxis) which have been known to be quite fatal. Protein-containing substances are the allergens (wool, hair, pollen, etc.), but allergic reactions may be experienced by a few individuals from exposure to almost any substance.

allergy

a hypersensitivity of the immune apparatus, a pathological immune reaction induced either by antibodies immediate hypersensitivity) or by living lymphoid cells (delayed type A).

allomones

allomones are chemicals produced by anorganism which include in a member of another species a behavioural or physiological reaction favourable to the emitter. These chemicals are involved in a variety of mutualistic and antagonistic relationships. The scents of flowers are mutualistic allomones; insects polinate plants from which they obtain nectar in return. Ventoms and repellents, which organsims use in defense against predator, are antagonistic allomones.

allophycocyanin

a red accessory pigment of algal chloroplasts that consists of a protein conjugated to a phycoblin.

allosteric enzyme

any of the regulatory bacterial enzymes, such as those involved in end-product inhibition.

allosteric inhibitors

low molecular mass compounds, though not resembling with substrate, which bind on the inhibitor sites of a regulatory enzyme. Thus the inhibitors could either decrease the affinity for the substrate at the catalytic site, or affect the catalytic efficiency of the enzyme, or do both.

allosteric protein

a protein that has two or more sites with which ligands bind and thus conformational changes occur in the protein.

allosteric site

a part of an enzyme to which a specific effector or modulator can be attached. This attachment is reversible. Allosteric enzymes possess an allosteric site in addition to their active site. This site is as specific in its relationship to modulators as active sites are to subsrates.

allostery

the property of an enzyme able to shift reversibly between an active and an inactive configuration.

alloteraploid

an allopolyploid whose chromosomes are derived from two different species and which therefore has four times the haploid number of chromosomes.

alloxan $C_4H_2N_2O_4$

crystalline oxidation product of uric acid; induces diabetes experimentally by selective destruction of pancreatic beta cells. Also known as mesoxyalyurea.

alluvial soil

a soil derived from marine, esturine or river deposits.

Such soils are usually very fertile with an undeveloped profile.

allysine

a derivative of lysine in which the ε-amino group has been converted to an aldehyde group; allysine undergoes an aldol condensation with hydroxyallysine during the cross-linking of collagen chains.

alternation of generations

production of independent haploid sexual, and diploid asexual, generations in life cycle. These two phases are known as gametophytic and sporophytic generations. If these generations are alike, it is known as homologous, and if they do not look alike, the alteration is antithetic.

alternative oxidase

an enzyme which catalyzes the oxidation of reduced ubiquinone which is not coupled to the phosphorylation of ADP. It is not inhibited by cyanide but sensitive to substituted hydroxamic acids.

alum precipitation

an immunochemical technique in which soluble antigens are mixed with aluminium adjuvants to form a precipitate. When injected into an animal, the precipitate forms a depot from which the antigen is slowly released.

alveolate or alveolar

surface covered with pits, and resembling honeycomb.

amaryllidacease alkaloids

a group of complicated alkaloids found only in plant family Amarylliaceae. Their biosynthesis is similar to that of the isoquinoline alkaloids, beginning with phenylamine or tyramine and a carbonyl compound. The main alkaloid galanthamine is isolated from Caucasians nowdrops, Galanthus woronowil, and is used therapeutically as an inhibitor of acetylcholinesterase.

amber suppressor

gene that prevents polypeptide chain termination as a result of an amber mutation. Such genes usually act by coding for transfer RNA which inserts an amino acid at the site of the UAG nonsense codon produced by the amber mutation.

ambiguous enzyme

an enzyme whose distribution between soluble and particulate forms varies with the metabolic state of the cell.

ameiosis

having one division (instead of two) of the nucleus at meiosis, so that the chromosome number is not reduced.

amethopterin

a folic acid analogue that inhibits the enzyme dihydrofolate reductase and that is used in the treatment of leukemia.

amidinotransferases, transamidinases EC 21.4

a group of enzymes catalysing transamidination. They are involved in the biosynthesis of creatine.

aminases

enzymes that catalyzes the hydolysis of amines.

amination

the introduction of the amino group (-NH_2) into an organic compound.

amino acid

any of the organic compounds that contain one or more amino groups and one or more acidic carboxyl groups and that are polymerized to form peptides and proteins; only 20 of the more than 80 amino acids found in nature serve as building blocks for proteins; examples are tyrosine and lysine.

amino acid arm

it is just opposite to anticoden arm of t-RNA. On this arm aminoacyl group is esterified by the amino acyl synthetases.

amino acid oxidase

an enzyme that catalyzes the oxidative deamination of amino acids; an L-amino acid oxidase is specific for L-amino acids and is a flavoprotein having FMN as a prosthetic group; a D-amino acid oxidase is specific for D-amino acids and is a flavoprotein having FAD as a prosthetic group.

amino acid pool

the collection of amino acids constituted by amino acids present in blood and extra cellular fluid. Amino acids enter this pool from dietary proteins, after synthesis from keto acids (non essential amino acids) and from tissue protein breakdown. Amino acids from this pool are used for synthesis of tissue proteins and synthesis of certain other important compounds like coenzymes, hormones etc. From some of the latter categories of compounds amino acids do not return to the pool. Amino acids over and above the above synthetic needs are deaminated and degraded. There is only limited storage of amino acids as protein in certain tissues. After deamination carbon skeletons of amino acids are used for oxidation (for energy), and for synthesis of glucose and fats.

amino acid reagents

reagents for the colorimetric identification and quantitation of amino acids. One of the most important is the ninhydrin reaction, in which a blue-violet dye, called Ruhemann's Purple (absorbance maximum at 570 nm, for proline at 440 nm) is formed by the reaction of 2, 2-dihydroxy-1-H-indene-1; 3 (2H)-dione (ninhydrin) with the amino acid.

In the flourescamine technique, the amino acids have been converted by reaction with 4-phenyl (furan-2 H (3H)-1' -phthalane)-3, 3'-dione (fluorescamine) into strongly fluorescing compounds which can be detected even in nanomole quantities at 336 nm. The reagent itself is not fluorescent, and in contract to ninhydrin, it is not sensitive to ammonia.

Other highly sensitive reagents have been 2, 4, 6-trinitrobenzosulfonic acid, 1, 2-naphthoquinone-4-salfonic acid (Folin's reagent) and 4, 4'-tetramethyldiaminodiphenylmethane (TDM). Intensely fluorescing amino acid derivates are formed by reaction with o-phthaladehyde in the presence of reducing agents with pyridoxal and $zinc^{2+}$ ions; and with dansyl chloride (5-dimethylaminophthalene sulfonyl chloride).

amino acid residue

the portion of an amino acid that is present in a peptide or a polypeptide. The amino acid loses a hydrogen atom, hydroxyl group or a molecule of water as it becomes linked to the other amino acids.

aminoacyladenylate, activated amino acid

the product of the first enzymatic reaction of protein biosynthesis. It consists of an amino acid linked by an acid anhydride bond to the phosphate of AMP.

aminoacyl-tRNA

transfer RNA molecule together with its relevant amino acid. The two are covalently bonded, and the bond is broken when the amino acid is linked by peptide bonds to other amino acids during protein synthesis.

3'-amino-3'-deoxyadenosine

a purine antibiotic synthesized by cordyceps militaris and Helminthosporium species. It has antitumor activity.

aminoglycoside antibiotics

a group of antibiotics that includes streptomycin, kanamycin, and neomycin.

amino hydroxy synthase

an enzyme which catalyses the conversion of 2-oxybutyrate or pyruvate to 2-acetohydroxybutyrate or 2-acetolactate during isoleucine or valine synthesis respectively.

aminolevulinic dehydrates

an enzyme which catalyzes the condensation of two molecules of d-aminolevulinic acid to porphobilinogen which provides the basic pyrrole units of porphyrins. It is competitively inhibited by the levulinic acid.

amino oxidase

an enzyme which catalyses the oxidation of spermine and spermidine only at terminal amino group with the formation of the corresponding aldehyde.

aminopeptidase

an enzyme which catalyzes the liberation of an amino acid from the end of a peptide having a free amino group.

aminopolypeptidase

a proteolytic enzyme that cleaves polypeptides containing either a free amino group or a basic nitrogen atom having at least one hydrogen atom.

aminoprotease
an enzyme that hydrolyzes a protein and unites with its free amino group.

amino sugar
a monosaccharide in which a non-glycosidic hydroxyl group is replaced by an amino or substituted amino group; an example, is D-glucosamine.

amino terminal
the end part of a polypeptide chain which contains a free α-amino group.

aminotransferase
an enzyme that catalyzes the transfer of an amino group from an amino acid to a keto acid (e.g., α-ketoglutarate) to form a new amino acid and keto acid. The various enzymes in this class have different specificites towards the initial amino acid; all use pyridoxal phosphate as a cofactor. Also known as transminase.

amitosis
the division of nucleus without normal mitosis. The chromosomes do not become visible and it is unlikely that two identical nuclei results.

ammonia, NH_3
a colourless gas with a sharp smell.

NH_3 is the product of nitrate reduction, biological nitrogen fixation, and deamination of amino acids and various catabolic pathways, for example oxidation purine degradation and reductive pyrimidine degradation.

ammonia assimilation
the utilization of ammonia in the net synthesis of the nitrogen-containing group of nitrogenous cell constituents, e.g., amonia acids, amides, carbamyl and guanido compounds. Incorporation of ammonia into the amide group of glutamine, catalysed by glutamine synthetase (EC 6.3.1.2) is of central importance: L-glutamate + NH_3 + ATP → L-glutamine + ADP + P_r. The amide nitrogen of L-glutamine is then used in various syntheses:

1. L-glutamine + α-ketoglutarate + 2 H^+ + 2 e^- → L-glutamate (Glutamate synthase).
2. L-glutamine + HCO^-_3 + 2 ATP + H_2O → carbamyl phosphate + L-glutamate + 2 ADP + P_r.
3. the amide group of glutamine is used in purine synthesis, where it provides N-3 and N-9 of purine ring, and the 2-NH_2, group of guanine.
4. in several syntheses, nitrogen is derived directly from the amide group of L-glutamine, e.g., histidine synthesis; conversion of chorismate into anthranilate; the synthesis of amino sugars; amination of UTP to CTP.
5. in some organisms, the amide group of glutamine is transferred to asparate by the action of asparagine synthetase (glutamine hydrolysing) (EC 6.3.5.4).

ammonia detoxification
the detoxification of the toxic,

non-dissociated compound by formation of ammonium salts and nitrogen-excretion compounds. The ammonia produced by catabolism in animals is either excreted directly, or it is converted into other nitrogenous compounds for excretion; it is not reassimilated.

ammonia volatilizati
the process by which gaseous NH_3 is released from the soil surface to the atmosphere. A wide variety of NH_4^+-forming compounds dissolved in soil solution and NH_4^+ ions are produced, NH_4^+ ion interacts with the cation-exchange complex of the soil and becomes 'fixed' in the clay lattices. NH_4^+ ions in soil solution also enter into equilibrium reactions with NH_3 of the atmosphere. The range of such losses are 0-25% of applied N.

ammonification
the conversion of organic nitrogen to ammoniacal nitrogen. It is mainly performed by wide variety of bacteria.

amount
total quantity of solute present in given solution. It is calculated by multiplying concentration with the volume of solution.

amphibian toxins
a group of chemically very heterogeneous toxins (biogenic amines, peptides, alkaloids, steroids) produced by toads, salamanders, frogs and newts. Pharmacologically, they include heart, muscle and nerve toxins, sympathicomimetica, local anaesthetics and hallucinogens.

amphipathic
a molecule having well separated polar and nonpolar groups due to the length of molecule e.g., lipids and protein are amphipathic membrane constituents.

amplify
to produce multiple copies of a gene is plasmids or any collections of these molecules.

amygdalin
glucose having a cyanide radical giving the characteristic flavour to almonds.

amygdalin $C_6H_5CH(CN)OC_{12}H_{21}O_{10}$
a glucoside occurring in the kernels of certain plants of genus Prunus.

amyloclastic method
a method of assaying for the enzyme amylase by determining the amount of unhydrolyzed starch that remains after incubation of the starch with the enzyme.

amyloid protein
a pathological, fibrillar, low-molecular-weight protein. In amyloidosis, it is deposited together with glycoproteins and proteoglycans, primarily in the spleen, liver and kidneys.

amylolysis
the enzyme-catalyzed hydrolysis of starch to soluble products.

amylolytic enzyme
a type of enzyme capable of denaturing starch molecules; used in textile manufacture to remove starch and slash sizing agents.

amylometric method
a method of assaying for the enzyme amylase by determining the amount of starch that is hydrolyzed during incubation of the starch with the enzyme.

amylopectin
a highly branched, high-molecular weight carbohydrate polymer composed of about 80% of corn starch.

amylopsin
an enzyme in pancreatic juice that acts to hydrolyze starch into maltose.

amylose
a linear starch polymer.

anabasine
a nicotiana alkaloid. It is isolated in the L-form, primarily from Nicotiana glauca and the asiatic Anabasis aphylla, in which it is the main alkaloid. Its physiological effects are similar to those of nicotine, and like nicotine, it is used as an insecticide.

anabolic steroid
a steroid hormone or synthetic steroid that promotes growth and formation of new tissue. It is used in the treatment of wasting diseases and, controversially, in sport to build up athlete's muscles. Most androgens have anabolic activity, but when used by women they lead to masculinization.

anaerobic glycolysis
a metabolic pathway in plants by which, in the absence of oxygen, hexose, is broken down to lactic acid and ethanol with some adenosinetriphosphate synthesis.

anakinesis
a process in living organisms by which energy-rich molecules, such as adenosinetriphosphate are formed.

analog computer
a computer that receives information in the form of continuous variables, such as pressure, temperature and flow, and that processes the information by translating each variable into an analogous related mechanical or electrical variable such as voltage.

analytical reagent
reagent with producer's certificate guaranteeing content of specified impurities below given limits. Also known as analytical grade reagent; analytically pure reagent.

analytical separation
here separation techniques resolve the smallest quantity of the compounds and frequently it is not necessary to recover the compound after separation. These techniques are highly sensitive and loading capacity is very limiting.

anaplasia
loss by a cell of its

characteristic structure accompanied by its reversion to a more primitive embryonic type.

anaplerotic reaction
a reaction whereby a metabolic intermediate is replenished; this is generally achieved through the insertion of either a one-carbon fragment, in the form of carbon dioxide, or a two-carbon fragment, in the form of acetyl-CoA, into the appropriate metabolic reaction.

andre reagent for alkaloids
an aqueous solution of potassium dichromate, which precipitates many alkaloids.

androgen
a class of steroid hormones produced in the testis and adrenal cortex which act to regulate masculine secondary sexual characteristics.

androsin $C_{15}H_{20}O_6$
a glucoside found in the herb Apoeynum androsaemifolium; yields glucose and acetov nillone on hydrolysis.

androstanazole
a synthetic and highly active anabolic steroid. It is used, in the therapy of inflammation and tumours and in reconvalescence.

androsterone
metabolite of androgens, used as diagnostic indication of male sex hormone when present in urine.

androstane $C_{19}H_{12}$
the parent steroid hydrocarbon for all androgen hormones. Also known as etioall cholane.

androstenedione $C_{19}H_{26}O_2$
any one of three isomeric androgens produced by the adrenal cortex.

androsterone $C_{19}H_{30}O_2$
an androgenic hormone occurring as a hydroxy ketone in the urine of men and women.

angular velocity
the central angle (measured in radians) transvered per unit time during the course of rotation.

angustmycins
the purine antibiotics synthesized by various species of Stretomyces. It is specific for mycobacteria. Gram positive and Gram negative bacteria and fungi are not sensitive to angustmycin A. It acts by inhibiting the formation of 5-phosphoribosy 1-1-pyrophosphate in purine biosynthesis.

anhydrase
any enzyme that catalyzes the removal of water from a substrate.

anion-ion exchangers
ion exchangers having positively charged groups and attract negatively charged solute molecules. These are also known as basic ion exchanger materials.

anion respiration
the phenomenon that exposure of plant tissues to salt solutions frequently leads to an increase in respiration which appears to be proportional to the rate of

anion absorption by the plant.

ankyrin, anchorin syndein
an erythrocyte membrane protein which binds Spetrin.

anoxia
absence or very low oxygen availability to the root system during flooding or complete anaerobic condition in rhizosphere by supplying nitrogen in place of oxygen.

anthesis
(i) opening of flower bud.
(ii) the duration of life of a flower from the opening of the bud to the setting of the fruit.
(iii) dehiscence of anthers.

anthocyanin
any of the intensely coloured, sap-soluble glycoside plant pigments responsible for most scarlet, purple, mauve, and blue colouring in higher plants.

anthranilate synthetase
an enzyme which catalyses the synthesis of anthranilate from chorismate during amino acid formation.

anthraquinone pigment
colouring material which occurs in plants, fungi, lichens and insects; consists of about 50 derivatives of the parent compound, anthraquinone.

anthraquinones
yellow, orange, red, red-brown or violet derivatives of anthraquinone (9, 10-anthracenedione), the largest group of naturally occurring quinones.

anthrone reaction
a colorimetric reaction for carbohydrates, particularly hexoses, that is based on the production of a green colour on treatment of the sample with anthrone.

antiauxins
compounds which inhibit competitively the action of auxins. These have structural similarity with auxins. The inhibition can be overcome by increasing concentration of auxins.

antibiotics
substances produced by microbes which kill or inhibit the growth of other microorganisms. In contrast to general cell poisons, the antibiotics are selective.

antibody
a protein molecule formed within the body of an animal in order to neutralize the effect of a foreign invading protein (called an antigen). These serum proteins (immunoglobulins) are produced by certain cells of the lympocyte series in response to the presence of antigens. Antibodies bind specifically to molecules of the eliciting antigen but not to other antigens. Antibodies are produced by lymphocytes in response to the presence of antigens. Each antibody has a molecular structure that exactly fits the structure of one particular antigen molecule, like a lock and key (i.e., they are specific). Antibody molecules attach themselves to invading antigen

molecules (on or from bacteria, transfused red blood cells, or grafted tissue of another animal) and so render them inactive. It may also assist in the ingestion of antigenic matter by phagocytes (opsonization) and also activate complement. Immunoglobulin molecules each comprise two parallel heavy chains (of high molecular mass) and two light chains, all united by disulphide bonds. The amino acid sequence in certain regions of both heavy and light chains is highly variable. These variable regions contribute to the three-dimensional structure of the two antigen binding sites on each molecule, and confer specificity on the antibody. There are several classes of antibodies, according to the nature of the invariable regions of their heavy chains. IgM antibodies have mu(μ) heavy chains; they are a polymerized form of the antibody secreted during the early response to antigens. IgG antibodies, with gamma (γ) heavy chains, appear later in the immune response and are the most abundant immunoglobulin class in normal blood serum. IgA antibodies, with alpha (α) heavy chains, are secreted with mucous surfaces, especially in the alimentary and respiratory tracts. IgE, with epsilon heavy chains, has a special role in relation to mast cells and in the mediation of Type I hypersensitivity. Maternal IgG antibody passes to the fetus across the placenta before the birth in primates and rodents. In most herbivores mammals, antibody transfer take place in the first 2 days of life of newborn, which absorbs the IgG and IgA antibodies in colostrum across the gut mucosa. Antibody can be detected and estimated by means of the reactions they undergo with antigens in vitro. They are also now used in a wide range of assays and tests to label specific antigenic components.

antibody heterogeneity

the state of a given preparation of antibodies in which the antibodies differ with respect to size, structure, charge, or other properties.

anticodon

a specific sequence of three nucleotides in a transfer RNA, complementary to a codon for an amino acid in a messenger RNA. For a specific triplet nucleotide sequence of codon in a mRNA, there is always corresponding complementary acticodon in t-RNA e.g., for AUU codon in the mRNA there is UAA anticodon in t-RNA.

anticodon arm

the portion of t-RNA having anticodon base sequence for a specific amino acid.

antidepressants

the drugs with stimulatory and antidepressant action. They decrease fatigue, reduce appetite and decrease sleeping time. These effects are the results of reduced autonomic activity, especially of cholinerig systems, and of central sympathetic activation.

anti-enzyme
one of a group of substances analogous to the antitoxins, which are produced by the organism following the injection of various enzymes into the blood. These anti-enzymes are able to inhibit the normal action of the enzymes from which they are formed to a remarkable extent and, like the antitoxins, are selective in their action. Antibodies for many enzymes trypsin, pepsin, lipase, emulsin, urease, lactase, tryosinase, thrombase, and rennin.

antifertilizin
an immunologically specific substance produced by animal sperm to implement attraction by the egg before fertilization.

antifibrinolysin
any substance that inhibits the proteolytic action of the fibrinolysin.

antiflorigen
a hypothetical transmissible flower inhibiting stimulus synthesised under non-inductive photoperiod. It may inhibit florigen synthesis, interferes with intercellular membrane transport of one of the reactant of florigen or it may compete for crucial site of action or it is transmitted to the shoot apex to inhibit flowering. Isolation and estimation have not been achieved.

antigen-antibody reaction
abb. AAR: together with phagocytosis, the most important protective mechanism of the animal organism against invading foreign substances.

antigen binding capacity
the total antibody concentration in an antiserum based on a determination of the amount of antigen bound by a given volume of the antiserum.

antigenic determinant
an area on the surface of an antigen which combines with the antigen binding site of an antibody.

antihemolytic
an agent that prevents the destruction, or loss from the organism, of red blood corpuscles.

antihemophilic factor
a soluble protein clotting factor in mammalin blood. Also known as factor VIII; thromboplastinogen.

anti-insulin
a compound, such as a sex hormone or a corticosteroid, that decreases the activity of insulin.

antilymphocyte serum
abb ALS : an immune serum which has an opsonizing and cytotoxic effect on lymphocytes, thus producing immune suppression.

anti-matter

hypothetical matter consists of antiparticles. Contact between anti-matter and matter would result in the annihilation of both with the production of annihilation radiation.

antimitotic

an agent that causes disruption of cells division (mitosis). Antimitotics have a wide variety of mechanisms, with activity at specific phases during the cell cycle. Rapidly dividing cells, such as neoplastic cells, of the bone marrow, and gastrointestinal epithelial cells, are more susceptible to the effects of such agents. Examples of antimitotic drugs are colchicine, 5-fluorouracil, cytosine arabinoside, vincristine, vinblastine, and alkylating agents (e.g., cyclophosphamide). These drugs are used in the treatment of cancer. Their side-effects are due to the disruption of mitosis in areas of rapid cell division (e.g., the bone marrow and gastrointestinal tract), causing immunosuppression, vomiting, and diarrhoea.

antiseptic

1. a drug or other substance used to oppose sepsis by its action upon microorganisms. 2. any substance which will destroy or inhibite growth of bacteria or other infective organisms when in contact with the tissue of humans or animals. Antiseptics should be distinguished from disinfectants, which are applied to non-living objects rather than to people because of their high toxicity (e.g., inorganic mercury compounds, cresol), and also form sterilants, which include agencies such as heat and ultra-violet radiation as well as chemical substances. The most commonly used antiseptics are the organic mercury compounds (thiomersal), essential oils (thymol and menthol), silver compounds (argyrol, silver sulphadiazine), and oxidizing materials (such as hydrogen peroxide and potassium permanganate). Alcohols also exhibit antiseptic properties; iodine solution in ethyl alcohol (3%) has been widely used, but is considered to be too drastic for most applications.

antiserum, immune serum

the serum of an animal (including humans) which has been immunized against an antigen. It can be monovalent or polyvalent, i.e., contain one or more specific antibodies, depending on whether the animal was immunized with a purified antigen or a mixture of antigens.

antisigma factor

a protein that is produced during the infection of Escherichia coli and T4 phage and that prevents recognition of the promoter by the sigma factor of DNA-dependent RNA polymerase.

antitermination

a transcriptional control mechanism that applies to intercistronic termination sites present in some operons. Transcription continues bypassing the termination site in presence of antitermination factor which is a protein.

antithrombin

a substance in blood plasma that inactivates thrombin.

antitumor proteins

the proteinaceous antibiotics isolated from culture filtrates of various streptomyces strains which inhibit tumour growth.

antiviral protein

a protein, induced by interferon, that binds to ribosomes and inhibits the translation of either viral RNA or of the messenger RNA which is derived from viral DNA.

antivitamin

any substance that prevents a vitamin from normal metabolic functioning.

antizymotic

a substance that prevents, inhibits, or retards fermentation, and is frequently used for that purpose in medicine, in food products, etc. Antizymotic agent reduces fermentation and gas formation in the gastrointestinal tract or reduces the stability of foam and allows the release of gas. Antizymotics that reduce the number of gas-producing organisms in the digestive tract include oil of turpentine, linseed oil, formalin, and antibiotics. Antifoaming agents, which are used especially to prevent and treat frothy bloat, include poloxalene, polyemerized methyl silicone, polythylene glycol, and various vegetable oils. Polyoxypropylene-polyoxyethylene polymer series derivatives (PPD) give fast relief in case of frothy bloat and protect against reformation for the next 12 hours. They can be used in dairy cattle because they are not excreted in the milk. Turpentine oil is liable to taint milk and should not be used in lactating cattle.

apical meristem

when meristem is present at the apex of shoot i.e., stem or root apical meristems. The activity of apical meristem gives rise to linear growth or primary growth.

apoenzyme

polypeptide moiety of a conjugated enzyme after removal of its prosthetic group. As the activity of conjugated enzymes depends on their prosthetic groups an apoenzyme is inactive, but its presence can sometimes be demonstrated by binding of specific antibodies raised against the whole enzyme (holoenzyme).

apomixis

embryos resulting from without the fusion of gametes

in fertilization, but because of development of unreduced egg cell. In this case embryo develops from cells other than the fertilized egg e.g., nuclear embryo in citrus.

apomyglobin

myglobin devoid of its haeme group. It was first obtained by lowering the pH of a myoglobin solution to 3.5. The haeme groups binds only weakly to the protein at this PH, and can be removed by extraction with an organic solvent.

apurine acids

polynucleotides which have been subjected to short treatment with mild acid, which removes the purines and leaves the phosphate, pentose and pyrimidines.

apurinic acid

a DNA molecule from which the purines have been removed by milk acid hydrolysis, and still retaining the pyrimidine bases and the sugar-phosphate structure.

aqueous vapour pressure

the pressure exerted by water vapour in equilibrium with liquid (or solid) water at given temperature.

arachidonic acid

5, 8, 11, 14-icosatetraenoic acid, CH_3-$(CH_2)_4$-CH=CH-CH_2-CH=CH.CH-CH_2-CH=CH-CH_2=CH.$(CH_2)_3$-COOH. An essential fatty acid. M_r 30.45, m.p. 49.5°C. This is an esterified component of fish liver oil and of animal phosphatides.

arachin

the peanut protein composed of 6 sub-units, M_r 345000. Each subunit is composed of 2 equal-sized, convalently bound polypeptide chains. A. is very similar to edistin.

arboviruses

the group of single-standed RNA viruses possessing an envelope around the capsid and causing diseases in man such as yellow fever and encephalitis. They are carried by insects and frequently replicate in both the insect and human host.

arecoline

1, 2, 5, 6-tetrahydro-1-methyl-3-pyridinecarboxylic acid methyl ester, the most important of the areca alkaloids. The compound is the methyl ester of the alkaoid arecaidine (M_r 141.19, m.p. 232°C). It is responsible for the physiological effect of betel nuts. It acts as a parasympatheticomimetic, but due to is high toxicity, it is used only in veterinary medicine.

arenchyma

a tissue of thin walled cells surrounding large airspaces. The cells walls are perforated so that the air spaces are continuous throughout the organ. Such tissues are associated with hydrophytes.

arginase

an enzyme that catalyzes the splitting of urea from the amino acid arginine.

l-arginine
abb. Arg. 2-amino-5-guanidovaleric acid, the most strongly basic amino acid. It is unstable in hot alkaline solutions and forms nearly insoluble nitrates, picrates and picrolonates, and a particularly insoluble salt with flavianic acid. The Sakaguchi reaction is used for the detection and quantitative determination of Arg.
It is found in particularly large amounts in protamines and histones.

arginine $C_6H_{14}N_4O_2$
a colourless, crystalline, water-soluble, essential amino acid of the α-ketoglutaric acid family.

Armani-Barboni test for caffeine
the sample to be tested is heated with potassium hydroxide solution; cooled and phosphomolybdic acid is added to it until a white precipitate forms. Then 50% potassium hydroxide solution is added until the precipitate dissolves. An intense blue colour indicates the presence of caffeine.

arnold solution
a mixture of one part of a 1% aqueous solution of sodium nitrate, with two parts of a 1% aqueous solution of P-aminoacetophenone hydrochloride. This is a reagent for testing acetoacetic acid in urine. A brownish-red colour, in ammoniacal solution, indicates the presence of acetoacetic acid.

Arnold test for proteins
upon the addition to 1-2 ml of protein solution, of 2-4 drops of a 5% solution of sodium nitroprusside, and a few drops of ammonia, a purple-red colour is formed.

aromatic amino acid
an organic acid containing at least one amino group and one or more aromatic groups; for example, phenylalanine, one of the essential amino acids.

aromatic compounds
highly unsaturated cyclic hydrocarbons generally having 3 double bonds and general formula C_6H_6.

arreguine test for citric acid
the dilute solution to be tested is acidified with sulphuric acid and oxidized with a 4% acidic potassium permanganate solution; 0.1 g resorcinol is added, followed by the addition of sulphuric acid until a red colour develops. The solution is then extracted with ether, a few drops of ammonia are added to the extract. An intense blue fluorescence indicates the presence of citric acid.

arrow poisons
the natural toxins used for coating arrows, spears or blow pipe darts. In ancient Greece, extracts of aconitin were used. Ouabain and similar cardiac glycosides were (are) used in Africa. The jungle Indians of South America use various

kinds of Curare alkaloids and tribes in Columbia use Batrachotoxin from the Columbian arrow poison frog.

artificial plasmid

vectors constructed by a complex series of cutting and joining reactions.

arylamidases

an ubiquitous group of aminopeptidases which preferentially cleave amino acid arylamides, e.g., alanine β-naphthylamide. Determination of arylamidases in the serum and urine is considered to have a certain diagnostic value in some liver diseases.

ascending chromatography

a technique for the analysis of the mixtures of two or more compounds in which the mobile phase rises through the fixed phase.

ascorbic acid oxidase

an enzyme which catalyses the oxidation of ascorbic acid to dehydroascorbic acid by using oxygen.

ascospore

a spore resulting from meiosis and borne in an ascus (ascomycetes fungi).

asparagine

one of the 20 common amino acids. It is unchanged, but carries a polar side-chain.

aspartate transcarbamylase

a regulatory enzyme that catalyzes the first step in the biosynthesis of pyrimidines in which N-carbamyl aspartic acid is formed from carbamyl phosphate and aspartic acid. The enzyme consists of two classes of subunits referred to as catalytic and regulatory subunits.

assimilate

in the wider sense, a product of assimilation. In the narrower sense, a stabilized end product of photosynthesis.

assimilation number

the amount of photosynthesis taking place in unit mass of a leaf in an hour and considering the weight of chlorophyll in the tissue. It is expressed as the ratio of weight of CO_2 (in mg) absorbed/time (in hours/ weight of chlorophyll (in mg) in the tissue.

astacin $C_{40}H_{48}O_4$

a red carotenoid ketone pigment found in crustaceans; as in the shell of a boiled lobster.

astaxanthin $C_{40}H_{52}O_4$

a violet carotenoid pigment found in combined form in certain crustacean shells and bird feathers.

asymmetrical factorial experiment

when number of levels and the factors are not identical or equal.

asymmetry

a molecular arrangement in which each bond of the central element (usually carbon) is attached to different elements or group. This results in three-dimensional optical isomers having mirror-image configurations called enatiomorphs or enantiomers. Carbon is the most common asymmetric element, but the phenomenon also exists with sulphur, nitrogen, cobalt, and others. A compound may contain several asymmetric carbons is 2 to the nth power, where n equals the number of asymmetric carbons. Each isomer displays optical rotation to the left or right under polarized light, a property of many sugars, amino acids, aldehydes, and terpenes. An asymmetric atom is conventionally denoted by an asterisk, for example, C*. It is possible for a molecule to be asymmetric even in the absence of an asymmetric atom, i.e., by having two different organic groups attached to one end of a carbon chains, as in allenes.

atavism
situation in which a genetic trait, evident in a parent organism, is not expressed in the progeny nor in the cimmediate future, but is expressed only in distant generation. The phenomena is understandable as a pattern of inheritance of a recessive gene. The term is now rarely used.

atom percent excess
the concentration of an isotope in a sample of element expressed as the difference between the percent of the atoms existing as the isotope in sample and the percent of the atom existing as isotope in the element found in its natural state.

ATP regenerating system
an enzymatic system for the synthesis of ATP from ADP that is used in cell-free amino acid incorporation experiments for replenishing the ATP that is used up in the course of amino acid activation. The system consists either of phosphocreatine and creatine kinase or of phosphoenolpyruvate and pyruvate kinase.

atractyloside
a glucoside from the Mediterranean thistle Atractylis gummitera. It is a competitive inhibitor of adenine nucleotide binding and transport across the inner mitochondrial membrane.

attached X chromosome
genetic phenomenon in drosophila that segregates as a single gene mutation and involving the failure of the two X chromosomes to separate at meiosis. This means that eggs from affected females carry either two or no X chromosomes. The failure of chromosomes to separate at meiosis is termed as non-disjunction.

attenuation
a regulatory mechanism employed by the bacterial cell. Whereas Enzyme repression allows the cell to respond to extreme concentrations of metabolites, it probably

represents a means of "fine tuning" to relatively mild fluctuations in the concentrations of metabolites.

aurora borealis

a display of mainly red and green light, visible at North and South Poles. It is probably caused by streams of electrified particles from the Sun, most prominent when large Sun spots are observed.

autoantigen

an antigen that is a normal constituent of an individual and that has the capacity of producing an immune response against itself in the same individual.

autoicous

when male and female inflorescences are present on the same plant.

autoimmunel diseases

conditions resulting from a lack of immune tolerance for the organism's own components.

These diseases include neurological conditions like multiple sclerosis, bacterial eye inflammation (ophthalmia sympathica), myasthenia gravis, erythematodes (a skin disease), chronic rheumatism, chronic liver inflammation and certain forms of chronic kidney inflammation.

autoimmunity

a disease state in which antibodies are formed and react against a normal component of the animal's own tissues. Autoimmunity is a contributory factor of a number of diseases (autoimmune diseases), such as rheumatoid arthritis and some forms of gout.

autolytic enzyme

a bacterial enzyme, located in the cell wall that causes disintegration of the cell following injury or death.

autonomic control

regulation of growth and development which may operate spontaneously within the plant itself. Autonomic control is expressed at both the intercellular and intracellular levels.

autoxidation

an oxidation that takes place spontaneously in a substance exposed to air or oxygen at temperatures below 150°C. It is activated by a free radical chain mechanism (autocatalysis) and is characteristic of many hydrocarbons; thus it is supplied to a number of industrial operation in the chemical industry, such as the production of acetone and phenol from cumene. Autoxidation also is responsible, at least in part, for development of its rancidity in food products, the drying of certain types of vegetable oils, the formation of 'gum' in petroleum products, and the deterioration of vulcanized rubber.

auxilliary enzyme

an enzyme that is added to a

reaction mixture to assay a second enzyme that is not readily assayed directly. It converts the product formed by the second enzyme, quantitatively to a substance which can be determined by some analytical method. The entire system is known as coupled assay.

auximone

any of certain growth-promoting substances occurring principally in sphagnum peat decomposed by nitrogen bacteria.

auxin

any organic compound which promotes plant growth along the longitudinal axis when applied to shoots free from indigenous growth-promoting substances.

auxin antagonists

inhibitors of auxins whose effects can be at least party reversed by auxins.

available water

water which given sufficient time, a plant could extract from the soil mass.

avermectin

any of a group of macrocyclic lactones, first isolated from the actinomycete bacterium Streptomyces avermitilis, with activity against helminth parasites. They include the commercially available anthelmintic ivermectin.

avidin

a protein constituting 0.2% of the total protein in egg white; molecular weight is 70,000 daltons; combines firmly with biotin but loses this ability when subjected to heat.

avidity

a term used to describe the total affinity of an antibody for its specific antigen as a summation of all possible binding sites.

avoparcin

a glycopeptide antibiotic produced by a strain of the bacterium Streptomyces candidus. It is active against Gram-positive bacteria and is used in feed for pigs, cattle, and poultry as a growth promoter. Absorption from the gastrointestinal tract is extremely low and most of the drug is excreted unchanged in the faeces. Development of resistance by bacteria is not widespread and there is not cross-resistance with other antibiotics.

axial bond

one of the six bonds parallel to three-fold axis in symmetry in chair form of cyclohexane. Axial bond direction are alternately upwards and downwards, parallel to each other and perpendicular with respect to 'mean' plane of ring, i.e., plane bisecting all C-C ring-forming bonds.

axoplasm

the cytoplasm of the axon. It contains many neurofilaments and microtubules but not the dark-staining Nissl granules seen in the neurone cell body. These axoplasmic structures convey proteins produced in the cell body of the neurone to the peripheral parts of the axon.

8-azaguanine, pathocidin

a purine antagonist which is shown to be identical with pathocidin, in antibiotic from Streptomyces spectabalis. 8-Azaguanine affects many different enzymes of purine metabolism and synthesis. In particular it inhibits translation and causes errors of translation, due to its incorporation into mRNA.

azeotrophe

a mixture of two or more liquids that has a constant boiling point. It is distilled without a change in composition. The boiling point of the mixture is below the boiling point of the component liquids.

azine

any heterocyclic compound of six atoms in the ring, one or more of which is nitrogen, and the ring structure resembling benzene in terms of aromaticity; for example, pyridine is an azine.

azoprotein

a modified protein in which a tyrosine residue has been coupled to an aromatic diazo compound. Diazotization is often employed to form protein-heptan conjugates.

azulene, cyclopentacycloheptene

the parent compound of a group of blue to violet, nonbenzoid aromatics. These compounds are artefacts, however, produced from colourless sesquiterpens, the product lines. The compounds have antiinflammatory properties.

bacitracins

branched, cyclic peptides produced by various strains of Bacillus licheniformis. They are effective against Gram-positive bacteria. It has little antimicrobial activity.

back cavity

widened opening between the inside faces of the two guards cells of a stoma.

back to back emission

once positron has dissipated its energy it interacts with electrons and then annihilated. The mass and energy of the two particles are converted to two gamma rays emitted at 180° to each other.

bacteria

a large and diverse group of organisms, which, in terms of numbers and variety of habitats, includes the most successful life forms. In nature, bacteria are important in the nitrogen and carbon cycles, and some are useful to man in various industrial processes, especially in the food industry. However, there are also many harmful parasitic bacteria that causes dieases such as botulism and tetanus. Bacterial cells are simpler than those of the animals and plants and do not contain complex organelles such as chloroplasts and mitochondria. They may divide every 20 minutes and can thus reproduce very rapidly. They also form resistant spores. Bacteria include all prokarytoic organisms except the blue-green algae, from which they can be distinguished by the latter's ability to photosynthesize aerobically. They include the eubacteria, actinomycete, spirochetes, rickettsiae, slime bacteria, iron bacteria, and sulphur bacteria.

balata

a rubber-like polyterpene of low molecular weight obtained from the latex of tropical trees, especially from mimusops balata.

bacteriochlorophyll

chlorophyll-like compound found in some autotrophic bacteria. It is structurally similar to chlorophyll.

bacteriostat

a substance that prevents the growth and multiplication of bacteria but doe not kill them. The use of such agents to treat infections depends on a component host immune system to kill the organisms. Also, it is essential to maintain an effective concentration of the bacteriostat during the course of treatment or the organisms may recover and resume reproduction.

baert test

a test for reducing sugars in raw sugars made by dissolving approximately 10 g of the sugar in 50 ml of Fehling solution and 2 ml of 1% methylene blue solution. A funnel is placed at the mouth of the flask and the mixture is brought to a boil in 2-3 minutes. The blue colour is discharged if the sample contains more than 0.05% of invert-sugar.

baeyer's test for glucose

1. when a solution containing glucose is boiled with a solution of *o*-nitrophenyl-propiolic, acid in aqueous solution carbonate, indigo precipitates. 2. alkaline potassium permanganate is reduced by glucose to produce a green colour. Several modifications of these reactions have been developed.

balanced chromosome

chromosome having several overlapping inversions which impede recombinations with a homologus chromosome.

bamberger test for *o*-diketones

the addition of potassium hydroxide solution, in the absence of air, to a heated alcoholic solution of the *o*-diketone gives a dark red to black colour, which disappears on shaking in presence of air.

band spectra

in a molecule, ground and excited states are really subdivided into a number of energy sublevels. Such molecular spectra are known as band spectra.

barbache reagent for glycerol

a solution of 0.25 ml phenol in

1 litre water, to which a few drops of saturated solution of ferric chloride are added. It is used in testing for glycerin, which decolourizes this reagent.

barbiturates

a group of drugs that are derivatives of barbituric acid (malonyl urea), so called because it was first prepared on St Barbara's day in the 1863. Barbituric acid itself is inactive. The thiobarbiturates are prepared from thiourea and have sulphur in place of oxygen as the substituent on carbon-2.

Those barbiturates that are, or have been, therapeutically useful exert a depressant action on the central nervous system (e.g., phenobarbitone, amylobarbitone, thiopentone, methohexitone), but stimulant barbiturates have been synthesized. Depressant barbiturates exert sedative, hypnotic, antiepileptic and anesthetic activity. Their uses are sedatives or hypnotics are now largely obsolete, but the longacting ones (e.g., phenobarbitone) remain in use as anticonvulsant drugs in epilepsy, and the short-acting ones (e.g., sodium thiopentone and sodium methohexitone) are used as intravenous anaesthetics. Their main mechanism of action is probably exerted at GABA receptors, where they act to potentiate GABA. The problem with barbiturates that have led to a substantial reduction in their use as sedatives and hypnotics include serious tolerance and drug dependence, and enzyme induction.

base

a base is a substance that:

(i) liberates hydroxyl ions when dissolved in water (Arhenius).

(ii) that liberates negative ions of various kinds in any solvent (Franklin);

(iii) that receives a hydrogen ion (proton) from a strong acid to form a weaker acid (Bronsted-Lowry);

(iv) that gives up two electrones to an acid, forming a covalent bond with the acid (Lewis); Lewis bases are considered hard if they have high electronegativity and are difficult to oxidize and soft if they have low electronegativity and are easily oxidized. These properties relate to the presence or absence of vacant orbitals. Bases react with acids to form salts and water; when the proper proportions are used, neutralization occurs. All bases give solutions having a PH of more than 7.0. the neutral point.

base analogue

a purine or pyrimidine base that is similar in its chemical structure to the normal base occurring in nucleic acids. It may be incorporated into the nucleic acids in place of the normal base e.g., 8-Azoguanine, thiouracil etc.

base composition
the relative amounts of the various purines and pyrimidines in a nucleic acid; generally expressed in terms of mole percent.

baseline resolution
separation at the peak base, that is, no overlap of any peak area.

base pairing
the linking together of the two helical strands of DNA by bonds between complementary bases, adenine pairing with thymine and guanine pairing with cytosine. The specific nature of base pairing enables accurate replication of the chromosomes and thus maintains the constant composition of the genetic material. In pairing between DNA and RNA the uracil of RNA pairs with adenine.

base ratio (base composition)
ratio of the number of guanine and cytosine bases (G+C) to adenine and thymine bases (A+T) in the DNA of a particular organism, or in some sub-fraction of the DNA, such as the mitochondrial DNA or the ribosomal DNA. For any one organism or cell the mount of G will always equal to T, and similarly the sum of A+G will equal T+C. The base ratio is, however, widely divergent. Differences in base composition underlie the differing melting temperatures of different DNA fractions. Due to the frequent variation in the third base of a coding triplet, considerable differences in overall base composition may occur in closely related species.

basic dye
dye (e.g., methylene blue) that specifically stains negatively charged material since the dye carries a positive charge.

bathochrome
atom or group of atoms which, when substituted into molecule or organic compound, shifts its absorption spectrum towards longer wavelengths.

bathochromic shift
presence of double bonds lower the energy required for electronic transition and hence causes an increase in the wavelength at which chromophore absorbs.

bauer test for milk
one drop of a 0.25% aqueous solution of Nile blue sulphate is added to 3 ml of the milk, cow's milk becomes green-blue, while human milk turns violet. On shaking with ether, cow's milk changes to blue, and human milk becomes colourless.

B-chromosomes
extra copies of the normal chromosome or aberrant and supernumary chromosome which is normally heterochromatic.

bdellins
a group of protease inhibitors from the leech. They inhibit trypsin and plasmin, and they

show a strong inhibitory activity towards the trypsin-like protease, acrosin, present in the acrosomes of spermatozoa.

Bechi-Hehner solution

a solution of 1 g silver nitrate in 250 ml ethanol, with the addition of 50 ml of diethyl ether and 0.1 ml concentrated nitric acid. The reagent gives a dark red colour only mixtures if cottonseed oil is present.

Bechmann mixture

an oxidizing reagent consisting of 60 parts (by weight) potassium dichromate, 80 parts concentrated sulphuric acid, and 270 parts water.

bee toxin

a defense secretion which is produced in an abdominal gland of queen and worker bees and delivered by the sting. It contains three types of active principle :

(i) biogenic amines, including histamine, which cause pain and dilate the blood vessels, allowing wider penetration;

(2) biologically active peptides such as Mellitin and apamin, and

(3) enzymes like hyaluronidase and phospholipase A. B. t. is applied intracutaneously or percutaneously for treatment of neuralgias, rheumatism and allergies.

Bellier reagent for wheat

I. a solution of 5 g potassium hydroxide in 15 ml glycerine and 85 ml water. II. A mixture of 100 ml of (I) and 5 ml glycerin. III. A mixture of I part of (I) and 3 parts water. These reagents are used to differentiate starches from various sources by their swelling properties.

bence-jones proteins

the proteins excreted in the urine of patients with multiple myeloma, a malignancy of antibody-producing cells.

benda solution

a mixture of 4 parts of 2% aqueous solution of osmic acid, 15 parts of 1% aqueous solution of chromic acid, and a small amount of glacial acetic acid; used as a fixative.

benedict-hopkins-cole reagent

add 250 ml saturated oxalic acid solution, slowly and with cooling, to 10 g magnesium powder. Filter and acidify with acetic acid, and dilute to 1 litre. This reagent is used to test for tryptophane or proteins yielding. The substance to be tested is mixed with the reagent, and a ring-test is performed with concentrated sulphuric acid. A red-violet ring indicates the presence of tryptophane.

benedict uric acid reagent

a solution of 1g of sodium tungstate and 3 g of arsenic pentoxide in 70 ml water, which is then boiled with 5 ml concentrated hydrochloric acid and made up to 100 ml. This reagent gives a blue colour with solutions containing uric acid, upon the addition of sodium carbonate solution.

benson model
the model of a biological membrane according to which the proteins are largely globular and are located in the interior of the membrane, and the lipids are intercalated into the folds of the protein chains, with the polar portions of the lipid molecules at the exterior surfaces of the membrane.

benzoyl group
the univalent radical C_6H_5 CO-

benzyl group
the univalent radical $C_6H_5CH_2$-

benzylisoquinoline alkaloids
a group of alkaloids found mainly in poppy plants (Papaveraceae). The benzyl substituent on the CI atom of the isoquinoline radical can enter various secondary cyclizations through phenol oxidation.

benzylviologen
low potential electron acceptor and carrier. Oxidised from colourless to pale yellow, reduced from blue to violet. Reduced from very readily oxidised by O_2. It is used either anaerobically or as carrier to O_2 or nonautoxidisable acceptors. Reduced compound used as an electron donor. Reduced by dithionite, borohydride.

berg reaction for aldehyde sugars
the reaction based on the conversion of the aldose into a hydroxy acid by bromine water and then adding berg reagent to produce an intense yellow colour.

beta carotene $C_{40}H_{56}$
a carotenoid hydrocarbon pigment found widely in nature, always associated with chlorophylls; converted to vitamin A in the liver of many animals.

betacyanin
a group of purple plant pigments found in leaves, flowers, and roots of members of the order Caryophyllales.

beta globulin
a heterogeneous fraction of serum globulins containing transferrin and various complement components.

betaines
inner anhydrides of amino acid derivatives containing a hydroxyl attached to the nitrogen atom which split out water with the carboxyl group, thus joining the nitrogen to the carboxyl carbon atom.

betain
an anthocyanin that contains nitrogen and constitute the principle pigment of garden beets.

betalain
the name for a group of 35 red or yellow compounds found only in plants of the family Caryophyllales, including red beets, red chard, and cactus fruits.

betalaminic acid
the skeleton of the betalains. It is biosynthesized from tyrosine via dopa. Boding to various amino acids, such as

cyclodopa or proline, gives rise to the Betacyanins and Betaxanthins.

betanantins

yellow betalain plant pigments with absorption maxima between 474 and 486 nm.

betulinic acid

a pentacyclic triterpene carboxylic acid found in many plants e.g., Gratiola officinalis, Melaleuca spp., various cacti, the bark of Platanus spp. and the bark of the pomegranate tree, Punica granatum.

biennial

a plant that completes its life cycle in two years or seasons. In the first year or season it grows vegetatively and produces food storage organ and flowers in the second year only e.g., radish, cabbage.

bifunctional oligomeric enzymes

the bifunctional enzymes such as tryptophan synthetase of E. coli. This enzyme consists of two proteins designated A and B. Protein A has a molecular mass of 29,500 and consists of one subunit, α. Protein B has a molecular mass of 90,000 and has two pyridoxal phosphate binding sites per mole of B. In the presence of 4M urea solution, protein B dissociates into two β subunits, each containing one pyridoxal phosphate binding site and each having a molecular mass of 45,000. The complete tryptophan synthetase consists of two A proteins and one B protein designated as α_2, β_2. The association of the subunits to form fully active and associated synthetase is greatly increased by the presence of both pyridoxal phosphate and the substrate L-serine.

bile

a complex organic liquid secrted by the liver of vertebrate animals and comprised chiefly of cholic acid and its derivatives. It is a mixture of bile salts, bile pigments, (bilirubin and biliverdin), cholesterol, and traces of other substances. It functions in the body as an emulsifying agent of ingested fats and is stored in the gall bladder. The bile salts aid digestion by facilitating the emulsification of fats, while the bile pigments are merely excretory products, playing no part in digestion.

bile acid

any of the liver-produced steroid acids, such as taurocholic acid and glycocholic acid, that appear in the bile as sodium salts.

bile alcohols

a group of polyhydroxylated steriods which are derived structurally from cholestane. They occur as sulfuric acid esters in the bile of lower vertebrotes.

bile pigments

a mixture of the pigments bilirubin and biliverdin, which are present in bile and colour it yellow, green, or brown, depending on their relative proportions. They are excretory products produced by the degradation of haemoglobin and other haem-containing proteins. When haemoglobin is destroyed in the body the protein portion, globin, is degraded to amino acids, while the porphyrin or haem portion gives rise to the bile pigments. The green pigments biliverdin is the first of the bile pigments; it is easily reduced to the red-brown pigment bilirubin. Bilirubin is the major pigments in human bile, there being only slight traces of biliverdin, which is the chief pigment in the bile of birds. A specific enzyme, biliverdin reductase, catalyzes the reduction of biliverdin to bilirubin. The formation of biliverdin and bilirubin from haem takes place in the reticuloendothelial cells of the liver, spleen, and bone marrow. The pigments are then transported to the liver where they are excreted in the bile into the duodenum. In the intestine, bilirubin undergoes further chemical modification and is secreted in the faeces.

bile salt
the sodium salt of glycocholic and taurocholic acids found in bile.

bilicyanin
a blue pigment found in gallstones; an oxidation product of bilverdin or bilirubin.

biliprotein
the generic name for the organic compounds in certain algae that are composed of phycobilin and a conjugated protein.

biliproteins, phycobilins
chromophores which serve as photosynthetic pigments in the blue bacteria (Cyanophyceae and red algae (Rhodophyta) and are responsible for the colours of these organisms.

bilirubin $C_{33}H_{36}N_4O_6$
an orange, crystalline pigment occurring in bile; the major metabolic breakdown product of heme.

biliverdin $C_{33}H_{34}N_4O_6$
a green, crystalline pigment occurring in the bile of amphibians, birds, and humans; oxidation product of bilirubin in humans.

binding protein
one of several proteins that specifically and reversibly, bind a number of substances e.g., amino acids, sugars, inorganic ions and vitamins. These do not have enzyme activity and are believed to function in the transport of the bound substance.

binomial nomenclature
system of giving two names to an organism. The first name is generic and the second is species. These names are italicized or underlined.

biobenzyllsoquinoline alkaloids
a group of isoquinoline alkaloids with a skeleton

formed by fusion of two isoquinoline units by a phenol oxidation. The curare alkaloids, for example tubocurarine, belong to this class.

biocatalyst

a biochemical catalyst, especially in enzyme.

biochemical lesion

a biochemical alteration, such as the inactivation of an enzyme, that leads to a pathological condition; may be caused by a mutagen, a carcinogen, or other factors.

biochemical marker

a mutable site on a chromosome that when mutated, leads to a specific enzyme defect which can be detected by biochemical means.

biochemical oxygen demand, BOD

refers to the rate at which the oxygen dissolved in water is consumed for the oxidation of organic compounds in the water by microorganisms.

biochrome

any naturally occurring plant or animal pigment, such as chlorophyll, haemoglobin.

biocolloid

a general term including all biochemically active aggregates in the colloidal size range, such as protein macromolecules, nucleic acid complexes, and various coenzymes, bacteria, and viruses.

biodegradability

the susceptibility of an organic material to decomposition as a result of attack by microorganisms. The term is applied especially to detergents and insecticides, which vary widely in this respect. For ecological reasons, a high degree of biodegradation is desirable to minimize the adverse environmental effect of such materials. Sewage is highly biodegradable, and present methods of treatment are based on this property. Phosphate compounds and chlorinated hydrocarbons such as DDT are not biodegradable, and it is largely for this reason that their use is restricted. Biodegrdable plastic containers have been developed to get rid of the solid waste problem.

bioenergetics

the branch of biology dealing with energy transformations in living organisms.

bioflavonoid

a group of compounds obtained from the rinds of citrus fruits and involved with the homeostasis of the walls of the small blood vessels; in guinea pigs a marked reduction of bioflavonoids results in increased fragility and permeability of the capillaries; used to decrease permeability and fragility in capillaries in certain conditions. Also known as citrus flavonoid compound; vitamin P complex.

biogenic amines

refer to a biologically and pharmacologically important

class of compounds characterized by the presence of an amine group. They occur widely in plants and animals. they can be precursors of alkaloids (which is why they are also called protoalkaloids) and hormones. In addition, some are Neurotransmitters or components of phospholipids, vitamins, ribosomes and bacteria.

the biosynthesis and metabolism of the biogenic amines are generally similar. Some B a. are hallucinogens, e.g., mescaline and psilocybin. Many are toxic, cadaverine and putrescene.

biological oxidation-reduction

1. the oxidation-reduction reactions in aerobic cellular respiration whereby nutrients are oxidized in the citric acid cycle, electrons are transported by the electron transport system, and ATP is synthesized through oxidative phosphorylation. 2. Any oxidation-reduction reaction occurring in a living system.

biological value

a measurement of the efficiency of the protein content in a food for the maintenance and growth of the body tissues of an individual.

biomass

the amount of organic substance in living organisms on a given area. The term is used in ecology.

biomaterial

any of the various materials, used either within the body or as a prosthetic device in contact with external tissue under the supervision of a surgeon or dentist. Such materials must meet standards of tissue compatibility, resistance to degradation, toxicity, and functional dependability. Among the materials used are titanium, tantalum, cellulose, graphite, and reprocessed animal bone; alloys (amalgams, stainless steel); many kinds of plastics, including nylon; ceramics, composites, and elastomers of various kinds.

biome

a large community of plants and animals, characterized by its particular type of dominant vegetation and its associated animals e.g., Tropices.

biomolecules

the molecules of organic nutrients and other structural, functional components of living organisms e.g., carbohydrates, proteins, nucleic acids etc.

bionics

the term used for the application of structural and functional principles discovered in organisms to man-made objects, especially in electronics. The goals of the discipline are the optimization of technological processes and the development of new ones.

biophile

any element concentrated or

found in the bodies of living organisms and organic matter; example are carbon, nitrogen and oxygen.

biopolymer, biomacromolecule

a naturally occurring substance which can be regarded as a chain (polymer) of identical or similar subunits (monomers).

synthesis of biopolymers begins with the transfer of an activated monomer to a primer molecule (initiation). It continues with the addition of more activated monomers, one at a time (elongation). At some point the growth terminates, for reasons which have not been entirely elucidated. The biopolymer is not necessarily complete at this point (Post-translational modification); it may be further modified.

biopotency

capacity of a chemical substance, as a hormone, to function in a biological system.

bioregulators

biologically active low molecular weight compounds, either naturally occurring or synthesized, which regulate biosynthetic and/or metabolic system and thus affects the expression of biological response in living tissue.

biosynthesis

production, by synthesis or degradation, of a chemical compound by a living organism.

biosynthesis, biogenesis

the biological synthesis of a compound, i.e., an enzymatic synthesis.

it can occur in vivo, that is, in a living organism or in a cultivated part of it (such as perfused organ), or in vitro, in cell homogenates, extracts, enzyme preparations and reconstituted systems.

The sum of all biosynthesis, in an organism is referred to as anabolism.

biotechnology

the various industrial processes that involve use of biological systems. It includes, but not limited to, the industrial aspects of genetic engineering, fermentation and hybridoma technologies, plants and animals transformations. In broader sense it pertains to studies of relationship between living organisms and machines, especially in terms of physiological, psychological and technological requirements.

biotest, biological assay

refers to a procedure in which the biological activity of a compound is tested by observing its effect on an appropriate organism.

these are frequently used for hormones, inhibitors, and antibiotics. The test objects are usually whole organisms, or isolated organs or tissues, sometimes in tissue culture.

biotin $C_{10}H_{16}N_2O_3S$

a colourless, crystalline vitamin of vitamin B complex occurring widely in nature, mainly in bound form.

biotin carboxylase

in case of prokaryotes made up of three different proteins, two enzymes and a biotin containing coenzyme. Two enzymes are biotin carboxylase carboxyltransferase. It catalyzes the combination of biotin carboxyl carrier protein with CO_2 using ATP yielding 1-N' carboxybiotin carboxyl carrier protein.

bisubstrate reactions

when an enzyme catalyzes reactions with two interacting substances; the enzyme kinetics is more complex than simple one substrate reaction e.g., transferases: Km and Vmax are calculated by keeping one substrate at saturated concentration and 2nd substrate amount is gradually changed. Then 2nd substrate concentration is fixed and Ist taken at different concentration. These may be single or double displacement reactions.

bitter peptides

refers to the bitter tasting peptides that may spoil the palatability of certain foodstuffs, e.g. These sometimes arise during the ripening of certain types of cheese, and they have also been found in fermented soyabean products.

blackman reaction

reactions of CO_2 fixation in the matrix of chloroplasts and do not require light. However, depend upon ATP and $NADPH_2$ produced during light reaction. Here CO_2 is reduced through Kelvin cycle to glucose, fructose etc.

blanching

a term used in the food industry to describe the mild heating of fruits and vegetables at 93-100°C primarily to inactivate enzymes that would cause deterioration or loss of flavour. This process usually precedes canning, dehydration, freezing, and other preservation methods. Notwithstanding the name, it has little effect on colour.

blastomere

any of the cells produced by the cleavage of the zygote, during the earliest stages of embryonic development until the formation of the blastocyst. Blastomeres divide repeatedly without overall growth and so decrease in size.

blocking antibody

1. a protective antibody that prevents anaphylaxis by combining with the allergen; it is formed during desensitization and is primarily of the IgG type. 2. An incomplete antibody that actively inhibits agglutination.

blood (human)

a heterogeneous suspension, considered to be liquid tissue, containing the following:

(i) red cells, or erythrocytes, which contain hemoglobin, an iron-protein complex; they are not actually living cells, but rather are aggregates of haemoglobin, liquids, and water.

(ii) white cells, or leukocytes, which are true biological cells, they contain nucleoproteins and liquids and function as a protective mechanism against infections.

(iii) platelets, made up of cephalin and other proteins, which play a part in blood clotting.

Besides these major components, blood contains many proteins, sugars, cholesterol, fatty acids, and inorganic substances in ionized form. Blood acts in the body as a transport agent for nutrients and for oxygen and carbon dioxide. It is strongly buffered system and maintains a PH of from 7.3 to 7.5. The coagulation mechanism involves protein fibrinogen; serum is the fraction remaining after coagulation.

The blood is the vehicle for metabolic communication between the organs of the body. It transports nutrients from the small intestine to the liver and other organs and transports waste products to the kidneys for excretion. The blood is also the vehicle for transport of oxygen from lungs to the tissues and for the transport of carbon dioxide generated during the respiratory metabolism of the tissue to the lungs for excretion. Moreover, the hormones are transported from the endocrine glands via the blood to their specific target organs, in their function as chemical messengers. The blood in the vescular system of an adult human has a volume of about 5 to 6 litres. Almost half of its volume is occupied by cells, which consists largely of red blood cells (erythrocytes), much smaller number of white blood cells (leukocytes), and blood platelets. The liquid portion is the blood plasma, which is about 90% water and 10% dissolved matter. Over 70% of the plasma solids is constituted by plasma proteins. About 20% consists of organic metabolites, which are passing between various organs, and the waste products urea and uric acid, which passes to the kidneys to be excreted into the urine, the remaining 10% of the plasma solids consists of inorganic compounds.

Some of the blood components normally vary in concentration, depending upon the nature of the nutritional intake. The blood glucose level, for example reaches a maximum just after the meal, especially if it is rich in sugar, and then may decline below the mean level after several hours. Similarly, the blood varies during the period between the meals. The concentrations of the various components of the blood plasma are maintained at characteristic levels by certain regulatory systems.

blood clotting

process in which fibrinogen, a protein present in blood plasma, is acted upon by the enzyme thrombin and, by the removal of a terminal peptide, is modified to form fibrin. This protein is capable of rapid polymerization to form clot. Thrombin is not normally free-by available in blood, but becomes so by the conversion of prothrombin, a process requiring calcium ions a lipoprotein factor released from broken platelets and a special antihaemophilic globulin molecule. Also known as blood coagulation.

blood group antigens

refers to the specific oligosaccharide structures attached to glycoproteins in the membranes of blood cells which are recognized as antigens by the immune systems of other individuals or organisms. The antigens get attached to the protein glycophorin in erythrocytes and to both proteins and lipids in other parts of the body. In humans, five systems of antigens could be identified, the ABO system, the MN, P, rhesus and Lutheran systems. Only the ABO and rhesus systems affect blood transfusions, between humans; the other systems have been identified using animal antibodies against human blood.

blood group substance

a genetically determined particulate isoantigen that is attached to surface of red blood cells and that may be attached to the surface of other cells; related blood group substances represent alternative antigens, specified by allelic genes.

blood serum

blood plasma from which clotting factors, such as blood platelets, have been removed by centrifugation.

blood sugar

the carbohydrate, principally glucose, of the blood.

blotting

any number of techniques whereby chromatographically or electrophoretically separated DNA, RNA or protein molecules can be transferred from the support medium e.g., a gel, to another medium such as filter paper or membrane matrix.

blue-green bacteria, cyanobacteria, blue-green algae, cyanophyta, cyanophyceae

refer to a group of photosynthetic prokaryotic organisms using H_2O as hydrogene donor (Photosynthesis). Many are also able to fix atmospheric nitrogen (Nitrogen fixation). Since they are prokaryotes, they have no nucleus, mitochondria or chloroplasts. There are two major classes of blue-green the chroococcals, in which the cells are solitary (e.g., Anacystis) or colonial, held together by mucoid hulls; and the hormogonals, which grow in filaments (trichomas), often enclosed in a sheath.

blue tetrazolium
an electron acceptor; oxidized form; reduced from (bisformazen) blue to black. Reduced by flavoprotein enzymes, rate increased by intermediate electron carriers such as phenazine methosulphate: Hydrogen acceptor in Hill reaction.

boat form
labile (flexible) conformation in saturated six-membered carbocyclic and heterocyclic compounds, e.g., cyclohexane. In this conformation carbon bond angles maintain value of 109.5°; however, C-C bond system at two pairs of adjacent carbon atoms is ecliptic and repulsion between substituents is observed at 1, 4-flag-pole position.

bolting
in most of biennial rosette plants there is rapid elongation of stem after one season of growth and then plant flower e.g., lettuce, radish.

bone seeker
any element that tends to concentrate in the bones and teeth of animals and men. Most important are calcium, an essential components of bony structure, and fluoride, which in very low concentration (1mg/L) can inhibit tooth decay. Strontium also belongs to this class; the radioactive isotope strontium-90 is extremely dangerous, as it replaces calcium and cause radiation damage in blood- and marrow-forming structure. It occurs in the fallout from atomic bombs, is picked up by vegetation, and finds its way into the body via milk.

bongkrekic acid
the 3-carboxymethyl-17-methoxy-6, 18, 21-trimethyldocosa-2, 4, 8, 12, 14, 20-heptaenedioic acid, M_r 486.61. One of two toxic antibiotics produced by Pseudomonas cocovenenans in spoiled bongkrek (a coconut product consumed in Indonesia). It is an inhibitor of adenine nucleoside translocation and affects carbohydrate metabolism.

boot
the sheath-like leaf structure on the upper end of the grain or grass plants which encloses inflorescence prior to its emergence.

bound auxins
when indole-3-acetic acid or any other auxins get bounded with various types of metabolites. In this form higher level of free auxins is reduced and kept as physiological concentration. Free auxins are released from bound auxins by hydrolysis either enzymologically or

autolysis e.g., Ascorbigen, glucobrassicin and auxin peptides etc.

bound metabolites

the metabolites which are not free, conjugated with other compounds to form physiologically inactive complex.

bovine serum albumin (BSA)

a protein isolated from serum of bovine. Used at 0.1-1.0% in isolation of mitochondria and chloroplast as phenol and quinone absorbent or to bind free fatty acids and inhibit further lipolytic activity.

branched metabolic pathway

a sequence of metabolic reactions that diverges and that can give rise to two or more end products.

branching enzyme

an enzyme which catalyzes the synthesis of branch points in a polymer.

brassinosterone

it occurs most frequently and isolated from 12 sources. It is C-28 compound having a ketone group and are of 6 types.

break point

the water potential of the incubating medium, of the incubating solution of PEG, in which no change in strips dimensions occurs.

brewing

the production of beer and ale be enzymatic conversion of the starches contained in barley malt to wort, or malt extract. This is then hydrolyzed to sugars and proteins by a process known as mushing, followed by boiling with hops and fermentation with yeast. These processes (all of which are of the batch type) involves complex reactions induced by enzymes and require extremely close control and careful selection of ingredients. Barley is the grain chiefly used as a source of malt; its enzymes are activated by controlled cycles of water absorption and aerating, white induce partial germination of the barley. Beer and ale also contain colloidally suspended proteins which cause farming; they are clarified by filtration through adsorptive clays or diatomite.

bromelain

a thiol enzyme (EC 3.4.22.4) from the stems and fruits of the pineapple plant. The stem enzyme is a basic glycoprotein (M_r 33000; IP 9.55) which is structually and catalytically similar to papain%. It is an endopeptidase and is used in protein chemistry to hydrolyse polypeptide chains into large fragments.

bronsted test

to test for tartaric acid, add calcium acetate solution to a 0.15 aqueous solution of the acid. A precipitate of calcium tartrate forms after standing for hours; however a precipitate of calcium racemate appears immediately if 1 drop of an *l*-tartrate solution is added.

brown fat

a type of adipose tissue containing small fat cells with multiple small fat droplets in their cytoplasm. Brown fat tissue is particularly abundant in rodents and in new born and hibernating animals, occurring in various parts of the body, including the axillary and neck regions. Compared to normal white fat, deposits of brown fat are more richly supplied with blood vessels and have a higher proportion of unsaturated fatty acids. They can also be more rapidly converted to heat energy, especially during arousal from hibernation and during cold stress in young animals. Since the deposits are strategically placed near major blood vessels, the heat they generate warms the blood returning to the heart. It is also postulated that brown fat turnover may be used to dispose of excess fat intaken in the food, rather than increasing the whote fat deposits. In this view, highly obese individuals may have a defect in brown fat metabolism.

brucellergen
a nucleoprotein fraction of brucellae used in skin tests to detect the presence of Brucella infections.

budding yeast
type of yeast that can reproduce by budding as well as by sexual means. The common budding yeast used for baking and brewing is Saccharomyces cerevisiae.

bufadienolide
a steroid that is a 24-carbon homologue of a cardenolide and occurs as a cardiac glycoside in plants and toads.

buffer
a solution of weak acid and its salt which resists changes in its pH.

buffy coat
the layer of white cells that is formed between the red cell layer and the plasma, when unclotted blood is centrifuged at moderately lower temperatures.

bufotoxin
the main toxin in the venom of the European toad Bufo vulgaris. M_r 757. It is a steroid derivative.

bulk density
the ratio of weight of water free soil to its bulk volume. It is expressed in pounds per cubic foot or grams per cubic centimetre.

bundle-sheath
the sheath of parenchyma around the vascular bundle of a leaf. The elongated cells conduct materials between the bundle and the leaf parenchyma.

bunyavirus
a family of RNA viruses that have enveloped helical capsids and contain segmented negative-strand RNA. The most notable veterinary example is the agent of Nairobi sheep disease.

buoyancy

the upward thrust exerted upon a body immersed in a fluid, equal to the weight of the fluid displaced.

busch theory

a theory of carcinogenesis that postulates three stages of disease referred to as initiation, promotion, and acceleration. According to this theory a portion of the DNA is responsible for carcinogenesis and is inhibited in normal cells by combination with a suppressor protein. The carcinogen binds to the cancer DNA-suppressor complex in the initiation stages, releases the DNA in the promotion stage and allows it to form cancer RNA in the acceleration stage.

butyric fermentation

type of oxidative fermentation of hexoses, e.g., of glucose, caused by Bacillus butylicus, leading to decomposition of carbohydrate with formation, of *n*-butanol, butyric acid, ethanol, formic acid, acetic acid, lactic acid and carbon dioxide.

butyrinase

an enzyme that hydrolyzes butyrin, found in the blood serum.

buxus alkaloids

a group of steroid alkaloids which are characteristic of plants in the boxwood genus (Buxus).

C-3 photosynthesis or Calvin cycle

in most of the crops which are C-3 plants the Ist product of dark fixation of CO_2 is C_3 compounds i.e., 3-phosphoglyceric acid. CO_2 is accepted by ribulose-1, 5-bisphosphate. Ribulose biscarboxylase/oxygenase catalyses this step.

cachet

any lenticular edible capsule that encloses a dose of medicine.

cadaverine $C_5H_{14}N_2$

a nontoxic, organic base produced as a result of the decarboxylation of lysine by the action of putrefactive bacteria on flesh.

caffeine, 1, 3, 7-trimethylxanthine

a purine derivative which is found in coffee beans and leaves, tea leaves and cola nuts. It is usually produced from tea leaves (1.5 to 3.5% caffeine content) and as a byproduct from the production of caffeine-free coffee.

caine-

a combination form used in naming synthetic alkaloid anesthetics, such as isocaine, metycaine, neurocaine.

calcifuge or calciphobe or calcifobous

plant species which do not thrive on a lime soil. They prefer an acid soil.

calcium

an essential element for animal and plant growth. It is present between plant cell walls as pectate, and is found in the bones and teeth of animals. Calcium ions, Ca^{2+}, are important in triggering muscle concentration where their rapid release from the cisternae of the sacroplasmic reticulum is thought to set off the reaction between ATP and the myofilaments. Calcium is important in resting muscles in maintaining the relative impermeability of the cell membranes. If the calcium concentration falls, the potential difference across the membrane also falls so that muscles may spontaneously contract without activation by acetylcholine, giving twitching and spasms. The concentration of calcium ions is also important in influencing the breakdown of glycogen in muscles. Calcium is important in the clotting of blood in the conversion of prothrombin to thrombin. In mammalian stomach it is also important in precipitating casein from milk.

calcium ion pump

chemical pump, which in some cases is operated by ATPases, that is responsible for:

(a) keeping the calcium concentration of the cytosol lower than the extracellular concentration by a ratio of approximately 10^{-7} M inside to 10^{-3} M outside; and

(b) pumping calcium ions from the cytosol through the sarcoplasmic reticulum of muscle cells to balance the loss of calcium due to nerve impulse depolarization of the muscle cell membranes.

calcium metabolism

biochemical and physiological process involved in maintaining the concentration of calcium in plasma at a constant level and providing a sufficient supply of calcium for bone mineralization.

calibration

the graduation of an instrument to enable measurements in definite units to be made with it.

callose

a carbohydrate component of plant cell walls; associated with sieve plates where calluses are formed.

callose special wall

callose layer deposited around microspores after they have completed meiotic division, and effectively separating them from each other while the pollen grain wall proper is laid down.

calmodulin

a widely distributed intracellular protein that binds calcium ion with high affinity and specificity. It exists as a monomer of molecular weight 17000 daltons. It resembles, but is not identical with, the troponin C of skeletal and cardiac muscle. Binding of Ca^{2+} results in a conformational change which causes the calcium ion-calmodiulin complex to activate a number of cellular enzymes and so modulate a range of cellular functions including secretion, motality, mitosis, cyclic nucleotide metabolism and glycogen metabolism.

caloric value

the quantity of heat that is produced when a foodstuff is subjected to complete oxidation. It is generally expressed in kilocalories per gram.

camphor

a bicyclic monoterpene ketone found widely in plants. It is obtained commercially from camphor trees (Cinnamomum camphora) native to the coastal areas of Eastern Asia. The partial synthesis from pinene is also important, although the product is a racemic mixture used mostly in plastics.

l-canalin

2-amino-4-aminoxy-butyric acid. It is a hydrolysis product of L-Canavanine and is found in a few canavanine-containing legumes.

cancer research

scientific study of :

(1) the factors which lead to the formation of the various malignant tumours.

(2) the continuous growth of the malignant tumours, and

(3) of their inhibition by anti-cancer agents, in order to find effective methods of therapy.

canavanine $C_5H_{12}O_3N_4$

an amino acid found in the jack bean.

cane sugar

sucrose isolated from sugar cane.

canopy structure

amount and organization of aboveground plant material. It includes size, shape, orientation and positional distribution of various plant organs such as leaves, stem, branches, flowers and fruits.

caoutchouc

elastic, high-polymer hydrocarbons (elastomers) which become rubber on vulcanization.

capping

1. concentration of a specific protein at a localized region of the surface of a cell. The process is energy dependent and can be shown, by the use of fluorescent antisera, to commence with generalized binding to all parts of the cell surface, followed by flow of the bound molecules to form a cap or accumulation at one location on the surface. 2. one of the post-transcriptional modifications to much of the hnRNA and mRNA synthesized in eukaryotic cells. Capping consists in the addition of a methylated guanosine residues of the 5'- end of the RNA.

N-caproic acid, decanoic acid

a fatty acid, CH_3-$(CH_2)_8$-COOH. Occurs in milk fat (2%), coconut oil (<1%) and various other seed and essential oils.

capsanthin

a carotenoid pigment isolated from paprika (Capsicum annuum). It is characterized by a terminal five-membered ring.

capsid

the protein coat, composed of capsomers, that surrounds the nucleic acid of a virus and determines the overall shape of the virus.

capsule

(i) a nonliving layer of material, usually polypeptide or polysaccharide, laying outside some bacterial cell wall.
(ii) a fruit type.

caramel

a brown substance of complex composition, formed by the action of heat on sugar or other carbohydrate materials. Its chemical nature is not fully known, and its reactions vary its method of preparation. It is used as a colouring agent for foodstuffs and drinks.

carbamic acid NH_2COOH

an amino acid known for its salts, such as urea and carbamide. Also known as amidocarbonic acid; aminoformic acid.

carbamino

a compound formed by the combintaion of carbon dioxide with a free amino group in an amino acid or a protein.

carbaminohaemoglobin

the carbamino compound that is formed by the reaction of hemoglobin with carbon dioxide and that represents one of the forms in which carbon dioxide is transported by the blood.

carbamyl phosphate $NH_2COPO_4H_2$

the ester formed from reaction of phosphoric acid and carbamyl acid.

carbo-di-imides

water soluble carbo-di-imides are used to modify -COOH of proteins. Reaction is usually performed at PH 4.5-5.0 in the presence of amine. The -COOH group is converted to amide of the added amine. These react at similar rate with -SH group and more slowly with tyrosine -OH.

carbohydrase

any enzyme that catalyzes the hydrolysis of carbohydrates.

carbohydrate

any of the group of organic compounds composed of carbon, hydrogen, and oxygen, including sugars, starches and celluloses.

carbohydrate productivity

amount of carbohydrate produced per square metre of the area on which light is falling. It is equal to carbohydrate assimilation rate into duration of full light interception.

carbohydrates metabolism

the constant formation, transformation and degradation of the carbohydrates in the organism. The most important reactions in carbohydrate metabolism are :
(1) interconversions of the polymeric storage forms (glycogen and starch) and the monomeric transport and substrate form (glucose),
(2) reactions of carbohydrate degradation and

interconversion, and
(3) reactions for the synthesis of glucose from noncarbohydrate substances (glucogenic amino acids, fats). Glucose 6-phosphate has a central position in the entire carbohydrate metabolism.

carbon anhydrase
an enzyme which catalyzes the equlibrium of carbon dioxide with bicarbonate ior in a solution. It is of two types, i.e., stromal and cytosolic present in chloroplast and cytoplasm respectively.

carbon dioxide assimilation
in the narrower sense, the fixation of atmospheric carbon dioxide in photosynthesis. It is part of photosynthesis; it is often incorrectly used as a synonym for photosynthesis.

carbon dioxide reductase
a latent enzyme present in potato tubers and activated by light. It catalyzes the fixation of carbon dioxide, CO_2 in formulate as primary product in potato chloroplast.

carboligase
the enzyme that catalyzes the formation of acetoin from acetaldehyde and active acetaldehyde.

carbonic anhydrase
an enzyme which helps in release and transport of carbon dioxide by catalyzing the synthesis, and the dehydration, of carbonic acid from, and to, carbon dioxide and water.

carboxylase
any enzyme that catalyzes a carboxylation or decarboxylation reaction.

carboxylation
the first step of dark reaction of photosynthesis. Here a 5-carbon compound ribulose 1-5-bisphosphate acts as carbon dioxide acceptor and β-oxido acid is formed. β-oxido acid is a 6-carbon compound and it is hydrolyzed to form two molecules of 3-phosphoglyceric acid.

carboxylation resistance
resistance associated with photosynthetic reactions at CO_2 fixation sites.

carboxylic acids
organic compounds containing the carboxyl group, COOH. Alkane and alkene monocarboxylic acids are also called fatty acids. They are synthesized from activated acid derivatives, such as anhydrides or thioesters (for d le, acetyl-coenzyme A).

caroboxylic esterases
1. a sub-group of esterases acting on carboxylic esters;
2. carboxylesterase, (EC 3.1.1.1), a class of enzymes with wide specificity, usually for a short-chain acid and an alcohol with only one hydroxyl group.

carboxyl transferase
an enzyme which catalyzes the transfer of CO_2 moiety of carboxybiotin to acetyl-coenzyme A and thus malonyl-CoA is formed during palmitate synthesis. It is one of the

active components of acetyl-CoA carboxylase complex.

carboxypeptidase

any enzyme that catalyzes the hydrolysis of a peptide at the end containing the free carboxyl groups.

carcinogenic index

a term used in biochemistry to measure the activity of a carcinogen; equal to 100 A/B, where A is the number of animals bearing a tumour divided by the number of animals living on the day of appearance of the first tumour, and B is the mean time in days of the appearance of tumours.

cardiac glycosides

cardiotoxins in the narrower sense, a group of poisonous vegetable glycosides with specific carniac effects and related chemical structures.

carminic acid

a red glucoside pigment from the scale insect Coccus cacti L. which lives on Central American cacti of the genus Opunita. It is the principle component of cochineal, which was formerly one of the most prized dyes for wool and silk.

carnitine $C_7H_{15}NO_3$

α-Amino-β-hydroxybutyric acid trimethylbetaine; a constituent of striated muscle and liver, identical with vitamin B_T.

carnitine barrier

the limited ability of long chain fatty acids to cross the inner mitochondrial membrane in the form of fatty acyl-CoA, as contrasted with their ability to cross the membrane in the form of fatty acyl carnitine.

carnosine $C_9H_{14}N_4O_3$

a colourless, crystalline dipeptide occurring in the muscle tissue of vertebrates.

carorenoids

a large class of yellow and red pigments which are highly unsaturated aliphatic and alicyclic hydrocarbons and their oxidation products. These arise biogenetically from isoprene units (C_5H_8) and therefore have the methyl branches typical of isoprenoid compounds.

carotene $C_{40}H_{56}$

any of several red, crystalline, carotenoid hydrocarbon pigments occurring widely in nature, convertible in animal body to vitamin A, and characterized by preferential solubility in petroleum ether. Also known as carotin.

carotenoid

a class of labile, easily oxidizable, yellow, orange, red, or purple pigments that are widely distributed in plants and animals and are preferentially soluble in fats and fat solvents.

carotol $C_{15}H_{25}OH$

a sesquterpenoid alcohol in carrots.

carrier gas

an inert gas which pushes the sample through the column. Common carrier gases are helium, nitrogen, argon and argon/methane mixture. It is of ultra high pure grade.

carrier free
a radioactive nucleide that is essentially free of its stable isotopes.

carr-price test for vitamin A
1. on adding 1 ml of the Carr-Price reagent to 0.1 ml of the oil to be tested, a blue colour indicates the presence of vitamin A. 2. Stannic chloride, dissolved in chloroform, gives a deep blue colour changing to purple with vitamin A. 3. Anhydrous ferric chloride, on addition to an oil containing vitamin A, dissolved in chloroform, gives a fluorescent red-violet colour. 4. Powdered anhydrous aluminium chloride gives red-violet colour fading to brown with an oil containing Vitamin A.

casein
a phosphoprotein that is present in milk (as calcium caseinate). It belongs to a group of proteins whose main function is to store amino acids as nutrients and as building blocks for growing animals. It is precipitated from milk by the action of rennin, a process utilized in the manufacture of cheese.

catabolism
the degradative processes by which complex molecules are broken down into simpler ones. Generally energy is released in such reactions e.g., respiration.

catabolism, dissimilation
the sum of all degradative metabolic processes. Amino acids, purines, pyrimidines, etc. formed in the turnover of cell components can be degraded, in some cases to inorganic compounds (water, carbon dioxide, ammonia, etc.). Catabolic processes are linked with the formation of ATP by substrate phosphorylation and respiratory chain phosphorylation. C. is therefore, in a certain sense, identical to energy metabolism.

catabolite activator protein
a dimeric protein in E. coli that binds to, and is activated by, cyclic AMP and that is necessary for the efficient transcription of certain operons which are subject to catabolite repression.

catalase
an enzyme responsible for the breakdown of hydrogen peroxide, which is toxic, to water and oxygen. Its prosthetic group contains iron, and its pH optimum is 6.5-7.0.

catatoxic steroid
a steroid that protects an animal against a drug by stimulating the activity of drug-metabolizing enzymes.

catecholamine
any one of a group of sympathomimetic amines containing a catechol moiety, including especially epinephrine, norepinephrine (levarterenol), and dopamine.

catechol estrogens
2-hydroxylated derivatives of estrogens, are hydroxylated by

the action of the microsomal cytochrome P450 system of the silver. The 2-hydroxyl group then becomes methylated by the action of a methyl transferase and Sadenosyl-L-methionine in the liver cytosol. The corresponding methoxy derivatives are excreted in the urine.

catemer

an oligomeric nucleic acid molecule in which complete genomes are held together in an end-to-end manner by either covalent or noncovalent bonds.

cathepsin

any of several proteolytic enzymes occurring in animal tissue that hydrolyze high-molecular weight proteins to proteoses and peptones.

cation

an ion bearing a net positive charge. It accepts electrons and becomes neutral. It gets accumulated at cathode.

causal analysis, induction

the scientific method of reasoning in which a generalization (subsumptive generalization) is postulated on the basis of previous experiments and verified or falsified through the experimental analysis of a single case derived from it strictly in accordance with the rules of logic.

caustic

a term which has the general meaning of corrosive and is applied to the water-soluble hydroxidase of the light metals to distinguish them from their carbonates. It is also used in medicine to designate substance that destroys body tissues; thus lunar caustic is silver nitrate.

cell

the smallest living unit of an organism. Living organisms are classified as prokaryotic (prokaryotes) or eukaryotic eukaryotes, depending on their type.

cell and tissue culture

a technique of regenerating whole plant from a single cell/ tissue. It includes (i) Establishment of aspetic culture. (ii) Multiplication of callus and differentiation into root and shoot. (iii) Establishment of plants in soil. These techniques are used to multiply and to get disease-free plants.

cell-free amino acid incorporating system

a reconstituted cell-free system for the in vitro study of protein synthesis. It generally consists of ribosomes, messenger RNA (natural or synthetic), transfer RNA, enzymes, amino acids, ATP, GTP, an ATP regenerating system, buffer, and other inorganic and organic compounds.

cell line

a heterogenous groups of cells derived by first subculturing, or at any stage during the serial subculturing, of a primary culture.

cell strains
some primary cultures which are capable of regrowth when cells are reinoculated into fresh medium and may be subcultured several times before becoming moribund. These cells have high degree of fidelity to the *invivo* state.

cell surface antigen
antigen, often a protein or a polysaccharide, inserted into the plasma membrane (or attached to a plasma membrane insert), and protruding from it in such a way as to elicit an immune reaction by non-self immunocopetent cells. Cell surface antigens include histocompatibility antigens, allotypically and idotypically non-self surface immunoglobulins, and blood group antigens such as those derived from H substance or erythrocytes.

cellulase
any of a group of extracellular enzymes, produced by various fungi, bacteria, insects, and other lower animals, that hydrolyze cellulose.

cellulose
a plant polysaccharide built of glucose units liked β-1, 4. The chains are not branched and have M_r between 300 000 and 500 000, corresponding to 3000 to 5000 glucose units.

cell wall
the dead part of cell external to protoplast often thick, inert, elastic and acts as an envelop for the cell. It is made of cellulose. However, hemicellulose, lignin, suberin and cutin are also present in the cell wall: It provides free apparent space for ion absorption. Main function is protection of protoplast.

cell wall yield stress of threshold
difference between water potential of the incubating medium and osmotic potential of the cell.

cembranes, cembranoids
monocyclic diterpenes isolated from several plants, especially from the gums resins of pines. They have also been found in marine coelenterates and insects.

central metabolic pathway
the metabolic pathway composed of the reactions of the citric acid cycle and some of the reactions of glycolysis. The pathway occupies a central position in metabolism, since it can be used either catabolically for the oxidation of metabolites to carbon dioxide and water, or anabolically for the synthesis and inter-conversion of metabolites.

centrifugation
the separation of the components on the basis of their size, shape and density. Here a solution or a suspension is subjected to a centrifugal force to separate the various components.

centrifuge
an apparatus in which suspensions may be rotated at very high speeds in order to separate the component solids by centrifugal force. If different components have different sedimentation coefficients then they may be separated by removing pellets of sediments at given intervals.

centriole
the paired, body found near the nucleus in some motile plant cells and in many animal cells. Similar in structure to a basal body. Thought to be associated with spindle formation.

cephalin
any of several acidic phosphatides whose composition is similar to that of lecithin but having ethnolamine, serine, and inositol instead of choline; found in many living tissues, especially nervous tissue of the brain.

cerebroside
any of a complex group of glycosides found in nerve tissue, consisting of a hexose, a nitrogenous base, and a fatty acid. Also known as galactolipid.

ceroid
a lipid granule that may be formed in an animal, particularly in the liver, as a result of either the injection of oils rich in unsaturated fatty acids or the ingestion of various experimental diets.

ceruloplasmin
a blue, copper-containing glycoprotein found in mammalian blood plasma. It consists of 4 subunits (α_2/β_2) and contain 8 cu^2 + ions per molecule.
it is phylogenetically related to lecease (EC 1.10.3.2) and ascorbic oxidase (EC 1.10.3.3), which are both tetrameric, blue, copper oxidases. C is both a storage and a transport protein for copper (II). It has a central hole in the metabolism of copper-containing enzymes, such as phenol oxidases, and in copper-dependent reactions, for example hemoglobin synthesis. When the organism has no C, as in congenital Wilson's disease copper is deposited in the tissue, which causes death.

chalcone
yellow flavonoid pigment found in plant cell vacuoles and providing colour in many flowers.

chalones
antitemplate substances, tissue-specific; endogenous mitosis inhibitors. These are proteins produced by mature or differentiated cells which inhibit cell division in primordial cells by a kind of negative feedback.

channel protein
a protein capable of mediating passive transport across a biological membrane by forming an aqueous channel through which the solutes of appropriate size and charge

can diffuse.

charged tRNA

a transfer RNA molecule to which an amino acid has been covalently linked; as aminoacyl-tRNA molecule.

charge-relay system

a network of hydrogen bridges in the catalytic centre of chymotrypsin and other serine proteases which is responsible for the high degree of nucleophilicity of the ser_{195}hydroxyl group.

charging

the covalent attachment of an amino acid to a transfer RNA molecule to form an amino-acyl t-RNA molecule.

chase

(i) the effective stoppage of the incorporation of either an isotopes or a labelled compound into a substance by the addition of large amount of either the non-radioactive element or the unlabelled compounds.

(ii) the amount of non-radioactive element or unlabelled compound used to stop the incorporation of an isotope or a labelled compound.

chemical immobilisation

the enzymes are immobilised on the supporting matrix by atleast one covalent bonding between amino acid residues in the active site of the enzyme and the matrix.

chemical potential gradient

ratio between chemical potential and distance. Diffusion of solvent depends on energy gradient. If the gradient is steep down hill diffusion will be rapid. Diffusion will cease when the gradient no longer exists i.e., at equilibrium chemical potential gradient is affected by concentration, pressure, and temperature.

chemical score

a measure of the nutritional quality of a protein based on a comparison of its amino acid composition with that of egg, which has a nearly ideal balance of essential amino acids. The amount of each amino acid in the protein is expressed as a percent of the amount of the same amino acid in egg; the lowest value, or score, is given by the essential amino acid that is limiting for growth and is a measure of the nutritionally quality of the protein.

chemical shifts

in shielded or deshielded nuclei displacement in the spectral lines are known as chemical shifts.

chemiosmotic hypothesis

a hypothesis of the coupling of ATP synthesis to the electron transport system in oxidative phosphorylation. According to this hypothesis, the transport of electrons generates an energy-rich proton gradient across the mitochondrial membrane and the protein motive force associated with this gradient then drives the phosphorylation of ADP to ATP.

chemosterilant

a chemical compound which adversely affects the reproductive ability of an insect exposed to it. Such compounds have been successfully used on both male and female insects of several species, including the screw-worm fly. This method of control may eventually considerably reduce the need for insecticides. The chemicals used so far, are mainly antimetabolites, organo-tin, and boron compounds.

chemosynthesis

1. chemical synthesis.

2. the utilization of inorganic compounds or ions (ammonia, nitrite, hydrogen sulfide, thiosulfate, sulfide, iron(II) or manganese(II) ions) and of hydrogen or elemental sulfur to obtain reducing equivalents and ATP.

chemotherapy

c. was used by its founder, Paul Ehrlich, as "the use of a drug to combat an invading parasite without damaging the host". The term is also used for treatment of cancer with chemicals which are more damaging to dividing cells than to differentiated ones.

chicken pancreas hormone

a polypeptide hormone which occurs in the amide form. It consists of 36 amino acid residues.

chimeric protein

covalently joined proteins from different species; made in response to chimeric DNA.

chip

a common name for an integrated circuit; a single package (a slice of silicon; a Wafer) holdings innumerable microscopic components and used in computers.

chitin

a white or colourless amorphous polysaccharide that forms a base for the hard outer integuments of crustaceans, insects, and other invertebrates.

chitinase

an externally secreted digestive enzyme produced by certain microorganisms and invertebrates that hydrolyzes chitin.

chlorin

one of the basic structures of the porphyrins. Chlorin is 17, 18-dinphyoporphyrin.

chlorobium chlorophyll $C_{51}H_{67}N_4N_4Mg$

either of two spectral forms of chlorophyll occurring as esters of farnesol in certain photosynthetic bacteria. Also known as bacterioviridin.

chlorocruorin

a hemoglobin-like, respiratory pigment of invertebrates that has a molecular weight of 3.5×10^6 and that contains 190 haeme groups per molecule.

chlorocruoroheme

the heme prosthetic group of the chlorocruorins, green respirator pigments of certain invertebrates, such as the annelid spirographs.

chloroethyl choline chloride, abb. CCC, 2-chloroethyl trimethyl ammonia chloride [Cl-CH_2-CH_2-$N^+(CH_3)_{2]}$ C^{1-}

a synthetic growth retardant used on grain to produce shorter, thicker straw and to prevent lodging.

chlorogenic acid $C_{16}H_{18}O_9$

an important factor in plant metabolism; isolated from green coffee beans; the hemihydrate crystallizes in needlelike crystals from water. Also known as 3-caffeoylquinic acid; 3-(3, 4-dihydroxycinnamoyl)quinic acid.

chlorophyll

the generic name for any of several oil-soluble green tetrapyrrole plant pigments which function as photoreceptors of light energy for photosynthesis.

chlorophyllase

(EC 3.1.1.4). A plant carboxy-esterase which catalyses the reversible transformation of chlorophyllides to chlorophyll in the last step of chlorophyll biosynthesis.

chlorophyll$_a$ "core" antenna complex

a special form of chlorophyll, complex which is tightly bound to the reaction centre of photosystem I. It collects and transfers excitation energy to the photochemical centre. Here 70 KD tetramer protein binds with 130 chlorophyll, and 16 carotenoid molecules.

chlorophyll b c_{55} $H_{70}O_6N_4Mg$

an ester similar to cholorphyll α but with a—CHO substituted for a —CH_3; occurs in small amounts in all green plants and algae.

chlorophyll, core antenna complex

a special form of chlorophyll II, complex which is tightly bound to the reaction centre of photosystem I. It collects and transfers excitation energy to the photochemical centre. Here 70 KD tetramer protein binds with 130 chlorophyll and 16 carotenoid molecules.

chlorophyll synthetase

an enzyme which catalyzes the esterfication of propionic acid side chain on ring D of the porphyrin with long chain alcohol.

chloroplasts

the photosynthesis organelles of higher plants. The whole chloroplast is lens-shaped and contains stacks of membranes (thylakoids) embedded in an aqueous phase (stroma). The chlorophyll is embedded in the thylakoids, and here the transformation of light energy to ATP and reductive equivalents (NADPH) occurs (both are required for reduction of CO_2).

chlorosis

condition in green plants in which levels of chlorophyll are reduced, leading to pale green or yellow colour in the leaves. Chlorosis may be caused by a number of factors, including a deficiency of iron, magnesium or copper, poor light conditions or infection with virus or other pathogens.

cholane $C_{24}H_{42}$

a tetracycle hydrocarbon which may be considered as the parent substance of sterols, hormones, bile acids, and digitalis aglycons.

cholate

any salt of cholic acid.

cholecystokinin

a hormone produced by the mucosa of the upper intestine which stimulates contraction of the gallbladder.

choleglobin

combined native protein (globin) and open-ring iron-porphyrin, which is bile pigment hemoglobin; a precursor of biliverdin.

cholera toxin

protein complex (molecular mass about 87,000) that increases adenyl cyclase activity in the gut mucosa, resulting in loss water and ions by the gut epithelial cells into the gut. It is produced by the causative organism of cholera vibrio cholerae.

cholestanol

5-α-cholestan-3β-ol. A zoosterol. It is a 5, 6-dihydroderivative of cholesterol and occurs in small amounts with cholesterol in animal cells.

cholesterol $C_{27}H_{46}O$

a sterol produced by all vertebrate cells, particularly in the liver, skin and intestine, and found most abundantly in the nerve tissue.

cholic acid $C_{24}H_{40}O$

an unconjugated, crystalline bile acid.

choline $C_5H_{15}O_2N$

a basic hygroscopic substance constituting a vitamin of the B complex; used by most animals as a precursor of acetylcholine and a source of methyl groups.

choline acetylase

an enzyme which catalyzes the synthesis of acetylcholine from phosphatidic acid and choline by using ATP.

choline kinase

an enzyme which catalyzes the phosphorylation of choline by using ATP to form phosphatidyl choline.

choline phosphotransferase

an enzyme which catalyses the combination of phosphorycholine with CTP in the presence of Mn^{++} to form CDP-choline and pyrophosphate.

cholinesterase pseudocholinesterase (EC 3.1.1.8)

an unspecific acylcholinesterase which hydrolyses butyrol and propionoyl choline much faster than acetylcholine. C is found primarily in the serum of the liver and pancreas. It is also found in cobra venom.

choline sulphatase

an enzyme which catalyzes the hydrolysis of choline sulphate to choline and free sulphate ions.

chondrin

a horny gelatinous protein substance obtainable from the collagen component of cartilage.

chondroitin

a nitrogenous polysaccharide occurring in the cartilage in the form of condroitinsulfuric acid.

chondroitin sulfate

a water-soluble mucopolysaccharide found in animals. Chondroitin A and C consist of equimolar amounts of D-glucuronic acid and N-acetyl-D galactosamine linked in alternating β-1, 3 and β-1, 4 bonds; they differ in the position of the sulfate ester.

chondromucoid

a mucoid found in cartilage; a glycoprotein in which chondroitinsulfuric acid is the prosthetic group.

choriogonadotropin, placental gonadotropin, human chorionic gonadotropin, abb. hCG

the most important hormone formed in the placenta during pregnancy. It is a glycoprotein containing about 30% carbohydrate and an α-and β-polypeptide chain of 92 and 139 amino acids, respectively.

christensen reagent for quinine

a solution of 1.0 g iodine in a mixture of 1.0 g, 50% hydriodic acid, 0.8 g sulphuric acid, and 50 g 70% ethyl alcohol. This solution is used as a test reagent for quinine. Characteristic coloured crystals are obtained.

chromatid

one of a pair of replicated chromosomes found during the prophase and metaphase stages of mitosis and meiosis. During mitosis, sister chromatids remain joined by their centromer until anaphase. In meiosis it is not until anaphase II that the centromer divides, the chromatids being termed daughter chromosomes after separation. Although in most cells chromatids are only visible during mitosis or meiosis, the two sisters copies will be present in the cell following DNA replication at the S phase of the cell cycle.

chromatin

the stainable material of the interphase nucleus, consisting of the uncoiled chromosomes (DNA).

chromatin-positive

descriptive of an individual whose cell nuclei exhibits the highly compacted X chromosomes called the barr body. Normal females in the human are chromatin-positive.

chromatophore

any pigmentary cell or colour producing plastid, such as those of the deep layers of the epidermis; a chlorophyll-containing granule in certain bacteria. The chromatophores are molecular aggregates that can be isolated from photosynthetic bacteria and contain the photosynthetic pigments of the cell.

chromium, Cr.

an essential dietary constituent for animals. Cr is known to be a constituent of glucose tolerance factor (GTF), a water-soluble, relatively stable organic complex of Cr, with M_r about 500, which is essential in animals and humans for normal glucose tolerance. The earliest symptom of Cr deficiency is impaired glucose tolerance. More severe deficiency leads to glycosuria, fasting hyperglycemia, impaired growth, shortening of life span, cases of diabetes refractory to insulin may be the result of Cr deficiency.

chromomere

granular complex of condensed chromatin seen in the relatively uncoiled chromosomes of the leptotene and zygotene stages of meiosis.

chromoplast

a chromatophore filled with carotenoids, and therefore red-orange to yellow in colour.

chromoproteins

a class of protein substances characterized by being coloured. The prosthetic group is a coloured compound in such cases. Haemoglobin and hemocyanin are the best known examples of this class of proteins.

chromosomal walking

a tecnnique for mapping and sequencing a chromosome. Here large restriction fragments are produced and a single point is identified; new probes are synthesized from sequences of the same fragment that are adjacent to the starting point. The procedure is used repetitively, working toward the ends of the chromosomes away from the starting point.

chromosome

a thread like structure made up of nucleohistone, DNA and is bearer of the hereditory material. Chromatin is isolated from chromosomal preparation.

chromosome loss

process in which, following formation of artificial cell hybrids, chromosomes are spontaneously lost. Such loss may also occur spontaneously at a very low incidence in normal cell division.

chromosome rearrangment

chromosomal aberration that involves novel association of sequence due to inversion of translocation.

chyle

the lymphatic fluid is taken up by the lymph vessels from the intestine during digestion and that is characterized by its high content of fat globules.

chyme

the semifluid mass of partially digested material that is passed from the stomach into the intestine.

chymopapain (EC 3.4.22.6)

an enzyme from the latex of the papaya tree. It is made up of several equal sized segments (C A and B, M_r 35000).

chymotrypsin

proteloytic enzyme found in mammalian gut. Chymotrypsin consists of a single small polypeptide (molecular mass ~ 21, 600) comprising 245 amino acids. It has been studied in great detail by several techniques including X-ray crystallography. The amino acid sequence is known, the active site has been mapped and substrate specificity established with considerable precision. Amino acid residues involved in catalysis has been identified, and chymotrypsin strands out as one of the best understood of all enzymes in terms of its mechanism of action at the molecular level.

cinchona alkaloids

a group of about 30 alkaloids from the bark of tropical trees, especially Cinchona succiruba. They are included among the indole alkaloids on account of their precursors, although the main representatives have a quinoline structure. Cinchona, the dried bark, contains 7 to 10% alkaloids. The main alkaloid is quinine which makes up 5 to 7% secondary alkaloids including quinidine, epiquinine and epiquinidine. Other important C. a. are cinchonine, and its stereoisomers, and cinchonamine.

cinnamic acid 2-hydroxylase

an enzyme which catalyzes the formation of *o*-coumarate from cinnamate during synthesis of secondary product derived from phenyl propanoids.

cinnamic acid 4-hydroxylase

an enzyme which catalyses the conversion of cinnamate to para-coumarate during synthesis of secondary products derived from phenyl propanoids. Its activity is photocontrolled.

circular deoxyribonucleic acid

a single or double-stranded ring of deoxyribonucleic acid found in certain bacteriophages and in human wart virus. Also known as ring deoxyribonucleic acid.

circular DNA

a DNA molecule that has a closed ring type structure, not necessarily that of a geometric circle.

cirrhosis

disease of the liver in which fibrous connective tissue proliferates all the expense of the hepatocytes, often as a consequence of insult to the liver cell by alcohol or other poisons.

citral

a doubly unsaturated monoterpene aldehyde. A mixture of the cis and trans isomers is a component of many essential oils.

citramalase

an enzyme that is involved in

fermentation of glutamate by Clostridium tetanomorphum; catalyzes the breakdown of citramalic acid to acetate and pyruvate.

citrate

a salt or ester of citric acid.

citric acid

a colourless crystalline or white powdery organic, tricarboxylic acid occurring in plants, especially citrus fruits, and used as a flavouring agent, as an antioxidant in foods, and as a sequestering agent; the commercially produced form melts at 153°C.

citrostadienol

4α-methyl-5α-stigmasta-7, 24(28)-diene-3B-ol, a phytosterol. It is found in the oils of grapefruit and orange peels. It is also considered one of the tetracyclic triterpenes and is an intermediate in the synthesis of sterols.

civetone $C_{17}H_{30}O$

9-Cycloheptadecen-1-one, a macrocyclic ketone component of civest used in perfumes because of its pleasant odour and lasting quality; believed to function as a sex attractant among civet cats.

class

taxonomic group which includes one or more orders and is a subdivision of a phylum. Thus insecta is a class of Anthropoda.

clarification

removal of colloidally dispersed solids from a liquid either by coalescence and sedimentation or by adsorption on active material surfaces. For example, aluminium sulphate causes flocculation and settling of solid particles in purification of potable water; finely divided clays, carbon and certain proteins effect clarification of vegetable oils, sugar solutions, beverages. The operation is sometimes called decolorization.

clenbuterol

a selective agonist for β_2 adrenergic receptor that acts on smooth muscle in the bronchi, uterus, and skeletal muscle vasculature, causing muscle relaxation at these sites; it has no significant effects on the heart.

clinical chemistry

clinical chemical laboratory diagnostics, part of clinical and medical biochemistry. Their results are important for the diagnosis, therapy and prophylaxis of diseases.

clone

(i) a group of individuals developed from the same stock. From such clone new individuals are propagated vegetatively, usually by stem cuttings or multiplication or bulbs or tubers.

(ii) a family of cells of genetically identical constitution derived asexually from a single cell by repeated division.

cloning vector

unlimited production of any particular fragment of DNA by

introducing vector or carriers DNA in a suitable host cell, where it is replicated as the cell grows and divides.

clupeine

a protamine found in salmon sperm, mainly composed of arginine (74.1%) and small percentages of threonine, serine, proline, alanine, valine, and isoleucine.

coacervation

the process of producing, by coagulation of a hydrophilic sol, of a liquid phase, which often appears as a viscous drops, instead of forming a continuous liquid phase, e.g., during salting out with electrolytes. One constituent of separated phase is a concentrated sol, and the other, a dilute soil.

coadaptation

interaction between different genes or alleles of genes that optimizes fitness. The selection of such harmoniously interacting genes leads to their becoming established in a population.

cobalt co.

an important bioelement which is present in traces in plants, animals and microorganisms. The ligands in cobalt complexes in living cells are often the corrin ring system of vitamin B_{12}, benzimidazole or sugar components. As a component of certain coenzymes, Co. is also required for the symbiotic fixation of atmospheric nitrogen. Traces of Co. are required for microbial growth. Co. can also serve as cofactor of several enzymes, e.g., in pyrophosphatases, peptidases and arginase.

cobamide

the conenzyme form of vitamin B-12 in which a 5' - deoxyadenosyl group is attached to the sixth coordination position of the cobalt atom.

cocaine

an alkaloid derived from the leaves of the coca plant, Erythroxylon coca. It can be used as a local anaesthetic, but such use is greatly restricted because of its addictive properties in humans. In animals it was formerly administered topically in the eye or on mucous membranes. Due to its sympathomimetic activity it constricts small blood vessels at the site of application and causes dilation of the pupil. It may also produce clouding of the cornea and is more irritant than agents now in use.

cocarboxylase

obsolete term for the prostheic group of the decarboxylating yeast enzyme pyruvate decarboxylase.

cocktail

(i) the mixture of reagents required for the cell free amino acid incorporating system; excludes the mRNA, ribosome and enzyme fractions.

(ii) the solution of fluors used

for liquid scintillation counting.

coding ratio
the ratio of the number of nucleotides in a messenger RNA molecule to the number of amino acids in the polypeptide chain that is coded for by the messenger RNA; the number of nucleotides in a codon.

coding sequence
that portion of a gene which directly specifies the amino acid sequence of its protein product. Non-coding sequences of genes include control regions, such as promotors, operators, and terminators as well as the intron sequences of certain eukaryotic genes.

coding strand
the strand of double stranded DNA that serves as template for transcription i.e., sense strand.

codogenic strand
the strand of a DNA double helix from which the genetic information is transcribed onto RNA.

codon
the nucleotide triple in a mRNA molecule, that is responsible for the incorporation of a specific amino acids into an polypeptide. It is universal, unambiguous, commaless, degenerate; third base is less specific than the first two. There are 64 codons.

codon code triplet
the linear sequence of three adjacent nucleotides in RNA which specify a particular amino acid.

coefficient of solar energy utilization
the ratio of the energy fixed in plant dry weight to the incident solar energy. This coefficient indicates how economically a stand uses the solar radiation available during an interval between two harvests.

coenzyme
the nonprotein portion of an enzyme; a prosthetic group which functions as an acceptor of electrons or functional groups.

coenzyme A $C_{21}H_{36}O_{16}N_7P_3S$
a coenzyme in all living cells; required by certain condensing enzymes to act in acetyl or other acyl-group transfer and in fatty-acid metabolism. Abbreviated CoA.

coenzyme Q_{10}
an electron-carrying coenzyme active in the electron-transport chain. Coenzyme Q_{10} serves as an acceptor of electrons not only from NADH dehydrogenase, but also from the flavin components of succinic dehydrogenase, glycerol phosphate dehydrogenase, and fatty acyl-CoA dehydrogenase.

cofactor
a non-protein substance that helps an enzyme to carry out its activity. Cofactors may be cations or organic molecules, known as coenzymes. Unlike enzymes they are, in general, stable to heat. When a catalytically active enzyme

forms a complex with a cofactor a holoenzyme is produced. An enzyme without its cofactors is termed an apoenzyme. Cofactors include metal ions, coenzymes and prosthetic groups. Prosthetic groups remain attached to the enzyme during the complete catalytic cycle, whereas coenzymes must be dissociated from the enzyme in order to function.

cognate tRNA

transfer RNA recognized by a particular aminoacyl-tRNA synthetase.

coherent

intermolecular attraction between similar molecules in the liquid state, i.e., water-water attraction.

coiled coil

structure found in proteins such as keratin, myosin and fibrin in which the alpha-helix is itself further coiled, usually by the interwining of two or more individual α-helices. Nucleic acids can also adopte a coiled coil configuration.

colchicine

an alkaloid, obtained from the autumn crocus, Colchicum autumnalem, that has antimitotic properties. It acts as anti-inflammatory agent in gout arthritis and may occasionally be used in cancer therapy. Colchicine is a mitotic poison, inhibiting aggregation of microtubules to form the mitotic spindle. It is widely used to yield a large number of cell in mitosis by mitotic arrest (since the cells cannot progress beyond metaphase) and has also been used to produce polyploid varieties in horticulture. Colchicine binds to microtubular proteins within cells causing disruption of the mitotic spindle and microtubular structures. Apart from interfering with cell division, this prevents the release of histamine-containing granules from mast cells, inhibits insulin secretion from pancreatic cells, and inhibits the movement of melanin granules in melanophores.

colchicum alkaloid

a group of Isoquinoline alkaloids in which the nitrogen is present as a substituted amino group on a tricyclic skeleton.

these are biosynthesized via a 1-phenylethysoquinoline alkaloid from which androcymbin is formed by hydroxylation, methoxylation, attack of phenol oxidase and oxidative couplings. Androcymbin is then converted to demecolcine and further to colchicine.

cold hemagglutinin

a hemagglutinin that causes agglutination of red blood cells at lower temperatures but leads to their dispersion at higher temperatures.

colineariry

the order of amino acids in a polypeptide chain corresponds

to the order of nucleotides in the gene sequence that specifies its structure. Although originally an hypothesis, it is now so strongly supported by observation (such as the correspondence between the position of an altered base in a DNA sequence and the position of a new amino acid in the protein sequence, e.g., in sickle cells globine) that it is regarded as a rule. Because of the existence of intron sequences within eukaryotic genes, however, the genetic code should be understood as an interrupted linear code rather than a simple colinear one.

collagen

a protein occurring in the connective tissue of the body, having a fibrous polypeptide chain comprised of many amino acids; possesses the unique property of shrinking in hot water within a specific temperature range from 62-65°C. This behaviour is a critical factor in leather tannage, for leather, the shrinkage temperature increase within the extent of tannage. In addition to leather, it is used to some extent in the manufacture of animals glues and in many medical applications such as dialysis membranes, sutures, etc. Collagen is converted into gelatin by hydrolysis, after purification it is used as a protective colloid and gel-former in food products, for sausage casings, and for coating photographic film. Collagen is synthesized, primarily by fibroblasts, as tropocollagen (molecular mass ~360,000; length ~ 280 nm). About one-third of the molecule is glycine and about one-third is glycine and about one-third is proline or hydroxyproline. The secondary structure of collagen is a triple helix. The macromolecule polymerizes to form native collagen fibres which have a repeat period of 70 nm due to the overlapping arrangement of the collagen macromolecules. Collagen contains about 35% glycine, 11% alanine, 12% proline, and small percentages of other amino acids. Collagen is chemically inert which suggests that its reactive side groups are immobilized by ionic bonding. Collagen fibrils are highly complex and have a variety of orientations depending on the biological function of the particular type of connective tissue. The secondary structure of collagen is that of a triple helix of peptide chains. Its tertiary structure is of three alpha helices in a 'super helix', which is responsible for its role in support tissues.

collagenase

a proteolytic enzyme, the only enzyme capable of degrading native collagen to soluble, low-molecular weight peptides.

colligative properties
the properties of a solution which depend only on the number of solute particles in a given amount of solution. Due to the presence of solute, freezing point is depressed and boiling point is alleviated.

column capacity
the amount of solute, which can be loaded on a column, resolved efficiently by a column. It depends upon length and width of the column.

column chromatography
a chromatographic procedure in which a sample dissolved in a small amount of solvent is placed on the top of a chromatographic column. In the course of the elution process, the different materials in the sample separate out on the column as discrete bands. The chemical nature of both the sorbent and the eluting solvent exert primary control over the degree in which individual mixture components are retained on the column.

comicellization
the solubilization of an insoluble or a slightly soluble compound through the formation of a mixed micelle that consists of the compound and of an amphipathic compound. The process occurs at concentrations of amphipathic compound which are considerably below its critical micelle concentration.

command voltage
the selected voltage that maintains a fixed membrane potential in the voltage clamp technique.

commensalism
the close spatial coexistance of two organisms of different species which is neither beneficial for the partners (commensals), as in symbiosis, nor detrimental to either partner, as in parasitism.

compatible
mixable in the formulation or in the spray tank for application together in the same carrier without undesirably altering the separate effects of components.

compensator gene
gene present on the X chromosome of Drosophila, which in the female reduces the activity of other sex-linked genes that she possesses in double dose. No X chromosome interaction occurs in Drosophila. Since the male only possesses one X-chromosome, no active on the part of the compensator gene is necessary.

competition
the attempt by neighbouring plants to utilise the same unit of light, water, mineral nutrients or space.

competitive enzyme inhibition
prevention of an enzymatic process resulting from the reversible interaction of an

inhibitor with a free enzyme.

competitive inhibition
enzyme inhibition in which the inhibitor competes with the natural substrate for the active site of the enzyme; may be overcome by increasing substrative concentration.

competitive inhibitor
an inhibitor that produces competitive inhibition and that generally bears a structural similarity to the substrate of the inhibited enzyme.

complementary base sequence
the sequence of bases in a single-stranded molecule of DNA or RNA that is precisely complementary to that on another single strand and therefore capable of specific hybridization to it with consequent hydrogen bonding.

complementary bases
bases that normally pair up when DNA or RNA adopts a double-stranded configuration. Guanine pairs with cytosine, and adenine with either thymine or uracil (depending on whether DNA or RNA is involved), the former pair having three hydrogen bonds between the bases, and the latter two pairs having only two hydrogen bonds between the bases.

complementary colour or primary colour
refers to yellow, red and blue that in mixture give other colours.

complementary genes
non-allelic genes that complement one another in their expression in the phenotype. This may occur in either the dominant or recessive condition. When dominant complementarity is involved, the dominant alleles of two or more genes are essentially involved in the expression of some trait (e.g., the ability of an organism to synthesize a complex molecule. In the case of recessive complementarity, the trait is only apparent in the homozygous double recessive since the dominant expression of either gene will prevent expression.

complementation test
a test for determining whether the mutations of two mutan chromosomes occurred in the same gene so that complementation between the gene is possible; performed by introducing the two mutant chromosomes simultaneously into the same cell.

complement binding reaction
the binding of the Cl component of complement to the Fe fragments of antibodies which are bound to the surface antigens of erythrocytes or bacteria. The complement system is activated by this step.

complete randomised design (CRD)
experimental design where treatments are applied to

experimental unit in complete random way. It is used when material is homogenous and treatments are less than six. It is less accurate.

complex I
one of the four complexes derived from the electron transport particles that, by itself can catalyze the oxidation of NADH by coenzyme Q.

complex II
one of the four complexes derived from electron transport particles that, by itself, can catalyze the oxidation of reduced coenzyme Q by cytochrome C.

complex III
one of the four complexes derived from electron transport particles that, by itself, can catalyze the oxidation of reduced coenzyme Q by cytochrome C.

complex IV
one of the four complexes derived from electron transport particles that, by itself, can catalyze the oxidation of reduced cytochrome c by molecular oxygen.

composite transposon
DNA sequence flanked by insertion sequences which facilitate its transposition.

computer language
a computer programming systems: a set of conventions specifying how to instruct a computer what to do.

concentration polarization
it happens when protein solution is concentrated beyond a certain limit. In this the protein concentrates at the membrane surface, which reduces the solute flux and makes recovery of the protein fraction difficult. It can be minimised by placing a stirrer or agitator just above the membrane.

concentration variables, fundamental variables, primary variables
those substances in an enzymatic system whose concentration can be directly controlled by the experimenter, for example the substrates, products and effectors.

conceration
when in a chemical reaction formation and breaking of bonds are occurring simultaneously.

conchiolin
a nitrogenous substance that is the organic basis of many molluscan shells.

configuration
arrangement in space of substituent groups in stereoismores. Such structure cannot be interconverted without breaking one or more covalent bond.

conglutinin
a protein that is present in normal serum and that causes the agglutination of antigen-antibody-complement complexes; conglutinin is not an antibody.

conjugase
any of a group of enzymes which catalyze the breakdown

of pteroylglutamic acid.

conjugated auxins
when auxins bind with glucose, amino acid to form glucosyl ester, or peptide respectively. There are physiologically inactive.

conjugated cytokinins
ribosides and ribotides of cytokinins and are physiologically less active.

conjugated phenols
the phenols which are combined with a non-phenolic compound.

conjugated protein
a protein combined with a nonprotein group, other than a salt or a simple protein.

conserved sequence
a base sequence in a nucleic acid (or amino acid sequence in a protein) that has changed only slightly in the course of evolution.

constitutive enzymes
when a set of enzymes is present throughout the life cycle of a plant, although operating at different rates at various phases e.g., carbon reducing enzymes of photosynthesis and respiratory enzymes.

constitutive mutation
a mutation that results in extensive synthesis of an inducible enzyme in the absence of an inducer and that involves an alteration in either the operator or the regulator gene of the enzyme.

contamination
(i) the mixing of an impurity, such as heavy metal ion or radioactive substance.
(ii) an impurity that is present in the sample.

continuous buffer system
during electrophoresis when the buffer present in both reservoirs is normally the same buffer which is used to saturate the supporting medium.

continuous transpiration rate
continuously rate of transpiration is monitored to avoid errors due to short term changes in environmental conditions. It is determined by gasometric methods using transpiration chambers, IRGA or psychrometer or hygrometers to detect humidity changes.

contractile proteins
proteins, present in plant cells, involve in streaming of cytoplasm in several systems. When such proteins e.g., Actin and myosin like are present in sieve elements due to persistaltic movement of these contractile proteins and material may be transported.

control
(i) untreated plants in an experiment.
(ii) exercise of restraint of control upon. It is wide in scope than regulation.

convection
transfer of heat by mass movement of air usually vertically, such as the heat flows away from a hot radiator.

Cook's formula
a relationship for calculating the acetyl number of an organic substance from the saponification titers before and after acetylation. It is equal to their difference, divided by a correction factor that approaches unity as the initial saponification value decreases.

cooperative feedback inhibition
the feedback inhibition of an enzyme that is produced by two or more end products such that the inhibition caused by a mixture of two end products present together is greater than that caused by either end product present alone at the same total specific concentration (i.e., the concentration relative to the inhibitor constant).

cooperativity
this is displayed by oligomeric or monomeric enzymes which possess more than one binding site for a certain ligand. The cooperative binding may be negative or positive, and it may occur for the same ligand (homotropic cooperativity) or for a different ligand (heterotropic cooperative).

coordinated enzyme
enzymes of a metabolic pathway that retains a constant concentration ratio with another enzyme whatever the degree of induction or repression of the pathway. Coordinated enzymes synthesis is associated with those bacterial enzymes produced from a common messenger RNA molecule transcribed from a cluster of genes in an operon.

copolymer
a polymeric molecule containing more than one kind of monomer unit. An example would be a synthetic polynucleotide obtained by incubation of two or more nucleoside di- or triphosphates with the appropriate polymerase. Using RNA polymerase, khorana was able to synthesize C. according to the following scheme (the choice of starter molecule was arbitrary and could be varied according to need) :

RNA polymerase
AUGAUGAUG....

copper cu
an important bioelement in plants and animals, which is frequently involved in electron transport processes in membranes and particles (mitochondria). In plants, Cu is necessary for the synthesis of chlorophyll and is a component of a number of enzymes, such as cytochrome oxidase, ascorbic acid oxidase, tyrosinase and monophenol monoxygenase.
the blood contains a number of copper proteins. The synthesis of hemoglobin is dependent on Cu, although it does not contain the metal.

copper number
an expression of the quantity of a reducing carbohydrate, in terms of the number of milligrams of metallic copper required for reduction of that quantity of Fehling's solution, which is reduced by one gram of the sample.

copper proteins
metalloproteins, often blue in colour, which usually contain a mixture of mono and mostly divalent copper in their molecules.

coprecipitation
when impurities present in salt get precipitated with the precipitation of mineral. The precipitated element is solubilised. It is a method of purification.

core enzyme
1. the portion of the enzyme RNA polymerase that consists of an aggregate of five subunits and that possesses catalytic activity, but that requires the attachment of the sigma factor before it can recognize an initiation site of transcription.
2. the smallest aggregate of DNA-dependent DNA polymerase that has the enzymatic activity.

core particles
the particles released from chromatin by partial enzymatic digestion. They contain about 140 base pairs of DNA and 2 molecules each of the "inner histones" H2A, H2B, H3 and H4.

corepressor
a small molecule that combines with an aporepressor to form an active repressor which binds to the operator and inhibits transcription in enzyme repression. It is generally either the end product of the enzymatic reaction or a compound that is structurally similar to the product.

corrinoids
the chemical compounds based on the corrin ring, which is similar to the porphyrin ring. It consists of four pyrrole rings linked in a large ring. Three of the links between pyrroles are methenyl groups; the fourth is a direct bond between the two pyrroles. The pyrroles carry acetate, propionate and methyl substituents.

corrin ring system
the ring structure of vitamin B-12 in which a cobalt atom is chelated.

cortexone, reichstein's substance Q, 11-deoxycorticosterone abb. DOC
21-hydroxypregn-4-ene-3, 20-ditone. A mineralocorticoid hormone from the adrenal cortex. Its acetetate or glucoside is used in treatment of Addison's disease and of stock. It is biosynthesized from progesterone, which can also be converted into C. by partial synthesis, or microbiologically.

corticosteroid
1. any steroid hormone

secreted by the adrenal cortex of vertebrates. 2. any steroid with properties of an adrenal cortex steroid.

corticosterone $C_{21}H_{30}O_4$

a steroid hormone produced by the adrenal cortex of vertebrates that stimulates carbohydrate synthesis and protein breakdown and is antagonistic to the action of insulin.

corticotropin

a hormonal preparation having adrenocorticotropic activity, derived from the adenohypophysis of certain domesticated animals.

cortisone

a steroid hormone, closely related biochemically to hydrocortisone and corticosterone, found in extracts of adrenal tissue. One of the first adrenal steriods to be isolated and synthesized, it has potent glucocorticoid activity and some mineralocorticoid action; it acts after being converted to hydrocortisone in the body.

cortisone, reichstein's substance F, kendall's substance E

11-dehydro-17 α-hydroxycorticosterone, 17 α, 21-dihydroxypregn-4-ene-3, 11, 20-trione. A glucocorticoid hormone from the adrenal cortex. Like cortisol, it stimulates the formation of carbohydrate from proteins, promotes glycogen storage in the liver and raises the blood sugar level. It is biosynthesized from cortisol by enzymatic dehydrogenation of the 11 β-hydroxyl group. It can be obtained by partial synthesis from other pregnase compounds, bile acids and steroid sapogenins.

cosmides

the vectors for transforming insert of about 40 KD in length. These contain cos sites plus essential features of a plasmid and several unique restriction sites for insertion of DNA to be cloned.

co-transduction

transducing phages carry some host DNA either in place of the phage genome or integrated within it. Two host genes are said to undergo co-transduction if they are both transferred with the same phage particle. Co-transduction frequencies are used for mapping genes.

co-transmitter

a substance that is released from a nerve ending by nerve impulses along with the main transmitter, and that serves to modulate the efficiency of the main transmitter. Many central axon, in addition to the main transmitter, contain one or more polypeptides that may function in this way, and it has been proposed that ATP or neuropeptide Y may serve a co-transmitter function in some noradrenergic nerve fibres.

cot value

product of the mole

concentration of nucleotide residues and time of renaturation (in seconds).

cotyledons

in most of the dicots seed reserve food material is stored in bulky tissue. In many cases these become first leaf structure and in others just storage organ. During germination either cotyledons remain under the soil or come out of the soil. The former is due to elongation of hypocotyl and in latter one epicotyl elongates.

coupled mitochondria

when isolated mitochondria show oxidative phosphorylation i.e., electron transport and ADP phosphorylation are joined together such that one cannot occur without the other.

coupled pump

a pump for the transport of one solute across a membrane that also derives the transport of a second solute across the same membrane in the opposite direction and in such a fashion that the transport of the second solute is physically dependent on the pump.

coupled reactions

these are endergonic and exergonic reactions linked energetically, the endergonic reaction is driven by the exergonic reaction which occurs simultaneously. These are also known as 'driven reactions'.

coupling factors

a group of mitochondrial proteins which, when added to specially treated mitochondria, can partially restore the capacity of the mitochondria to synthesize ATP. The mitochondria are treated in such a way that they can carry out electron transport but are incapable of ATP synthesis.

covalently closed circle (CCC)

a double-stranded DNA molecule with no free ends. The two strands are interlinked and will remain together even after denaturation. In its native form a CCC will adopt a supercoiled configuration.

cozymase

an early designation of a heat-stable, fraction-consisting chiefly of ATP, ADP, AMP,and NAD^+, that was isolated from yeast and participated in the reactions of alcoholic fermentation. Subsequently, cozymase I was used to denote NAD^+ and cozymase II was used to denote $NADP^+$.

C_3 plants, calvin plants

the green plants which produce C_3 compounds as the first product of CO_2 fixation. The reaction is catalysed by the ribulose 1, 5-bisphosphate carboxylase (EC 4.1.1.39): ribulose 1, 5-bisphosphate + $CO_2 \rightarrow 2$ (3-phosphoglycerate). The products of the light reaction, ATP and NADPH, are used to reduce the 3-phosphoglycerate to 3-phosphoglyceraldehyde which enters the Calvin cycle. The vast majority of green plants are C_3 plants.

crabtree effect

a reduction in the rate of respiration after addition of glucose. The cause is the increased intracellular glucose 6-phosphate level, which inhibits hexokinase, the first enzyme in glycolysis. Glucose also inhibits the enzymes of the tricarboxylic acid cycle and the respiratory chain.

c-reactive protein

a protein that reacts with the pneumococcal type C polysaccharide and that is present in plasm during some bacterial infections.

creatine $C_4H_9O_2N$

α-Methylguanidine-acetic acid; a compound present in vertebrate muscle tissue, principally as a phosphocreatine.

creatine kinase, creatine phosphokinase

a phosphotransferase, EC 2.7.3.2. C.k. is a dimeric enzyme, of M_r 82000 found specifically in heart and skeletal muscle. It catalyses the formation of ATP from ADP and creatine phosphate in a reversible reaction dependent on magnesium (II) or manganese (II). When ATP is present in excess, creatine kinase makes possible to storage of the chemical energy of the ATP in the energy-rich creatine ATP $\rightleftharpoons$ creatine p hosphate + ADP. When there is damage to the skeletal or heart musculature, the level of creatine kinase in the serum is increased. It is therefore used in the early diagnosis of heart infraction, the detection of muscle wastage and to distinguish heart infraction from a lung embolism in which there is no increase in the creatine kinase concentration in the serum.

creatine phosphate

compound that acts as a reservoir of high-transfer potential phosphoryl groups in vertebrate muscle; that is, it is a phosphogen. When ATP is required for muscle contraction, creatine kinase catalyzes the transfer of phosphoryl groups from creatine phosphate to ADP. The same enzyme regenerates creatine phosphate from ATP and creatine when ATP is plentiful. Also known as phosphocreatine.

creatinine $C_4H_7ON_3$

a compound present in urine, blood and muscle that is formed from the deyhydration of creatine.

critical photoperiod

the length of photoperiod beyond which flowering is promoted in LDP and inhibited in SDP.

crocetin

a brick-red C_{20} dicarboxylic acid with seven conjugated trans double bonds, 4 methyl branches and two terminal carboxyl groups. It is an apocarotenoid, an oxidation product of carotenoids.

crossover

1. the chromosome resulting from crossing over. 2. the individual resulting from crossing over.

cross-reacting antibody

an antibody that can combine with antigens that are specific for stimulating the production of different antibodies.

cross-reactivation

the restoration of the activity of a mutuant virus, which carries a lethal mutation as a result of previous exposure to a mutagen, by the simultaneous infection of a host cell with both the mutant virus and with one or more active viruses. The mutant virus is activated by a genetic exchange that leads to a replacement of its damaged DNA.

crotamine

a basic polypeptide toxin isolated from the venom of the rattlesnake Crotalus durissus terrificus var. crotaminicus. It appears to act by activating sodium channels in muscle fibre membranes, thereby producing depolarization and contracture. Its action is prevented by tetrodotoxin.

crude extract

a preparation that has not been extensively purified; used particular by to describe a preparation of either homogenised tissue or broken cells from which unbroken cells and cell debris have been removed commonly by centrifugation.

crustecdysone $C_{27}H_{44}O_7$

20-Hydrocedyhsone, the molting hormone produced by Y organs in crustaceans.

cryptic plasmid

a plasmid whose presence causes no discernible change in the phenotype of the host.

cryptoxanthin $C_{40}H_{57}O$

a xanthophyll carotenoid pigment found in plants; convertible to vitamin A by many animal livers.

crystallins

group of proteins synthesized in the cells of the vertebrate lens (of the eye). Their variation is one means of altering the refractive index of different parts of the lens. Crystallins, even those synthesized in embryonic life, are preserved in the inner lens fibres, are preserved in the inner lens fibres, and so sectioning and crystallin assay of a lens permits study of the types of crystallin produced throughout onotgeny.

cumulative feed back inhibition

when end product of a pathway is utilized for the synthesis of various compounds. Individually these compounds inhibit enzyme activity partially. But when present simultaneously the inhibitory effects are cumulative.

curare alkaloids

the toxic principles of arrow and

bait poisons used by South America Indians.

Calabash curare is obtained from plants of the Strychnos genus and is packed in hollow gourds. It contains a large number of alkaloids and is extremely poisonous. The alkaloids are derived from indole and can be divided into types, the yohimbine type (e.g., mavacurine), the strychnine type (e.g. Wieland-Gumlich aldehyde and the bisindole type (e.g. calabash toxiferin - I).

these alkaloids interrupt nervous impulses, at the end plates of motor nerves by displacing acetylcholine, which leads to paralysis of the striated muscles.

Curie

the amount of radioactive material which undergoes 3.700 X 10^{10} disintegration per second.

cutin

the plant material composed of a group of substances chemically related to fatty acids forming a continuous layer called the cuticle on the epidermis · of plants, interrupted only by stomata or lenticels. Being fatty in nature, cutin is water-repellent, therefore helping to reduce transpiration. It is also protective, for example preventing invasion by parasites.

cut-out

a stage of cotton plant when flowering is stopped the 2nd axillary bud grows vegetatively. The nutrients are diverted to these branches devoiding bolls.

cyanides

salts of hydrogen cyanide (HCN) with the general formula Me'CN. The soluble cyanides are hydrolysed in water to the metal hydroxide and hydrogen cyanide, and are thus highly poisonous. HCN and alkali cyanides are often components of insecticides and other biocides.

cyanoalanine synthase

during conversion of ACC to ethylene, amino group of ACC gives rise to hydrocyanic acid (HCN) which is detoxified by this enzyme in presence to cysteine to β-cyanoalanine.

cyanobacteria

group of bacteria, previously known as blue-green algae. They are unicellular and non-motile, often coated with mucilaginous slime, and the photosynthetic membranes occur as thylakoids within the cell cytoplasm rather than being in a membrane bounded chloroplast.

cyanogen bromide

selectively cleaves peptide bonds on carboxyl side of a methionine residues at room temperature, under strongly acidic conditions. Solid cyanogen bromide is volatile at room temperature; vapours extremely toxic.

cyasterone

a phytoecdysone. It has been isolated from various plants, including Cyathula capitata, family Amaranthaceae, and Ajuga decumbens, family Labiatae.

cyclase

an enzyme which catalyzes the cyclization of an unknown intermediate to imidazoleglycerol phosphate during histidine synthesis.

cyclic adenylic acid $C_{10}H_{12}N_5O_6P$

an isomer of adenylic acid; crystal platelets with a melting point of 219-220°C; a key regulator which acts to control the rate of a number of cellular processes in bacteria, most animals, and some higher plants. Abbreviated cAMP.

cyclic form

tautometric form of cyclic structure, existing in equilibrium with its open-chain form. Tautometric equilibrium often exists in several cyclic forms, differing in size, e.g., open chain D-ribose exists in tautometric equilibrium with α- and β-D-ribofuranose and with α- and β-ribopyranose.

cyclic nucleotides

mononucleotides in which phosphate moiety is attached to both the third and the fifth carbon atoms of the ribose component of the molecule, thus forming a cyclic diester. They are more correctly referred to as 3′, 5′-mononucleotides, but the usage of the adjective cyclic is very common.

cyclitols

carbocyclic compounds with several hydroxyl group e.g., inositols, quercitols.

cycloartenol

9, 19-cyclo-5α, 9B-lanost-24-en 3β-ol. A tetracyclic triterpene alcohol. It is found in many plants, including the latex of Euphorbiacease, the potato (Solanum tuberosum) and nux vomica (Strychnos nuz vomica). It is biosynthesized from squalene via 2, 3-epoxysqualene.

cyclohexantriones

new growth retardants; they inhibit GA synthesis in higher plants beyond GA_{12} -aldehyde. These are structurally similar to 2-oxoglutarate.

cycloleucine

non-metabolizable synthetic amino acid; valine antagonist, inhibits amino acid transport.

cyproterone acetate

17α-acetoxy-6-chloro-1α, 2α-methylenepregna-4, 6-diene-3, 20-dione. An antiandrogen steroid derived from pregnane. It counteracts the effects of the male sex hormone testosterone and is used in cases of hypersexuality ("hormonal castration").

L-cysteine

abbreviation Cys. L-2-amino-3-mercapto-propionic acid, HS-CH_2-$CH(NH_2)$-COOH. A sulfur-containing, proteogenic amino acid which is the central compound in sulfur metabolism.

Cys is synthesized in the course of sulfate assimilation or from Methionine by Trans-sulfuration. It is presumably the precursor of the nonproteogenic sulfur-containing amino acids. It is degraded either reductively or oxidatively. The end products of Cys degradation are usually oxidized sulfur compounds like taurine, NH_2-CH_2-CH_2SO_3H.

cysteine $C_3H_7O_2NS$

a crystalline amino acid occurring as a constituent of glutathione and cystine.

cystine $C_6H_{12}N_2S_2$

a white, crystalline amino acid formed biosynthetically from cysteine.

cytase

any of several enzymes in the seeds of cereals and other plants, which hydrolyze the cell-wall material.

cytide

pyrimidine nucleoside found in nucleic acids. Strictly speaking it occurs only in RNA as a D-ribose linked to cytosine base, whereas in DNA the equivalent molecule is cytosine deoxyriboside.

cytidine $C_9H_{13}N_3O_5$

cytosine riboside, a nucleoside composed of one molecule each of cytosine and D-ribose.

cytidine phosphates, phosphoric esters of cytidine

cytidine 5-mono-phosphate, abbreviation. CMP, cytidylic acid, cytidine 5' diphosphate, abbreviation CDP, and cytidine 5'-triphosphate, abbreviation CTP are important in Phosphatide biosynthesis. CDP has been called the coenzyme of this synthesis. Activated choline is CDP-choline, and the sugar alcohol ribitol is also activated by bonding to CDP.

the reduction of ribose to deoxyribose in the synthesis of deoxyribonucleotides also occurs most often at the level of CDP.

cytidyl diphosphate (CDP)

derived from CTP by reacting with phosphatidate to form CDP-diacylglycerol. This step is catalysed by phosphatidase cytidyl transferase.

cytidylic acid $C_9H_{14}O_8N_3P$

a nucleotide synthesized from the base cytosine and obtained by hydrolysis of nucleic acid. Also known as cytidine monophosphate.

cytochalasin

one of a series of structurally related fungal metabolic products which, among other effects on biological systems, selectively and reversibly block cytokinesis while not affecting karyokinesis; the molecule with minor variations consists of a benzyl-substituted hydroaromatic isoindolone system, which in turn is fused to a small macrolide-like cyclic ring.

cytochemistry

a branch of biochemistry which deals with the chemical nature of the living cells and the behaviour of its components, such as membranes, nucleus, protoplasm, etc., including nutrient and metabolic factors. Both plant and animal cells are studied in this science.

cytochrome

any of the complex protein respiratory pigments occurring within plant and animal cells, usually in mitochondia, that function as electrone carriers in biological oxidation.

cytochrome a

a cytochrome in which the heme prosthetic group contains a formyl side chain; a cytochrome which contains heme A.

cytochrome b

a cytochrome that contains protoheme or a related heme (without a formyl group) as its prosthetic group and in which the prosthetic group is not bound covalently to the protein.

cytochrome c

a cytochrome in which there are covalent linkages between the side chains of the heme and the protein. Cytochrome c is a ubiquitious protein found in all aerobic organisms. Its sole function is to transport an electron from a donor of lower reduction-oxidation potential to an acceptor of higher reduction-oxidation potential. The heme group in cytochrome c has a polypeptide chain of 104 amino acids attached and wrapped around it. All cytochromes have in their structure the sequence Cys_{14}-x-x-Cys_{17}-His_{18} in which the two cyestine sulphydryl groups are covalently linked to the heme by thioether bridges. In addition, the imidazole ring nitrogen atom of histidine-18 is coordinately bonded to one of the side of heme iron as the fifth ligand. Methionine-80 extends its sulphur atom as the sixth iron ligand on the other side. Thus, unlike the iron in hemoglobin further coordination. Cytochrome c therefore cannot react by simple coordination but must react indirectly by an electron-transfer mechanism. It can reduce the oxygen and transmit its oxidizning power toward the burning of food and release of energy in respiration.

Cytochrome c of vertebrates possesses N-acetyl glycine as the terminal group, and 103 additional amino acids. Cytochrome c from insects and fungi do not have an acetylated NH_2-terminal amino acid. Cytochrome c from higher plants, has at the amino terminus, N-acetyl alanine and seven additional residues.

Cytochrome c's of the two primates monkey and man are almost identical; they differ by an average of 10 amino acids fromother mammals such as dog or whale, by about 15 residues from cold blooded vertebrates, by about 30 residues from insects, and by about 50 residues from plants and procaryotes.

cytochrome d

a cytochrome with a tetrapyrolic chelate of iron as a prosthetic group in which the degree of double bonds is less than that is porphyrin; dihydroporphyrin is an example.

cytochrome oxidase

the last member of the electron transport chain. It normally reacts with oxygen, but can be inhibited by reaction with CN^- or CO. Its prosthetic group is hemin a, or cytohemin, which has a lipophilic C_{12} side chain, an aldehyde and a vinyl group on the porphyrin ring. The reaction with O_2 involves both the heme iron and copper :

$$2\,Fe^{2+} \xrightarrow{\frac{1}{2}O_2} 2\,Fe^{3+}$$

$$\text{and } 2\,Cu^{2+} \xrightarrow{2e^-} 2\,Cu^{+}.$$

electron microscopic studies have shown that the protein part of the molecule undergoes conformational changes during the redox process; the oxidized form is crystalline, but the reduced form is amorphous.

cytochrome P_{450}

the cytochrome component of an electron trasnport chain that is present in the endoplasmic reticulum of liver and some other cells. It is unique to the endoplasmic reticulum, being absent from the mitochondrial electron transport chain. The 450 denotes the fact that the reduced form of the cytochrome has an absorption band at 450 nm. ATP is not synthesized by the endoplasmic reticulum system, its primary function is in the hydroxylation of various metabolities, and it plays an important part in the metabolism of certain drugs (such as phenobrbitone, steroids, sterols, fatty acids, polycyclic hydrocarbons and certain amino acids).

cytodifferentiation

differentiation of cells and tissues; used in a confined sense to distinguish between the differentiation of the cell in terms of proteins produced in the cytoplasm and morphological characteristics developed, disregarding any changes which may be found in the nucleus or the chromosomes.

cytokinin

any of a group of plant hormones which elicite certain plant growth and development responses, especially by promoting cell division.

cytokinin antagonist

a substance which inhibits synthesis of cytokinin in the tissue e.g., N-benzyl-N' phenylurea and N-benzyl N'-3-4 diphenylurea.

cytokins, phytokinis, kinins

a group of plant hormones which promote cell division and generally stimulate plant metabolism, in particular RNA

and protein synthesis. They are generally N-substituted derivatives of adenine. Together with other plant hormones (gibberllins and auxins), they mediate the plant's response to environmental factors, such as light.
they are synthesized mainly in the roots of higher plants, and they are not subject to much translocation.

cytoplasmic control principle
coordination of chloroplast and nuclear gene expression by cytoplasmic translational products. This regualtion may be negative feed back control of free or unassembled subunits.

cytoplasmic inheritance
transmission of inherited characters via DNA of extranuclear organelles of mitochondria and chloroplasts. Also known as extrachromosomal inheritance.

cytosine
abb. C or Cyt, 6-amine 2-hydroxypyrimidine. One of the pyrimidine bases of DNA and RNA. It is synthesized as the triphosphate from UTP by an ATP-dependent amination.

cytosol
the soluble fraction of cytoplasm remaining after all particles have been removed by centrifugation.

cytotaxis
(i) the attraction or repulsion of cells from one another that leads to the ordering and arranging of new cell structures under the influence of prexisting ones.
(ii) the reorientation of cells resulting from an internal or external stimulus.

cytotoxic drugs
the drugs that are capable of killing cells. Many antitumor drugs widely used clinically are cytotoxic drugs, and own their selective antitumorigenic properties to the fact that they are most effective against rapidly dividing cells.

cytotoxic T cells
T lymphocyte that has the capacity to recognize and kill foreign tissue cells, as in a graft, or cells infected with virus, and therefore carrying novel antigen on its surface.

D-amino acids
related to D-glyceraldehyde. These are mirror images of L-amino acids, and are not present in proteins and occur in other chemical forms.

damping effect
when free-running cycle of endogenous rhythm does not maintain normal amplitude.

dansyl amino acid
an amino acid derivative formed by the reaction of 1-dimethylaminonaphthalene-5-sulphonyl chloride with the alpha amino group of amino acid. These derivatives are fluorescent and used for the estimation of amino acid by fluorometry.

dansyl chloride
reacts with - NH_2 groups to attach a fluorescent dimethylamino-naphthalene sulphonyl group. Used for the amino end group analysis and sequence analysis of proteins on an ultramicroscale.

dark break or dark interruption
if dark period of SDP is interrupted by flash of light prior to critical dark period flowering is inhibited whereas in LDP night break promotes flowering.

dark fixation of carbon dioxide
the fixation of carbon dioxide by the carboxylation of keto acids in plant roots. The energy for dark carbon dioxide fixation arises from ATP and NADH provided by respiration. It plays significant role in root growth and germinating seeds. Carbon dioxide is fixed from phosphoenolpyruvate via oxaloacetate to malate. The sequence of reactions and enzymes are the same as in C_4 and CAM metabolism.

dark reactions of phytochrome
dark reversion and destruction processes. Here pfr is converted to pr.

dark reactivation
the enzymatic repair of DNA, previously damaged by exposure to a mutagen, that does not require light and entails an excision-repair mechanism. This characteristic distinguishes these repair enzymes from other polymerases carrying out somewhat similar functions, but which require visible light, a process called photoreactivator or light repair. Also known as dark repair.

Davis U-tube
a U-tube containing a porous filter in its lower portion so that bacterial cultures may be placed in either one or both arms of the tube. The filter prevents passage of bacteria but allows passage of diffusible substances.

day position
the situation adopted by leaves of plants during the day. They alter this position when the light intensity decreases.

deacetylation
the removal of an acetyl grouping from a molecule.

deactivation of excited state
loos of excitation energy of atom or molecule due either to non-radiative or radiative transitions or to chemical reaction.

dead volume
in chromatography, the volume of mobile phase contained between the lower end of the bed of stationary phase and outlet of the column.

dealkylation
elimination of alkyl group from molecule of organic compound.

deaminase
an enzyme that catalyzes the hydrolysis of amino compounds, removing the

amino group.

deamination

removal of the amino group, -NH_2 from a chemical compound :

(a) oxidative D is catalysed by Flavin enzymes and pyridine nucleotide enzymes. Amino acids may be oxidatively deaminated to keto acids.

(b) transmination involves the transfer of an amino group from an amino to a keto compound, and is important in the synthesis of amino acids from tricarboxylic acid cycle intermediates.

Dean and Webb method

a method for determining the equivalence zone of a precipitation reaction by mixing a constant amount of antiserum with varying dilutions of antigen and taking the tube in which precipitation occurs most rapidly to be indicative of the equivalence zone.

decalescence

absorption of heat, usually by an alloy, without rise in the temperature, due to an allotropic transformation.

decarbonization

removal of carbon from any system which contains it. The substitution of oxygen for carbon dioxide in the blood in the lungs is termed decarbonization, as is also the burning out of a portion of the carbon in cast iron to make steel.

decarboxylase

an enzyme which catalyses the removal of CO_2 from different metabolites.

decarboxylation

the cleavage of the carboxyl group from a carboxylic acid to produce CO_2. The process accurs several times in the course of Tricarboxylic acid cycle.

decontamination factor

ratio of amount of radioactive impurities present in substance before purification to that present after purification.

defective lysogenic strain

a strain of mutant bacterial cells that have incorporated, a prophage that cannot replicate upon inductionand that cannot give rise to intact phage particles.

defective virus

a virus that cannot synthesize one or more of its structural proteins and that can only form intact virus particles in the host cell when it is in the presence of a helper virus.

deflagration

excessive local heating within the glowing mass. It occurs during dry ashing of plant material when ashing is done quickly.

defloculation

the reverse process of flocculation, or the process of preventing flocculation, i.e., the process of breaking up dispersing agglomerates to form a stable compound.

deformylase

an enzyme which catalyzes the removal of formyl group from the N-terminal N-formalmethionine during post-translational modification of proteins.

degenerate

when there is more than one code word for an amino acid. For most of the amino acid degeneracy is not uniform.

degradation of acids

a method of reducing the number of carbon atoms in the molecule of an acid; especially a fatty acid by the decomposition of its calcium or barium salt in the presence of a salt of acetic acid, followed by oxidation of the resulting methyl ketone.

dehydrase

an enzyme which catalyzes the removal of water from a substrate.

dehydratases

the enzymes catalyzing the reaction in which dehydration precedes deamination. For example, the a-amino group of serine and threonine can be directly converted to NH_4^+ because each of these amino acids contains a hydroxyl group in its side chain. These direct deaminations are catalyzed by serine dehydratase and threonine dehydratase, in which pyridoxal phosphate is the prosthetic group.

dehydrocholesterol $C_{27}H_{43}OH$

a provitamin of animal origin found in the skin of man, in milk, and elsewhere, which upon irradiation with ultraviolet rays becomes vitamin D.

dehydrogenases

redox enzymes which extract hydrogen ($2H^+ + 2e^-$) from a substrate (hydrogen donor) and transfer it to a second substrate (hydrogen acceptor).

dehydrogenation

removal of hydrogen from a reduced substrate, which thereby becomes oxidized. Enzymatic dehydrogenation is catalysed by dehydrogenases or oxidases.

delayed inheritance

when each successive generation has the genotype of the female parent for a particular character.

delayed-type hypersensitivity

an allergic response that occurs a few hours or a few days after the administration of an antigen. The response depends on the sensitization of certain cells, especially lymphocytes, rather than on circulacing antibodies.

deliberate immunization

the purposeful introduction of antigens, antibodies, or lymphocytes into an organism to either stimulate the production of antibodies by the organism or provide the organism with antibodies.

deletion

1. the removal of one or more nucleotides from the nucleic acid strand. 2. A chromosomal

aberration in which there is a loss of genetic material from the chromosome.

delipidised protein

a lipoprotein from which part or all of the lipid has been removed.

delphinidin $C_{15}H_{11}O_7Cl$

a purple or brownish-red anthocyanin compound occurring widely in plants.

delta assay

the construction of a thermal denaturation profile by measurements of the system at the various ambient conditions; the assay measures the extent of the transition.

demethylation

elimination of methyl group, -CH_3 from the molecule of an organic compound.

demissine

one of the Solanum alkaloids, a steroid found in wild potatoes (Solanum demissum). It is a glycoalkaloid, consisting of the steroid base demissidine, 5α-solanidan-3β-ol.

denatured alcohol

ethyl alcohol containing, sufficient amount of methyl alcohol, acetone, methyl iso-butyl ketone, hydroxybutyraldehyde, or other organic compounds to render it unsuitable for bevarage use.

density gradient

the change of density with distance; refers particularly to a solution in which there is such a change from end of the tube or the cell which holds the solution to the other. A density gradient may be set up in an ultracentrifuge cell by virtue of the variation of the centrifugal force with distance from the centre of rotation, so that the density increases from the meniscus to the bottom of the cell; solutions of cesium chloride are commonly used for such experiments. A density gradient may also be set up in a centrifuge tube by layering solutions of different densities above each other so that the density increases from the top to the bottom of the tube; solutions of sucrose are commonly used for such experiments.

deoxy-

1. combining form indicating a compound that contains 2-deoxy-D-ribose. 2. Combining form indicating a compound that contains less oxygen than the parent compound.

5'deoxyadenosylcobalamine, B_{12} coenzyme, DBC coenzyme (DBC = dimethylbenzimidizole cobamide)-

the coenzyme form of vitamin B_{12}. In this compound, the 6th coordination position of the cobalt atom in the centre of the corrinoid ring is covalently bound to the 5'C atom of the deoxyadenosine. Other cobamide coenzymes contain an N-heterocyclic base other than dimethylbenzimidazole.

deoxyribonuclease I (EC 3.1.21.1)

an enzyme which preferentially attack double-stranded DNA and produces 5'-phosphodi- and -oligonucleotide by endonucleolytic cleavage. It is inhibited by a protein.

deoxyribonuclease II (EC 3.1.22.1)

an enzyme that catalyzes the hydrolysis of DNA to mono-and oligonucleotides consisting of, or terminating in, a 3'-nucleotide.

deoxyribonucleoprotein

a conjugated protein that contains DNA as the nonprotein portion.

deoxyribose phosphates

the phosphorylated derivatives of the doxypentose 2-deoxy-D-ribose. They are synthesized biologically by reduction of ribose phosphates in the course of nucleotide synthesis.

deoxyribosyltransferases

enzymes which catalyse the transfer of deoxyribose from purine and pyrimidine deoxyribosides to free bases in the synthesis of deoxynucleosides.

deoxy sugar

a sugar in which oxygen has been lost by replacement of a hydroxyl group (-OH) with hydrogen (H). The most important example is deoxyribose, the sugar component of DNA.

depsipeptide

the polypeptides, which contain ester bonds as well as peptides. The naturally occurring D. are usually cyclic peptide, also called peptolides, which generally have α- or β-hydroxyacids as heterocomponents.

depurant

a drug used to effect purification of the system and its normalization by stimulating excretion.

derepression

any modification that eliminates the repression of a gene and permits the synthesis of the gene product. Possible modifications include a decrease in the repressor concentration produced by starving the organism of a required nutrient, a reaction of the inducer with the repressor, a mutation of the regulator gene, or a mutation of the operator gene.

dermatan sulfate

formerly called β-heparin, and chondroitin sulfate B. It is a mucopolysaccharide containing L. iduronic acid linked αl, 3 to N-acetyl-D-galactosamine 4-sulfate; the letter is linked to αl, 4 to the next iduronic acid residue.

desalanine insulin

insulin from which the alanine residue at the carboxyl end of the B-chain has been removed by the action of the trypsin.

desensitized enzyme

a regulatory enzyme that has been so altered by either mutation or chemical modifications that, while it is still catalytically active, it no longer responds to an effector.

desmin
the muscle protein forming the Z lines in striated muscle.

desmolase
any of a group of enzymes which catalyze rupture of atomic linkages that are not cleaved through hydrolysis, such as the bonds in the carbon chain of D-glucose.

desmotropism
obsolete term denoting tautomerism in which equilibrium rate is relatively low, thus enabling isolation of tautomers, e.g., ketonic and enolic forms of ethyl acetoacetate, were called desmotropes.

desulfuricants
anaerobic bacteria of the genera Desulfovibrio and Desulfortomaculum, whose Sulfate respiration contributes to the process of Desulfurication.

determinate nodule
rounded nodule with closed vascular system and absence of meristematic tissue. These are urides producing in nature e.g., peanut, cowpea and soybean.

determination
quantitative estimation of content of a given component in studied sample. Also known as estimation.

detoxification
the enzymatic reactions in an organism whereby foreign compounds, produced within the organism or introduced in it, are converted to less harmful forms and to more readily excrete products; the foreign compounds are either chemically altered or conjugated to normally occurring metabolites of the organism.

dextran
one of a group of branched chain polysaccharides of D-glucose found in yeast and bacteria. It is used in isolation of cell organelles.

dextrin
a polymer of D-glucose which is intermediate in complexity between starch and maltose.

dextrorotatory
describing compounds that rotate the plane of polarized light to the right (clockwise as viewed facing the oncoming light); such compounds usually exist in the form of so-called optical isomers, one of which is dextrorotatory and the other levorotatory, the latter turning the plane of polarized light to the left. Dextroroptatory is dictated either by the Italic letter d prefixed to the name, or by a plus ring (+); levorotatory isomers are indicated by Italic *l*, or by minus sign (-). The use of + and - signs is now preferred.

dextrin 6-α-D-glucanohydrolase, oligo-1, 6-glucosidase (EC 3.2.1.10)
a glycosidase present in the digestive juices of the small intestine; formerly known as limit dextrinase, or

isomaltase; It is specific for the hydrolysis of the α-1, 6 bonds in isomaltose and in the oligosaccharides produced by the action of α-amylase on starch and glycogen.

dextrose $C_6H_{12}O_6H_2O$
a dextrorotatory monosaccharide obtained as a white, crystalline, odourless, sweet powder, which is soluble in about one part of water; an important intermediate in carbohydrate metabolism; used for nutritional purposes, for temporary increase of blood volume, and as a diuretic. Also known as corn sugar; grape sugar.

dia-
a prefix having several meanings: 1. passing through, as in dialysis, diaphragm, diameter. 2. opposite to, an in diamagnetic. 3. complete or throughout, as in diagnosis it is not a prefix in the word diamond.

diacetyl, butane-2, 3-dione CH_3-CO-CO-CH_3
a diketone produced as a byproduct of carbohydrate degradation. It is a component of the butter aroma, and has been found in many biological materials.

dicarboxylic acid cycle
a cyclic pathway for the utilization of glyoxylic acid or one of its precursors (e.g., glycolic acid) as a carbohydrate source for the growth of microorganisms. The D. a.c. includes some of the reactions of the tricarboxylic acid cycle, and malate synthase (EC 4.1.3.2), of the glyoxylate cycle, acts here as a respiratory enzyme. It also provides starting materials for the synthesis of cell components.

diacytic
a type of stomata in dicots in which each stoma is surrounded by two subsidiary cells their common walls being at right angles to the long axis of the stoma. It is also known as caryophyllaceous type.

diaheliotropic movement
leaf movement in which the leaf lamina remain oriented perpendicular to the sun's direct rays.

diamine oxidase
a flavoprotein which catalyzes the aerobic oxidation of amines to the corresponding aldehyde and ammonia.

diaminopimelate $C_7H_{14}O_4N_2$
a compound that serves as a component of cell wall mucopeptide in some bacteria and as a source of lysine in all bacteria. Abbreviated DAP. Also known as diaminipimelic acid.

diaminopimelate pathway
a pathway for the biosynthesis of lysine that proceeds by way of diaminopimelic acid and occurs in bacteria and higher plants.

diaphorase
mitochondrial flavoprotein enzymes which catalyze the reduction of dyes, such as methylene blue, by reduced

pyridine nucleotides such as reduced diphosphopyridine nucleotide.

diastase

an enzyme that catalyzes the hydrolysis of starch to maltose. Also known as vegetable diastase.

diatom

a number of the algal class Bacillariophyceae a characteristic of which is the possession of a silica cell envelope or frustule.

diauxie

the biphasic growth curve that is obtained when an organism is exposed to two substrates that are utilized by the organism in such a fashion that one of the substrates is metabolized by constitutive enzymes while the other substrate is metabolized by inducible enzymes. The substrate requiring the constitutive enzymes is utilized first and repress the induction of the enzymes required for the utilization of the second substrate. Only after the first substrate is used up, can the enzymes be induced by the second substrate which is then metabolized.

diazole

a cyclic hydrocarbon with five atoms in the ring two of which are nitrogen atoms and three are carbon atoms.

diazonium salt

the salt of a compound that contains diazonium group ($-N^+ = N$). It is prepared by reacting nitrous acid with a primary aromatic amine.

dicarboxylate translocator

a translocator present on the inner envelop of chloroplast. It regulates the counter exchange of dicarboxylates such as L-malate, succinate, 2-oxoglutrate, aspartate and glutamate.

dicyclohexylcarbodiimide

a compound used as a condensing agent for either amino acids or nucleotides; in this reaction, water is split out between the two condensing molecules and the reagent is converted to dicyclohexylurea. Dicyclohexylcarbodiimide is also an inhibitor of ATPase.

differential boundary

the boundary formed between two solutions that contain the same components but at different concentration.

differential gene activation

plant cells are totipotent, however all the genes are not expressed. Different genes are expressed at different rates at different times in response to some inducers or repressors.

differential spectrophotometry

spectrophotometric method of determination of concentration of investigated solutions by the measurement of its absorption with respect to standard solution of substance to be determined and of known and similar concentration. Also known as differential colorimetry; differential absorptiometry.

differential thermogravimetric analysis
thermal analysis in which the rate of material weight change upon heating versus temperature is plotted; used to simplify reading of weight-versus-temperature thermogram peaks that occur close together.

diffraction
the effect of an aperture or an opaque edge upon a beam of light or electrons such that the imaged beam appears as a pattern of intensity of maxima and minima owing to the effect of interference. This is a phenomenon associated with the wave nature of both light and electrons and is a fundamental limitation to resolution in light and electron microscopes.

diffusion
the mutual permeation of two or more substances due to the kinetic activity of their molecules so that a uniform mixture of solution results. Gases of different densities will mix uniformly counter to gravity. For gases, the rate of diffusion is inversely proportional to the square roots of their densities. Two metals in close contact also show a slight tendency to diffuse. Diffusion also takes place when a barrier or film of a microporous solid (metal or cellulosic) is placed between two gases or between two liquid solutions of different concentrations; in the latter case, the rate depends on the relative strength of the concentrations.

diffusion potential
the electrical potential difference due to diffusion of ions across a membrane. It is caused by slight separation of ions.

digestion of food
the digestion of food begins in the mouth and stomach, and the final stages of digestion of all major food components into the blood takes place in small intestine. During digestion in the gastrointestinal tract of mammals the three major nutrients (carbohydrates, lipids and proteins) undergo enzymatic hydrolysis into their building block components. This is necessary for their utilization, since the cells lining the intestine are able to absorb into the blood stream only relatively smaller molecules. For example, polysaccharides and even disaccharides must be completely hydrolyzed into monosaccharides by digestive enzymes before they can be absorbed. Similarly, proteins and lipids must also be hydrolyzed into their building block components.

digestion of proteins
ingested proteins are enzymatically hydrolyzed into their constituent amino acids

in the gastrointestinal tract. When protein enters the stomach, it stimulates the secretion of the hormone gastrin, which in turn stimulates the secretion of hydrochloric acid by the parietal cells of the gastric glands, and pepsinogen by the chief cells. The gastric juice (PH 1.5-2.5) acts as an antiseptic and kills most bacteria and other cells, and also causes globular proteins to undergo denaturation or unfolding in strongly acidic conditions, rendering their internal peptide bonds more accessible to enzymatic hydrolysis. Pepsinogen, an inactive precursor or zymogen is converted into active pepsin in the gastric juice by the enzymatic action of the pepsin itself. In this process 42 amino acid residues are removed from the amino-terminal end of the polypeptide chain of pepsinogen as a mixture of small peptides. As the acid stomach contents pass into small intestine, the low pH triggers the secretion of the hormone secretin into the blood. Secretin stimulates the pancreas to secrete bicarbonate into the small intestine to neutralize the gastric HCI. The PH then rises from 1.5 and 2.5 to about PH 7. In the small intestine the digestion of proteins continues. The entry of amino acids into the duodenum releases the hormone cholecystokinin which stimulates secretion of several pancreatic enzymes, whose optimum PHs are near 7. Three of these trypsin, chymotrypsin, and carboxypeptidase are made by exocrine cells of the pancreas as their respective enzymatically inactive zymogens trypsinogen, chymotrypsinogen, and procarboxypeptidase. Synthesis of these enzymes as inactive precursors protects the exocrine cells from destructive proteolytic attack. Chymotrypsinogen has a single polypeptide chain with a number of intrachain disulphide bonds. When it reaches the small intestine, it is converted into chymotrypsin by trypsin, which cleaves the single long polypeptide chain of the chymotrypsin at two points by excision of dipeptides. Chymotrypsin hydrolyzes those peptide bonds involving phenylalanine; tyrosine, and tryptophan residues. Degradation of the short peptides in the small intestine is completed by other peptidases. The first is carboxypeptidase, a zinc containing enzyme. It removes successive carboxyl-terminal residues from short peptides. The small intestine also secretes an aminopeptidase, which can hydrolyze off successive amino-terminal residues from short peptides.

The ingested proteins are ultimately hydrolyzed to yield a mixture of free amino acids, which are then transported across the epithelial cells lining the small intestine. The free amino acids enter the blood capillaries in the villi and are transported to the liver.

digestive enzyme

any enzyme that causes or aids in digestion.

digicitrin $C_{21}H_{21}O_{10}$

a flavone compound that is found in foxglove leaves.

digitanols, digitanol glycosides

a group of plant glycosides with pregnane type Steroids as aglyca, for example, Diginin and digifolein. They occur together with cardiac glycosides, but have no cardiotomic themselves. They are biosynthesized from pregnenolone.

digitonin

a mixture of four different steroid saponins from the seeds of the purple foxglove, Digitalis purpurea. It is a strong hemolytic poison, due to its affinity to blood cholesterol. It is used as a precipitating agent for cholesterol and other sterols, in their isolation and quantitative determination.

diglucoside

a compound containing two glucose molecules.

diglycosides

when disaccharides are combined among themselves or react with the non-carbohydrates with the formation of glycosidic linkage e.g., Gentiobiose.

dihydrolipoyl dehydrogenase

an enzyme with FAD prosthetic group; catalyzes the regeneration of the oxidized form of lipoamide.

dihydroorotase

an enzyme which catalyzes the ring closure of N-carbamyl aspartic acid and leads to the formation of dihydroorotic acid.

dihydroxyphenylanine $C_9H_{11}NO_4$

an amino acid that can be formed by oxidation of tyrosine; it is converted by a series of biochemical transformations, utilizing the enzyme dopa oxidase to melanins. Also known as dopa.

diluent

any gas, solid or liquid materials used to reduce the concentration of an active ingredient in a formulation.

dinucleotide fold

a characteristic folded protein structure constituting part or all of the structure of four NAD-dependent dehydrogenases, and certain other enzymes, some of which do not bind nucleotides.

diose

a member of a class of monosaccharides that have two carbon atoms; the only compound that belongs to this class is glycoaldehyde.

dioxygenase

any of a group of enzymes which catalyze the insertion of both atoms of an oxygen molecule into an organic substrate according to the generalized formula $AH_2 + O_2 \rightarrow A(OH)_2$.

dipeptidase

an enzyme that hydrolyzes a dipeptide.

dipicolinic acid

the compound, pyridine-2, 6-dicarboxylic acid, that is present in large concentrations in spores and that is related to the heat resistance of the spores.

dipolar potential

the membrane potential that arises from the orientation of polar molecules at the surface of the membrane and the ionic double layer of the membrane.

direct acting bilirubin

the watersoluble conjugated form of bilirubin, bilirubin diglucuronide, that gives an immediate reaction with diazotized sulfanilic acid to yield a diazo dye.

direct induction

a phenomenon wherein only photoperiodically induced part of a plant is capable of causing flowering when grafted on to the vegetative test plant e.g., Perilla.

directed application

placement of herbicide or fertilizer to avoid or minimise contact with the crop.

directing effect

the effect of substituent groups already present in benzene and other aromatic derivatives which forces new substituent groups, about to enter the molecule, into definite positions relative to the original groups.

disaccharidases

a group of enzymes which hydrolyse disaccharides. They are most abundant in ripe fruits, microorganisms (yeast) and the intestinal mucosa.

disaccharide

any of the class of compound sugars which yields two monosaccharide units upon hydrolysis.

disease

disturbance in the structure and/or the function of an organ, a tissue, or an organism, as that produced by either a viral or bacterial or fungal infection.

dispersion medium

in colloidal system the continuous phase in which disperse phase is distributed is known as dispersion medium. It can be solid, liquid, or gas. It is intermicellar fluid.

dispersive replication

a mode of replication for double-stranded DNA in which the parental strands are broken into segments that are incorporated equally, together with newly formed segments, into the two daughter DNA molecules.

displacement

1. a chemical reaction in which one molecule, atom, or radical is replaced by another. 2.

Chromatographic method that consists in washing out of mixture of components from column with the help of agent whose affinity to stationary phase is greater than that of any of components being separated.

distillation

the process whereby a liquid is purified by boiling and the vapours are condensed and collected.

disulfide bridges, cystine bridges

a term referring to disulfide bonds, -S-S-, in proteins and peptides formed by oxidation of two sulfhydryl groups : 2-SH → S-S-. These are the major factors responsible for formation and maintenance of secondary structure in proteins. Proteins which contain a large number of these bridges are very resistant to denaturation by heat, acid or alkali, detergents, etc. and to hydrolysis by proteolytic enzymes.

diuretic hormone

a neurohormone that promotes water loss in insects by increasing the volume of fluid secreted into the Malpighian tubules.

diurnal acid rhythm

the fluctuation in the content of organic acids in the chlorophyll-containing parts of succulent plants, such as cacti. At night, CO_2 is fixed by carboxylation of phosphoenolpyruvate to oxaloacetate, which is then reduced to malate, leading to a considerable acidification of the tissue. By day, the malate is oxidatively decarboxylated to pyruvate, and the CO_2 is fixed photosynthetically. The mechanism allows the plants to absorb CO_2 from the air at night, when they can open their stomata without suffering the high water loss which would occur during the day. It is thus an adaptation to a hot, arid climate.

diurnal variation

the changes in rates of reaction as influenced by dark and light cycle of 24 hrs.

divergent transcription

transcription in which sections of DNA that are being transcribed have opposite orientation, relative to a central region.

DNA-Agar technique

a technique for measuring the extent of hybridization between the nucleic acid molecules. Nucleic acid fragments from one source are trapped in an agar gel and are allowed to hybridize with radioactive labelled nucleic acid fragments from a second source. The amount of radioactivity in the agar is then determined.

DNA chimera

a DNA containing genes from two different species.

DNA gyrase

enzyme that increases or introduces positive supercoiling in covalently closed circular DNA molecules generated by DNA replication. This is achieved by breakage of at least one DNA strand followed by untwisting and subsequent resealing of the duplex. DNA gyrase is an alternative term for a type II topoisomerase. Also known as swivelase.

DNA helicase

an enzyme which binds ahead of the replicating fork in the discountinuous replication of DNA and it catalyzes the energy-dependent unwinding of the duplex. The enzyme has ATPase activity and hydrolyzes 2 molecules of ATP/DNA base pair broken.

DNA like RNA

an RNA molecule that resembles DNA in its overall base composition and base ratios; the RNA is generally rich in adenine and uracil and has an adenine/uracil ratio of approximately 1.0.

DNA methylase

an enzyme which catalyzes the methylation of the bases in DNA; methylation occurs subsequent to, rather than prior, to the incorporation of the bases into the polynucleotide strand.

DNA polymerase I

a DNA-dependent DNA polymerase,originally thought to function in the replication of DNA but now believed to function in the repair-synthesis of DNA. It is a 109-kdal single polypeptide chain. It catalyzes the step-by-step addition of deoxyribonucleotide units to a DNA chain. DNA polymerase I adds deoxyribonucleotides to the 3'-hydroxy terminus of a preexisting DNA (or RNA) strand. DNA polymerase I can also hydrolyze DNA strating from the 5' end of the chain. It can also add deoxyribuncucle-otides to a primary chain, but it cannot catalyze the joining of two DNA chains, or the clourse of a single DNA chain.

DNA polymerase II

a DNA dependent DNA polymerase that is sensitive to sulfhydryl reagents and that is believed to function in the replication of DNA.

DNA polymerase III.

a DNA-dependent DNA polymerase that is sensitive to sulfhydryl reagents and that is believed to function in the replication of DNA. Under certain assay conditions the enzyme behaves as a reverse transcriptase and utilizes polyriboadenylic acid preferentially. DNA polymerase II and III are like polymerase I in certainrespects, such as:

(a) they catalyze a template-directed synthesis of DNA from deoxyribonucleoside triphosphate precursors.

(b) A primer with a free 3'-OH group is required.

(c) synthesis is in the 5' $\rightarrow$ 3' direction.

(d) they possess 3' $\rightarrow$ 5' exonuclease activity. DNA polymerase III, but not II, also a 5' → 3' exonuclease.

These polymerases differ in their template preferences. Polymerases II and III act optimally on double-stranded DNA templates that have short gaps. In contrast, extensive single-stranded regions near double helical regions are preferred templates for polymerase I.

DNA replicase system

the entire complex of enzyme and specialized proteins required in biological DNA replication.

DNA-RNA hybridization

pairing of DNA with RNA molecules by specific hydrogen bonding between complementary bases. DNA-RNA association by annealing can be favoured relative to DNA-DNA association by appropriate manipulation of the conditions.

DNA-RNA hybrids

double-stranded molecules, of which one strand is DNA, and the other of the complementary RNA. They are presumably the intermediate form in RNA transcription and in the multiplication of on cogenic RNA viruses but they can also be produced in vitro by Hybridization. They are resistant to ribonuclease.

DNA synaptase

an enzyme which catalyzes the fusion of the double-stranded DNA molecules at a region of homology and that may play a role in genetic recombination.

dolichol

any of a group of long-chain unsaturated isoprenoid alcohols containing up to 84 carbon atoms; found free or phosophorylated in membaranes of the endoplasmic reticulum and Golgi apparatus.

dolichol phosphate

a coenzyme involved in the glycosylation of proteins and lipids. It is a membrane bound polyprenol phosphate which accepts glycosyl units from soluble donors (uridine-or guanosine-diphosphate glycosides) and donates them in turn to membrane proteins or lipids.

donar position

the binding site for the peptidyl-tRNA on the ribosome during protein synthesis.

Donnan ratio

the ratio of concentration of a diffusible cation on one side of the membrane to the concentration of the same ion on the other side of the membrane in a Gibbs-Donnan equilibrium. For an anion, the ratio of the two concentration terms is reversed.

dopamine

a catecholamine neurotransmitter in the central nervous system which might also have a neurotransmitter role at some ganglia in the autonomic nervous system. It is formed by decarboxylation of D O P A (dihydroxyphenylalanine). An alternative name for dopamine is 3-hydroxytyramine. Dopamine is the immediate precursor of noradrenaline and is also the transmitter of dopaminergic nerve fibres. It is believed to be released into the synaptic cleft by exocytosis. Dopamine release is a calcium-dependent process and occurs in response either to action potentials reaching nerve terminals or to drugs.

dopa oxidase

an enzyme that catalyzes the oxidation of dihydroxylalanine to melanin; occurs in the skin.

doping

the administration of foreign substances to increase the performance of athletes.

dormancy or rest

state of arrested growth due to presence of dormant organs. Dormancy is means to overcome adverse climatic conditions. The perennating organs such as seeds or buds show dormancy.

dose response curve

a curve that describes the relation between the dose that is given to an organism and either the number or the percentage of organisms that show a response.

double carboxylation

an early hypothesis to explain malate formation in CAM plants. Accordingly in dark first RuBP is carboxylated to produce 3-phosphoglyceric acid which is further converted to phosphoenolpyruvate. PEP is carboxylated to form malate.

double code

a genetic code in which an amino acid is specified by two adjacent nucleotides in mRNA; thought to have been a forerunner of the present genetic code.

double fertilization

in angiosperms while one male gamete fuses with egg. The other fuses with secondary nucleus. This is called double fertilization.

double lysogeny

the phenomenon in which a bacterium is infected twice with the same temperature phage, the two prophage of which are inserted in tandem into the host bacterial DNA.

double sigmoid growth curve

in stone fruits like cherry, plum, and peach and in non-stone fruits such as fig, grape, etc. The pericarp and ovule growth and development are not synchronised. There exist two sigmoid growth curve. The first sigmoid curve is due to the growth of the pericarp and the second curve is associated with seed development.

double strand break

a break in a double-stranded DNA molecule in which both strands are broken without separating from each other.

drought

less availability of water to the plant due to decrease in soil water content below the permanent wilting percentage or due to the presence of excess salts in soil.

drought resistance

the capacity of plants to survive conditions of drought with little or no injury.

dry ice

solid carbon dioxide having temperature of 194K used to refrigerate foodstuffs in transit, for carbonation of liquids and for cold traps in laboratories. It sublimes from solid state to gaseous state with liquerfying.

dry point

in a laboratory distillation the thermometer reading observed when the last drop of liquid evaporates from the lowest point in the flask.

dry weight

the weight of material, in g or mg, remaining after drying tissues, organisms, etc. at temperature somewhat above 100°C.

dulcitol, galactitol

an optically inactive sugar alcohol derived from galactose. It has 6 C atoms. It is found in algae, fungi and the sap and bark of various higher plants. It is produced synthetically or by reduction of galactose by isolation from dulcite or madagascar mannu (melampyrum nemorosum L.).

duplex DNA

DNA in the double-stranded form, forming a double helix as described in the Waston-Crick model, that is with two polynucleotide chains lying in opposite 3'- to 5'-polarities, interwined and hydrogen-bonded together. Such DNA can be made single stranded by denaturation of DNA melting.

duplication

the union of a fragment of a chromosome with a whole chromosome of the same sort.

dye

a chemically coloured compound used to stain a specific metabolite or organelle of cell in extract or tissue section.

dye-sensitized photo-oxidation

the oxidation of a biologically important molecule that occurs in the absence of oxygen but in the presence of a photosensitizing dye and an appropriate electron and/or hydrogen acceptor.

dynamic steady state

when a relatively higher rate of synthesis is exactly counter balanced by a relative higher rate of degradation. It is synonomous to equilibrium which is dynamic in nature.

dynorphin

a heptadecapeptide which stimulates opiate receptors and may act as an endogenous ligand of such receptors. It is found in the pituitary and in the duodenum.

dysmyelination

the formation of a myelin that has a faulty structure.

Ebolic test

many alkaloids give characteristic colours when 1-2 mg of the alkaloid is treated on a watch glass with 5-6 drops of a 50% (w/w) sulphuric acid solution, followed by addition of a small piece of potassium dichromate.

ecdysone
the molting hormone of insects.

ecgonine
the principal part of the cocaine molecule and the basis of many Coca alkaloids.

economic yield
economically useful part of total dry matter, produced by a plant or crop in unit land area.

ectoenzyme
an enzyme that is an integral protein of the cell membrane but has its active site located on the outside surface of the cell so that its activity is directed outward.

ectopic hormone syndrome
the syndromes in which there is a production of hormones by the 'wrong tissue', such as production of parathyroid hormone (PTH) and ACTH by malignant cells in the case of lung cancer.

ectopic protein
a protein produced by a neoplasm that is derived from a tissue that is not normally engaged in the synthesis of that protein.

edestin
a haxameric, globular protein from hemp seeds, Cannabis sativa. Each of the 6 subunits consists of two nonidentical polypeptide chains joined by disulfide bridges.

editing enzyme
enzyme responsible for proof-reading the DNA and correcting errors in replication or following from mutation.

edman degradation technique
in protein analysis, an approach to amino-end-group determination involving the use of a reagent, phenylisothiocyanate, that can be applied to the liberation of a derivative of the amino-terminal residue without hydrolysis of the remainder of the peptide chain.

effector
a small molecule either synthesised on a specified structural gene or end product of reaction which combines with repressor to form repressor effector complex. This complex attaches to operator and thus genes are repressed. During induction repressor is inactivated by effector molecules and thus operator is switched on.

effervescence
the formation of gas bubble in a liquid as a result of chemical reaction. It occurs during fermentation, during the action of acids upon carbonates, etc. Boiling is not regarded as effervescence, nor is the frothing produced in such actions as that of the

concentrated sulphuric acid upon sugar.

effusion

a process taking place when a gas under pressure escapes through a small orifice. Graham's law applies to effusion as well as to diffusion of gases, and it is often more convenient to measure rates of effusion rather than rates of diffusion.

eflux

release of ions from tissue into the medium. It is measured from quasisteady wash out curves of ions from pre-loaded tissue.

Ekkert test for alcohol

two ml of alcohol containing 0.01 g resorcinol gives a pale pink to red ring-test with 1 ml sulphuric acid. With more acid and less alcohol, a deepening red colour is obtained on heating.

Ekkerts test for glycerin

a mixture of glycerin, sulphuric acid, and codeine becomes deep blue on heating. If codeine is replaced by resorcinol, the colour formed is deep-red.

Ekkert test for lactic acid

when a lactic acid solution is floated on a 1% solution of pyrocatechol in sulphuric acid, a blood-red ring test is obtained.

Ekkert test for saccharin

on shaking 1-2 ml water with 0.2 g saccharin and adding 3-6 drops 30% hydrogen peroxide and 0.02-0.04 g sodium nitrite, a yellow colour is produced which changes to brown-red with ammonia.

elastase (EC 3.4.21.11)

an endopeptidase specific for the elastin in animal elastic fibres. Its inactive precursor, proelastase, is formed in the vertebrate pancreas and transformed in the duodenum to elastate by the action of trypsin.

elasticity

when cell wall is stretched by stress if deformation is not permanent i.e., stretching is reversible the strain is known as elastic. It is intimately connected with turgor and is not of much significance in cell elongation.

elastin

an elastin protein composing the principal component of elastic fibres.

Elbs persulphate oxidation

oxidation of monohydroxyphenols to dihydroxyphenols by the action of potassium persulphate in alkaline medium, followed by the hydrolysis of persulphate compound formed.

electrochemical

conversion of chemical energy to electric energy e.g., as an electrochemical cells.

electrocratic

a term used to denote a dispersion of solid particles of colloidal size in a liquid, whose stability is maintained by either positive or negative electric charges on the particles.

electrode potential

(i) a measure of the tendency of an oxidation-reduction half reaction to occur by either loss or gain of electrons.

(ii) the potential across a chemically reactive electrode that participates either in the formation of ions from atoms or in the formation of atoms from ions.

electrodialysis

the separation of ionizing substances from other materials in a solution, and also from the solvent, by use of one or more semipermeable membranes, and an electric current (electrolysis).

electrogenic pump

ionic pumps which transport net charge. Inhibition of these pumps leads to rapid depolarization of the membrane. These are uniport in nature.

electromotive force

the directly measurable electrical energy that can be derived from an electrical cell composed of two half-cells.

electron acceptor

a species having vacant orbitals to accept electrons. Molecule within, for example, the electron transport chain of mitochondrial energy conversion, which takes up electrons. NAD is a major electron acceptor.

electron affinity

the energy released when an electron is added to a gas phase atom or ion. It is a measure of the hold that an atom or anion has on an additional electron.

electron dense

description of a substance, such as heavy metal ion or concentrated macromolecular matter, that has the tendency to scatter impinging electrons and to prevent their passage through it e.g., in an electron micrograph some areas of cell are electron dense.

electron impact

bombardment of electrons on the molecules in the gaseous phase to produce ions in the mass spectrometer.

electron probe microanalysis EPM

a method of analyzing a very small quantity of a substance by directing a finely focused electron beam on to it so that an X-ray emission is produced characteristic of the elements present in the sample. The diameter of the beam is usually about 1 mm and quantities as small as 10^{-14} can be detected by this method. The method may be used quantitatively for elements whose atomic numbers exceed 11.

electron transfer flavins abb. ETF

the flavoproteins which mediate electron transport from reduced FADH to the cytochrome system. Flavoproteins can oxidize those substrates of the respiratory chain whose oxidation does not involve pyridine nucleotides.

electron transfer flavoprotein

an electron carrier that serves as a link between the reduced form of fatty acyl coenzyme A dehydrogenase and the electron transport system.

electron transfer potential

the free energy change per mole for an oxidation-reduction reaction.

electronic transition

the transition of electrons of an atom or molecule from one atomic orbital to another. It requires large amount of energy and can be induced by visible light, ultraviolet light, and X-rays.

electron transport particles abb. ETP

fragments of mitochondria, obtained by ultrasonic or detergent treatment, which are capable and transporting electrons. ETP contain the complete electron transport system of the respiratory chain. In the electron microscope, ETP appears as membrane-enclosed vesicles, which are thought by some authors to be a giant molecule of defined composition.

electrophilic addition

an addition reaction in which the first step is the attack by an electrophile on the electron rich site of the molecule.

electrophilic substitution

a substitution reaction in which the first step is the attack by an electrophile. The electrophile substitute is a feature of reactions of benzene in which a positively charged species approaches the delocalized π-electrons on the benzene or any other aromatic ring.

electrophoretic mobility

a characteristic of living cells in suspension and biological compounds (proteins) in solution to travel in an electric field to the positive or negative electrode, because of the charge on these substances.

electrophoretic variants

phenotypically different proteins that are separable into distinct electrophoretic components due to differences in mobilities; an example is erythrocyte acid phosphatase.

electrostriction

contraction of a solution with the addition of small amount of certain salts.

elongation

the phase of protein biosynthesis in which the amino acid chain is extended by addition of new residues.

elongation factor

protein which, following its binding to ribosomes, promotes elongation of the polypeptide chain during translation. These are designated either as T and G, or as I and II. Elongation factor T is required for the binding of aminoacyl-tRNA to the ribosome and is dissociated into a stable and an unstable subunit referred to as T_s and T_U; elongation factor G is the translocase.

elution

in general, a process for extracting a solid substance from a mixture of solids by means of a liquid; as in the recovery of a vitamin absorbed on an adsorbent by means of a solution. Specifically, a process for the recovery of sucrose from molasses.

elution profile

a plot of some property of a column eluate, such as absorbance or radioactivity, as a function of either the eluate fraction number or the cumulative volume of the collected eluate.

elution volume

the volume of eluate collected in column chromatography from the time of sample application to the time at which as given component is eluted at maximal concentration.

embryo

a young microscopic plant developing from an egg cell, with or without fertilization.

embryonal inducers

compounds which induce the differentiation of organs in the course of embryonic development.

emerson effect, enhancement effect

an increase in the photosynthetic quantum yield from long-wave red light (700 nm) obtained by simultaneous irradiation with shorter wavelengths (< 670 nm). There is a sharp drop-off in photosynthetic efficiency around 700 nm, but light of this wavelengths can be utilized synergistically with light of shorter wavelength.

emission

electrons in a molecule may change their energy level only when distinct quanta of radiation are emitted. The frequency of emitted radiation is direct function of the change in energy of the electron.

encephalitogenic protein, myelin protein A 1'

the most important myelin protein of the mammalian central nervous system. On injection into guinea, pigs, rabbits, or rats it induces allergic autommune encephalomyelitis, abb. EAE, an inflammation of the brain and spinal column.

end-labelling

the introduction of a radioactive atom at the end of a DNA or RNA molecule. A commonly used method is to use T 4 polynucleotide kinase to introduce a ^{32}p atom on the 5' end.

endocrine

pertaining to ductless glands,

or to their products or secretions.

endocyclic compounds

unsaturated cyclic derivatives in which the double bond or bonds occur in the nucleus.

endogenous

relating to the metabolism of nitrogenous tissue elements.

endoenzyme

an intracellular enzyme, retained and utilized by the secreting cell.

endogenous pyrogen

a fever-inducing substance (protein) produced by cells of the host body, such as leukocytes and macrophages.

endogenous switch

here switch behaviour may occur in constant environment or in a varying environment regardless of the precise details of the environment thus discontinuity may form part of the unperturbed developmental dynamics of the system.

endonuclease

any of a group of enzymes which degrade deoxyribonucleic acid or ribonucleic acid molecules by attracting nucleotide linkages within the polynucleotide chain.

endopeptidase

an enzyme that acts upon the centrally located peptide bonds of a protein molecule.

endorinlogy

the study of hormones. It includes the chemistry, metabolism, effects on cells, organs, individuals and populations of hormones. Ecoendocrinology is concerned with the interactions of endocrine system with the environment.

β-endorphin

a 31-amino acid peptide fragment of pituitary β-lipotropic hormone having morphinelike activity.

endorphins

the endogenous peptides with morphine-like effects (endogenous morphine), the natural ligands for the opiate receptors. The enkephalins are pentapeptides isolated from pig brain. There are two of these, Met enkephain (Tyr-Gly-Gly-Phe-Met) and Leu enkephalin (Tyr-Gly-Gly-Phe-Leu). The sequence of Met eukephalin is the same as the amino acids 61 to 65 of β-lipotropin, and other segments of this hormone have been found to be E.

endotoxins

toxic substance formed inside the cells of the gram-negative bacteria, (e.g., Samonella) and released on disintegration of the cell. They are heat stable polysaccharide-protein complexes causing nonspecific effects in their hosts, e.g., fevers.

endotransglycosylases

these catalyse, in addition to breaking of glycosylic linkages, the transfer of a portion of a polysacchaarides to itself thus triggering the synthesis of cell wall material during cell wall elongation.

energy

capacity or potential capacity to do work.

energy converter

any element or compound having the ability to convert the radiant energy of sunlight into electrical, thermal or chemical energy. Prominent among them are silicon, and tellurium, as well as the chlorophyll of plants in photosynthesis.

energy metabolism

the chemical reactions involved in energy transformations within cells.

energy-rich phosphates, high energy phosphates

the phosphorylated compounds which have high energies of hydrolysis of the phosphate ester. Chemical energy in biological systems is stored in energy-rich phosphates. These may be acid anhydrates of phophoric acid (e.g., ATP), enol phosphate (e.g., phosphoenolpyruvate) or amidine phosphates (e.g., phosphagens). A high energy phosphate bond is represented as R ~ p, instead of the usual hyphen between groups.

energy transfer

the transfer of excitation energy from one chromophore of one molecule to another by a radiationless process. It is strongly dependent on the distance between the chromophores.

enkephalin

a mixture of two polypeptides isolated from the brain; central mode of action is an inhibitor of neurotransmitter release.

enolase

an enzyme that catalyzes the reversible dehydration of phosphoglyceric acid to phosphopyruvic acid.

enteropeptidase, enterokinase (EC 3.4.21.9)

a highly specific duodenal protease which acts only on trypsinogen. It consists of two covalently bound glycopeptides. It removes the N-terminal peptide from trypsinogen (Val-[Asp_4-Lys) to activate it to trypsin.

entrance resistance

total of boundary layer, stomatal pore and substomatal cavity resistances.

entropic dome

reaching of the universe to a state of complete randomness due to increase in free energy of organisms. It is only speculative approach.

enzyme

a protein that acts as a catalyst in biochemical reactions. Each enzyme is specific to a particular reaction or group of similar reactions. Many require the association of certain nonprotein cofactors in order to function. The molecule undergoing a reaction (the substrate) binds to specific active site on the enzyme molecule to form a short-lived intermediate; this greatly increases the rate at which the reaction proceeds to form the product. Many other molecules may compete for the active site, causing inhibition of the enzyme or even irreversible destruction of its catalystic properties. Enzyme production is governed by a cell's genes. Enzyme activity is further controlled by PH changes, alterations in the concentrations of essential cofactors, feedback inhibition by the products of the reaction, and activation by another enzyme, either from a less active form or an inactive precursor (zymogen). Such changes may themselves be under the control of hormones or the nervous system.

Enzymes are characterized by their specificity; each initiates a certain chemical reaction, but is of little significance for other reaction. There are four types :

(a) those which effect removal of water;

(b) those which aid transfer of electrons;

(c) those which transfer radicals; and

(d) those which act on a single carbon-carbon bond without removal or transfer of radicals.

All enzymes are proteins of high molecule mass ranging from about 10,000 to more than 1,000,000. An enzyme molecule may contain one or more polypeptide chains. The sequence of amino-acids within the polypeptide chain is characteristic for each enzyme and is believed to determine the unique three-dimensional conformation in which the chains are folded. This conformation, which is necessary for the activity of the enzyme, is stabilized by interactions of amino-acids in different parts of the peptide chains with each other and with the surrounding medium. These interactions are relatively weak and may be disrupted readily by temperature or PH variations, or changes in the polarity unfolding of the peptide chains and a concomitant loss of enzymatic activity, solubility and other properties characteristic of the native enzyme. Enzymes have a vast number of specific, among which are synthesis of proteins, conversion of starches to sugars, catalysis of fermentation processes, promotion of digestive reactions, etc. They act by lowering the overall activation energy of a reaction sequence by involving a series of intermediates, or mechanism different from the spontaneous uncatalyzed reaction. Most enzymes show their activity within a narrow PH range and at around 300-310 K and are destroyed at higher temperatures. Enzyme production is governed by a cell's genes.

The names of most enzymes terminate in either -ase or -in, for example, rennin, diastase, amylase, phosphatase, cholinesterase, and epimerase. There are six classes of enzymes, namely :

(a) oxidoreductase, which catalyze oxidation-reduction reactions;

(b) transferases, which catalyze group transfer reactions;

(c) hydrolases, which catalyze bond cleavage by hydrolysis;

(d) lyases, which catalyze the removal of a group, leaving a double bond; or the

(e) reverse; isomerases, which catalyzes the formation of isomers; and

(f) ligases, or synthetase, which catalyze the combination of two molecules with the combination of hydrolysis of a high-energy bond (e.g., in ATP).

Enzymes are similar to protein in their chemical nature and often are closely assocaited with them (coenzymes). An example is ribonuclease, composed of 124 amino acids arranged in a specific sequence and having four disulphide cross-links.

enzyme blotting

the blotting of enzymes to nitrocellulose paper and their subsequent detection by reactions with specific substrate. It is used for the detection of proteinases.

enzyme induction

synthesis of an enzyme by a bacterial cell in response to the presence of its substrate or some other inducing agent. This property of bacterial cells is engineered by a special gene regulatory mechanism, with a number of different enzymes often being coordinately produced in response to one inducer. Also known as adaptive enzyme synthesis.

enzyme kinetic parameters, enzyme parameters

the paramters of the rate equations which remain constant, so long as temperature, pressure, pH value and buffer composition are constant. They are derived from the rate constants of the rate equations, and are frequently used to characterize the enzyme functionally.

enzyme labelling

a method for locating antigens or antibodies in tissues; based on binding the antigen or the antibody to an enzyme and then determining the location of the enzyme in the tissue by making use of the known properties of the enzyme.

enzyme multiplicity

the occurrence of two or more forms of the same enzyme, all of which catalysis the same reaction.

enzyme repression

the process whereby the synthesis of a respressible enzyme is decreased in response to either a repressor or a repressor-corepressor complex. The repressor or the repressor-corepressor complex binds to and blocks an operator and thereby prevents the transcription of the structural gene of the enzyme which is controlled by that operator.

enzyme species intermediates

all covalent and noncovalent complexes between an enzyme and a substrate and or product or effector, and all the various enzyme isomers (Enzyme isomerization). The concentrations of the E.s. cannot be measured directly by means of steady state Enzyme kinetics but their steady-state concentrations can be calculated from the kinetic equations for definite values of the concentration variables. In principle, the concentration of the E.s. could be determined by the methods of presteady-state kinetics.

enzyme unit

the amount of enzyme that, under defined conditions, will catalyze the transformation of 1 mole of substrate per minute, or where more than one bond of each substrate molecule is attacked, 1 eq of the group concerned per minute.

enzymology

a branch of science dealing with the chemical nature, biological activity, and biological significance of enzymes.

epicotyl

the portion of embryo axis above the cotyledenary node. In hypogeal germination of seed the epicotyl elongates and cotyledons remain under soil. The epicotyl ends into plumule.

epinephrine

a substance secreted by the adrenal medulla as a result of stressful stimuli (such as fear, excitement, hyperglycemia, etc.) and leads to glycogenolysis in liver and muscles, owing to stimulation of phosphorylation.

epiphyte

a plant growing on another plant, but not deriving food from it e.g., orchids.

equatorial positions

in cyclic compounds when hydrogen atoms lie in the plane of molecules. These positions are as far away as possible from ring hydrogen.

equilenin

3-hydroxyestra-1, 3, 5(10), 6, 8-pentaen-17-one, an estrogen. It found together with Equilin in the urine of pregnant mares. It has 1/25 of the biological activity of estrone.

equilibrium potential

the membrane potential that arises from the differences in the concentration of ions across a membrane and that exactly balances the tendency of these ions to diffuse from the more concentrated to the more dilute solution.

equivalence point, equivalence zone

the region of the precipitation curve in which all the antibody binding sites are saturated with the antigenic determinants, and the antibodies have been quantitatively precipitated.

equivalent of acid

the number of parts by weight of the acid that contain 1.008 parts by weight of hydrogen replaceable by a metal.

equivalent of oxidizing agent

the number of parts weight of the compound that will furnish 8 parts by weight of oxygen for the oxidizing reaction.

erepsin

an outdated term for the amino and dipeptidases secreted by the mucous membranes of the small intestine.

ergosterol $C_{28}H_{44}O$

a crystalline, water- insoluble, unsaturated sterol found in ergot, yeast, and other fungi, and which may be converted to vitamin D_2 on irradiation with ultraviolet light or activation with electrons. Also known as ergosterin.

ergot-alkaloids, claviceps alkaloids, ergoline alkaloids

a group of over 30 indole alkaloids, possessing the ergoline ring system. They are produced by various species of the fungal genus Claviceps (family Ascomycetes) which parasitize rye and wild grasses. Following infection by spores of Claviceps purpurea, the ears of rye develop 1-3 cm long dark violet (almost black), highly poisonous sclerotia, containing up to 1% E.a. More recently, E.a. have been found in higher plants.

error-prone repair

type of DNA repair in which DNA chain growth occurs across damaged DNA segments, but some of these new strands are themselves defective. Such error-prone repaire appears to be the chief source of genetic mutation in the bacteria in which it occurs.

error sum of square

total sum of square-treatment sum of square.

erythrina alkaloids

a group of isoquinoline alkaloids, usually tetracyclic, found exclusively in the legume genus Erythrina.

erythrocruorin

a hemoglobin-like protein found in many invertebrates. In some snails and worms it is a high-molecular-weight extracellular respiratory pigment.

erythro form

diastereoisomer having two adjacent non-equivalent chiral centres i.e., two identical or similar atoms (or groups of atoms) situated on the same side of Fischer's projectional formula.

erythrophleum alkaloids

a group of terpene alkaloids from Erythrophleum guineense and Erythrophelum ivorense.

They are esters or amides of the diterpene cassainic acid with substituted ethanolamines.

erythrulose

a ketose sugar occurring as an oxidation product of erythritol due to the action of certain bacteria.

escherichia coli

an intestinal bacterium of the family Enterobacteriaceae. It is the most experimental organism in molecular biology. A single cell has dimensions of about $1 \times 1 \times 3$ µm, a volume of about 2.25 μm^3, and a wet weight of about 10^{-12}g, which corresponds, to a dry weight of about 2.510^{-13}g. Under optimal conditions, the organism doubles about every 20 minutes. The wild type can grow on a completely synthetic medium containing salts, glucose and ammonia. The chemical composition, biosynthetic capacity and energy expenditures are listed in the table. The majority (70%) of the dry mass is protein, but the number of (smaller) lipid molecules is much larger. When the cell is growing logarithmically, it must synthesize 12500 lipid molecules and 1400 protein molecules per second. Assuming an average of 400 peptide bonds per protein, this amounts to 560000 peptide bonds per second for which the cell expends 88% of its biosynthetic energy.

essential amino acid

an amino acid that an organism is unable to synthesize in sufficient quantities. It must therefore be present in the diet. In man the essential amino acids are arginine, histidine, lysine, threonine, isoleucine, leucine, valine, phenylalanine, and tryptophan. These are required for protein synthesis and deficiency leads to retarded growth and other symptoms.

essential enzyme

an enzyme without which a cell or an organism cannot grow or survive.

estrogens, oestrogens

a group of female sex hormones. The ring system of E. is estrane (Steroids). They have an aromatic A ring with a phenolic 3 hydroxy group, and an oxygen function on C-17. The chief estrogens are Estrone, Estradiol, and Estriol.

estrone oestrone

3-hydroxyestra-1, 3, 5 (10) trien-17-one. An estrogen, which occurs in human urine, ovaries and placenta, and it has also been found in pomegrane seeds (17 mg/kg) and palm oil.

essential oils

an extremely heterogeneous mixture of volatile, lipophilic plant products with characteristic odours. The International Standard Organization (ISO) has defined the E o, in the strict sense as the steam distillates of plants or oils obtained by pressing out the rinds of a few citrus fruits. However, in practice the products of extraction with organic solvents, enfleurage or maceration of blossoms (flower oils) and the resinoids which can be extracted from other plant parts, resins and balsams are included by the term E.o.

ester

a molecule formed by the condensation reaction between an acid and an alcohol with the elimination of water. The acid involved may be organic, for example acetic acid as in acetylcholin, but many esters of biological importance as derivatives of inorganic phosphoric acid, for example AMP, glucose-6-phosphate, phospholipids, and nucleic acids. Triesters, molecules containing three ester groups, are major constituents of oils and fats.

esterolytic protease

a proteolytic enzyme that catalyzes the hydrolysis of ester bonds in appropriate substrates at a faster rate than it catalyzes the hydrolysis of natural peptide bonds.

ethanolamine, aminoethanol H_2N-CH_2-CH_2-OH

a biogenic amine produced by decarboxylation of L-serine. It is a common constituent of phospholipids in which it is esterfied to an acyl glycerol phosphate moiety to form phosphatidyly ethanol-amine.

ethionine $C_5H_{13}O_2N$

an amino acid that is the ethyl analog of and the biological antagonist of methionine.

ethylation

the formation of a compound by introduction of the ethyl group.

ethylene antagonists

compound which interfere with ethylene action. Silver nitrate, carbon dioxide and $KMnO_4$.

ethynyl hydrogen

the hydrogen attached to the terminal triple bond. The ethynyl hydrogen atoms are weakly acidic, and insoluble salts of silver and copper are formed, when terminal ethynyl compounds are treated with alkaline solutions of these metal ions.

etioplast

development of plastid in etiolated leaves. These have pro-lamellar bodies.

etamycin, viridogrisein

a cyclic peptide lactone antibiotic from streptomyces griseus and related species. It is effective against Gram-positive bacteria and Mycobacterium tuberculosis.

euchromatin

the diffuse chromatin that is active in RNA synthesis and that stains weakly during interphase, but stains strongly during metaphase.

euglobulin

true globulin; a simple protein that is soluble in distilled water and dilute salt solutions.

eumelanins

brown or black melanin pigment found in animals. These are heterogeneous, cross-linked polymers built of 5, 6-dihydroxyindole units, and usually linked to proteins. They are very widespread in skin, hair, feathers, insect cuticula etc.

evapotranspiration

loss of water vapours due to evaporation and transpiration.

exchange reaction

1. process of transformation of two or more substrate molecules, involving mutual exchange of their atoms or ions.

excitation spectrum

a plot between fluorescence and excitation wavelength. Emission wavelength is fixed. Excitation spectrum is independent of emission wavelength. It is used to find out the wavelength at which maximum excitation occurs.

exclusion

removal of damaged section of DNA strand, generally 10-100 nucleotides long, prior to repair. The types of DNA damage include the base modification by chemical mutagens, single-strand breaks and adjacent base dimerization through the action of ionizing or ultraviolet radiation. The excision is carried out by a number of specialized enzymes including DNA glycohydrolases and nucleases probably including (in bacteria) DNA polymerase I.

exergonic

of or pertaining to a biochemical reaction in which the end products possess less free energy than the starting materials; usually associated with catabolism.

exocellular enzyme

an enzyme that may readily be isolated from association with living cells, e.g., pepsin, maltase, zymase. Also known as extracellular enzyme.

exoenzyme

(i) an enzyme which catalyses a reaction involving the end of a polymer rather than internal positions.

(ii) an enzyme that is released outside the cell.

exon

the sequence of a gene that is represented as mRNA. It is the coding region of DNA. Most mammalin genes are more complicated, in that the coding regions are interrupted by noncoding regions, that are eliminated when the primary RNA transcript is processed into mature mRNA.

exopeptidase

an enzyme which catalyses the sequential hydrolysis of amino acids from one end of the polypeptide chain.

exoswitch

controlling switch operated by external environmental conditions. Supply of water, nutrients and gases are regulated.

expressor protein
a protein produced by a regulator gene, that is required for the expression of one or more genes.

extensin
a protein, rich in hydroxyproline, that is attached to cellulose fibrils in plant cell walls.

extinction point
the critical O_2 tension for a green plant below which aerobic fermentation occurs as part of the metabolism of the plant, and above which aerobic respiration occurs exclusively.

extrachromosomal genes
DNA molecules located outside the nucleus. The most important are in the Plastids and Mitochondria. The corresponding extra chromosomal genes in bacteria are the plastids.

extrinsic fluorescence
fluorescence that is caused by a small molecule which is bound to the protein, and not by the protein itself.

extrinsic heterogeneity
the heterogeneity of antibodies that results from extrinsic factors, such as the large number of antigen determinants in any particular antigen.

eyespot or stigma
an organelle containing organge or red globules. Found in some motile and colonial algae and it acts as photoreceptor.

face B
freeze-fractured grana facing towards the outer side. It retains very little membrane mass and is covered with particles which are 175 Å diameter and 90 A in height. There are about 1500 particles per μm^2.

facilitated diffusion
the passive transport, the movement of specific compounds across a bio-membrane from higher to lower concentration, but at a rate greater than simple diffusion.

factitious protein
a product of genetic engineering; a protein designed for a specific purpose or for its expected properties.

factor
a term used chiefly by biochemists to indicate any number of a biologically active complex, especially if its exact chemical nature is unknown or if its function in cellular metabolism has not been elucidated. Several of the B-complex vitamins were originally referred to as factors until their identity had been established by research.

factor IV
calcium ions involved in the mechanism of blood coagulation.

factor VII

a procoagulant, related to prothrombin, that is involved in the formation of a prothrombin-converting principle which transforms prothrombin to thrombin. Also known as stable factor.

factor XI

a procoagulant present in the normal blood but deficient in hemophiliacs. Also known as plasma thromboplastin antecedent (PAT).

factor XII

a blood clotting factor effective experimentally, only in vitro; deficient in hemophiliacs. Also known as Hageman factor.

fallow

farm-land, unused during a growing season. Such land generally restores fartility.

Fanconi's anemia

a disease in which the patient shows anemia, leukopenia, hyperpigmentation of the skin, and a high incidence of leukemia. Cells isolated from these persons have a normal response to ultra violet and ionizing radiation.

fast reaction

a reaction or step in a reaction sequence that has a very high rate constant and that proceeds very rapidly; special techniques are required for analysis of such reaction.

fat biosynthesis, triacylglyceride synthesis

refers to biosynthesis of neutral fats from fatty acids and glycerol. Fatty acids and glycerol are synthesized by separate pathways and then combined in a series of reaction in which the acyl moieties of fatty acyl -CoA molecules get transferred to glycerol phosphate.

fat degradation

refers to the hydrolysis of the ester bonds in neutral fats to form fatty acids and diacyglycerol, which is further degraded to fatty acids and glycerol. The enzymes responsible are lipases.

fatliquor

a mixture of neatsfoot oil and water, emulsified with a fatty acid or sulphonated oil; the neatsfoot oil is derived from water extraction of animal tendons. Fatliquors are used primarily in the leather industry to lubricate skins and hides, which tend to become hard and dry as a result of tanning. This treatment enables the finished leather to bend easily without cracking and to withstand the stresses it receives during fabrication into shoes and other products.

fatty acid activation

the conversion of a fatty acid to a fatty acyl coenzyme A ester which is the first step in the reactions of beta oxidation. The fatty acyl coenzyme A ester can be formed in a reaction catalyzed by a thiokinase or in a reaction catalyzed by a thiophorase.

fatty acid degradation

the catabolic pathways for fatty acids. The most common to β-oxidation; minor pathways are α- and γ-oxidation.

1. β-Oxidation, the stepwise degradation of fatty acids from the carboxyl end. In each turn of the cycle, two carbon atoms are removed as acetyl-CoA, and the β-carbon atom is oxidized; R-CH_2 CH_2-CO-SCoA HS-CoA R-Co-CoA + CH_3-CO-CoA.

2. α-oxidation of fatty acids occurs in germinating plant seeds. A fatty acid peroxidase (EC 1.11.1.3) catalyses the decarboxylation and stimultaneous formation of an aldehyde, in which H_2O_2 acts as hydrogen acceptor. The aldehyde can either be oxidized to a fatty acid or reduced to a fatty alcohol R-CHOH-COO → R-CO-COO^- → R-COO^- + CO_2.

3. the terminal methyl group of a fatty acid may be oxidized (ω-oxidation) enzymes localized in the microsomal fraction of animal and microbial cells. The substrate is usually a C_8 to C_{12} fatty acid, which is converted to the decarboxylic acid in two steps. The first is hydroxylation to an ω-hydroxy fatty acid which requires oxygen and NADPH. The second step is catalysed by a soluble, non-microsomal enzyme, which is usually NAD^+ -dependent.

fatty acid peroxidase

an enzyme present in germinating plant seeds which catalyzes the oxidation of the carboxyl carbon of fatty acids to carbon dioxide.

fatty acid synthetase complex

a cytoplasmic, multienzymic complex that catalyzes a cyclic set of reactions from one molecule of coenzyme A and successive molecules of malonyl coenzyme A; the complex consists of six enzymes and the acyl carrier protein.

fatty acyl carnitine

transport from of fatty acids which allows them to cross the mitochondrial membrane; formed by reaction of fatty acyl-coenzyme A with carnitine by employing the enzyme carnitine acyltransferase. Also known as acyl carnitine.

fatty alcohols

unbranched, aliphatic mono-alcohol with 10 to 20 C atoms. They are found in nature as components of waxes. They are produced by reduction of fatty acids, and are used in the production of surface-active agents and emulsifiers.

fatty aldehyde dehydrogenase

an enzyme which catalyses the oxidation of fatty aldehyde to fatty acid using NAD and water during oxidation of saturated fatty acid.

fatty oil

a nonvolatile oil of vegetable or animal origin, and consisting of glyceryl (and other) esters of fatty acids (sometimes other organic acids), often with some of the free acid present.

Fd fragment

the fragment of the IgG immunoglobin molecule that is obtained by treating the molecule with the enzyme papain, followed by reduction. The fragment consists of that portion of the heavy chain that is joined to an intact light chain in the Fab fragment. Two Fd fragments are obtained per molecule of IgG.

febrifugine

a quinolazine alkaloid isolated from the shrub dichroa febrifuga, which has been used in Chinese folk medicine since ancient times. It is a strong antimalerial and fever-sinking agent, but is too toxic for human use.

fed-batch culture

a closed system, but fresh medium is added periodically, thereby increasing the total culture volume and stimulating further growth.

Fenton reagent

aqueous solution containing hydrogen peroxide and ferrous ions. System generates free hydroxyl radicals (-OH) without radiation of high energy.

ferment

a material which catalyzes certain organic reactions and which consists of an enzyme (a catalyzst which is the product of a living organism or organisms, and which has an organic chemical composition) in association with other substances produced by the living organism, or with the organism or cell itself.

fermentation

a form of metabolism in which the end products could be further oxidized. Per unit of substrate. It yields far less energy than respiration. For example, a yeast cell obtains 2 molecules ATP per molecule of glucose when it ferments it to ethanol, while complete respiration would yield 38 molecules of ATP.

fermentation, acetic

a fermentation which produces acetic acid, commonly in the dilute form (vinegar) from alcohol-containing solutions or substances.

fermentation, butyric

a fermentation reaction which produces butyric acid.

fermentation techniques, microbial production techniques

techniques for large-scale production of microbial products. These must both provide in optimum environment for the microbial synthesis of the desired product and be economically feasible on a large scale. They can be divided into surface (emersion) and submersion techniques. The latter may be run in batches on continuously.

ferreira de silva solution

a solution of 0.5 g ammonium selenite in 10 g concentrated sulphuric acid; used as a test reagent for alkaloids; characteristic colour reactions are obtained.

ferrihemoglobin

hemoglobin in the oxidized state. Also known as methemoglobin.

ferritin

the main storage form of iron in the animal body, comprising a complex of the protein apoferritin and ferrous iron. It is most abundant in the liver.

ferromagnetism

magnetism due to unbalanced electron spin in the inner electron orbits of the element concerned which gives the atom a resultant magnetic moment in ferromagnetic metals i.e., iron, cobalt, nickel and certain alloys.

ferroporphyrin

a red complex of porphyrin and iron in which the iron is in the 2 + oxidation state.

Feulgen reaction

a staining reaction that is specific for DNA and that is based on converting the DNA to apurinic acid and treating the apurinic acid with Schiff's reagent for aldehydes. The tissue section under investigation, after hydrolysis with dilute hydrochloric acid, is treated with Schiff's reagent. A purple coloration develops in the presence of DNA.

fibrin

the protein end product of blood coagulation. It is generated from the plasma protein Fibrinogen by thombin in the presence of Ca(II) ions. Thrombin removes two fibrinopeptide pairs A_2 and B_2 from fibrinogen. After the A peptide has been removed, the protein polymerizes in a pH-dependent, linear fashion. Thereafter, the B peptide is removed. At this point the fibrin bundle is still soluble in urea and has a cross-banding pattern visible in the electron microscope. It is establized by factor XIII, which must first be activated by thrombin and Ca^{2+}, factor, XIIIa removes the carbohydrate and generates two intermolecular E-(γ-glutamyl) lysinebonds per molecule between the γ and α chains of fibrin bundle. A cross-linked fibrin clot is insoluble both in water and in 8 M urea, and provides a stable would closure (Blood coagulation). It can be degraded to soluble eleavage products by Plasmin.

fibrinogen

a plasma protein synthesized by the parenchymall cells of the liver; the precursor of the fibrin. Also known as factor I.

fibrinoid

a homogeneous, refractile, oxyphilic substance occurring in degenerating connective tissue, as in term placentas, rheumatoid nodules, and Aschoff bodies, and in pulmonary alveoli in some prolonged pneumonitides.

fibrinopeptide

one of two peptides, denoted A and B, that are removed from fibrinogen during its conversion to fibrin by the action of thrombin.

fibroin

a protein secreted by spiders and silk worms which rapidly solidifies into strong, insoluble thread that is used to form webs or cocoons.

fibronectin

the group of large proteins secreted by many type of cells, and which form a fibrillar matrix linking cells to other extracellular proteins, such as collagen.

fibrous protein

any of a class of highly insoluble proteins representing the principal structural elements of many animals tissues.

Fick's second law

concentration of some solute changes with position and time as result of diffusion dj/dx = dcj/dt where dj = gradient of flux of j in the dx direction, dcj/dt = volume element in unit time.

field ionisation

uses potentials of upto 10 KV, to give rise to predominantly to the molecular ion of the organic compound.

filtrate

the soluble portion separated from the precipitate by filtration.

filtration

in most common sense, an operation involving liquid-solid separation, used in chemistry and chemical engineering; it consists essentially of either gravity or forced flow of a liquid containing dispersed solid particles through a structure having a pore size small enough to retain the particulates. Filter paper, glass fibre mats, and similar materials are used for laboratory filtration.

fine chemical

a chemical produced in comparatively small quantities and in a relatively pure state. Pharmaceutical and biological products, perfumes, photographic chemicals, and reagent chemicals are examples of fine chemicals.

fingerprint region

spectral range in infrared from 650 to 1480 cm^{-1} with a number of bands characteristic for separate functional groups.

first excited singlet state

when one electron of a pair absorbs red light, the electron is excited for a very short period and return to its normal level in approximately 10^{-5} seconds.

first-step-transfer DNA. FST-DNA

a DNA fraction of T5 phage that is injected into the bacterial host during the first few minutes of infection and that controls the breakdown of the host DNA and the injection of the remainder of the phage DNA.

Fischer peptide synthesis

a method of synthesis of peptides in which α-amino acids (or peptides containing a free amino group) react with acid halides of halo-acids, followed by amination with ammonia.

Fischer reagent for aldehydes and ketones

a solution of 1 part phenylhydrazine hydrochloride and 1 part sodium acetate in 10 parts water. It forms hydrazones with aldehydes and ketones.

fixation

in general, the act or process of making secure or permanent. Examples are found in microscopy, where the term is applied to the preparation of slides from specimens or sections cut from them; in photography, the term is applied to the removal from photographic film or other media, after exposure of the unchanged light-sensitive substances, to prevent further change and hence marring the picture; in immunology, the term is applied to the method of preventing hemolysis by the complement; in perfume and flavour formulation, to the use of high boiling components to make the evaporation of the mixture uniform; and in chemistry, it refers to the reactions and processes by which free nitrogen enters into chemical combination.

fixative

a reagent which will bring about fixation. Commonly used fixative is F.

fixed

as applied to nitrogen, the term refers to the atmospheric nitrogen that has been made available to plants by soil bacteria or has been combined by synthetic processes into useful chemical compounds, especially ammonia.

fixed oil

a nonvolatile oil of animal or vegetable origin, consisting usually largely of fatty acids, and their esters. Fixed oils may be solid, semi-solid or liquid at atmospheric temperature.

flagellin

the main protein component of bacterial flagella. The filaments of flagella have an a-keratin structure, which is reversibly converted to the β-keratin structure on stretching of the aggregate. It has 304 amino acids residues, but no cysteine or tryptophan and only traces of proline and histidine.

flanking DNA

segments of DNA immediately adjacent to the two ends of a DNA region under consideration.

flash evaporation

very rapid evaporation, especially as applied in industrial processes, in which liquids are heated under pressure is subsequently suddenly reduced causing the liquid, which is then superheated, to evaporate rapidly. Also known as flash drying.

flash photolysis

photolysis generated by very short but high-intensity flash of light. Flash photolysis is a method of investigating the mechanism of extremely rapid photochemical reactions involving the formation of free radicals (both inorganic and organic).

flavin adenine dinucleotide

a coenzyme important in various biochemical reactions. It comprises a phosphorylated vitamin (B_2) molecule linked to the nucleotide adenine monophosphate (AMP). It is usually tightly bound to the enzyme forming a flavoprotein. It functions as hydrogen acceptor in hydrogenation reactions and is reduced to $FADH_2$, which in turn is oxidized to FAD by the electron transport chain, thereby generating ATP. A key part of the structure of FAD is its isoalloxazin ring which is able to gain two hydrogen atoms, thus producing the reduced form $FADH_2$. FAD is the prosthetic group of some membrane-bound flavoprotein dehydrogenase such as succinate dehydrogenase. It is also the prosthetic group of some oxidases that react directly with oxygen, the two hydrogen atoms of $FADH_2$ reacting to give hydrogen peroxide. Examples of these are δ-amino acid oxidase and yeast alcohol oxidase.

flavin mononucleotide FMN

a derivative of riboflavin (vitamin B_{12}) that is the immediate precursor of FAD and functions as a coenzyme in various oxidation-reduction reactions. It is the prosthetic group of the membrane bound NADH dehydrogenase, a complex flavoprotein which is the first complex involved in the electron transport chains for oxidation of NADH by oxygen. The hydrogen atoms of $FMNH_2$ are released as protons, the electrons being transferred to the iron-sulphur centre of the enzyme complex.

flavin enzymes, flvoproteins, yellow enzymes

a diverse group of more than 70 oxidoreductases found in animals, plants and microorganisms which have Flavin adenine dinucleotide or Flavin mononucles tide as prosthetic groups. There coenzymes can be reversibly reduced by hydrogen atoms, which they can accept either directly from a substrate (for example, succinate dehydrogenase) or from NAD(P)H. The group name refers to the yellow colour of the oxidized riboflavin portion. The properties of the flavin dinucleotide (FAD) or flavin mononucleotide (FMN) are strongly dependent on the protein molecule around them. This group of proteins is structurally and functionally very heterogeneous, and there is no single generalized type of flavin enzyme. The metalloflavin enzymes (metalloflavoproteins) also contain metals, such as Fe, Mg, Cu or Mo, which are involved in the binding of the Fe, to the mitochondrion and in the redox reaction.

flavoprotein

a compound concerned with electron transfer and associated with the cytochrome system.

fleig blood reagent

a test reagent for testing the presence of blood in the urine, made by adding 10 g powdered zinc to the solution of 0.25g fluorescein and 20 g potassium dehydroxide in 100 ml water. A fluoresnce, in the presence of hydrogen peroxide, indicates the presence of blood.

flip-flop

(i) the transverse rotation diffusion of a molecule through the lipid bilayer of a biological membrane; involves a rotation of the molecule through the plane of the lipid bilayer so that it moves from one monolayer to the other.

(ii) a model proposed to explain the anticooperative effects of cartain oligomeric enzymes.

(iii) any oscillating mechanism involving two molecular forms.

floral evocation

the events occurring in the shoot apex that commit to flower formation. For this purpose the meristem should be competence, proper gene expression leading to drastic molecular changes which culminate in conversion of vegetative meristem to reproductive one.

flowering hormone, anthesin florigen vernaline

a principle which has been demonstrated physiologically but never isolated or chemically characterized.

flow quenching

a rapid flow technique in which the enzyme and the substrate are mixed in the usual manner, but the mixture then flows into a second mixing chamber rather than into an observation cell. The enzymatic reaction is stopped rapidly in the second chamber by mixing a chemical quenching reagent with the enzyme and the substrate. A reactant or a product of the reaction is then determined by any convenient method.

flow sheet

a chart, involving symbols and abbreviations that is used to outline the steps and the order in which they are to be used for the synthesis of a compound, the purification of an enzyme, the isolation of a protein, or some other multistep process.

fluence rate

dose of irrdiance on per unit exposed area in photomorphogenic work. Its units are Jm^{-2} or Wm^{-2}.

fluorescamine

a reagent capable of detecting nanogram quantities of amino acids. Like a ninhydrin, it forms a complex with amines, other amino acids. All primary amines react with fluorescamine under alkaline conditions (pH 9-11) to form a fluorescent product. The fluorescence is unstable in aqueous solution, and therefore the reagent must be prepared in acetone. The secondary amines, proline and hydroxyproline, do not react unless they are first converted to primary amines which can be done using N-chloro-succinimide.

fluorescence analysis

methods of analysis based upon irradiation with ultraviolet light, and observation of the colour and intensity of the fluorescent radiation emitted by the sample. Also known as fluorometric analysis; fluorimetry; fluorophotometry.

fluoride, F^-

an anion found in bone and tooth apatite. Small quantities are beneficial in lowering the incidence of caries, and this cariostatic effect of F^- has been clearly demonstrated in humans. Fluoridation of water is now a public health measure (optimal level in drinking water 1-2 ppm F^-). F^- affects several enzymes. Excess F^- decreases fatty acid oxidase in rat kidney, and partially inhibits intestinal lipase. Fatty acid utilization is generally impaired in fluorosis. Carbohydrate metabolism is also affected, probably due to inhibition of enolase and a shift of the NAD/NADH ratio in favour of NADH.

fluoroimmunoassay (FIA)

antigen is binded to a fluorescent and reacts with specific antibody. The uncoupled antigen is detected with fluorescent meter.

fly agaric toxins

the toxins of Amanita muscaria. Poisonings by this mushroom are rarely fatal. These toxins include Muscarin and other quaternary ammonium bases, such as muscaridin; indole compounds, ibotenic acid and its easily derivatives, Muscimol and Muscazone. Muscimol and ibotenic acid inhibit motor functions, and muscimol is psychotropic.

fodder

coarse grasses which are harvested whole and cured in an erect position e.g., Corn and sorghum.

fodrin

a spectrin-like protein that lines the cortical cytoplasm of neurons and which appears to link actin filaments to the membrane. Fodrin is thought to down-regulate the number of receptor bindings sites on the neuronal membranes. Its breakdown by the Ca^{2+} dependent protease, calpain 1, leads to the exposure of more receptors. Studies to date have been concerned with glutamate receptors, but there may well be a similar fodrin-mediated mechanism under lying the down and up-regulation of the other types of neuronal receptors. It has been suggested that the increase in receptor number arising from fodrin breakdown plays a part in memory storage.

fold back DNA

short repeated sequences of the eukaryotic genome which can 'fold back' on themselves to form duplexes following denaturation. These sequences can be either dispersed or found in clusters. Also known as snap back DNA.

foliar multiple fertilization

in most of legumes, nutrient demand far exceeds supply. At this stage, if nutrient solution, whose composition equals the NPKS of seeds, are sprayed will improve grain yield.

folic acid $C_{19}H_{19}N_7O_6$

a yellow, crystalline vitamin of the B complex; it is slightly soluble in water, usually occurs in conjugates containing glutamic acid residues; and is found especially in plant leaves and vertebrate livers. Also known as pteroylgutamic acid (PGA).

Folin-McEllroy reagent

a solution of 50g sodium carbonate, 100 g sodium pyrophosphate, and 30 g disodium phosphate dissolved in 1 litre of water, the resulting solution being then mixed with a solution of 13 g cupric sulphate dissolved in 1 litre water. This reagent is used for testing the presence of glucose in urine. A greenish-yellow or red precipitate indicates the presence of glucose.

follicle-stimulating hormone

the gonadotrophic protein hormone secreted by the anterior lobe of the pituitary gland, that stimulates the growth of ovarian follicles in the female and spermatogenesis in the male. In the absence of FSH, the testes are atrophic and sperm production is absent. FSH also stimulates estradial production in isolated Sertoli cells. Plasma FSH concentrations increase through puberty from the low levels of infancy.

food

a substance used to maintain certain essential biological processes in living organisms, notably to furnish cell and tissue-building materials, and to provide heat and energy, as well as to supply auxiliary substances needed for the functioning of these processes. The basic food requirements of animals and man are fats, carbohydrate, proteins, vitamins, and minerals, all of which are obtained by the ingestion of plants or their assimilated forms (meat, milk). The energy stored in the food is made available by oxidation, hydrolysis, and similar chemical reactions.

food additive

a substance that is added to, and not naturally present in, a food; includes those substances that are added in the preparation of a fortified food exclusive of sugar, salt and vinegar.

food preservation

the prevention of chemical decomposition and the development of harmful bacteria in foods. It is generally affected by the sterilization of the food (i.e., by the destruction of bacteria in it) by heating in sealed vessels, i.e., canning, or by making the conditions unfavourable for the development of bacteria, by pickling, drying, freezing, smoking etc.

form

of a living organism mean external and internal morphology along with structure and organisation of cells, tissues, and organs to make an organism.

formaldehyde

agent frequently used to preserve biological tissue, usually in the form of the aqueous solution, formalin. It is also used to denature DNA and RNA to single-stranded form by removal of intra-molecular bonding.

formamidase

an enzyme involved in tryptophane catabolism; catalyzes the conversion of N-formylkyn-urenine to kynurenine and formate.

formycins

a group of pyridine antibiotics (Nucleoside antibiotics) synthesized by Nocardia interforma.

fortification

a term used in the food industry to describe the addition of essential nutritional factors (vitamins, minerals, proteins etc.) to certain food products to replace losses incurred in the processing of raw materials, and to meet standard nutritional requirements. It is practiced especially with milled wheat flours, prepared mixes, meat and fish by-products, margarine, and infant foods. In cases where the food is baked after fortification, a large percentage of the vitamins so added may be inactivated by heat.

fractional distillation

the slow distillation of a liquid that allows the collection of fractions which distill at different temperatures.

fragment length mapping

a technique that aids in determining the base sequence of a nucleic acid molecules that is synthesized in vitro by a nuclease free polymerase.

The incubation of the polymerase with substrate for varying lengths of time results in the synthesis of polynucleotide fragments of different size, all of which contain the same 5'-terminal. The fragments are separated according to their size by means of polyacrylamide gel electrophoresis, and a specific oligonucleotide is then located in the nucleic acid by determining the minimum fragment length that is required to ensure the presence of the oligonucleotide.

fragment reaction

a reaction used to assay the activity of peptidyl transferase. In a cell-free system containing 70 or 80S ribosomes, the growing peptide chain is transferred to Puromycin and released as peptidyl-puromycin.

free electron

an electron which is not attached to an atom, molecule or ion, but is free to move under the influence of an electric field.

free-etching

technique used in the preparation of biological material for electron microscopy. Specimens are frozen in a cold liquid such as liquid nitrogen or freon, fractured under vacuum, and exposed surfaces allowed to sublime so that surface irregularities become evident. A carbon replica is then made, stripped away, and examined in the electron microscope.

free radical quenchers

free radical intermediates produced during normal mitochondrial processes, but are too reactive and toxic to be tolerated in living tissue. Several mechanisms have evolved to deal with them. In addition, several exogenous chemicals may act as free radical quenchers.

free-running cycles

after the transient cycle normal period is taken for completion of circadian rhythm under constant environment.

Freeze-Clamp Technique

a technique used for *in vivo* determining the concentration and the compartmentation of various metabolites.

freeze-thawing

the disruption of cells by repeated freezing and thawing of a cell suspension.

frequency

the number of vibrations or cycles per unit time; for electromagnetic radiation, the speed of light is divided by the wavelength.

Fritzmann test

nitrate in the milk is detected by a blue to violet ring which appears when milk containing formaldehyde and nitrate is floated over concentrated sulphuric acid. Various modifications of this test have been developed.

fructans
high-molecular-weight polysaccharides of D-fructose linked 1, 2- or 1, 6-glycosidically. They are common in plants. Examples are inulin and phlein, and the branched triticin, hordecin and graminin.

fructose-1,6-diphosphate phosphate
a regulatory enzyme which, together with phosphofructokinase plays a key role in regulating the flow of carbon up and down the glycolytic sequence. Regardless of the source, however, the phosphatase is strongly inhibited by AMP.

fruit
the ripened ovary often along with accessory floral parts of an angiosperms.

fruit-ripening hormone ethylene $CH_2 = CH_2$
gaseous plant hormone. It occurs widely in plant tissues, and accelerates the ripening of the fruit dropping of leaves and fruit and aging of the plant.

L-fucose $C_6H_{12}O_5$
a methyl pentose present in some algae and a number of gums and identified in the polysaccharides of blood groups and certain bacteria. Also known as 6-deoxy-L-galactose; L-fucopyranose; L-galactomethylose; L-rhodeose.

fucoxanthin
a carotenoid pigment with an allene, an epoxy and a carbonyl group, and three hydroxyl groups, one of them acetylated. It is found in many algae, especially brown algae (Phaeophyta), and it is the most abundant of the naturally occurring carotenoids.

fumarase
the enzyme catalyzing the reaction between fumaric acid and water to form L-malic acid in the citric acid cycle. The enzyme has been crystallized from pig heart. It is a tetramer of four identical polypeptide chains.

fumarase, fumarate hydratase (EC 4.2.1.2)
the tricarboxylic acid cycle enzyme which converts fumarate to malate by adding water to the double bond. The reaction is reversible.

functional group analysis
methods of analysis of organic compounds consisting in identification and determination of the compounds according to their functional groups.

functional nutrient requirement
the minimum concentration of ion in the plant at which the plant can maintain its metabolic functions at rates which do not limit growth.

funtumia alkaloids
a group of steroid alkaloids characteristic of the genus Funtumia of the dogbane Apocynaceae family. The F.a. are derived from pregnane and

have an amino or methylamino group on carbon 3 and/or 20. These are biosynthesized from cholesterol and pregnenolone.

furanose

a sugar having a five-membered ring containing four carbon atoms and one oxygen atom.

fused gene

a hybrid gene produced by linking a gene of interest to some other gene using methods of recombinant DNA technology.

fusel oil

unpleasant-tasting side product of alcoholic fermentation. It consists mainly of amyl, isoamyl, isobutyl and propyl alcohols. The compounds are formed from amino acids, especially leucine, isoleucine and tyrosine, by deamination and decarboxylation. Tyrosol, which is formed from tyrosine, is a component of beer.

fusidic acid

a tetracyclic triterpene antibiotic. It is isolated from culture filtrates of Fusidium coccineum and, like structurally related antibiotics Cephalosporin P_1 and helvolic acid, it is effective against Gram-positive organism. It is biosynthesized from squalene via 2, 3-epoxysqualene. It inhibits protein synthesis by preventing the reaction of the elongation factor EFG with the small ribosomal subunit.

fusion of gene

a hybrid gene consisting parts of two others genes. A fusion of gene can be formed by deletion of chromosomal segment between two genes or by crossing over.

fusion protein

protein molecule produced by recombinant DNA technology, usually when a novel gene is inserted into a recipient plasmid vector in such a way that a terminal stop codon in a plasmid gene is deleted. Thus translational read-through occurs with the new fusion protein beginning with a plasmid sequence and continuing with the protein sequence of the inserted novel gene.

GABA modulin

a polypeptide associated with GABA receptors. It is probably located in the postsynaptic membrane, and it is thought to down regulate the GABA recognition site allosterically. GABA modulin inhibits the facilitation of the benzodiazepine binding to GABA receptors that is elicited by GABA itself.

GABAergic nerve fibre

a nerve fibre that release gamma-aminobutyric acid (GABA) is a neurotransmitter.

galactans

refers to polysaccharides of D-galactose found in plants. They are usually unbranched and have high molecular weights.

Examples are agar-agar and carrageenan.

galactoglucomannan

any of a group of polysaccharides which are prominent components of the coniferous woods; galactoglucomannan consists of D-glucopyranose and D-mannopyranose units.

galactokinase

an enzyme which catalyses the conversion of galactose to galactose 1-phosphate using ATP.

galactomannan

any of a group of polysaccharides which are composed of D-galactose and D-mannose units.

D-galactosamine, chondrosamine, 2-amino-2-deoxy-D-galactose

an amino sugar. $[\alpha]^{20}/D + 125^\circ \rightarrow +98^\circ$ (water). It is derived from D-galactose by replacement of the OH group on C2 by an amino group. It is usually found in nature as the N-acetyl derivative and is a component of few mucopolysaccharides such as chondroitin sulfate, blood group substance A, etc. It is also found in mucoproteins.

galactosidase

enzyme that hydrolyses galactosides to galactose plus a second molecule having a hydroxyl group.

galactosyltransferase

any one of a group of enzymes that help to make mature complex oligosaccharides from more simple sugars. Many of these complex sugars are finally attached to proteins, and much of this assembly occurs in vesicles of the Golgi apparatus. Indeed these enzymes are used as specific markers for the Golgi vesicles.

galanin

a 29 amino acid neuropeptide isolated from porcine upper small intestine. It is present in nerve fibres in the mucosa, smooth muscle, intramural ganglia and around blood vessels of the gastrointestinal tract.

galegine, (3-methyl-2-butenyl) guanidine

a guanidine derivative found together with 4-hydroxygalegine in the seeds of goat's rue, Galega officinalis. It is synthesized in the shoot and accumulated in the seeds.

gamete

a cell which is capable of fusion with another gamete during sexual reproduction to produce a zygote.

gamma chain

1. the heavy chain of the IgG immunoglobulins. 2. One of the two types of polypeptide chains present in fetal hemoglobin.

gamma-globulin

species of the protein globulin of the blood which is employed as antibody.

ganglioside

one of a group glycosphingolipids found in

neuronal surface membranes and spleen.

gap detection

mechanism in the seed that can detect potentially competing plants and inhibit germination until these plant disappear. It is of considerable survival value, particularly for species that depend on open space for regeneration from seed.

gas chromatography

refers to a separation technique which is based on the distribution of gaseous compounds between a mobile gaseous phase and a stationary adsorbant phase. A prerequisite for separation is that the compounds in question can be vaporized or reproducibly converted to volatile-derivatives.

gas hold up

volume of carrier gas which passes through the column in order to elute a substance which does not interact with the stationary phase.

gastrin

a polypeptide hormone secreted by the duodenum in response to gastric dilatation or the ingestion of peptides and amino acids. Gastrin promotes gastric acid and pepsinogen secretion, motility of the pyloric antrum, and gastric mucosal growth.

gastrin inhibitory peptide, GIP

a polypeptide hormone (for structure, Secretin), purified from crude preparations of cholecystokinn-pancreozymin. It shows potent enterogastrone activity, i.e., it inhibits secretion of acid and pepsin by the stomach, and inhibits gastric motility.

gating

the opening and closing of a channel in a biological membrane, believed to be brought about by conformational changes of the integral membrane proteins, lining the channel, as a result of the binding of substrates or other ligands.

GC content

the amount of guanine + cytosine in nucleic acids, expressed in mol % of the total bases. The GC content plus the AT (adenine + thymine) content of a nucleic acid is thus equal to 100 mol %, provided that the molecule is double stranded.

gel permeation chromatography

a separation technique involving passage of a liquid moving phase through a column containing the stationary phase which consists of a porous material (gel). Gel permeation chromatography (GPC) affords a rapid method of separating high molecular weight material, with separation based on differences in molecular size.

gene

a section of DNA coding for a

single polypeptide chain (structural gene), a particular species of transfer or ribosomal RNA, or a sequence which is recognized by and interacts with regulator proteins (regulatory gene).

gene activation, gene expression

gene activation deals with the mechanisms which determine which genes will be expressed at a given time. In prokaryotes, the genes for the enzymes of a single metabolic pathway are often regulated as a unit, a the Operon.

in multicellular organisms, it is crucial to growth and differentiation.

it can be initiated by various effectors, which probably combine with specific nuclear proteins rather than acting directly on the genes. Such effectors may control the rate of transcription of particular genes, in addition to initiating or terminating transcription.

gene amplification

the selective replication of specific genes disproportionately to the extent of their occurrence in the genome.

gene mutation

an alteration in the DNA molecule that results in the replacement, addition or loss of nucleotide bases.

gene tagging

here transposon induced mutant allele of a desired gene is physically isolated through the use of transposon specific sequences as a hybridization probe. A gene may be cloned without knowing the gene product.

gene therapy

diseases caused by deficiency of a gene product are amenable to replacement therapy. The strategy is to close a gene into a vector that will readily be taken up and incorporated into the genome of a host cell. The introduced gene would begin to direct the expression of its protein product, and this corrects the deficiency in the host cell.

genetic block

a metabolic block that results from a mutation.

genetic code, code

the relationship between the sequence of bases in a nucleic acid and the sequence of amino acids in the polypeptide synthesized from it.

genetic cross

1. the mating of two organisms that results in the formation of genetic recombinants. 2. the production of progeny containing genotype of two or more parents, as in the simultaneous infection of bacteria with several types of phages. 3. the progeny derived from two or more parents by mating or by other means.

genetic damage

damage to DNA. This may be of two types: chromosome

damage and gene mutation. Genetic damage may be produced by exposure to certain chemicals. Mutagenicity tests are applied in attempts to detect compounds with this potential toxicity.

genetic material

the carrier of hereditary information. In higher organisms, bacteria and some virus, it is double-stranded DNA, in other virus it is single stranded DNA and in still other virus, it is RNA.

genetic system

the genetic material of a given species, includes the genetic components. Their organisation, and the method of transmission of genetic information.

gentiana alkaloids

terpene alkaloids with a pyridine skeleton (they therefore are also pyridine alkaloids) found primarily in gentian (Gentiana) species. The biogenetic precursors of these alkaloids are probably bicyclic monoterpenes.

gentianose

a nonreducing triaccharide composed of two D-glucose and D-fructose units. One glucose and the fructose are joined as in sucrose; the second glucose is linked β-1, 6 to the first. G. is a storage compound found in the roots of gentians.

genus

a taxonomic rank containing related species. Similar genera are collected into a family.

geomorphology

study of the characteristics, origin and development of land forms.

geraniol, 2, 6-dimethylocta-2, 6-dien-8-ol

the most important of the doubly unsaturated monoterpene alcohols. Nerol is the double bond isomer with the cis configuration at position 2. The structural isomer linaool has its OH group on C3 instead of C1. It is a component of many essential oils, and makes up to 60% of oils of roses. It has the fragrance of roses. It is used, primarily as the acetate (b.p. 242°C), in the perfume industry.

germinal centre

a spherical aggregation of lymphocytes and lymphoblasts of the B lymphocyte line together with follicular dendritic cells and tingible body containing macrophages.

gerontology

the study of aging, or those processes which occur progressively in the life of an organism, especially those which begin after it has reached maturity. Geriatrics is the branch of medicine concerned with old people. Aging consists of a gradual decline of physiological functions, eventually causing death. For humans, the probability of a neutral death increases logarithmically with increasing rate.

ghost

1. an erythrocyte that has lost some or all of its cytoplasmic content; prepared by allowing the erythrocyte to swell in distilled water so that its permeability is increased and the cytoplasmic material leaks out. 2. a T-even phage that has lost some or all of its DNA; prepared by subjecting the phage to an osmotic shock and digesting the DNA of the ruptured phage with deoxyribonuclease. 3. a spheroplast that has lost essentially all of its intracellular material; prepared by growing gram-negative bacteria in the presence of penicillin or by digesting the cell wall of the gram-negative bacteria with lysozyme.

giant chromosome, polytene chromosome

an especially large type of chromosome present in the Diptera. Giant chromosomes in the salivary glands of Drosophilia have been extensively studied. They have a cable-like appearance, without separation of the chromatids. They may consist of many thousand single chromosomes, and may reach a length of 0.5 mm and a thickness of 25 μm. The supercoiled DNA molecules are much more extended than in ordinary chromosomes, and the duplicated molecules remain in register as they lie side by side. This gives rise to a banded structure, consisting of DNA-rich bands with DNA-poor regions in between.

gibbane or gibberellene

the 4 ring structural skeleton necessary for gibberellins. All gibberellins have basic gibbane or ent-gibberellen structure with substitution at different positions.

gibberellic acid $C_{18}H_{22}O_6$

a crystalline acid occurring in plants that is similar to the gibberellins in its growth-promoting effects.

gibberellin

any member of a family of naturally derived compounds which have a gibbane skeleton and a broad spectrum of biological activity but are noted as plant growth regulators.

Gibbs effect

after the brief photosynthetic assimilation of $^{14}CO_2$ by Chlorella, the resulting fructose bisphosphate is labelled symmetrically, as expected from the operation of the Calvin cycle. In contrast, glucose phosphates and the glucose moiety of starch are asymmetrically labelled, C-4 containing significantly more ^{14}C than C-4, and C-1 and 2 containing significantly more than C-5 and 6. This apparently anomalous labelling of glucose is known as the Gibbs effect.

girdle lamella

the outermost lamella of an algal chloroplast when it

completely or partially envelope other lamellae.

gitonin

a steroid saponin. The aglycon is gitogenin (25 R)-spirostan-2α, 3β-diol, the sugar chain consists of 2 galactose, 1 glucose and 1 xylose units. Gitogenin differs from digitogenin in lacking the 15 β-hydroxyl group. It has been isolated from Digitalis purpurea and digitalis germanicum. Free gitogenin has also been isolated from agave and yucca species.

globins

polypeptide chains that form the protein components of haemoglobin, myoglobin and chlorocruorin.

globular proteins

a major group of proteins which perform a multitude of functions. A typical globular protein may be described as an extensively folded and compact polypeptide chain with little if any space for molecules of water in its interior. In general all the polar R groups of the amino acids are located on the outer surface and are hydrated, whereas nearly all the hydrophobic R groups are in the interior of the molecule. The polypeptide chain may have extensive α-helicityas in myoglobin, or it may have little as in cytochrome c and possess the β-extended forms of β-keratin.

globulins

these proteins are insoluble or sparingly soluble in water but soluble in dilute salt solutions and coagulate when heated e.g., storage seed proteins.

glucagon

a hormone, secreted by the islets of Langerhans in the pancreas, that increases the concentration of glucose in the blood by stimulating the metabolic breakdown of glycogen. It thus antagonizes the effects of insulin.

glucamine $C_6H_{15}O_4N$

an amine formed by reduction of glucosylamine or of glucose oxime.

glucan

a polysaccharide composed of the hexose sugar D-glucose.

glucobrassicin

bound form of IAA present in cruciferous plant. On hydrolysis free IAA is produced.

glucocorticoid

a corticoid that affects glucose metabolism; secreted principally by the adrenal cortex.

glucogenic amino acids

amino acids whose carbon chain can be metabolically converted into glucose or glycogen.

glucogenesis

formation of glucose within the animal body from products of glycolysis.

glucokinase

an enzyme that catalyzes the phosphorylation of D-glucose to glucose-6-phosphate.

glucolipid
a glycolipid that yields glucose in hydrolysis.

glucomannan
a polysaccharide composed of D-glucose and D-mannose; a prominent component of coniferous trees.

gluconeogenesis
the synthesis of glucose from pyruvate or amino acids. It cannot occur by a simple reversal of Glycolysis because the equilibria of those reactions are too unfavourable under physiological conditions. Instead, the pyruvate is carboxylated to oxaloacetate (either directly or indirectly, via malate).
the oxaloacetate is then decarboxylated and phosphorylated simultaneously by the phosphoenolpyruvate carboxykinase (ATP) (EC 4.1.1.49) to form phosphoenolpyruvate. Reversal of the glycolytic reactions then yields fructose 1, 6-bisphosphate from the phosphoenolpyruvate. The phosphofructokinase reaction is not reversible; instead fructose-bisphosphatase (EC 3.1.3.11) removes one phosphate group to form fructose 6-phosphate. This is converted readily to glucose 6-phosphate. If the blood sugar level is low, glucose 6-phosphate is hydrolysed to glucose by glucose 6-phosphate (EC 3.1.3.9). Otherwise, the glucose 6-phosphate is used directly for glycogen synthesis. Overall reaction : 2 pyruvate (2 CH_3COCOO^-) + 2 NADH + 4 H^+ + 6 ATP → glucose ($C_6H_{12}O_6$) + 2 NAD^+ + 6 ADP + 6 P_i. The energy required for G. can be obtained by oxidizing 20 to 30% of the lactate to CO_2 and H_2O.

glucoplastic amino acids
amino acids whose degradation products can contribute to gluconeogenesis.

glucopyranoside
any glucoside that contains a six-membered ring.

glucosamine
an amino sugar; the most abundant in nature, occurring in glycoproteins and chitin.

glucose $C_6H_{12}O_6$
a monosaccharide; occurs free or combined and is the most common sugar. Also known as cerelose; D-glucopyranose.

glucose hexokinase
an enzyme which catalyses the phosphorylation of glucose to glucose-6-P using ATP in glycolysis.

glucose-1-phosphate $C_6H_{12}O_8P$
an ester of glucopyranose in which a phosphate group is attached to carbon atom 1; there are two types: α-D- and β-D-glucose-1-phosphates. Also known as Cori ester.

glucose-6-phosphate $C_6H_{13}O_9P$
an ester of glucose with phosphate attached to carbon

atom 6. Also known as Robisonester.

glucose-6-phosphate dehydrogenase, GPDH (EC 1.1.1.49)

the key enzyme of the pentose phosphate cycle. It occurs widely in plants and animals and has been shown to be formed from inactive precursor subunits. It is a tetrameric enzyme with M_r ranging from 206000 in neurospora to 240000 in erythrocytes. In humans, 50 hereditary variants of the erythrocyte GPDH are known.

glucose tolerance test

a measure of the rate at which glucose is metabolized; used as a screening test for diabetes. A dose of glucose is administered to a fasting individual and the blood glucose concentration is then determined as a function of time. In normal individuals the glucose concentration rises to a maximum within about 30 minutes and drops back to the initial level within about 2 hours. In diabetic individuals, the glucose concentration rises to a higher value and does not drop back as rapidly as is the case for normal individuals.

glucosidase

an enzyme that hydrolyzes glucosides.

glucoside

one of a group of compounds containing the cyclic form of glucose, in which the hydrogen of the hemiacetal hydroxyl has been replaced by an alkyl or aryl group.

glucosyltransferase

an enzyme that catalyzes the glucosylation of hydroxymethyl cytosine; a constituent of bacteriophage deoxyribonucleic acid.

glucuronic acid $C_6H_{10}O_7$

an acid resulting from oxidation of the CH_2OH radical of D-glucose to COOH; a component of many polysaccharides and certain vegetable gums. Also known as glycuronic acid.

glucuronidase

an enzyme that catalyzes hydrolysis of glueuronides. Also known as glycuronidase.

glucuronide

a compound resulting from the interaction of glucuronic acid with a phenol, an alcohol, or an acid containing a carboxyl group. Also known as glycuronide.

glucuronyltransferase

membrane bound enzyme which catalyses the synthesis of glucuronoxylan.

glutamate-hydroxypyruvate aminotransferase

an enzyme which catalyses the conversion of serine into hydroxypyruvate in peroxysome during photorespiration.

glutamate receptors

receptors specifically sensitive to and operated by glutamic acid. Glutamate receptors are coupled to Na^+ channels. Influx are sensitive to both D-

and L- isomers.

glutamine antagonists glutamine analogs

the structural analogs of L-glutamine which competitively inhibit glutamine-dependent enzyme reactions. 6-Diazo-5-oxo-L-norleucine and Albizzin are members of this group of substances.

glutamyl tRNA glutamate dehydrogenase

an enzyme which catalyses the reduction of chloroplastic glutamyl tRNA glutamate to glutamyl tRNA and glutamyl-1 semialdehyde using NADPH.

glutaraldehyde

protein cross-linking agent widely used in the preparation of biological material for light or electron microscopy.

glutathione $HOOC\text{-}CH(NH_2)\text{-}CH_2\text{-}CO\text{-}NH\text{-}CH(CH_2SH)\text{-}CO\text{-}NH\text{-}CH_2\text{-}COOH$

a naturally occurring peptide with a γ-peptide bond. It serves as a biological redox agent, as a coenzyme and cofactor, and as a substrate in certain coupling reactions catalysed by glutathione S-transferase.

glutelin

1. one of the two major proteins of wheat gluten. Maize glutelin is one of the two main proteins of the maize (corn) kernel, along with zein. 2. a general name for a class of proteins which are insoluble in water, alcohol or neutral salt solutions, but readily dissolve in dilute acids and alkali. Glutelins are mixture of various similar proteins.

gluten

a mixture of about equal parts of the simple proteins glutelins and prolamins. It makes flour capable of rising when made into bread.

glycan

a polysaccharide made up of a single type of sugar unit (i.e., >95%). As a class the glycans serve both as structural units (e.g., cellulose in plants and chitin in invertebrates) and energy stores (e.g., starch in plants and glycogen in animals). The most common homoglycans are made up of D-glucose units and called glucans.

glycerate pathway

an anaplerotic pathway for utilization of glyoxylate in plants and microorganisms. Two molecules of glyoxylate are converted to tartronate semialdehyde by tartronate semialdehyde synthase (EC 4.1.1.47). The semialdehyde then gets reduced to D glycerate and phosphorylated by glycerate kinase (EC 2.7.1.31) to 3-phosphoglycerate. This is converted by phosphoglyceromutase (EC 2.7.5.3) and enolase (EC 4.2.1.11) to phosphoenolpyruvate, which enters the general metabolism. Balance :

2 glyoxylate + ATP + NAD(P)H

+ H^+ →
phosphoenolpyruvate + ADP + CO_2 + NAD(P).

glyceric acid

an acid formed by the oxidation of both the terminal —CHO group and the terminal —CH_2OH group of an aldose to —COOH group.

glycerate kinase

an enzyme which catalyses the phosphorylation of glycerate to 3-phosphoglyceric acid in chloroplast during photorespiration.

glycine, abb. glu, aminoacetic acid H_2N-CH_2-COOH

the simplest proteogenic amino acid. Gly is not essential in the diet. Its amino nitrogen can easily be exchanged, so it added to amino acids diets in large amounts to provide nitrogen for the synthesis of other amino acids. Gly is converted by transmination or oxidative deamination to glycoxylic acid, which is further metabolized to formic acid.

glycine allantoin cycle, purine cycle

a series of reactions leading to the synthesis of urea in the lungfish (Dipnoi) and certain urea-accumulating plants. The glyxylate and urea produced by purine degradation are reassimilated at different rates.

glycine aminotransferase

an enzyme which catalyses the formation of glycine from glyoxylate during amino acid synthesis.

glycine receptors

receptors specifically sensitive to glycine. Glycine receptors present on spinal cord neurons are coupled to CI channels. Influx of CI^- through these channels causes hyperpolarization of the postsynaptic cell. Glycine receptors are blocked by the strychnine.

glycinin

the chief protein component of soybeans. It is stored in subcellular particles, the "protein bodies". The dimer (M_r 350000) consists of 12 subunits (M_r 28500 each), 6 of these chains are acidic (IP 3.0 to 3.4) and 6 are basic (IP 8.0 to 8.5). It is structurally related to the protein arachin.

glycinuria

metabolic disorders of glycine catabolism, is characterized by excess urinary excretion of glycine in association with a tendency to formation of oxalate renal stones, although the amount of oxalate secreted in the urine is normal, it appears to be inherited as a dominant, possibly X-linked, trait. The plasma glycine levels are normal, while the urinary excretion of glycine ranges from 600 to 1000 mg/day. Consequently, glycinuria is attributed to a defect in renal tubular reabsorption of glycine.

glycocholate

the major bile salt, formed as a breakdown product of cholesterol. Cholesterol is converted in to trihydroxycoprostanoate and then in to cholyl CoA. The activated carboxyl carbon of the cholyl CoA then reacts with the amino group of glycine to form glycocholate.

glycogen

a storage polysaccharides with a highly branched structure. Approximately 12 glucose units from a repeating moiety. Mainly found in animals and the fungi.

glycogenic amino acid

an amino acid that can serve as a precursor of pyruvic acid, glucose, and glycogen in metabolism.

glycogen metabolism

the formation and breakdown of glycogen. The process has been well studied in mammalian muscle. Glycogen is synthesized from uridine diphosphate glucose (UDPG) and a starter molecule of the structure (α-1, 4-glucosyl)$_n$ by glycogen synthase (EC 2.4.1.11). The branching of the molecule is accomplished by 1, 4-α–glucan branching enzyme (EC 2.4.1.18), which transfers a segment of chain from a 4-OH to a 6-OH. (The enzyme is sometimes called Q enzyme).

glycogen phosphorylase

the enzyme that catalyzes the successive hydrolytic removal of glucose residues, in the form of glucose-1-phosphate, from the nonreducing end of glycogen; this reaction is the first step for the utilization of glycogen in glycolysis.

glycolic acid, hydroxyacetic acid $HOCH_2$-COOH

an hydroxycarboxylic acid found in young plant tissue and green fruits, such as gooseberries, grapes and apples. It is an intermediate in photosynthesis. Its precursor is active glycoladehyde, which is formed in Transketolation reactions.

glycolipid

any of a class of complex lipids which contain carbohydrate residues.

glycolysis

the enzymatic breakdown of glucose or other carbohydrate, with the formation of lactic acid or pyruvic acid and the release of energy in the form of adenosinetriphosphate.

glycolysis, embden-meyerhof-parnas pathway

the main pathway for anaerobic degradation of carbohydrates found in all groups of organisms. For each mole of glucose consumed, 150.7 kJ (36 kcal) energy is released. The organism obtains a net yield of 2 moles ATP per mole glucose. The starting material is glycogen or starch, which is hydrolysed to glucose 1-phosphate or glucose monomers. It can be divided into four phases :

1. the formation of two molecules of triose

phosphate(glyceraldehyde 3-phosphate and dihydroxyacetone phosphate) from one molecule of hexone. Two molecules of ATP are consumed in this step.

2. dehydration of the triose phosphates to 2-phosphoglycerate; NAD^+ is oxidized in the process to NADH. One molecule ATP is generated per triose phosphate, which makes up for the ATP invested in step 1.

3. conversion of 2-phosphoglycerate to Pyruvate via phosphoenolpyruvate. Another ATP is generated here for each molecule of pyruvate.

4. the reduction of pyruvate to regenerate NAD^+. In muscle, the pyruvate is converted to lactate, and in yeast, it is reductively decarboxylated to ethanol. In an aerobically respiring cell, the NADH is oxidized ultimately by the respiratory chain (Hydrogen metabolism), and the pyruvate is further oxidized in the Tricarboxylic acid cycle. Under anaeraboic conditions, G. can only be maintained continuously by the redox reactions.

balance : glucose ($C_6H_{12}O_6$ + 2 P_i + 2 ADP $\rightarrow$ 2 lactate $C_3H_6O_3$) + 2 ATP.

if the starting material is glycogen, which is degraded to glucose 1-phosphate, the yield is 3 ATP per glucose 1-phosphate consumed.

glycolytic pathway

the principal series of phosphorylative reactions involved in pyruvic acid production in phosphorylative fermentations. Also known as Emben-Meyerhof pathway; hexose diphosophate pathway.

glyconeogenesis

the metabolic process of glycogen formation from noncarbohydrate precursors.

glycoproteins

proteins that consists of a protein covalently linked to a carbohydrate polymer via an N or O-acyl glycosyl amine linkage. These are differentiated on the basis of their carbohydrate composition and the linkage of the carbohydrate to the protein. Glycoproteins fall in to three basic groups :

(a) plasma glycoproteins over 40% of which are found in the blood sera;

(b) mucin glycoproteins that are associated with various secretions such as saliva and make up the highly characteristic blood group substances associated with surface layers of cells; and

(c) mucopolysaccharides, which consists of a short peptide chain to which long unbranched polysaccharides are attached and which are found widely distributed in cartilage, eyes, tendons, skin etc.

A most unusual function of glycoproteins is found in the freezing resistance of some

Antarctic fish which survive in an environmental temperature of 271 K, because of the presence in their blood at a concentration of about 2.5% of a group of freezing point depressing glycoproteins ranging in molecular mass from 10,000 - 20,000.

glycosidase

an enzyme that hydrolyzes a glycoside.

glycoside

any of a member of a large class of carbohydrate derivatives characterized by the replacement of the hydrogen atom of the hemiacetal hydroxyl group than an alkyl or aryl moiety, the aglycon, the glycosidea are stable compounds and, do not undergo many of the reactions of sugars, e.g., they show no reducing properties, they do not mutarotate etc. The non-sugar part of a glycoside is known as the aglycon. Natural glycoside constitute a large and biologically important class of sugar derivatives. Many natural pigments and dyestuffs, poisons and drugs, are glycosides. Glycosides are classified according to the sugar formed during their hydrolysis as glucosides, fructosides, rhymnosides, galactosides, mannosides, arabinosides, xylosides, sorbosides, glucoheptosides, etc., or as aldosides, or ketosides if formed from aldoses or ketoses. Other classifications are based upon the nature of the non-sugar or aglycone group formed when glycosides are hydrolyzed.

glycosylation

attachment of an oligosaccharide to the asparagine amine groups of proteins. The process is only known to take place in the proximity of the rough endoplasmic reticulum of the cell.

glycosyl group

a sugar residue that is linked to another group or molecule by means of glycosidic bond.

glucosylation

post-transcriptional modification of a protein by addition of a carbohydrate moiety.

glycotropic

acting to antagonize the action of insulin.

glycyrrhetic acid, glycyrrhetin

a pentacyclic triterpene with carboxylic acid and ketone functions. It is the aglycon of glycyrrhizic acid, an extremely sweet principle from the root of licorice Glycyrrhiza glabra L. It is the aglycon of Saponins from other plants, e.g., the bark of Pradosia latescens and rhizomes of the fern polypondium vulgare.

glyoxalase

an enzyme present in various body tissues which catalyzes the conversion of methylglyoxal into lactic acid.

glyxylate bypass enzymes

the existence of isocitrate lyase and malate synthase enzymes in micro-organisms to catalyse degradation of fatty acid to acetate which can be used for growth.

glyoxylate cycle

a sequence of biochemical reactions related to respiration in germinating fatty seeds by which acetyl coenzyme A is converted to succinic acid and then to hexose.

glyoxylic acid $CH(OH)_2COOH$

an aldehyde acid found in many plant and animal tissues, especially unripe fruit.

glyoxylic acid, oxoacetic acid, glyoxalic acid CHO-COOH

a carboxylic acid found in green fruits, seedlings and young leaves. In some plants families (maple, borage, horse chestnut). It is present in the form of allantion and allantioc acid, which arise in the course of purine carbolism. It is synthesized by transamination or oxidative determination of glpcine, or from sarcosine. Decarboxylation of this acid yields active formate. It is the starting point of the glyoxylate cycle.

GMP reductase (EC 1.6.6.8)

a flavin enzyme which catalyses the conversion of guanosine 5'-monophosphate to inosinic acid in a single step.

G myeloma protein

an abnormal IgG immunoglobulin that is produced by individuals suffering from multiple myeloma.

goitrogenic agents

agents that induce goiter, an enlargement of the thyroid gland. The cause is usually insufficient synthesis of thyroid hormone, so that the pituitary is stimulated to release thyrotrophin which acts on the thyroid to cause enlargement. Goitrogenic agents include goitrin (present in turnips and related plants), the antituberculous drug s-aminosalicyclic acid and lithium salts (used in manic depression).

golgi apparatus

a structural element of eukaryotic cells which is stainable with osmium tetroxide. Its functions are the synthesis, concentration and storage of secretions. It is not present in prokaryote.

gonadal hormones, sex hormones

a biologically important group of steroid hormones which are produced in the male (testes) and female (ovaries) gonads. These determine the male or female character of an organism, in that they effect the normal development and function of the sex organs and the expression of the secondary sexual traits.

gonadorelin

a synthetic analogue of gonadotrophin releasing

hormone (GnRH) that acts on the anterior pituitary causing the release of endogenous gonadotrophins (FSH and LH). It is injected intramuscularly. In cattle it is used to treat ovarian cysts, stimulate ovulation in the postpartum period, and induce ovulation (usually given on the day of artificial insemination). Gonadorelin is not effective in the mare, but the related synthetic analogue suberlin, which has greater potency and a longer half-life, is effective in stimulating ovulation of mature follicle in the mare.

gonadotrophin releasing hormone GnRH
a hormone that causes the release of both luteinizing hormone and follicle-stimulating hormone from the adenohypophysis of the pituitary gland; it is often referred to as luteinizing hormone-releasing hormone (LHRH).

gorgonin
the protein, frequently containing iodine and bromine, composing the horny skeleton of members of the Gorgonacea; contains iodine and bromine.

gossypol
an aromatic triterpene from cotton seed (Gossypum hirsutum) which is synthesized from mevalonic acid via neryl pyrophosphate and cis, cis farnesyl pyrophosphate.

gradient elution
in order to increase the resolving power of the eluant, it is necessary to change its pH, ionic concentration of polarity.

gram molecular weight
the formula weight expressed in grams; the amount of a compound, element etc.; containing the same number of molecules or ions etc., as these are atoms in 12 g of C^{12} (avogadro's number).

gram positive bacteria
designating a bacterium that retains the initial gram stain and is not stained by the counterstain. Gram-positive bacteria generally possess a relatively thick and rigid cell wall that is readily digested by the enzyme lysozyme, and that consists of a layer of peptidoglycan.

gram stain
a set of two stains that are used to stain bacteria; the staining depends on the composition and the structure of the bacterial cell wall.

grand period of growth
the period of enlargement of a cell, tissue, organ or organism. This starts slowly immediately after differentiation, increases to a maximum rapidly, and finally falls off to zero.

gravitropism
growth movements induced by either gravitational stimulus or by mass acceleration e.g., by centrifugation.

grisein
an iron-containing antibiotic

synthesized by Streptomyces griseus. It is a cyclic polypeptide containing cytosine. The iron ions are strongly bound as hydroxamate-iron (III) complexes. It is especially effective against Gram-negative bacteria, but is not effective against fungi.

group transfer

the enzymatic transfer of a functional group from one molecule to another. In both anabolism, and catabolism, small groups of atoms are handled as units. Coenzymes often serve as corriers of the groups, hence the term "transport metabolites". Hydrolysis and phosphorolysis can be regarded as special cases of G.t. in which the group is transferred to water or a phosphate ion.

group transfer potential

the free energy change for the hydrolysis reaction in which a given group of atoms is removed from a compound.

growth

irreversible increase in volume and weight of cell, organ or organism. It is an active, intrinsic orderlyness from randomization. Growth is due to cell elongation and cell division. Assimilation of nutrients leads to quantitative increase in biomass.

growth correlations

the plant parts to not grow in isolation but follow an orderly pattern due to control of one part of plant over the other. The controlling effects by one part on the growth of other parts.

growth factor, growth supplement

a supplementary substance required in the Nutrient medium for growth of a specific organism. Growth factors are required, e.g., by Auxotrophic mutants; these have lost the ability to synthesize an essential metabolite, which then becomes a growth factor.

growth movement or tropism

when movement of plant organ is due to differential elongation of cells leading to different growth rates on opposite sides.

growth retardants

synthetic plant growth inhibitors, often used in agriculture for the control of plant growth. In particular, they cause stalk shortening in grassed, and some growth retardes are used for controlling stalk length in cereal crops.

guanidinium phosphates

the energy rich compounds that play a vital role in energy transfer and storage. It is found as phosphocreatine and phosphoarginine in muscles of vertebrates, respectively. The guanidinium phosphates, as represnted by phosphocreatine, are not inherently less stable because of the bond strain as in the case of ATP and ADP.

guanine
one of the purine bases found in DNA and RNA. Guanine has a purine ring structure.

guanosine, abb. Guo
9-β D-ribofuranosylguanine, a β-glycosidic nucloside containing D-ribose and guanine. The guanosine phosphates play an important role in the metabolism of all organisms.

guanosine phosphates
phosphoric acid esters of guanosine. They are nucleotides and are of great importance in metabolism. The biologically important derivatives are those esterified on C-5' of the ribose. According to the phosphoric acid component, the compounds are classified as guanosine mono-, di- and triphosphates.

guanosine-5'-triphosphate GTP
a high-energy compound that is required for peptide bond formation in protein synthesis.

gum
solutions of complex polysaccharides, gumarabic have methylpentose, hexose and uronic acid. These are exudates on the dark.

gutta
a rubber-like polyterpene of about 100 isoprene units in which the double-bonds are in the trans configuration. Gutta is less elastic than rubber, but it is more resistant to chemicals and environmental influences (insulating material). Depending on its source, it occurs in mixtures with other terpenes. The mixture with resins is called guttapercha, and that with triterpene alcohols is chicle (starting material for manufacture of chewing gum).

guttation
the oozing out of water in liquid form from turgid, uninjured leaves through the hydathodes. This occurs under moist and humid conditions during early hours of morning.

haemagglutination inhibition
the inhibition of haemagglutination; used for assaying haemagglutinating viruses by adding antiviral antibodies to a mixture of virus particles and red blood cells.

haematinic
a substance that promotes the formation of red blood cells. They are used to treat anaemia. Ferrous or ferric salts are given orally as haematinics in many species. Neonatal piglets are routinely given an intramuscular injection of iron-dextran to prevent piglet anaemia.

haemerythrin
a respiratory pigment similar to haemoglobin, and occurring in blood corpuscles of some invertebrate. Unlike haemoglobin, haemerythrin has two iron atoms bound directly to the polypeptide chains of the molecule.

haemocyanin

a blue copper-containing blood pigment found in many molluscs and arthropod. Haemocyanin is the second most abundant blood pigment after haemoglobin and functions similarly in acting as an oxygen-carrier in the blood.

haemoerythrin

a red oxygen-carrying blood pigment similar to the haemoglobin in containing iron. However, whereas haemoglobin is the blood pigment in all vertebrates and a wide range of invertebrates haemoerythrin is confined to several closely related minor groups of invertebrates, e.g., brachiopods.

haemoglobin C

type of haemoglobin with an abnormal beta-globin chain, in which lysine has replaced glutamic acid at position 6.

haemoglobin H disease

if three of the four genes that code for α–globin on chromosome 16 in all human cells, are deleted, the result is severe anemia that must be treated by transfusion. This state is called haemoglobin H disease.

haemolysin

one of a group of metabolic products of bacteria, some plants, snakes, toads, bees, spiders etc., which have the power of producing hemolysin. Certain of these exist normally in blood serum or are produced during immunization.

haemosiderin

an iron-containing storage complex found in animals that are receiving excessive amounts of dietary iron. It occurs principally in the liver, spleen, and bone marrow and has no fixed composition, containing variable amounts of iron along with protein and polysaccharides.

haine reagent

a solution of 8.314 g cupric sulphate and 40 ml glycerol in 400 ml water, to which is added 500 ml 5% aqueous potassium hydroxide solution. It is a test reagent for glucose, yielding a precipitate of cuprous oxide.

half-life

(i) the time required for the removal of half of the amount of a particular substance present in a given system.

(ii) the time required for the radioactive decay of half of the atoms in a given population.

half-value dose

the dose of radiation or toxic compound that produces deaths in 50% of the cells, or loss of infectivity of 50% of the virus particles, in a test group within a specified time; analogous to the median lethal dose for the animals.

half-value thickness

the depth of material which reduces the intensity of a radiation beam by one half.

halphen reagent for linseed oil

a solution of sufficient bromine in 10 ml carbon tetrachloride to bring the volume to 15 ml, used in detecting linseed oil. One ml of the reagent is added to 0.5 ml of the oil tested and 30 ml ether at 300 K. A turbidity which appears in 2 minutes is given by linseed oil.

haploid state

the chromosome state in which each type of chromosome is represented only once.

hapten

a small molecule which exhibits no intrinsic immunogenecity but will do so when coupled to a larger molecule (often a protein e.g., Bovine serum albumin) known as the carrier.

hapten protection

the shielding of the combining sites of an antibody by allowing a hapten to bind to them. The reaction may be used to specifically label the combining site of an antibody by reacting the antibody-hapten complex first with an unlabelled reagent and, after removal of the hapten, with the same, but labelled, reagent.

haptens

refers to the partial or incomplete antigens. These are either chemically defined molecules, e.g., dinitrophenol, or part of an antigen. They can bind especially to the corresponding antibodies (immunoglobulins), but they do not act by themselves as antigens. Only after coupling to a carrier protein do the haptanes become full antigens which are capable of eliciting an immune response.

hard water

water that contains sufficient concentrations of calcium, magnesium and iron ions; these ions form insoluble soaps that are ineffective as surface-active agents.

hartnup disease

a condition caused due to hereditary abnormality in metabolism of tryptophan; characterized by a pellagra like skin rash, intermittent cerebellar ataxia, and mental deterioration.

hashish

the dried resin from the glandular hairs of the female hemp plant (Cannabis sativa L). Due to the psychoactive Δ^3-tetrahydrocannabinol (2 to 8%) which it contains, it is one of the most common Narcotics. Marihuana (often used synonymously with hashish) is the dried and chopped tips of the shoots of the female hemp with a content of 0.5 to 2% Δ^3-tetrahydrocannabinol. Both hemp drugs have been used for millenia in folk medicine, due to their intoxicating action. Today they are, along with alcohol, the most widely used drugs; the number of consumers is estimated as 300 million. The drugs are usually smoked alone or mixed with tobacco in cigarettes ("joints") or pipes.

hay's test

this test is based on the fact that bile salts when present in the urine lower the surface tension. Place some fresh clear urine in a small beaker at room temperature. Sprinkle a little dry, finely powdered flowers of sulphur on to the surface. The sulphur particles sink in the presence of bile salts but remain floating if they are absent. Urines preserved with thymol may give a false positive and so should not be used.

HCG

abbreviation for Human chorionic gonadotropin, same as Chorionic gonadotropin.

heartwood

the central xylem of tree trunks, frequently impregnated with tannins, resinsetc. which can be considered to be excretory products. It contains non-functional xylem.

heat shock response

the transcriptional and translational activity of an organism induced by a heat shock. The response includes complete repression of the synthesis of some proteins, synthesis of some proteins not made at the lower temperature at all, and increased rates of synthesis of other proteins.

heavy isotope

an isotope that contains a large number of neutrons in the nucleus than the more frequently occurring common isotope of that element.

heliangin

a sesquilactone and a growth inhibitor, first isolated from the leaves of the Jerusalem artichoke (Helianthus tuberosus). It is a gibberelin antagonist and inhibits the growth of oat coleptiles, and stimulates root growth in beans (Phaseolus spp.).

helical content

the proportion of hydrogen bonded base pairs in a nucleic acid, or the proportion of hydrogen-bonded amino acid residues in a protein.

helix

the spiral arrangement of a biopolymeric compound, e.g., starch, some proteins and DNA.

helix-destabilizing proteins

proteins that bind to single-stranded regions of duplex DNA and induce unwinding further regions of the double helix. Helicase which unwinds bacterial DNA ahead of the DNA polymerase in one such enzyme.

helminthosporal

a natural product from the phytopathogenic fungus. Helminthosporium sativum (syn. Bipolaris sarokiniana, Shoemaker), which has a physiological effect on plants similar that of gibberellins.

helotism

a form of symbiosis, in which one partner benefits more than the other e.g., fungus growing in lichen thallus.

helvolic acid

refers to one of the tetracyclic triterpene antibiotics. It differs structurally from Fusidic acid in having a Δ^1-3. 6-diketo and a 7α-acetoxy function, and in lacking the 11α-hydroxyl group. It is produced by Aspergillus fumigatus and related fungal species. Like the structurally related triterpene antibiotics, fusidic acid and cephalosoporin P_1, it is effective against Gram-positive organisms.

hematein $C_{16}H_{12}O_6$

a brownish stain and chemical indicator obtained by oxidation of hematoxylin.

hematochrome

a red pigment occurring in green algae, especially when plants are exposed to intense light on subaerial habitats.

hematopoletin

a substance which is produced by the juxtaglomerular apparatus in the kidney and controls the rate of red cell production. Also known as hemopoietin.

heme iron

iron which is coordinately bound in porphyrins. It is present, for example, in the Hemoproteins.

hemes

1. metalloporphyrins, which act as the prosthetic groups of hemoproteins, e.g., cytochromes, hemoglobin, nitrite reductase, etc.
2. iron complexs with nonporphyrins with related tetrapyrrole structures, e.g., verdoheme biliverdine heme.
3. iron complexes of Chlorins.

hemicellulose $(C_6H_{10}O_5)_n$

a type of polysaccharide found in plant cell walls in association with cellulose and lignin; it is soluble in and extractable by dillute alkaline solutions. Also known as hexosan.

hemidesmosome

cellular structure morphologically resembling half a desmosome, occurring on the basal aspect of epithelial cells and assumed to serve a comparable adhesive function, in this case, anchoring the cells to the basal lamina. Recent evidence indicates certain compositional differences from a true desmosome but these may turn out to be minor.

hemiterpene

one of a class of substances related to terpenes of the formula C_5H_8, e.g., isoprene.

hemocyanin

an oxygen-transport copper protein. It does not contain porphyrin and is not particle-bound. It is oxidized state, it is blue. It occurs in molluscs and crustacea.

hemopexin

a heme-binding protein in human plasma that may be a regulator of heme and drug metabolism, and a distributor of heme.

hemoproteins
refers to the ubiquitous chromoproteins, which, as respiratory pigments, are involved in oxygen transport and in oxygen storage. As catalase and peroxidase, they effect the reduction of peroxides, and as cytochromes, they are involved in electron transport between dehydrogenases and terminal acceptors.

hemosiderin
an iron storage protein of the mammalian organism, functionally related to Ferritin. It is deposited in the liver and spleen (hemosiderosis), particularly in diseases associated with increased blood destruction, such as pernicious anemia, or with increased iron resorption (hemochromatosis), or even in hemorrhages.

hemotrophe
the nutritive substance supplied via the placenta to embyos of vivioparous animals.

heparitin sulfate heparan sulfate
a monosulfate ester of an acetylated (N-acetyl) heparin. As isolated from animal tissues (liver), it is probably a mixture of mucopolysaccharides with varying degrees of sulfatation or amino group acetylation.

heptose
any member of the group of monosaccharides containing seven carbon atoms.

herbalism
the practice that deals with herbs, parts of which are used for the benefit of the man as medicines or food, or for their scent of flavour.

hercogamy or herkogamy
the condition of a flower, when the stamens and stigma are so placed, that self-pollination is impossible.

hetero-
a prefix having the meaning 'different' or 'unlike', as in heterogeneous (different kinds) and heterocyclic (different atoms in the ring).

heteroatom
a term applied to the members of a ring structure other than carbon atoms; as in puridine, the nitrogen atom, and in thiophene, the sulphur atom, are heteroatoms.

heterobaric
when network of vascular bundles causes the effective isolation of sections of intercellular spaces, there is restricted lateral diffusion of carbon dioxide between the sections.

heteroduplex
a double-stranded nucleic acid molecule in which the two strands are complementary except for one or more regions in which they are not complementary. A double stranded phage DNA molecule that if formed by hybridizing one stand from a wild-type

phage with one strand from a mutant of this phage is an example.

heterogenity

(i) of a population containing several different species.

(ii) lack of agreement between different bodies of data in regard to the value of one or more parameters of which they are capable of yielding estimates.

heteroglycans

the polysaccharides, composed of two or more different carbohydrate residues, for example, pectins, plant mucilages, plant gums and mucopolysaccharides.

heteroimmunity

1. the immune reactions in which the antigens and the antibodies are derived from different animal species. 2. the immune reactions in which the antigens are derived from plants, microorganisms, or synthetic reactions.

heteronuclear

a condition in which two (or more) substituents occur in different rings or nuclei of compounds which contain two or more rings, as e.g., 1, 8-dichloronaphthalene. When substituents are both located in the same ring condition is termed isonuclear.

heteropycnosis

the variation of the degree of condensations of either different chromosomes or of parts of the same chromosome; used as the basis for classifying chromatin into euchromatin and heterochromatin.

heterosis or hybrid vigour

the increase in vigour, size and fertility of a hybrid as compared with its parents, resulting from the union of genetically different gametes and assumed to be due to special recombination of dominant and recessive genes.

heterotropic

dependent upon a supply of organic materials for its nutrition. Most bacteria, all fungi, and few higher plants are heterotropic as these are unable to synthesise food from simple inorganic substances.

heuristic model

one which enables the modeller to discover things about the system he is modelling that are not immediately obvious to him as properties of the system's components.

hexitols

sugar alcohols with 6 C-atoms. Of the 10 possible isomers D-sorbital, dulcital, D-mannitol, iditol and allitol are found in nature.

hexon bases

the amino acids lysine, arginine, and histidine which contain six carbon atoms.

high-density lipoprotein

a lipoprotein that contains approximately 30% protein, 30% neutral lipids, and 40%

phospholipids; these lipoproteins have molecular weights of the order of 100,000 to 400,000 and a density of about 1.062 to 1.21 g/I.

high energy bonds

the special bonds in ATP in which free energy is trapped and stored. On hydrolysis, which is very rapid, free energy is released from breaking of 3rd and 2nd phosphate bonds. It is represented by ~.

high energy bonds, energy-rich bonds

the chemical bonds which releases more than 25 kJ/mol on hydrolysis. They are usually esters (enol, thio and phosphate esters), acid anhydrides, or amidine phosphates.

highly repetitive DNA

sequence of DNA that occurs repeatedly in a given genomic sample of DNA. Such DNA is chiefly contromeric and palindromic DNA. DNA reassociation and cot plot analysis reveal the respective amounts of repetitious DNA in a sample.

high porosity gels

when amount of gel substance is low i.e., less than 2%, such gels offer least resistance to the passage of larger molecules. Thus macromolecules can easily be separated.

high salt plants

when plants are grown in a nutrient solution containing generous nutrients. Root excised from such plants show poor absorption of nutrients from the medium.

hill reaction

the light-dependent production of oxygen by the photosynthetic system in the presence of an artificial oxidizing agent (electron acceptor). R. Hill first observed this reaction in illuminated isolated chloroplasts, in the absence of CO_2, and using iron (III) oxalate as oxidizing agent. Iron (III) oxalate (Fe^{3+} is reduced to Fe^{2+} in the reaction) can be replaced by potassium ferricyanide, quinone and other compounds (Hill reagents). Spinach chloroplasts catalyse the following H :

$4K_3Fe(CN)_6 + 2H_2O + 4K^+ = 4 K_4 Fe(CN)_6 + 4H^+ + O_2$

the "natural" Hill reaction is the photolysis of water, and the "natural" Hill reagent is oxidized NADP.

hindrance

partial or complete blocking of a reaction resulting from the three dimensional structure of a molecule, often referred to as steric hindrance. For example, difference in the geometric arrangement of alkyl groups in saturated acids may cause substantial retardation of their rates of esterification; trimethylacetic acid esterifies at only a small fraction of the rate of the acetic acid because the reaction is hindered by three methyl groups attached to the first carbon atom.

histamine release

numerous stimuli are known to cause calcium dependent histamine release. Tissue injury such as trauma, heat and chemicals can cause histamine release, occurring through cell disruption or through a secretory process. During injury, released bradykinin and substance P can themselves release histamine. Plant poisons and animal venoms release histamine as well as other autacoids. Vagal stimulation and acetylcholine stimulate gastrin release, which by independent actions activates histidine decarboxylase, releases histamine and directly stimulates gastric acid secretion.

histaminergic nerve fibre

a nerve fiber that releases histamine as a neurotransmitter.

L-histidine abb. His

imidazolyalararine, a half-essential amino acid used in protein synthesis. The proportion of His in hemoglobin is especially high. It is also a component of carnosine and anserine. His is part of the active centers of many enzymes, and is an important buffer in the physiological pH range.

histidinemia

a metabolic disorder of histidine catabolism, in which the affected enzyme is histidase, is inherited as an autosomal recessive trait. Due to inadequate activity of liver histidase, conversion of histidine to urocanate does not take place. An alternate route of histidine metabolism, i.e., transamination to imidazolepyruvate, is then favoured and the excess imidazolepyruvate is excreted in the urine. Imidazole acetate and imidazolelactate, the reduction products of imidazolepyruvate, have also been detected in the urine of histidinemic patients.

histidinol phosphate phosphatase

an enzyme which catalyses the removal of phosphate group from histidinol phosphate giving rise to histidinol.

histoincompatibility

immunlogical intolerance to transplanted tissue that results from antigenic differences between the donor and the recipient of a transplant.

histological stains

the dye solutions used to produce contrast which aid resolution. Most of the stains rely on anionic or cationic reactions.

histone acetylation

attachment of an acetyl group (CH_3 CO-) to some amino acids of certain histone molecules. Two distinct types of histone acetylation are known, each correlated with a different aspect of histone function.

(a) Histones H1, H2A and H4 have the serine residues at their N-terminals irreversibly acetylated. This modification is associated with the histone synthesis.

(b) Reversible acetylation of N-terminal lysine residues of histones H2A, H2B, H3 and H4 may occur, and there is some evidence to support the view that genes which are being actively transcribed are associated in chromatin with histones which have highly acetylated lysines. This modification of histone molecules is rendered reversible by the activity of deacetylases in living cells.

Histone gas

one of a family of genes that code for histone proteins. They are distinguished by a complete absence of intron sequences.

holarrhena alkaloids, kurchialkaloids

a group of steroid alkaloids which are the characteristic active substances in plants of the dogbane (Apocynaceae) genus Holarrhena. The representatives so far isolated (about 50) are formal derivatives of the hydrocarbon pregnane which is substituted in the 3 and 20 positions with amino or methylamino groups, e.g., holarrhimine and conessine.

these alkaloids are biosynthesized via cholesterol and pregnenolone.

holocellulose

the total polysaccharide fraction of wood, straw, and so on, that is composed of cellulose and all of the hemicelluloses and that is obtained when the extractives and the lignin are removed from the natural material.

holoenzyme

a catalytically active complex made up of an apoenzyme and a coenzyme. The former is responsible for the specificity of the holoenzyme wiliest the latter determines the nature of the reaction.

holothurines

a group of highly toxic compounds from sea cucumbers (holothurioidea). They are triterpene saponts which contain holothurinogenins as aglycons and D-glucose, D-xylose, 3(O)-methyglucose and D-quinose as sugars.

homocyclic

a ring or nucleus composed of atoms of the same element which is usually carbon. This is true of cycloparaffins, cycloolefins, benzene and its derivatives, and cyclic terpenes. The term carbocyclic is also used for rings composed only of carbon.

homocysteine methyl tranferase

an enzyme which catalyzes the regeneration of methionine by the transfer of methyl group from N^5-

methyltetrahydrofolate.

homogenetic induction
the pattern of differentiation in one cell may induce similar changes in an adjacent cell.

homogentisase
the enzyme that catalyzes the conversion of homogentisic acid to fumaryl acetoacetic acid.

homogentisic acid $C_8H_8O_4$
an intermediate product in the metabolism of phenylalanine and tyrosine; found in excess in person with phenylketonuria and alkaptonuria.

homologous proteins
the proteins which are same or have similar functions, almost similar structure and molecular weights but immunologically not identical.

homoglycans
strainght or branched chain polysaccharides containing only one kind of monosaccharide residue. They are widespread in the vegetable kingdom.

homopolymer
a polymer built up of identical monomeric units, for example, amylose and polyphenylalanine. In a narrower sense, homopolymers are synthetic polynucleotides in which all the nucleotides contain the same base, for example polyadenylic acid. Polyuridylic acid, polydeoxyadaylic acid Homopolymers in the narrower sense are synthesized in vitro from nucleosides di-or triphosphates using the appropriate polymerases without a matrix.

homopolymeric nucleic acid
a nucleic acid chain containing only one type of nucleotide.

homopolymer tailing
use of terminal transferare to add a series of identical bases to the 3'- end of a DNA molecule, in the test-tube it often involves the addition of a string of poly A to carrier DNA and a string of complementary poly T to the DNA to be carried following the base pairing (or vice versa) or the use of the poly G and poly C in a similar way.

homosteroid
a modified steroid that contains one or several $-CH_2$ groups more than the parent compound; a homologous steroid.

horizontal resistance
the resistance that is pathotype non-specific and generally polygenic.

hormonal control of amino acid metabolism
insulin and the somatomedians enhance the active transport of amino acids across cell membranes. Insulin inhibits gluconeogenesis from amino acids and it promotes protein synthesis. Thyroid hormones also promote a positive nitrogen balance by stimulating

protein synthesis. Glucocorticoids like methylprednisolone, enhances gluconeogenesis from amino acids. Therefore, highdose glucocorticoid therapy leads to thinning of the skin and osteoporosis.

During fasting, the glucocorticoids predominate and insulin virtually disappears. The protein in skeletal muscle and in the viscera is lost daily by gluconeogenesis process to provide glucose.

hormone

1. a chemical messenger produced by endocrine glands and secreted directly into the bloodstream to exert a specific effect on a distant part of the body. 2. An organic compound that is synthesized in minute quantities in one part of a plant and translocated to another part, where it influences a specific physiological process.

horse radish peroxidase

enzyme used to identify endocytotic vesicles since the enzyme reacts with the contents of such vesicles and the products of the reaction are readily stained by osmium tetroxide for electron microscopy.

host-induced modification

a change in the properties of a virus that is brought about by the propagation of the virus in the host cells. In phages, the change amounts to a chemical alteration such as that produced by glucosylation or methylation of the phage DNA; in animal viruses, the change amounts to an incorporation of host cell membrane components into the viral envelope.

hot spot

a site on the DNA molecule at which mutational changes or recombinational events occur at a much higher frequency than is the case for average site.

human menopausil gonadotropin, HMG, castration gonadotropin

a glycoprotein of the anterior lobe of the pituitary. Carbohydrate content 30%. HMG has a similar action to follicle stimulating hormone. Its primary structure is not yet known.

hyaluronic acid

a polysaccharide found as an integral part of the gellike substance of animal connective tissue.

hyaluronidase

any one of a family of enzymes which catalyze the breakdown of hyaluronic acid. Also known as hyaluronate lyase: spreading factor.

hybrid enzyme

a form of polymeric enzyme occurring in heterozygous individuals that shows a hybrid molecular form made up of subunits differing in one or more amino acids.

hybridization
hybridization of nucleic acid molecules is a molecular biological technique for comparison of the nucleotide sequences and characterization of the information contents of differing nucleic acids. The filter, or gel technique is important.

hybridoma
a hybrid cell produced by the fusion of two cells and used for the production of monoclonal antibodies. Antibody producing lymphocytes of limited life span in cell culture are fused with tumour lymphocytes that are "immortal" in cell culture. Specific hybrides are selected and multiplied indefinitely in tissue culture.

hydramine
one of a series of amines derived from the glycols in which one hydroxyl is replaced by an amino group, e.g., oxythylamine, CH_2OH. CH_2NH_2

hydration
(i) the process whereby water molecules surround and bind to, solute ions and solute molecules in solution. (ii) the formation of hydrate.

hydro-
a prefix derived from the Greek word for water; in many chemical terms such as hydrocarbon and hydrogenation, it merely indicates the presence of hydrogen. Closely related is the prefix hygro, meaning dampness or moisture, as in hygroscopic (absorbing moisture).

hydrocarbon degradation, microbial hydrocarbon degradation
some microorganisms are able to degrable hydrocarbons and use them as their sole source of carbon and energy. The degradation of hydrocarbons depends highly on their structure. The most important pathway is the oxidation of one end to the corresponding fatty acid via the alcohol and aldehyde as intermediates. Further degradation of the fatty acids is achieved by β-oxidation. Ring cleavage is always preceded by the formation of a phenol by an oxygenase. Further degradation proceeds via pyrocatechol, cis, cis muconic acid and α-ketoadipic acid to the components of the tricarboxylic acid cycle, acetic acid and succinic acid.

hydrocortisone $C_{21}H_{30}O_5$
the generic name for 17-hydroxycorticosterone; an adrenocortical steroid occurring naturally prepared synthetically; its effects are similar to cortisone, but it is more active. Also known as cortisol.

hydrocyanic acid, hydrogen cyanide, HCN
a highly poisonous compound found widely in nature in the form of Cyanogenic glycosides.

It is released from these by β-glucosidases (such as emulsin) and oxinitrilases. A number of plants, especially those which contain cyanogenic glycosides, can metabolize HCN, usually by binding it to serine or cysteine to form cyanoalanine. Addition of water converts the latter to asparagine.

hydrodynamic

the motion of fluids and the forces on, as well as the motion of particles that are immersed in these fluids.

hydrogenase

enzymes that catalyzes the oxidation of hydrogen.

hydrogen ion equilibrium

the dissociation and association reactions of hydrogen ions, particularly those pertaining to functional groups in a protein.

hydrogen metabolism

1. metabolic redox reactions, involving pyridine nucleotide and flavin coenzyme.

2. all metabolic reactions involving hydrogen, i.e., hydrogenation, dehydrogenation, transhydrogenation, activation and formation of molecule hydrogen.

hydrolases

enzymes responsible for hydrolysis of organic compounds by adding water e.g., amylase, invertase, pectinase, phosphatases, proteases etc.

hydrolysis

reaction in which a compound is split by adding the elements of water across a chemical bond. For example, hydrolysis of peptides leads to the production of the constituent amino acids; hydrolysis of polysaccharides gives monosaccharides; hydrolysis of polynucleotides (e.g., DNA) leads to mononucleotides. The enzymes catalyzing hydrolysis reaction are called hydrolases; these include peptidase, glycosidases, nucleases, lipases, phosphatases, deaminases etc. Hydrolytic reactions in living organisms are not usually reversible; they are exergonic.

hydrolytic enzyme

a catalyst that acts like a hydrolase.

hydrophobic interaction

the attractive force between non-polar molecules or non-polar groups of molecules which leads to the association of these molecules or groups in an aqueous environment. These are unique in that their strength increase as the temperature is raised in the range of 0 to 60°C.

hydroxy acid

a carboxylic acid in which one or more hydrogen atoms of the alkyl group has been replaced by a hydroxyl group e.g., Lactic acid.

hydroxylamine

a powerful mutagen but only with isolated systems, since the normal components of a cell would readily scavenger the reagent. This reagent specifically reacts with cytosine.

hydroxylapatite or hydroxyapatite (HAP)

a form of calcium phosphate which can bind nucleic acid. Under certain conditions it will bind double stranded but not single-stranded DNA. It can, therefore, be used to fractionate DNA preparation to determine the extent of hybridization of two classes of single-stranded molecules. It is a calcium phosphate-calcium hydroxide complex $Ca_{10}(PO_4)_6(OH)_2$ that is also used as an adsorbent for purification of proteins.

hydroxylysine

an α-amino acid that is derived from lysine and occurs in colagen and gelatin.

hydroxyurea

a specific inhibitor of DNA synthesis in vivo; RNA and protein synthesis are not affected. DNA repair synthesis is not inhibited.

hypercalcinuria

an excessively high calcium concentration in the urine, usually occurring as a result of hypercalcaemia.

hyperchromic effect

increase in the extinction of a solution at a particular wavelength due to structural changes in the solute molecules. It is important in the denaturation of DNA when the double helix held together by hydrogen bonds is transformed into a disordered random coil.

hypersensitive sites

specific region in eukaryotic DNA that are cleaved by deoxyribonclease at higher rates than the bulk regions of the DNA; these sites frequently correlated with transcriptional activity of particular genes and may constitute regulatory regions in the DNA.

hyperuricaemia

the presence of an abnormally high concentration of uric acid in the blood.

hypervariable codon

a codon that has undergone an excessive number of mutations when it is considered in the context of the biochemical evolution of proteins.

hypervitaminosis

disease caused by excessive intake of a vitamin. It tends to occur more readily with the fat soluble vitamins, which are stored in the liver, but is less common with water soluble vitamins which can be excreted in the urine.

hypochromic effect

optical phenomenon in molecules with several chromophores, in which the sum of the optical densities of the individual components is greater than the optical density of the whole molecule. This effect depends on the content of adenine and thymine and is therefore greater in DNA than in RNA. Double-stranded polynucleotides have a greater effect than single-stranded, because the effect is intensified by hydrogen bonds.

hypocotyl

the portion of embryo axis below the cotyledonary node that it ends in root. In epigeal germination of seed the hypocotyl elongates and cotyledons come out of the soil.

hypokalaemia

an abnormally low concentration of potassium in the blood. It most commonly occurs as part of a complex metabolic disturbance known as metabolic alkalosis.

hypophysis, pituitary gland

a vertebrate organ for hormone production. In humans, it weights 0.7 g and lies at the base of the brain. It is connected to the midbrain by the hypophyseal stalk. It is composed of two parts with different ontogenies.

hypotonic

a solution having lower osmotic pressure. The solvent diffuses from such solutions till at equilibrium two solutions are isotonic.

hypoxanthine $C_5H_4ON_4$

an intermediate product derived from adenine in the hydrolysis of nucleic acid.

hypsochromic shift

a shift in the absorption spectrum of a compound toward shorter wavelength. Absence of double bonds, caused for example by protonating a ring nitrogen atoms, leads to a decrease in wavelength.

hysteresis

the fact that the water content at a given water potential is higher during a drying or desorption cycle during a wetting cycle.

hysteretic enzyme

an enzyme that appears to undergo very slow changes in either kinetic or molecular properties after the addition or the removal of a ligand; believed to be due to conformational changes of the enzyme as a result of the change in ligand concentration.

-ic

a suffix used in naming inorganic compounds to indicate that the multivalent positive element in the compound is in its highest valence state.

ideal solution

a dilute solution in which all of the solutes follow Raoult's law. Here chemical potential of each component is given by $u_i = u_i^o$ + RT in Xi where u_i^o is the standard chemical potential, R is gas constant, T is the absolute temperature, X_i is mole fraction of component.

IgA

an immunoglobulin that is present in serum in moderate

concentrations, has a variable sedimentation coefficient of 10 to 17S, and is a small multimer of the 7S immunoglobulin, and is incapable of passing the placenta. Secretory IgA consists of a dimer of two basic four-chain immunoglobin units. Each unit has two alpha heavy chains and two kappa or two lambda light chains.

IgE

an immunoglobulin that has a sedimentation coefficient of 8S, is present in serum in very low concentrations, and constitutes the reaginic antibody. It is found in mammals and possibly birds. It occurs at very low concentrations (17-450 ng/ml) in plasma; and is normally bounded by its C-terminal end to mast cells (basophils).

image processing system

interpretation of dynamics of vegetation from aerial photographus using imaging spectrophotometer. There are four major tasks; image digitization, scale correction feature identification and data display.

imidazole alkaloids

alkaloids of sporadic occurrence, possessing the imidazole ring system. The biosynthesis of these alkaloids is coupled to histidine metabolism.

immiscible

a term used to describe sustenances of the same phase that cannot be uniformly mixed or blended. It usually applies to liquids, such as oil and water, but may also refer to solids in powder form which differ widely in some physical property, such as magnesium carbonate and barium sulphate. In the case of liquids, immiscibility is due to differences in their chemical nature, which can often be overcome by addition of a third substance called an emulsifier or detergent.

immobolized enzyme

enzyme that is physically confined while it carries out its catalytic function. This may occur naturally, as in particulate enzyme, or it may be produced artificially by chemical or physical methods.

immune response

a uppecific protective or defense reaction against foreign substances. These foreign substances, known as antigens, release from the surface of the lymphocytes the signal for cellular or humoral immune response.

immune respression

the specific suppression of the immune response by corticosteriods, antimetabolites (purine analogs, folic acid antagonists), alkylating substances like cyclophosphamide ionization radiation or antilymphocyte serum. It is an important form of therapy for autoimmune disease and for preventing the rejection of transplanted organs.

immunoadsorbent

an insoluble material that is used for the purification of antibodies by adsorbing them from a serum; a gel for trapping antibodies, or an inert solid, to which either antigen or haptens have been covalently linked.

immunoconglutinin

an antibody that is specific for antigenic determinants which are exposed in fixed complement, but are unavailable for reaction in free complement.

immunoelectrophoresis

the technique which combines the specificity of immunoprecipitin reactions with the separation of molecules by electrophoresis in a molecular sieving medium.

immunoglobulin

any of a set of serum glycoproteins which have the ability to bind other molecules with a high degree of specificity.

immunoreactive insulin

that fraction of serum insulin that is not protein bound and is readily neutralized by anti-insulin serum; the bulk of this insulin is called little insulin and a smaller fraction is called big insulin.

immunosuppressants

agents that suppress the immune response. These include cytotoxic drug (such as cyclophosphamide, metotrexate, azothioprine, cytaribine, and actinomycin D) which inhibit proliferation of lymphocytes, anti-inflammatory steroids which act at the recognition phase of the immune response as well as on the proliferative stae, and cyclosporin A.

immunotolerance

the lack of an immune response to :

(a) the body's own substances or antigens with which the body has had contact since before or shortly after birth (natural) and

(b) larger or smaller amounts of certain antigens (tolerogens), which the body does not recognize as foreign and therefore tolerates (acquired I). The acquired immunotolerance can only be maintained when the tolerogens are constantly present; otherwise the immune response to this antigen arises again. Immunosuppressive measures facilitate the induction of an I. in adults.

implantation

the artificial introduction of materials, such as a tissue transplant or an encapsulated enzyme, into an organism.

incipient plasmolysis

osmotic pressure of solution in which plasmolysis just fails to occur. It is used to estimate OP and DPD of cell sap. At this stage turgor pressure is zero.

incomplete antibody

an antibody that does not give the serologic reactions of precipitation and agglutination, and can only be demonstrated either indirectly by means of special techniques or by means of special techniques or by means of its in vivo biological effect.

incomplete oxidation

the oxidation of organic compounds such that partially oxidised organic compounds are the final products.

independent variable

a quantity that can assume any arbitrarily chosen value independent of the values of other related variables.

indicator plant

a native plant that indicates the nature of soil conditions with regard to moisture, salinity and minerals.

indirect induction

in this the parts of an induced plant which are not directly exposed to inductive photocycles, could cause flowering when grafted onto the vegetative test plant e.g., Xanthium.

indolealkylamines

synthetic or naturally occurring compounds, or derivatives of the latter, containing an indolealkylamine nucleus in their chemical structures. They possess hallucinogenic activity.

indolepyruvic acid decarboxylase

an enzyme which catalyses the removal of CO_2 from indolepyruvic acid to form indole-3-acetaldehyde during auxin synthesis.

inducer

a chemical compound which stimulates the synthesis of enzymes (Enzyme induction). Inducer may be the substrate of the enzyme or another, effector, such as a hormone.

inducible

a gene or gene product is said to be inducible if its transcription or synthesis is increased by exposure to the cells to an effector.

inducible enzyme

enzyme formed in bacteria only when the cells are grown in the presence of its substrate.

industrial fermentation

a process in which products are synthesized or improved using micro-organisms. Discontinuous fermentation processes consist of the following steps : production of the nutrient medium, sterilization, innoculation, monitoring of the fermentation, separation and work-up of the product.

industrial microbiology, technical microbiology

a main area of technical biochemistry. It is concerned with the application of microbial production and processes in industry. The microbial production of products in industry, is called product synthesis. Industrial microbiology has an important role in the following branches of industry : fermentation industry, pharmaceutical industry (production of antiboitics, vitamins, and enzymes), chemical industry (production of proteins, enzymes and biochemicals), and food industry (baker's yeast). Industrial microbiology is also very important for sewage treatment and composing of garbage.

influx

net flux of ion into the tissue. It is determined by using tracer. Although tracer flux may not be equal to net flux.

informational molecules

molecules containing information in the form of specific sequences of different building blocks; include proteins and nucleic acids.

informosomes

according to Spirin, nucleoprotein particles containing mRNA which can be isolated from the cytoplasm of eukaryotic cells. They can be separated from ribosomes and polyribosomes by density-gradient centrifugation. They are thought to be transport particles for mRNA. They pick up the mRNA formed in the cell nucleus, probably at the nuclear membrane, and make it available in the cytoplasm for the formation of polyribosomes.

infusion

(i) an extract made by soaking a substance such as seed or plant, in water.

(ii) helping the penetration of a substance into seed with organic solvents.

inhibition coefficient

the lowest concentration of a bacteriostatic agent that inhibits bacterial growth under defined conditions.

inhibition index

a measure of the potency of an antimetabolite; equal to the ratio of the concentration of antimetabolite that is required to inhibit the effect of an essential metabolite, to the concentration of the metabolite.

inhibitor proteins

for the most part, low molecular weight, resistant proteins with compact structures and a lack of species specificity. Inhibitor proteins inhibit reversibly or irreversibly either, at the molecular level, certain anabolic or catabolic metabolic processes, or at the cellular level, growth and maturation processes of normal and malignant cells. The best known group or inhibitor proteins are the protease inhibitors, a group of protease-insensitive, disulfide-rich polypeptides widely distributed in the animal and plant kingdoms. They are especially frequent in the nutritional protein (egg white) of many eggs and in plant seeds. A large number of animal proteinase inhibitors are secretory proteins like the trypsin inhibitor of the mammalian pancreas, blood and seminal plasma, milk, colostrum, salivary, and snail mucous.

initial

(i) a cell which gives rise to further cells within a meristem, some of which form permanent tissues while others will remain meristematic.

(ii) the precursor of a organelle (especially plastids and mitochondria).

initial rate technique

a graphic method to determine the initial reaction rate from the reaction kinetic curves. The slopes of the tangents passing through the origin t = O for the reaction curves at various substrate concentrations are the initial rates at those concentrations.

initiation tRNA, starter tRNA, formylmethionyl-tRNA, abb. F-met-$tRNA_F$

a tRNA specific for methionine which differs in its primary and tertiary structure from the tRNA (Met-$tRNA_M$) which supplies the methionine incorporated into the middle of a polypeptide chain. The Met is formylated after esterification to $tRNA_F$ by a formyltransferase which transfers the formyl group from formyltetrahydrofolic acid. This enzyme is apparently absent from the cytoplasm of eukaryotes, so the initiation tRNA for protein synthesis on 80S ribosomes is Met-$tRNA_F$. F-Met or Met is removed from most proteins during their synthesis (post-translational modification of proteins).

inner volume

the volume of solvent that is trapped within the gel particles of the bed in gel filtration chromatography.

inosine phosphates

nucleotides, phosphoric acid esters of inosine :

1. inosine 5'-monophosphate, abb. IMP : inosinic acid, hypoxanthine riboside 5'-phosphoric acid is made up of the purine base hypoxanthine, D-ribose and phosphoric acid. Inosine phosphate is the precursor of all the other purines. It is the first intact purine compound in the course of Purine biosynthesis and all other purine nucleotides arise from it. Together with guanylic acid, IMP serves as a flavoring principle and is isolated from this purpose either from meat extract or from hydrolysates of yeast nucleic acids, or it is produced on a large scale by muntans of certain microorganisms, for example Corybacterium glutamicum.

2. inosine 5'-triphosphate, abb. ITP : can, as an energy-rich phosphate, replace ATP in certain metabolic reactions (carboxylations). It is formed by phosphorylation of IMP via inosine 5'-diphosphate, abb. IDP.

3. cyclic inosine 3, 5'-

monophosphate, abb. cyclo-IMP, cIMP. A structural analog of cyclic adenosine 3', 5',-monophosphate (Adenosine phosphates) which like the adenosine derivative, inhibits the growth of certain transplantable tumours.

inositol

carbohydrate that is an essential growth substance in some microorganisms and animals. Since it can normally be synthesized in adequate amounts by organism it is not classed as a vitamin.

inositol kinase

an enzyme which catalyses the conversion of myo-inositol to inositol-1-phosphate during phytic acid synthesis.

insect hormones

substances responsible for directing the life cycle of insects, mostly of low molecular weight. Three hormones are involved in the direction of post-embryonic development of insects :

1. activation hormone (brain hormone, adenotropic factor),
2. molting hormone (Ecdysone), and
3. juvenile hormone.

insertion

a mutation in either DNA or RNA in which one or more extra nucleotides are inserted into a polynucleotide chain.

inside-out protein

a protein that has an organisation of amino acid residues that is opposite to that of typical soluble globular proteins; a protein in which polar amino acids tend to be concentrated in the interior of the molecule while non-polar amino acids predominate on the exterior side of the molecule.

instantaneous transpiration rate

rate of transpiration at particular time and can be measured easily with; (i) short term weighing of detached parts of plants and (ii) short-term gasometric measurements.

insulin

a polypeptide hormone, secreted by the islets of Langerhans in the pancreas, that promotes the uptake of glucose by body cells and thereby controls its concentration in the blood. Insulin was the first protein whose amino-acid sequence was fully determined. It is a polypeptide produced by the β–cell of the islets of Langerhans of the pancreas. Its secretion is stimulated by high blood levels of glucose and amino acids after a meal. Glucose uptake is then stimulated by the action of the insulin on various tissues (e.g., muscles, liver and fat). It also stimulates glycogen and fat synthesis. Insulin is used therapeutically in the treatment of diabetes mellitus. Underproduction of insulin results in the accumulation of the large amounts of glucose in the blood and its subsequent excretion in the urine. This condition, known as diabetes mellitus, can be treated successfully by insulin injections. Insulin decreased blood glucose level by increasing glucose utilization and decreasing glucose formation. Glucose utilization is increased in the following way :

(a) in the presence of insulin, tissues start getting energy from glucose instead of fatty acids and ketone bodies. Even the formation of these fuel molecules (fatty acids and ketone bodies) is reduced. This is, partly, because lipolysis in the adipose tissue is, inversely, related to glucose utilization in this tissue. There are plasma membrane receptors for insulin in tissues. Insulin binds to these receptors to produce its effects. It increases glucose transport into the insulin sensitive cells except in the liver cells which are permeable to glucose without insulin. Activities of glycolytic enzymes, glucokinase, phosphofructokinase and pyruvic kinase are increased by insulin. Pyruvate dehydrogenase appears to be activated.

(b) Insulin promotes glycogenesis both in the liver and muscle. It activates synthase by activating phosphatase which dephosphorylates synthase.

insulinase

an enzyme produced by the liver which is able to inactivate insulin.

integral proteins

membrane proteins containing hydrophobic regions which attach to hydrocarbon chain of membrane lipids. These are like icebergs almost completely submerged in the phospholipid bilayer and insoluble in low ionic strength neutral solutions, however, soluble in low polarity or in detergent containing aqueous solutions.

integrated rate equation

an equation which represents the concentration of the substrate or product as a function of time. The corresponding plots are called the progress curves, which can also be obtained by direct measurement (Enzyme kinetics). By integrating the Michaelis-Menten equation, one obtains for example, with $(S_o-S) = P$, the integrated velocity equation $P(t) = V_m t + K_m InS/S_o$, where P is the product concentration, S the substrate concentration, so the substrate concentration at t = 0, and V_m and K are the maximal velocity of michaelis constant, respectively.

integration

the incorporation of one DNA segment into another as in :

(a) the incorporation of donor DNA into recipient DNA in

genetic recombination; (b) the incorporation of episomal DNA into chromosomal DNA; and (c) the insertion of the prophage DNA into the host bacterial DNA.

integrator

an instrument used to determine the area under a chromatographic peak. The measurement is either made mechanically or electronically providing a continuous digital read-out.

intercalary meristem

in most of the monocot some meristem remains undifferentiated either above or below the nodes. Activity of intercalary meristem helps in the elongation of internodes.

intercoversion

in biochemistry in general, the changing of one intermediary metabolic product into another; in enzymology, in particular, transformation of the active form of an enzyme into the inactive form, and vice versa, as a possibility for physiological regulation of metabolism.

integrator gene

hypothetical type of DNA sequence that controls a subset of other genes following its own stimulation.

interference

the property by which one cross over interferences with the occurring of another cross over in its neighbourhood.

interferometric

an optical system that focuses UV light passing through a solution in such a way that a photograph of interference fringes is obtained.

intergenic complementation

complementation that is produced by two mutant chromosomes which carry a mutation in different genes. The unmutated gene of one chromosome makes up for, or complements, the mutated gene of the other chromosome so that the necessary gene products of both genes are formed, and the wild type allele of each gene is expressed.

interkinesis

short interphase which occurs between the first and second meiotic divisions. Unlike a premitotic interphase, no DNA replication occurs in interkinesis.

interleukin-1

a polypeptide (or a group of closely related polypetides) synthesized in, and related from, mono-nuclear phagocytes during the early stage of the inflammatory response. Interleukin-1 induces several metabolic and immunological changes that are characteristic of the acute phase in inflammatory or immunologically mediated responses, *e.g.*, fever, increased synthesis of hepatic acute-phase proteins, increased white blood cell count, decreased serum iron and zinc levels, negative nitrogen balance.

interleukin-2

a lymphokine synthesized and secreted by some T-cells following activation with antigen or mitogen in the presence of monocytederived interleukin-1. Interleukin-2 permits long-term growth in vitro of T cell populations serving helper and cytotoxic functions and it augments natural killed cell activity. It is being evaluated for therapeutic use in patients with certain neoplasms or with acquired immune deficiency syndrome (AIDS).

interleukin-3

a substance derived from concanavalin A stimulated lymphocytes which appears to be involved in the maturation of stem cell subpopulation of T-cells.

intermediary metabolism

a term from early physiological chemistry, signifying all those metabolic reactions occurring between the uptake of foodstuffs and the formation of excretory products. In modern usage, it is essentially identical with primary metabolism.

intermediate

a compound that participates in a reaction and that occurs between the starting materials and the final products of the reaction.

intermedin

a hormonal substance produced by the intermediate portion of the hypophysis of certain animal species which influence pigmentation; similar to melanocyte-stimulating hormone in humans.

international standard

1. components added or already present in the same concentration in standard and investigated samples whose spectral line(s) is (are) used as reference lines for measurement of spectral line intensities of determined elements. 2. in NMR spectroscopy, reference substance dissolved in investigated solution; used for determination of the chemical shifts.

intersome

a collective term for the intermediate-size particles that either are naturally occurring precursors of ribosomes or are produced from ribosomes by the stepwise removal of proteins.

intervent

a solute that intervenes in, and reduces, the interactions between macromolecules.

intestinal hormone

either of two hormones, secretin and cholecystokinin, secreted by the intestine.

intracellular enzyme

an enzyme that remains active only within the cell in which it is formed. Also known as organized ferment.

intragenic suppression
the restoration of a genetic function, which was lost by mutation, through a second mutation in the same gene that sustained the primary mutation but at a different site in that gene.

intrinsic factor
a substance, produced by the stomach, which combines with the extrinsic factor (vitamin B_{12}) in food to yield an antianemic principle; lack of the intrinsic factor is believed to be a cause of pernicious anemia. Also known as Castle's intrinsic factor.

intron, or intervening sequence
a sequence within eukaryotic gene which is not represented in the protein product of that gene. Intron sequences are transcrbied into mRNA and must be excised and the RNA molecule religated, before it can be translated.

inulin
a polysaccharide made up of polymerized fructofuranose units.

invagination
(i) the process of infolding and pocket formation.
(ii) the structure formed by infolding, as that produced by an infolded membrane.
(iii) constriction of the cell resulting in division.

invertebrate hormones, hormones of invertebrate animals
the best studied of these are the insect and crustacean hormones. Many of these have not been chemically characterized, but the structures and biochemical effects of two are known : icdysone and juvenile hormone.

inverted repeat
two regions of a nucleic acid molecule which have the same nucleotide sequence but in the opposite orientation to one another.

invert sugar
a mixture of equal parts D-glucose and D-fructose which, in contrast to dextrorotatory sucrose, is levorotatory. Invert sugar is generated by acid or enzymatic hydrolysis of sucrose.

iodide pump
the active transport mechanism that concentrates iodine in the thyroid gland. Also known as iodide trapping mechanism.

iodopsin
the visual pigment found in the retinal cones, consisting of retinene, combined with the photopsin.

ion atmosphere
the region surrounding a charged atom, a charged group of atoms, or a charged molecule in which there is a statistical preference of ions of opposite charge.

ion channel block
blockade of ionic current flow

through membranes by chemical agents that bind to some components of the ion channels. A number of agent act selectively on particular channels. For example, tetrodotoxin and saxitoxin selectively block voltage dependent N channels, and blockade of such channels incardiac muscle is the main mechanism of action of class I antidysrrhythmic drugs. Tetratethyl ammonium and 4-aminopyridine block voltage-dependent KL - channels, and calcium channel blocking drugs are selective for CA channels. Block of the cholinoceptor-linked cation channels at the motor endplate is a special case, in the some of the drugs capable of producing this effect exert their main pharmacological action at a different site. Examples of channels include barbiturates, local anaesthetic drugs, phencyclidine, perhydrohistrionicotoxin and certain antibiotics. A surprising observation is that some neuromuscular blocking drugs, notably tubocurarine and gllamine, may block endplate ion channels under certain conditions. Their usual action is to block the recognition sites of the cholinoceptors.

ion exchange chormatography

a liquid-solid phase chromatographic method for analytic and preparative separation and purification of mixtures of substances. It is based on electrostatic binding between cations or anions of the substance to be studied or separated and the corresponding ion exchanger. (The components of an electrolyte solution are separated by successive adsorption and desorption through ion exchange. It can be run as a front, replacement or elution process. Ion exclusion and ion retardation are special techniques of ion exchange chromatography. It can be used to separate ionized from nonionized substances or substances ionized to different extents, e.g., inorganic from organic acids. Ions appear in the eluate sooner than nonions, because the latter penetrate the interstial and the interior resin phases and thus pass through the column more slowly.

ion exchanger

insoluble substance containing ions that can be exchanged for other ions from solution. Many insoluble substances, both inorganic and organic which have an interlocking molecular structure (case) can act as ion exchanger, e.g., aluminosilicates (clays) cross-linked organic polymers (ion exchanger resins), sulphonated coal and cellulose, and to some extent, proteins and nucleic acids. Ion exchange is a reversible phenomenon with many uses: water softening (zeolite), chromatographic analysis, elimination of ionic impurities (demineralization) of rare earth separations, acid removal, etc. Because of their predominantly siliceous nature, they have an important bearing on fertilizer application mixed-bed de-ionization.

ion-filtration chromatography

a chromatographic technique that is based on the combined use of the gel filtration and ion-exchange chromatography; performed by eluting macromolecules in the sieving range from a cross-linked ion-exchange gel under precisely controlled conditions of pH and ionic strength.

ionophore

a compound which increases the permeability of membranes to ions. Ionsphores act by delocalizing the charge of the ion and shielding it from the hydrophobic region of the lipid bilayer. They possess both hydrophobic (confers lipid solubility) and hydrophilic (binds the ion) regions.

ion-pair

(i) the positive ion formed by the action of ionising radiation together with the orbital electron that was ejected from the uncharged atom when the ion was formed.

(ii) the two ions consisting of either an anion and a cation that has remained in the secondary hydration shell of the anion, or a cation and an anion that has remained in the secondary hydration shell of the cation.

ionic double layer

the region encompassing the charges on an atom, a group of atoms, or a molecule together, with the layer of counterions that surrounds these charges.

ionophore

any of a class of compounds, generally cyclic, having the ability to carry ions across lipid barriers due to the property of cation selectivity; examples are valinomycin and nonactin.

ion pair chromatography

ion pair separation can be visualized as an ion exchange process wherein the ion exchanger (stationary phase) is dynamically maintained by the adsorption of relatively hydrophobic charged species from the mobile phase on to the hydrophobic surface of the reverse phase column. Thus, ion pair chromatography confers to a much greater degree of flexibility than does conventional fixed-site ion exchange. Both the identity of the ion exchange sites and the capacity of the system can readily be modified as necessary to meet new analytical conditions.

ipomoeamarone

a Phytoalexin with a sesquiterpene structure. It is

formed when sweet potatoes are infected by phytopathogenic microrganisms. Biologically, it is synthesized from mevalonic acid via farnesol.

iridoids

a group of natural products characterized by a methylcyclopentanoic monoterpene skeleton. Iridoids used to be called, incorrectly, pseudoinicans, because some of them can be transformed into intensely blue compounds in the presence of air and acids. This process has not been elucidated, but it is not chemically related to the transformation of indican glycosides into indigo.

irin

a mixture of substances (now known to be prostaglandins) released from the iris and associated structures during inflammation of the eye.

iron

an essential nutrient for animal and plant growth. It is contained in the protein haemoglobin, which gives the colour to red blood cells and is responsible for oxygen transport from the lungs. Iron deficiency leads to anemia. Iron is found in other porphyrins and in cytochromes, which are important components of the electron-transport chain. It is also required as a cofactor for certain enzymes, e.g., catalase and peroxidase. Certain iron-containing proteins are essential for the fixation of nitrogen by bacteria.

iron -binding prote:n

a seıum protein, such as hemoglobin, for the transport of iron ions.

iron metabolism

the chemical and physiological processes involved in absorption of iron from the intestine and in its role in erythrocytes.

iron-sulphur proteins

proteins that contain iron-sulphur clusters and participate in single-electrons transfer reactions; best known are the ferredoxins. They are involved in the functioning of such diverse enzymes as NADH dehydrogenase, succinate dehydrogenase, pyruvate dehydrogenase in anaerobes and nitrogenase. Three known types of iron-sulphur proteins are those in which:

(a) a single iron atom is liked to four cysteine sulphur atoms as in ruberdoxin;

(b) two iron atoms are linked to four cysteine sulphur atoms and to two bridging, acid-labile sulphur atoms as in plant-type ferredoxin; and

(c) four iron atoms are linked to four cysteine sulphur atoms and to four bridging, acid-labile sulphur atoms as in bacterial-type ferredoxin and in high potential iron-sulphur proteins.

irrational number
the number which can not be expressed as the quotient of two integers.

irritability of plant
the ability of plant or its parts to respond physically to an environmental factor.

isoagglutinin
an agglutinin, present in the blood, that reacts with blood group antigens of other members of the same species.

isoagglutinogen
a blood group antigen, that is capable of eliciting and/or binding specific antibodies in members of the same species.

isoalloxazine
the heterocyclic ring structure that occurs in riboflavin and in the flavin nucleotides.

isochorismate synthase
an enzyme which catalyses the transformation of chorismate to isochorismate which is precursor for vitamin K_i and anthraquinones.

isocitrate dehydrogenase (E.C. 1.1.91 or 1.1.1.92)
an enzyme belonging to the class of dehydrogenases which reduces isocitrate as the secondary hydroxyl group during the operation of the tricarboxylic acid cycle. It simultaneously catalyses the reversible decarboxylation of the resulting oxalosuccinate to 2-oxoglutarate. It transfers the hydrogen to NAD^+ or $NADP^+$. The NAD^+ -specific form is found, only inside the mitochondria, is allosterically activated by ADP, inhibited by ATP, and catalyses the reaction only in the direction of 2-oxoglutarate. The $NADP^+$ -dependent cytoplasmic enzyme requires manganese (II) ions and produces hydrogen for syntheses. Isocitrate dehydrogenase is allosteric and therefore serves as a regulatory enzyme.

isodynamic enzyme
one of two or more different enzymes or enzyme forms that catalyze the same reaction but differ in their properties.

isoelectric point
the pH at which an amphoteric substance will not migrate toward either pole in an electric field.

isoenzymes, isozymes
multiple forms of an enzyme with the same substrate specificity, but genetic differences in their primary structure. If there are no differences in primary structure, one speaks of Pseudoisoenzymes.

isoform
one of a group of proteins of related function but slightly differing amino acid sequence. Many isoforms are a result of differential exon splicing.

isofunctional enzymes
two or more different enzymes that catalyse the conversion of the same substrate to the same product. Such enzymes may be

involved at the first step of a branched metabolic pathway and may be subjected to feed back. inhibition; the end product of one branch inhibits one of the enzymes while the end product of the second branch inhibits the other enzyme.

isogenic

(i) having the same genetic constitution.

(ii) propagating entirely by means of apogamy.

isohydric shift

a set of two reactions, occurring in the red blood cell, whereby the oxygenation and deoxygenation of haemoglobin during respiration are lined to the reversible ionization of carbonic acid. As a result, the intracellular PH of the red blood cell remains essentially constant despite the fact that protons participate in both reactions.

isoionic protein

a protein that has an equal number of protonated basic groups and deprotonated acidic groups; operationally defined as a protein from which all bound ions have been removed by electrolysis or by mixed-bed ion-exchange chromatography. Such a protein contains no ions other than those arising from dissociation of solvent.

isolation

(i) the condition in which individuals of common ancestry are separated into two mating groups. It may be geographic by space, or genetic by genotype.

(ii) the condition in which chromosomes or parts of chromosomes of common ancestry are prevented from undergoing effective recombination.

(iii) separation of specific type of substance.

isomaltose

a reducing disaccharide, composed of two molecules of D-glucopyranose linked 1, 6-glycosidically. It is formed by the enzymatic degradation of branched polysaccharides, e.g., amylopectin.

isomerism

occurrence of substances with same molecular formula, but having different structural formulae.

isometric

an adjective used to describe a muscle contraction in which the muscle length remains constant while the tension developed increases.

isopeptide bond

a covalent cross-linking bond between the εamino group of lysine and the side-chain carboxyl group of glutamate or aspartate, formed by condensation :

$$H_2N-CH(COOH)-CH_2-CH_2-COOH+H_2N-CH_2-CH_2-CH-CH_2-CH(NH_2)-COOH \xrightarrow{H_2O} N_\varepsilon$$

γ-glutamyl-lysine. It has been found in polymerized fibrin and native wool. It is not hydrolysed by the body's own digestive proteases, but only by the bacteria in the large intestine. Its presence in nutritional proteins therefore reduces their nutritional value.

isoprene unit

a complex alkenes containing multiple double bonds. It is non-cyclic 5 carbon compound. All terpenes are isomeric forms of isoprene units.

isoquinoline alkaloids

a large group of alkaloids occurring widely in the plant kingdom. The heterocyclic skeleton is usually synthesized in vivo by a mannich condensation between a phenylethylamine derivative and a carbonyl component. The resulting tetrahydroisoquinoline derivatives are converted by dehydrogenation into isoquinoline derivatives.

isoreceptors

a term (analogous to isoenzyme or isozyme) sometimes used in referring to subtypes of a more major class or receptors. (Isoceptors is an alternative name). For example, β_1-adrenoceptors and β_2-adrenoceptors are isoreceptors of the general class of the β-adrenoceptors.

isosemantic substitution

the incorporation of an amino acid into a polypeptide chain that results from a mutation in which the normal codon of an amino acid has been mutated to a synonym codon; consequently, the amino acid that is incorporated into the polypeptide chain is identical to the normal one, but is incorporatey in response to one of its synonym codons.

isotope

atomic species with the same atomic number but different mass numbers. In such cases number of neutrons/atom will differ in various species of the element. The atomic weight is also different e.g., C^{-11}, C^{-14}.

isotopic number

the difference between the number of neutrons in an isotope and the number of protons.

Isotopic Trapping

a method for demonstrating that compound X is an intermediate in a metabolic pathway. A labelled precursor of the pathway is added to the *in vivo* or the *in vitro* system, followed by the addition of large amount of unlabelled X. The appearance of label in X indicates that it is intermediate of the pathway at position subsequent to that of the labelled precursor.

isotopically enriched

a substance in which the relative amounts of one or more isotopes has been increased.

isotype

one of two or more antibodies produced by the same species;

the IgA, IgD, IgE, IgG, and IgM immunoglobulins of a given species are examples.

isovaleraldehyde $(CH_3)_2$ CH-CH_2-CHO

a naturally occurring aldehyde p=0.7977, m.p. 92.5°C. It is a colourless, sharp smelling liquid which is very reactive and polymerizes easily in the presence of acid. It occurs in many aromatic oils, especially in eucalyptus oils, and is obtained synthetically by oxidation of isoamyl alcohol.

Jablokoff test

to detect mineral oils in fatty oils, mix 1 part of the oil with 4 parts of aniline. The presence of mineral oils causes turbidity.

Jacquemart reagent

an aqueous solution of mercuric nitrate acidifed with nitric acid; used as a test reagent for ethyl alcohol. A black precipitate, produced upon addition of concentrated ammonium hydroxide, indicates the presence of ethyl alcohol.

Jager test for cholesterol

on heating with isobutyric anhydride cholesterol forms its isobutyrate.

jasmonates

proposed as naturally occurring growth regulators and thought to be ubiquitous in higher plants e.g., Jasmonic acid.

jaundice

the condition when bilirubin accumulates in the blood, and when it reaches a certain concentration, it diffuses in to the tissue, which then become yellow.

jervine

a jeveratrum type of Veratrum alkaloid with a C-nor-D-homo structure. It is the main alkaloid of white and green hellebore (Veratrum album and veratrum viride).

joro spider toxin (JSTX)

a toxin from the venom glands of the Japanese Joro spider (Nephila clavata). It has the property of blocking glutamate receptors in crustacea and mammals.

juction potential

the potential that arises either across the junction between two half cells or across the boundary between two solutions of different concentrations; it is due to differences in diffusion rates of the ions on the two sides.

juvenile hormone

a hormone secreted by endocrine glands associated with the brain in insects that prevents metamorphosis into the adult form and maintains the presence of larval characteristics. The exact mechanism of juvenile-hormone action is not clear, but it appears to modify the effect of the moulting hormone, ecdysone. The concentration of juvenile hormone possibly decreases gradually during development, declining below a threshold level during the final instar to allow ecdysone to promote differntiation into the adult.

juvenile leaf

the form of leaf found on sporeling or seedling. When it differs markedly from the leaf of the adult plant.

juvenile myxedema

a condition developed due to the lack of sufficient thyroid hormone in the later life. This is characterized by decreased bone growth and slowing of mental development.

kaempferol

a flavonoid with a structure similar to that of quercetin but with only one hydroxyl in the B ring; acts as an enzyme cofactor and causes growth inhibition in plants.

kafirin

storage protein of sorghum. On SDS-PAGE it has been separated into 1 or 2 bands with molecular weight 20-25 KD and one or more minor bands of lower molecular weight.

kairomones

the chemical substances that benefit the recipient living organism rather than the organism emitting it. These compounds elicit positive responses of predators to their prey, herbivores to their food plants, and parasites to their hosts.

kaliuretic action

an action that promotes kaliuresis; i.e., the excretion of potassium ions in the urine. Many diuretic drugs, e.g., thiazide drugs, possess a kaliuretic action as an unwanted effect.

kallikrein kininogenin, kininogenase

a proteolytic enzyme (EC 3.4.21.8) which preferentially cleaves Arg and Lys peptides. There are at least three types.

kappa chain

one of two types of light chain found in immunoglobulins which differ by about 60% in their constant region amino acid sequences. In any one immunoglobulin molecule both light chains are either kappa (κ)- or lambda (λ)- type.

karyoplasm

the gel state of the nucleoplasm.

kendall's compound

a designation for some steroids; Kendall's compounds B,E, and F refer, respectively, to corticosterone, cortisone, and cortisol.

keratin

any of various albuminoids characteristic of epidermal derivatives, such as nails and feathers, which are insoluble in protein solvents, have a high sulfur content, and generally contain cystine and arginine as the predominating amino acids.

keratolytic agents

agent that promotes keratolysis, i.e., softening or peeling of the horny (keratin) layer of the epidermis. Keratolytic agents are applied topically and include resorcinol, salicylic acid and sulphur.

keratoplastic agents

agents that promote the growth of the superficial layers, the keratin, of the epidermis. Such agents include coal tar, ichthamol, and tretinoin.

kermesic acid

a bright red insect dye belonging to the group of anthraquinones, m.p. 250°C (d). It is structurally closely related to Carminic acid; it possesses the identical structure of a tetrahydroxylated methylanthraquinone carboxylic acid, but the C-glycosidic glucose on C-2 is absent. It makes up 1 to 2% of kermes, the dried bodies of female scale insects Kermococcus ilicis.

keto acids

several α-keto acids are important metabolic intermediates; these include pyruvic acid and α-ketoglutaric acid. Keto acids are produced from the corresponding amino acids in transmination reactions. β-Keto acids in bound form are intermediates in fatty acid oxidation metabolism.

keto-enol tautomerism

the tautomerism that is due to a shift of a hydrogen atom so that one of the isomers is a ketone and the other is an enol.

α-ketoglutarate pathway

the catabolic pathway whereby arginine, proline, histidine, glutamine, and glutamic acid enter the citric acid cycle by way of α-ketoglutaric acid.

a-ketoglutaric acid dehydrogenase

an enzyme that catalyzes the succinyl-CoA by the oxidative α-decarboxylation of α-ketoglutaric acid. This reaction requires TPP, Mg^{2+}, NAD^{+}, FAD, lipoic acid, and coenzyme A as cofactors.

ketone

a class of unsaturated and reactive compounds whose formula is characterized by a carbonyl group to which two organic groups are attached; these groups may be either paraffinic (alkyl) or aromatic (aryl). The best-known example of this class is acetone, or dimethylketone. $(CH_3)_2$ C=O. Other important ketones are methyl ethyl ketone, accetophenone, and cyclohexanone. The reactions of ketones are generally similar to those of the aldehydes. Their major uses are in the solvent field, especially in the plastics, textile, paint, and lacquer industries. They are particularly good solvent for cellulose derivatives. The ketones are named in various ways :

(i) by combining the names of the radicals (alkyl or aryl) with

'ketone', as dimethyl ketone, ethyl methyl ketone, etc.
(ii) the Geneva names are formed by adding the suffix "one" to the root of the parent hydrocarbon. Thus, acetone is propanone, ethyl methyl ketone is butanone.
Simple ketones contain two alkyl or aryl groups of one kind; in mixed ketones the alkyl or aryl groups are different, e.g., ethyl methyl ketone.

ketone bodies

organic compounds produced by ketogenesis in the organism. Ketone bodies are acetoacetate and the compounds formed from it, β-hydroxybutyrate and acetone. The increased production of under certain pathological conditions, e.g., diabetes mellitus, leads to acidosis, because acetoacetate and β-hydroxybutyrate are present as anions, which reduces the concentration of HCO_3 in the blood. Other consequences are the excretion of the k.b. by the kidneys, production of acid urine, and damage to the central nervous system.

ketose

monosaccharide that contains a ketone group. The simplest example is dihydroxyacetone (a triose having three carbon atoms) and one of the most abundant in nature is fructose (a hexulose having six carbon atoms). The C-2 ketone in hexauloses can react rapidly and reversibly with the C-5 hydroxyl group to form an intramolecular ring structure consisting of four carbon atoms and an oxygen atom (furanose); it is the predominant form of hexuloses in solutions.

ketosis

an excessive accumulation of ketone bodies in the tissues, blood, and urine. Ketone bodies are formed by the oxidation of fatty acids by the liver. The simplest form of ketosis occurs in starvation and involve depletion of available carbohydrate coupled with mobilization of free fatty acids. Thus, ketosis arises as a result of a deficiency in available carbohydrates.

key enzyme

an enzyme that is unique to a metabolic pathway which has several enzymes in common with other pathways.

killed vaccine

a vaccine that consists of originally infectious bacteria or viruses that have been rendered noninfectious; a vaccine of either killed bacteria or of inactivated viruses.

kindling

a term applied to a lasting change in brain function that results from repeated focal electrical stimulation and leads to a predisposition to epileptiform convulsions.

kinetic data evaluation

data evaluation by computer is performed by a nonlinear regression analysis, using an objective procedure, in which the sums of the squares of the differences between calculated and experimental values are minimized (method of least squares).

kinetic energy

energy of motion is known as kinetic energy. Any mass in motion possesses kinetic energy. It is shown in a number of forms i.e., mechanical, radiation, electrical and ionic energies.

kinetin $C_{10}H_9ON_5$

a cytokinin formed in many plants which has a stimulating effect on cell division.

kinins

1. chemical substance which stimulate differentiation of plant cells that otherwise may have lost permanently the power of differentiation. The kinins contain adenine, which seems to give these substance their biological activity. 2. Group of blood-borne polypeptides that causes smooth muscle contraction and blood vessel dilation, the best known is bradykinin.

Klotz plot

a plot of binding data in which the average binding number (V) is plotted as a function of the logarithm of the free ligand (S) concentration.

kornberg enzyme

the DNA-dependent DNA polymerase, from Escherichia coli, that is believed to function in the repair-synthesis of DNA.

Kreb's cycle or Tricarboxylic acid cycle or citric acid cycle

reaction in which pyruvic acid is oxidative decarboxylated and CO_2 is released and it is dehydrogenated to reduced NAD and FAD coenzymes in the matrix of mitochondria. Electron undergoes oxidative phosphorylation and terminal oxidation thereby forming water. 15 moles of ATP are produced when one mole of pyruvic acid is completely oxidised through this cycle.

Kreb's solution

a physiological salt solution for bathing isolated in mammalian tissues. Its composition is (mmol/L); NaCl, 94; KCl, 4.7; $MgSO_4$ $7H_2O$, 0.45; $CaCl_2$ 2.5; KH_2PO_4, 1.2; $NaHCO_3$, 22; glucose, 13; pyruvic acid, 3.1; fumaric acid, 5.3; glutamic acid, 3.1; (the acids are converted to the sodium salts by the $NaHCO_3$). The solution is bubbled with 5% carbon dioxide in oxygen.

Kreb's-Henseleit solution

a psysiological salt solution used for maintaining mammalian tissues, especially when nerve evoked responses are to be recorded. It has the following composition (mmol/L):

NaCl, 11.8; KCl 4.7; $CaCl_2$ 2.5; $MgSO_4$ $7H_2O$ 1.2; NaH_2PO_4 1.2; (but sometimes replaced by KH_2PO_4), $NaHCO_3$ 25; glucose 11.1. It is obtained with 5% carbon dioxide in oxygen.

K system

a system composed of a regulatory enzyme and an effector, such that the effector alters the substrate concentration at which one half of the maximum velocity of the reaction is obtained but does not alter the value of the maximum velocity.

kynureninase

an enzyme that functions in tryptophan metabolism and requires pyridoxal phosphate as a coenzyme.

L-gluonolactone oxidase

an enzyme which catalyses the oxidation of L-gluonolactone to H_2O_2 and 3-Keto derivative which tautomerizes to form L-ascorbic acid.

label triangulation method

a method for determining the quaternary structure of protein complexes. The subunits of the complex are separated, labelled with heavy atoms, and allowed to aggregate and reform the complex. The distances between the subunits are then measured by some techniques such as X-ray diffraction, neutron diffraction, or spectroscopy.

labile phosphate group

a phosphate group that is readily liberated from a compound by hydrolysis at 100°C in 1 N hydrochloric acid for 7 to 10 minutes. The terminal phosphate group of nucleoside triphosphates and the phosphate groups of pyrophosphate fall into this category; the phosphate group of ordinary esters generally requires longer times for hydrolysis.

labile pool

fraction of stable element in the soil which is accessible to the plant. It includes nutrients which are in solution or can readily pass into it. It is determined by isotopic dilution.

labile sulphur

sulphur, such as that present in some iron sulphur proteins, that is readily released from the protein in the form of H_2S when the PH is lowered to about 1.0.

LAC operon

genetic system of E coli responsible for the uptake and initial catabolism of lactose. Also known as lactose operon. The operon and its regulatory gene consists of four key DNA regions:

(a) a number of structural genes that serve as templates for the mRNA's responsible for the translation in the ribosomes of information for the synthesis of enzymes involved in lactose metabolism, namely, β-galactsidase, galactoside permease, and thiogalactoside transacetylase, respectively;

(b) the operator gene adjacent to the first structural gene;

(c) the promoter region which consists of two subregions, namely, the CAP and the RNA polymerase interaction site, which is in turn contiguous to the operator gene; and

(d) the closely associated regulatory gene site.

lac repressor protein

the first repressor substance (product of a repressor gene) to be isolated and characterizud. It is an acidic (I.P. 5.6) allosteric protein of M_r 152000. It consists of four identical subunits (M_r 38000, 347 amino acids, sequence and spatial structure known). Its primary structure has recognizable similarities to histones or to β-galactosidase.

lactice acid bacteria

a group of bacteria that ferment carbohydrates in the presence or absence of oxygen, with lactic acid always a major end product. They have a high tolerance of acid conditions. Lactic acid bacteria are involved in the formation of yogurt, cheese, sauekraut, and silage. They can occur as spoilage organisms and some are pathogenic, causing infections of the nasophrynx. They include members of the genera Lactobacillus, Steptococcus, and Leuconostoc.

lactose

a sugar comprising one glucose molecule linked to a galactose molecule. Since it has a potentially free carbonyl group on the glucose residue, lactose is a reducing disaccharide. Lactose is manufactured by the mammary gland and occurs only in milk. For example, cow's milk contains about 4.7% lactose. It is less sweet than sucrose (cane sugar). The first step in its metabolism is by way of hydrolysis to the component monosaccharides. It is an excellent example of an inducer compound. The inducible enzyme is β-galctosidase and it catalyzes the conversion of lactose into galactose and glucose. In directly, E. coli utilizes lactose. First, a galactoside permease which permits entry of lactose into the cell must be induced; and second, the β-galactosidase which hydrolyzes the disaccharide to galactose and glucose must be induced. A third enzyme, thiogalactoside transacetylase, is also induced, but its function is not fully understood. Thus, when E. coli is grown in the presence of lactose as the sole carbon source, these three enzymes are induced in large quantities in a coordinated manner.

laevorotatory

designating a chemical compound that rotates the plane of plane-polarized light to the left (anticlockwise for someone facing the oncoming radiation).

lagging strand

during semidiscontinuous synthesis of DNA one template strand is copied discontinously in segments. These segments are referrud to as lagging strand.

lambda chain

one of two types of light chains found in immunoglobulins which differ by about 60 percent in their constant region amino acid sequence.

lamp-brush chromosomes

very large chromosomes, up to 1 mm long, which occur in the meiotic prophase in newts and a few other animals. They form loops along the sides, which give them a brush-like appearance. The loops are not fixed structures. They represent unwound, individual chromomers, consisting of DNA protein and RNA. They appear at the sites of active RNA synthesis, thus indicating increased physiological activity in the particular chromosome section.

lanatoside

any of three natural glycosides from the leaves of Digitalis lanata; on hydrolysis with acid, it yields one molecular of D-glucose, three molecules of digitoxose, and one molecule of acetic acid, all three glycosides are cardioactive.

lanolin, wool, fat, wool wax

the fatty or more correctly waxy substance secreted by the skin of the sheep, m.p. 36-42°C. It is a complicated mixture of fatty acids, alcohols, fats and waxy substances.

laser

light amipliphication by stimulated emission of radiation. The laser produces a powerful, highly directional, monochrmoatic, and coherent beam of light.

latency

the phenomenon of an inactive particulate enzyme that either becomes active after it is exposed, while still attached to an insoluble matrix, or becomes active after it is detached from the insoluble matrix.

latent heat

gain or loss of heat caused by change in state, such as the loss when water evaporates or the gain when dew condenses.

layering

(i) the banding seen in thick cell walls, due to the presence of wall layers differing in water content, chemical composition and physical structure.

(ii) the grouping of vegetation in a wood into 2 or more well defined layers differing in height, as trees, shrubs, and ground vegetation.

(iii) a method of artificial propagation in which stems are peged down until they root and then detached from the parent plant.

laudanum

the name originally given to preparations of, or containing opium. The name laudanum, which is now obsolete, and is restricted to the simple alcoholic tincture of opium.

leader peptide

a peptide, coded by a sequence of nucleotides in the leader

segment of mRNA, and believed to function in the regulation of attenuation.

lead Pb

a highly toxic cumulative element in man and animals. It affects adversely nearly all steps in heme synthesis. It inhibits the mitochondrial enzyme 5-aminolevulinic acid synthase, but inhibits even more strongly 5-aminolevulinic acid dehydrase. The result of this inhibition is an increase in the blood level of 5-aminolevulinic acid, which is also detectable in the urine. Other enzymes inhibited by absorbed Pb are cytochrome P_{450} (liver), adenyl cyclose (brain and pancreas), enzymes of collagen synthesis, some ATPases, and lipoamide dehydrogenase.

leaf area index

ratio between leaf area and land area. LAI determines NAR and CGR. It is affected by stand density water and nutrient supply, light and other environmental factors. LAI is similar to chlorophyll index. LAI is used in calculating CGR and NAR under high radiation conditions when CO_2 is limiting.

leaf primordium

a localised mass of meristematic tissue near the apical meristem. It ultimately divides to form a leaf.

least square analysis

method by which an estimation procedure is determined by minimising the sum of squares of difference between observed and estimated values. If one is estimating a single number on the basis of a set of observations, the least squares gives the means.

lecithin

any of a group of phospholipids having the general composition of CH_2OR_1. $CHOR_2$. $CH_2.OPO_2.OHR_3$, in which R_1 and R_2 are fatty acids and R_3 is choline, and with emulsifying, wetting, and antioxidant properties.

lecithinase

an enzyme that catalyzes the breakdown of a lecithin into its constituents.

lectins

group of phytohaemagglutinins synthesised in legumes and responsible for host-rhizobial specificity during nodule initiation due to their unique ability of binding specifically to carbohydrate groups. These are conjugated to fluorochromes and to colloidal gold and used as cytochemical probes at both the light microscope and electron microscope levels.

leghemoglobin legoglobin

an autoxidizable hemoprotein, present in the root nodules of leguminous plants. It is structurally and functionally related to hemoglobin and myoglobin. Amino acid sequence of L, shows homology with that of animal myoglobin X-ray crystallography shows similar topology and three dimensional structure of it and animal myoglobins. It is essential for symblotic nitrogen fixation in the root nodules of leguminous plants, where it is responsible for the rapid flow of oxygen to the bacteroids (cf. role of myoglobin in transport of oxygen to respiratory enzymes of muscle).

legumin

major storage protein of pea having sedimentation coefficient of 11-13 S and the molecular weight ranging from 380-410 KD. It is having 6 monomers. These are not glycoprotein and made up of hexamers of disulphide bridge. These are also isolated from various leguminious sources.

leptocurares

a term used to denote the type of neuromuscular blocking drugs the produce block by depolarization. It has been pointed out the molecules of such drugs are thin and flexible with relatively small groups (usually methyl) on the quaternary nitrogen atoms. Diagrammatically, the molecules might be represented as $Me_3\ N^+ \sim N^+Me_3$. Decamethonium is a typical example (Me_3N^+-$(CH_2)_{10}$-N^+Me_3).

leucine aminopeptidase LAP

an aminopeptidase that acts on most amino acids and that catalyzes the sequential hydrolysis of a polypeptide chain from the N-terminal.

leucoanthocyanidins

a group of flavonoid natural products derived from flavan-3, 4-diol, and differing in their degree of hydroxylation. They are common in plants, especially in wood, bark and the rinds of fruits The dimers, oligomers and polymers of with cathechols (flavan-3-ols) form polyphenols which have the properties of taning agents.

leucomaine

one of a number of protein degradation products, formed in animal tissues.

leucoplasts

colourless plastids in plant cells, generally those which are not exposed to light. These include the starch-storing amyloplasts, the protein-storing aleurolasts, the fat-storing elaioplasts and the estioplasts, which are the colourless chloroplasts of sprouts and stolons (for example, potato shoots) which have been kept in the dark etiolated).

level of significance

indicates the probability of occurrence of particular events. Two commonly used levels of significance are 5 and 1% indicating 95 and 99% respectively the chances of probability and the differences at these levels are significant and highly significant.

levulose

levulose is a name applied in earlier years to D-fructose.

This name had the advantage of calling attention to the levorotatory property of one of the two simple sugars derived from sucrose by hydrolysis, in contrast to the dextrorotatory property of the other hydrolysis product which was called dextrose (now D-glucose). These names dextrose and levulose are not acceptable chemical names partly because both sugars have optical antipodes for which the names levo-dextrose or dextro-levulose would seem unfortunate.

liebermann burchard reaction

a reaction used for colorimetric determination of sterols. The substance to be tested is dissolved in chloroform and treated with sulfuric acid and acetic anhydride. A colour change from pink to blue to greedin dicates unsaturated sterols and is the basis for the quantitative determination of cholesterol in blood.

life

the sum of all the chemical and physical processes occurring within an organism and enabling it to maintain its structural identity. Life includes the complex interactions and the integration in time and space of these processes.

ligase

an enzyme that catalyzes the union of two molecules, involving the participation of a nucleoside triphosphate which is coverted to a nucleoside diphosphate or monophosphate. Also known as synthetase.

light chain

one of two polypeptide chains that are linked to two heavy chains to form the immunoglobulin molecule. The molecular mass of a light chain is about 25,000 and that of a heavy chain is about 50,000. The light chains of type K and type L immunoglobulins are known, respectively, as κ(kappa) and λ(lambda) chains.

light harvesting Chl. a/b protein (LHC)

the complex, composed of chlorophylls a and b, carotenoid, and one or more polypeptides, that functions in conjuction with photosystem I and II in photosynthesis of green plants.

light interception capacity

the extent of radiation absorbed by canopy. It provides energy for canopy processes and thus determines the production of assimilates.

light meromyosin

the smaller of two fragments obtained from the muscle protein myosin following limited proteolysis by trypsin or chymotrypsin.

light strand

1. a polynucleotide chain that is either not labelled with a heavy isotope or that is labelled with a light isotope. 2. The

naturally occurring polynucleotide chain of a duplex that has a lower density than the complementary chain.

lignin

a substance that together with cellulose forms the woody cell walls of plants and cements them together; a colourless to brown substance removed from paper-pulp sulfite liquor.

lignoceric acid

n-tetracosanoid acid, CH_3-$(CH_2)_{22}$-COOH. A fatty acid. It occurs as a component of glycerides (usually less than 3%) in many seed oils, such as ground nut and rape seed oil. It is a component of certain cerebrosides (e.g., kerasin), phosphatides and waxes.

Linde test for glycerol

in the presence of glycerol, borax colours the flame green. A borax solution, to which litmus has been added, changes from blue to red with glycerol.

line

(i) abbreviation for long interspersed repeated sequence.

(ii) a pure-breeding group of homozygous individuals that have a distinctive phenotype.

linear transformation

a mathematical transformation of an equation into one for a straight line e.g., conversion of the Michaelis-Menten equation into its Line weaver-Burk formulation.

linked enzyme assay procedure

a method for the detection of proteins and proteinase inhibitor; involves coupling a reporter enzyme to a substrate protein which, in turn is immobilized on a particulate support. Upon incubation with a proteinase peptides containing an active enzyme label are released from the support. The labelled peptides are collected by centrifugation or filtration and are used in a second incubation, to transfer molecules of the reporter enzyme substrate, thereby providing great amplification of the initial peptide bond hydrolysis by the proteinase.

linker

(i) DNA is located on the surface of nucleosomes. DNAs of nucleosomes are interconnected with each other with the help of small length of DNA is known as linker.

(ii) a short chemically synthesised double-stranded DNA molecule that contains the recognition sequence for a restriction endonuclease. They are ligated to large, blunt ended DNA molecules, and then cleaved with the recognition enzyme whose recognition sequence the linker bears. In so doing the cohesive ends are formed on the originally blunt ended DNA molecules.

linker DNA

1. segment of DNA between adjacent nucleosomes. Its length is variable, averaging

about 50 base pairs, and it is probably an attachment site for histone H_1. 2. DNA sequence used in recombinant DNA technology to join together two other DNA fragments or the ends of one fragments.

linoleic acid $C_{17}H_{31}COOH$

a yellow unsaturated fatty acid, boiling at 229°C (14 mm Hg), occurring as a glyceride in drying oils; obtained from linseed, safflower, and tall oils; a principal fatty acid in plants, and considered essential in animal nutrition; used in medicine, feeds, paints, and margarine. Also known as linolic acid; 9, 12-octadecadienoic acid.

linolenate

a salt or ester of linolenic acid.

linolenic acid $C_{17}H_{29}COOH$

one of the principal unsaturated fatty acids in plants and an essential fatty acid in animal nutrition; a colourless liquid that boils at 230°C (17 mm Hg or 2266 newtons per square meter), soluble in many organic solvents; used in medicine and drying oils. Also known as 9, 12, 15-octadecatrienoic acid.

lipase

an enzyme that catalyzes the hydrolysis of fats or the breakdown of lipoproteins.

lipid

one of a class of compounds which contain long-chain aliphatic hydrocarbons and their derivatives, such as fatty acids, alcohols, amines, amine alcohols, and aldehydes; includes waxes, fats, and derived compounds. Also known as lipin; lipoid.

lipid acyl hydrolase

an enzyme which catalyses the hydrolysis of acyl group from several classes of lipids, including glycolipids, phospholipids, sulpholipids and mono and diacylglycerols, but is inactive on triacylglycerols.

lipid crystalline or fluid phase

bilayer membrane lipid phase in young functioning cells. Fatty acid chains possess motional freedom, due to which the embedded proteins, like buoys in a lipid sea, show maximum physiological activity. Excess of unsaturated fatty acids increases the fluid phase.

lipid digestion

in the small intestine fat is hydrolyzed by pancreatic lipase. As such pancreatic lipase is inactive and is activated by calcium salt and bile salts. Bile salts are essential for emulsification of fat. Soluble proteins also help in the emulsification land absorption of fatty acid. Intestinal juice also contains lipase which can act upon any fat unaffected by pancreatic lipase.

Partially hydrolyzed lipid is readily absorbed in the last portion of duodenum and proximal part of jejunum.

Lipids are also absorbed by pinocytosis process, lipids pass through the membrane by diffusion. Lipids, whether absorbed as such or re-synthesized in the epithelial cell enter the lymphatic vessels as a milky emulsion called chyle. The minute droplets of fat are chylomicron. Chylomicron consists of triglycerides, phospholipid. Free fatty acid and they are surrounded by thin layer of protein. These particles pass through lymphatic duct of abdominal cavity and then enters into blood.

lipid metabolism

the physiological and metabolic processes involved in the assimilation of the dietary lipids and the synthesis and degradation of the lipids.

lipoamide

the dipeptide-like structure, formed by linking a molecule of lipoic acid through its carboxyl group to the ε-amino group of a lysine residue, that is part of the enzyme for which lipoic acid serves as a coenzyme.

lipochrome

any of various fat-soluble pigments, such as carotenoid, occurring in natural fats. Also known as chromolipid.

lipofuscin

any of a group of lipid pigments found in cardiac and smooth muscle cells, in macrophages, and in parenchyma and interstitial cells; differential reactions include sudanophilia, Nile blue staining, fatty acid, glycol, and ethylene.

lipoic acid $C_8H_{14}O_2S_2$

a compound which participates in the enzymatic oxidative decarboxylation of α-keto acids in a stage between thiamine pyrophosphate and coenzyme A.

lipoid

a fatlike substance.

lipolysis

the breakdown of storage lipids in living organisms. Most long term energy reserves are in the form of triglycerides in fats and oils. When these are needed, e.g., during starvation, lipase enzymes convert the triglycerides into glycerol and the component fatty acids. These are the transported to tissue and oxidized to provide energy. Lipolysis is under hormonal control. Lipolysis is effected in the body, largely in the gut, by the lipase enzymes. Hormones (e.g., ACTH and adrenaline) increase lipolysis from adipose tissue thus making more fatty acid available in the blood plasma.

lipolytic enzyme

an enzyme that catalyzes the hydrolysis of fats and other esters to yield alcohols and acids Also known as lipase, stearolytic enzyme.

lipopolysaccharide

any of a class of conjugated polysaccharides consisting of

a polysaccharide combined with a lipid.

lipoprotein

any of a class of conjugated proteins consisting of a protein combined with a lipid.

lipoprotein lipase

the lipase that catalyzes primarily the hydrolysis of triglycerides which are associated with proteins, as those present in serum lipoproteins and in chylomicrons.

lipoproteins

conjugated proteins in which the prosthetic groups are lipid. They occur in blood plasma and cell cytoplasm, in the membranes of the cell and cell organelles, and in egg yolk Blood plasma lipo-proteins are responsible for the transport and distribution of lipids (lipid hormones; lipids absorbed by the intestine, such as neutral fats, phospholipids, free and esterifeid cholesterol, free fatty acids, and fat-soluble vitamins) via the lymph and blood system to the liver and other organs.

liposome, phospholipid bilayer vesicle

an aqueous compartment enclosed by a completely sealed lipid bilayer. Liposomes are formed by ultrasonic irradiation (sonication) of phosphoglycerides (or other suitable lipids) and water.

liposomes

microscopic phospholipid vesicles used as drug carriers. Liposomes are composed of naturally occurring phospholipids and are therefore non-immunogenic and biodegradable. The liposome containing the drug may be taken up into cells by endocytosis and there fuse with the lysosome, it may fuse with the cell membrane and release its contents intracellularly, or it may become adsorbed to the cell surface and the drug may slowly diffuse across the lipid boundaries to the inside of the cell.

lipotropic

having an affinity for lipid compounds.

lipotropic hormone

any hormone having lipolytic activity on adipose tissue.

lipoxidase

an enzyme catalyzing the oxidation of the double bonds of an unsaturated fatty acids.

lipoxygenase

an enzyme which catalyses the oxidation of unsaturated fatty acids with are end products of phospholipases action. In action free radical of oxygen is involved. Lipoxygenase is responsible for free radical formation during oxidation of polyunsaturated fatty acid. During senescence, a marked increase in lipoxygenase activity is noticed.

liquid chromatography

chromatography employing

liquid as mobile phase. The moblie phase is percolated through the column by means of either gravity or the under pressure pumps. The two principal forms of liquid chromatography are ion-exchange chromatography and gel chromatography.

liquid flow porometer

an apparatus to monitor stomatal conductance of leaf epiderman peel. Here flow of bathing solution through the epidermis is used as an indirect measure of stomatal response. With this apparatus large populations of stomata can be observed rapidly and conveniently. The same epidermal peel can be used again and again. Relatively small area of epidermis is required.

lithocholic acid $C_{24}H_{40}O_3$

a crystalline substance with a melting point of 184-186°C; soluble in hot alcohol; found in ox, human, and rabbit bile.

liver

the largest metabolic gland of vertebrates. Liver and pancreas arise from the midgut in the course of embryonic development. The human L. weights 1.5 kg and lies in the abdominal cavity in the right sulphrenic space. 1 to 2 blood per minute is supplied by the portal vein and the liver arteries, and leaves via the liver veins. The liver secretes bile, which flows out into the duodenum through a system of vessels, of which the gall bladder is a side arm. The functional unit of the liver is the hepatocyte, which is surrounded by blood vessels and bile capillaries. Metabolically, the liver is the most versatile organ in the body. Nearly all the products of digestion which are absorbed by the intestine are carried to the liver by the portal vein, there to be transformed or degraded.

liver phosphorylase

an enzyme that catalyzes the breakdown of liver glycogen to glucose-1-phosphate.

loading dose

a large initial dose given so that the effective concentration in the biophase is reached quickly. This is followed by smaller maintenance doses given to maintain the concentration at the desired level. The size of the maintenance doses is therefore determined by the rate of elimination of the drug. Examples of drugs which are often adminsitered in the form of a large loading dose followed by smaller maintenance doses include sulphonamide antimicrobial drugs and cardiac glycosides. The adminsitration of the initial loading dose of a cardiac glycoside is termed digitalization.

load test

a tolerance test in which an individual is given a dose of a specific metabolite and the urinary concentration of this metabolite, or of a related compound, is determined as a function of time. A phenylalanine load test is used as a diagnostic tool for phenylketonuria, and a tryptophan load test is used as a diagnostic tool for schizophrenia.

lobelin

(-)-lobelin, cis-8, 10 diphenyl-lobelionol. The main lobelia alkaloids. Structurally, it is a lobelionol, in which both R_1 and R_2 are phenyl ($-C_6H_5$) groups. L., crystallizes as colourless needless, m.p. 130-131°C, $[\alpha]_D^{15}$ - 43° (c = 1, ethonol). It is used medicinally as a respiratory analeptic. On account of its nicotine-like properties, it is also used in the treatment of smoking addiction.

Locke solution

a physiological salt solution originally devised for perfusing the isolated mammalian heart. It has the following composition (mmol/L): NaCl 1,54; KCl, 5.4-5.6; $CaCl_2$, 1.1-2.2; $NaHCO_3$, 1.8-6.0; glucose, 5.5-11.1. Air or oxygen is bubbled through the solution.

loculus

a small chamber or compartment used to describe the space surrounded by lamellae (partitions) in the chloroplast grana.

logarithmic transformation

when standard deviation, mean and observations are very large, and are whole number. Then log of original data are taken and Anova performed.

long day plants

plants flowering under long day conditions above the critical light period. The dark period should be less than the critical dark period, LDPs are either qualitative or quantitative.

long terminal repeat LTR

sequence of several hundred bases found at either end of some DNA molecules, especially the genomic DNA of retroviruses. The sequences at either end are identical to one another, or in at least some cases, are inverted repeats.

low-energy phosphate acceptor

a low energy compound that can function as an acceptor for the phosphoryl group transferred from high energy phosphate donors by way of the ADP-ATP phosphoryl group carrier system.

low porosity gels

when amount of gel forming substance is high from 8-15% pore size is small and hence offers resistance to the passage of large molecules. Low molecular weight compound can be easily separated.

luciferase

a low molecular weight oxidoreductase, which catalyses the dehydrogenation of iuciferin in the presence of oxygen, ATP and magnesium ions. During this process, 96% of the energy released appears as visible (mostly blue) light. This is the basis of Bioluminescence.

luciferin

a species-specific pigment in many luminous organisms that emits heatless light when combined with oxygen.

lunularic acid decarboxylase

an enzyme which catalyses the decarboxylation of lunularic acid in liverworts. The product is lunularim.

lupin alkaloids

a group of quinolizidine alkaloids containing a ring system variously known as quinolizidine, octahydrophyridocoline, norlupinane, or 1-azabiocyclo [0, 4, 4] decane. This ring system may be further condensed with other N-containing ring systems, so that tri- and tetracyclic, as well as bicyclic lupins are known. Chief representatives are lupine, lupanine; sparteine and cytisine (ICHS).

luteinizing hormone

a glycoprotein hormone secreted by the adenohypophysis of vertebrates which stimulates hormone production by interstitial cells of gonads. Also known as interstitial-cell-stimulating hormone.

luteinizing hormone releasing factor

a small peptide hormone released from the hypothalamus which acts on the pituitary gland to cause release of luteinizing hormone.

lyase

an enzyme that catalyzes the nonhydrolytic cleavage of its substrate with the formation of a double bond; examples are decarboxylases.

lycopene $C_{40}H_{50}$

a red, crystalline hydrocarbon that is the colouring matter of certain fruits, as tomatoes; it is isomeric with carotene.

lymphocytes

colourless, nucleated blood cells, approximately the same size as erythrocytes. They are immunologically component i.e. they recognize antigens, and they play a central role in the immune response (an average human possesses about 10^{12} L.), which make up 1.3 kg. Only 3 g are present in the blood, the majority being found in bone marrow, spleen, lymph glands and lymph.

lymphokine

a biological response modifier produced by activated lymphocytes that acts to modulate the immune system. It includes a group of soluble glycoproteins, produced by activated lymphocytes, that have various roles in promoting and regulating the activity of lymphocytes and macrophages. They include interleukins, interferon, and migration inhibition factor, which mediates Type IV hypersensitivity.

lyotropic series

an arrangement of cations and anions in a series according to their effect on the solubility of proteins; the ions are ordered according to decreasing salting out efficiency and decreasing extent of hydration.

lysergic acid

a tetracyclic indole derivative. The D-form is one of the Ergot alkaloids. (Change of configuration at C-8 produces biologically inactive isolysergic acid). It is a close structural relative of LSD.

lysine $C_6H_{14}O_2N_2$

an essential, basic amino acid obtained from many proteins by hydrolysis.

lysogenic cycle

the sequence of reactions whereby a bacterial cell becomes infected with a temperate phage, incorporates the prophage into the bacterial DNA, and then divides.

lysogenic repression

prevention of incorporation of the prophage DNA into bacterial DNA.

lysogenic response

the incorporation of phage DNA into the bacterial DNA that follows the infection of the bacterium by a temperate phage.

lysosomes

organelles, 0.2-2 nm diameter, found in the cytoplasm of eukaryotic cells. They are bounded by a single lipoprotein membrane, but otherwise show no fine structure. Under the light of electron microscope, they are markedly polymerphic. They can be characterized biochemically or histochemically, but not morphologically. They are sites of intracellular digestion particularly of biological macromolecules, such as proteins, polynucleotides, polysaccharides, lipids, glycoproteins, glycolipids, etc. Approximately 40 different lysosomal hydrolases are responsible for this degradative activity; they all show optimal activity at acidic pH values.

lysostaphin

a bacteriolytic enzyme which is specific for members of the genus Staphylococcus. It lyses viable and killed staphylococcal cells and isolated cell walls. The unit of lysotaphin has been designated as the amount required to reduce the optical density of a standard suspension of S, aureus FDA 209P 50% in 10 minutes at 37°C. Lysostaphin has proved to be highly active in vitro against all of the more than 500 coagulase-positive isolates of S. aureus tested. It has proved inactive against all of 72 viable isolates of 53 species of 21 genera of bacteria other than staphylococci. Coagulase-negative staphylococci are attacked at a more variable rate than coagulase-positive isolates. Efforts are in progress to correlate this variable lysotaphin susceptibility of coagulase-negative staphylococci with their relative virulence.

lysozyme

an enzyme present in certain body secretions, principally tears, which acts to hydrolyze certain bacterial cell walls.

lysozyme, endolysin, muramidase, n-acetylmuramide glycanohydrolase (EC 3.2.1.17)

a widely occurring hydolase, found in phases, bacteria, plants, invertebrates and vertebrates. In the latter, it is found particularly in egg white, saliva, tears and mucosas.

lysyl oxidase

any of a group of enzymes found in bone and connective tissue which oxidize terminal amino groups of lysine residues in tropocollagen molecules to aldehyde residues.

lytic cycle

1. the sequence of reactions whereby, a virulent phage infects a bacterial cell, multiplies inside the cell, and ultimately leads to the lysis of the cell. 2. The sequence of reactions whereby a prophage is induced in an infected bacterial cell, multiplies inside the cell and ultimately leads to the lysis of the cell.

D-lyxose

aldopentose, a constituent of a lyxoflavin, isolated from human heart muscle.

macrocortin

an endogenous glycoprotein which is inhibitor of the enzyme phospholipase-A which catalyzes the release of arachidonic acid from membrane phospholipids. The synthesis and release of macrocortin is stimulated by the glucocorticoids which inhibit eicosanoid synthesis by this mechanism. Macrocortin is so called because it is a large molecule originally obtained from rat macrophages, and because it mimics the effects of glucorticoids (alternative names are renocortin and lipomodulin although lipomodulin may not be identical with macrocortin).

macroenvironment

complex of factors that is not affected by the vegetation. It includes weather processes and climate, taken over extended periods of time and over large areas of the globe. These factors control vegetative plant life and soil forming processes. It covers temperature, day length, wind and precipitation.

macroglobulin

an gamma globulin with a sedimentation constant of 195.

α_2-macroglobulin, α_2-antiplasmin

an α_2-plasma protein. The first

reported M_r determination by sedimentation diffusion gave a value of 820, 000. Later determination by sedimentation equilibrium gave values of 725,000. These results, together with studies of subunits composition, indicate that the true M_r lies in the range 650,000-725000. α_2-M is a glycoprotein containing 8.2% carbohydrate. The carbohydrate moiety contains mannose, fucose, N-acetylglucosamine and sialic acid. Electron microscope studies of the protein reveal a structure resembling two beans facing each other; these two identical subunits are bound noncovalently. Each subunit consists of two peptide chains linked covalently by a disulfide bridge. α_2-M, binds tightly and inhibits a number of proteases of varying specificity and origin, e.g., trypsin, plasmin, thrombin, kallikrein and chymotrypsin. It is therefore a natural inhibitor of plasmin.

macroglobulinemia

the presence of excessive amounts of macroglobulins, specifically IgM immunoglobulins, in the blood.

macrolide antibiotics

one of a number of antibiotics that are similar in their structure, action, and antimicrobial spectrum, and that are characterized by having a large lactone ring that contains anywhere from 14 to 20 carbon atoms. Two representative compounds are erythromycin A and methymycin. Certain of these lactones, known as macrolides, are clinically valuable antibiotic drugs; erythromycin is widely used in the therapy of infectious diseases of bacterial origin.

It is likely that the biological ring-closure reaction by which these large ring compounds are formed is not the energetically improbable lactonization of the free open-chain hydroxy acid. Since these compounds are the metabolic products of living organisms, and thus are synthesized under enzymatic catalysis, it is probable that one of the functions of the enzyme is to provide a specific binding site at which the hydroxyl and carboxyl groups are fixed in close proximity prior to the intramolecular esterification reaction. Also known as macrolides.

macronutrient

an element, such as potassium and nitrogen, essential in large quantities for plant growth.

macrophage

morphologically dissimilar relatively long lived, phagocytic cells, which may be sessile or motile, and which play an important role in the immune response by processing antigens and presenting them to B and T lymphocytes.

madder dyes

refer to the plant dyes from madder (Rubia tinctorum) and other members of the madder family (rubiaceae). Important representatives are the glycosidically bound component alizarin and purpurin.

maintenance pathway

glycolysis and gluconeogenesis reactions of respiration.

maintenance respiration coefficient

rate of resynthesis to maintain degradable structural component of dry mass at a constant level without growth. In other words it is ratio between maintenance respiration and growth rate.

major elements, or macro-elements

the essential elements required in large quantities by plants for structural purposes. The range of requirement is mg/g. These are C, H, O, N, P, K, Ca, S, Mg and Fe.

major-minor code

an early version of the genetic code according to which the central nucleotide of a codon is the major factors in positioning the correct amino acid on the template, while the two adjoining nucleotides are minor factors in selecting the amino acid.

malic acid $COOH \cdot CH_2 \cdot CHOH \cdot COOH$

hydroxysuccinic acid; a dibasic hydroxy acid existing in two optically active isomers and a racemic form; found in apples and many other fruits.

malic dehydrogenase

an enzyme in the krebs cycle that catalyzes the conversion of L-malic acid to oxalo-acetic acid.

malic enzyme

an enzyme which utilizes nicotinamide-adenine dinucleotide phosphate (NADP) to catalyze the oxidative decarboxylation of malic acid to pyruvic acid and carbon dioxide. Also known as malate dehydrogenase.

malonic acid $HOOC\text{-}CH_2\text{-}COOH$

a dicarboxylic acid, which has been found in the free form in plants, but is of only sporadic occurrence, m.p. 135.6°C. A metabolically important derivative of malonic acid is malonyl-CoA, an intermediate of fatty acid biosynthesis.

maltase

an enzyme that catalyzes the conversion of maltose to dextrose.

maltose $C_{12}H_{22}O_{11}$

a crystalline disaccharide that is a product of the enzymatic hydrolysis of the starch, dextrin, and glycogen; does not appear to exist free in nature. Also known as maltobiose; malt sugar.

mammogenic hormone

any hormone that stimulates or induces development of the mammary gland.

mammotrophic drugs

the drugs that produce breast enlargement and galactorrhoea as unwanted side-effects in women (usually associated with amenorrhoea). The usual mechanism is through excessive secretion of prolactin from the pituitary, arising from interference with the hypothalamic dopaminergic mechanism that normally serves to inhibit prolactin release.

manganese, Mn

a bioelement present in all living cells, which usually contains less than 1 ppm. on a dry weight basis or less than 0.01 mM in fresh tissue. Bone contains 3.5 ppm. Mn (II) is necessary for sporulation in Bacillus subtilis, and these bacteria can maintain an intracellular Mn concentration of 0.2 mM against an external concentration of 1 μM. Mn is an essential nutrient for animals and plants. Mn deficiency in animals leads to degeneration of the gonads and to skeletal abnormalities; the characteristic skeletal abnormality in chickens is called slipped tendon disease, or perosis. In plants, Mn deficiency results in chlorosis and mottling.

Mn may also be important in the regulation of enzyme activity, e.g., nonadenylylated glutamine synthetase requires Mg (II), but the adenylylated form binds Mn (II). Also the specificity of nucleases and DNA polymerases is changed when Mg (II) is replaced by Mn (II). The physiological significance of these differences is not clear.

mangrove

an association of plants on the muddy swamps at the mouth of rivers and elsewhere in the tropics; over which the tide flows daily, leaving the mud bare at low tide.

mannan

any of a group of polysaccharides composed chiefly or entirely of D-mannose units.

D-mannitol, mannite, manna sugar

a hexitol related to D-mannose. M, 182.17, HOH_2C-CHOH-CHOH-CHOH-CHOH-CH_2OH. It is found widely in plants and plant exudates, and in fungi and seaweeds. Mannitol is used as a sugar substiture for diabetics.

mannose $C_6H_{12}O_6$

a fermentable monosaccharide obtained from manna.

map-genetic

to determine the relative positions of genes or restriction sites of a DNA molecule. Genetic mapping is done by carrying out mating experiments to determine the linkage relationships between genes and the frequency of recombination between them.

maple syrup urine disease

a hereditary disease, the most striking feature of which is the characteristic odour of the urine, which resembles maple syrup of burnt sugar. Plasma and urinary levels of the branched chain amino acids leucine, isoleucine, and valine, and their corresponding α-keto acids are highly elevated. For this reason, the disease is also termed as branched chain ketourea.

market enzyme

an enzyme, the intracellular location of which is known, so that an assay of the enzyme can be used as an aid in following the isolated and purification of subcellular fractions.

mass number

the sum of the number of protons and neutrons per atom of a given nucleide.

mast cell

a basophilic cell of connective tissue that has heparin and histamine and that functions in immediate type hypersensitivity.

maturase

protein that catalyzes the removal of the introns. It is likely that such proteins are not enzymes, but act as factors that modify the activity of the splicing enzymes. Many maturases are themselves products of the sequences whose correct splicing they help to control and at least some are coded on introns (e.g., maturases found in yeast mitochondria).

maturation-defective mutant

a phage mutant that can synthesize DNA but not the viral structural proteins.

maximum potential yield

the yield harvestable component of the crop in the absence of water or mineral/ nutrient deficiencies when losses of the component through physiological, pathological and mechanical causes have been minimised.

M chain

one of the two types of polypeptide chain of lactate dehydrogenase isozymes; denoted M, since the tetramer of M chains is found predominantly in muscle tissue.

McN-A-343

a compound that selectively stimulates a particular subclass of muscarinic cholinoceptors. McN-A-343 stimulates muscarinic receptors on sympathetic ganglia. These receptors mediate excitation of the ganglion cells and a rise in blood pressure results. As well as being blocked by atropine, they are blocked by mianserin.

M-current

a current carried by outward-flowing K^+ ions passing through a particular class of calcium-independent, voltage-sensitive K^+ channels in the membrane of ganglion cells. It is inhibited by acetylcholine acting on muscarinic cholinoceptors, hence the term M-current. The M-current in frog ganglion cells, for example is switched on progressively between -70 mV and 0 mV. It is non-inactivating and therefore forms a major component of the steady membrane conductance. Inhibition of the M-current by acetylcholine causes a slow membrane depolarization which does not directly activate the cell but which may facilitate the cell's response to signals mediated through nicotinic cholinoceptors.

median

a value which is located in the middle of a series when the observations are arranged in order of magnitude and it divides the series into two equal halves.

melanin

any of a group of brown or black pigments occurring in plants and animals.

melanogen

a colourless precursor of melanin.

melanogenesis

the formation of melanin.

melanoprotein

a conjugated protein in which melanin is the associated chromagen.

melanotropin, melanocyte stimulating hormone, MSH

a polypeptide hormone produced by the polygonal cells of the pars intermedia of the hypophysis, except in species that lack this structure, e.g., chicken, porpoise, whale, where MSH is produced by the neurohypophysis. The production of MSH is under the control of MRH and MIH of the hypothatamus. MSH causes the melanophores to expand, thus producing a generalized darkening of the skin. The function of MSH in humans is not clear.

melatonin

a hormone, produced by the pineal gland, that has no known action in man but produces marked lightening of the skin in embryonic fish and larval amphibians.

melissic acid

n-triacontanoic acid, CH_3-$(CH_2)_{28}$-COOH. A higher monocarboxylic fatty acid. It is present as an ester in beeswax and montan wax.

membrane enzymes

the enzymes present on the surfaces of the many different types of biological membranes. There are, e.g., glucose 6-phosphatase of the endoplasmic reticulum, galactosyl transferase of the Golgi apparatus, oligomycinsensitive. ATPase of inner mitochondrial membrane, monoamine oxidase and rotenone-insensitive NADA-cytochrome c-reductase of the outer mitochondrial membrane and the sodium-independent ATPase and the 5-uncleotidase of the cell membrane. A very large number of reactions occur on membranes, and the membrane enzymes play a central part in cell metabolism.

membrane families
the groups of membrane, which during membrane flow processes, may fuse or be derived from each other. Membranes not belonging to the same family never come into direct contact with each other e.g., plasmalemma and tonoplast; smooth and rough endoplasmic reticulum. Golgi membrane, cytosomes, mitochondria and plastids outer membrane etc., belong to one family whereas inner membrane of mitochondria, plastids and thylakoid belong to other family.

membron
a functioning, regulatable, transaltion complex of a polysome and a specific surface area of a biological membrane.

membranochromic pigments
the plant pigments which impregnate the cell wall, e.g., the phenols and quinones that give colour to heart wood.

2-mercaptoethanol
a sulfhydryl group containing compound that is used to protect the sulfhydryl groups of enzymes and other proteins against oxidation.

meristemoid
isolated locations of maintained embryonic potency and thus of continued divisions, in an otherwise maturing tissue. These do not form all tissues but rather highly specialized structures which do not change under known circumstances e.g., rays cells, stomata, hairs and secretory glands etc.

merocrine gland
a gland that produces a secretion without significantly damaging its secreting cells.

meromyosin
protein fragments of a myosin molecule, produced by limited proteolysis.

mesobilirubin $C_{33}H_{40}O_6N_4$
yellow, crystalline by-product of bilirubin reduction.

mesons
a group of unstable elementary particles with rest masses between those of the electron and the proton. Positive, negative and neutral mesons exist. These are found in cosmic rays and are emitted by nuclei under bombardment by high energy particles.

mesotocin
a peptide hormone that is related to oxytocin in its structure and in its function; it is secreted by the posterior lobe of the pituitary gland and occurs in reptiles and amphibia.

metabolic control, metabolic regulation
metabolism is subject to control and an analogy may be drawn with electronic and

mechanical regulation processes used in technology. In a purely formal way, living systems can be regarded as cybernetic machines. Control is a fundamental principle in the organization of living organisms, and depending on the nature of the signal or method of information transfer, there are four broad types :

1. neural (nervous) control. The nerve impulse is an electrical signal, and the regulatory response may also be electrical (e.g., further nerve impulse to a muscle) or chemical (e.g., production of a hormone). The nervous system may be considered as a physiological broadcasting system.
2. hormonal (humoral) control. Hormones act as chemical signals in a regulation system that is superimposed on the more basic levels of M.c.
3. differential gene expression. The signals (or triggers) of differential gene expression may be chemical (hormones) or environmental (e.g., light). Differential gene expression is responsible for the regulation, at a molecular level, of differentiation and development.
4. feedback and feedforward mechanisms, in which metabolites themselves act directly as signals in the control of their own breakdown or synthesis. Feedback is negative or positive. Negative feedback results in inhibition of the activity or synthesis of an enzyme or several enzymes in a reaction chain by the end product.

metabolic cycle

a catalytic series of reactions, in which the product of one bimolecular reaction is regenerated :

$$A + B \longrightarrow C + A$$

thus A acts catalytically and is required only in small amounts, and A can be considered as a carrier of B. The catalytic function of A and other members of the metabolic cycle ensure economic conversion of B into C; B is the substrate of the metabolic cycle and C is the product. If intermediates are withdrawn from the metabolic cycle, e.g., for biosynthesis, the stationery concentrations of the metallic cycle intermediates must be maintained by synthesis. Replenishment of depleted metabolic cycle intermediates is called anaplerosis.

metabolic cycles are anabolic, catabolic, or amphibolic. The calvin cycle is an anabolic (synthetic) cycle.

metabolic inhibitors

usually refers to agents that inhibit ATP production in the mitochondria.

metabolic quotient

a measure of the rate of uptake or discharge of a metabolite by a tissue or an organism. The uptake of oxygen, denoted by

Q O_2, and the evolution of carbon dioxide, denoted by Q CO_2 are the examples. The rate at which O_2 is consumed or CO_2 is released expressed on dry weight, nitrogen, protein or DNA. Metabolic quotient may also be determined in atmospheres of different or varying gas composition. It is represented by Q_x where X is the gas being measured.

metabolite

a substance that takes part in a metabolic reaction, either as reactant or product. Metabolites are thus intermediates in metabolic pathways. Some are synthesized within the organism itself, whereas others have to be taken in as food.

metachromatic dye

a dye that stains cells or tissues with two or more different colour depending on the extent to which the dye molecules are stacked on the chromotrope.

metalloenzyme

enzyme consists of a protein molecule complexed with one or more metal atoms. Carboxypeptidase A, for example, contains an atom of zinc.

metalloporphyrin

a compound, such as heme, consisting of a porphyrin combined with a metal such as iron, copper, silver, zinc or magnesium.

metalloprotein

a protein enzyme containing a metallic atom as an iherent portion of its molecule.

metallothionein

one of a group of proteins that bind heavy metals, especially copper, cadmium and zinc. They have two important functions: homeostasis, ensuring that metal-requiring enzymes are provided with these atoms; protection, binding excess heavy metal and thus, by the excretion of the complex, reducing the heavy metal content of the cell or tissue. These proteins are probably ubiquitous and are remarkable in that they are specifically inducible by heavy metals which they bind. They are also characterized by their low molecular mass and high glycine content.

metanephrine

an inactive metabolite of epinephrine (3-*O*-methylepinephrine) that is excreted in the urine; it is recovered and measured as a test for pheochromocytoma.

metaphloem

completely developed primary phloem, consisting of sieve tubes, fibres and parenchyma.

metarhodopsin

a structurally altered form of rhodospin that is produced after the exposure of rhodopsin to light and prior to its dissociation into opsin and retinal.

metastable state

(i) an excited state of an atom or nucleus which has an appreciable life time.

(ii) the state of supercooled water or of supersaturated solutions in which the phase, which is normally stable under the given conditions, does not form unless a small amount of the normally stable phase is already present.

methanogenesis

the biosynthesis of the hydrocarbon methane; common in certain bacteria. Also known as bacterial methanogenesis.

methanol dehydrogenase

the enzyme responsible for the oxidation of methanol to formaldehyde in methylotrophic bacteria. It has an unusual prosthetic group, pyrroloquinoline quinone. It is also unusual in being a dehydrogenase that interacts with the electrons transport chain at the level of cytochrome c, thus by passing the quinones and b-type cytochromes which are usually involved in the oxidation of organic molecules. The result of this arrangement is that only one molecule of ATP is synthesized for every molecule of methanol oxidized to formaldehyde.

methionine $C_5H_{11}O_2NS$

an essential amino acid; furnished both labile methyl groups and sulfur necessary for normal metabolism.

methods of biochemistry

usually method for the study of metablic processes, but in the widest sense including isolation, identification and characterization of natural substances. Methods for the study of metabolism are classified into 3 types :

1. in vivo methods employ whole organisms, their organs or cells, or populations of cells or micro-organisms. In balance studies, substances are administered to the organism and the time course of their conversion to various products is determined by analysis of body material or excretory products (feces, urine, expired gases).

2. in vitro methods are performed outside the whole organism. They are essentially "test tube" methods, employing crude cell homogenates, sub-cellular fractions thereof, or purified enzymes. For methods of cell disruption, subcellular fractionation and enzyme purification. Proteins and Density gradient centrifugation.

3. the techniques of histochemistry and cytochemistry are also in vitro methods; the sites of metabolites, enzymes or metabolic reactions are identified in organ or tissue slices and in cells by characteristic chemical reactions, e.g., specific colour reactions.

methonium compounds

the name given to a series of polymethylene bistrimethylammonium compounds of the general structure Me_3N^+ -(CH_2)- $^+NMe_3$. The two most important members of series are hexamethonium (where n=6) and decamethonium (where n=10). Hexamethonium blocks transmission through autonomic ganglia by a non-depolarizing mechanism (probably receptors block plus ion channel block), whereas decamethonium blocks neuromuscular transmission in skeletal muscle by depolarization block (although phase II neuromuscular block may also occur).

methyl-accepting chemotaxis proteins, MCP

the cell membrane proteins in Escherichia coli involved in the iniation and control of chemotractic behaviour. There are at least 3 different MCP in E. coli, each responsive to stimuli from different types of chemoreceptor, including both attractants and repellants.

methylase

a DNA modifying enzyme which covalently attaches methyl (CH_3) group to the specific nucleotide bases within a DNA molecule e.g., a methyl transferase.

methylated cap

methylated guanine nucleotide that is added to the 5'- end of eukaryotic hnRNA and mRNA after transcription but prior to later processing and translation.

methyl containing compounds and their biological significance

a great variety of methyl-containing compounds occurs in microrganisms as well as in the tissue and body fluids of higher plants and animals. A tentative list of these compounds includes:

(a) qualitatively and quantitavely important constituents of cell structures, such as methionine-containing proteins, lecithins and nucleic acids;

(b) substances involved in the storage of energy or in certain metabolic reactionism, such as creatine phosphate and carnitine;

(c) hormones (e.g., epinephrine) and vitamins (e.g., vitamin B12);

(d) compounds which are believed to play special roles (physiological or structural) for certain organisms (such as alkaloids in plants; cyclopropane- or branched fatty acids in bacteria);

(e) excretory products, resulting from the catabolism of physiologically active compounds (e.g., metanephrine, methylnicotinamide) or from the detoxication of foreign materials (e.g., methylpyridine). Some preformed methyl-containing substances are obtained from the diet or from the environment, either directly or after digestion.

Generally, the methyl groups arise in living bodies by two distinct mechanism; net synthesis from one-carbon metabolites (methylneogenesis) or transfer from other methylated compounds containing labile methyl groups (transmethylation).

methylene glutamine synthetase

an enzyme which catalyses the formation of methylene glutamine from methylene glutamate.

methylglytoxal

an intermediate of carbohydrate degradation in certain organisms. In some bacteria (pseudomnas spp.) methylglyoxal which is converted to lactate (precursor of pyruvate) by a catalytic cycle involving gluthione.

methyl transferase

any of a group of enzymes which catalyze the reaction of S-adnosyl methionine with a suitable acceptor to yield the methylated acceptor molecule and S-adenosyl homocysteine.

mevalonate kinase

an enzyme which catalyses the phosphorylation of mevalonate to mevalonate 5-phosphate using ATP.

Michaelis constant

a constant K_m such that the initial rate of reaction V, produced by an enzyme when the substrate concentration is high enough to sature the enzyme, is related to the rate of reaction v at a lower substrate concentration c by the formula $V = v(1+K_m/c)$.

microbiological assay

the assay of a biochemical compound, such as a vitamin or an amino acid, that is based on measuring the growth of microorganisms for which the compound is an essential growth factor.

microbiological preservation

the preservation of plant material by lactic acid produced by lactic acid fermentation. The lactic acid fermentation is used in the preparation of silage and sauerkraut.

microbodies

glyoxysomes, peroxisomes and spherosomes are small 1-2 nm in diameter, dense structures bounded by single unit membrane.

microchemistry

the chemistry of individual cells and minute organisms.

microencapsulated enzyme

an enzyme that is immobilized in a microcapsule, equipped with a semipermeable membrane, such that substrates and products, but not the enzyme, can diffuse across the membrane.

micronutrient

trace elements and compounds

required by living system only in minute amounts.

microsomal electron transport

the endoplasmic reticulum membranes have a number of electron transport chains built into them which is not linked to phosphorylation of ADP but utilises oxygen.

microsomes

a heterogeneous fraction of sub-microscopic vesicles, 20-200 nm diameter, formed during disruption of the cell by the resealing of fragments of the endoplasmic reticulum (and to some extent of the plasma membrane). Under the electron microscope, Ribosomes can be seen attached to the outside of the microsomes. Preparation of microsomes is by differential centrifugation of disrupted, homogenized cells; following the sedimentation of larger fragments, microsomes are sedimented at 100, 000 g.

microtubules

an integral component of the cellular cytoskeleton. They consist of cytoplasmic tubes 25 nm in diameter and of indefinite length. These are necessary for the formation and function of the mitotic spindle and thus are present in all eukaryotic cells. They are responsible for the intracellular movement of endoytotic and exocytotic vesicles. A number of important alkaloids can prevent microtubule assembly. These include colchicine and its derivative demecolcine.

milk factor

a filtrable, noncellular agent in the milk and tissues of certain strains of inbred mice; transmitted from the mother to the offspring by nursing. Also known as Bittner milk factor.

Miller experiment

an experiment in which organic compounds are synthesized under conditions believed to simulate those that have existed during the early stages of chemical evolution on the earth. The experiment demonstrates the formation of amino acids and other compounds from a mixture of reducing gases that have been subjected to an electric discharge.

million reaction

a colorimetric reaction for tyrosine and other phenolic compounds that is based on the production of a red colour upon treatment of the sample with a solution of mercurous and mercuric nitrates in concentrated nitric acid.

mineralisation

the conversion of organic matter to inorganic matter, and the infiltration of organic matter by inorganic matter.

mineralocorticoid

a corticosteriod that is relatively more powerful in its action on electrolyte and water balance than on carbohydrate metabolism. Aldosterone is the most potent endogenous mineralocorticoid, although hydrocortisone has a significant effect because of its relatively high concentration. Deoxycortisterone is the major mineralcorticoid in many animals, it has a lesser role in electrolyte metabolism in humans.

minimal stable length

the minimum size of the segment of nucleotide pairs that must be formed during renaturation with the base-pairing in perfect register to lead to the formation of duplex DNA or RNA.

minimum protein (or nitrogen) requirement

the amount of complete protein required daily to compensate the nitrogen lost by excretion. Adults require 25 to 35 g complete (containing the optimal amounts of essential amino acids) protein per day. The absolute minimum protein requirement is the amount of nitrogen excreted on a protein-free but calorically adequate diet, about 2.4 g N = 15 g protein per day for adults.

miraxanthins

yellow betaxanthins found in Mirabilis jalapa.

M-I : betalamic acid conjugated with methionine sulfoxide.

M-II: betalamic acid conjugated with aspartic acid.

M-III : betalamic acid conjugated with tyramine.

M-IV : betalamic acid conjugated with dopamine.

mispairing

the occurrence of a base in one strand of a double-stranded nucleic acid molecule that is not complementary to the base in the corresponding position in the second strand, resulting in incomplete base-pairing.

missense mutation

a missense mutation substitutes one amino acid for another. If the amino acids are similar, this may produce a functional protein. If the amino acids are dissimilar, the protein may be completely inactive.

missing plot techniques

when in randomized block design (RBD) or Latin square design (LSD) one or more observations are missing, then value is estimated from remaining block or treatment total or by iterative method. Missing value is substituted with estimated value and the ANOVA performed.

mist

droplets of water, formed by the condensation of water-vapour on dust particles.

mitogen

a substance that stimulates mitosis and therefore cell division. An example is the leucoagglutinin PHA- L, a lectin from red kidney beans, which stimulates mitotic division of isolated lymphocytes.

mitosis

normal process of cell division

in which each chromosome splits longitudinally and the halves pass onto the two daughter cells, each of which is identical to the original, keeping the same number of chromosomes.

mixed acid fermentation

the fermentation of glucose that is characteristic of E. coli and related bacteria and that yields formic, acetic, lactic and succinic acids, as well as a number of other products.

mixed cryoglobulin

a cryoglobulin with a monoclonal component made of immun globulin belonging to two different classes, one of which is monoclonal.

mixed function oxidase

an enzyme which reduces molecular oxygen by incorporating one atom into water and the other into another substrate e.g., Phenylalamine hydroxylase.

mixed inhibition

the inhibition of an enzyme that cannot be fully described in terms of one of the basic types of inhibition. In the Cleland nomenclature of enzyme kinetics most mixed type inhibitions are considered to be varieties of noncompetitive inhibition.

mobile elements

these can be retranslocated from the older parts. The deficiency symptoms of these elements will be in older organs or from the base of organs. Since to meet the demand of nutrients retranslocation from older tissue is very easy and fast e.g., N, K, P and Mg.

mode of action

the manifestation of measurable effect (biochemical or physiological response e.g., cell elongation) of hormone. The direct and specific molecular interaction are followed by succeding series of steps which lead to the response.

modification

any change to a nucleic acid or protein molecule made after its initial synthesis, DNA methylation, and the methylation, acetylation, and phosphorylation of histones are examples of such modification.

modified base

base other than those bases from which DNA and RNA are normally synthesized (i.e., thymine, cytosine, adenine, guanine, and uracil). Modified bases result from postsynthetic changes in nucleic acid and include 5-methylcytosine and 6-methyladenine.

modulating codon

a codon that codes for a rare tRNA molecule and that does not lead to the insertion of an amino acid into the growing polypeptide chain during translation. Instead such a codon acts as a regulatory agent, leading either to release of the ribosome and interruption of translation, or to slowing down of the rate of translation.

modulation

1. the regulation of the frequency with which a specific gene is transcribed. 2. the decrease in the rate of translation of a messenger RNA brought about by a modulating codon. 3. the control of a regulatory enzyme by means of an effector.

mole

the amount of substance which contains as many elementary units as there are atoms in 0.012 kg of carbon-12. The elementary units must be indicated and these may be atom, molecule, ion, radical, electron etc.

molecular biology

the science that deals with the study of biological processes at the molecular level, particularly with respect to the physical chemical properties and the relationship of these properties and changes to biological phenomena. Nerve impulse conduction, vision, membrane transport, and molecular genetics are some of the topics of molecular genetics; the replication and transcription of both DNA and RNA, and the translation of RNA.

molecular genetics

a component of genetics and of Molecular biology. Classical genetics defined the gene, on the basis of its phenotypic expression and its mathematical distribution, as a hypothetical unit of inheritance. M.g. recognizes genes as defined segment of DNA, and shows the molecular basis for the causal relationship between the gene and its phenotypic expression.

molecule

the smallest portion of a substance capable of existing independently and retaining the properties of the original substance.

molting hormone

any of several hormones which activate molting in arthropods.

monoamine oxidase

a flavoprotein enzyme which catalyses the oxidative deamination of monoamine.

monoclonal antibody

a specific antibody produced by one of numerous identical cells derived from a single parent cell. (The population of these cells comprises a clone and each cell is said to be monoclonal). The antibody-producing cells are specially prepared lymphocytes, made by fusing a normal antibody-secreting lymphocyte with an actively dividing cell from a myeloma, which also has a specific enzyme deficiency. The resultant hybrid cell (hybridoma) has the antibody-secreting properties of the lymphocyte and the multiplication potential of the myeloma.

monokine
a biological response modifier produced by monocytes.

monomer
(i) the repeating unit in a polymer.
(ii) the basic unit in a molecular aggregate, regardless of the number of polypeptide chains or the number of subunits of which it is composed; thus the 70 S ribosome is monomer while the 30 S and 70 S ribosomes are subunits and the 100 S ribosome is a dimer.
(iii) the individual polypeptide chain in an oligomeric protein.
(iv) a protein that is composed of a single polypeptide chain.

monopodium (pl, ia)
an indeterminate branch in cotton which grows vegetatively very vigorously and later on converted to reproductive branch. Monapodia varies from 0-10 in different cotton varieties. In each monopodium branching by similar lateral branches occurs in acropetel succession.

monosaccharide
a carbohydrate which cannot be hydrolyzed to a simpler carbohydrate; a polyhedric alcohol having reducing properties associated with an actual or potential aldehyde or ketone group; classified on the basis of the number of carbon atoms, as triose (3C), tetrose (4C), pentose (5C), and so on.

monosome
1. the complex that consists of a single ribosome attached to a strand of messenger RNA.
2. a chromosome that lacks a homologue.

monozygotic twins
twins that are genetically identical and that are derived from one fertilized egg; they are formed by a division of the embryo into two halves at some stage of its development.

mood stabilizer
a term used to describe the beneficial effect of lithium salts (usually lithium carbonate) in manicdepressive illness. Lithium salts taken orally are effective in normalizing a manic episode and in reducing the recurrence of attacks of manic-depressive illness. The mechanism of action is uncertain. Speculation is concerned with effects on neuronal membranes where Li^+ may partially replace Na^+, and on its ability to modify central turnover of noradrenaline and dopamine.

MOPP
a particular combination of anticancer drugs; mustine, oncovin, procarbazine and prednisone. It is also known as MVPP.

morphine
medically the most important, and quantitatively the chief member of the opium alkaloids. It is isolated in large quantities from opium. It acts as an anesthetic without

decreasing consciousness, and it is the most powerful analgesic known. High doses cause death by respiratory failure.

morphine like drugs

drugs producing the type of analgesia produced by morphine. They are more commonly called narcotic analgesic drugs, opioids or opiates.

morphogene

a gene that functions, either directly or indirectly in growth control and morphogenesis e.g., genes for hormones, inducers and mitogene.

morphogenesis

the genesis of form and shape; the ability of a molecule, group of molecules, an organ or organism to assume a certain shape.

motor system

any system which causes or allows movements. These are of three types; (i) having non-living tissues which move suddenly e.g., for dehiscence; (ii) parts capable of differential growth e.g., tendrils. (iii) Movement by alternation of turgor e.g., pulvini.

M-protein

1. a galactoside carrier protein in the permease system of E. coli. 2. a structural protein present in the M line of the myofibrils of striated muscle.

mucilage

a gum-like substance frequently present in the cell walls of aquatic plants and in the seed coats of certain other species. Mucilages are hard when dry and slimy when wet. Like gums they probably have a general protective function or serve to anchor the plant. Some organisms (e.g., certain bacteria) are completely covered with mucilage and in such cases it probably prevents water loss.

mucin

a glycoprotein constituent of mucus and various other secretions of man and lower animals.

muclgen

a substance from which mucin is derived; contained in mucus-secreting epithelial cells.

mucoid

1. any of various glycoproteins, similar to mucins but differing in solubilities and precipitation properties and found in cartilage, in the crystalline lens, and in white of egg. 2. resembling mucus.

mucopolymer

a polysaccharide of nitrogen containing sugars, cross linked with short chains of amino acids. Characteristic of prokaryotic cell wall.

mucoprotein

any of a group of glycoproteins containing a sugar, usually chondroitinsulfuric or mucoitinsulfuric acid, combined with amino acids or polypeptides.

multienzyme system
the structural and functional entity that is formed by the association of several different enzymes which catalyze a sequence of closely related reactions; the aggregate may contain one or more molecules of a given enzyme.

multifunctional protein
a protein that has two or more different catalytic and/or binding functions on a single polypeptide.

multiple correlation
when dependent variate is correlated to more than one independent variate. It is represented by R, multiple correlation coefficient which is the square-root ratio of the regression sum of squares to the total sum of squares. It is always positive and less than one.

multiple forms of an enzyme
a collective term for all the proteins that possess the same enzyme activity and that occur naturally in a single species; includes genetically independent proteins, heteropolymers, genetic (allelic) variants, proteins conjugated with other groups, proteins derived from one polypeptide chain, polymers of a single subunit, and forms differing in conformation.

multivalent allosteric inhibition
the inhibition of a regulatory enzyme by two or more negative effectors; the inhibition of a multivalent regulatory enzyme.

muramic acid
an organic acid found in the mucopeptide (murein) in the cell walls of bacteria and blue-green algae.

muramidase
lysozyme when acting as an enzyme on the hydrolysis of the muramic acid-containing mucopeptide in the cell walls of some bacteria.

murein
the peptidoglycan of bacterial cell walls.

muropeptide
the repeating unit in peptidoglycan that consists of N-acetyl-glucosamine, N-acetylmuramic acid, and a tetrapeptide side chain.

muscaaurins
orange betalains present in the cap of the fly agaric. All muscaaurins are derivatives of betalamic acid.

muscimol
the enol betaine of 5-aminomethyl-3-hydroxyisoxazole. It is strongly polar, and it is probably not a native constituent of the agaric (amanita muscaria). It is pharmacologically very potent, and is most tests it is more active than ibotenic acid. The primary pharmacological effect is an inhibitor of motor function.

mutagen
an agent that causes an increase in the number of

mutants in a population. Mutagens operate either by causing changes in the DNA of the genes, so interfering with the coding system, or by causing chromosome damage. Various chemicals (e.g., colchicine) and forms of radiation (e.g., X-rays or gamma rays emanating from radioactive substances) have been identified as mutagens.

mutagenesis

the production of mutations. Mutagenesis is said to be direct if the mutagenic agents lead to mutation only at the site of the DNA damage. Mutagenesis is said to be indirect if mutation occurs at other sites as well because of relaxed fidelity of replication or other causes.

mutagenic action

an action that produces an abnormality of the genetic material so that a permanent change in inherited constitution (a mutation) occurs. Mutagenic actions of drugs are unwanted side-effects that may be associated with carcinogenicity.

mutants

organisms, which as a result of Mutation show characteristic differences from the parent or wild type organisms, e.g., morphological differences (change of defects in cell wall formation), physiological differences (e.g., change in temperature sensitivity), or new nutritional requirements. Auxotrophic mutants are obtained in pure culture by suitable enrichment and selection techniques, e.g., the Penicillin selection technique. The precise growth requirements of mutants are determined by growth studies on supplemented minimal media.

the mutation rate represents the probability of a mutation occurring in the generation of one cell; its value lies between 10^{-6} and 10^{-10}.

mutant technique

an important area of biochemical methodology, employing mutants in particular auxotrophic mutants of microorganisms. An auxotrophic mutant has a metabolic block at a certain point in the biosynthetic pathway of an essential product (e.g., an amino acid or coenzyme). Such a block is caused by an enzyme.

mutase

an enzyme able to catalyze a dismutation or a molecular rearrangement.

mutator gene

a gene that increases the mutation rate of other gene, as in a system where the mutator gene produces a DNA polymerase that makes errors during replication.

mycobactin

any compound produced by some strains, and required for growth by other strains, of

Mycobacteria.

mycolic acid

one of a group of long-chain hydroxy fatty acids that contain from 60 to 90 carbon atoms and that have varying degrees of branching and unsaturation.

mycoside

a lipid composed of a long chain, highly branched and hydroxylated hydrocarbon that is terminated by a phenol to which a trisaccharide is linked by means of a glycosidic bond.

myelin

a complex material formed of protein and phospholipid that is laid down as a sheath around the axons of certain neurons, known as myelinated (or medullated) nerve fibres. The material is produced and laid down in concentric layers by neurilemmal cells at regular intervals along the nerve fibre. Myelinated nerve fibre conduct impulses more rapidly than nonmyelinated fibres.

myoglobin

a hemoglobinlike iron-containing protein pigment occurring in muscle fibres. Also known as muscle hemoglobin; myohemoglobin.

myohematin

a cytochrome respiratory enzyme allied to hematin.

myotropic activity

the anabolic effect of androgens on nitrogen metabolism that leads to nitrogen retention by the body and to a limited increase in muscle strength and development.

myrcene

a triply unsaturated acyclic monoterpene hydrocarbon. It is a component of many essential oils, and it is prepared for the perfumery industry by pyrolysis of β-pinene (from oil of turpentine).

myristic acid $C_{14}H_{28}O_2$

a saturated fatty acid that contains 14 carbon atoms; occurs as glycerides in milk and in certain vegetable oils. Also known as n-tetradecanoic acid.

myrosinase

an enzyme which catalyses the breakdown of glucobrassicin in the members of family Brassicaceae during auxin synthesis through indoleacetaldoxime pathway. The product in indoleacetonitrile.

NADH

abbreviation for nicotinamide adenine dinucleotide hybride.

Nadi reagent

a reagent that consists of a mixture of a-naphthol and p-penylenediamine and that is used for the detection of certain oxidases.

Na, K-ATpase

the adenosine triphosphatase that is located in the cell membrane and that is implicated in the membrane transport of sodium and potassium ions. The enzyme is vectorial in its action, is greatly stimulated by the addition of both sodium and potassium ions, but is only slightly stimulated by the addition of either sodium or potassium ions alone.

narcotic analgesic drug
a drug that produces narcosis (reversible depression of the central nervous system) as well as analgesis. Usually restricted to drugs of the morphine type, and a more precise, although perhaps less literal, definition is, an agent producing naloxone-reversible analgesia.

narcotic drug
literally, a drug that produces narcosis; i.e., reversible insensibility or stupor. In practice, the term is often used to mean a dependence-producing drug. No contradiction arises when dependence-producing drug of morphine type, for example, are referred to, because these drugs to produce depression of the central nervous system. However, the term is sometimes less appropriately applied to dependence-producing drugs which stimulate the central nervous system. The misuse of the term in so far as it literal nervous system.

narcotios, narcotic drugs
substances which act predominantly on the central nervous system. Depending on the dose, these show different phases of activity; small dose have a sedative action, somewhat higher doses are stimulatory, while even higher doses cause loss of consciousness (narcosis).

nascent polypeptide chain
a polypeptide chain that is in the process of being formed and that is attached to a transfer RNA molecule which, in turn, is bound to a ribosome.

nastic movement
when response of a plant is not related to the direction of stimulus but here stimulus may be diffuse e.g., opening and closing of flowers with change in light intensity. These are photonastic movements.

native
(i) a protein or a nucleic acid molecules in its natural in vivo state as opposed to its denatured state.

(ii) a protein or nucleic acid molecule that has been isolated by mild procedures so that it is undenatured, or only slightly denatured, and is taken to represent the in vivo state of the molecule.

natural abundance
the relative proportion of an isotope in nature, based on the sum of the concentration of all other isotopes of that particular element.

natural product
(i) a secondary metabolite that has no known function.

(ii) any organic compound produced by a living organism.

natural product chemistry

a branch of chemistry concerned with the identification, isolation and structural elucidation of natural compounds.

negative control

the prevention of a biological activity by the presence of a specific molecule; the prevention by a repressor of either inducible enzyme synthesis or initiation of messenger RNA synthesis are two examples.

negative feedback

a feedback mechanism in which a large output of the system leads to a decrease in the subsequent output while a small output of the system leads to an increase in the subsequent output.

negative staining

(i) a heavy metal stain, often phosphotungstic acid, is allowed to dry in a puddle around the surfaces of isolated cell particles. During drying the stain molecules deposit onto surface crevices and thus ghost image is produced in which the specimen will appear light against a dark background.

(ii) in electrophoresis the gel is mixed with the substrate e.g., starch, after run the gels are stained with the specific reagent e.g., potassium iodide-iodine, the bands in which enzyme activity will hydrolysis the substrate and will appear transparent against dark background.

negatron

the negatively charge beta particles ejected from a neutron. The neutron is converted to a proton and negatron. Negatron is similar to electron.

nephrolysin

a toxic substance capable of disintegrating kidney cells.

nephrotoxic drugs

drugs that may produce kidney damage as an unwanted effect. Such drugs include, amongst many others, the antibiotic gentamycin, the anaesthetic methoxyflurane, the antiarthritic group of gold salts, and the solvent carbon tetracloride.

nerol

a doubly unsaturated acyclic monoterpene alcohol. It is an oil with an odour of roses. It is a structural isomer of linalool and a cis-trans-isomer of Geraniol. It is the most valuable acyclic monoterpene alcohol used in perfumery. The pyrophsphate ester of N, neryl pyrophosphate is an intermediate in the biosynthesis of the monoterpenes.

neuberg fermentation

neuberg's first form of fermentation is the normal “unsteered” fermentation by yeasts, i.e., all the reactions and side reactions of the anaerobic degradation of carbohydrate, with the production of ethyl alcohol.

neuberg's second form of fermentation (or sulfite fermentation) occurs in yeasts in the presence of sodium hydrogen sulfite. The acetaldehyde, which would normally act as a hydrogen acceptor is converted to its bisulfite addition compound. The resulting excess NADH reduces dihydroxyacetone phosphate to glycerol 1-phosphate (or 3-phosphate), a reaction catalysed by glycerol 1-phosphate (or 3-phosphate) dehydrogenase (Baranowski enzyme) EC 1.1.1.8). The oxido-reduction cycle (i.e., reduction of NAD and its regeneration from NADH) is thus maintained. The glycerol 1-phosphate is dephosphorylated by a phosphatase (EC 3.1.3.21) and free glycerol is produced. The process is therefore also known as a glycerol fermentation.

neuberg's third form of fermentation proceeds under alkaline conditions. Two molecules of glucose are converted into two molecules of glyceraldehyde and two molecules of acetaldehyde (via pyruvate by decarboxylation). The glyceraldehyde becomes reduced to glycerol, and the acetaldehyde undergoes a dismutation to produce equivalent amounts of ethanol and acetate.

neuraminic acid $C_9H_{17}NO_8$
an amino acid, the aldol condensation product of pyruvic acid and N-acetyl-D-mannosamine, regarded as the parent acid of a family of widely distributed acyl derivatives known as sialic acids.

neurine CH_2=$CHN(CH_3)_3OH$
a very poisonous, syrupy liquid with fishy aroma; soluble in water and alcohol; a product of puterfaction of choline in brain tissue and bile, and in cadavers. Also known as trimethylvinylammonium hydroxide.

neurohormone
a hormone that is produced by specialized nervous tissue. Examples are noradrenaline, serotonin, vasopressin, and oxytocin.

neurohumor
a hormonal transmitter substance, such as acetylcholine, released by nerve endings in the transmission of impulses.

neurosporene
a hydrocarbon carotenoid, containing 12 double bonds, nine of them conjugated. It is a direct biosynthetic precursor of lycopene, and it is found in Neurospora crassa.

neurotensin
a tridecapeptide originally isolated from the bovine hypothalamus, but later found to have a characteristic distribution in the gastrointestinal tract, mainly within mucosal N-cells in the terminal ileum. Its

pharmacological action include vasodilation, reduced gastric acid secretion, delayed gastric emptying, inhibition of gut motility, and stimulation of exocrine pancreatic secretion.

neurotoxin

a poisonous substance in snake venom that acts as a nervous system depressant by blocking neuromuscular transmission by binding acetylcholine receptors on motor end plates, or on the innervated face of an electroplax.

neutral

(i) being neither acidic nor basic; a neutral solution has a pH of 7.0.

(ii) being neither positively or negatively charged; a neutral atom has an equal number of protons and orbital electrons.

neutral ion pump

it transports zero net charge across the membrane. Under such conditions potential across the membrane is due to the gradient of the ions which are able to diffuse across it. This potential is known as diffusion potential. Inhibition of such pumps has little immediate effect. These are symport or antiport in nature.

neutral lipids

the lipids that do not have a hydrophilic end and do not form micelles or bilayers with water; e.g., cholesterol esters and triglycerides.

niacinamide

a member of the **vitamin B_2** complex.

niche

the home of a species. A plant's niche is an abstraction compounded of its spatial, functional and temporal relationships within a community. Evolution of differences in niche minimises interspecific competition and allow the development of a complex community such as woodland.

nickase

an endonuclease that introduces single-strand breaks into double stranded DNA.

nicked DNA

a DNA molecule having one or more breaks in either one or both of its strands.

nickel, Ni

Ni occurs only in traces in living system. In particular, it seems to be associated with RNA. A nickel metalloprotein named "nickeloplasmin"has been isolated from human and rabbit serum, but its function is not known.

nicking

breaking of a phosphodiester bond on one of the two strands of a native DNA molecule. Nicking can be brought about by physical or chemical damage and by specific enzymes.

nick translation

a technique for labelling DNA based on the ability of the DNA polymerase from E. Coli to degrade a strand of DNA that has been nicked and then to resynthesize the strand, if a radioactive nucleoside triphosphate is employed, the rebuilt strand becomes labelled and can be used as a radioactive probe.

nicotiana alkaloids, tobacco alkaloids

a group of pyridine alkaloids occurring mainly in the tobacco plant (Nicotlana). These contain a pyridine ring system substituted at position 3 by pyrrolidyl or piperidyl residues. the pyridine ring system of these alkaloids is derived biosynthetically from nicotinic acid (or a closely related derivative). The pyrrolidine ring is derived from ornithine or closely related compound in the ornithine-proline-glutamic acid family of amino acids.

nicotinamide $C_6H_6ON_2$

crystalline basic amide of the vitamin B complex that is interconvertible with nicotinic acid in the living oranism; the amide of nicotinic acid. Also known as niacinamide.

nicotine

chief representative of the Nicotiana-alkaloids Oxidative degradation of nicotine produces nicotinic acid. It is present in all parts of the tobacco plant (Nicotiana).

it has many different physiological effects. Owing to its toxicity, it is not used therapeutically.

nicotinic acid $C_6H_5NO_2$

a component of the vitamin B complex; a white, water-soluble powder stable to heat, acid, and alkali; used for the treatment of the pellagra. Also known as niacin.

ninhydrin

a reagent used for the detection of amino acids. A blue colour is produced with proteins and all amino acids except for proline, which gives a yellow colour. Ninhydrin also react with amino acids to give yellow colour.

ninhydrin reaction

the reaction of ninhydrin (triketo-hydrinden hydrate) with free alpha amino acids, peptides or proteins, the reaction yields coloured compounds that are used for chromatographic detection and for the quantitative determination of amino acids and peptides.

nitrate dissimilation, dissimilatory nitrate reduction

microbial reduction of nitrate to various products, which are not assimilated.

nitrate reductase

the enzyme that catalyzes the reduction of nitrate to nitrite in nitrate assimilation by plants and fungi; it is a molybdenum-containing flavoprotein.

nitrite reductase quotient

the ratio of nitrate reductase induced in the presence of nitrate/initial activity. It indicates the nitrogen nutritional status of plant tissues. Higher the value lower is the nitrate supply to the plant.

nitrilase

an enzyme which catalyses the conversion of indoleacetonitrile to IAA. It has been isolated from members of gramineae, cruciferae and musaceae.

nitrogen

an essential element found in all amino acids and therefore in all proteins, and in various other important organic compounds, e.g., nucleic acids. Gaseous nitrogen forms about 80% of the atmosphere but is unavailable in this form except to a few nitrogen-fixing bacteria. Nitrogen is therefore usually incorporated into plants as the nitrate ion, NO_3; absorbed in solution from the soil by roots. In animals, the nitrogen compounds urea and uric acid form the main excretory products.

nitrogen balance

difference between the total nitrogen intake of an organism and its total nitrogen loss. Young growing animals are in positive nitrogen balance i.e., they retain more nitrogen (as protein added during growth) than they excrete. Mature, healthy adults show a zero nitrogen balance i.e., nitrogen intake is exactly balanced by nitrogen excretion. A negative nitrogen balance results from a deficiency of an essential amino acid; a decrease in the concentration of any proteogenic amino acid in the body's amino acid pool impairs total protein synthesis, so that the concentration of all other free amino acids in the pool is increased; this leads to an exaggeration of degradative pathwaays and an increase in urea formation.

nitrogen cycle

the cyclic set of reactions involving plants, animals, and bacteria, whereby (i) Atmospheric nitrogen is converted to inorganic compounds and these are then converted to complex organic compounds and (ii) The organic compounds are broken down to inorganic compounds which ultimately yield atmospheric nitrogen.

nitrogen mustards

a group of alkylating agents that alkylate various nucleophilic cell constituents, e.g., the 7N of guanine which is the main purine base of DNA that is alkylated. They are used as cytotoxic agents in cancer chemotherapy, and include such drugs as mustine, chlorambucil, melphalan, and cyclophosphaide.

nitroprusside reaction

a colorimetric reaction for cysteine and free sulphydryl groups in a protein that is based on the production of a red colour upon treatment of the sample with sodium nitroprusside and ammonia.

nitrosamines
simple alkylamino compounds that are potent oncogens. They may be formed in the stomach after ingestion of nitrites. They are metabolized in the liver with the production of alkylating agents that are the active oncogens. For example, dimethyl-nitrosamine is hydroxylated to produce methylhydroxynitrosamine.

nitrous acid mutant
a mutant produced by treatment of a nucleic acid with nitrous acid; such mutants have been produced, for example, by treating the RNA from tobacco mosaic virus with nitrous acid, infecting tobacco leaves with the mutated RNA, and isolating the mutant viral particles formed in the infected leaves.

noble metals
metals like silver, gold and platinum which do not corrode or tarnish in air or water, and are not easily attacked by acids.

nomogram
an alignment chart for the rapid determination of a variable from the given values of two or more variables. A typical nomogram consists of a minimum of three scales such that when known values of two scales are connected by a straight line, the line intersects the third scale at the sought value.

non-coding DNA
DNA that is in the nonsense strand (negative strand) of the DNA duplex, or is out with the coding sequence of any gene. It may or may not be taken to include intron sequences. Centromeric region DNA is non-coding.

noncompetitive inhibition
enzyme inhibition in which the inhibitor can combine with either the free enzyme or the enzyme-substrate complex so that the inhibitor does not compete with the substrate for the enzyme.

non-crystalline
when arrangement of molecules is completely without any order. It forms the wall matrix which appears relatively featureless in the electron microscope.

non-essential enzyme
an enzyme that is not required for either the growth or the survival of a cell or an organism.

nonheme iron proteins, NHI-proteins
proteins containing iron that is not bound in a heme system. In these proteins, the iron is bound by the sulfur of cyteins residues, and it is often also associated with inorganic sulfur. They are also called iron-sulfur proteins.

non-mediated transport
transport across a biological membrane that does not involve a transport agent; simple diffusion.

nonproductive complex
an enzyme substrate complex in which the substrate is bound to the enzyme in such a

fashion that catalysis is impossible and products cannot be formed.

non-protein amino acids
in addition to the 20 common and many rare amino acids of proteins, over 150 other amino acids are known to occur in free or bound forms. These are never present in proteins. Most of them are important precursors of intermediates in metabolism e.g., β-alanine, ornithine, citrulline etc.

nonprotein nitrogen
the nitrogen fraction in the body tissues, excretions, and secretions, not precipitated by protein precipitants.

non-reducing end
in a polysaccharide or monosaccharide chain, the end(s) which does not act as a reducing agent. Branched chains have more than one non-reducing end.

non sense proteins
the functional enzymes containing mistake amino acid sequence produced during senescence. These are produced due to error either at transcriptional or translational levels. Their functions are degradation of enzymes which have been used in various reactions, cell metabolism becomes erratic and leads to senescence.

nonsense suppressor
gene that codes for a molecule of tRNA which is able to respond to one or more nonsense codons.

non-steroidal anti-inflammatory drug
a drug, not based on a steroid nucleus, that is used to control the inflammatory response. In general they act by inhibiting the synthesis of prostaglandins. Aspirin is the classical example but the group also includes other salicylates and pyrazolone derivatives.

noradrenaline
a catecholamine, which is secreted as a hormone by the adrenal medulla, that regulates heart muscle, smooth muscle, and glands. It is also secreted by nerve endings of the sympathetic nervous system in which it acts as a transmitter of impulses. In the brain, levels of noradrenaline are related to mental function; lowered levels lead to mental depression. Also known as norepinephrine.

noradrenalin, norepinephrine, arterenol
dihydroxyphenylethanolamine, a hormone with activity on the nervous system and the vascular system. It is a catecholamine and a biogene amine. Together with adrenalin it is synthesized from L-tyrosine via Dopa (Dopamine) in the adrenal medulla and in the nervous system. In the sympathetic nervous system, acts as an adrenergic Neurotransmitter. It causes contraction of blood vessels, with the exception of the

coronary vessels; it therefore causes an increase in the peripheral vascular resistance, with a consequent rise in blood pressure. The effect of noradrenalin on carbohydrate metabolism and blood sugar is similar to, but weaker than that of adrenalin.

norepinephrine $C_8H_{11}O_3N$

a hormone produced by chromaffin cells of the adrenal medulla; acts as a vasoconstrictor and mediates transmission of sympathetic nerve impulses. Also known as noradrenaline.

normal enzyme

an enzyme, the substrate of which are metabolites normally occurring within the organism, as distinct from a drug-metabolizing enzyme, the substrates of which are compounds foreign to the organism.

normal solution

when gram equivalent weight of acid or base is sufficient to neutralise 17.008 g of -OH or 1.0008 g of -H ions. The solution is said to be one normal (IN).

normality

the number of equivalents of solute per litre of solution.

norsteroid

a modified steroid that lacks one or more carbon atoms compared to the number of carbon atoms in the parent compound.

notexin

a polypeptide neurotoxin from the Australian tiger snake. It acts to prevent the release of acetylcholine from cholinergic nerve fibre endings.

nuclear fission

a reaction in which a heavier atomic nucleus is broken up into two or more lighter and more stable nuclei with the release of large amount of energy e.g., Uranium splited into two approximately equal parts, at the same time emitting neutrons and releasing very large amount of nuclear energy.

nuclear isomer

one of two or more nucleides that have the same atomic number and the same atomic mass but have nuclei that are at different energy levels.

nuclease

an enzyme that catalyzes the splitting of nucleic acids to nucleotides, nucleosides, or the components of the latter.

nucleases

a group of hydrolytic enzymes, which cleave nucleic acids. Exonucleases attack the nucleic acid molecule at its terminus, whereas endonucleases are able to catalyse a hydrolytic cleavage within the polynucleotide chain. Deoxyribonuleases (DNAases) are specific for DNA, and ribonucleases (RNAases) for RNA. All N. are phosphodiesterases. They catalyse the hydrolysis of either the 3' or 5' bond of the 3', 5'-phosphodieser linkage.

nucleic acid
a large, acidic, chainlike molecule containing phosphoric acid, sugar, and purine and pyrimidine bases; two types are ribonucleic acid and deoxyribonucleic acid.

nucleic acid bases
the heterocyclic nitrogenous weakly basic compounds found in nucleic acids as nucleotides. These strongly absorb ultraviolted light from 250 to 280 nm. Free bases are relatively insoluble in water. There are two types of bases, purine, and pyrimidine. Free bases are in traces.

nuclealus (plur. nucleoli)
a compartment of the nucleus. It contains the nucleolus organizer. The number of nucleolus per nucleus varies widely. The main components of the nucleolus are proteins (over 80% of the dry weight), RNA (over 50%) and DNA.

nucleolus organizer
a portion of the chromosome that is associated with the nucleolus and that functions in the synthesis of the ribosomal RNA.

nucleonics
the application of nuclear phenomena to other fields.

nucleoprotein
any member of a class of conjugated proteins in which molecules of nucleic acid are closely associated with molecules of protein.

nucleosidase
an enzyme that catalyzes the hydrolysis of a nucleoside to its component pentose and its purine or pyrimidine base.

nucleoside
the glycoside resulting from removal of the phosphate group from a nucleotide; consists of a pentose sugar linked to a purine or pyrimidine base.

nucleoside diphosphate compounds
compounds containing a nucleoside diphosphate grouping. This grouping has an activating effect, so that the molecule has a high group transfer potential. Examples of these are nucleoside diphosphate sugars and cytidine diphosphate choline.

nucleoside phosphorylase
an enzyme which catalyses the formation of nucleoside from the combination of a base and ribose-5-P.

nucleotidase
any of a group of enzymes which split phosphoric acid from nucleotides, leaving nucleosides.

nucleotide
an ester of a nucleoside and phosphoric acid; the structural unit of a nucleic acid.

nucleotide coenzyme
a coenzyme containing a nucleotide structure. Nucleotide coenzymes are Pyridine nucleotide coenzymes the nucleoside diphosphate moieties of Nucleoside diphosphate sugars and coenzyme A.

nucleotide exchange reaction
the reaction, catalyzed by the enzyme nucleoside diphosphate kinase, in which a nucleoside diphosphate and a nucleoside triphosphate are converted to the opposite pair of nucleoside di- and triphosphates by the transfer of a phosphate group.

nucleotides, nucleoside phosphates
the phosphoric acid esters of Nucleosides. o-phosphoric acid is esterified with a free OH-group of the sugar. If the sugar is D-ribose the nucleotide is called a ribonucleotide or ribotide. If the sugar is D-2-deoxyribose, the N is a deoxyribonucleotide, deoxynucleotide or dexyribotide. The phosphate may be present on position 2', 3' or 5' (in deoxy-ribonucleotides, only the 3'- and 5'- phosphate are possible). The 5'-nucleoside phosphate are metabolically very important; they may be mono-, di-ortriphosphorylated e.g. guanosine 5'-monophosphate, cytidine 5'-diphosphate and adenosine 5'-triphosphate.

NUL lymphocyte
a lymphocyte which has no detectable immunoglobulin or T lymphocyte on its surface.

numerical hybrid
hybrid whose parental gametes differed in respect of the number of chromosomes.

nurse tissue
a tissue which provides nutrient to developing embryo e.g., nucellar.

nutation
(i) the spiral growth of the apex of a plant organs e.g., shoots, tendrils, etc. It is caused by variation in the rate of growth of the meristematic areas.
(ii) the lateral swaying of the tip of a growing organ.

nutrient
the raw inorganic or organic materials from which complex compounds are synthesised, e.g., N, P, K, sugar, amino acids etc. These are low molecular weight compounds with simple structure and are used in building complex structural components of a cell.

nutrient intensity
the nutrient concentration of the soil solution. It is affected by soil conditions i.e., pH, temperature, aeration and moisture level which influence the labile pool of ions. It is the buffer factor and it indicates how intensity varies with quantity.

nutrient quantity
the availability of nutrient. It is very much dependent on climatic and soil conditions. All factors influencing the distribution of roots in the profile contribute to the quantity factor.

nutritional physiology of microorganisms
the terms autotrophy and heterotrophy are too broad to

distinguish between all the different forms of microbial nutrition. Different types of nutritional physiology are classified according to :

1. the nature of the carbon source;
2. the source and mechanism of formation of ATP;
3. the source of reducing power for the synthesis of cell constituents.

nux vomica

a plant product having about 1.8-5.3% of the total alkaloidal base. The main alkaloids of therapeutic importance are strychnine (1.25%) and brucine (1.5%) which are present in the large thick-walled cells of endosperm. The high concentration of strychnine is present in cells near the centre of the seeds while brucine is concentrated in the outer cells near the epidermis. The other minute alkaloids present in the drugs are α-colubrine, β-colubrine, icajine, 3-methoxyicajine, protostrychnine, vomicine, novacine, N-oxystrychnine, pseudostrychnine, and isostrychnine. The seeds also contain chlorogenic or igasuric or caffeotannic acid (a condensation product of caffeic acid and quinic acid), loganin (a glycoside), fixed oils (3%) and proteins. Loganin is also present in the fruit pulp upto 5% along with secologanin. Hemicellulose consisting of mannan and galactan are present in the thick cell wall of the endosperm. Aleurone grains are present in the endosperm of the seed.

obligate anaerobe

(i) an organism or a cell that can grow only in the absence of molecular oxygen.

(ii) an organism or a cell that lacks the ability to synthesise an oxygen linked respiratory chain and must, therefore, utilise fermentation.

ochratoxin A $C_{20}H_{18}ClNO_6$

a toxic metaboite from Aspergillus ochraceus: a crystalline compound which exhibits green fluorescence; melting point is 169°C; inhibits phosphorylase and mitochondrial respiration in rat liver.

ochre codon

the UAA sequence in mRNA. Like the amber codon, it signals the end of the protein biosynthesis. The synthesized polypeptide chain is released after the incorporation of the amino acid encoded immediately before the ochre codon and the one most widely employed by all living systems.

ocimene

a triply unsaturated monoterpene hydrocarbon. It is a double bond positional isomer of Myrcene, and a component of many essential oils.

octopamine

the product of β-hydroxylation of tryamine by dopamine-β-hydroxylase. It occurs in the vesicular fraction of noradrenergic nerves. It is also found in mammalian sympathetically innervated tissues, and in the central nervous system, where it is unevenly distributed. It has been classified as a false transmitter in the mammalian nervous system, since it is a cotransmitter of noradrenaline. Octopamine stimulates an adenylate cyclase which appears be senstive only to amine.

oestradiol
most important naturally occurring oestrogen.

oestriol
oestrogen hormone which can be detected in the urine of pregnant woman and is produced by the ovary and placenta.

oligo dA
homopolymer of deoxyriboadenylate that can be made as an artificial polymer in vitro and used as a synthetic template for polymerases.

oligo (dT) cellulose
short lengths of deoxythymidylic acid (dT) homopolymer convalently attached to powdered cellulose. Oligo (dT) cellulose is used in the purification of eukaryotic mRNA by affinity chromatography.

oligomeric enzymes
when enzyme consists of 2 or more polypeptide chains that are held together by weak noncovalent forces to occasionally by disulphide bridges. Such enzyme does not show simple Michaelis-Menten kinetics, but gives a sigmoidal relationship between initial rate and substrate concentration.

oligomeric protein
a protein composed of two or more polypeptide chains.

oligosaccharides
oligosaccharides are composed of two or more (arbitrarily up to about 10) monosaccharides, covalently bonded by glycosidic linkages between the monosaccharides. Some oligosaccharides occur naturally; these and many others may appear in partial hydrolysis of higher oligosaccharides or polysaccharides.

oncogenes
genes that, when expressed abnormally, may lead to cancerous growth. These were first found in tumour viruses (viral oncogenes) but is now known that normal vertebrate cells also possess such genes (cellular oncogenes). Indeed, during evolution, the viruses may have acquired them from vertebrates rather than vice versa. The normal function of the cellular oncogenes may be to direct the synthesis of enzymes or other proteins that play an essential role in cell growth and multiplication. One such enzyme is a protein kinase that phosphorylates

tyrosine subunits in proteins; another is a DNA-binding protein that is essential for DNA replication. It is only when there is augmented expressions (e.g., cause by chemical mutagens or carcinogens or radiation), that the cell is overwhelmed and becomes transformed into a cancer cell.

on-line working
the use of a device which is connected directly to a computer so that it becomes a peripheral device. In off-'line working' the device produces information in readable form for subsequent processing by a computer.

onium type compounds
compounds having charged ammonium, phosphonium or sulphonium groups. Inhibit GA synthesis before ent-kaurene step and most of them are retardant e.g., CCC, AMO-1618, chlorophonium chloride and mepiquat chloride etc.

ontogenesis
the development of the organism by cell growth and differentiation from the zygote onwards; i.e., production of the existing form.

open gas exchange system
here an air stream of known properties is passed through the assimilation chamber at a measured, constant flow rate. All or part of it is then passed through the gas analyser before it exhausts from the system.

open-promoter complex
the conformation in transcription that follows the initial binding of RNA polymerase to the promoter and in which the RNA polymerase has undergone a conformational change and the two DNA strands have become locally unwound.

open system
1. a system in dynamic equilibrium with its surroundings, i.e., there is a continual exchange of material, energy and information with the environment.
2. in biology, plants are considered to be O.s., whereas animals are closed systems. The plant is theoretically capable of unlimited growth; certain cells remain embryonal and able to divide and differentiate, so that growth occurs from vegetative sites, such as the meristematic regions of the shoot and root tips, intercalary meristems, etc.

operon hypothesis
the model, proposed by Jacob and Monod, according to which enzyme induction and repression result from the control of one or more structural genes by an adjacent operator genes. During repression a repressor, a small molecule either product or similar to the product, binds with operator. An inducer binds to the repressor, and thus preventing

the blocking of operator. The synthesis of repressor is controlled by a regulator gene which need not be adjacent to the operon. Inducers are generally substrates of the enzyme or compounds similar to the substrates.

opiate

an analgesic drug derived from the opium poppy; e.g., morphine, codeine. Also includes morphine derivatives, such as heroin (diacetylmorphine) which is prepared from morphine.

opine

the gall cells are induced to synthesise organic compounds derived from amino acids, keto acids and sugars. These are rich sources of C and N for Agrobacterium e.g., nopaline, agropine, octopine etc.

opioid

an analgesic drug with pharmacological similarities to opium (morphine). Includes both synthetic morphine-like drugs (e.g., buprenorphine) and endogenous peptides (e.g., metenkephalin). More specifically, it refers to any directly acting opiod receptor agonist, not from opium, that is stereospecifically antagonized by naloxone. An opioid peptide is an opioid drug that is a polypeptide. Metenkephalin is an example.

opiopeptins

a generic term that covers the three distinct families of endogenous opioid peptides; enkephalin family, dynorphin family and endorphin family.

opsin

the protein component of the retinal pigment rhodopsin, which is localized in the red cells of the retina. Opsin is released from rhodopsin when light strikes the retina.

opium

the congealed or dried latex of Papaver somniferum. The chief active constituents of opium are the Opium alkaloids. The action of opium is essentially similar to, but weaker than that of its constituent Morphine.

opium alkaloids

the Papaveraceae alkaloids that occur in Opium. There are about 40 different O.a.; the chief representatives are Morphine (opium alkaloids) Codeine and Papaverine.

opsonization

coating of microorganism and other antigenic particles with opsonins thus facilitating their phagocytosis.

optical test

a method introduced in 1936 by Otto Warburg for the determination of the enzymatic activity of NAD and NADP-dependent dehydrogenases. Absorbance at 340 nm (or another suitable wavelength in that region) in measured as an index of the degree of reduction of NAD or NADP. The principle of this method is now widely used for measuring enzyme activities and the concentration of metabolites. Determinations of dehydrogenase activities by this test are now conveniently performed in an automatic recording spectrophotometer, so that the change in absorbance at 340 nm is monitored continuously with time, e.g., the activity of malate dehydrogenas is measured from the rate of increase of absorbance at 340 nm due to the production of NADH in the reaction : NAD^+ + Malate→ Oxaloacetate + NADH + H^+.

orcinol reaction
a colorimetric reaction for carbohydrates that is based on the production of a green colour upon treatment of the sample with orcinol and with ferric chloride dissolved in concentrated hydrochloric acid. The reaction is used particularly for pentoses and for RNA estimation.

organophosphate phosphate anticholinesterases
a class of long-lasting compounds which have been mainly used as insecticides and as potential agents of warfare. Di-isopropyl fluorophosphate (DFP) is an example of this group of compounds.

origin of replication
replication of DNA in host cell will not occur if it is not having a sequence which is recognized by the cell as origin of replication.

ornithine $C_5H_{12}O_2N_2$
an amino acid occurring in the urine of some birds, but not found in native proteins.

ornithine cycle
cyclic series of biochemical reactions responsible for the conversion and detoxification of the nitrogenous products of protein metabolism. Ammonia and urea are derived from the metabolic pathway, the ammonia being used to convert ornithine to citrulline and the innocuous urea being largely excreted. Some genetic mutants in the human have blocks in the cycle, resulting in, for example, the citrullinuria and ornithine transcarbamylase deficiency. Also known as urea cycle.

orotic acid $C_4H_4O_4N_2$
a crystalline acid which is a growth factor for certain bacteria and is also pyrimidine precursor.

orthogenesis
the theory of the mechanism of evolution which postulates that variation is determined by the action of the environment on the fixed constitution of the organism, so that the possibilities of variation are limited to certain definite lines.

orthomolecular conformation
a high energy conformation of mitochondria that occurs in mitochondrial preparations containing little or no ADP and that is characterized by a mitochondrial matrix which is

squeezed together tightly and which stains heavily.

orthostichy
a given leaf is generally connected via the vascular system to other leaves directly above or below it on the stem. The number of internode between leaves on the same orthostichy varies with species. Generally photosynthates from a source leaf is translocated to the sink leaf of the same orthostichy.

osmotic agents
agents used to raise the osmotic pressure of the tissue fluids in order to withdraw water from the CSF when there is high interacranial pressure, or from the eye in glaucoma. Hypertonic dextrose, urea, mannitol, sorbitol and glycerol may be used for these purposes.

osmotic potential
the change in free energy of water produced by the addition of solute. Addition of the solute decreases the osmotic potential. It is affected by ionisation of the solute and temperature of solution.

osmotic pressure
the pressure required to inhibit osmosis. It is directly proportional to the number of solute molecules in a given amount of solution e.g., one molal solution of a undissociated solute at 0°C has a O.P of 22.4 atm.

ototoxicity
toxicity manifested in the functions of the ear. For example, aminoglycoside antibiotics may produce deafness as a consequence of damaging the eighth cranial nerve.

outer volume
the volume of solvent that is contained in the spaces among the gel particles of the bed in gel filtration chromatography.

ovalbumin
the major, conjugated protein of egg-white.

overwinding
situation in which the DNA double helix, already wound in a right handed spiral, is placed under additional torsional stress in the same direction resulting in positive supercoiling of the double helix upon itself.

ovulation inhibitors
a group of steroids, which inhibit ovulation by feedback inhibition of the production of Luteinizing hormone and/or Follicular stimulating hormone. They are used extensively as oral contraceptives (otherwise known as "the pill").

oxalic acid HOOC-COOH
it occurs widely in plants as its calcium, magnesium, and potassium salts. Owing to its ability to bind calcium, large amounts of oxalic acid are poisonous. By forming insoluble calcium oxalate in the intestine, it hinders the absorption of calcium. Animals cannot metabolize oxalic acid.

Higher levels may lead to kidney damage (formation of oxalate kidney stones).

oxaloacetate pathway

a metabolic pathway whereby aspartic acid and asparagine are catabolized through conversion to the oxaloacetic acid, which then feeds into the citric acid cycle.

oxidase

an enzyme that catalyzes oxidation reactions by utilization of molecular oxygen as an electrone acceptor.

oxidative deamination

a method of preparing α-keto acids in which two hydrogen atoms are probably removed to produce an amino acid, which is hydrolyzed to ammonia and a keto acid.

oxidative phosphorylation, respiratory chain phosphorylation

formation of ATP coupled with the operation of the respiratory chain. Energy available from the flow of electrons from substrate to oxygen via the respiratory chain drives the synthesis of ATP from ADP and inorganic phosphate. Oxidation of one molecule of reduced nicotinamide adenine dinucleotide ($NADH+H^+$) generates three molecules of ATP, while reduction of one molecule of reduced flavin adenine dinucleotide ($FADH_2$) yields two ATP. Complete oxidation of one molecule glucose yields 38 ATP, 2 from glycolysis and 36 from O.p. the mechanism of oxidative phosphorylation i.e., the nature of the energy transducing mechanism that coverts the energy of electron flow into the chemical energy of ATP, has always been a controversial area of biochemistry.

oxidoreductase

an enzyme catalyzing a reaction in which two molecules of a compound interact so that one molecule is oxidized and the other reduced, with a molecule of water entering the reaction.

oxygen debt

a physiological state that occurs when a normally aerobic animal is forced to respire anaerobically during a temporary shortage of oxygen (anoxia), e.g., due to violent muscular excretion. Pyruvate, a product of the first stage of internal respiration, is converted anaerobically to lactic acid, which is toxic and requires oxygen for its breakdown, thereby building up an oxygen is made available and allows oxidation of the lactic acid in the liver.

oxygen evolving complex (OEC)

the site on the photosystem II responsible for oxygen evolution during photolysis of water. Due to absorption of light by the chlorophylls (4 positive charges) and pool of plastoquinone is reduced. S_4 is converted to S state by removing 4 electrons- and 4 protons from water, with the concomitant evolution of oxygen. Manganese has been shown to be the species of OEC, accumulating positive charges.

oxygen metabolism
metabolic reactions involving oxygen, including :
1. general oxidation of metabolites by Dehydrogenation, removal of electrons (oxidases, Flavin enzymes), and addition oxygen to the substrate.
2. oxidation of reduced coenzyme via the respiratory chain.

oxygen toxicity
when activated form of O_2 induces destructive oxidation of cellular components in an uncontrolled fashion by producing superoxide and hydrogen peroxide.

oxygen quotient
the rate of oxygen consumption of an organism or tissue. It is usually expressed in μL of oxygen per mg of dry weight per hour. Small organisms tend to have higher oxygen quotients than larger ones.

oxyhemoglobin
the red crystalline pigment formed in the blood by combination of oxygen and hemoglobin, without the oxidation of iron.

oxysome
inner membrane subunits on the mitochondria membrane, involves in electron transport chain and thus ATPs are produced.

oxytocic agents
agents that hasten evacuation of the uterus by stimulating contraction of the myometrium.

oxytocin $C_{43}H_{66}O_{12}N_{12}S_2$
a polypeptide hormone secreted by the neurohypophysis that stimulates contraction of the uterine muscles.

Oz group
a group of allotypic antigenic sites in the constant region of the lambda chain of human immunoglobulins. Oz^+ λ chains have lysin at position 191 whereas Oz chains have arginine at the same position.

pH-stat
a device of maintaining a system at constant pH by continuously monitoring the pH and responding to deviation by automatically adding a sufficient volume of solution (e.g., an acid) to restore pH to the preselacted value.

pacemaker enzyme
an enzyme that catalyzes a reaction that is essentially irreversible in the chemical sense; such enzymes frequently catalyzes either the initial, the final, or a branch point reaction of a metabolic pathway.

pair production
results when very high gamma-rays react with the nucleus of an atom and all the energy of the gamma-ray is converted to a positron and

negatron.

paleoproteins

a group of proteins from fossils, in particular the exoskeleton of molluscs (snail and mussel shells, and cuttle bone).

pale or pales or palet

(i) the inner bract of a grass floret.

(ii) a general name for the glumes associated with grass flower.

(iii) the scales which form the ramentum on ferns.

palindrome

a nucleic acid sequence that is identical to its complementary strand (when both are read in the same 5' - 3' direction). In the region of a palindrome there is therefore a two fold rotational symmetry.

palmitic acid $CH_3(CH_2)_{14}COOH$

a saturated fatty acid; glycerides of palmitic acid occur widely in plant and animal oils and fats. Also known as hexadecanoic acid.

pancreas

a vertebrate organ producing a digestive secretion which enters the adjacent duodenum in response to the hormones Secretin and Cholecystokinin. It also contains about 1 million islets of Langerhans, which have a diameter of 150 µm, a rich supply of blood and are innervated with unmyelinated nerve fibres. The islets contain various types of hormone-producing cells, the A cells which produce Glucagon the B cells which make Insulin and the D cells which manufacture gastrin.

pancreatic juice

the digestive juice that consists of the secretion of the pancreas and that is discharged into the small intestine; contains proteolytic enzymes, secreted as zymogenus, nucleases, carbohydrases, and lipase.

pancreatin

a cream-coloured, amorphous powder obtained from the fresh pancreas of a hog; contains amylopsin, trypsin, and other enzymes.

pancreozymin

a crude extract of the intestinal mucosa that stimulates secretion of pancreatic juice.

papain

an enzyme preparation obtained from the juice of the fruit and leaves of the papaya (Carica papaya); contains proteolytic enzymes.

papaveraceae alkaloids, papaver alkaloids, poppy alkaloids

a group of Benzylisoquinoline alkaloids occurring especially in species of poppy (Papaver). They include the important Opium alkaloids.

papaveretum

a solution of the total pure alkaloids of opium as the hydrochlorides for oral use or for subcutaneous or intramuscular injection.

papaverine
an opium alkaloid occurring with morphine in various species of poppy. Physiologically it acts peripherally, and causes relaxation of smooth muscle; it is therefore used for the treatment of spasms in the gastrointestinal tract.

paracrystalline
of a substance when true crystallinity is not seen, but some regularity, often in two dimensions, is present. Cellulose chains are held in such forms within the microfibril.

parameter
a technical term originally coined to have precise meaning in various branches of mathematics. It is included here because it is frequently misused in many disciplines, including biochemistry, pharmacology and medical science generally, simply to mean any measured factor. An acceptable meaning in medical science arising through common usage, may be a variable, the measurement of which is indicative of a function that cannot itself be precisely measured by the direct methods.

paramylum
a reserve, starchlike carbohydrate of various protozoans and algea.

paranemic joint
region in which complementary DNA sequences are associated like trame lines rather than interwined in a helix.

parasite
when two or more dissimilar organisms living together in more or less intimate association. Only one of them will have advantage over the other. The benefitted partner is parasite and the losing partener is host e.g., most of the pathogens.

parasympathomimetic action
a term used to describe drug actions that resemble those of the parasympathetic nervous system.

parathromone
a polypeptide hormone that functions in regulating calcium and phosphate metabolism. Also known as parathyroid hormone.

parathormone, parathyrin
a hormone produced by the parathyroid gland, which influences the metabolism of calcium and phosphate. It is a single chain proteohormone with 84 amino acid residues of known primary structure.

partial agonist
a term used to denote an agonist that fails to produce a maximal response of a tissue when all the receptors are occupied by it. Partial agonists also possess antagonistic activity in the sense that they reduce the response to more active agonists.

partial derivative
determination of change in the

dependent variable when only one of the independent variables is allowed to vary, which leads to a quantity known as partial derivatives.

partial pressure

the pressure exerted by a gas when it is a part of a mixture of gases; it is equal to the pressure that gas would exert if it alone occupied the entire volumes occupied by the mixture at the same temperature.

particulate antigen

an antigen that is part of an insoluble structure of a microbial or other cell, a virus, or some other particle.

partition

(i) to distribute between two phases; often, a distribute between two immiscible liquid phases.

(ii) the lamellae which separate the loculi of the grana in a chloroplast.

partition or distribution coefficient (Kd)

(i) the ratio of solute distributed itself between two immiscible phases. These two phases are not only solvents, but also by its distribution between any two phases, such as solid/liquid or gas/ liquid phases. Kd is constant at a given temperature and it is equal to concentration of solute in solvent A/ concentration of solute in solvent B.

(ii) of an organ is the ratio of the total gross dry matter increment of the whole plant.

passive transport

the movement of a solute across a biological membrane that is produced by diffusion, is directed downward in a concentration gradient, does not require carriers, and does not require the expenditure of energy.

pause

the reduction in the rate of RNA chain elongation that occurs during the transcription of DNA by RNA polymerase at specific regions of the DNA. These regions are known as pausing sites.

pA value

the negative logarithm p of the molar concentration of antagonist, A in the presence of which the potency of the agonist is reduced to x times; that is x times more agonist is required to produce a given response in the presence than in the absence of the antagonist.

pectate lyase

the enzyme that catalyzes the degradation of pectins whereby the glycosidic bonds between the monosaccharide residues are cleaved and water molecules are eliminated.

pectic acid

a complex acid, partially demethylated, obtained from the pectin of fruits.

pectic substances

polymers of galacturonic acid. These are polysaccharide like compounds present in the middle lamella of cell walls.

pectin

a purified carbohydrate obtained from the inner portion of the rind of citrus fruits, or from apple pomace; consists chiefly of methoxylated polygalacturonic acids.

pectinase

an enzyme that catalyzes the transformation of pectin into sugars and galacturonic acid.

pectinesterase

an enzyme that catalyzes the hydrolytic breakdown of pectins to pectic acids.

pelargonidin

an anthocyanidin pigment obtained by hydrolysis of pelargonin in the form of its red-brown crystalline chloride. $C_{15}H_{11}ClO_5$.

pelargonidini

3, 5, 7, 4'-tetrahydroxyflavylium cation. An aglycon of many Anthocyanins. It is widely distributed in higher plants as its various glycosides, which are responsible for the rose, orange-red and scarlet colours of petals and fruits.

pelargonin

an anthocyanin obtained from the dried petals of red pelargoniums or blue cornflowers in the form of its red crystalline chloride, $C_{27}H_{31}ClO_{15}$.

penicillinase

a bacterial enzyme that hydrolyzes and inactivates penicillin.

penicillin selection technique

an aid to the isolation of chosen auxotrophic mutations in a bacterial population. It is based on the fact that penicillin kills growing bacterial cells, but does not affect nongrowing cells.

pentosan

a hemicellulose present in cereal, straws, brans, and other woody plant tissues; yields five-carbon-atom sugass.

pentose

a monosaccharide with five carbon atoms. The importance of pentoses in metabolism derives from the fact that:

(a) D-ribose and D-2-deoxyribose are components of all cells, occurring particularly in nucleic acids and coenzymes,

(b) they are intermediates in important metabolic pathways such as the pentose phosphate pathway and the photosynthetic cycle, and

(c) the utilization of dietary pentoses ad pentitols requires the existence of suitable metabolic reactions for the conversion of pentoses into useful products.

pentose phosphate isomerase

an enzyme which catalyses the equilibrium between the ribose-5-phosphate and ribulose-5-phosphate.

pentose phosphate pathway

a pathway by which glucose is metabolized or transformed in plants and microorganisms;

glucose-6-phosphate is oxidized to 6-phosphogluconic acid, which then undergoes oxidative decarboxylation to form ribulose-5-phosphate, which is ultimately transformed to fructose-6-phosphate.

pepsin

an enzyme that catalyzes the partial hydrolysis of proteins of polypeptides. It is secreted by the gastric glands in an inactive form, pepsinogen, and is activated by hydrogen ions. At pH values of 4.6 and less pepsin activates pepsinogen, i.e., it is autocatalytic. Pepsin initiates the digestion of proteins, splitting them into smaller fragments. The extent of this action is proportional to the length of time the protein is in contact with the enzyme.

pepsin inhibitor

a polypeptide fragment that inhibits pepsin and that has a molecular weight of about 3000; it is removed, together with other peptides, from pepsinogen in the course of its activation to pepsin.

peptide

a compound of two or more amino acids joined by peptide bonds.

peptide antibiotic

an antibiotic e.g., Gramicidin or actinomycin D, that consists largely on entirely of a peptide.

peptide bond

joining of a-carboxyl group of one amino acid to the α-amino group of another. Formation of the bond involves loss of a water molecule from the two amino acids, and the bond can be broken by hydrolysis. The equlibrium is in favour of hydrolysis; the reverse reaction, as in protein synthesis, requires an input of energy and information with respect to the sequence of amino acids. The orientation of the carbonyl group in the peptide is usually trans to the amino group, and because the bond has a partial double bond character (due to resonance) the bond is rigid and planar. This rigidity limits the number of configurations of a polypeptide chain and is a major determinant of the shape of proteins.

peptides

organic compounds consisting of two or more amino acids joined covalently by peptide bonds (peptide bond). Those containing ten or fewer amino acids are called aligopeptides while more than ten amino acid residues constitutes a polypeptide.

peptidyl-puromycin

a peptide attached to puromycin; formed between a growing polypeptide chain and puromycin when protein synthesis is inhibited by puromycin.

peptone

large protein fragment produced form a protein molecle

following partial hydrolysis by a degradative enzyme.

peribacteriodal space

the space between bacteroids and the peribacteroid membrane in leguminous root nodules. During period of high nitrogenase activity nitrogen and carbon metabolizing enzymes are present in this space. However, during nodule sensescence the activity of acid phosphatase is also localised here.

periodate oxidation

the oxidative cleavage by periodate of the bond between two adjacent carbon atoms carrying any combination of hydroxyl, aldehyde, ketone or primary amine group. The periodate ion is reduced to the iodate ion and the reaction mixture is analysed by titration. The reaction is used to find out the structure of unknown carbohydrates.

periodic acid-Schiff (PAS) reaction

a test for the presence of glycoproteins, polysaccharides, certain mucopolysaccharides, glycolipids, and certain fatty acids in tissue sections. The tissue is treated with periodic acid, followed by Schiff's reagent. A positive reaction is the development of a red or magenta coloration.

peripheral proteins

the membranal proteins associated with cytoskeleton of cells. These are literally floating on the surface of the phospholipid bilayer sea. These are easily soluble in aqueous buffers and may be rapidly separated from membranes by increasing the ionic strength of the solvent or by using chelates such as EDTA or by repeated washing with low strength ionic buffers.

periplasmic enzyme

a bacterial enzyme that exists either in free or in bound form in a region between the cell wall and the cell membrane.

peristomatal transpiration

the guard cells are free of plasmadesmata but there are very permeabile regions in the outer walls and cuticle of the epidermal layer, particularly over guard cells. Water loss through these regions is known as peristomatal transpiration.

permanent wilting

wilting of plant which would not recover during night. Only when plants are watered turgidity will be regained and such plants will recover from wilting.

permease

any of a group of enzymes which mediate the phenomenon of active transport.

peroxisome

a membrane-enclosed, cytoplasmic organelle that contains a variety of oxidoreductases, such as urate oxidase, catalase, and D-amino acid oxidase.

pesticides

chemicals which control the infestation of pest and pathogens on the crop plants. These are contact and systemic in nature e.g., fungicides, insecticides.

petite mutants

yeast mutants characterized by slow growth, so that the colonies they form are much smaller than those of wild-type cells. Such mutants are best known in the budding yeast saccharomyces cervices, but are not confined to that species.

petunin

a blue anthocyanin present in the flowers of the blue garden petunia. The structures of more than 10 other naturally occurring glycosides of petunidin have been determined.

PGB

a prostaglandin that has one double bond between carbon atoms 8 and 9 and another between carbon atoms 13 and 14.

phaeophytin

a yellow-grey coloured pigment of chlorophyll appearing in organic solvent extracts of chlorophyll and often seen during paper chromatography of such extracts.

phage development

entry of phase DNA (or RNA) into the host cell initiates a series of processes leading to new phage progeny. They can be divided into three phases :
1. synthesis of early phage RNA and early phage proteins, and termination of the synthesis of all host nucleic acids and proteins;
2. synthesis of late RNA and late proteins;
3. morphogenesis of new phages. This complicated interaction of host cell and phage is regulated largely on the level of gene expression.

phage lysozyme

the enzyme, present in many phages, that has a specificity similar to that of lysozyme and that functions in the injection of phage nucleic acid into, and the release of progeny phage from, the bacterial cell.

phagocytin

a type of bactericidal agent present within phagocytic cells.

pharmacy

the study and practice of pharmaceutical preparation and analysis, involving a knowledge of dispensing techniques and the laws governing the use and sale of pharmaceuticals.

phaseolic acid

isolated from Phaseolus seed. It is a keto carboxylic acid, which resembles gibberellic acid.

phaseolin

glycoprotein storage molecule from the bean phaseolus vulgarus, making up some 50% of the cotyledon storage protein. These proteins are coded by a small gene family of about 10 genes.

phellogen or cork cambium
a layer of meristematic cells, lying in the cortex of a stem or root. It forms cork on the outside and phelloderm on the inside.

phenol
a strong and inexpensive disinfectant with a characteristic pine odour. At low concentration it is bacteriostatic, but higher concentrations (1-2%) are bactericidal and fungicidal. Activity is lowered by cold, alkalinity, or the presence of lipids and soaps. It is thought to act by denaturing protein and is able to penetrate skin, causing inflammation and local precipitation of protein with necrosis. Also known as carbolic acid.

phenylalanine $C_9H_{11}O_2N$
an essential amino acid, obtained in the levo form by hydrolysis of proteins (as lactalbumin); converted to tyrosine in the normal body. Also known as α-aminohydrocinnamic acid; α-amino-β-phenyl-propionic acid; β-phenylalanine.

phenylanine ammonia-lyase
an enzyme which catalyses the conversion of phenylalanine to cinnamate during synthesis of secondary products derived from phenylpropanoids. Its activity is phytochrome mediated.

phenylketonuria
disorder of amino acid metabolism in humans and occurring as an inherited trait in individuals homozygous for the gene, who represent about one in 11,000 of the human population in the western world. Affected individuals cannot convert phenylalanine in tyrosine due to lack of a functional phenylalanine hydroxylase in the liver. Brain abnormally will result unless dietary intake of phenylalaine is drastically restricted from an early age.

phenylpyruvic acid $C_6H_5CH_2$ CO COOH
a keto acid, occurring as a metabolic product of phenylalanine.

phorbol esters
the parent alcohol of tumour-promoting esters in croton oil (from crotontiglium, family Euphorbiaceae). The tumour-promoting phorbol esters act as analogues of diacylglycerol and cause long-lasting stimulation of protein kinase C.

phosphagen
a high-energy phosphate compound, such as phosphocreatne or phosphoarginine, that serves as a storage form of free energy. It is found in animal tissues and provides a reserve of chemical energy in the form of high energy phosphate bonds. The most common phosphagens are creatine phosphate, occurring in vertebrate muscle and nerves, and arginine phosphate, found

in most invertebrates. During tissue activity (e.g., muscle contraction) phosphagens give up their phosphate groups, thereby generating ATP from ADP. The phosphagens are then reformed when ATP is available.

phosphatase
an enzyme that catalyzes the hydrolysis and synethesis of phosphosic acid esters and the transfer of phosphate groups from phosphoric acid to other compounds.

phosphate translocator
a 29-30 KD translocator situated on the inner envelope of chloroplast regulating export of fixed carbon in the form of triosephosphate, from the chloroplast into the cytosol and inorganic phosphorus from cytosol is shuttled back to stroma. Its activity is affected by light.

phosphatidyl choline
a major phosphoglyceride in higher plants and animals; consists of choline that is esterified to the phosphoric acid residue of phospatidic acid. Also known as lecithin.

phosphatidylserine
a phospholipid containing the amino acid serine.

phosphocreatine $C_4H_{10}N_3O_5P$
creatine phosphate, a phosphoric acid derivative of creatine which contains an energy-rich phosphate bond; it is present in muscle contraction and other tissues, and during the anaerobic phase of muscular contraction it hydrolyzes to creatine and phosphate and makes energy available. Abbreviated PC.

phosphodiester
a phosphate ester in which two hydroxyl groups of the phosphoric acid are esterified with organic residues :

$$RO — PO_2H — OR'$$

for example, R and R' may be nucleosides. All polynucleotides and nucleic acids are P. in which the 3' and 5' positions of neighbouring pentose units are linked by esterification with a phosphate residue.

phosphodiesterases
enzymes that catalyze the hydrolysis of phosphodiesters such as cyclic nucleotides and phosphatidylinositol-4, 5-biphosphate.

Cyclic nucleotide phosphodiesterases occur as a number of isoenzymes, exhibiting distinct kinetic properties, substrate specificities and cellular localizations. Three basic forms of the enzyme occur in mammals. One is membrane-bound with a high affinity for cyclic AMP. The other two forms are cytosolic and are capable of hydrolyzing both cyclic AMP and cyclic GMP. One of these has about equal affinities for cyclic AMP and cyclic GMP, and cyclic GMP stimulates the hydrolysis of cyclic AMP. The other displays a higher affinity for cyclic GMP than for cyclic AMP, and is dependent upon calmodulin for activity.

phosphoenolpyruvic acid CH_2=O(OPO_3H_2)-COOH

a high-energy phosphate formed by the dehydration of 2-phosphoglyceric acid; it reacts with adenosinediphosphate to form adenosinetriphosphate and enolpyruvic acid.

phosphoglucomutase

an enzyme that catalyzes the conversion of glucose-1-phosphate to glucose-6-phosphate.

phosphoglycerate kinase

an enzyme which catalyses the addition of phosphate group to-3-phosphoglyceric acid which in presence of NADPH + H^+ and triose phosphate dehydrogenase is reduced to 3-phosphoglyceraldehyde.

phospholipase

an enzyme that catalyzes a hydrolysis of phorspholipid, especially a lecithinase that acts in this manner on a lecithin.

phospholipase A_2 inhibitors

chemicals that inhibit the enzyme phospholipase A_2 (phosphatide-2-acyl-hydrolase) which specifically hydrolyses the 2-acyl linkage of phosphoglycerides to produce a free fatty acid and a lysophosphoglyceride. In mammalian cells the phosphoglycerides are the main source of arachidonic acid for the synthesis of prostanoids. Inhibitors of the enzyme include:

1. a series of *n*-alkylphosphoryl- cholines which alkylate the active site.
2. Ca^{2+} chelating compounds which remove Ca^{2+} a necessary co-facto from the enzyme.
3. cholesterol and general anaesthetic drugs which modify the properties of the surrounding lipids of the membrane.
4. local anaesthetic drugs which possibly act through their ability to block Ca^{2+} binding sites on calmodulin.
5. certain butyrophenones which produce a non-competitive enzyme inhibiton.
6. glucocorticoids which cause the release of proteinaceous phospholipase A_2 inhibitor called macrocortin from macrophages and neutrophils.

phospholipid

any of a class of phosphoric acid, containing one or two molecules of fatty acid, an alcohol, and a nitrogenous base. Also known as phosphatide.

phospholipid transfer proteins

the proteins present in cytosol and involved in membrane synthesis by catalysing intermembrane exchange. These contain non-specific hydrophobic crevices into which the transferred phospholipids acyl chains are embedded, while the head group may be associated with a specific polar site. During senescence content of these proteins are decreased.

phospholipoprotein
a conjugated protein that contains phospholipid and that is soluble in aqueous solutions.

phosphomonoesterase
an enzyme catalyzing hydrolysis of phosphoric acid esters containing one ester linkage.

phosphoproteins
conjugated proteins, containing phosphate esterified with the hydroxyl groups of serine or (less often) threonine residues. Well known examples are casein and ovalbumin.

phosphorescence
an excited triplet electron reverses its spin and become metastable and thereafter returns to ground state. During this process, excess of energy is given out as radiation of very long wavelength. Decay of phosphorescence is slow.

phosphoribulokinase
an enzyme which catalyses the addition of phosphate group to Ist carbon of ribulose-5-phosphate to form ribulose-1, 5-bisphosphate using ATP.

phosphorolysis
a reaction by which elements of phosphoric acid are incorporated into the molecule of a compound.

phosphorylase
an enzyme that catalyzes the formation of glucose-1-phosphate (Cori ester) from glycogen and inorganic phosphate; it is widely distributed in animals, plants and microorganisms.

phosphorylase a
the active form of glycogen phosphorylase of skeletal muscle; consists of four subunits, each of which contains a phosphoserine residue that is essential for activity.

phosphorylases
the enzymes that catalyze phosphorolysis, i.e., the cleavage of a bond by the introduction of a phosphate group. Many enzymes of this type are found in cells, but the term phosphorylase usually applies to glycogen phosphorylase, which cleaves glycogen to glucose 1-phosphate.

phosphorylation
addition of phosphate group to form high energy bonds. Phosphorylation is of two types; (i) Photophosphorylation and (ii) Oxidative phosphorylation.
The former occurs during light reactions of photosynthesis and the latter in respiration.

phosphoserine aminotransferas
an enzyme which catalyses the formation of phosphoserine from 3-hydroxypyruvate during serine synthesis.

phosphotransacetylase
an enzyme that catalyzes the reversible transfer of an acetyl

group from acetyl coenzyme A to a phosphate, with formation of acetyl phosphate.

phosphovitin
phosphoprotein that is abundantly present in yolk. Along with lipovitellin, it is a product of the large precursor molecule vitellogenin, which is synthesized in the liver.

photoblastic seeds
the seeds whose germination is affected by light. These are either positive or negative photoblastic.

photochrome
a molecule, or a group in a molecule, that is sensitive to light and shows the phenomenon of photochromism.

photoelectron effect
the ejection of an orbital electron from an atom as a result of the impingement on the atom of a photon of sufficient energy; all of the energy of the photon is used to eject the electron and to impart kinetic energy to it.

photolysis of water
cleavage of water by the light reaction of photosynthesis. It is a property of photosystem II. It is not a simple photodissociation of water, but is the physiological counterpart of the Hill reaction. Electrons are withdrawn from water or OH- ions, then-transported to $NADP^+$ via an electron transport chain; this result in the production of molecular oxygen with the formation of NADPH + H^+. Since Hill reagent oxidize water by withdrawal of electrons, $NADP^+$ is the natural Hill reagent.

photolyte
an old concept of photosynthesis where active form of CO_2 which is produced during photosynthesis reacts in air with a special form of chlorophyll. It absorbs one quantum of light and is split into oxygen, reduced carbonic acid and free chlorophyll. Photolyte is regenerated in a dark reaction.

photometric measurement
light measuring system where units are based on highly spectral selectivity of eye. Such units are lux and lumen. These are not in current use and replaced with radiometric units.

photon flux
rate of propagation of radiant photons. It is replaced with radiant flux.

photophosphorylase
an enzyme that is associated with the surface of a thylakoid membrane and is involved in the final stages of adenosinetriphosphate production by photosynthetic phosphorylation.

photoreactivation
reversal of UV induced damages in DNA with blue light irradiance.

photorespiration
the light respiration i.e., light induced reducing power is

used for the reduction of O_2. There is no oxidative phosphorylation. It is active in C_3 plants where it can be reduced to very low rate under low O_2 tension. Here glycollic acid is oxidised to glyoxylic acid which is further metabolised to glycine, oxalate, formate or CO_2. Its rate is about 5 times that of dark-respiration. Glycollate is oxidised in peroxisomes and synthesised in chloroplast. Most of crop plants show photorespiration which consume about 25 per cent of current photosynthates. Metabolic event of photorespiration are confined to chloroplast, peroxysome and mitochondria.

photosensitizer

(i) a substance that when added to a biological system, will increase the damage to the system when it is exposed to a subsequent dose of radiation.

(ii) a substrate that brings about photosensitization.

(iii) the coloured compounds which absorb light of a specific wavelength and transfer energy to an acceptor molecule e.g., chlorophyll, methylene blue and eosine etc.

photosynthesis

synthesis of chemical compounds in light, especially the manufacture of organic compounds (primarily carbohydrates) from carbon dioxide and a hydrogen source (such as water) with stimultaneous liberation of oxygen, by chlorophyll-containing plant cells.

photosynthetic experimental organisms and systems

for technical reasons, certain systems are preferred for the investigation of photosynthesis, e.g., green algae such as Chlorella photosynthetic bacteria and isolated chloroplasts. Green algae and eugleoids (e.g., Euglena gracilis) can be cultured under defined conditions in an illuminated chemostat and they can also be grown in Synchronous culture. It is relatively easy to obtain chlorophyll-deficient mutants of these organisms, which must grow heterophically Mutant technique. The production of plastids can be prevented by culture in the dark.

photosynthetic number

the ratio between the number of grams of CO_2 absorbed per hour by a unit of a leaf to the number of grams of chlorophyll which that unit contains.

photosynthetic organisms

photosynthesis occurs not only in green plants but also in lower eukaryotic organisms such as algae, euglenids, dinoflagellates, and diatoms. Photosynthesis also occurs in prokaryotic organisms such as cyanobacteria, green sulphur bacteria and the purple sulphur bacteria. Photosynthetic organisms can be divided into two classes: those which produce oxygen and those which do not. The green leaf cells of higher plants are oxygen producers. With the exception of cyanobacteria, which have an oxygen producing photosynthetic system resembling that of green plants, photosynthetic bacteria do not produce oxygen. In fact, many of them are anaerobes and cannot tolerate oxygen. As hydrogen donors some photosynthetic bacteria use inorganic compounds. For example, the green sulphur bacteria use hydrogen sulphide as hydrogen donor. These bacteria, instead of giving off molecular oxygen, extrude elemental sulphur as the oxidation product.

photosynthetic unit
the number of chlorophyll molecules that are required for the fixation of one molecule of carbon dioxide in photosynthesis.

photosystem I
one of two reaction sequences of the light phase of photosynthesis in green plants that involves a pigment system which is excited by wavelengths shorter than 700 nanometers and which transfers this energy to energy carriers such as NADPH that are subsequently utilized in carbon dioxide fixation.

photosystem II
one of two reactions sequences of the light phase of photosynthesis in green plants which involves a pigment excited by wavelengths shorter than 685 nanometers and which is directly involved in the splitting or photolysis of water.

photosystem pigment systems
structural functional units of the light reaction of photosynthesis. The quantum efficiency of photosynthesis in chloroplasts falls sharply at wavelengths longer than 680 nm, although chlorophyll still absorbs light longer than 680 to 700 nm. This phenomenon is known as the "red drop". However, the quantum efficiency of light above 680 nm is increased by the simultaneous presence of shorter wavelength light. This Emerson effect led to the proposal that photosynthesis depend upon the interaction of two light reactions (i.e., two photosystems), both driven by light less than 680 nm, but only one by light of longer wavelengths.

phototropism
growth movement in response to unilateral light stimulus. Stem and other aerial parts are + vely and root and other underground parts are-vely phototropic.

phycobilin
any of various protein-bound pigments which are open-chain tetrapyrroles and occur in some groups of algae.

phycobilisomes
the supramolecular pigment aggregates which serve as the primary light gathering antennae in red algae and in cyanobacteria.

phycocyanin
a blud phycobilin.

phycocyanobilin $C_{31}H_{38}O_2N_4$
phycobilin with an ethylidene side chain (=CH—CH_3) and only one asymmetric carbon atom (C_1).

phycoerythrin
a red phycobilin.

phycoerythrobilin $C_{31}H_{38}O_2N_4$
phycobilin with seven conjugated double bonds, an ethylidine side chain (=CH-—CH_3), and two asymmetric carbon atoms (C_1 and C_7).

physiological dwarf
when internode elongation differs only in light grown seedling and not in etiolated seedling e.g., No. 9 variety of pea.

phytase
an enzyme occurring in plants, especially cereals, which catalyzes hydrolysis of phytic acid to inositol and phosphoric acid.

phytic acid
the reserved compound in phosphorous metabolism. It is synthesised from myo-inositoal, after phosphorylation inositol hexaphosphate is thus produced.

phytoalexins
substances produced by a wide range of plants in response to bacterial of fungal infections or, less commonly, following chemical exposure or injury. They are non-specific antibiotics. More than 20 have been characterized and have been shown to be mostly phenolic compounds. They include pisatin from the pea (Pisum sativum), phaseolin from the French bean (phaseolus spp.) and rishitin from the potato (Solanum tuberosum).

phytochrome
a photoreversible, photochromic molecules undergoing photo and non-photochemical (thermal) inter-conversion responsible for slow and fast photomorphogenetic processes. It is chromoprotein existing in two major forms i.e., red and far red forms. The protein part has a molecular weight of 12 KD whereas chromophore is a tetrayprrole.

phtyofluene
an aliphatic polyisoprenoid hydrocarbon carotenoid. It contains ten double bonds (five of them conjugated), six branch methyl groups and two terminal isopropylidene groups. It is an intermediate in lycopene.

phytohaemagglutinin PHA
lectin derived from the seeds of phaseolus vulgaris or P. communis. It binds to N-acetyl-β-D-galactosamine on red blood cell surfaces and so

agglutinates them. It is a potent mitogen for human and mouse T lymphocytes.

phytohormone or plant hormone
an organic substance which is produced in cells in one part of the plant and transferred to other parts where it produces an effect. It is present in very low amount.

picrotoxin $C_{30}H_{34}O_{13}$
a poisonous, crystalline plant alkaloid found primarily in Cocculus indicus; used as a stimulant and convulsant drug. Also known as cocculin.

pigment
any colouring matter in plant or animal cells.

pigment 700 P_{700}
a chlorophyll with an absorption maximum at 700 nm. P. 700 is a component of photosystem I and serves as an energy sink or trapping center in the light reaction of this system. It is important in the primary energy transformation of photosynthesis.

pig-pong reaction
the non-sequential enzymic reaction which proceed via modified form of the enzyme which may take the form of acylated enzyme.

pinching
removal or suppression of apical buds in order to stimulate the production of lateral branches.

plane polarized light
light of single wavelength i.e., monochromatic light is obtained after passing through Nicol Prism. The emerging light vibrates only in one plane. When such light passes through optically active solution plane polarised light is rotated either on left or right side.

planimeter
(i) a mechanical integrating instrument for measuring plane areas, consisting of a movable tracing arm, the movement of which are recorded on a dial, and the fixed arm for fixing movable arm on the board.
(ii) a device for measuring the area under a curve, a graphical integrator that is used in chromatography and electrophoresis for estimating the relative amount of separated components.

plant hormone
an organic compound that is synthesized in minute quantities by one part of a plant and translocated to another part, where it influences physiological processes. Also known as phytohormone.

plant mucilages
high Mr, complex, colloidal polysaccharides, which form gels and have adhesive properties. They are widely distributed in the plant kingdom, being found as secondary membrane thickening and as intercellular and interacellular material.

They occur in root, bark, cortex, leaves, stalks, flowers, endosperm and seed coat. Some bulbs contain special muciage cells.

plasma cells
the while blood cells (leucocytes) derived from lymphocytes in the lymphoid tissue. They have clear cytoplasm and a large nucleus and they produce antibodies important in defence against disease.

plasmalemmasome
an invagination of the plasmalemma containing vesicles or tubules derived entirely from elaboration of plasmalemma itself.

plasma-specific enzyme
an enzyme that is present in blood plasma and that has a specific function in plasma; an enzyme that functions in the reactions of blood clotting is an example.

plasmin
a proteolytic enzyme in plasma which can digest many proteins through the process of hydrolysis. Also known as fibrinolysin.

plasminogen
the inter precursor, or zymogen, of plasmin. Also known as profibrinolysin.

plasticity
when cell wall is stretched by stress, if deformation is permanent i.e., cell wall stretching is irreversible. The strain is known as plastic. It is involved in cell elongation. Auxins elogate cell by changing plasticity of cell membrane.

plastid genome
in vascular plants plastid genomes are circular, and in most are 120-180 Kbp in size. Plastids have been reported to contain 22-900 genome copies. The DNA molecules are associated with the inner membrane of the envelope or with internal thylakoid membranes in aggregates of 10-20 DNA molecule.

plastids
organelles in the cells of eukaryotic plants. These contain DNA, and are self replicating. Division of P. and replication of P. DNA are not synchronized with nuclear division and replication of nuclear DNA. They are usually elipsoid, 1-10 μm long.

plastogene
a gene present in a self-replicating plastid. Inheritance studies have shown that plastogenes control leaf colour in some plants, e.g., yellow leaved primula sinensis.

plastoquinone
a lipid-soluble compound used as an electron carrier in photosynthesis. It is closely related to coenzyme Q and that functions as a hydrogen donor and acceptor in the photosynthetic electron transport systems.

plate height
the length of the theoretical plate in the column and is represented by H. Efficiency of

the column depends upon the number of theoretical plates that are involved. If number of theoretical plates is more, the separation of the solute will be very sharp and the peak will be very narrow.

pleromer

a component that can replace another component in a polymer with respect to the overall balance of components in that polymer. Thus in a DNA molecule in which the mole percent of guanine equals that of cytosine plus 5-methylcytosine, the components cytosine and 5-methylcytosine are considered to be pleromers.

plus and minus strands (+ and - strands)

conversion for designating strands of DNA or RNA. Messenger RNA and other strands with the same sequence polarity are called plus strands, whereas the coding strand is a minus strand. Some single-stranded viruses are genomes of, for example plus strand DNA, which must be first replicated to provide minus strand DNA from which transcription can occur.

podsol

a type of soil profile developed under good drainage, relatively cool climate, and high rainfall. These conditions lead to leaching so that this soil is typified by having a layer of humus on top, below which is a greyish, leached zone, followed by a dark layer where the leached salts have accumulated

pol I

RNA polymerase I. Enzyme responsible for catalyzing the synthesis of the large ribosomal RNA (rRNA).

pol II

RNA polymerase II. Enzyme responsible for catalyzing the synthesis of heterogenous nuclear RNA (hn RNA) and messenger RNA (mRNA).

pol III

RNA polymerase III. Enzyme responsible for catalyzing the synthesis of small ribosomal RNA (5S rRNA) and transfer RNA (tRNA).

polar groups

a part of molecule which possesses a permanent dipole e.g., two small, point electric charges of opposite sign separated by a short distance.

polarography

a method for electroanalytical studies of chemical substances, including the reduction of anions and cations and for qualitative and quantitative microanalysis; based on measurements of the current produced at a microelectrode as a function of the changing potential applied to an electric cell.

pollution

when natural environment is contaminated by the addition of toxic air or water which are harmful to man and animal e.g., SO_2, CO, radioactive fallout, insecticides, factory effluent etc.

polyandry

(i) having a large and indefinite number of stamens.

(ii) the qospores formed when more than one functional antheridium is present.

polycentric

(i) having many centres of growth and development and more than one reproductive organ.

(ii) a chromosome or chromatid which has several centromeres.

polycistronic message

the molecule of messenger RNA that is a product of transcription of a series of randomly located genes on the DNA. Although some polycistronic messages are later processed by cleavage into separate messages, some are translated intact. The message of bacterial operons such as the lac operons of E. coli are polycistronic.

polydeoxyribonucleotide

a linear polymer of more than 10 deoxyribonucleotides that are linked by means of 3', 5'-phosphodiester bonds; a polynucleotide.

polyethylene glycol

osmotically active, metabolically inert, soluble macromolecules with varying mol. wt. These are used in isolation of cell organelles, simulation of water stress and fusion of protoplast.

polygalacturonase

an enzyme that catalyzes the hydrolysis of glycosidic linkage of polymerized galacturonic acids.

polyketides, acetogenins

natural products containing several recurring two-carbon units, formally equivalent to the condensation products of several molecules of acetate, Biosynthesis of these alkaloids occur on a multienzyme complex. examples of P. are tetracyclines, griesofulvin, macrolide antibiotics, cycloheximide, and various fungal products such as orsellinic acid, 6-methylsalicyclic acid and cyclopaldic acid.

polymerase

an enzyme that links nucleotides together to form polynucleotide chains.

polynucleotide

a linear sequence of nucleotides.

polynucleotide ligase

enzyme that catalyzes phosphodiester bond formation between adjacent 3'-hydroxyl and 5'-phosphorus terminal in nucleic acids.

polynucleotide ligase, DNA-ligase

an enzyme that joins two DNA fragments by catalysing the formation of an internucleotide ester bond between phosphate and deoxyribose. These are active in the repair of damaged DNA, and in the linkage of okazaki fragments during DNA replication.

polyploid

cell or nucleus containing more than two complete sets of chromosomes.

polyprotein

a polyfunctional protein; a large protein molecule that serves as a precursor for a number of biologically active peptides or proteins. Polyproteins are made from a polycistronic mRNA molecule and are cleaved by proteolytic enzymes after synthesis of the polypeptide chain has been completed.

polysaccharide

a carbohydrate composed of many monosaccharides.

polysaccharide sulfate esters, polysaccharide sulfates

sulfate esters of polysaccharides, synthesized by the action of sulfokinase. There are two possible mechanisms of biosynthesis :

1. sulfation of the polysaccharide chain by phosphoadenosinephosphosulfate (PAPS).
2. polymerization of sugar sulfates, which occur as sulfated sugar nucleotides.

polyvalent

(i) having more than one valency.

(ii) containing more than one type of antibody and therefore effective against more than one type of micro-organisms.

porometers

instruments to measure the diffusive flux of water vapour in an amphistomatous leaf. These are water vapour diffusion (ventilated and unventilated), steady-state diffusion mass flow, resistance and pressure drop types.

porous packing

packing materials which are porous throughout the entire structure of the particle.

porphin

a heterocyclic ring consisting of four pyrrole rings linked by methine (—CH=) bridges; the basic structure of chlorophyll, hemoglobin, the cytochromes, and certain other related substances.

porphobilinogen $C_{10}H_{14}O_4N_2$

dicarboxylic acid derived from pyrrole; a product of hemoglobin breakdown that gives the urine a Burgundy-red colour.

porphyrin

a class of red-pigmented compounds with a cyclic tetrapyrrolic structure in which the four pyrrole rings are joined through their a-carbon atoms by four methene bridges (=C—); the porphyrins form the active nucleus of chlorophylls and hemoglobin.

positive cooperativity

when conformational changes in allosteric enzyme result increased activity towards substrate molecules.

positive effector

a metabolite, when bound to an allosteric enzyme acts as an

activator and leads to an increase in the binding of the substrate and other effectors.

positive staining

a staining technique, used in electron microscopy, in which components of the sample are visualized through their binding of an electron-dense material; the staining of nucleic acids with uranyl acetase and the staining of antigens with ferritin-labeled antibodies are two examples.

post-translation

after protein is synthesised, it undergoes conformational changes, to facilitate the processing of proteins.

post translational modification of proteins processing

in a general sense, any differences between a functional protein and the linear polypeptide sequence encoded between the initiation and termination codons of its structural gene can be regarded as a post translational modification of proteins. Thus, the folding of the polypeptide chain, stabilized by weak, noncovalent interactions and the association of the subunits of an oligomeric protein both represent a modification that occurs after translation.

potassium

one of the essential elements in plants and animals. It is absorbed by plant roots as the potassium ion, K^+, and in plants is the most abundant electropositive ion in the cell sap. Potassium ions are required in high concentration in the cell for efficient protein synthesis, and for glycolysis in which they are an essential cofactor for the enzyme pyruvate kinase. In animals the gradient of potassium and sodium ions across the cell membrane is responsible for the potential difference across the membrane, which is important for the transmission of nerves impulses.

precipitation curve

an increasing quantity of antigen is added to a constant amount of antibody. The resulting precipitate is removed by centrifugation, and antibody and antigen are determined in the supernatant.

precipitin reaction

if increasing amounts of antigen are mixed with aliquots of suitable antibody solution a precipitate forms in some of the cases. These reactions are used for qualitative and quantitative analysis of antigen in the zone of equivalence.

precusor

(i) simple, low molecular weight compounds obtained from environment and converted into living matters made up of building block biomolecules.

(ii) in metabolism precursor is a simple compound which forms the end product via various intermediates.

Molecular weight varies from 18-100.

precursor rRNA

the giant precursor RNA molecule from which the various species of rRNAs are cleaved off by post-transcriptional processing.

prednisolone $C_{21}H_{28}O_5$

a glucocorticoid that is a dehydrogenated analog of hydrocortisone.

pregnenolone $C_{21}H_{32}O_2$

a steroid ketone that is formed as an oxidation product of cholesteroil, stigmasterol, and certain other steroids.

pre-planting or pre-emergence

applied before sowing or before emergence of seedling.

pre-proprotein

a precursor in the biosynthesis of a secretory protein which possesses an N-terminal signal peptide sequence in addition to the proprotein sequence, e.g., pre-proinsulin, preprotrypsin, pre-proparathormone, pre-promellitin, etc.

Pressure Chamber or 'Bomb'

it is thick walled metal vessel sealed with a rubber gasket and connected to a pressure gauze and supply of compressed air or nitrogen. Leaves of twigs are placed insidse the chamber with a portion of petiole or stem remaining outside. Pressure required to ooze out sap is noted and it is equal to water potential of the xylem tissue.

pressure dialysis

dialysis in which there is either an application of pressure to the dialysis sac or an application of vacuum to the space surrounding the dialysis bag.

primary cell wall

the cell wall that surrounds the protoplast until it is nearly mature, and fully grown. It is thin, usually non-stratified and contains less cellulose and more protein than the mature wall. It later on perists as the middle lamella.

primary immunization

the first injection of the antigen to the animal for raising specific antibodies.

primary isotope effect

an isotope effect in which the isotope itself is involved in bond cleavage, such that the bond to the isotope is broken in the transition state of the reaction.

primary solvent

the solvent used in scintillation counting for transfer of energy from the radioactive sample in the flour e.g., Toluene, dioxan.

primary xylem or wood

the xylem formed from a procambium strand and present in a primary vascular strand. It consists of protoxylem and metaxylem.

primase

bacterial polymerase probably also found in eukaryotes that makes the precursor primer RNA molecule on the lagging strand during DNA replication, in E. coli, it is protein of molecular mass about 60,000 and, unlike RNA polymerase, is not inhibited by rifampicin.

prime end

the end of macromolecule that functions as the starting point for the polymerization of nucleotide e.g., 5' and 3' end of RNA and DNA.

primer

1. a small polymer that is required as a starter for the synthesis of a larger biopolymer. In nucleic acid synthesis for example, an oligonucleotide serves as a primer, and it is extended by the enzyme-catalysed addition of further nucleotide units from nucleoside triphosphates. 2. a Pheromone that causes a long term physiological change.

proaccelerin

a labile procoagulant in normal plasma but deficient in the blood of patients with parahemophilia; essential for rapid conversion of prothrombin to thrombin. Also known as factor V; labile factor.

processing

(i) the series of chemical reactions whereby a primary RNA transcript is converted to functional mRNA tRNA, or rRNA molecule. (ii) the series of chemical reactions whereby a newly synthesised polypeptide chain is converted to a functional protein.

procoagulant

any of blood clotting factors V to VIII; accelerates the conversion of prothrombin to thrombin in the presence of thromboplastin and calcium.

production value

the mass of a compound that can be synthesised from one unit of substrate used for carbon skeleton and the energy required for biosynthesis.

productivity of transpiration

the reciprocal of transpiration coefficient is known as productivity of transpiration which is ratio between photosynthetic assimilation rate of CO_2 and transpiration rate.

proenzyme

the inactive form in which some enzymes are synthesized and secreted, particularly by the pancreas. This prevents self-digestion of tissues, which can happen in certain diseases, such as pancreatitis. Activation usually occurs by limited proteolysis of the proenzyme to yield the active form of the enzyme. For example, the proenzyme trypsinogen is converted to trypsin by the enzyme enterokinase.

progestational hormone

1. the natural hormone progesterone which induces progrestational changes of the uterine mucosa. 2. Any derivative or modification or progesterone having similar actions.

progesterone $C_{21}H_{30}O_2$

a steroid hormone produced in the corpus luteum, placenta, testes, and adrenals; plays an important physiological role in the luteal phase of the menstrual cycle and in the maintenance of pregnancy; it is an intermediate in the biosynthesis of androgens, estrogens, and the corticoids.

progestogen

one of a group of naturally occurring or synthetic hormones that maintain the normal course of pregnancy. The best known is progesterone. In high doses progestogens inhibit secretion of luteinizing hormone, thereby preventing ovulation, and alter the consistency of mucus in the vagina so that conception tends not to occur. They are therefore used as major constituents of oral contraceptives.

proinsulin

prohormone of the hormone insulin. It is synthesized in the β-cells of the islets langerhans and consists of a polypeptide chain of about 80 amino acids. The central section of 30 amino acids is cleaved out by specific proteolytic action, leaving the two terminal peptides which, by association, from the active insulin molecule.

projection formula

a two dimensional representation of a molecule in which bonds projecting forward with respect to the plane of paper are indicated by horizontal lines, and bonds projecting backward are indicated by vertical lines.

prolactin

a protein hormone produced by the adenohypophysis; stimulates lactation and promotes functional activity of the corpus luteum. Also known as lactogenic hormone; luteotropic hormone; mammary-stimulating hormone; mammogen; mammogenic hormone; mammotropin.

prolamin

any of the simple proteins, such as zein, found in plants; soluble in strong alcohol, insoluble in absolute alcohol and water.

prolamines

a group of simple (unconjugated) proteins. They occur in cereals, and contain up to 15% proline and 30-45% glutamic acid, but they have only low contents of essential amino acids. The chief representatives are gliadin (wheat and rye), zein (maize; contains no tryptophan or lysine) and hordein (barley; contains no lysine). Olats and rice do not contain P.

proline $C_5H_9O_2$

a heterocyclic amino acid occurring in essentially all proteins, and as a major constituent in collagen proteins.

promitosis

the special type of nuclear division during the growth

stage in the plasmodiophoraceae.

promoter

(i) the site on the DNA molecule to which RNA polymerase attaches and at which transcription is initiated.

(ii) a carcinogenic agent that brings about the second stage in a two-stage or multistage mechanism of carcinogenesis.

propionic acid

one of the volatile fatty acids produced by the rumen microglora and absorbed directly from the rumen into the bloodstream of the animal. The propionate (propanoate) is carried to the liver where it is converted to glucose; this represents a significant source of energy for ruminants.

proprotein

an inactive precursor of a protein that is converted to the active form by removal of a peptide fragment.

prostaglandin synthase

fatty acid cyclo-oxygenases, or simply cyclo-oxygenases.

prosthetic group

nonproteogenic. In an enzyme, this group is a catalytically active group attached to the enzyme protein (aboenzyme).

protamine

any of the simple proteins that are combined with nucleic acid in the sperm of certain fish, and that upon hydrolysis yield basic amino acids; used in medicine to control hemorrhage, and in the preparation of an insulin form to control diabetes.

protean

an insoluble, primary derived protein that is obtained by treatment of a protein with heat, acid, enzymes, or other agents.

protease

an enzyme that digests proteins.

protecting group

a chemical group that is reacted with, and bound to, a functional group in a molecule to prevent the functional group from particulating in subsequent reactions of the molecule.

protective layer

a layer of suberised cells lying across the place where a leaf comes away at leaf fall. It checks water loss, and the entry of parasites.

proteinase

a type of protease which acts directly on native proteins in the first step of their conversion to simpler substance.

protein-bound iodine

iodine bound to blood protein. Abbreviated PBI.

protein deficiency diseases

the result of long-term nutritional deficiency in the form of too little complete protein. In small children it is called kwashiorkor. The symptoms are swelling of the legs, face and liver (starvation edema), liver damage, gastrointestinal malfuntion, anemia and osteoporosis. It is often fatal.

protein detection

proteins exhibit a variety of colour reactions; some of the common reactions used to detect the presence of proteins in different matrices are :

1. Biuret reaction :— To alkaline solution of protein a dilute solution of copper sulphat is added. A red or violet colour is formed with peptides containing at least two peptide linkages. A dipeptide does not give this test.

2. Xanthoproteic reaction :— Proteins usually form a yellow colour when warmed with concentrated nitric acid. This colour becomes orange when the solution is made alkaline. The colour is due to nitration of aromatic ring present in phenylalanine, tyrosine and tryptophan.

3. Millon's reaction :— Millon's reagent (mercuric nitrate in nitric acid containing traces of nitrous acid) usually yields a white precipitate on addition to a protein solution which turns red on heating. This reaction is characteristic of phenols (e.g., the phenolic amino acid tyrosin).

4. Ninhydrin test :— To an aqueous solution of a protein an alcoholic solution of ninhydrin is added and then heated. Red to violet colour is formed.

5. Nitroprusside test :— Proteins containing sulphur group form red colour with nitroprusside solution.

6. Lead sulphide test :— Alkaline solution of sulphur containing proteins, on addition to lead acetate, produces a black precipitate.

protein factor

the factor 6.25 that, when multiplied by the weight of nitrogen (in grams) derived from a sample containing protein, gives the approximate weight (in grams) of the protein in the sample.

protein folding

the processes involved in the conversion of an ensemble of newly synthesised (or denatured) polypeptide chain conformations to the unique, three dimensional conformation of the native protein.

protein fractionation

the separation of a mixture of different proteins for the purpose of the isolating one particular type of protein; requires the use of one or more physical-chemical techniques such as precipitation, centrifugation, or electrophresis.

protein kinases

enzymes that phosphorylate proteins. Protein kinase A is cyclic AMP-dependent, protein kinase G is cyclic GMP - dependent and protein kinase C is Ca^{2+} - dependent.

proteinosis

the accumulation, in a tissue, of excessive amounts of

normal proteins or of abnormal proteins.

proteolysin
a lysin that produces proteolysis.

proteolysis
fragmentation of a protein molecule by addition of water to the peptide bonds.

proteolytic enzyme
any enzyme that catalyzes the breakdown of protein.

proteosome
the structural entity in eukaryotes with a sedimentation coefficient of 19S. It is homologous with a large proteinase complex. Capable of hydrolysing protein ubiquitin conjugates.

prothrombin
an inactive plasma protein precursor of thrombin. Also known as factor II; thrombinogen.

protochlorophyllide reductase
an enzyme which catalyses the reduction of protochlorophyllide to chlorophyllide using NADPH. Here D-ring of porphyrin is reduced.

protomer
one of the polypeptide chains composing an oligomeric protein. Also known as subunit.

proton pump
the structure and/or the mechanism that mediates the active transport of hydrogen ion across a biological membrane.

protopectin
insoluble pectic substances, including cross-linked chains of pectic acid as well as their salts with such metals as calcium, magnesium and iron. These molecules are still larger than pectic acid and pectins, and have higher molecular weight. These are insoluble in water and degree of methylation varies. Protopectins are found in apples and oranges.

protoplasmic poison
an obsolete expression sometimes formerly used to describe a depressant drug whose mechanism of action was unknown; for example, quinidine was formerly described in the way with respect to its depressant action on the heart.

protoxylem
the xylem derived from the apical growing point. Its elements are extensible and becomes partially thickened before elongation is complete.

pseudoalkaloids
the isoprenoid alkaloids in which nitrogen is inserted into a non-amino acid residue. The isoprenoid residues involved in the formation of pseudoalkaloids are mono, sesqui-, di- or triterpenoid.

pseudoisoenzyme
one of two or more different forms of an enzyme that catalyses the same reaction but are not true isoenzymes since they do not have genetically determined

different primary structures.

pseudouridine

an unusual nucleoside, occurring in transfer RNA, in which the normal base uracil is linked to ribose through carbon atom 5 of the uracil.

pseudoverification

the deacylation of a correctly acylated, but noncognate, transfer RNA molecule by an amino-acyl-tRNA synthetase; can be brought about under special conditions in a mixed solvent.

pteroic acid $C_{14}H_{12}N_6O_3$

a crystalline amino acid formed by hydrolysis of folic acid or other pteroylglutamic acids.

ptyalin

a diastatic enzyme found in saliva which catalyzes the hydrolysis of starch to dextrin, maltose, and glucose, and the hydrolysis of sucrose to glucose and fructose. Also known as ptyalase; salivary amylase; salivary diastase.

puberulic acid $(HO)_3(C_7H_2O)COOH$

a keto acid formed as a metabolic product of certain species of Penicillium; has some germicidal activity against gram-positive bacteria.

pure line

(i) the descendents obtained from self fertilization of a single homozygous parent.

(ii) an inbred homozygous strain.

pure substance

a material with an unchanging composition structure, and behaviour. It may be composed of elements or compounds.

purine

a heterocyclic compound containing fused pyrimidine and imidazole rings; adenine and guanine are the purine components of nucleic acids and coenzymes.

purine antibiotics

purine derivatives with antibiotic activity. They occur as nucleosides polypeptides or free bases (8-azaguanidine).

purity

(i) the state of preparation in which all the molecules are those of a single type in terms of ions, molecules, macromolecules.

purpurin

1, 2, 4-trihydroxyanthraquinone. A red anthraquinone pigment, m.p. 263°C. Its glycoside occurs in madder root (rubia tinctorum) (accompanied by alizarin), and in other members of the Rubiaceae. It is formed from its glycoside during storage, and there is no appreciable quantity of this in the fresh root. It is used as a reagent for the detection of boron, for the histological detection of insoluble calcium salts, and as a nuclear stain. It forms coloured lakes with various metal salts, and is used as a fast dye in cotton printing.

putrefaction

decomposition of organic matter particularly the anaerobic breakdown of proteins by bacteria, with the production of foul-smelling compounds.

pyrenoid

a spherical protein body found in the chloroplasts to many algae. Pyrenoids are associated with the storage of starch; layers of the starch are often found around them.

pyridine alkaloids

a group of alkaloids containing the pyridine ring system, which occur in various unrelated plants, and as metabolic products of microorganisms. Important examples are nicotiana alkaloids, Areca alkaloids, Gentiana alkaloids, and Valeriana alkaloids. They are biosynthesized either from nicotinic acid, or as products of terpene synthesis.

2, 3-pyridinedicarboxylic acid $C_7H_5NO_4$

an odourless, crystalline compound with a melting point of 190°C, soluble in water; inhibits glucose synthesis. Also known as quinolinic acid.

pyridine nucleotide

any one of the oxidized or reduced forms of nicotinamide adenine dinucleotide phosphate; NAD^+(NADH) or $NADP^+$(NADPH).

pyridoxal phosphate

coenzyme of transaminating enzymes and of amino acid decarboxylation.

pyridoxine hydrochloride $C_8H_{11}NO_3$ HCl

a crystalline compound, decomposing at about 208°C; used in medicine in vitamin therapy. Also known as pyridoxal hydrochloride; vitamin B_6 hydrochloride.

pyrimidine $C_4H_4N_2$

a heterocyclic organic compound containing nitrogen atoms at position 1 and 3: naturally occurring derivatives are components of nucleic acids and coenzymes.

pyrimidine antibiotics

structurally modified pyrimidine derivatives with antibiotic activity. They occur as nucleosides polypeptides (e.g., albomycin and grisein), or free bases (e.g., bacimethrin). The P.a. Toxoflavin and Fervenulin, are biosynthesized from purines.

pyrolysis

the transformation of one substance into another that is brought about by heat alone; includes such processes as thermal decomposition, isomerization and synthesis.

pyrophosphatase

an enzyme catalyzing hydrolysis of esters containing two or more molecules of phosphoric acid to form a simpler phosphate ester.

pyrroles pyrrole derivatives

the compound containing the pyrrole ring. They are subdivided into mono, di, tri and tetrapyrroles. The tetrapyrroles may be noncyclic or cyclic. Bile pigments and the chromophores of Biliproteins are linear, while Porphyrins and Corrinoids are cyclic tetrapyrroles.

pyruvate carboxylase

the enzyme that catalyzes the anaplerotic reaction whereby pyruvic acid is carboxylated to oxaloacetic acid.

pyruvate decarboxylase

an enzyme which catalyses the conversion of pyruvic acid in the presence of magnesium ions to acetaldehyde by removing CO_2. This reactionoccurs under anaerobic conditions.

pyruvate decarboxylase, carboxylase (EC 4.1.1.1)

a thiamine pyrophosphate (TPP)-dependent lyase, absent from animals, and present in high activity in yeasts and wheat seedlings. It is a specific enzyme of alcoholic fermentation, which catalyses the cleavage of pyruvate (via actiue acetaldehyde) into acetaldehyde and CO_2. The cofactors are Thiamine pyrophosphate and magnesium ions.

pyruvate dehydrogenase system

a multienzyme system, consisting of a large number of three different enzymes and five different coenzymes, that catalyzes the conversion of pyruvic acid to acetyl coenzyme A. Also known as pyruvate dehydrogenase complex.

pyruvate translocator

a translocator present on the inner envelope of chloroplast of C_4 plants. It controls light dependent and uncoupler-sensitive active transport of pyruvate in mesophyll chloroplast but not in bundle sheath chloroplasts. Its activity is inhibited by the -SH reagent and pyruvate analogs.

pyruvic acid

important intermediate in protein and carbohydrate metabolism; liquid with acetic-acid aroma; melts at 11.8°C; miscible with alcohol, ether, and water; used in biochemical research. Also known as acetyl formic acid; α-ketopropionic acid; pyroracemic acid.

Q notation

a method used in the past to denote enzyme activity, especially that of respiratory enzymes. The Q_8 value of an enzyme was taken to be the number of microliters, at standard temperature and pressure, of the substrate used up per hour per milligram of enzyme.

qualitative SDP

when a short day plant requires specific critical dark period. If dark period exceeds the plant grows vegetatively e.g., Glycine max, Chenopodium rubrunm and Xanthium pennsylavanicum.

quantal response

a response that is capable of existing in only one of two states. For example, dead or not dead in a test to find the lethal dose, and convulsions or no convulsions in an insulin bioassay. The response is measured as the percentage of animals responding in each group. If the percentage responding in each group is plotted against the logarithm of the dose given to each group an S-shaped curve is produced. The curve is converted into a straight line by rescaling the percentages into units called probits.

quantasome

an elementary photosynthetic particle that is believed to be present in the thylakoid disks of chloroplasts and to contain both photosystems I and II as well as the electron transport system.

quantitative inheritance

the inheritance of characters where the variation is continuous.

quantum requirement

the number of light quanta required for the formation of one molecule of O_2 in Photosynthesis. Two quanta are required per electron. The theoretical value of quantum requirement is eight, since the production of one molecule of O_2 proceeds according to the following equation, with transfer of four electrons from water to $NADP^+$.

$$2H_2O \rightarrow O_2 + 4H^+ + 4e^-$$

it is influenced by the physiological state of the experimental system.

quantum theory

the theory that energy can be radiated and absorbed only in discrete particles, called quanta, the energy of which is proportional to the frequency of the radiation.

quaternary structure of proteins

the arrangements of multichain of oligomeric proteins. When a protein is made up of more than one type of polypeptides, between these similar polypeptides covalent bonding is absent but still each chain fit well with another to form stable compact structure.

quenching

(i) the process whereby secondary and subsequent ionistion in ionisation detector are stopped so that the detector becomes again sensitive to new, incoming ionising radiation.

(ii) a decrease in fluorescence that results from an absorption of some or all of the emission energy.

(iii) interference in the energy transfer process in scintillation. It may be due to optical, colour and chemical reason.

quercetin $C_{15}H_5O_2(OH)_5$

a yellow, crystalline flavonol obtained from oak bark and douglas fir bark; used as an antioxidant and absorber of ultraviolet rays, and in rubber, plastics, and vegetable oils.

quiescent centre

a group of cells in the centre of the apical meristem in which mitotic divisions are rare or absent. The cells may begin dividing if another part of the meristem is damaged.

quinacrine
derivative of acridine use as an antimalarial drug and also in cancer chemotherapy. Quinacrine dyes (quinacrine mustard or quinacrine hydrochloride) are also used as chromosomes stains and will fluoresce under UV light.

quinine
the most important of the cinchona alkaloids. In quinine a quinoline ring system is connected via a secondary hydroxyl on C4 to a quinuclidine structure. It occurs in nature in association with its stereoinsomers quinidine, the C-9 empimer and epiquinine and epiquinidine, the C 8' epimers. It is used therapeutically as a drug against malaria and bacterial influenza. By reducing the rate of tissue respiration, it has an antipyretic effect.

racemase
any of a group of enzymes that catalyze racemization reactions.

Racker band
an absorption band that is produced by the binding of NAD^+ to a dehydrogenase and that is thought to be due to the formation of a charge transfer complex.

radiation biochemistry
the study of the response of the constituents of living matter to radiation.

radiation chimera
a chimera produced experimentally by first irradiating an organism so as to destroy its antibody producing cells, and then by injecting it with antibody-producing cells from a different source.

radiationless transition
a transition, involving an exicted atom or molecule, in which no visible or ultraviolet radiation is emitted.

radicle
(i) the embryonic root of seedplants.
(ii) any very small root.
(iii) a rhizoid of a moss.

radioactive decay
the changes occurring in the nucleus of a radioactive atom that lead to transformation of the nucleus into a different one and to the emission of ionising radiation.

radioimmunoassay
an immunoassay which involves the competition of radioactivity-labelled and unlabelled antigen for the antibody.

radiophosphorus decay
the radioactive disintegration of P^{32}, particularly that in P^{32}-labeled phage nucleic acid. The disintegrations lead to breaks in the sugar-phosphate backbone of the nucleic acid. Single-stranded nuceic acid is inactivated when a chain break occurs, but double-stranded nucleic acid is inactivated only when a break occurs in both strands.

raffonase

an enzyme that hydrolyzes raffinose, yielding fructose in the reaction.

raffinose $C_{18}H_{32}O_{16}$ $5H_2O$

a white, crystalline trisaccharide found in sugarbeets, cottonseed meal, and molasses; yields glucose, fructose, and galactose on complete hydrolysis. Also known as gossypose; melitose; melitriose.

rancidity

the development of unpleasant odours and taste from fats and oils by the oxidation of the unsaturated fatty acid components and/or the hydrolysis of the triglycerides to diglycerides, monoglycerides, glycerol and free fatty acids.

range

(i) of a distribution is the difference between the largest and the smallest observations. It indicates variability in observations.

(ii) the area over which a species is spread in the wild.

(iii) minimum and maximum amount of a substance which can be estimated with an instrument.

ranitidine

an antihistamine that acts as a reversible competitive antagonist of histamine as H_2 receptors. It has similar actions to but greater potency than cimetidine.

rapid flow kinetics

the kinetics of a chemical reaction that are determined by means of rapid growth techniques.

rare bases

purine and pyrimidine nucleosidse phosphates that occur infrequently in nucleic acids. They include such compounds as 1-methylguanosine, ribothymidine and 5-ribosyluracil which are found in the molecules of transfer RNA.

rate equation

in enzyme kinetics, an equation expressing the rate of a reaction in terms of rate and the concentrations of enzyme species, substrate the product. When it is assumed that steady state conditions obtain, the Michaelis-Menten equation is a suitable approximation.

Rate-Zonal Technique

in this method separation is based upon differences in size or sedimentation rates. After layering the sample on density gradient, it is centrifuged until the desired degree of separation is achieved. Discrete zones or bands are formed depending upon the velocity of particles. Centrifugation is termined before pellet formation at the bottom. It is used for the separation of enzymes, hormones, RNA-DNA hybrids, ribosomal subunits, subcellular organelles etc.

reactive residue

an amino acid residue in a

protein that is accessible to and can undergo a reaction with a specific reagent.

reading-frame

mRNA molecules have their nucleotide sequence translated in groups of three nucleotides by the ribosome. Each codon is represented by a single amino acid in the protein synthesised.

read-through protein

a protein that is produced as a result of a failure in the termination of translation of a polycistronic messagner RNA; such a protein consists of the regular amino acid sequence specified by its cistron plus a sequence of amino acids that corresponds to a translated inter-cistronic region.

reannealing

the renaturation of DNA; the joining of dissociated, complementary single-strand to from duplex molecules.

receptor

a site or structure in a cell which combines with a drug or other biological to produce a specific alteration of cell function.

reclamation

the process of removing excess soluble salts or excess exchangeable sodium from soils.

recognition

a specific binding interaction occurring between the macromolecules, as that between a transfer RNA molecule and an aminoacyl-tRNA synthetase, or that between an immunocyte and an antigen.

recombinant DNA

DNA that contains genes from the different sources that have been combined by the techniques of genetic engineering rather than by breeding experiments.

recombination repair

a post replicative repair mechanim of DNA that involves an exchange of good for bad segments between two damaged, homologous, duplex molecules.

recon

the unit of genetic recombination; the smallest section of a chromosome, which may be as small as single nucleotide, that is capable of recombination and that cannot be divided by recombination.

red drop phenomenon or Emerson effect

when a plant is exposed to red and far red region of light above 680 nm, the quantum yield of photosynthesis decreases. This decrease in quantum light is known as red drop.

reducing end

the end of an oligo or polysaccharide that carries the hemiacetal or the hemiketal groupings and thus acts as a reducing agent. There can only be one reducing end per molecule.

reductant cistron

a cistron that is present in

multiple copies on the same chromosome.

redundancy

1. the occurrence (frequent in eukaryotes, only in isolated instances in prokaryotes) of linearly arragned, largely identical, repeated sequences of DNA.
2. terminal redundancy. The existence of identical genetic information at each end of viral chromosome.

reflection coefficient

the measure of the extent to which solutes are reflected at the membrane. It gives considerable information about cell membranes and in particular the passage of water and solute across them. It is determined using pressure probe.

regeneration phase

the third stage of the Calvin cycle in which ribulose-1, 5-bisphosphate is regenerated by a series of reactions, beginning with glyceraldehyde-3-phosphate.

regulator gene

a gene that is responsible for the synthesis of a repressor that, in turn, controls an operator. The regulator gene need not be adjacent to the operator.

regulatory enzyme

an enzyme that has a regulatory function in metabolism and that has the capacity of having its catalytic activity modified. It is frequently the first enzyme in a reaction sequence or the enzyme at a branch point of metabolic pathway. These are of two types: (i) Allosteric enzyme, and (ii) Convalently modified enzyme.

regulatory sequence

a segment of DNA that functions in regulating the expression of structural genes in an operon e.g., operators, promoters and attenuators.

regulatory site

a site on a regulatory enzyme to which an effector binds, as distinct from a catalytic site to which the substrate binds. Also known as allosteric site.

relative humidity

the actual amount of water vapour present in an atmosphere expressed as percentage of atmosphere saturated with water vapour at the same temperature.

relaxation effect

the retardation of the electrophoretic mobility of a charged particle that results from the electric field set up by the differential movement of the charged particle and its ion atmosphere.

relaxation time

the time that a plant takes to recover to its original position after the stimulus has been removed, as in tropisms.

relaxed control

the continued synthesis of RNA that occurs in some bacterial mutants after removal of an essential amino acid from the medium.

relaxin

a hormone found in the serum of humans and certain other animals during pregnancy; probably acting with progesterone and estrogen, it causes relaxation of pelvic ligaments in the guinea pig.

releasing hormones, releasing factors, liberins, statins

a group of peptide neurohormones, synthesized in various distinct nuclei of the hypothalamus. They are released into the capillaries of the portal vessels in the median eminence of the hypothalamus, then carried to the anterior pituitary (adenohypophysis) where they regulate the production and secretion of tropic hormones (e.g., thyretropin, somatotropin, gonadotropins).

rennin

an enzyme found in the gastric juice of the fourth stomach of calfs; used for coagulating milk casein in cheesemaking. Also known as chymosin.

renninogen

the zymogen of rennin. Also known as prorennin.

reovirus

a family and genus of RNA viruses, distinguished by having double stranded RNA (all other RNA viruses are single-stranded). The reoviruses have an enveloped icosahedral capsid containing segmented RNA. There are three main genera; the orbiviruses, reoviruses, and rotaviruses.

repeating unit

the structural unit of a polymer, a large number of which are linked together to form the polymer; repeating units may be either identical or dissimilar.

repetitious DNA

a DNA that consistutes a significant fraction of the total DNA of eucaryotic cells and that is characterized by its content of an extremely large number of copies of different nucleotide sequences; the number of copies of a given nucleotide sequence may be as high as one million. Also known as repetitive DNA.

replicate

division of experimental material to which treatment is given in a random way. Larger the replicate size less heterogenity in experimental material.

replication

(i) the equal incorporation of all treatments and combinations two or more times in an experimental design, which is then said to be replicated.

(ii) a technique used for electron microscopy of surface. A replica of surface is taken and either viewed directly or used to prepare further replica. The final replica is often of carbon.

(iii) duplication of a part, or all, of an organism from an

existing structure of the same kind.
(iv) or duplication. Copying of DNA to form identical daughter molecules. It occurs in nucleus.

replicon
a functional unit of replication, analogous to the operons which is a functional unit of transcription. The replicon is genetic element, of either DNA or RNA, that behaves as an autonomous unit during replication. In eukaryotes, each chromosome consists of many replications. Each replicon contains two locus. For DNA replication, the initiator locus represents the site to which RNA polymerase binds and the replicator locus is the site at which DNA replication begins. The RNA primer synthesised by RNA polymerase is known as initiator.

repressible enzyme
enzyme formed in bacteria only when the cells are grown in the absence of its product (or the final product of the metabolic pathway of which the repressible enzyme is a component).

repression
when transcription of DNA is prevented due to the presence of an end product of a reaction. The end product will act as repressor molecule and thus further synthesis of enzyme is also stopped.

reproduction
the process of generating new individuals whereby the species is perpetuated.

repressor
an end product of metabolism which represses the synthesis of enzymes in the metabolic pathway.

reserpine
therapeutically the most important Rauwolfia alkaloids. Hydrolysis of reserpine with alcoholic KOH produces reserpinic acid (structurally similar to yohimbine), trihydroxybenzoic acid and methanol. It is found widely in the genus Rauwolfia, and is responsible for the sedative properties of these plants.

resin acids
the mixture of oxyacids, carboxylic acids and phenols. They are present in the free state or as esters. They are soluble in acqueous alkaline solutions which form soap-like froth on shaking. Abietic acid in Rosin or Colophony, copaivic acid and oxycopaivic acid in Copaiba, guaiaconic acid in Guaiac, pimaric (pimarinic) acid in Frankincense, sandaracolic acid in Sandarac, aleuritic acid in Shellac and commiphoric acid in Myrrh are the examples of resin acids.

resin composition
purified resins are amorphous, brittle, translucent, hard solids. On heating they are softened and then melt. They are practically insoluble in water but dissolve in organic

solvents like alcohol, ether and chloroform. Varnish-like film is formed on evaporation of the solvent. They produce smoky flame on burning. Chemically, resins are complex mixtures of many compounds including resin acids such as abietic acid, copaivic acid, and sandaracolic acid; resin alcohols and resenes.

resolution

(i) the separation of enantiomers from a racemic mixture.

(ii) the degree of separation between two components in a mixture as achieved by chromatographic, electrophoretic or other separation techniques.

(iii) the cutting process that separates the two participating DNA molecules during genetic recombination.

(iv) capacity of a microscope to render two objects as separate entities. Resolution of visible light microscope is about 0.2 µm and for electron microscope it is 1 nm.

resonance transfer

the transfer of light energy through tightly packed light harvesting chlorophyll molecules. Such transfer of quantum energy occurs preferentially from a pigment with a shorter wave absorption to a pigment with longer wave absorption band.

respiration

an oxidative process where energy in the form of ATP is released during oxidation of substrates. It is of two types; (i) Aerobic acid (ii) Anaerobic.

respiratory acidosis

a primary acidosis that is caused by a decrease in respiration which leads to an increase in the carbon dioxide and carbonic acid concentrations of the plasma.

respiratory inhibitor

a compound which interferes in some way with the respiratory chain. There are three types :

1. uncouplers which prevent the synthesis of ATP without stopping the flow of electrons.
2. inhibitors of oxidative phosphorylation in the narrower sense, and
3. inhibitors of electron transport along the respiratory chain.

respiratory pigment

any of various conjugated proteins that function in living organisms to transfer oxygen in cellular respiration.

respiratory repression

the regulation of the synthesis of enzyme by an exogenous electron acceptor that is independent of either specific or catabolic repression.

resistance

the capacity of bacteria to resist infection by phage particles; results from the inability of the phage particles to adsorb to, and to inject their DNA into, the bacterial cells.

restriction enzymes

the endonucleases

synthesised by many bacteria. Each enzyme recognises a specific sequence within double-stranded DNA which is typically 4 to 6 nucleotides in length with two fold axis of symmetry. These enzymes protect bacteria against invading foreign DNA molecules by degrading them. Thus important in molecular biology. Type II is most commonly used class of such enzymes.

restriction fragment

when restriction enzyme recognises a specific sequence of nucleotides and thus cleaves the DNA within this restriction site and resulting in production of restriction fragments.

retention time (tR)

the time required for a substance to pass through the column. It is measured from the time of injection of the sample to the time at which the top of the peak appears. Units cm or units of time.

retinene

a pigment extracted from the retina, which turns yellow by the action of light; the chief carotenoid of the retina.

retinoid

the set of molecules composing vitamin A and its synthetic analogs, such as retinal or retinyl acetate.

retroregulation

the regulation of mRNA translation by DNA segments that lie down-stream from the segment that codes for the mRNA.

retrosteroid

a synthetic steroid that has a structure at carbon atoms 9 and 10 which is opposite to that is progesterone. Retrosteroids are made from lumisterols and are extremely active as progestogens.

reverse transcriptase

an RNA-dependent DNA polymerase that catalyzes the synthesis of DNA from deoxyribonucleoside-5'-triphosphates, using RNA as a template. The enzyme has been found in RNA-containing tumour viruses and is thought to be related to the tumorigenic properties of these viruses.

reversible reaction

a chemical reaction that :

(i) establishes an equilibrium and can be made to proceed in either directions by a change in the conditions or

(ii) has an equilibrium constant of the order of 1.0, or

(iii) proceeds equally well in both directions because of other factors.

reversible sink

when in a sink reserves are remobilized at different times i.e., unmodified stem. Here import of assimilate is reversible and its unloading can be switched from symplastic to apoplastic.

rhabdovirus

a family of RNA viruses characterized by having a virion with a bullet-shaped envelope and which contain segmented negative-stranded RNA. The two main genera are the lysaviruses and vesiculoviruses, which include, respectively, the viruses responsible for rabies and vesicular stomatitis.

rhamnose $C_6H_{12}O_5$
a deoxysugar occurring free in poison sumac, and in glycoside combination in many plants. Also known as isodulcitol.

rhesus factor, abb. Rh-factor
several closely related, blood group-specific erythrocyte antigens, present in 85% of europeans (Rh-positive). The antigen is absent from the remaining 15%, who are Rh-negative. The natural antibody does not normally occur in humans, but is formed, in rabbits or guinea pigs after immunization with rhesus monkey erythrocytes. If Rh-negative individuals come into contact with Rh-antigen, e.g. by blood transfusion, or from an Rh-positive fetus (the antigen crosses the placenta), Rh-antibodies are formed. Repeated transfusion may then lead to hemolysis, or an Rh-positive fetus may suffer hemolytic damage (erythroblastosis of the newborn).

rhizobium
the sapropytic, aerobic and facultative bacteria, which symbioses with legume root to form nodules. These are specific for different legumes species and are of two types; (i) fast growing (ii) slow growing.

rhodoxanthin $C_{40}H_{50}O_2$
a xanthophyll carotenoid pigment.

α-ribazole
the compound, 1-α-D-ribofuranozyl-5,6-dimethyl-benzimidazole, that forms part of the structure in which an uncommon nitrogenous base is linked to the sugar by means of an a-glycosidic bond.

riboflavin $C_{17}H_{20}N_4O_6$
a water-soluble, yellow-orange fluorescent pigment that is essential to human nutrition as a component of the coenzymes flavin mononucleotide and flavin adenine dinucleotide. Also known as lactoflavin; vitamin B_2; vitamin G.

riboflavin 5'-phosphate $C_{17}H_{21}N_4O_9P$
the phosphoric acid ester of riboflavin. Also known as flavin phosphate; flavin mononucleotide; FMN; isoalloxazine mononucleotide; vitamin B_2 phosphate.

ribonuclease $C_{587}H_{909}N_{171}O_{197}S_{12}$
an enzyme that catalyzes the depolymerization of ribonucleic acid.

ribonuclease P
a bacterial ribonuclease which cleaves on oligonucleotide from precursor tRNA, thereby, producing the 5'-terminus of mature tRNA.

ribonucleic acid
a long-chain, usually single-standard nucleic acid

consisting of repeating nucleotide units containing four kinds of heterocyclic, organic bases; adenine, cytosine, quanine, and uracil; they are conjugated to the pentose sugar ribose and held in sequence by phosphodiester bonds; invohed intracellularly in protein synthesis. Abbseviated RNA.

ribonucleoprotein
any of a large group of conjugated proteins in which molecules of ribonucleic acid are closely associated with molecules of protein.

ribose $C_5H_{10}O_5$
a pentose sugar occurring as a component of various nucleotides, including riboncleic acid.

ribose phosphates
the phosphorylated derivatives of ribose of Ribose 1-phosphate, and ribose 5-phosphoribosyl 1-pyrophosphate are metabolically important. Ribose is phosphorylated in position 5 by the action of ribokinase (EC 2.7.1.15) and ATP. Ribose 5-phosphate is also produced in the pentose phosphate cycle, and in the calvin cycle of photosynthesis. Phosphoribomutase catalyses the interconversion of ribose 5-phosphate and ribose 1-phosphate, and the cosubstrate of this reaction is ribose 1, 5-bisphosphate.

riboside
any glycoside containing ribose as the sugar component.

weight 600,000; and 18-22S RNA with molecular weight 1,200,000. Abbrevated r-RNA.

ribonucleotide reductase
an enzyme which catalyses the conversion of ribonucleoside diphosphates to deoxyribonucleoside diphosphates.

ribosomal editing
the hypothesis that errors in protein synthesis, resulting from the transfer of a peptide to an inappropriate aminoacyl-tRNA, are detected by the ribosome; this detection then leads to the preferential dissociation of the inappropriate peptidyl-tRNA from the ribosome.

ribosome cycle
the set of reactions whereby ribosomal subunits combine to form the intact ribosome during initiation of translation, travels along the mRNA as an intact ribosomes, and dissociated back to the subunits during the termination of translation.

ribosome receptor
a receptor in the membrane of the rough endoplasmic reticulum to which a ribosome becomes bound during protein synthesis according to the signal hypothesis. The receptor is believed to be adjacent to a membrane pore and the ribosome becomes bound to the receptor after the signal sequence has become detached from the signal recognition protein.

ribozyme
RNA sequence with enzyme like activity. It is an internal guide sequence contained within an intron of a eukaryotic transcript which is able to catalyse the splicing of that intron in vitro in absence of any enzyme or other protein molecule.

ribulose $C_5H_{10}O_5$
a pentose sugar that exists only as a syrup; synthesized from arabinose by isomerization with pyridine; important in carbohydrate metabolism. Also known as D-erythropentose; D-riboketose.

ribulose diphosphate $C_5H_{12}O_{11}P_2$
the phosphate ester of ribulose.

ribulose-5-phosphate epimerase
an enzyme which catalyses the formation of ribulose-5-P from xylulose-5-P of C_3 pathway of CO_2 fixation. It also catalyses the same reaction in oxidative pentose phosphate pathway.

ribulose-1, 5P_2 oxygenase
an enzyme which catalyses the oxidative reaction of ribulose-1, 5-P_2 to glycerate-3-P and glycollate-2-P. It is 20-30% of carboxylase activity of Rubisco.

rifamycins
a group of antibiotics produced by Streptomyces mediterranel. They contain a naphthalene ring system bridged between position 2 and 5 by an aliphatic chain. Rifamycin SV and rifampicin inhibit DNA-dependent RNA synthesis in prokaryotes, chloroplasts and mitochondria, but not in the nuclei of eukaryotes.

RNA-dependent DNA polymerase
an enzyme which catalyses the synthesis of DNA from deoxyribonucleoside triphosphate using RNA as a template. It is also known as reverse transcripatase.

RNA maturation
in eukaryotic nucleus the 3 types of rRNA are made as a single, very long precursor strand that subsequently is cleaved and further processed to yield that final finished products, in a process known as RNA maturation.

RNA polymerases classes
muitiple forms of DNA-dependent RNA polymerase that occur in eukaryotes. All are high molecular weight proteins and all are found in the nucleus. Each form is responsible for the synthesis of a particular type of RNA and various enzymes can be distinguished by their sensitivity to inhibition by α-amanitin.

RNA-synthetase, RNA-replicase, RNA-dependent, RNA-polymerase
an enzyme that appears in bacterial, animal and plant cells, following infection with RNA viruses. Using a template of single stranded (viral) RNA, the enzyme catalyses the synthesis of a complementary

strand of RNA.

root

(i) that portion of a quantity which, when multiplied by itself a specified number of times, yields the quantity in question.

(ii) the organ developed from the radicle of seedling. Responsible for anchoring of plant in medium, absorption of water and minerals.

rotation spectra

changes in vibration energy levels may be accompanied by changes in rotational energy levels. These occur in the short microwave region.

rotational transition

the rotation of molecules about their axis that results in their achieving a random orientation.

rubredoxin

a redoxin, functionally similar to Ferredoxin. It was isolated from Clostridium pasteurianum; synthesis of R, appears to be promoted by a relative deficiency of iron. It contain less iron than ferredoxin, usually containing one F atom/molecule of protein. Under acid conditions it is more stable than ferredoxin, and it has more positive redox potential (E_o-0057 V).

runaway replication

uncontrolled replication of plasmid molecules which multiply within host building up of several thousand copies. This usually halts cell division but is a very powerful way of amplifying a gene product.

running gel

small pore polyacrylamide gel over which actual separation of proteins occurs on the basis of their molecular sizes and charges.

ruthenium red

an non-competitive inhibitor of Ca^{++} transport into mitochondria. About 50% inhibition is achieved with 7 mmole mg^{-1} protein concentration.

S-100 protein

(i) an acidic protein involved in the process of leaking and other neurophysiological functions. Its molecular weight is 20 KD and rich in aspartic and glutamic acids.

(ii) one of a group of low molecular weight, Ca^{++} binding, modulator proteins that function in cell cycle progression, cell differentiation and cytoskeletal membrane interactions.

sabininic acid

12-hydroxylauric acid, $HOCH_2$-$(CH_2)_{10}$-COOH. A fatty acid, present as a typical wax acid in the wax of many pines.

salt linkages

interaction between the amino group of the basic amino acids and the side chain carboxyl group of the acidic amino acids.

saltation

the movement of medium sized soil particles by wind. Sand particles are picked up by Eddy winds into the horizontal air stream. The vertical lift is dissipated and particles fall back to the ground, throwing up more particles.

salvage pathway

a pathway that utilises compounds formed in catabolism for biosynthetic purposes, even though these compounds are not true intermediates of the corresponding normal biosynthetic pathway e.g., free purines may be salvaed from the hydrolysis of nucleotides and then used for the biosynthesis of nucleotides.

sample error

error due to sampling. It can be reduced by taking unbiased optimum sample size and by stratification.

saponification

formation of soaps, i.e., salts of fatty acids produced on alkaline hydrolysis.

saponins

a large and widely distributed group of plant substances, named from their ability to form strongly foaming, soap-like solutions with water. They are all glycosides, and are classified according to the nature of aglycon (also called a genin). i.e., steroid, triterpene and steroid-alkaloid saponins; the latter are also known as glycoalkaloids. Aglycons of the steroid saponins are also called sapogenins; these are spirostane-type, C_{27}-steroids. They all possess a 3β-hydroxyl group (spirostanols), which forms a glycosidic linkage with the sugar, e.g., D-glucose, D-galactose, or L-arabinose. The triterpene saponins are less well studied; their aglycons are chiefly tetra and pentacyclic triterpenes.

S. are powerful surfactants, cause hemolysis and are potent plasma toxins and fish poisons, but they have no toxic effects when ingested by humans, because they are not absorbed.

sarmentocymarin

a cardioactive, steriod glycoside from the seeds of Strophanthus sarmentosus; on hydrolysis it yields sarmentogenin and sarmentose.

sarmentogenin $C_{23}H_{34}O_5$

the steroid aglycon of sarmentocymarin; isometric with digitoxigenin, and characterized by a hydroxyl group at carbon number 11.

satellite DNA

DNA fractions that can be separated from the main DNA by CsCI-gradient centrifugation. It has been demonstrated in the nuclei of many eukaryotes, accounting for about 1% of nuclear DNA in man, and about 10% in the mouse. It consists of a linear double helix, and differs markedly from the rest of the nuclear DNA with respect to base composition and density.

saturated fatty acids

fatty acids in which the carbon

bonds are fully saturated. The general formula is $C_nH_{2}n + 1$ COOH e.g., Formic, acetic and propionic acids.

saturated solution

a solution containing maximum amount of solute dissolved at a specific temperature and pressure. Slight increase in temperature will further dissolve some solute and thus resulting into super saturated solutions; but such solutions are unstable.

saturation thickness

the thickness of a radioactive sample such that any additional increase in its thickness will not increase the observed counts any further.

scanner

(i) an instrument for measuring the distribution of either colour intensity or radio-activity on a chromatogram or on an electrophoretogram.

(ii) a photoelectric scanning attachment for the analytical ultracentrifuge that provides a plot of absorbance versus radial distance and that is used in conjunction with the UV absorption optical system.

scanning tunneling microscope

a powerful microscope that produces three dimensional images of surface; it enables one to "see" surfaces, atom by atom, and it can resolve features that are a fraction of the size of an atom.

schardinger dextrin

any of several water-soluble, nonreducing, dextrorotatory polysaccharides that have a low molecular weight and that are obtained by the action of Bacillus macerans on a starch solution.

Schlieren Optical system

an optical system that focuses UV light passing through a solution in such a fashion that a photograph is obtained that represents a plot of refractive index gradient as a function of distance in the solution. A boundary in the solution appears as a peak on the photographic plate and measurements are made on this photographic plate with microcomparator. The optical system is used in analytical ultracentrifuge and the Tiselius electrophoresis apparatus.

scion

(i) a portion of a plant, usually a piece of young stem which is inserted into a root stock in grafting.

(ii) a young plant formed at the end of, or along the course of, a runner.

(iii) a stolon.

sclerenchyma

mechanical tissue consisting of dead cells with thick lignified walls and small lumens. If the cells are elongated they are known as fibres, and have pointed ends usually occurring in bundles. When the cells are oval or rounded, they are called sclerides. They occur singly or in groups.

scleroprotein
any one of a class of proteins, such as keratin, fibroin, and the collagens, which occur in hard parts of the animal body and serve to support or protect. Also known as albuminoid.

scorpion venoms
secretions of the scorpion stinging apparatus. Active principles of S.v. are the neurotoxic scorpamines. They are similar to cobra toxins with respect to M_r (M_r 6800-7200; 4 disulfide bridges; 63-64 amino acid residues of known sequence), amino acid composition (high contents of basic and aromatic amino acids) and activity (both peripheral and central nervous system).

secalose
a polysaccharide consisting of fructose units; occurs in green rye and oats, and in rye flour.

second meassenger
3'-5' cyclic AMP is proposed to act as second messenger in explaining the mechanism of action of growth regulator on various physiological processes. Now-a-days active Cacalmodulin complex is more favoured as second messenger.

secondary colour
mixture of two primary colours e.g., Orange, green or violet.

secondary growth
when lateral or intercalary meristem undergoes cell division and elongation resulting increase in diameter. Secondary growth is very common in dicots and very rare in monocots.

secondary isotope effect
an isotope effect in which the isotope itself does not participate in bond cleavage; the bond to the isotope, though not broken, has a different energy during the transition state than it does in the ground state.

secondary structure
the regular folding of a polypeptide chain or of a polynucleotide strand along one axis of the molecule, as in a helix, that is due to the formation of intramolecular hydrogen bonds along the length of the chain or strand; the local spatial arrangement of segments of the polynucleotide strand without regard to the conformation of side chains or to the relation of one segment to other segments.

secretin
a basic polypeptide hormone produced by the duodenum in response to the presence of acid; acts to excite the pancreas to activity.

secretion
(i) a substance produced within a cell and passed out through the plasma membrane, and having a special function in the organism.
(ii) the passage of the substance from the cell. In contrast to simple diffusion, the cell does work against the forces of diffusion.

(iii) a general term for the transport of protein across any membrane, either into some cellular compartment or into the medium.

secretory protein
protein such as enzyme amylase or trypsinogen or the polypeptide hormone insulin or growth hormone, that is secreted by cell by means of exocytosis.

sedimentation
(i) the movement of molecules in solution under the influence of a centrifugal field and away from the centre of rotation.
(ii) the settling out of molecules from a solution under the influence of a gravitational field.

sedimentation potential
the electrical potential produced by the sedimentation of particles through a liquid as a result of gravity or the application of a centrifugal force.

sedoheptulose
a seven-carbon ketose sugar widely distributed in plants of the Crassulaceae family; a significant intermediary compound in the cyclic regeneration of D-ribulose.

sedum alkaloids
a group of piperidine alkaloids from sedum spp. They are 2- or 2, 6-substituted piperidine derivatives, similar in structure and biosynthesis to the Punica and Lobelia alkaloids.

seedling
the young plant developing from a germinating seed. It is well differentiated phase having root, stem and leaves etc.

segment
(i) a portion of the lamina of a leaf, when it is deeply lobed, but not divided into leaflets.
(ii) a daughter-cell, cut off from a single apical cell.
(iii) the free part, when a calyx or corolla consists of partially fused lobes.
(iv) a multinucleate portion of a filament or hypha, which is cut-off by a cross wall.

selectivity
(i) the tendency of a detector to respond to certain classes of compounds to a greater degree that other classes of compounds.
(ii) the discriminatin power of the system, i.e., membrane, permeability, weedicides etc.

self-priming
not requiring a primer. The synthesis of RNA by DNA-dependent RNA polymerase is a self-priming reaction as opposed to the synthesis of DNA by DNA-dependent DNA polymerase which requires the 3' -OH end of a primer.

self-sterile
the inability of a gametes of opposite sex, but produced by the same individual, to fuse.

semiconservative replication
one of the manners of DNA replication; each new DNA

duplex contains one original parental strand and one newly synthesized strand.

semipermeable

when membrane allows passage of one type of ions and impermeable to others.

semisynthetic

descriptive of a compound of which part of the structure has been isolated from natural sources and part of it has been synthesized. Semisynthetic penicillins and cephalosporins are examples of such synthetically modified antibiotics.

senscence

it is a last stage in life of plants or organs, where degradation is faster than synthesis, chlorophyll, proteins and nucleic acids are degraded. Synthetic capacity is decreased. Senescence is of different type; (i) sequential (ii) simultaneous or synchronised.

sensitized fluorescence

the fluorescence that occurs when a photon excites a molecule which then excites a second molecule by means of an energy transfer, and the second molecule dissipates the excitation energy by fluorescence.

sequence homology

to identify the similarities in sequence of either the amino acids in segments of two or more proteins, or the nucleotides in segments of two or more nucleic acid.

sequence hypothesis

the hypothesis that sequence of nucleotides in a nucleic acid specifies the sequence of amino acids in a protein.

sequential feed back inhibition

here the first step of a branched pathway is not inhibited by the ultimate end products. Accumulation of branch chain point metabolic inhibits the activity of the Ist enzyme of the pathway. The other steps are inhibited by the accumulation of the end products.

serine $C_3H_7O_3N$

an amino acid obtained by hydrolysis of many proteins; a biosynthetic precursor of several metabolites, including cystein, glycine, and choline.

serine convention

a method for assigning configurations to compounds by a comparison with the configuration of serine; thus (+) tartaric acid is designated as L_G when compared to glyceraldehyde, and as D_S when compared to serine.

serine proteases

a group of well studied animal and bacterial endopeptidases which have a similar action mechanism, and a catalytically active serine residue in their active centers (serine residue 195 in chymotrypsin). In all serine proteases catalysis involves formation of an ester between the hydroxyl group of the catalytically active serine and the carboxyl group of the cleaved peptide bond (acyl-enzyme intermediate); this is hydrolysed in the deacylation stage of the reaction, restoring the free hydroxyl group of the serine and releasing the cleavage peptide.

serine transhydroxymethylase
an enzyme which regulates reversible conversion of serine glycine during amino acid synthesis.

serotonin $C_{10}H_{12}ON_2$
a compound derived from tryptophan which functions as a local vasoconstrictor, plays a role in neurotransmission, and has pharmacologic properties. Also known as 5-hydroxytryptamine.

serum
in biochemistry, the fluid expressed from a blood clot as it contracts after coagulation of blood. The essential difference between plasma serum is that the latter does not contain fibrinogen.

serum albumin
the principal protein fraction of blood serum and serous fluids.

serum blocking power
the capacity of an immunoadsorbent to adsorb antibodies from a serum and to decrease the antibody titer of the serum.

serum globulin
the globulin fraction of blood serum.

severe combined immunodeficiency syndrome SCID
the most severe form of congenital immunological deficiency state in which the thymic agenesis with lymphocyte depletion coexists with deficiency of plasma cells and antibody deficiency syndrome.

sex determination
the process by which a haploid spore or egg or diploid zygote comes to develop the properties of one or other sex.

sex hormone
any hormone secreted by a gonad, but also found in other tissues.

sex ratio
the ratio of the males to females in a population at a given time. It is usually expressed as the number of males per 100 females.

sexual attractants
natural products involved in sexual interaction.
they are usually produced by the sexually mature female in order to attract and predispose the male to copulation.
plant sexual attractants are called gamones, or palnt sex hormones.

shear
(i) the deformation experienced by a liquid as a result of the variation in the velocity of flow of different layers. Shear is associated with the flow of a liquid through a capillary with the forcing of a liquid through a pipette and with the homogenisation of a suspension.

(ii) to fragment DNA molecules into smaller pieces. DNA, as a very long and fairly stiff molecule, is very susceptible to hydrodynamic shear forces. Forcing a DNA solution through a hypodermic needle will fragment it into small pieces. The size of the fragments obtained is inversely proportional to the diameter of the needle's bore.

shift down

a shift experiment in which the change in the medium leads to a decrease in the rate of growth of the cells.

shikimic acid $C_7H_{10}O_5$

a crystalline acid that is a plant constituent, and an intermediate in the biochemical pathway from phosphoenolpyruvic acid to tyrosine.

shikimic acid pathway

it is most important pathway for the biosynthesis of phenols. Aromatic amino acids like tryptophan, tyrosine, cinnamic acid are obtained via shikimic acid intermediate. Here shikimic acid is formed from phosphoenolpyruvate and D-Erythrose-4-phosphate.

shuttle

a mechanism whereby reducing equivalents are removed from cytoplasmic NADH and passed to the electron transport system in the mitochondrial membrane by way of intermediate compounds, since NADH itself cannot pass through the membrane.

sialic acid

any of a family of amino sugars, containing nine or more carbon atoms, that are nitrogen- and oxygen-substituted acyl derivatives of neuraminic acid; as components of lipids, polysaccharides, and mucoproteins, they are widely distributed in bacteria and in animal tissues.

side reaction

a secondary reaction that occurs simultaneously with the major reaction.

siderophilins

nonheme, iron-binding, single chain animal glycoproteins, carbohydrate content about 6%. On the basis of their occurrence, they are classified as transferrin (vertebrate blood), lactoferrin (mammalian milk and other body secretions) and conalbumin or ovotransferrin (avain blood and avain egg white). They differ in their physical, chemical and immunological properties, but each possesses two iron-binding sites for iron (III).

sigma cycle

the set of reactions composed of:

(a) the attachment of the sigma factor to the core enzyme of RNA polymerase at the initial site of transcription;

(b) the release of the sigma factor from the core enzyme during chain elongation; and

(c) the subsequent binding of the sigma factor to the same, or to another, core enzyme at an initiation site.

sigma structure

(i) the DNA structure formed during the replication of double-stranded circular DNA according to the rolling circle model.

(ii) the RNA structure formed during the splicing of pre-mRNA in eukaryotes.

sigmoid growth curve or grand growth curve

a graph in which rate of some characteristics i.e., weight, area or dimension is plotted against time or age or stage of plant. The Ist part is linear followed by exponential phase. After that the rate fall off at about the same rate to zero.

signal to noise ratio

the ratio of the electrical response of an instrument during the measurement of a sample to the response from random background electrical fluctuations.

simple immunodiffusion

here diffusion of antigen from a solution into the gel containing antibody occurs. In these methods diffusion is allowed either in one or two dimensions.

simple lipids

these do not have fatty acids and therefore, non-saponifiable. These are of two types; (i) Terpenes. (ii) Steroids.

simple protein

one of a group of proteins which, upon hydrolysis, yields exclusively amino acids; included are globulins, glutelins, histones, prolamines, and protamines.

single displacement reactions

the bisubstrate reaction in which both substrates must be presented on the enzyme active site simultaneously to make a ternary complex in order for the reaction to proceed. There are two forms of single displacement reactions; (i) random and (ii) ordered.

single-substrate enzyme

an enzyme which catalyses a reaction involving only one substrate.

siroheam

an unusual heam compound having tetrahydro-porphyrin in which adjacent pyrrole rings is reduced and possessing 8 carboxylate side chains. It is associated with nitrite reductase of green plants.

sistrand

the translational unit of mRNA as opposed to the genetic unit, the sistrand is that unit of RNA that lies between an initiation and termination signal.

site heterogeneity

the heterogeneity of antibodies that results from the antigen molecule possessing several antigenic determinants; consequently, one antigen leads to the production of several types of antibodies.

slope

(i) the slope of any function at

the particular point is simply 'Rise over Run'. For a straight line the slope is constant. It is used in calculating the magnitude of a parameter from its standard curve.

(ii) the tangent of the angle a line (extended, if necessary) makes with the X-axis; hence, dy/dx.

slow component

that fraction of DNA that reassociates last in a reassociation kinetics experiment.

small-nuclear RNA

a class of small RNA molecules, consisting of 100-300 nucleotides, that are located in the nucleus of eukaryotic cells. Their distinguishing feature is their association with specific protein molecules to form small nuclear ribonucleoproteins; some of the latter participate in RNA processing.

snake venomes

a mixture of toxins produced in the venom glands (parotid gland, or salivary gland of the upper jaw) of venomous snakes (asps or blood snakes, e.g., the cobra; sea snakes; vipers, e.g., puff adder, rattlesnake). They consist of highly toxic, antigenic polypeptides and proteins (which cause paralysis and death of the prey), and enzymes (which facilitate the spread of the toxins, and initiate digestion of undivided swallowed prey).

snapback

the rapid renaturation of heat denatured double-stranded DNA or RNA that occurs when the nucleic acid contains a short segment in which the nucleotide pairs are intact, with the base pairing in perfect register. The minimum size of this segment varies with the composition of the nucleic acid; the segment generally consists of between 12 and 20 nucleotide pairs.

sodium error

the apparent decrease in the pH of a solution that is measured with most glass electrodes when they are used at high pH values; the effect is due to the fact that most glasses that are responsive to protons are also somewhat responsive to sodium ions.

sodium dithionite

a powerful reducing agent, used to reduce many physiological and artificial electron carriers including NAD, NADP, flavin and cytochromes. Oxidises in air, readily when damp or in solution.

solar constant

the integrated flux density of solar radiation incident upon a surface perpendicular to the sun's rays at the outer edge of the earth atmosphere. Its value is about 1400 W m^2 (2.0 cal cm^{-1} min^{-1}).

solubility curve

a plot of the amount of solute in solution as a function of the amount of solute added.

soluble enzyme

an enzyme that exists in the free state in the cytoplasm in contrast to a particular enzyme, is readily extracted from cells, and can be purified by the general method of protein fractionation.

solvent demixing

the separation of a solvent system into its constituent components.

solvolysis

a generalized concept for the reaction between solvent and a solute by which new substances are produced. In most cases the solvent donates a proton to, and/or accepts a proton from the solute. When the solvent is water, the reaction is known as hydrolysis.

somatomedians

a collective term for a group of peptides comprising somatomedians A, B and C. In particular, it causes an increased incorporation of sulfur into cartilage and is therefore called sulfation factor. All these have insulin-line activity.

somatotrophin

a hormone, synthesized and stored in the adenohypophysis, that promotes bone growth and stimulates protein synthesis (via somatomedin). Its release is controlled by the opposing actions of growth-hormone releasing factor and somatostatin.

sorbose $C_6H_{12}O_6$

a carbohydrate prepared by fermentation; produced as water-soluble crystals that melt at 165°C; used in the production of vitamin C. Also known as sorbin; L-sorbose.

source

an organ which supplies nutrients or photosynthates to developing organs e.g., fully expanded and mature leaves.

space

(i) part of the universe lying outside the limits of the earth atmosphere.

(ii) the volume occupied by the various atoms in a molecule to give a definite shape of structure. It has three dimensions i.e., length or height, width and depth. It is of two types :—

(i) perceptual and

(ii) conceptual space.

Physical space is a relative space.

space filling model

a compact molecular model that shows the full bulk of each atom and the effective shape of the molecule. In this model, the bond angles are correct and the distance between the atoms are to scale based on their Van der Walls radii.

spacer DNA

a segment of DNA that does not code for any identifiable RNA species; spacer DNA, rich in adenine and thymine, occurs between transcribable segments of the DNA that codes for ribosomal RNA.

spatial
the arrangement of atoms or groups in space to describe structure of a compound.

specific adsorption
the adsorption of specific ions to a surface that results from the formation of consideration complexes between groups of atom on the surface and the ions.

specific gravity
the ratio of the weight of a given volume of a substance to that of an equal volume of water; it is numerically equal to density.

specific retention volume
the volume of liquid per gram of adsorbent, that passes through a column in displacement chromatography before a particular substance is eluted from the column.

specific rotation
it is proportional to obs/Cl where obs is the observed rotation of plane polarized light by a solution. C is the concentration of the solute in grams per millimeter, 1 is the length of the light path through the sample in decimeters.

specificity factor
a protein that associates temporarily with the core component of RNA polymerase, and thereby determines to which promoter the enzyme will bind and which genes will be transcribed.

S-peptide
a short fragment of the enzyme ribonuclease that is obtained by a subtilis in catalyzed cleavage of the molecule between amino acid residues 20 and 21.

spermaceti
a solid animal wax, obtained from the head of the sperm whale, physeter macrocephalus. It consists chiefly of cetyl palmitate, accompained by smaller quantities of cetyl laurate and myristate. It is used in the pharmaceutical and cosmetic industries as a basis for creams.

spermatin
an albuminoid material occurring in semen.

spermatocyte
a cell which differentiates into a spermatozoid.

s p e r m i d i n e $H_2N(CH_2)_3NH(CH_2)_4NH_2$
the triamine found in semen and other animal tissues.

spermine $C_{10}H_{26}N_4$
a tetramine found in semen, blood serum, and other body tissues.

spherical aberration
an intrinsic aberration of lenses such that rays passing through the lens at different distance from the centre are brought to a focus at different planes. This aberration is not easily avoidable in electron microscopes, thus limits resolution.

sphingolipid
any lipid, such as sphingomyelin, that yields sphingosine or one of its

derivatives as a product of hydrolysis.

sphingomyelin
a phospholipid consisting of choline, sphingosine, phosphoric acid, and a fatty acid.

sphingosine $C_{18}H_{37}O_2N$
a moiety of sphingomyelin, cerebrosides, and certain other phosphatides.

spinochrome
a type of echinochrome; an organic pigment that is known only from sea urchins and certain homopteran insects.

spin decoupling
a technique used in nuclear magnetic resonance in which the effect of spin coupling with nucleus A on the spectrum of nucleus B is eliminated by irradiation with the resonance frequency of nucleus A.

spindle
a collection of fibers (microtubules) but usually a little narrower (200 Å diameter); concerned with chromatid separation during nuclear division.

split protein
a protein that has been removed from ribosomes, such as one removed in the diassembly of ribosomes by concentrated salt solutions.

split-split design
when more than two factors are to be investigated, the 3rd factor is designated as sub-sub treatments. Plot size for sub-sub treatment will be smallest.

spongin
a scleroprotein, occurring as the principal component of skeletal fibres in many sponges.

sporophyte
the spore forming phase of a plant which shows alternation of generations. The main generation in pteridophytes, gymnosperms and angiospersms. It is formed by the union of sexual cells produced by the gametophyte.

sporopollenin
a substance related to suberin and cutin but more resistant to decay that is found in the exine of pollen grains.

spring wood
secondry xylem formed during the spring and early summer. It is distinguished by the large, thin walled element of which it is composed.

spurious counts
counts of radioactivity that are not caused by the sample but that result from outside factors such as malfunctioning of the apparatus.

squalena $C_{30}H_{50}$
a liquid triterpene which is found in large quantities in shark liver oil, and which appears to play a role in the biosynthesis of sterols and polycyclic terpenes; used as a bactericide and as an intermediate in the synthesis of pharmaceuticals. Also known as spinacene.

stacking interactions
the hydrophobic interactions between two base pairs are

arranged in parallel planes in the interior of a double-helical nucleic acid structure.

stacking gel

the large pore polyacrylamide gel over which protein sample in a suitable buffer is layered. It is essential for uniform initial migration of protein to form disc or zone at the interface of stacking and running gels.

standard amino acids

the 20 amino acids that occur in proteins as distinct from other amino acids (non-protein amino acids) that function only in various areas of metabolism.

starch

a polysaccharide consisting of various proportions of two glucose polymers, amylose and amylopectin. It cccurs widely in plants, especially in roots, tubers, seeds, and fruits, as a carbohydrate energy store. Starch is therefore a major energy source for animals. When digested it ultimately yields glucose. Starch granules are insoluble in cold water but disrupt if heated to form a gelatinous solution.

starch phosphorylase

an enzyme which catalyses the hydrolysis of starch to form glucose-1P in glycolysis.

statolith

the membrane bound solid inclusions in a plant cell, often a starch grain, free to move under the influence of gravity. It may be means whereby position in respect to gravity influences a plant organ.

steady-state stacking

in a stacking gel when current is fed, proteins present in the sample gel stacked over the chloride ion according to their decreasing mobility. On the top of the protein bands glycine molecules are present.

steapsin

an enzyme in pancreatic juice that catalyzes the hydrolysis of fats. Also known as pancreatic lipase.

stele

the vascular cylinder. The cylinder or core of vascular tissue in the centre of stems and roots. It consists of xylem, phloem, and pericycle, and in some cases with the medullary rays. It is surrounded by an endodermis. The detailed structure differs in different groups of plants.

stercobilin

urobilin as a component of the brown fecal pigment.

stercobilinogen

a colourless reducting product of stercobilin found in feces.

stereoisomer

one of two or more isomers that have same molecular composition and the same atom-to-atom sequence, but that differ from each other in the spatial arrangement of the atoms in the molecule; stereoisomers cannot be distinguished on the basis of their two-dimensional structures.

steroid
a compound composed of a series of four cabon rings joined together to form a structural unit called cyclopentanoperhydrophenanthrene.

steroid conjugate
a steroid breakdown product that is conjugated to either glucuronic acid or sulphuric acid and that is excreted in this form.

sterol
any of the natural products derived from the steroid nucleus; all are waxy, colourless solids soluble in most organic solvents but not in water, and contain one alcohol functional group.

stickland reaction
an amino acid fermentation involving the coupled decomposition of two or more substrates.

sticky ends or cohensive
the action of restriction enzymes to produce single-strand cuts. These ends are not only identical, but complementary and will base-pair with each other.

stigma
(i) an eyespot in algae.
(ii) the surface of the carpel of higher plants which receives the pollen grains.

stigmasterol
5 α-stigmasta-5, 22-diene-3 α-ol, a widely distributed phytosterol, first isolated from calabar beans, and later from many other sources, e.g., soybeans, carrots, coconut oil and sugar cane wax. It is used as a starting material in the technical synthesis of steroid hormones.

stomatal resistance (r_s)
the resistance offered by stomatal pore to CO_2 and H_2O vapour diffusion. Its values vary from 0.6 to 20 s cm^{-1}, it is function of level of irradiation, temperature, leaf water status, age and general physiological condition of the plant.

stomatal transpiration
the transpiration through stomata. It is major loss responsible to create transpirational pull necessary for the ascent of sap.

strain
(i) a natural or artificial mating group, uniform in some particular characters.
(ii) a variety of species, with distinct morphological or physiological characters.
(iii) the relative amount of distortion. It is effect of stress. Strain may be reversible or irreversible.
(iv) a deformation in a molecule.
(v) to pass through a coarse filter as cheese cloth.

streak
(i) to apply material as a strip to either a chromatographic or an electrophoretic support, usually for preparative purposes.
(ii) to apply a bacterial inoculum as a strip to the surface of a solid nutrient medium.
(iii) a layer of tissue differing

in colour or structure from the tissue on each side of it.

(iv) a furrow.

(v) a kind of virus disease in which necrotic streaks develop.

strepogenin

a factor, possibly a peptide derivative of glutamic acid, reported to exist in certain proteins, acting as a growth stimulant in bacteria and mice in the presence of completely hydrolyzed protein. Also known as streptogenin.

streptoblosamine $C_{13}H_{23}NO_9$

a nitrogen-containing disaccharide, obtained when streptomycin undergoes acid hydrolysis; in the streptmycin molecule it is glycosidally linked to streptidine.

streptodornase

a largely obsolete term for a mixture of enzymes obtained from cultures of Streptococua.

streptogenin peptides

natural products (e.g., liver extracts, peptones, partial hydrolysates of proteins) or synthetic peptides, which stimulate the growth of microorganisms, especially lactic acid bacteria. The unknown growth stimulant is called streptogenin.

streptokinase

an enzyme occurring as a component of fibrinolysin in cultures of certain hemolytic streptococci.

streptolysin

any of a group of hemolysins elaborated by Streptococcus pyogenes.

streptomycin

inhibits intiation, elongation and termination of protein synthesis in prokaryotes and induces misreading.

stress tolerance

the stress resistance by an ability to come to thermodynamic equilibrium with the stress without suffering injury. The plant is able to prevent, decrease, or repair the injurious strain induced by the stress.

stripping

(i) the hydrolytic removal of an amino acid from an aminoacyl tRNA molecule.

(ii) the removal of ribosomal proteins from ribosomes, resulting in the production of ribosomal particles.

strong electrolyte

an electrolyte that is completely dissociated into ions in water.

structural protein

protein that has, as its chief function, a contribution to the shape and structure of cells and tissues (e.g., collagen, actin, myosin). The term is slightly misleading since many structural proteins also have enzymic functions.

strychnine

a strychnos alkaloids. It is the chief alkaloid in the seeds of tropical strychnos spp., from which it is obtained commercially, the total synthesis by woodward is uneconomic and only of scientific interest. It has many therapeutic properties, but its high toxicity precludes its extensive use in medicine.

stuart factor

a procoagulant in normal plasma but deficient in the blood of patients with a hereditary bleeding disorder; may be closely related to prothrombin since both are formed in the liver by action of vitamin K. Also known as factor X; Stuart-power factor.

subcloning

a variation of the molecular cloning technique in which a DNA segmen is cloned, isolated and then cut into successively smaller fragments by the use of several restriction enzymes. A specific fragment is then recloned in a suitable plasmid.

suberin

a fatty substance found in many plant cell walls, especially cork.

substance P

an undecapeptide widely distributed in the central nervous system and found in highest concentrations in superficial layers of the dorsal horn of the spinal cord, in the trigeminal nerve nucleus, and in the substantial nigra; acts as a neurotransmitter.

substituated enzyme

the modified enzyme that is produced by the reaction of the original enzyme molecule with the first substrate in a ping-pong mechanism.

substomatal cavity

the space filled with water vapour and carbon dioxide, between stomatal pore and mesophyll cell walls.

substrate inhibition

inhibition of the activity of an enzyme by the substrate of the enzyme; generally most pronounced at higher substrate concentrations.

subunit

1. in protein chemistry the smallest protein or polypeptide unit that can be separated from an oligomeric protein without breaking covalent bonds. In allosteric enzymes, e.g., aspartate transcarbamylase, non-identical subunits can be further classified into regulatory and catalytic subunits.

2. the term is also applied to two subunits of ribosomes.

subunit exchange

the association of small ribosomal subunit from one ribosome with the large subunit from a different ribosome, the vice-versa, as a result of the operation of ribosomal cycle.

succinate pathway

a catabolic pathway where-by methionine, isoleucine, and valine are converted to succinic acid which then enters the citric acid cycle.

succinic acid

a symmetrical dicarboxylic acid that is an intermediate in the citric acid cycle where it is formed from α-ketoglutaric acid.

succinic acid dehydrogenase
an enzyme that catalyzes the dehydrogenation of succinic acid to fumaric acid in the presence of a hydrogen acceptor. Also known as succinic dehydrogenase.

succinoxidase
a complex enzyme system containing succinic dehydrogenase and cytochromes that catalyzes the conversion of succinate ion and molecular oxygen to fumarate ion.

sucrose
a sugar comprising one molecule of glucose linked to a fructose molecule. It occurs widely in plants and is particularly abundant in sugar cane and sugar beet (15-20%), from which it is extracted and refined for table sugar. If heated to 200°C sucrose becomes caramel. Also known as cane sugar, beet sugar, saccharose.

sucrose phosphatase
an enzyme which catalyses the removal of phosphate from sucrose-6-phosphate thus yielding sucrose and Pi.

sugar
a generic term for a class of carbohydrates usually crystalline, sweet, and water soluble, examples are glucose and fructose.

sugar alcohol
an alcohol derived from a monosaccharide by reduction of its carbonyl group (C=O) so that each carbon atom of the sugar has an alcohol group (-OH). For example, glucose yields sorbitol, common in fruits and mannose yields mannitol.

sulfatase
any of a group of esterases that catalyze the hydrolysis of sulfuric esters.

sulfate esters
products formed by the transfer of a sulfuryl group to the oxygen function of organic compounds. Donor for the sulfuryl transfer is phosphoadenosinephosphosulfate (PAPS). Naturally occurring sulphate esters are polysaccharide sulfate esters, and sulfate esters of phenols, steroids, choline, cerebrosides and flavonoids. Synthesis of phenol sulfate esters in mammalina liver was the first biological sulphate ester synthesis to be recognized, and the first to be performed in vitro.

sulfhemoglobin
a greenish substance derived from hemoglobin by the action of hydrogen sulfide; it may appear in the blood following the ingestion of sulfanilamide and other substances.

Sullivan reaction
a colorimetic reaction for cysterine that is based on the production of red colour upon treatment of the sample with sodium 1, 2-naphthoquinone-4-sulphonate and sodium sulphite.

sulphate respiration

the dissimilatory reduction of sulphate in the course of cellular respiration in which sulphate replaces oxygen as the terminal electron acceptor; the sulphate is reduced to hydrogen sulphide which is excreted.

sulphatide

cerebroside which contains a sulphur group esterified to the C-3 atom of the galactose molecule. Sulphatides are abundant in the white matter of the brain.

sulphite oxidase deficiency

a genetically inherited metabolic defect in man that is associated with mental retardation and that is due to a deficiency of the enzyme sulphite oxidase.

sulphite reductase

an enzyme which catalyses the formation of free sulphide from sulphite without the involvement of bound inermediate. In chloroplast it is Fd dependent.

superamolecules

when various macromolecules interact with other class of such compounds, supermolecular systems are produced which are made up of supermolecules e.g., Lipoproteins, nucleoproteins, ribosomes etc. molecular weight varies from 10^6-10^{10}.

supermolecular complex

(i) a complex composed of several of many molecules such as a ribosome, a biological membrane, or a virus.

(ii) multienzyme system.

(iii) metabolon.

superoxide

a free radical of O_2 and is spontaneously formed in photo-oxidative processes or enzymatically. It is involved in lipoxygenation of polyunsaturated fatty acid during senescence.

suppression

the partial or complete restoration of genetic function lost as a result of a mutation, by means of a second mutation occurring at a different site on the chromosome.

suppressor

with reference to Amber mutants and Ochre mutants, a S. mutation is a secondary mutation in a tRNA to recognize the nonsense codon. The resulting new tRNA is called suppressor tRNA. The nonsense codon then becomes a sense codon and codes for a specific proteogenic amino acid during translation.

surface tension

the tension exerted by the surface of a liquid as a result of the intermolecular attractive forces between the molecules of the liquid.

suspension

the presence of small sized solute particles in liquid phase which settle down on standing under the force of gravity.

switch site

a short sequence of DNA 5' to each heavy chain C-region gene which act as a recognition site for translocation of the V-region gene during switching of the gene expression from one class of heavy chain to another.

sym-coupled translocation
involve equilibrium of two solutes across an osmotic barrier and translocation of the one solute is coupled to the translocation of other solute in the same direction. Such carriers are known as symport.

synalbumin
an insulin-inhibitory polypeptide in the blood; may be identical to the B chain of insulin which binds to albumin under certain conditions and which acts as an inhibitor of insulin in that form.

synaptonemal complex
a complex protein structure that forms between, and parallel to, the two paired homologus chromosomes during the early stages of meiosis.

synergism
positive interaction between two or more compounds which is more than the additive effects of individual compounds. Some time one compound is not effective, but when given in combination with some other compound effectiveness is increased.

syngenetic
a term meaning 'genetically identical', usually applied to grafts made within an inbred stain.

synthetic

polyribonucleotide
an RNA molecule made in vitro in the absence of a nuceic acid template; this may be accomplished either by using the enzyme polynucleotide phosphorylase or by chemical synthesis.

synzyme
a synthetic enzyme; a synthetic macromolecule that has enzymatic activity.

systematic name
a name created on the basis of definite rules of nomenclature to distinguish clearly one item from related ones.

systemic
when applied chemical moves inside the plant and can affect parts of the plant remote from point of application (as opposed to contact).

tachysterol
the precursor of calciferol in the irradiation of ergosterol; an isomer of ergosterol.

tactoid
a particle that appears as a spindle-shaped body under the polarizing microscope and occurs in mosaic virus, fibrin, and myosin.

tailing
(i) the addition of a stretch of identical nucleotides of the ends of a restriction fragment using the enzyme terminal transferase.
(ii) a peak characterized by a rapid rise to its peak, followed by a gradual return to the base line.

tailward growth

a polymerization mechanism in which the activated head of a monomer adds to the passive tail of a chain, thereby making its own tail the receptor for the next addition of monomer.

tanda effect

when excised root tips are floated on distilled water in petri dishes. The root tip starts moving toward negatively charge glass. It involves fast reactions of phytochrome, which are due to changes in membrane permeability when exposed to red and far-red light.

tannase

an enzyme that catalyzes the hydrolysis of tannic acid to gallic acid; found in cultures of Aspergillus and Penicillium.

tannins

water soluble polyphenolic compounds, with molecular weights in the range of 500-3000, naturally occurring with chemical and physical properties akin to those converting raw hide to leather. Tannins are of two types; (i) Hydrolyzable and (ii) Condensed tannins.

T antigen

1. an antigen occurring in the nuclei of cells that are infected with, or transformed by, certain oncogenic viruses, such as polyoma virus or SV-40; thought to be a virus-specific protein. 2. an antigen that is present on normal human red blood cells but that is unreactive unless the cells are first treated with the enzyme neuraminidase.

tape

an informational molecule that functions in replication, transcription and translation; used specifically for mRNA.

tau proteins

proteins that have molecular weight of about 60-70 KD and that are associated with and enhance the polymerization of microtubules.

taurine

a component of bile, in which it occurs combined with cholic acid to form taurocholic acid - a bile salt. It is formed from cysteins by oxidation and decarboxylation. There is some evidence that taurine may function as an inhibitory transmitter or modulator in the brain. It is a central depressant with antiepileptic activity and attempts to make analogues that might serve as useful antiepileptic drugs are underway. Taurine may also be involved in the control of Ca^{2+} fluxes in cardiac muscle cells. Also known as 2-amino ethyl sulphonic acid.

taurocholic acid $C_{26}H_{45}NO_7S$

a common bile acid with a five-carbon chain; it is the product of the conjugation of taurine with cholic acid; crystallizes from an alcohol ether solution, and decomposes at about 125°C. Also known as cholaic acid; cholytaurine.

teichoic acid

a polymer of ribitol or glycerol

phosphate with additional compounds such as glucose linked to the backbone of the polymer; found in the cell walls of some bacteria.

telophase

the terminal phase of mitosis or meiosis during which nuclei revert to the resting stage.

temperature

a measure of the intensity of heat but specifies nothing about quantity of heat. It is measured in degrees i.e., Fahrenheit, Celsius or Kelvin.

template

a micromolecule that determines the structure of another micromolecule. In protein translation, 3 nucleotides in the mRNA determine the nature of the amino acid at each position in the polypeptide (Genetic code).

template-primer

a macromolecule that functions as both a template and a primer e.g., a double-stranded DNA molecule that is replicated in vitro with DNA polymerase I uses one strand as a template and then switches (Jumps) to use the second displaced strand as a template.

teratogenic

the property of a substance or mixture of substances to produce or induce functional deviation or developmental anomalies, not heritable, in or on an animal embryo or foetus.

terminal

the end of a polymeric chain, such as the C- or N-terminal of a polypeptide chain, or the 3' or 5' - terminal of a polynucleotide strand. Also known as terminus.

terminal enzyme

an enzyme that catalyzes the addition of nucleotides to the terminal of a nucleic acid strand in the absence of a template, with nucleoside triphosphates serving as substrates.

terminal transferase

an enzyme which catalyses the sequential addition of deoxyribonucleotides to the 3' -OH end of a DNA strand without any requirement for a template. The enzyme is used to add homopolymer tails. It is used in incorporating DNA into the DNA of the cloning vector.

termination codon, stop codon punctuation codon

a sequence of three nucleotides in mRNA, which signals the end of polypeptide synthesis and release of the polypeptide in the process of protein biosynthesis 5'-UAA, S'-UAG (Amber condon) and UAG are rermination codons.

ternary mixture

a mixture of three solvents in proportions such that all are mutually soluble in one another but which will form two phase when one of the solvent is added in excess.

terpenoid

a polyisoprenoid compound that may be linear or cyclic and in which the isoprene units are usually linked in a head to -tail manner.

tertiary structure
the characteristic three-dimensional folding of the polypeptide chains in a protein molecule.

testicular hormone
any of the various hormones secreted by the testes.

testosterone $C_{19}H_{28}O_2$
the principal androgenic hormone released by the human testis; may be synthesized from cholesterol and certain other sterols.

19-nor-testosterone
a synthetic anabolic steroid. It differs from Testosterone by the absence of the C 19 methyl group. It has a higher anabolic but lower androgenic activity than testosterone.

tetanolysin
a hemolysin produced by Clostridium tetani.

tetracyclines
a group of broad-spectrum antibiotics that inhibit the binding of aminoacyl transfer RNA to 70S ribosomes. Chemically they are based on the tetracycline nucleus, and various substituent groups are introduced to produce chlortetracycline, dimethyl-chlorotetracycline, doxycycline, methacycline, minocycline, oxytetracycline, and tetracycline. The first tetracyclines (chlortetracycline, oxytetracycline and demeclocycline) were obtained from Streptomyces species. The remaining members of the group (tetracycline, rolitetracycline, methacycline, doxycycline, clomocycline, lymecycline, minocycline) are either prepared from the naturally occurring compounds or are totally synthetic.

tetrad division
the nuclear and cell division occurring when a spore mother cell divides to form 4 spores.

tetrodotoxin $C_{11}H_{17}N_3O_8$
a toxin that blocks the action potential in the nerve impulse.

tetraterpenses
terpenes comprising eight isoprene units ($C_{40}H_{61}$). Naturally occurring tetraterpenes are almost all carotenoids, and the group contains no polycyclic compounds.
tail-to-tail condensation of two molecules of geranyl-geranylpyrophosphate gives phytoene, which undergoes stepwise dehydrogenation to produce the all-transconfiguration of the true caretenoids.

tetrodotoxin
a non-protein toxin present in the ovaries and liver of the Tetroadontidae (puffer fish), and in the skin, muscle and blood of the Salamandridae.

tetrose
any of a group of monosaccharides that have a four-carbon chain; an example is erythrose, $CH_2OH\ (CHOH)_2$ CHO.

the error catastrophe theory

a senescence hypothesis proposed by Orgel accordingly ageing is due to accumulation of error committed by molecular genetic system during protein synthesis. When amount of error products excessed a certain threshold value, disorder, senescence and death occur. Errors are in the form of non-sense protein.

theoretical yield
the expression of full potential of yield under controlled environmental conditions i.e., in a phytotron.

thermal death time
the minimum time required for the sterilization of a standard suspension of bacteria at a given temperature.

thermal emissivity
the loss of heat from a leaf by radiation, conduction and convection.

thermogenic tissue
a tissue where heat is generated through cyanide-resistant respiration e.g., Arum maculate, Victoria sauromatum gauttaum, flowers or inflorescence.

thermogenicity
the generation of heat through cyanide resistant respiration in thermogenic tissues. Thermogenicity helps to volatilize the odoriferous compounds formed in them. These compounds serve to attract pollinating insects.

thermolysin
a proteolytic enzyme from the thermophilic bacterium Bacillus termoproteolyticus Rokko.

thermostable enzymes, heat stable enzymes
a small number of enzymes, mostly hydrolases, whose temperature optima lie between 60 and 80°C. They usually have a compact structure, stabilized by many disulfied bonds and/or extensive hydrophobic regions, and a low α-helix content.

theta replication
the bidirectional replication of double-stranded circular DNA.

thiamine $C_{12}H_{17}ClN_4OS$
a member of the vitamin B complex that occurs in many natural sources, frequently in the form of cocarboxylase. Also known as aneurine; vitamin B_1.

thiokinase
an enzyme which catalyses the conversion of fatty acid to fatty acetyl Co-A in glyoxysome.

thiol group, sulfhydrl group, mercapta group
SH. the functional group of thiols (mercaptans), RSH, where R is the remainder of the molecule. The functional form of lipoic acid and thioredoxin is a dithiol.

third order curve
an algebraic plane curve which has an equation in Cartesian coordinates of the form f (X,Y) = o, where f is a polynomial in X and Y. If f has degree n and it is of third degree, it is known as a cubic etc.

three point attachment
the concept that there must be

at least three points of contact (binding sites) between an enzyme and its substrate in order to account for the different reactivity of identical groups that are either parts of a symmetrical substrate molecule, or are attached to a meso carbon of the substrate. Also known as three-point landing; polyaffinity theory.

threonine $CH_3CHOHCH(NH_2)COOH$

a crystalline α-amino acid considered essential for normal growth of animals; it is biosynthesized from aspartic acid and is a precursor of isoleucine in microorganisms.

threshold

that intensity of stimulus below which there is no response by a given irritable tissue.

thrombokinase

a proteolytic enzyme in blood plasma that, together with thromboplastin, calcium, and factor V, converts prothrombin to thrombin.

thromboplastin

any of a group of lipid and protein complexes in blood that accelerate the conversion of prothrombin to thrombin. Also known as factor III; plasma thromboplastin component (PTC).

Thunburg technique

a technique used to study oxidation of a substrate occurring by dehydrogenation reactions; methylene blue, a reversibly oxidizable indicator, substitutes for molecular oxygen as the ultimate hydrogen acceptor (oxidant), becoming reduced to the colourless leuco form.

thymidine $C_{10}H_{14}N_2O_5$

a nucleoside derived from deoxyribonucleic acid; essential growth factor for certain microorganisms in mediums lacking vitamin B_{12} and folic acid.

thymidine kinase

an enzyme which catalyzes the conversion of thymidine to thymidine monophosphate by phosphorylation.

thymidylate synthetase

the enzyme which catalyzes the methylation of deoxyridine monophosphate to the thymidine monophosphate.

thymidylic acid $C_{10}H_{15}N_2O_8P$

a mononucleotide component of deoxyribonucleic acid which yields thymine, D-ribose, and phosphoric acid on complete hydrolysis.

thymine $C_5H_6N_2O_2$

a pyrimidine component of nucleic acid, first isolated from the thymus.

thyroglobulin

an iodinated protein found as the storage form of the iodinated hormones in the thyroid follicular lumen and epithelial cells.

thyroid gland

glandula thyreoidea, a well vasculated gland at the front of the neck. It is paired in amphibians and birds, and unpaired in elasmobranch fish and mammals, synthesizes, stores (in the thyroid follicles) and secretes thyroxin and triodothyronin, under the influence of the anterior pituitary hormone thyrotropin.

thyroid hormone
commonly, thyroxine or triiodothyronine, or both; a metabolically active compound formed and stored in the thyroid gland which functions to regulate the rate of metabolism.

thyroid-stimulating hormone TSH
a hormone, synthesized and secreted by the adenohypophysis, that stimulates the thyroid gland to produce the hormones thyroxine and triiodothyronine. The production of TSH is itself controlled by negative feedback from the thyroid hormones. Also known as thyrotrophin.

thyroprotein
a protein secreted in the thyroid gland, such as thyroxine.

thyrotropic hormone
a hormone produced by the adenohypophysis which regulates thyroid gland function. Also known as thyroid-stimulating hormone (TSH).

thyrotropin
a thyroid-stimulating hormone produced by the adenohypophysis.

thyroxine $C_{15}H_{11}I_4NO_4$
the active physiologic principle of the thyroid gland; used in the form of the sodium salt for replacement therapy in states of hypothyroidism or absent thyroid function.

time constant of a reaction
a measure of the duration of a reaction; for an exponential decay, the time constant is the time required for 63% of the total change to occur.

time facot effect
the effect of exposure time on the results produced by irradiation when reciprocity does not hold, so that the product of dose rate and exposure time is not constant, under these conditions, a short time of radiation at a high intensity is frquently more effective than a long time irradiation at a low intensity.

tissue tension
the mutual compressions and stretching exerted by the tissue of a living plant.

topological isomers
isomers that differs in their topological structure; duplex DNA molecules that are relaxed have positive, or negative superhelicity.

total inhibition
the inhibition of the activity of an enzyme in which a saturating concentration of inhibitor can cause the reaction velocity to become zero.

total soil moisture stress (TSMS)
a sum of the osmotic pressure of the soil solution and soil moisture tension. TSMS

includes gravitational, adsorptive and hydrostatic forces holding water to the soil.

toxic proteins

mostly low M_r single chain, nonenzymic proteins, produced especially by snakes and invertebrate animals, but also by some plants (phytotoxins) and virulent strains of bacteria. With the exception of bacterial enterotoxins and Botulinus toxins these show practically no oral activity, and are only toxic when injected, i.e., when the digestive tract it bypassed.

toxigenicity

the production of a toxin, particularly the production of a toxin by bacteria.

toxin

any of various poisonous substances produced by certain plant and animal cells, including bacterial toxins, phytotoxins, and zootoxins.

toxohormone

a toxic substance that inhibits the activity of the enzyme catalase; apparently a polypeptide that can be extracted from cancer cells and that may also occur in normal cells.

toxoid

a toxin that has lost its toxic properties as a result of denaturation or chemical modification but that has retained its antigenic properties.

toxoplasmin

the Toxoplasma antigent; used in a skin test to demonstrate delayed hypersensitivity to toxoplasmosis.

trace elements, microelements

elements required in very small quantities by living organisms. They act catalytically, or are components of catalytic systems and other mineral nutrients is not always possible.

tracer

an isotope incorporated into a compound of biological importance, so that the passage of the isotope atoms can be followed through the physiological processes of the plants.

tracking dye

a dye used as a marker in gel electrophoresis.

transacylase

an enzyme that catalyzes the transfer of an acyl group from one compound to another.

transaldolase

an enzyme that catalyzes the transfer of a dihydroxyacetone group from a ketose phosphate to carbon number one of an aldose phosphate.

transamidation

the reaction in which the guanido group of arginine is transferred to glycine thereby forming guanidinoacetic acid.

transaminase

one of a group of enzymes that catalyzes the transfer of the amino group of an amino acid to a keto acid to form another amino acid. Also known as aminotransferase.

transduce

(i) to transfer genetic material from one bacterium to another by transduction.

(ii) to transform one form of energy into another.

transduction

the transfer of DNA from one bacterium to another by means of a bacteriophage (phage). Some bacterial DNA is incorporated into the phage. When the host bacterium is destroyed the phage infects another bacterium and introduces the DNA from its previous host, which may become incorporated into the new host's DNA.

transferase

any of various enzymes that catalyze the transfer of a chemical group from one molecule to another.

transfer cells

these are characterized by protuberances of the cell wall which may extend for a considerable distance into the cell, increasing the surface area of plasmalemma, responsible for phloem loading and situated at the end of minor vein. Transfer cells are of two types. Type A and Type B.

transferrin

any of various beta globulins in blood serum which bind and transport iron to the bone marrow and storage areas.

transformation

conceptually the simplest form of genetic transfer. "Naked" DNA from a donor cell enters a recipient cell and is incorporated into the recipient DNA by genetic recombination. There is no other carrier substance or structure involved; small fragments of the donor DNA simply penetrate the membrane (and wall if it is present) of the recipient cell.

transgenesis

an organism that contains some genetic material that has been experimentally transferred into it from some other source.

transition

in replication or transcription, an error in which one purine is substituted for another or one pyrimidine for another.

transition state

the state of activated condition of molecules at any given instant having some energy. At this state formation or breakdown of a chemical bond is very easy.

transketolase

an enzyme that cleaves a substrate at the position of the carbonyl carbon and transports a two-carbon fragment to an acceptor compound to form a new compound.

translation

in the wider sense equivalent to Protein biosynthesis. In the narrower sense, it is the decoding process whereby each codon in mRNA is translated into one of 20 amino acids during protein synthesis on polysomes.

translation error model

a model for the evolution of the genetic code according to which the code evolved so as to minimize errors during translation.

translocase

the enzyme that catalyzes the GTP-dependent translocation reaction in protein synthesis in which the peptidyl transfer RNA is shifted from the A site to the P site on the ribosome, and in which the messenger RNA is shifted simultneously by one codon.

translocators

the carriers situated on the surface of plasma membrane or organelle membrane responsible for transport of ions across the membrane.

transmethylase

a transferase enzyme involved in catalyzing chemical reactions in which methyl groups are transferred from a substrate to a new compound.

transmethylation

a metabolic reaction in which a methyl group is transferred from one compound to another; methionine and choline are important donors of methyl groups.

transplant

(i) the part of an animal that is transferred within the same, or to a different, animal by transplantation.

(ii) planting of the seedling from nursury bed into the field.

transplantation

(i) the transfer of a part of an animal to another site of the same animal or to a site of a different animal.

(ii) act of transferring the seedling from nursury into the field.

transplantation immunity

the reactions of the immune response that occur in the recipient of a transplant and that are caused by the antigens of the transplant.

transposable elements

the mobile segments of DNA which inactivate or alter gene-expression by insertion into a genetic locus. These induce mutation of specific target genes. In brief it is also known as transposon.

transversion

a point mutation in either DNA or RNA in which there is a replacement of a purine by a pyrimidine or vice versa. In double-stranded nucleic acids, a complementary base is then inserted into the second strand so that a new base pair is produced.

trehalose

a non-reducing disaccharide of glucose that occurs in the hemolymph of many insects. Almost 30% of the cocoon of the parasitic beetle Larinus maculates consists of the carbohydrate trehalose. Upon acid hydrolysis, the trehalose gives D-glucose as the major product.

tree diagram

a graphical representation of nuclear magnetic resonance data; shows the individual effects of each coupling constant on the overall nuclear magnetic resonance pattern.

tricholomic acid

erythro-dihydroibotenic acid, a compound isolated from the Basidomycete (mushroom) Tricholoma muscarium. It possesses flavor promoting activity similar to, but much more active than, that of sodium glutamate. It also has a synergistic effect on the flavour improving property of inosinic acid and guanosine 5'-phosphate.

trichome

(i) a hair.

(ii) in cyanophyta, a single row of cells which with their sheath make up the filament.

trigger reaction

a reaction that initiates another reaction or a sequence of reactions.

triose

a group of monsaccharide compounds that have a three-carbon chain length.

triphosphopyridine nucleotide $C_{12}H_{28}N_7O_{17}P_3$

a grayish-white powder, soluble in methanol and in water; a coenzyme and an important component of enzymatic systems concerned with biological oxidation-reduction systems. Abbreviated TPN. Also known as codehydrogenase II; coenzyme II; triphosphopyridine dinucleotide.

triple helix

a structure that is composed of three intertwined helical chains, as that of tropocollagen and certain synthetic polynucleotides.

triploid state

the chromosome state in which each of the various chromosomes, except the sex chromosome, is represented three time.

trisaccharide

a carbohydrate which, on hydrolysis yields three molecules of monosaccharides.

trivial name

a working or common name that is not based on rules of nomenclature.

tropic hormone

a peptide hormone that stimulates the target gland to secrete its hormone; for example, thyrotropin of the pituitary stimulates secretion of thyroxine by the thyroid.

tropocollagen

the fundamental units of collagen fibrils.

tropomyosin

a muscle protein similar to myosin and implicated as being part of the structure of the Z bands separating sarcomeres from each other.

troponin

a protein species located at specific stations every 36.5 nanometers on the actin helix in muscle sarcomere.

true solution

when solute particles are of molecular or ionic dimensions and do not settle down on standing. These pass through the perchment paper.

trypsin

a proteolytic enzyme which catalyzes the hydrolysis of peptide linkages in proteins and partially hydrolyzed proteins; derived from trypsinogen by the action of enterokinase in intestinal juice.

trypsinogen

the zymogen of trypsin, secreted in the pancreatic juice. Also known as protrypsin.

tryptophan $C_{11}H_{12}O_2N_2$

an amino acid obtained from casein, fibrin, and certain other proteins; it is a precursor of indoleacetic acid, serotonin, and nicotinic acid.

tryptophan 2, 3-oxygenase, tryptophan oxygenase, tryptophan pyrrolase, L-tryptophan : oxygen 2, 3-oxidoreductase (decyclizing), (EC 1.13.11.11)

an enzyme catalysing the oxidation of L-tryptophan to N. formylkynurenine, the first stage in the total degradation of L-tryptophan in animals and microorganisms; this is also the first stage in the conversion of L-tryptophan into the nicotinamide moiety of NAD and NADP in molds and in some mammals, and in the conversion of L-tryptophan into Ommochromes in insects.

trysinogen

relatively inactive form of trypsin; synthesized in the pancreas, and is converted to trypsin in the gut by enzymic removal of some terminal amino acids. Trypsinogen is converted into the active form by action of the enzyme enteropeptidase (enterokinase)

tumour antigens

carcinoembryonic antigens, which serves as an aid to the early recognition of liver carcinoma and teratoblastomas (tumours of reproductive cells, especially in the testes and ovaries). They are embryonal plasma proteins produce in the placenta during pregnancy and in some organs of the embryo, and on longer detectable shortly after birth. They can be formed again later in life in response to malignant tumours.

tungston lamp

a miniature bulb used in spectrophotometer as source of radiation in visible range.

turgor pressure

the actual pressure exerted by swelling protoplast on the cell wall as a result of osmosis. TP is always equal to wall pressure but opposite in direction.

turnover

(i) the rate at which a substrate is acted upon by an enzyme and measured by the turnover number.

(ii) the rate at which an

intracellular protein is renewed; the balance between the rate of degradation and the rate of synthesis.

turnover number

the number of molecules of a substrate acted upon in a period of 1 minute by a single enzyme molecule, with the enzyme working at a maximum.

twisting number

the total number of turns of the double-helix of DNA. It is equal to the number of base pairs in duplex DNA divided by the number of base pairs per turn of the double-helix.

type B transfer cells

these resemble in structure with parenchyma cells, does not always abut onto sieve, but when they do the convoluted will is most prominent on the sieve element side and there are few, if any, protoplasmic connections.

tyrosinase

an enzyme found in plants, molds, crustaceans, mollusk, and some bacteria which, in the presence of oxygen, catalyzes the oxidation of monophenols and polyphenols with the introduction of —OH groups and the formation of quinones.

tyrosine $C_9H_{11}NO_3$

a phenolic alpha amino acid found in many proteins; a precursor of the hormones epinephrine, norepinephrine, thyroxine, and triiodothyronine, and of the black pigment melanin.

tyrosinosis

a genetically inherited metabolic defect of tyrosine catabolism in man that is characterized by accumulation of metabolites that adversely affect the activities of several enzymes and transport system. The proposed metabolic defects is in fumarylacetacetate hydrolase.

tyvelose

a dideoxy sugar found in bacterial lipopolysaccharides.

ubiquinone

one of various benzoquinone derivatives with side chains of differing lengths that act as electron carriers in the mitochondria of the cells. Also known as coenzyme Q.

ubiquitin

one of the heat-shock proteins in plants. Process of ubiquitin formation i.e., ubiquitination tends to increase environmental stress tolerance.

ultradian

noncircadian rhythm with very short period cycles (minutes or hours) e.g., changes in metabolic components.

unavailable nutrients

minerals which for some reason such as insolubility, cannot be absorbed by the plant from the soil.

uncoupler

a chemical compound which prevents oxidative phosphorylation of ADP to ATP in the respiratory chain without affecting electron transport. It thus uncouples respiration and ATP formation; respiration continues or is even increased, but yields no energy. Some important U. are 2, 4 dinitrophenol (abb. DNP), dicumarol, carbonyl cyanophenylhydrazone, salicylanilide etc.

uncoupling

the separation of the two proceses that constitute oxidative phosphorylation such that ATP synthesis is dissociated from the electron transport system at one or more of the phosphorylation sites. As a result of uncoupling, ATP synthesis is inhibited but electron transport and respiration are allowed to proceed and may even be stimulated.

uncoupling agent

an inhibitor that binds about the uncoupling of ATP synthesis from the electron transport system at one or more of the phosphorylation sites.

unidentified reading-frame

an open reading-frame recognized from a DNA sequence for which no genetic function is known.

unit cell

the smallest group of atoms or molecules which defines a complete crystal lattice. By regular repetition in three dimensions the complete lattice can be built up from unit cell.

universal recipient

an individual of the AB type in the ABO blood group system, who can receive blood from any donor.

unstable isotopes

elements with high atomic number having neutrons to proton ratio in excess of one. These are generally artificially produced. Such is otopes emit particle and/or electro magnetic radiation.

upstream

describing a location or a sequence of units in the opposite direction to that in which a process occurs.

(i) during transcription, the location or sequence of deoxyribonucleotides on the transcribed strand of DNA from the 5' - to 3' -end.

(ii) during translation, the location or sequence of ribonucleotide on the mRNA from 3' -to-5' end.

(iii) during replication, the location in a direction that is opposite to that of the replication fork movement.

(iv) in a polypeptide chain, the sequence of amino acids in which they are linked together, from the C- to the N-terminal.

(v) in the electron transport system, the sequence of electron carriers in the direction opposite to the flow of electrons, from oxygen to metabolite.

uracil $C_4H_4N_2O_2$

a pyrimidine base important as a component of ribonucleic acid.

uracil-rich code
an early version of the genetic code according to which the codons of all the amino acids contain at least one uracil nucleotide.

urea cycle, arginine urea cycle, ornithine cycle, krebs-henseleit cycle
a metabolic cycle present in mammals and other ureotelic animals (e.g., adult amphibians), which results in the synthesis of urea from carbon dioxide, ammonia and the α-amino nitrogen of L-aspartic acid. The process is energy-dependent.

urease
an enzyme that catalyzes the degradation of urea to ammonia and carbon dioxide; obtained from the seed of jack bean.

ureide plants
plant families that accumulate allantoin and/or allantoic acid, and use these compounds as nitrogen metabolism. It is excrted in the urine in certain animal families, particularly birds and reptiles. It has been isolated from bird excrements (guano). It is generated from xanthine by the enzyme xanthine oxidase in aerobic purine catabolism.

uric acid $C_5H_4N_4O_3$
a white, crystalline compound, the excretory end product in amino acid metabolism by uricotelic species. Also known as 8-hydroxyxanthine.

uricase
an enzyme present in the liver, spleen, and kidney of most mammals except man; converts uric acid to allantoin in the presence of gaseous oxygen.

uricosuric acid
the substances which help in the enhanced excretion of excess uric acid through urination and thus reduce the urea concentration in the plasma. There are two important agents which are frequently used in hyperuricemia, which are sulphinpyrazone and probenecid, both of which enhance the level of penicillin in plasma by inhibiting secretion.

uridine $C_9H_{12}N_2O_6$
a crystalline nucleoside composed of one molecule of uracil and one molecule of D-ribose; a component of ribonucleic acid.

uridine diphosphate
the chief transferring coenzyme in carbohydrate metabolism. Abbreviated UDP.

uridine diphosphoglucose
a compound in which a-glucopyranose is esterified at carbon atom 1, with the terminal phosphate group of uridine-5'-pyrophosphate (that is, uridine diphosphate); occurs in animal, plant and microbial cells; functions as a key in the transformation of the glucose to other sugars. Abbreviated UDPG.

urobilin

a bile pigment produced by reduction of bilirubin by intestinal bacteria and excreted by the kidneys or removed by the liver.

urobilinogen
a chromogen, formed in feces and present in urine, from which urobilin is formed by oxidation.

urocanic acid $C_6H_6N_2O_2$
a crystalline compound formed as an intermediate in the degradative pathway of histidine.

urochrome $C_{43}H_{51}O_{26}N$
yellow pigment found in normal urine.

urokinase
an enzyme, present in human urine, that catalyzes the conversion of plasminogen to plasmin.

uronic acids
aldehyde carboxylic acids formed by oxidation of the terminal primary alcohol group of aldoses. They give the usual reactions for sugars and are widely distributed as components of glycosides, polyuronides, polysaccharides and mucopolysaccharides.

uropepsin
the end product of the secretion of pepsinogen into the blood by gastric cells; occurs in the urine.

uroporphyrinogen
an intermediate in the biosynthesis of the porphyrins that is formed by the linking of four molecules of porphobilinogen.

ursolic acid $C_{30}H_{48}O_3$
a pentacyclic terpene that catalyllizes from absolute alcohol solution, found in leaves and berries of plants; used in pharmaceutical and food industries as an emulsifying agent.

usnic acid $C_{18}H_{16}O_7$
yellow crystals, insoluble in water, slightly soluble in alcohol and ether, melts about 198°C; found in lichens; used as an antibiotic. Also known as usninic acid.

vaccine
a living or dead preparation used to stimulate active immunity in animals. Liver vaccines consists of living organisms, which replicate in the recipient animal. They comprise either attenuated strains of disease-producing organism, or a species of organism closely related to the disease-producing organism that causes the development of an immunity embracing the related organism.

vaculoe
a fluid-filled space in the cytoplasm of cell. A single vacuole, taking up most of the volume of the cell is present in many mature plant cells, and contains cell-sap which is isotonic with the cytoplasm. It is enclosed by a semipermeable membrane and acts as store house of materials. (i) that accumulates in excess from outside. (ii) produced in excess by

protoplasm. Its size is relatively small in meristematic cells.

vagotonine

an endocrine substance which is thought to be elaborated by cells of the pancreas and which regulates autonomic tonus.

valence

the relative combining capacity of an atom, ion or radical, including; (i) the number of electron pairs shared with another atom or atoms; and (ii) the number of electrons given or taken up by an atom or group of atoms.

valine $C_5H_{11}NO_2$

an amino acid considered essential for normal growth of animals, and biosynthesized from pyruvic acid. Also known as 2-aminoisovaleric acid; α-aminoisovaleric acid; 2-amino-3-methylbutyric acid.

vanadium V

a trace element required for normal growth by animals. Most dietary items contain less than 100 ng V/g. It stimulates the oxidation of phospholipids, and decreases cholesterol synthesis by inhibiting squalene synthase (a liver microsomal enzyme system); it also stimulates acetoacetyl-CoA deacylase in liver mitochondria. Its deficiency leads to abnormal bone growth.

Van-der-Waals or London forces

the weak attraction forces between electrically neutral or symmetrical molecules of liquid or gases. This attraction is weak about 1Kcal mol^{-1}, and effective only if molecules are very close together. In general, physical properties of liquids and gases depend upon these forces.

vascular ray initial

a cell of cambium which divides to give daughter cells which are converted into medullary ray cells.

vasopressin

a peptide hormone which is elaborated by the posterior pituitary and which has a pressore effect; used medicinally as an antidiuretic. Also known as antidiuretic hormone (ADH).

vasotocin

a hormone from the neurosecretory cells of the posterior pituitary of lower vertebrates; increases permeability to water in amphibian skin and in bladder.

vector

1. organism responsible for parasite transfer from one host to another.

2. plasmid or other self-replicating DNA molecule that transfers DNA between cells in nature or in recombinant DNA technology. In the latter connection it may be called a cloning vector or cloning vehicle.

veratrum alkaloids

a group of steroid alkaloids found in the solanaceae, and in the genera veratrum (hellebores) and Fritillaria (fritillary). They are structural derivatives of the parent hydrocarbon cholestane (steroids); in some members ring C is contracted and ring D is expanded (C-nor-D-homo type). These have a positive ionotropic action on the heart, and cause a decrease of blood pressure by reflex inhibition of the vasomotor centres. They were used for treatment of hypertension, but have been replaced by rauwolfia alkaloids and other drugs.

verification
the deacylation of a misacylated transfer RNA molecule by its aminoacyl-tRNA synthetase, thereby regenerating the uncharged transfer RNA molecule.

vernalin
a hypothetical factor synthesised during vernalization and is not diluted by vegetative growth that takes place during the time the plant is exposed to a non-inductive cycles. This factor is transmissible from a donor to the receptor plant across a graft union. It leads to change in the condition of the cells such that they are able to produce florigen when subsequently returned to favourable conditions.

vesicle
(i) a small sac; a membranous cavity.
(ii) a closed bilayer structure. The structure may consists of a single-bilayer (Unilamellar vesicle) of several bilayer (multimellar vesicle). Unilamellar vesicle may be small (SUV: 0.02-0.05 μm) or large (LUV; > 0.06 μm); multimellar vesicle ranges in size from 0.1 to 5.0 μm. Vesicles formed from synthetic surfactants are known as surfactant vesicles; those composed of phospholipids are called liposomes.

vigour
the efficiency of growth potentialities shown by seeds after storage. Viable seed shows variations in vigour. More vigourous seed establishes the crop stand very quickly.

villin
the calcium-dependent, actinfragmenting protein, also capable of nucleating actin assembly. It is abundant in intestinal brush border microvilli.

vincristine, leurocristine
a dimeric indole alkaloid closely related to vinblastine, from Vinca rose a (Vinca alkaloids). It is used mainly for the treatment of acute leukemia in children, and against various other neoplasmic growths.

viridicatine
a quinoline alkaloid from moulds of the genius Penicillium. It is biosynthesized from anthranilic acid, phenylalanine and the methyl group of

methionine. Biosynthesis is catalysed by the enzyme cyclopenase.

virus

one of a group of small particles of protein and nucleic acid which can produce disease in many plants and animals. Incapable of replication outside the host cells.

virus coat proteins, capsides

proteins with the largest known M_r values (up to 40 × 10^6). They comprise many, usually identical, subunits, called capsomeres (M_r 13000-60000). V.c.p. of tobacco mosaic virus consists of 2130 capsomers of M_r 17500. V.c.p. lie on the exterior of the virus particle, enclosing the DNA or RNA.

viscous

(i) possessing viscosity;
(ii) thick, sticky; glutinous.

visual cycle

a series of reactions occurring in the cone cells of the retina. These cells function in sensing new intensity light but do not sense colours. In the visual cycle, an oxidised form of retinol, retinal or vitamin A aldehyde, is the active component bound to a protein called opsin. The retinal-opsin complex called rhodopsin, is present in stacked intracellular membranes in the rod cells. When the rhodopsin is excited by the visible light, the retinal in which the double bond at the 11 position in the -*cis* form, undergoes a number of complex, rapid molecular changes and is finally isomerized to form II-trans-retinal. These alternations which change the geometrical configuration of the retinal are believed to accompany a change in the shape of entire rhodopsin molecule. This event is a molecular trigger producing in the optic nerve endings an impulse that is transmitted to the brain. The all-trans-retinal formed during illumination is then enzymatically converted back into 11-*cis* retinal in dark reactions.

visual pigment

any of various photosensitive pigments of vertebrate and invertebrate photoreceptors.

visual yellow

an intermediary substance, formed from rhodopsin in the retina after exposure to light; it is ultimately broken down to retinene and vitamin A.

vitamin

an organic compound present in variable, minute quantities in natural foodstuffs and essential for the normal process of growth and maintenance of the body; vitamins do not furnish energy, but are essential for energy transformation and regulation of metabolism.

vitamin A $C_{20}H_{29}OH$

a pale-yellow alcohol that is soluble in fat and insoluble in water; found in liver oils and carotenoids, and produced synthetically; it is a component of visual pigments and is essential for normal growth and maintenance of epithelial tissue. Also known as antiinfective vitamin; antixerophthalmic vitamin; retinol.

vitamin B_2

a vitamin of the B-complex that is a constituent of the flavoprotein coenzymes FMN (flavin mononucleotide) and FAD (flavin dinucleotide), which are essential to the transfer of hydrogen in the metabolism of carbohydrates, fats, and amino acids, and in cellular respiration. It is synthesized by most green plants and microorganism, including those in the gut of animals. Also known as riboflavin.

vitamin B_6

a vitamin which exists as three chemically related and water-soluble forms found in food; pyridoxine, pyridoxal, and pyridoxamine, dietary requirements and physiological activities are uncertain.

vitamin B_8

the nucleotide adenylic acid that is no longer classified as a vitamin.

vitamin B_9

a designation that has not been used for B vitamin.

vitamin B_{10}

an activity that promotes growth and feathering in the chicken and that is probably a mixture of folic acid and vitamin B_{12}.

vitamin B_{12}

a group of closely related polypyrrole compounds containing trivalent cobalt; the antipernicious anemia factor, essential for normal hemopoiesis. Also known as cobalamin; cyanocobalamin; extrinsic factor.

vitamin B complex

a group of water-soluble vitamins that include thiamine, riboflavin, nicotinic acid, pyridoxine, panthothenic acid, inositol, p-aminobenzoic acid, biotin, folic acid, and vitamin B_{12}.

vitamin C

a water-soluble vitamin, which is widely required in metabolism. It is required for metabolic oxidation-reduction reactions, transport of iron, synthesis of corticosteroids, and formation of intercellular substances and collagen in connective tissues, bone, cartilage, and dentine. In most vertebrates it is synthesized from glucose in quantities sufficient to meet normal requirements; exceptions include humans, other primates, guinea pigs, some species of fish, and possibly very young animals, such as newborn calves and newly hatched chicks. The absence of vitamin in human diet gives rise to scurvy, a disease characterized by edema, subcutaneous hemorrhage, anemia, and pathological changes in the teeth and gums. The biochemical role played by this vitamin is undoubtedly related to it being a good reducing agent. Its oxidized form, dehydroascorbic acid, is capable of being reduced again by various reductants including glutathione, and the two forms of the ascorbate constitute a reversible oxidation reduction system. Also known as ascorbic acid.

vitamin D

either of two fat-soluble, sterol-like compounds, calciferol or ergocalciferol (vitamin D_2) and cholecalciferol (vitamin D_3); occurs in fish liver oils and is essential for normal calcium and phosphorus deposition in bones and teeth. Also known as antirachitic vitamin.

vitamin E $C_{29}H_{50}O_2$

any of a series of eight related compounds called tocopherols, α-tocopherol having the highest biological activity; occurs in wheat germ and other oils and is believed to be needed in certain human physiological processes.

vitamin F

the essential fatty acids, which cannot be synthesized in the body. These include the unsaturated fatty acids, in particular linoleic, linolenic and arachidonic acid. They occur in high concentrations in vegetable oils. Deficiency of essential fatty acids in rats leads to loss of hair, disturbances of water balance, and reproductive failure.

vitamin H (biotin; bios II; coenzyme R)

a sulfur-containing water soluble vitamin. Chemically it is a cyclic urea derivative; 2'-oxo-3, 4-imidazoline-2-tetrahydrothiphene-n-valeric acid. It is most commonly known as biotin. Biotin is biosynthesized from cysteine, pimelic acid and carbamyl phosphate. It acts as the prosthetic group of carboxylation enzymes the carbonyl group of biotin forms an amide bond with the ε-amino-group of biotin forms an amide bond with the ε-amino-group of a lysine residue in the enzyme protein.

vitamin K

any of three yellowish oils which are fat-soluble, nonsterod, an nonsaponifiable; it is essential for formation of prothrombin. Also known as antihemorrhagic vitamin; prothrombin factor.

vitamin L_1

a liver filtrate whose activity is believed to be necessary for lactation and is probably related to anthranilic acid.

vitamin L_2

a yeast filtrate whose activity is believed to be necessary for lactation and is probably related to adenosine.

vitamin P

a substance, such as citrin or one or more of its components, believed to be concerned with maintenance of the normal state of the walls of small blood vessels.

vitamin R
an activity that promotes bacterial growth and that is apparently related to the folic acid.

vitamin S
an activity that promotes the growth of chicks and that is related to the peptide streptogenin.

vitamin T
a group of activities isolated from termites, yeasts, or molds and reported to improve protein assimilation in the rat.

volume rate
the amount of liquid applied per unit area. Spray volume rates are often described as high, medium, low, very low or ultra low (ULV), but to avoid confusion they are best specified, in litre per hectare.

volutin
a basophilic substance, thought to be a nucleic acid, occurring as granules in the cytoplasm and vacuoles of algae and other microorganisms.

vulgaxanthin
a yellow betaxanthin from sugar beet (Beta vulgaris).

wall effect
if rate of solvent flow differs between centre and wall of the column. Then spreading and curving of zone as it migrates downward occurs.

wall pressure
during expansion of cell, cell wall exerts inward pressure on the protoplast to maintain proper shape of cell.

Warburg's direct method
a manometric method for studying the cellular respiration of tissue slices or cells to which the only gases exchanged are oxygen and carbon dioxide, and in which respiration is measured by the absorption of carbon dioxide in alkali.

warfarin
a dicoumarol derivatives, used as a rat poison by a mechanism similar to dicoumarol, i.e., there is uncontrolled internal bleeding due to lack of the clotting factors II, VII, IX and X.

water
universal solvent and fluid of life has unique properties; (i) high specific and vapourisation heat; (ii) less dense when solid than as a liquid; (iii) high cohesion and adhesion. All these properties are due to hydrogen bonding.

water-soluble B
an early designation for a fraction of water-soluble vitamins prepared from egg yolk.

wave number
the number of waves per unit length; the reciprocal of the wavelength.

wet application
a method of sample application

in electrophoresis in which the sample is applied to a previously wetted support.

wetting agent
chemicals used to reduce surface tension of solutions so that these stick to leaf surface when sprayed.

Wilson disease
a disease in which free copper (instead of bound copper) is deposited in the liver, brain, and eye where it disrupts the function of these tissues.

wilting coefficient
the percentage water in a soil when a plant begins to wilt.

winter green plant
small plants which retain their green leaves throughout the winter.

Wolfson's method
an analytical procedure for determining γ-globulins in serum by precipitating them with ammonium sulphate and sodium chloride.

wood
a mixed polymer with lignin as a structural component. The deposition of lignin in the cellulose matrix of the cell wall is called lignification.

wound cork
a layer of cork formed below and around wounds, if not too large. It heals the damage, and prevents the entry of parasites into the plant.

xanthine
a purine that is an intermediate compound in the oxidative degradation of adenine and guanine to uric acid. The molybdenum-containing enzymes xanthine oxidase oxidizes xanthine to uric acid, and also hypoxanthine to xanthine. Elevated uric acid levels in blood can be treated with allopurinol, an inhibitor of xanthine oxidase.

xanthine oxidase
a flavoprotein enzyme catalyzing the oxidation of certain purines.

xanthophyll $C_{40}H_{56}O_2$
any of a group of yellow, alcohol-soluble carotenoid pigments that are oxygen derivatives of the carotenes, and are found in certain flowers, fruits, and leaves. Also known as lutein.

xanthoprotein reaction
a qualitative test for protein, using concentrated nitric acid. The resulting yellow colour is due to the nitration of aromatic amino acid residues.

xanthurenic acid $C_{10}H_7NO_4$
sulfur yellow crystals with a melting point of 286°C; soluble in aqueous alkali hydroxides and carbonates; excreted by pyridoxine-deficient animals after ingestion of tryptophan.

X-chromosome
the larger of the two types of sex chromosome, similar in appearance to the other chromosomes and carrying many sex-linked genes.

xenobiotic
(i) the non-biological production of free radical of oxygen e.g., from industrial

pollution, acid rain, urban transportation; cigarette smoke and bipyridilium herbicides.
(ii) a synthetic compound that is foreign to living systems, e.g., drugs, insecticides, anesthetics, and petroleum products.

xenogamy
pollination of a flower from a flower of the same but of another plant.

xerophyte
a plant which can live where water supply is scanty or there is physiological drought.

xylem
conductive tissue in higher plant through which water and solutes move from root and shoot. It is dead tissue and consists of vessels, and/or tracheid, fibres and some paraenchyma.

xylose $C_5H_{10}O_5$
a pentose sugar found in many woody materials; combustible, white crystals with a sweet taste; soluble in water and alcohol; melts about 148°C; used as a nonnutritive sweetener and in dyeing and tanning. Also known as wood sugar.

xylosyl nucleosides
nucleosides in which the sugar component is xylose. They may act as analogs of purine or pyrimidine ribosides.

X-Y-Z cell theory
a theory according to which immunocytes are classified into three categories: X-cells are immunologically competent cells that are not yet engaged in any specific immunological response; Y-cells are immunologically activated, or primed, cells as a result of an interaction between X-cells and antigen; and Z-cells are antibody-producing cells formed as a result of a second stimulation of the Y-cells by antigen.

Y-chromosome
the smaller of the two types of sex chromosomes, found only in the heterogametic sex.

yellow enzyme
one of a group of flavoprotein dehydrogenases that contain a yellow flavin prosthetic group.

yield coefficient
the weight of bacteria obtained from a culture divided by the weight of a limiting material that was utilized by the bacteria during their growth.

yield maximisation
it implies striving for the highest possible yield in purely quantitative terms.

yield optimisation
the best yield obtained by means of providing the best conditions. It includes quality of the yield.

yohimbine
a rauwolfia alkaloid. It has five chiralc enters and therefore many stereoisomers; seven of these occur naturally, the most important being Corynanthine, obtained chiefly from the bark of the tropical tree, Corynanthe yohimbe. It

is vasodilatory and has been used in the treatment of arteriosclerosis, in veterinary medicine and by African natives as an aphrodisiac.

yolk

1. nutritive material stored in an ovum. 2. The yellow spherical mass of food material that makes up the central portion of the egg of a bird or reptile.

Youngburg and Youngburg method

a method for determination of serum phospholipids, lipid phosphorus. The lipids are extracted into an ethanolether mixture and digested with sulphuric acid and hydrogen peroxide. The phosphorus, which has been oxidized to phosphate, is then determined colorimetrically by any standard method.

Z scheme

the series formulation for the photosynthetic reactions of photosystems I and II of chloroplast.

zein

the principal protein of maize (corn). It is deficient in the essential amino acids lysine and tryptophan.

zero mobility position

the position occupied by an uncharged substance in an electrophoresis experiment.

zero time binding DNA

the fraction of DNA that contains repeating sequences and, therefore, forms duplexes at the very start of the reaction.

zinc Zn

an essential bioelement for the growth and development of plants, animals and microorganisms. It has a high affinity for nitrogen and sulfur ligands, and occurs in the cell in association with many different compounds, e.g., proteins (insulin), amino acids, nucleic acids.

zinc sulphate turbidity test

a liver function test that is based on the production of turbidity when serum from individuals with one of several forms of hepatitis is treated with a barbiturate buffer containing zinc sulphate.

zippering

the formation of a helical DNA or RNA duplex from the two separated and complementary strands. Also known as zippering up.

zonal soil

a broad group of soils occurring in one of the main climatic regions of the world.

zonation

(i) the formation of bands of different colour on the surface of a plant.

(ii) the formation, by fungi in culture, or a concentric band of colour, texture, abundance of spores etc.

(iii) the occurrence of vegetation in bands each having its characteristic dominant species.

(iv) a stage in the development of an oogonium.

(v) when the contents are arranged in two or more well marked zones.

zone of equivalence

when increasing amount of a protein are added to the same amount of corresponding immune serum, the precipitates first increase in quantity and then decrease progressively. The part of the curve where proportion of antigens to antibodies gives maximum precipitation is referred to as zone of equivalence.

zoom lens

a cinematic or television camera lens whose focal length can be adjusted continuously to vary the magnification without loss of focus.

zoospore

an asexually produced motile spore.

zwitterion

a dipolar ion which has a positive charge on one pattern of molecule and a negative charge on another.

zygomatic gland

a salivary gland lying below the orbit in carnivores. It represents a condensation of the small dorsal buccal glands of other species.

zygotene

the second stage of the first prophase of meiosis, in which the homologous chrmosomes form pairs (bivalents).

zymase

a heat-labile enzyme fraction that is obtained from yeast and that catalyzes the reactions of alcoholic fermentation.

zymass

a complex of enzymes that catalyze glycosis.

zymogen

the inactive precursor of an enzyme; liberates an active enzyme on reaction with an appropriate kinose. Also known as proenzyme.

zymogen granules

granules of zymogen in gland cells, particularly those of the pancreatic acini and of the gastric chief cells.

zymosan

cell wall fractions of yeasts that are capable of activating the alternative complement pathway.

zymosterol $C_{27}H_{43}OH$

an unsaturated sterol obtained from yeast fat; yields cholesterol on hydrogenation.

PART 6

PHILOSOPHY

abadhita (unsublatability)
it is a state of experience wherein the object of experience cannot be sublated or contradicted by subsequent perception. According to Advaita Vedanta, the valid knowledge (prama) can never be sublated or contradicted.

abandonment
the term used for one of the central ideas of atheistic existentialists, like Sartre. As God does not exist there can be no objective values or meaning to life; thus man is thrust out into the world, "abandoned". He must make decisions, distinguish right from wrong, but as there is no guiding hand he is thrown back entirely on himself.

abbey
1. Monastic community governed by an abbot or abbess.
2. Building occupied by a community of monks or nuns so governed.

abduction
it is a syllogism in which the major premise is true but the minor premise is only probable.

abhihitanvaya-vada (the theory of restructuring of the spoken)
according to Bhatta Mimamsa, words have their independent meaning. When they are brought together in a sentence their meaning is restructured in such a way that it expresses one connected idea.

abhinava-anyatha-khyati (the neo-theory of apprehension otherwise)
it is a Dvaite theory of error. This error is a resultant effect of asat-khyati and anyatha-khyati. In asat-khyati, the object of the erroneous cognition is considered to be unreal, and in anyatha-khyati, the object of error appears to be as something other than what it is. In this way, what is seen in erroneous cognition, is unreal, but the substance in which it occurs is real.

abhinivesha
Sanskrit term signifying the love of life and fear of death. One of the five kinds of delusive attachment of the Yoga system.

ability
in its general sense, ability is a psychic capacity of an individual that regulates his behaviour and serves as the best condition for his actions. Senses are regarded as the most important ontogenetic abilities of humans.

absolute
a term which was used by post-Kantian idealist metaphysicians to cover the totality of what really exist, a totality thought of as a unitary system somehow both generating all apparent diversity.

absolute space
space considered as an entity within which bodies are placed, and which itself has real properties, such as shape or extension.

absolute suchness

ashvaghosa's name for reality.

absolutism

it is a philosophical doctrine that is opposed to any form of relativism. In epistemology, it proclaims that all knowledge is absolute and objective. For example, in Cartesian philosophy, the knowledge of innate ideas is universal, necessary and indubitable. Hence such knowledge is absolute. In ontology or metaphysics, this doctrine claims that reality is one and immutable. For example, in Hegle's Idealism, reality is Absolute spirit or idea. Similarly, in ethics this doctrine insists that values are objectively real.

absorption

it is a form of argument expressed as p q. thus, p (p.q.).

abstract ideas

if words are employed meaningfully then, surely, the user must have an idea of what they mean; indeed perhaps that idea is the meaning? Granted this seductively obvious assumption, then a question arises about such general words as 'man', or 'animal', or 'triangle'. Since they cannot refer to anything individual and particular, may be what is involved is abstract ideas conceived as special kinds of mental images.

abstraction

from the Latin abstractus, past participle of the verb abstrahere ("to draw from").

(1) In aristotelian and Scholastic philosophy abstraction refers to the process whereby universal ideas come to be appropriated by the mind. Abstraction is possible because of the hylomorphic nature of substance, i.e., that substance is composed of matter and form. The mind receives a sense datum or phantasm and draws out the form, thus providing a universal for intellectual use.

(2) For Locke abstraction takes place by drawing out what has been common to 8 groups of individual things, on the basis of a comparison of their similarities and differences.

absurdity

in its general sense, absurdity is nothing but a palpable falsity that stands in contrast to common-sense or reason.

academy of athens

in effect, the first university, established by Plato about 385 B.C.

academy of plato

an ancient philosophical school started by Plato near Athens. The influence of Pythagoreans was so conspicuous on Plato's Academy from its condition that those who do not know mathematics should not enter the Academy. The Academy was started between 387-385 B.C.

acceptance

one possible reaction to a

theory or to evidence. A philosopher of science who believes that evidence never decisively proves or refutes a scientific theory may conclude that acceptance of a theory ought always to be provisional or partial.

accident

from the Latin accidens, present participle of accidere, "to happen".

In Aristotelian and Scholastic philosophy, that mode of being which inheres in some other being, such as the mode of existence of the redness in an apple. To be contrasted with substantial being, such as the mode of existence of the apple itself. Not only a quality such as redness, however, but any of the nine Aristotelian categories other than substance itself.

Achates

faithful friend of Aeneas.

achilles

son of Peleus, king of the Myrmidons and the sea-goddess, Thetis, who dipped him in the Styx to make him invulnerable, but as she held him by the heel, this part remained vulnerable. He plays a principal role in Homer's 'Iliad'. Brought up with Patroclus, his bosom friend, at Phthia, he was educated by Phoenix and Chiron. He led the Myrmidons in 50 ships to Troy and during the early years of the Trojan war distinguished himself by many splendid exploits. When, however, Agamemnon, king of Mycenae, deprived him of Briseis, his favourite slave girl, Achilles, in dudgeon, withdrew from the fighting, with the result that the Greeks suffered heavy losses. They entreated him to take up arms again, but he refused. At length he agreed to let Patroclus stand in his place and lent him his own arms and armour. His friend was slain, and so determined was Achilles to avenge his death that he made up his quarrel with Agamemnon, returned to the war, and killed Patroclus' killer, Hector. In the 'Iliad' his own death by a poisoned arrow in the heel, at the hands of Paris and Apollo, is foretold.

acosmism

from the Greek a ("not") and kosmos ("world"). The term was coined by Hegel to refer to the doctrine that the world is unreal and that only God exists. Hegal applied the term to the philosophy of Spinoza, but that may be a mis-application. Terms fits more exactly the Acosmic Pantheism of Shankara.

acrasia or akrasia

a Greek term for 'weakness of the will'. Aristotle distinguished a man who is morally weak (akrates) from a man who can resist the temptations of sensuous pleasures (enckrates).

act

a Latin term which has been

derived from agree ("to do"). The Greek term is energeia.
(1) Aristotle contrasted act (energeia) with potency (dynamics), associating the former with form and the latter with matter.
(2) the same contrast in Scholastic philosophy is between actus and potentia. A distinction is made between first and second act. By "first act" is meant the form of a thing, and by "second act" the operation of the thing. "Act" suggests in this terminology both actually and activity. In contrast to other beings, God is regarded as actus purus.

Actaeon

hero from Boeotia, he chanced one day to catch sight of Artemis bathing. But he paid dearly for his pleasure; the huntress goddess turned him into a stag to be torn to pieces by his own hounds.

action

a word which is sometimes applied to things (for example, the action of acid on metal), but primarily relating to the doings of purposive agents. Aristotle distinguished an action—what a man does (poiesis)—from what merely happens to him (pathos : 'usually translated affection' or 'passion').

action at a distance

the use of the term implies a remote and instaneous influence by the body, without any apparent mechanism for transmitting the force produced.

activism

according to activism, reality (natural as well as social) can be explained in terms of action or praxis. In opposition to intellectualism, activism emphasizes that action precedes the intellect. For example, Marxism is a form of activism.

actuality and potentiality

actuality (Greek: energeia) refers to that mode of being in which a thing can bring other things about or be brought about by them; the realm of events and facts. By contrast, potentiality (Greek: dynamis) refers to not a mode in which a thing exists, but rather the power to effect change, the capacity of a thing to make transitions into different states.

actus purus

a Latin term which means "pure act" or "pure actuality". This is the appropriate name for God in Scholastic philosophy. As purely actual, God is the one being without potentiality; hence the highest, or only complete.

adam kadmon

the term used for the hermaphroditic, primordial man of the Cabala.

adaptation

a process of quick adjustment to the conditions of external or internal environment. This concept was made use of by scientists as well as sociolgists. In science, a rational interpretation of adoptation as the outcome of the struggle for existence was first explained by Darwin in his Origin of Species.

addition

it is a basic argument form expressed as p, thus p V q.

ad hoc

the Latin phrase, meaning "to this," suggest the directional character of the ad hoc. In the logic of explanation an ad hoc hypothesis is one formed to explain a given phenomenon, but different from powerful hypotheses in not being derivable from other phenomena or yielding other testable consequences.

adhvaryu

reciter at a sacrifice.

adhyasa (superimposition)

the imposition of quality or an attribute on a thing that does not belong to the thing. Adhyasa is of two types: svarupa-adhyasa, and samsarga-adhyasa. In the case of svarupaadhyasa, something illusory is imposed on something real. For example, the superimposition of an illusory silver on a shell. In the case of samsarga-adhyasa, an attribute is superimposed on an object.

a dicto simpliciter ad dictum secundum quid

it is a nonverbal, fallacy that occurs when a general rule is applied to a special case without taking special circumstances into consideration. For example, it is a general rule that killing a man is a crime. On this count a soldier cannot be condemned to death because he killed his enemy in the war.

Adonis

son, according to one version of the tale, of Cinyras, king of Cyprus, and renowned for his beauty. Aphrodite fell in love with him. He was killed by a boar while hunting, the anemone springing from his blood. According to another version he was, as a child, hidden by Aphrodite in a box which she gave to Persephone for safe-keeping in the Underworld. When, later, Persephone refused to surrender it, Zeus intervened; Adonis was to spend 6 months of the year with Aphrodite away from the Underworld.

adoptionism

the theological doctrine that Christ, born as a mortal being, became the son of God by adoption. The doctrine, appearing in several forms in the first three centuries A.D., led to the Adoptionist Controversy in 8th-century Spain, and was condemned in the Charlemagne-sponsored synods of 792, 794, and 799.

ad quem

from the Latin ad ("to") and quem ("which"). The phrase along with ad quod ("to what") is used in referring to the end point, tendency or goal of an argument or chain of reasoning. To be contrasted with a quo, referring to the corresponding beginning point.

advaita (non-dualism)

it is one of the six orthodox systems of Indian philosophy. It does not have any founder, but has its roots in the Upanisads. It asserts that there is no duality in the supreme Reality called Brahman.

adventitious ideas

refers to one of Descartes, three classes of ideas, along with "factitious" and "innate". Adventitious ideas come from experience, entering the mind through sensation.

Aeneas

son of Anchises and Aphrodite. The 'Iliad' portrays him as a leader of the Trojans. He is the hero of Virgil's 'Aeneid'. After the fall of Troy he fled, carrying his father and household gods on his back, and holding his son, Ascanius, by the hand; his wife he lost in the confusion. After many wanderings he came eventually to the coast of north Africa. Here he stayed for some years as guest and lover of Dido, queen of Carthage. In the end he left her and sailed to Italy, landing at the mouth of the Tiber. Cordially received by Latinus, king of Latium, whose daughter, Lavinia, he married, he founded the city of Lavinium.

Aeolus

ruler of the winds, dwelling, according to Homer, on a floating island.

aeon

among Valentinia Gnostics, especially, the name given to the semi-divine, spiritual intermediaries emanating from God and the material world, which meant—in their view—bridging between good and evil.

affect

a term used in the rational psychology of Spinoza to name the variety of feelings, purposes, and drives which motivate us. As the effects are internal their influence upon us would seem to allow a kind of self-determination.

affectivity

properties possessed by things affect the sense organs to generate percepts. Kant used the term 'affectivity' to denote the power of properties of things to act on the sense-organs.

affirmative

an affirmative sentence is a sentence in which there is no negative particle. For example, 'All rabbits are herbivorous'.

a fortiori

a Latin phrase which means "all the more" or "with the greater force". A type of argument in which two cases are compared, a lesser and a greater. The argument runs from the lesser to the greater case. If from the lesser case one is able to gain a certain consequence how much more certain one should be able to except this consequence, or a stronger result, in the greater case.

after image

refers to the visual version of what psychologists called 'after-sensation', wherein a visual image resembling an observed object persists after the external stimulus assumed to have caused it has been withdrawn.

Agamemnon

son of Atreus and brother of Menelaus. He was legendary king of Mycenae, though probably in origin an historical personage. In Homer he appears as commander-in-chief of the Greek expedition against Troy. He was personally brave, but somewhat irresolute and despondent. His quarrel with Achilles is a principal motif of the 'Iliad'. The 'Odyssey' relates how, on his return from the wars, he and his followers were treacherously murdered by his wife Clytemnestra the daughter of Priam, king of Troy, whom Agamemnon had brought back with him.

agape

Greek term which means "selfless love". The term is derived from the Agape or "love feast" of the early Christians, a common meal to promote "Christian fellowship" frequently associated with the sacrament.

agni

a Sanskrit term which means "fire". One of the most important of the Vedic gods, Agni was god of the alter fire; and also represented the trinity of the earthly fire, lightening, and sun. In this extended sense he was the mediator between the gods and man.

agnosticism

from the Greek a ("not") and gignoskein ("to know"). A term coined by T.H.Huxlay to express a position of suspended belief. Huxley used the term to apply to any proposition for which the evidence as insufficient for belief. It is usually, however, applied principally to suspension to belief with respect to God.

ahavaniya

type of fire.

ahimsa (non-injury)

it is one of the fundamental mottos of Jainism, Buddhism and other Hindu religions.

ajativada

Sanskrit which means "No-Origination." A doctrine of Gaudapada holding the sole reality to be the Absolute.

ajax

son of Telamon, king of Salamis. He sailed to Troy with 12 ships, gaining in the Trojan war a reputation for heroic deeds second only to that of Achilles. In a contest for Achilles' armour, however, he was beaten by Odysseus, and after a fit of madness killed himself.

aksara
from Sanskrit meaning "imperishable". Used in the Upanishads as, an alternative name for Brahman.

Alastor
son of Neleus and brother of Nestor.

Alcaeus
son of Perseus and father of Amphitryon.

Alcestis
daughter of Pelias. She was the wife of Admetus, king of Pherae in Thessaly, who won her by the aid of his friend, the god Apollo. When Admetus' death was approaching, Apollo induced the Fates to spare him if someone else would consent to die in his stead. Alcestis thereupon offered herself. She was saved, however' by Heracles, who after a struggle with Death carried her back from the Underworld.

alchemy
a medieval philosophy which combines an occult cosmology with practical chemical experimentation.

Alexandrian school
the term used for a centre of Neoplatonism in 5th and 6th century Alexandria. Unlike its rival at Athens the Alexandrian School became Christian, concentrating on scholarly commentary' rather than theurgy and metaphysical speculation. It survived the capture of Alexindria by the Arabs (641AD) and transmitted much Neoplatonist learning to the Middle Ages.

algebra of logic
the name applied in the 19th century to that development, influenced by mathematics, beyond traditional logic. Contributing significantly to this development were Boole, De Morgan. Jevons, Peirce, Venn and Schroder.

algorithm
derived from Al-Khwarizmi of Al-Korisimi, the surname of the author of a famous 9th-century Arabic work on arithmetic which was translated into Latin. All such books were called the Algorismus, and so the term came to mean the operations of arithmetic in Arabic notation. It now refers to any sort of logical or mathematical operation with any sort of notation.

alfenaus
a medieval term which distinguishes certain adjectives that are peculiarly tight relations with the nouns to which they are applied.

alienation
(1) Marx's view of alienation is described in his Economic and Philosophical Manuscripts of 1844 (q.v. Max 1). It is a process of the concretization of man's inner nature which then becomes property, and separates one man from another.
(2) in a more general sense the alienated individual is a theme often treated in existentialism

perhaps most clearly in the concept of inauthenticity.

allah

islamic name for God.

alogism

denial of logical thinking as a means to arrive at the truth. Alogism substitutes intuition, revelation, and faith in the place of logic.

altar

place of sacrifice, commemoration, or devotion, commonly shaped like a table. In Roman Catholic usage associated with the Mass. In Protestant churches it is usually alluded to as the 'holy table'.

alteration

for Aristotle one of three basic types of change, namely "change of quality," to be distinguished from growth and diminution which is "change of quantity," and locomotion which is "change of place".

altruism

from Latin alter which means "other". Coined by the French philosopher, Auguste Comte. The term implies regard for and devotion to the interest of others, even to the sacrifice of personal interest.

altruism and egoism

as a philosophical term 'altrusmi' may most usefully be seen in opposition to (ethical) 'egoism'. Egoism rests on the hypothesis that morality can be explained ultimately in term of self-interest, albeit so called enlightened self-interest. For the egoist, the apparent conflicts between the demands of morality and of personal gain are merely conflicts between different aspect of our self-interest-indirect v. direct or longterm v. short-term.

Amazons

the 'breastless ones', a mythical race of female warriors dwelling in Asia Minor. Their right breasts were said to have been cut off to facilitate use of the bow. They were ruled by a queen, and mated periodically with men of another race. Male children were exposed at birth.

ambiguity

a word, term, or expression is to be ambiguous, or to have the property, "ambiguity" when it is capable of having more than a single sense. Ambiguity can lead to the fallacy of Equivocation.

Amitabha

the term used for the Saviour of the Pure Land sect of Mahayana Buddhism also the reincarnated Pantshen Lama of Lamaism.

Amphitrite

sea-goddess, daughter of Nereus (Oceanus) and wife of Poseidon. Triton was her son.

Amphitryon

son of Alcaeus and grandson of Perseus. He married his cousin Alcmene. He died fighting in war against Erginna, the king of the Minyae.

ampliative

from Latin ampliare which means "to make wider".

"Ampliative judgement" and "synthetic judgement" have been identical in meaning, referrig to judgment whose predicates have been not implict in the meanings of their subject terms. "Synthetic judgement" contrasts with "analytic judgement" as "ampliative judgement" contrasts with "explicative judgement".

"Ampliative inference" on the other band refers to the type of inference in which something predicated in the conclusion is not found in the premises, i.e., that form of induction in which by analogy one affirms one affairs of the whole what was found to be true of a part of the whole.

amrita

heavenly drink that confers immortality.

Amyntor

king of Ormenium, father of Phoenix. He was killed by Heracles.

anacreontic

verse in praise of wine and women in the manner of the Greek poet Anacreon.

anagogical interpretation

from the Greek and ("up") and agoge ("a leading"). The term is used, to refer to interpretations, usually of Scripture, leading one "upward," i.e., toward the spiritual or mystical. The anagogical has been thus a type of allegorical interpretation.

analogia entis

a Latin term which means 'analogy of being'.

analogical interpretation

from the Greek and ("up") and agoge ("a leading"). The term is used to refer to interpretations, usually of Scripture, leading one "upward", i.e., toward the spiritual or mystical. The anagogical has been thus a type of allegorical interpretation.

analogies of experience

for Kant the a prior principles making possible the unity of human experience. The three principles deriving from the category of Relations, have been substance, causality and reciprocity. For Kant the principles have been derived from the basic types of propositions, and imply the orderings of substance, cause, and community according to which we interpret experience.

analogy

from Greek ana ("according to") and logos ("ratio, proportion"). This term refers to the relation of similarity between two or more things allowing the drawing of probable or necessary conclusions depending on the kind of relation in question.

analysis

it is a method used in philosophy to analyse complex sentences or concepts or locutions into simpler ones. Analysts of the 20th century generally believe that the problems or puzzles in philosophy appear due to muddled thinking. This muddled thinking is largely the product of the improper use of language. Thus they feel that analysis makes language more refined and intelligible. There are two types of analysis—world analysis, and word analysis. The world analysts such as Moore, Russell, early Wittgenstein, Carnap, and others indulged in analysing the facts of reality; while the word analysts such as Austin, Ayer, later Wittgenstein indulged in analysing the concepts of ordinary language and science.

analysis, intentional

a type of analysis which was introduced by Husserl taking the intentional aspect of experience to be fundamental, and exhibiting the development of all philosophy from this starting point.

analysis, philosophical

according to Ayer refers to analysis function of philosophy, and consists of translating sentences needing clarification into other sentences which contain neither the key words of the original sentences, nor synonyms for them.

analytic

from the Greek analytikos, derived from the verb analyein, "to resolve into its elements". (1) Aristotle used the term to name his logical treatise : the Prior Analytics containing his analysis of the syllogism, the Posterior Analytics containing analyses of the conditions of demonstrable knowledge.
(2) kant in the section of his first critique, called "Transcendental Analytic", analysed the functions of reason within experience, especially with respect to its contribution to the structured phenomena of our experience. The main burden of the transcendental analytic concerned with the deduotion of the categories present in experience.

analytic judgement, statement, or proposition

a judgement, statement, or proposition having the properties of necessity and universality by virtues of the fact that the predicate of the judgment is a result of analysis of the subject term.

analytic & synthetic

a sharp distinction between analytic and synthetic was first made by the German philosopher Immanuel Kant in his Critique of Pure Reason. According to him, an analytic judgement is a judgement in which the predicate is already 'contained' in the subject. For example, 'Body is an extended thing'. Whereas a synthetic judgement is a judgement in which the predicate is not there in the subject, and it is something new. For example,

'Bodies have specific gravity'. Even neo-positivists made a cleavage between analytic and synthetic propositions. According to them, all the propositions of logic and mathematics (exact sciences) are called analytic. These propositions are universal, necessary, and certain. Moreover they are conventional or verbal. They do not convey any new information about reality. These analytic propositions reassert what is already stated in the original propositions. For example, 'Roundsquares do not exist' can be analysed into 'No one thing can be both round and square'. Thus they are tautologies. As regards synthetic propositions, all the propositions of natural sciences come under this catogery. Such propositions are mere empirical hypotheses. They are not certain but highly probable e.g., 'Arsenic is poisonous'. However, neo-positivists do not agree with Kant's interpretation of the distinction between the analytic and synthetic on the grounds that Kant, according to them, has used a psychological criterion rather than a logical one. This is the reaon why Kant categorised and judgements of mathematics under 'synthetic a priori' judgement. For neo-positivists all the propositions of mathematics are analytic. Kant prefer to use the term 'judgement', while neo-positivists prefer to use the term 'proposition'.

anamnesis

a Greek term meaning, "to recall the memory". Plato's doctrine of knowledge as recollection of the ideas known to the soul in a previous existence, and forgotten in the trauma of birth.

anarchism

this term is used to designate a variety of doctrines centering on the belief that the organized state is the cause of injustice among men and should be eliminated. The means of its elimination varies with the anarchists; the point of view include evolutionists and revolutionists, those committed to violence and those committed to non-violence.

anarchy

a type of political trend in which every individual and every group goes against all authority and state. Anarchy has its philosophical foundations in individualism, subjectivism, and voluntarism. The chief exponents of the anarchist view are Proudhan and Bakunin.

anastokaya

Sanskrit term which means "nonphysical". Used in Jainism in the phrase anastikaya dravya ("nonphysical substance").

anaxagoras (500-428 B.C.)

an ancient Greek philosopher who believed that matter is infinitely divisible, and is the motive force behind all processes. He was charged with impiety and was sentenced to death.

anaximenes of miletus

a younger compatriot of Anaximander of Miletus. He held that air is the fundamental matter, which takes on other forms and apperances by condensation and rarefaction. These derivative substances, he may have thought became in their turn the elements of compounds. His other cosmological notions, being closer to popular traditions, are less interesting, but there was some meteorological speculation, using the conception of rarefying and condensing air.

ancestor-worship

cult of the dead, arising, arising from the belief—not universal—that the spirit or soul of the individual person survives physical decease.

Anchises

father of Aeneas.

Andromache

wife of Hector of Troy. When Troy fell the Greeks threw her infant son, Astyanax, from the city walls, she herself being forced to become the slave of Achilles's son, Neoptolemus. She is said to have married afterwards Helenus of Epirus.

Andromeda

daughter of Cepheus, king of Aethiopia. Her mother Cassiopeia claimed that she was more beautiful than even the Nereids, the sea-nymphs, whereupon Poseidon sent a seamonster to ravage the Aethiopian countryside. The oracle of Ammon, which Cepheus consulted, declared that deliverance would be won only if Andromeda herself were given to the beast, and her father chained her to a rock. There she was found by the hero Perseus, who released her, slew the monster, and obtained her as his wife.

anglicanism

the teaching and practice of the Church of England and sister or daughter churches (as, for example, the Anglican Church of Canada), known collectively as the Anglican Communion. It originated in the reforms brought about by Henry reforms brought about by Henry VIII's breach with Rome in 1532-4. The essential nature of Anglicanism as something of a via media between Roman Catholicism and the more extreme forms of Protestantism is to be found in the Book of Common Prayer, the basis which presupposes all variations in subsequent Anglican liturgies, and in the consistent adherence to the episcopal ministry. The Thirty-Nine Articles (1571), a classical formulation of Reformation teaching, now have only historical value although assent to them is still required of Church of England clergymen.

angst

German term which means "dread". A basic fact of human nature, according to existentialist philosophy, Angst is a nameless fear which has no object.

an hominem argument

(Latin for: argument directed at a man). The term is used for two kinds of argument. The first kind has been a fallacious argument whereby the premises merely attack a particular man (for example, for his unwholesome moral character) while the conclusion purports to establish the falsity of a thesis he holds.

The second kind is an argument taking as its premise something that has been accepted by the other party but not perhaps by the arguer and deducing a consequence unacceptable to that other party.

anima (Latin for : soul)

(in Jungian psychology). The part of the collective unconscious within an individual that represents the feminine aspect of man's nature.

animal soul

refers to an analogue in animals of the human soul or mind. In opposition to the Cartesian view that man alone possessed a soul, the doctrine of animal soul claimed that animal behaviour was not physicalistically explicable, but implied mental functioning and the existence of soul.

animism

a belief that soul and spirits affect the lives of humans and animals. They also exert influence on the phenomena and the objects of the world.

anirvacaniya-khyati (the indefinability of apprehension)

it is a theory of error advocated by Advalta. According to this theory, the object of error is neither real nor unreal. An object of error can be sublated. In this sense, it is not real. Since the object of error can be perceived, it cannot be said to be unreal. Thus it is neither real nor unreal.

an sich

(1) in the Kantian philosophy a thing or event independent of experience.

(2) in Hegal the term is also used, but there the an sich is not only separate from consciousness but therefore in large measure potential, latent, undeveloped or impoverished.

(3) the term is also used by Sartre, the French phrase being en soi. Sartre distinguishes between the en soi, or "in itself", and the pour soi, or "for itself". The former is applied to that which is without, and the latter to that which possesses, awareness.

antariksha
the atmosphere.

antecendent
in sentences, or propositions, of the form "if A, then B" A is called the antecendent, and B the consequent (q.v. Proposition 2).

anthrepocentrism
from the Greek anthropos ("man") and kentron ("center"). The view that man is, or must took upon himself as, the centre of reality. This not a philosophical concept in itself but the term has analogies to the view of Protagoras that "man is the measure of all things".

anthropology, philosophical
the term, literally means "philosophical knowledge of man". It applies to those studies which treat man as a "whole being", attempting to avoid or go beyond approaches in which man is regarded merely as a scientific object.

anthropomorphism
from the Greek anthropomorphos ("of human form"). This term refers to the attribution of human qualities to the divine; thus, the conceiving of God or the gods in human form.

anthropopathism
from the Greek anthropos ("man") and pathein ("suffering"). A term which was coined by the writer and critic John Ruskin to designate the state of mind leading to what he called the "pathetic fallacy", i.e., emotional strain or grief leading the poet to ascribe to nature the emotions of sympathy or cruelty.

anthroposophy
refers to an occult system which claim that the key to wisdom and to an understanding of the Universe lies in man himself.

antichrist
this term simply means one who denies Christ. In extension, however, the term signifies a great force, filling the world with evil, whose defeat will lead to the Second Coming. In the extended sense the Antichrist has been taken to be, at different times, the Roman Empire, specific emperors, Mohammed, and the popes themselves.

anticipations of experience
Kant's doctrine that all sensations are having some intensive magnitude or degree. According to Kant we can know this in advance of experience, although we cannot know in advance what the quality or degree would be.

Antigone
daughter of Oedipus by his mother Jocasta, wife of Laius, king of Thebes.

antilogism
from the Greek antilogismos which means "a countercharge". The term refers to a method of checking on the validity of a syllogism.

antinomianism
refers to the view that ordinary

moral laws are not applicable to Christians, whose lives, it is said, are governed solely by divine grace. Opponents of this position have always pointed, during its not infrequent recurrences, to its alarming ethical implications.

antinomy
refers to an obsolescent synonym for paradox or contradiction.

antithesis
from the Greek anti ("against") and tithenai ("to set"). Etymologically the term has been comparable in meaning to "antinomy" and "contradiction".

(1) in Kant's "Antinomies of Pure Reason" the "antithesis" is the negative member of the antinomy, the one opposing thesis.

(2) in Fichte and in Hegel "antithesis" is the middle member of the triad, opposing the thesis; the opposition of thesis and antithesis is resolved by the synthesis, and third member of the triad.

anu (atom)
the smallest individual material particle is called atom. Atoms are supposed to be eternal. Jainism claims that atoms are insensient. The four elements, namely, earth, water, fire, and air are atomic in their primary form.

anupalabdhi (non-cognition)
the Bhatta school of Mimamsa and Advaita admit anupalabdhi (non-cognition) as a valid source of knowledge. The absence of an object is known through non-cognition.

anuvaka
lesson.

anxiety
this notion is widely prevalent in existentialist literature. Anxiety is a physical state of an individual resulting from the awareness of uncertainity, guilt, meaninglessness in life, and finitude. Anxiety is not fear, but a kind of anguish and dreadfulness.

apagoge
from the Greek opo ("from") and agein ("to lead").

(1) in Aristotelian logic an abductive syllogism.

(2) the method of indirect demonstration whereby one demostrates the absuridity of the conclusion contradictory to one which to be established.

apathia
a Latin term from the Greek apatheia, which is derived from a ("not") and pathos ("suffering"). This Greek virtue of utter tranquility served as the most important valued for the Stoic. It has to be compared to the state of atarxia stressed among the Epicureans.

apeiron
a Greek term which means "boundless, indeterminate, infinite".

(1) in Anaximander that from which all determinate being comes, and into which it goes.

(2) for the Phythagoreans one of two principles : Unlimited

(apeiron) which opposes the limit (peras).

aphrodite

Greek goddess of love and fertility, born from the sea. Her Roman counterpart is Venus.

apocalypse

from the Greek apokaluptein ("to uncover or disclose"). The doctrine that the world is soon to be destroyed by fire, purified from evil, and that the righteous would be resurrected to live in a purified order of things. Popular in the last centuries before Christ, the doctrine generated a body of apocalyptical literature. Daniel, Revelation, and a number of the books of the Apocrypha belong to this literature.

apocatastasis

from the Greek apokatastasis which means "complete restoration". A concept of universal salvation held by Origen the theologian.

apodeictic

a proposition whose truth is established beyond all doubt. This term was first used by Aristotle to mean the absolute truth. For example, 'Five is less than eight'.

apodosis

a Greek term which means "a giving back" the term refers to the "then" clause of an if then statement. The conditional clause has been the protasis.

apollinarianism

the christological doctrine that in Jesus the Logos (a perfect divine nature) assumed a human body, exercising the functions ordinarily performed by a human mind.

Apollo

son of Zeus and Leto and brother of Artemis; he was the most Greek of gods and represented the ideal type of manly beauty. His special care was for music, prophecy, medicine, archery, and the tending of flocks and herds.

apologetics

a branch of theology that tries to justify a dogma by means of arguments addressed to reason. Apologetics is included in the Catholic and the orthodox systems of theology.

apology

refers to a form of discourse in defence of one's position. Among the most famous instances of such discourse one may cite Plato's Apology, giving Socrates' defence of his philosophic life and mission the entire movement of early Christian apologists and Cardinal Newman's Apologia pro Vita Sua, where he defends his philosophical and religious development, including his leaving the Anglican Church for Catholicism.

apophantic judgment

from the Greek apohansis ("proposition"). The subject-predicate form of judgement through by Aristotle to be basic.

aporetic

raising questions and objections, without necessarily

providing answers. Such a procedure is characteristic of Socrates in the early dialogues of Plato. A difficulty of this sort is sometimes labelled, by Ryle and others, and aporia (Greek for : puzzle).

apostasy

from the Greek apostasia ("a defection"). In Roman Catholicism a total desertion of, or departure from, one's faith or from holy orders or from the monastic state. A formal apostate has been subject to excommunication.

a posteriori

from the Latin a ('form') and posteriori ('the later'). The term is used to designate a kind of knowledge which can be gained only from experience; hence, it can be formulated only after observation or experiment.

apostle

Title given in the gospels to the 12 principal disciples of Jesus, but it is probable that in, the decades following Jesus' death the title was applied to a wider circle of christain officials. St. Paul certainly ranks as an apostle. The word is also used of the first Christian missionaries to a region or of one who evangelizes with conspicuous success.

apotheosis

from the Greek apo ("from") and theoun ("to deify"). The elevation of a mortal to the rank of a god. Virtually all cultures show evidence of the transformation of heroes and rules into divinities.

appeal to common consensus

it is an appeal made to a misplaced authority that tries to resolve the point at issue by bringing in an alleged general belief of mankind.

apperance

in the history of the philosophy the term stands in contrast to reality. At times the relation is that of illusion or falsity to truth. Most often, however, at least in Western philosophy, the relation is that of opinion-that which may or may not be true-to truth.

apperception

self-consciousness or inner awareness, in contrast with 'perception', denoting outer awareness.

appetites

from the Latin oppetere ('to strive after, long for'). The term applies to the dynamic, striving aspect of human nature.

appetition

the term is sometimes used to apply to the process of satisfying the appetites.

appropriation

refers to the subjective approach to truth favoured by Kiekegaard. He contrasted his view with objective approach of science, which he called "endless approximation," and which he opposed.

a priori

knowledge obtained prior to experience (sense-experience) is called a priori knowledge.

Contrary to a posteriori knowledge, a priori knowledge is universal, necessary, and certain. In Kant's philosophy, 'a priori' is the mark of necessity. Such necessity can never be explained in terms of experience. Both Rationalists and Empiricists are unanimous in claiming that analytical propositions are a prior in their nature.

apriorism

refers to the philosophical position, opposed to empiricism, held by those who characteristically consider that the mind is furnished with innate ideas and that there exists the possibility of genuine knowledge independent of experience.

aprthak-siddhi (internal relation of inseparability)

it is a key concept in Visistadvaita. It is a relation obtained between Brahman, the souls, and matter. This is also known as the soul-body relationship.

apsara

celesial nymph, dancer of heaven.

Aquinas, St. Thomas (1225-1274)

medieval philosopher theologian.

A QUO

from the Latin a ("from") and quo ("which"). The phrase, part of the vocabulary of Scholastic philosophy, refers to the point of origin of an argument, that is, to the principles, assumptions, and definitions, from which it is derived.

arani

stick used to generate a fire.

Aranyaka

Sacred test.

Arbor Porphyii

the tree of Porphyri, a manner of illustrating the relations of genus, species, and individuals, widely influential throughout the Middle Ages.

Arcadian

of Arcadia, ideally rural. By literary convention, the inhabitants of Arcadia were idealized shepherds who composed pastoral verses in which were mirrored the simplicities of an imaginary Golden Age.

archdeacon

an ecclesiastical dignatory next in rank below a bishop and deriving from him certain official powers of oversight in respect of the lower clergy.

arche

a Greek term with significy "that which was in the beginning".

Archelaus of Atheus

a pupils of Anaxagoras and teacher of Socrates. His small contribution, to cosmology rather than philosophy, seems to have consisted in amending the system of Anaxagoras, using elements drawn from other predecessors.

archetypes

in Plato's philosophy, Ideas or Forms are considered to be the archetypes or prototypes. Such archetypes are original and immutable. They represent Being, while all other objects or things are mere copies of those ideas or forms. These objects or things represent the state of 'becoming'. In Berkeley's philosophy, those ideas which potentially exist in the mind of God are archetypes.

architectonic
the term used to describe a philosophical system constructed according to a consistet plan.

arete
the Greek term for virtue. It is a fulfillment term. For Aristotle who may be taken to represent the Greeks in this respect, arete is the fulfillment of the function of being human.

argonauts
'sailors of the Argo', the 50 adventurers who sailed to Colchis with Jason to secure the Golden Fleece.

argumentum ad hominem
it is one of the forms of Ignoratic Elenchi. This fallacy consists in criticising the opponent rather than arguing against his reasoning. For example, the statement of Berkeley 'Reality is mind dependent' can be disproved by putting forward counter arguments but not by abusing him.

argumentum ad judicicum
an argument relying on the judicious sense or common sense of mankind.

argumentum ad populum
this is another form of Ignoratio Elenchi. This fallacy occurs when an argument is proved valid by appealing to the passions and sentiments of the pubic, instead of appealing to reason. Demagogues often follow this method to convince people.

argumentum ad rem
an argument which adheres to the point, hence avoiding the fallacies which involve moving away from the point at issue in one of a great variety of ways.

argumentum ad verecundiam
this is also a form of Ignoratio Elenchi. This fallacy occurs when the arguments of the opponent are proved invalid by putting him to all sorts of shame.

argumentum ex concesso
an argument which takes as its basis the propositions conceded to be true by one's opponent.

Ariadne
daughter of Minos of Crete. She fell in love with Theseus when he came to Crete, and gave him the clue of thread which enabled him to find his way out of the Labyrinth after slaying the Minotaur. On leaving the island he took Ariadne with him, but abandoned her on Naxos. There, according to Homer, she was killed by Artemis, but other versions tells of her subsequent marriage to

Dionysus.

arianism

4th cent. A.D. The name of a dispute which wracked the early church, continued from 318 to 381 A.D. The subject of the dispute was the meaning of the incarnatio in relation to the Christian premise of monotheism.

aristocracy

from the Greek aristos ("best", and kratein ("to rule"). One of the perennially formulated types of ideal government, aristocracy implies rule by the best in the interests of the whole society but without the participation of the governed.

(1) for Plato aristocracy was the ideal social structure, standing in contrast to four degenerate forms of government.

(2) for Aristotle on the other hand, aritocracy was one of three desirable forms of government, sharing Aristotle's commendation with monarchy and polity.

aristotelian logic

it is a form of logic that makes use of a categorical syllogism in order to provide an analysis of arguments using two categorical statements as premises and a categorical statement as a conclusion. It is also referred to as syllogistic logic.

Aristotle 384-322 B.C.

Greek philosopher. Born in Stagyra, Macedonia. Son of Nicomachus, physician to the king. At 18 entered Plato's Academy, and studied there nearly 20 years.

In Metaphysics Aristotle explicitly criticizes Plato's theory of Forms, alluding to the third man argument and complaining that the Forms are useless as explanatory devices and that the various arguments for accepting the Forms either prove nothing or establish the existence of unwelcome Forms such as negations and relations.

In the Categories, for example, individual things such as particular men and animals are called Primary substances; species and genera (genus) of primary substances are called secondary substances. The species and genera are what an individual thing is; Socrates is a man (species) and an animal (genus).

Aristotle adds that it is characteristic of both Primary and Secondary realities (substances) not to have contraries. Many of Plato's Forms come in contrary pairs, for example, the large and the small.

In the Posterior Analytics, a treatise on the logical structure of a science, Aristotle argues for the autonomy of various disciplines (geometry, astronomy, harmony) and against there being principles common to all sciences, from which the correct explanations given in those sciences could be deduced. Acceptance of this would undermine the hopes that Plato, at one stage at least, held of dialectic Plato's Republic speaks of dialectics as pursuing the most general principles from which even the principles of mathematics can be derived.

Aristotle does conclude that the best (and happiest) man spends as much time as possible in the purest activity of reason, theorizing (Ethics X). However, since he is a man, the rational part of his soul (psyche) is more than just an intellect, and intellectual excellence by itself does not make a good and happy man. Reason governs action as well as theorizing. Action is the response made to desire, and here, Aristotle insists, one can respond too much or too little. The correct response lies some where between the two extremes. This is the doctrine of the mean (golden mean). It does not pretend to provide a moral decision procedure. It is a (meta-ethical) statement about the form of certain moral concepts; to every virtue there are two distinct vices.

arithmetic, foundations of

(1) Peano demostrated that all of the natural numbers and their relationship can be Reduced from five postulates.

(2) Dedekind discovered how to define real numbers in terms of rational numbers.

(3) Frege demonstrated the possibility of defining rational numbers in terms of logical entities.

(4) Russell and Whitehead developed this program in their Principia Mathematica, thus basing arithmetic on logic.

armenians

the Armenian Orthodox Church, which uses classical Armenian as its liturgical language, its members speaking either Armenian, Turkish, or Arabic. Their head, the Catholicos of All Armenians, has his seat at Etchmiadzir in Soviet Armenia, but there are also patriarchates at Constantinople and Jerusalem, and in Egypt. The Church has a strong membership in North Aerica. A consip in North America. A considerable number of Armenian christians now belong to the Roman obedience and are known as Armenian Catholics. They have a patriarch of their own.

ars combinatoria

a Latin phrase which means the "combinatory art". The phrase was used by Leibniz (q.v. 11-12) to signify the general program of building complex concepts from simple ones according to rule.

art

from the Latin ars signifying any purposeful making or doing.

(1) in Plato art is the activity or object of any making or doing controlled by the movement down from theory to practice,

and contrasting with the upward movement toward theory.

(2) in Aristotle art is one of three branches of knowledge.

(3) Aquinas follows both of his predecessors, defining art as right reason in making thing.

artemis

originally a primitive earth-goddess; she appears in Greek mythology as daughter of Zeus and Leto and sister of Apollo; a virgin huntress and patroness of chastity, she was identified by the Romans with Diana.

articles of faith

propositions concerning the interpretation of a religion which have to be taken on faith.

artificial language

any non-natural language such as Esperanto or Ido. Natural languages are ordinary languages such as English, French, Chinese, Russian, etc.

asana

from the Sanskrit, which means "sitting". In Yoga and other systems of Indian philosophy, the emphasis on postures as one of the conditions of spiritual progress.

Asanga 4th or 5th century A.D

Indian philosopher. Founder of the Yogachara (Way of Yoga) or Consciousness-Only School. In the founding of the school, he was assisted by his younger brother, Vasubandhu who was known as the systemarizer of the position.

Principal writings: Mahayanabhidhar-masangiti-shastra; Mahayanasam-parigraha-shastra; Mahayanasutralankara-shastra.

(1) Like certain of his predeccessors in Mahayana Buddhism he held that reality is devoid of plurality, and that all phenomena are subjective in character. His addition was to hold that the nature of the real is pure consciousness.

(2) Surrounded by illusion-even the empirical ego is part of this illusion-the way of liberation requires the destruction of this illusion. One will first realize the imaginary nature of external objects; then the imaginary character of the individual mind. Third, one will grasp the nondual nature of pure consciousness as neither existence nor nonexistence, neither affirmation nor negation, neither identity nor difference. At last even this state will be transcended and the state of liberation, wherein all categories are merged, will be reached.

asat

from the Sanskrit which means "non-being". The opposite of "Sat" meaning "being". A theory of the origin of being from non-being dating back to Vedic times.

asatkarya-vada (the theory of non-preexistence of effect)

it is one of the theories of

causation, according to which the effect does not preexist in its cause. Thus the effect is something totally new. It is also known as arambha-vada. The chief exponents of this theory are Nyaya-Vaisesika.

asat-khyati (apprehension of the non-existent)

this theory of error was held by Madhyamika school of Buddhism. This school holds that the object of error is totally non-existent.

asceticism

from the Greek askesis which means "self-denial". The view, which has been an important theme of both Eastern and Western religion and has played a minor role in philosophy, that the body is to be denied, possibly mortified, so as to make possible the purification of the soul in its progress toward salavation.

Asclepius

Greek god of medicine.

ashramas, the four

in the Mahabharata and in Hinduism generally, the four stations of life, and their duties.

Ashvaghosa

1st century A.D. Indian philosopher. The chief expounder of Mahayana Buddhism-Claiming that after Buddha's death there were many errors of interpretation among those who sought to understand his teachings. Ashvaghosa set out to explain the fundamental teachings of the Buddha.

Principal writings: The Awakening of the Faith in the Mahayana.

(1) Ashvaghosa holds that reality is "Absolute Suchness", that which it is, beyond the categories of human understanding.

(2) But the "Absolute Suchness", trained by ignorance appears as "Conditional Suchness", i.e., as the manifold phenomenal word, including the apparent plurality of finite selves. In fact, as the calm water of the ocean, whipped by wind, appears as waves, so does consciousness, as the result of ignorance, appear as finite minds.

(3) The relative phenomenal world cannot be sublated by reason since this, too, is relative or relational. We must get beyond intellect and approach reality directly, and Buddha utilized words and definitions to lead the seeker beyond words and definitions.

(4) Following Buddha's example the bodhisattvas, those on the way to enlightenment, defer their ova Nirvaṇas in order to enable others to overcome their ignorance, and so end their suffering.

(5) In the state of enlightenment we are aware of our Absolute Suchness and identify with the self existent immortal reality.

asmita

a Sanskrit term which means "I am-ness". A false egoism which confuses the sensible self with the true self, or purusha. One of the five kinds of suffering to be overcome in the Yoga system.

assertion
any declarative statement that is uttered and put forward as true.

assertoric
the term used for describing a proposition that simply asserts that something is or is not the case. The term has been used to contrast such proposition with modal propositions.

assertoric judgment
refers to one of the three modes of judgment distinguished by Kant that one asserting the something is (or is not). The other two modes have been those of the problematic judgment and the Apodeictic judgment. The analysis of modality goes back at least tc Aristotle.

association of ideas
a term introduced into philosophy by John Locke. The term used for the view that complex mental phenomena are derived from the joining together of simple elements according to a small set of principles.

associationism
refers to a psychological rather than a philosophical theory, taking association to be the fundamental principle of mental life.

assumption
from the Latin ad ("to") and sumere ('take'). The taking for granted of the truth of a proposition for the sake of the argument.

assyrians
a small body of Eastern Christians, dwelling mainly in Iraq, who alone today perpetuate the Nestorian doctrine of the dual personality of Christ. They were much persecuted by the Turks. Their spoken language is a colloquial form of Syriac.

asura
demon.

atalanta
like Artemis, a huntress, and an athlete. Averse to marriage, she demanded that her suitors should each content with her in a race on foot, unsuccessful competitors being put to death. Her cousin Milanion, however, obtained 3 golden apples from Aphrodite and threw them in front of her. Stooping to pick them up, she lost the race.

ataraxia
the goal and inspiration of the Greek Sceptics. It was to be achieved by the clam and reasoned suspension of judgment (epoche) about contentious issues.

atheism
the rejection of belief in God, whether on the grounds that it is meaningful but false to say that God exists, or, as the logical positivists held, that it is meaningless and hence

neither true nor false (logical positivism).

Atlas

father of the Pleiades. As punishment for his part in the revolt of the Titans he was employed to support the heavens with his head and hands.

atman

Sanskrit term which means "self" or "soul". In the Upanishads which means and in the Vedanta philosophy, Atman as the individual soul and Brahman, the ruler of all things, are held to be identical. Shanara gives one of the standard analyses of this identity.

atomic proposition

it is also known as elementary proposition. It is a proposition in which there is no logical operator. Hence it is simple and further unanalysable.

atomic sentence

a sentence having no logical operator, and which is thus logically simple.

atomic uniformity, principle of

the name given by J. M. Keynes to the further assumption, additional to that embodied in the principle of limited independent variety, supposedly required to justify induction: "the material universe must consist........ of bodies.. such that each.. exercises its own separate, independent and invariable effect, a change of total state being compounded of a number of separate changes each of which is solely due to a separate portion of the preceding state".

atomism

the belief that matter consists of atoms. It is usually traced to the Greek philosophers. Leucippus and Democritus (5th century BC).

Atreus

father of Agamemnon.

attis, atys

youthful paramour of Cybele, the Phrygian mother-goddess. The latter, jealous that he should marry another woman, pestered him till he castrated himself.

attribute

any property, whether essential or accidental, that is affirmed or denied of a subject in question is called attribute. According to Spinoza, an attribute is something that is perceived by intellect or mind as constituting the essence of substance. For example, Spinoza's substance has two important attributes, namely, infinite thought and infinite extention.

attributive

denoting a particular placing of an adjective. The adjective "white" is in the attributive position in "Silver is a white horse" and in the predicative position in 'Silver, the horse, is white".

Augustine of Hippo

the greatest of the Latin

Church fathers, born in North Africa. He studied, and taught in Carthage, Rome, and Milan. Although many passages in Augustine's work, like the famous analysis of time in the Confessions, suggest outstanding technical ability, his philosophy was almost always auxiliary to religious preoccupations. He saw both philosophy and religion as essentially quests for wisdom and, through wisdom, beatitude; the crucial difference was that Christian faith succeeded in the quest, while the unaided human reason of the philosophical schools could not. He did not, however, deny that some truths, including theological truths, were attainable by reason alone. Neoplatonism certainly helped him to break free from Manichaen dualism, and Platonic concepts played an important role in his interpretations of Christian teaching. But the task of reason was essentially that of elucidating things already accepted by faith as divine revelation—an attitude late summed up in the formula "Credo ut intelligam" (I believe so that I may understand).

Augustine's writings, especially on divine grace and the role and the authority of the Church, profoundly influenced both medieval, and Reformation religious thought.

Aurobindo, Sri (Aurobindo Ghose)

1872-1950. Indian philosopher. A modern leader of the Advaita Vedanta philosophy in modern India, Aurobindo considered the illusionism of Shankara a misinterpretation of the Upanishads.

Principal writings : Essays on the Gita (E), 1926-44, 1950; The Life Divine (E), 2 vols., 1947; The Synthesis of Yoga (E), 1948 : The Supramental Manifestation upon Earth (E), 1952.

1. Reality exists in a graded series which begins in matter, and mounts to the Absolute itself, or Brahman. The essential power of Brahman requires his descent into the finite.

2. That some power requires the finite to struggle toward the infinite. On one level this struggle is the evolution of lower into higher forms. On another level man seeks, and must seek, identity with the Absolute by passing beyond the level of the mental into the divine life.

3. The means, of this passage is called 'integral yoya' providing a transformation of mind, life and body.

Austin, John Longshaw (1911-1960)

a contemporary British analytical philosopher who attempted to apply the method and the standards of a scholar of classical texts to ordinary language. His article on "Other

Minds" (1946) received an unqualified acclaim for his meticulous and incisive analysis of the term 'know'. His major works include: Sense and Senibilia, and Philosophical Papers (a posthumous publication).

authenticity

from the Greek authentes ("one who acts with authority, or what is done by one's own hand"). Anticipated in fiction by Goethe, the term has come into philosophic use with the existentialists, for whom it is an important value term.

autonomous and heteronomous ethics

two diametrically opposite views concerning the origion of the morality. Autonomous ethics maintains that moral principles are the outcome of certain idealistic notions of the internally inherent, a priori moral obligations. Kant is considered to be the champion of such a view. The heteronomous ethics tries to deduce the fund a mental moral principles from the causes independent of the will of the acting agent. These external causes are considered to be the laws of states, religious commandments, and also such motives as personal interest, etc.

autonomy

from the Greek autos ("self") and nomos ("law"). Hence, the reference is to that which gives law to itself, or is its own law.

autonomy of ethics

refers to the doctrine that the naturalistic fallacy is indeed a fallacy.

avadhi (supernatural cognition)

Jainism holds that an individual can perceive the things which have shape and form without the aid of sense-organs. Such an act of supernatural cognition is of three types, namely, desa-avadhi (limited by space and time), sarva-avadhi (apprehension of all modes of physical objects), and parama-avadhi (not limited by space and time).

avalokitesvara

the reincarnated Dalai Lama of Lamaism.

avatar

from the Sanskrit avatara ("descent"). The term is used to refer to the descent of a deity to earth and his incarnation in man or animal. In Hinduism the term applies mainly to Vishnu. Nine avatars of the god have already appeared, and a tenth is expected.

avenarius, Richard (1843-1896)

a Swiss philosopher and a chief advocate of empirio-criticism. According to Avenarius, experience is the bridge between psychic and physical phenomena. Thes he proposed the idea of the absolute interdependence of subject and object.

average

in one common sense, a word virtually synonymous with 'typical', 'ordinary,' or 'in no way distinguished'. More technically, the average is the arithmetic mean.

avernus

deep lake near Puteoli, believed to be an entrance to the Underworld.

avesta

avestan term which means "knowledge". The term applies to the sacred scriptures of the Zoroastrian religion.

avicenna

(Arabic name : Ibn Sina abu' Ali al-Husayn). (980-1037). Islamic philosopher. Main works : Kitab al-Shifa' (the Book of Healing (of the Soul), abridged by Avicenna in Kitab al-Najat (the Book of Salvation), and Qanun fit 'l-Tibb (the Canon of Medicine). (The latter two works were printed in Rome in 1593).

avidya

Sanskrit term which means "nescience" or "ignorance". A synonym is maya. Specifically, avidya is ignorance of the identity of self and Brahman in Indian philosophy, and therefore belief in the separate nature of self.

avowals

Gilbert Ryle used this term to denote first person utterances like 'I am in pain' to distinguish them from their third person counterparts like 'He is in pain'. Ryle felt that the third person statement are open to doubt as one cannot introspect into the feelings of others, while the first person statements (avowals) are infallible.

avyakta

from the Sanskrit meaning "unmanifest". A term used in the Upanishads and in the Bhagavad-Gita along with the term Prakriti to refer to the unmanifest power of God, or to Brahman before creation in the state of superabundance, or to the unborn universe.

axiological ethics

refers to one of the types of ethics to be contrasted with deontological, telelogical, intuitionistic, and formalistic types.

axiology

refers to the philosophical study of values, undertaken especially in the fields of ethics religion, and aesthetics.

axiom

any proposition that is considered to be self-evidently true. It does not require any proof to prove its validity. Axiomatic method is a popular method in Symbolic Logic.

axioma

the term used by Ramus as the general name for statements. He distinguished axioma simplex, axioma generale, axioma particulara, and axioma proprium.

axiomatic method

refers to a method of formalizing and studying a subject by using only the method of formal logic in order to derive the truths of the subject from a list of underfined terms and a list of axioms.

axiom of infinity

an axiom of set theory that asserts, in one form or an other, that there exists a set with infinitely many members.

ayam atma brahma

Sanskrit term which means "This self is Brahman."

ayana

period of six months.

baal

refers to a semitic term, i.e., one found in most semitic languages, meaning "possessor". A title of divinity in the history of many Semitic peoples, baal signifies the possessor of a place, object, or attribute, but not a person. Deities of individuals and tribes bear other names, such as "Elohim".

Bacon, Francis (1561-1626)

a well-known British philosopher, who is regarded as the pioneer of empiricist movement. Though a systematic account of empiricism was first given by John Locke, the seeds of empiricism are found in the writings of Bacon. He opposed all forms of scholasticism and dogmatism. His attitude towards ethics was utilitarian. One of the important works of Bacon is Novum Organum, where he wrote that the fist step to acquiring true knowledge is to cleanse the mind from all sorts of preconceptions and prejudices (Idols).

Bacon, Roger (1214-1292)

a British philosopher of middle ages, who was opposed to Scholasticism. He was a precursor of experimental science. He upheld the method of cognition based on experiment and mathematics. The aim of all learning, according to Bacon, is to have mastery over nature.

Badarayana

he is also known as Vyasa. He is the author of Brahma Sutra.

bad faith

in the existentialism of Sartre, a form of deception of self and others; the attempt to rationalize human existence through religion, science, or any belief in operative forces that impose meaning and coherence. Man shapes his own destiny through a succession of free choices for which he is totally responsible. In 'bad faith' he denies the necessity of relying on his own moral insight and fallible will, trying to escape the burden of responsibility by regarding himself as the passive subject of outside influences, and his actions as being predetermined by these rather than freely chosen by himself.

bahaism

a religious movement which was initiated by Baha u'llah, a schismatic Mohammedan who in the middle of the 19th century founded a new religion.

baptism

from the Greek baptein ("to dip in water"). The rite, religious or tribal, in which a liquid (usually water but somtimes oil, blood, urine, etc.) is applied to the human form by immersion, washing, pouring, or sprinkling, to ward off evil effects or purify from sin. The ritual has been world-wide, and is to be found in most religions. Baptims by water gained sacramental status in Roman Catholicism, and retains such status in most varieties of Protestantism.

baptists

the term used for a major Protestant organization of congregational form, originating within English Congregationalism in the early 17th century, over the issue of the proper form of Baptism. Baptists stress the importance of personal religious experience. The denomination is having many subgroups within it.

Barber paradox

a paradox which illustrates a problem in set theory. Suppose that the barber of Seville shaves all the men of Seville, except those who shave themselves. Does the barber shave himself ? If he does shave himself, he is not to be shaved by the barber, that is, himself, if he doesn't he should be shaved by the barber. Hence he both does and does not shave himself. So the original supposition has been false.

basic action

refers to a thing that we simply do without having to do anything else to make it happen. The contrast has been with those of our actions that involve causing things to happen (for example, exploding, a demolition charge by pressing the detonator). Raising one's arm is the stock example of a basic action.

basic propositions

they are also called protocol propositions. Their truth can never be challenged, since they are the translations of the data directly given in one's own sensory-experience. Ayer calls them basic propositions, while Neurath prefers to call them protocol propositions. In fact the sensedatum statements are called basic propositions.

basic statements

a phrase whcih was coined by Ayer in the context of arranging the beliefs of an individual. If epistemology is conceived as the project of arranging the statements we believe according to the reason we have for believing them, then we are likely, sooner or later, to come to beliefs for which no reason can be given.

battle of Gods and giants

an image in Plato's Sophist describing the perennial

conflict between two types of thinker: "One side drags down everything from heaven and the unseen to earth, rudely grasping rocks and trees in their hands. For they get their grip on all such things, and they maintain that alone exists which can be handled and touched. Terrible men... Those who battle against them defend themselves very carefully from somewhere above in the unseen, contending that true existence consists in certain incorporeal Forms which are objects of the mind". Plato himself is the first forefather of the gods, Leucippus and Democritus, Hobbes and Marx, fight in the front line for the giants.

beatification
from the Latin beatus ("blessed") and facere ("to make"). That stage in the Roman Catholic process of canonization whereby a candidate for sainthood is declared one of the "blessed" and entitled to public religious honor.

beatific vision
in Christianity the immediate vision of God which is enjoyed by the faithful in heaven.

beauty
refers to the sensible condition of aesthetic excellence considered to arouse the keenest pleasure.

becoming
in Plato's philosophy, becoming represents the world of sensible things. According to him, the transient sensory world is subjected to change. The classical representatives of this view was Heraclitus who claimed that reality is under constant 'flux'.

begging the question
refers to the procedure of taking for granted, in a statement or argument, precisely what is in dispute.

behaviourism
the theory, first propounded by the psychologist J.B.Watson in Behaviourism (1925), that psychological functioning has been definable in terms of observed behavioural data. Initially introduced in order to establish a firm scientific basis for psychology, the theory has since had extensive elaboration, notably in the writings of B.F.Skinner.

being
from the Greek ousia and ontos; in Latin esse, essentia, and substantia are the basic referents to "being".

In philosophy the search for what underlies apperance led in Parmendies to the claim that "being is and nonbeing is not". For Parmenides being is changeless, rational, and one.

being, the great chain of
the phrase, used by A.O.Lovejoy as the title of his influential book, serve introduced a concept of importance running from. Neoplatonism through the medieval period; that is, the

concept of a graded reality embodying all of the passibilities in a continuum running from pure matter to pure spirit, from sheer potentiality to pure actuality.

belief

it is a kind of feeling that makes an individual to accept something as true even when there is no conclusive evidence. In epistemology, belief is considered to be a claim to knowledge. However, it is not a mere opinion. According to Gettier, a justified true belief is nothing but knowledge. C.S. Peirce, the pioneer of Pragmatic movement, holds the view that the best way to fix or unfix a belife is to put it for a pragmatic test.

bellerophon

son of Glaucus, king of Corinth; slayer of Belerus of Corinth (from which deed he derived his name). After the murder he fled to Proetus, king of Argos, whose wife Antea tried to seduce him. When he repelled her she accused him to her husband of having affronted her chastity. Proetus then sent him to Iobates, king of Lycia, Antea's father, carrying with him a letter which besought Iobates to put him to death. Iobates therefore sent Bellerophon to slay a fearsome monster, the Chimaera; this, by aid of the winged horse, Pegasus, he did. Bellerophon was exposed by Iobates to further perils, but in every contest he was victorious. The king forgave him, accepted him as a son-in-law, and named him successor to his own throne.

bellona

Roman goddess of war.

benevolence

from the Latin bene ("well") and volens principle taken to support social interest and oppose self interest.

bentham, Jeremy (1748-1832)

a British moral philosopher who advocated utilitarian ethics. He reduced all the motives of human conduct to either pleasure or pain. According to him, pleasure or happiness is the highest good desirable by any individual. He preferred quantitative pleasure to qualitative one. His chief work is Deontology of the Science of Morality.

Berlin, Sir Isaiah (1909-)

a British moral and political philosopher who argued against the determinist philosophy of history. He stressed the importance of moral values only in the light of human responsibilities and freedom. One of his important works is Two Concepts of Liberty.

bernoulli's theorem

a concept in probability theory, also known as the law of large of numbers. Suppose that there is a sequence of *n* trials, and every one of which an outcome A is possible and on every one of which the probability of A is the same, say p. The theorem states that the probability that the proportion of As in the sequence lies within the range p ± h (where h is any small fraction) approaches 1 in n approaches infinity.

berry's paradox

refers to an informal version of Richard's paradox.

bertrands's box paradox

a paradox which suggests that different ways of describing alternative lead to different probability assignments.

best, principle of the

the Leibnizian principle of perfection, satirized by Voltaire in Candide through the hero's native belief that "everything is for the best in the best of all possible words".

Bhagavad-Gita

it literally means 'the song of the lord'. It is one of the most sacred books of Hindus. The philosophy of Gita is based on the philosophy of Karma which in turn is based on Jnana yoga, and supported by Bhakti yoga. According to Gita, the duty of man is to fight against all evil forces. Gita emphasizes on 'niskamya karma', that is to say, one should not aim at any fruits while performing an action for the sake of good.

bhairava

in Hinduism a name of Shiva meaning "fearful". The name of the third member of the Hindu trinity in his "fear" form. A dozen form of this Bhairava Shiva relationship are known, the most common being "Bhairava the Black" and "Bhairava the Dog".

Bhakti (sanskrit for devotion)

in the vedanta and other Indian systems, love of God, expressed in prayer and meditation and ultimately in total self-surrender to the divine nature. Bhakti came to prominence during the medieval theistic period of Indian thought; its philosophical basis was chiefly provided by Ramanuja.

Bible

from the Greek biblia ("the books"), derived from the name of the Phoenician city, Byblos, an important source of papyrus. The term refers to the scriptures of the Jews (divided into the Law, Prophets, and Writings) as well as to those of the Christians (39 books of the Old Testament and 27 of the New Testament).

Biblical criticms

refers to the application to the Bible of linguistic and historiographic tools in order to purify the text and provide a sound basis for its interpretation.

bibilicism

refers to the adherence to the Bible as authoritative in a literal sense.

biconditional

refers to a statement in which

it is asserted that possession of one property is a necessary and sufficient condition for possession of another, as in 'A number is prime if it has no divisors other than one and itself, on that the existence of one state of affairs is a necessary and sufficient condition for the existence of another, as in "He will be president if he wins the election".

binary operation

refers to a two place operation.

biography

history of the life and character of a person.

biology

from the Greek bios ('life') and logia ('knowledge of'). The study of biology was central to the Lyceum of Aristotle, and conducted on an experimental basis. Where the study of physics remained speculative and theoretical, knowledge of living forms was gained inductively and by dissection.

bishop

one having oversight of a congregation in the primitive Christian Church. Later, an ecclesiastical dignitary, of the highest of the 3 orders of ministry, presiding over a diocese.

bivalence, principle (or law) of

refers to the principle that states that every statement is either true or false; that is, that every statement has a truth value and that there are just two truth-values. In the presence of a negation operator, as standardly conceived, this principle entails that of the excluded middle, but since it makes no mention of negation is not equivalent to it. The law of excluded middle has been a logical law operating at the level of the object language, whereas the principle of bivalence is a semartic principle, one governing the interpretation of the language to which it is applied.

Blanshard, Brand (1892-)

an American rationalist philosopher who claimed that his entire work consists in the vindication of reason against any philosophical argument. His three main works are: Reason and Goodness; Reason and Analysis; and Reason and Belief.

bodhi

a Sanskrit term which means "wisdom" or "enlightenment". Widely used in Indian philosophy, the term's opposite is avidya or ignorance.

bodhisattva

in Sanskrit bodhi ('wisdom') and sattva ('existence in'). In Buddhism those who defer Buddhahood for the sake of others. The doctrine is to be found in both Hinayana and Mahayana Buddhism, but it is much more central to the latter.

body

for Descartes body is extended

and has reference to space, time, and motion, standing in contrast to mind, which altogether lacks the first reference retaining the third only in a metaphorical sense.

boo-hooray theory

refers to the apt and widely employed nickname of the view of moral, and indeed of all evaluative, utterance expressed in Ayer's Language, Truth and Logic (1936). Such utterances, or the evaluative elements in them, do not sate anything, but, like ejaculations, simply express the reactions of the speaker.

book of changes, the, (or I ching)

refers to one of the basic Chinese classics. The book arose in relation to the practice of divination and was formed between the 6th and the 3rd centuries B.C. The book consists of sixty-four hexagrams, based on eight trigrams of three lines each. The trigram for heaven is---. That for earth is---. A divided line stands for the concept of Y in. an undivided line stands for Yang. The trigrams are combined into all the possible hexagrams, and are supposed to symbolize all possible situations. The hexagram formed by placing the trigram for water--aver the trigram of fire---symbolizes conquest, triumph, or success.

book of dead

in Egyptian religion a book of formulae, prayers, and hymns designed to assist the decreased in meeting the challenges of passage into the after-world.

Boolean Algebra

the algebra developed by Georage Boole (1815-64) as a way of manipulating symbols by purely algebraic methods (for example, multiplication), without regard for any particular interpretation but merely reflecting basic laws of thought. The term now refers to abstracts systems, similar in many respect to the original Booleon algebra, which may be applied to such diverse areas as probability and computer design.

Boole, George (1815-1864)

a well-known British logician and mathematician, who invented algebra. One of his important work is, Mathematical Analysis of Logic.

boreas

the north wind personified; he is said to have helped the Athenians in the Persian war by destroying the enemy ships.

boundary situation

from the German Grenzsituation, a term used to refer to those situations which set the limits of man's historical being, i.e., death suffering, struggle, and guilt.

boundless, the

refers to a translation of the Greek apeiron. Underlying principle of change in the philosophy of Anaximander.

bouts-rimés

list of rhyming words which, by way of pastime, are used for rhymes for verses in the same order as in the list.

Brahma

along with Vishnu and Shiva the Gods making up the Hindu trinity. Brahma is the creator god.

brahman

Sanskrit term, etymology uncertain. The term may have meant 'magic', referring to the gaining of magical results through ritual and sacrifice.

brahmana

commentary on a veda, also a priest.

brain

a central part of the nervous system that consists of the cerebrum and the spinal cord. The upper most parts of the cerebrum are directly connected with the mental or psychic life of humans and animals. They are the organs of control through which various activities of the individual are regulated.

brahmacarya (celebacy)

the first stage of life, namely, student life.

breviary

a book containing the daily offices, or services, of the Roman Catholic church, consisting of psalms, lessons, hymns, and prayers. These services are known as, in order throughout the day: matins, lauds, prime, terce, sext, none, vespers, and compline. Matins and evensong in the Anglican prayer-book represent a conflation and condensation of certain of these.

Brhaspati

a heretical teacher, who is believed to be the traditional founder of Carvaka school of materialism. It is also believed that the founder of this Caravaka school was the same Brhaspati who was the teacher of Devas (Gods) and who propagated materialism among Asuras mainly to ruin that race. Carvaka, it is claimed, after whose name the Indian materialistic school is called, was the ideal disciple of Brhaspati.

brutes

all animals other than man. A famous passage in Descartes Discourse deals with 'the' difference between men and brutes: The crucial point about animals, for Descartes, is their lack of language; animal 'utterances' are always elicited by a specific stimulus and never amount to genuine speech.

Buddha, Gautama Siddhartha (560-480 B.C.)

founder of the Buddhist faith. Born in South Nepal India, in the foothills of the eastern Himalayas. Son of a king of the Shakya clan. He is said to have made the great renunciation after the birth of his first child. The Buddha is the typical title given to Siddhartha Gautama, founder or re-founder of the Buddhist tradition. It is among a number of epithets assigned to Gautama and to some other spiritual leaders of the period. The term meaning 'awakening one' or 'enlightened one' and is related to the word bodhi, meaning 'awakening' or 'enlightenment'. The latter expression has become the favourite translation of the word in modern English.

Siddhartha was his given name and Gautama his family or clan name. These spellings are the Sanskrit ones. In Pali the two names are Siddhattha and Gotama. Since the Theravada canon is composed in Pali and in some ways reflect an earlier tradition than many of the Sanskrit texts of the Mahayana, it is quite common in English writings to see the Buddha's names rendered in their Pali version. However, the materials which we have on the life of the Buddha are heavily encrusted with legendary and mythic material, and as well shall see, it is hard to be sure of much in the actual life of the Buddha. The quest for the historical Buddha is even more arduous than the quest of the historical Jesus. The term 'Buddha' is the same in both Pali and Sanskrit, fortunately. Because he came from a small people known as the Sakyas (Sanskrit; Pali: Sakya) he was also known as sakyamuni, or sage of the sakyas. Among other important epithets used of him are jina ('conqueror', 'victor'), tathagata ('thus-gone'), bhagavan ('lord') and sugata ('well-gone'). Jina was also a favourite title of the contemporary movement known as Jainas ('followers of the jina'). In parallel the Buddhist followers came to be called bauddhas.

The term 'the Buddha' is usually taken to refer to the historical figure; but in the Buddhist tradition there has virtually always been a belief in earlier Buddhas. In the Pali canon they are often simply referred to collectively.

There is great debate about the dates of the Buddha. Based on the Sri Lankan tradition, there is the commonly accepted pair of dates for the birth and death of the Buddha, namely 563 and 483 B.C. Other variants calculated by scholars are 484 and 485 as the death date. But such theories depend on Sri Lankan traditional calculations from the date of the accession of Asoka, which is also in dispute. Another strategy is to take the northern tradition, which has a different view of the time between the death of the Buddha and the accession of Ashoka namely 116 years instead of 218 according to Sri Lankan sources. This would have the Buddha die in 386 or 383.

Let us now rehearse the legendary account of the life of

the Buddha, and then estimate what of this is historically reliable. The legendary life is of course important, for it is that narrative that enters phenomenologically into the consciousness of most Buddhists up to modern times. He was born the son of Suddhodana, the king of the Sakyans and Mahamaya. Before his birth his mother dreamed that a beautiful white elephant passed through her side into her womb. This led to the prediction that when he grew up he would either be a universal monarch (cakravartin) or a spiritual cakravartin. His mother born him at Lumbini in Nepal, as it is now, where in the third century B.C. the emperor Asoka would implant an inscribed pillar, rediscovered in 1896, and a stupa or memorial shrine. A holy man called Asita, hearing of his birth, came down from the mountains and again predicted the dual choice in his destiny. A week after his birth his mother died, and he was raised by her sister.

Because of the predictions he was treated to great luxury, fitting for a prince. His classification in accord with his tribal origins was as a ksatria or warrior; in his later teachings, however, he was to set himself against the varna system of ancient Aryan India, which assigned people to four classes, headed by the Brahmins. Possibly the system was not functioning among the Sakyans. When he was 12, he was found during a festival sitting alone under a tree, having attained the first stage of meditation (dhyana, jnana). At 16, he was married to Yasodhra. It was not, however, till he was 29 that he made some harrowing discoveries which would impel him to leave home. These 'four signs' were the sight of an old man, bent and feeble, and a sick man, stewing in his own excrete; a corpse; and a shaven-headed man wearing a robe who had left home, to wander. He shortly heard of the birth of his first and only son, Rahula. He decided to leave home, and slipped away in the middle of the night, making his great renunciation. His desire was to find the good, and during the early part of his search he sat at the feet of two notable teachers who taught him different stages of meditation, incorporated later into the ascending scale of stages of dhyana in the Buddha's teaching. But both left him dissatisfied, and he tried to attain peace through the practice of the severe self-mortification, in the company of five fellow-seekers. But in due course he came to reject the path of extreme austeity, and his companions left him, disillusioned with him. He accepted food from a young woman named Sujata, and strengthened by this prepared to attain enlightenment, seated at the base of an asvattha or bodhi tree.

Gautama set forth to teach his former comrades, and delivered the first sermon in the deer park at a place called Saranath, close of Varansi (Banaras). The rest of his life was devoted to teaching and to the founding and nurture of his order of monks (later nuns too), known as the sangha. Later formulations would sum up the creed of the Buddhism as affirming that one went to the Buddha, the dharma and the sangha for refuge. These are the three jewels of Buddhism. The forty-five years of organizing and teaching involved his wandering over the Gangetic region, winding up in Kusinagara, a small town not far from his birthplace, where he died after a severe illness resulting from eating a meat given him by a smith called Chanda: probably of pork, though another translation of the once-used term is truffles. When he died his body was cremated and his ashes distributed to various sites, later important for pilgrimages. The most important pilgrimage locations, however, are the places associated with the crucial stages of his life - Lumbini, where he was horn, Bodh Gaya, where he gained bodhi, Sarnath where he set the wheel of the dharma in motion, and Kusinagara, where he deceased and so gained ultimate nirvana. Before his death he reminded his disciples that their teacher would not have disappeared but would live on in the teachings, and that they should diligently strive to attain liberation. Earlier he had remarked that he did not have the closed fist of the teacher, that is, he did not hold anything back: and so we may assume that he thought that the Dhrma was sufficient for salvation.

To these events may be added other legendary material relating to the extensive collection of stories of the previous lives of the Budha, when he was bodhisattva or buddha-to-be, in various forms at varying times as a king, a hare, and so on.

Among the peoples he associated with were the Vajjians and the Licchavis, who had republican type constitutions, and they served as rough models for the constitution of the sangha, which was also, however, bound tightly by a rule or vinaya, a later increasingly elaborated, which imposed upon monks and hermits rules designed to make them tread a middle path between luxury and harsh austerity.

More can be gleaned from the discourses of the Buddha as to his originality as a teacher. Although there are certain ritual elements evident in early Buddhism, and though ultimately his teachings were something to be confirmed by direct experience, it is in his philosophical and doctrinal teachings that his creativity shows through. There is a characteristic style about the Buddha's teachings as transmitted and of course greatly elaborated in the canonical texts which is striking: it is a style which is on the one hand highly analytical, and on the other hand full of the metaphors, parables and illustrations.

It is very likely that the Buddha himself formulated early versions of some of key ideas- the four noble truths, the eightfold path, the doctrine of the dependent origination, the analysis of the self into the five skandhas (khandhas), the Buddhist version of the rebirth and karma doctrine, the rationalistic ethics, the rejection of the varna system, the critique of Brahmin claims about the gods and about creation and the nature of the sangha.

The most original idea of the Buddha was his rejection of the permanent self, and more generally his analysis of the world without recourse to the idea of the substance. This related, it seems, to a conventionalist account of language. The growing Sanskrit tradition of the period appealed to the everlasting and primordial character of the Sanskrit language, which in the form of the recited Veda formed the backbone of a revelatory ritual tradition. The banddhas were characteristically nastika or nonorthodox, rejecting such a revelatory tradition. This goes back to the Buddha's having found the source of his knowledge from quite a different source, namely in inner contemplative experience. In addition he found it in analysis, not reliance on tradition handed down by sacred persons. There was an empiricist bent, no doubt, to the Buddha's outlook, althoug it was not a narrow empiricism he expressed which confines knowledge to what can be derived from the five senses, but included importantly, yogic perception also. That is, he included a type of religious experience, which of course had to be cultivated through the practice of dhyana and to be buttressed by some degree of moral development, as a source of empirical knowledge.

But he also perceived that from the empirical point of view it was not necessary to postulate permanent entities underlying the shifting phenomena which we encounter in experience.

This fitted in with a conventionalist view of language, since language could be held to be up to a point misleading, in suggesting that there are permanent things, and in particular a self, underlying changes. It would seem to be these insights which led him to his interpretation of nirvana, which is so crucial for understanding early Buddhist philosophy.

It was from this point of view that he was led to some other momentous ideas, namely the idea of the undetermined questions and the notion of the individual as a bundle of types of states or processes. The former questions relate above all to the status of the Tathagata after his death. It is inappropriate to say that he does exist, or does not, or both does and does not, or neither does nor does not. The analogy is with the question of where a fire goes when it goes out. It does not make sense. In so far as the Tathagata is defined by the empirical states which can be pointed to in this life, there is no Thathagata to point to once he has deceased after attaining nirvana in this life. Similarly the question of whether there is an end or boundary to the cosmos is unanswerable. In a certain sense there is, in so far as the saint ultimately disappears when he gains nirvana, and here we are led back to the concept of nirvana. It would seem that the fourfold negation was used creatively by him to eliminate radically transcendental questions, as being metaphysically unanswerable, given the analysis of the world as a series of processes and without a characterisable creator standing behind it. The Buddha produced what might be called, may be anachronistically, a non-substantialist variety of Sankhya.

His original view of nirvana led to his characterising the individual as being made up of the bundles of different kinds of processes, with nothing permanent or substantial underlying them. This doubtless is the root of the doctrine of the skandhas. We are made up of bodily processes, perceptions, feelings, dispositions and states of consciousness. The doctrine has a double effect: one is to make us see ourselves as composite beings, who are the result of different ingredients being put together; the other is to make us see ourselves as impermanent entities. The idea of us as a composite of ingredients has a typically Buddhist air, where so much is made of lists of ingredients and types of events.

Another piece of originality

seems to be the Buddha's reading of karma and rebirth. Generally speaking we may look on his doctrine of karma as being a psychological one. Sometimes, of course, it looks as if the whole of the Buddhist teaching is psychological. But unlike the Jainas he did not see the effects of karma as being automatic given a certain external act, such as crushing an insect. The crucial thing, on the contrary, was the mental disposition of the actor. That is why the very first verse of the Dhammapada claims that whenever anyone acts with an impure mind duhkha follows him or her as the plough follow the ox.

The Buddha accepted the notion of the rebirth, though, rather originally, he dispensed with the notion of an underlying jiva or atman carrying over from one life to the next. The causation of rebirth had to do with the dispositions of the individual. It looks as if he kept to the doctrine because he believed that it was based on memory of previous lives, which he, it was claimed, possessed. The triad of rebirth, karma and yogic practice seems to have belonged widely to sramanic religious movements of his time and no doubt had begun to penetrate Brahmins' thinking.

His rationalist ethic can be glimpsed in various primitive formulations of it as in the five precepts and the transcendental virtues of maitri or kindliness; karuna or compassion; mudita or joy; and upeksa or equanimity. Ethics was of course a vital ingredient in the eightfold path, and is the necessary accompaniment to meditative accomplishment as represented in the last three stages or aspects of the path.

In a special way the Buddha's attitude towards the gods seems to have been sceptical. In regard to Brahma he was ironic: Brahma, creator and patron of Brahmins, was the first being to emerge after a period of cosmic repose: he then thinks that other beings, which come into being later than he, occur because of him. So he fallaciously supposes himself to be creator. The rest of the gods may be some sort of the force within the cosmos, but Brahma and they are all ultimately impermanent. Moreover the Buddha knows them in his own experience, but Brahmins rely upon a handed-down tradition, which is like a chain of blind persons hanging on to one another.

There were some paradoxes in his position which were to generate, fruitfully, some new developments. Thus there is an obscurity in the position as sketched above about the relation between ethics and the pursuit of salvation. The aim of the saint (arhant) to liberate himself or herself could be interpreted as being ultimately selfish, however heroically the saint might relinquish this worldly aims. As we know, this tension was overcome in the Mahayana by the ideal of bodhisattva, who puts off his or her own liberation in order to work for the welfare of all living beings. There were issues too about the scope of early Buddhist critique of language. It seems clear that some core of scepticism about ordinary language existed from the earliest teachings. How far should criticism be taken? The notion that all substance talk is misleading would take us very far indeed in criticising all nouns whatsoever. The extreme outcome of this extension of scepticism was found in the dialectic of Nagarjuna.

The orginality and force of the Buddha's personality can be in little doubt. The power of his ideas has survived through many elaborations in the wide swathe of Asian civilization which his religion has penetrated. It was therefore not surprising that there was an increase in the tendency to deify him, from the time of the proto Mahayana Lokottaravadins. It would seem, though, that in the earliest teaching the transcendent aspect of Buddhahood had simply to do with his capacity for nirvana, and with the noncomposite and non-important character of that ideal.

buddhi (intellect)

it is the first evolute from prakrti. It is the basis for all the intelligence of the individual. According to Nyaya-Vaisesika, it is of two types—smrti (recollection), and anubhava (experience).

buddhism

the religion founded by Gautama Buddha in the 6th century B.C. Arising in the Eastern provinces, far from the Indus Valley, center of Vedic culture.

buddhism, hinayana 400-250 B.C. (formative period)

the earlier and more strict of the two interpretations of Buddhism which arose after Gautam Buddha's death. The term 'Hinayana' means "the small vehicle" and was given to this variant from by its chief rival which was self-styled as "Mahayana" or the great vehicle.

buddhism, mahayana

0-500 A.D. (formative period): the later, more popular and more elaborate of the two interpretations of Buddhism which arose after the death of the founder, Gautam, Buddha. Members of the movement gave themselves the name 'Mahayana' meaning 'the great vehicle'. To be contrasted with the term 'Hinayana' meaning the small vehicle which they applied to the earlier and more strict interpretation of the teachings of Buddha.

buddhist councils

two councils are accepted by all Buddhists, and three by most. The first was a seven-month session held in 483 B.C. following Buddha's death.

buddhist philosophy

buddhism is an originally Indian religion, founded in the 5th century B.C. by Siddhartha Gautama, the 'Buddha' (enlightened one).

burali-forti's paradox

the paradox of the greatest ordinal, and one of the logical paradoxes.

buridan's ass

the traditional illustrative example, first found in Aristotle but now associated with Buridan, of the problem of decision making when there is no reason for preferring one of the possible alternatives. The ass, faced with two equally desirable haybales, starves to death through indecision since, exhypothesi, there are no grounds for preferring one bale to the other.

Burke, Edmund (1729-97)

a British statesman and a philosopher who argued that our enjoyment of beauty consists in the way in which our imagination is engaged by obscurity and suggestiveness rather than by intellectual clarity.

bushido

from the Japanese bushi ('warror') and ('way' or 'principle'). The term refers to the chivalric code (Confucian and Zen. Buddhist in origin) of the warrior-knight in feudal Japan.

byzantine church

in a strict sense those congregations falling under the jurisdiction of the Church of Constatntinople. In a looser sense the entire group of Eastern Orthodox Churches.

cabala

the term is employed to designate a set of mystical doctrines which developed within Judaism between the last pre-Christian centuries and the 14th century, and the collection of books written in support of these doctrines. The Cabala developed in contrast to orthodox Jewish doctrine, emphasizing exactly the elements rejected by the orthodox.

Cadmus

son of Agenor, king of Phoenicia, who sent him in quest of his sister, Europe, when she was abducted by Zeus. His mission proved fruitless, but in following the advice of the Delphic oracle he founded the Cadmea, later the citadel of Thebes. To obtain water there he had to kill a dragon, an offspring of Ares, guarding the well. This done, Athena counselled him to sow the creature's teeth in the soil, from which there sprang up armed men, whom he killed by setting them to fight one another. The 5 survivors—the Spartoi (sown men)—became the ancestors of the Thebans. Cadmus married Harmonia, daughter of Ares and Aphrodite.

calchas

soothsayer with the Greek army at the siege of Troy.

calculus

refers to a system of symbols so organized that inferences can be made by manipulating the symbols of the system according to rule. The elements of any calculus : have been symbols, definitions, axioms, and rules of inference. Some of these symbols must be primitive, or underfined; the rest will be defined in terms of those which are undefined. Through the appropriate combination of symbols, well formed formulae and, through the manipulation of such formulae, the theorems of the calculus, can be gained.

calemes

valid syllogism in AEE mood, fourth figure.

callicles

5th century B.C. A Greek philosopher and politician. Callicles enters Plato's dialogue, Gorgias, as one of Socrates contemporaries. One of the Sophists, he argues that the natural expression of the natural justice. The conversion of the society attempt to enslave the strong and thus subvert natural justice. He also argues for pleasure as the goal of life.

callirrhoe

daughter of the river-god Achelous. A spring in Athens was named after her.

calvinism

refers to the movement of thought and practice following from Calvin's work.

Calypso

nymph who lived on the island of Ogygia, where she detained Odysseus for 7 years.

cambridge platonists

an English intellectual movement centering in Cambridge University in the third quarter of the 17th century. Centering around problems in the philosophy of religion, the group stood largely in the tradition of Neoplatonism, citing especially Plato, Proclus, and Plotinus. Jacob Boehme, Descartes, and malebranche also received attention.

Camus, Albert (1913-1960)

a French existentialist philosopher who won the Nobel prize for literature. He was influenced by Kierkegaard, Nietzsche and Dostoyevsky. However, he remained as an atheist. His philosophy was concerned with the meaning of human existence. According to him, man's existence is 'absurd', thus he made the category of the 'absurd' as the basis of his philosophy. One of his famous novels is The Rebel.

canon
a Latin term which means "measuring line", "rule", or "model", derived from the Greek kanon ("rule" or "rod").
(1) canons of scripture are those writings regarded as authoritative for a given religion. The Jewish or Hebrew canon consists of the Law, Prophets, and Writings. The Christian canon, or Bible consists of 39 books of the Old Testament and 27 of the New.
(2) canon law. The most authoritative law of the Roman Catholic Church, bearing the authority of Scriptures, pope, or council. To be distinguished from decrees of bishops, church-state concordats, and church law resting on custom. The body of Canon Law was published in 1582 by Gregory XIII as the Corpus Juris Canonici. A new codification, known as the Codex Juris Canonici, was promulgated under Benedict XV in 1917.

canonization
in Roman Catholicism the decree placing a person in the catalogue or canon of saints and commending that he be venerated. Necessary to canonization is the prior achievement of beatification and the authentication of at least two miracles by intercession of the person, always deceased, under consideration.

Canter, George (1845-1918)
a German mathematician who has been regarded as the father of the set theory. By means of a diagonal theory he proved that the set of all natural numbers is not equivalent to the set of real numbers. Thus there are more than one infinite number.

cantor's paradox
refers to a paradox in set theory which was discovered by George Cantor. The paradox is generated by the question of whether the set of all sets has been (a) equal to or (b) greater than its own power set. If (a), a contradiction arises in that it can be proved that the power set of any given set is greater than the set itself. If (b), a contradiction arises since the power of any set is itself a set of sets and therefore a subject of the set of all sets, and it can be proved that the subset of any given set is not greater than the given set.

capitalism
refers to that economic system which stresses the role of capital, i.e., wealth of all sorts including economic goods utilized in the production of other goods.
(1) the classical expression of the capitalism is credited to Adam Smith who argued for the free play of a self regulating market and who believed that, given competition, the operation of an "invisible hand" would move prices to "natural" levels and induce labour and capital to move from

less to more profitable enterprises. In sort, man's competitive striving would be transmuted automatically into the common good.

(2) the French term laissez-faire ("let do" or "let make"), derived from the Physiocrats (q.v.), came to be attached to "capitalism" as a qualifying phrase. The total phrase "laissez-faire capitalism" emphasized the point that in this system economic interests where to be let alone to continue their development without government control and with a minimum of regulation.

(3) Mex Weber found the rise of capitalism and that of Protestantism to be related, the former standing as a secularized version of the latter's emphasis on individualism, and the necessity that one work out his own salvation.

cardinal

a prince of the Roman Catholic Church.

cardinality

the cardinality of a set, X, refers to any property possessed by all and only those sets equivalent to X. (Two sets are equivalent if members of one set can be paired off with members of the other set in such a way that each member of either set is paired with exactly one member of the other, that is, there is a one-to-one correspondence between members of the two sets.) The set of all those sets equivalent to X is sometimes taken as a cardinal number. Intuitively, two sets share the same cardinality if they have the same number of members.

cardinal virtues

a term introduced by St. Ambrose, having come across Plato's classification of the natural virtues in the writings of Cicero.

(1) among the Greeks, and for Plato, the virtues were "wisdom", "courage", "temperance" and "justice".

cartesian

of or relating to Rene Descartes.

cartesianism

the doctrine of Descartes is known as Cartesianism. It became very popular in France and Netherlands.

Cassandra

daughter of Priam and Hecuba of Troy. For her beauty Apollo bestowed upon her the gift of prophecy—provided she gratified his desires. She refused, and the god decreed that, though she might retain the gift, her utterances would never be believed. Carried off to Mycenae by Agamemnon after Troy's fall, she was murdered there by his adulterous wife, Clytemnestra.

Cassiopeia

beautiful mother of Andromeda.

casualism

from the Latin causes ("tall",

"accident"). Taken literally, although the usage tends to be obsolete, the doctrine that all things result from chance.

casuistry

in ethical realm, casuistry is regarded as a systematic discussion of the applicability of the general moral laws to particular cases of conduct. In the process, it accommodates new ideas that challenge the existing social order.

catechism

from the Greek katexein ("teach by word of mouth"). A compendium of essential religious instruction arranged in the form of questions and answers. Although it is common to many religions, in Western usage the term refers to practices of Jewish Eastern Orthodox, Roman Catholic, and Protenstant religious instruction.

categorematic

in traditional logic, a denoting term or word that can stand on its own apart from its usage in a sentence or statement. Example: blue, Socrates, bird etc.

categorical imperative

a term which was introduced into ethics by Kant to distinguish the guidance to action given by morality that of other forms of prescription.

category

the most important concepts are called categories. All the sciences (exact, natural as well as social) are based on certain fundamental categories of their own subject-matter. For example, physical is based on certain fundamental categories like matter, motion, change, space and time, etc. Similarly there are certain philosophical categories which are very important for the better understanding of the subject-matter of philosophy. For example, form and content, freedom and necessity, cause and effect, determinism and indeterminism, etc. However, in Aristotle's philosophy the term 'category' covers all the modes of classes which in turn explain all the modes of existence (being). Thus, a predicate belonging to one category may not be applicable to a subject belonging to another category. In modern times, it was Kant who focused his attention on the categories of understanding. Unlike Aristotle, Kant did not restrict categories to mere 'subject and predicate' of a statement rather extended the categories of understanding to entire 'judgements'. All in all Kant recognised twelve categories of understanding which can be reduced to four basic or fundamental categories or understanding. They are—quantity, quality, relation and modality.

category mistake

Gilbert Ryle first introduced this term in his The Concept of Mind. According to him, we often commit category mistake by attributing same qualities or properties to the entities belonging to two different logical types. For example, Descartes advocated the view that mind exists independent of mind. Here mind and body, Ryel holds, belong to two different logical types, still the notion of existence is attributed to both. This results, according to Ryle, in a category mistake.

cathedral

the principle church in a diocese, containing the bishop's cathedra or throne.

catholicism

literally, the faith and practice of the whole Church, the expression 'catholic Church being first found in a letter of St. Ignatius of Antioch. In time the term came to be used in the further meaning of true or authentic, in contrast with schismatic or heretical. The Roman Catholic Church claims for itself the exclusive right to this epithet and stresses the authority and continuity of the historic Church, the importance of organized ministry (the fount of authority being the Papacy), and the absolute indispensability of the sacraments.

causa

Latin term which means "cause". Among Latin phrases embodying the term the following have to be noted. Causa cognoscendi refers to the cause of our knowledge of an event, and has to be distinguished from causa essendi, the cause of the event itself.

causa sui

a Latin term for 'cause of itself'. According to Spinoza, substance is a causa sui. In his philosophy, substance is identified with the God, and God is identified with the Nature. Thus, God, for Spinoza, exists in every object. Such a God is uncaused.

causation

refers to the relationship between two events or states of affairs such that the first brings about the second.

cave, image of the

Plato's illustration in the Republic (Book VII) of the difference between knowledge and illusion, reality and apperance. Men chained in a cave, facing a blank wall, with a fire burning behind them, can only shadows, which they take for real objects.

Cecrops

in Greek legend the first king of Attica (as distinct from Athens).

centaur

lecherous and drunken creature, half horse, half man, inhabiting Mt. Pelion in Thessaly. The Centaurs are famous in Greek myth for their fight with the Lapithae (depicted on the Parthenon metopes).

cerberus

monster with 3 (or 50) heads; the watchdog of Hades.

Ceres

Roman goddess of corn, identified with the Greek Demeter.

certainity

from the Latin cernere and the Greek krinein ('to decide').

(1) logical certainty is a property of valid conclusions in deductive inference (q.v. logic), the property being simply that the conclusion follows necessarily from the premises. Since one is interested in true conclusions, however, it is necessary to have true premises as well as valid reasoning.

(2) psychological certainty is a state of belief in the truth or falsity of a given proposition; and this state does not insure truth in one's conclusions, even should the latter be gained by valid reasoning.

certainity and doubt

concepts that play an important part in Cartesian theory of knowledge. In the first of his Meditations, Descartes argued that if one is know that a proposition P is true, then (a) one must be certain that p, and (b) one must be unable to doubt that p. So if one is to say, with justification, 'I know that p', one must not be in a position in which one may at some time have to take back one's assertion that p; the assertion that p, must be such that one cannot doubt the truth of what one says.

ceteris paribus

Latin phrase which means 'other thing being equal'.

chain of being

a metaphor for the order, unity, and completeness of the created world, thought of as a chain extending to include all possibilities of existence, from God to the tiniest particle of inanimate matter.

chaldeans

a small sect of Eastern Christians in communion with the See of Rome but having a patriarch of their own, styled the Patriarch of Babylon. They use Syriac as their liturgical language. About half their number live in Syria.

change

refers to the opposite of permanence, and one of the basic categorials ideas.

(1) heraclitus held to the universality of constant change, explaining that it takes place by opposites. His example was the tension of the drawn bow.

(2) Parmenides, Zeno and Nagarjuna argued for the permanence and against the possibility of change.

(3) Aristotle distinguished three types of change : alteration, growth or diminution, and locomotion.

(4) Bergson and Whitehead made the category of becoming or process central to their philosophies.

chaos

the term first used in the Theogony of Hesiod (8th century BC) to describe the gap resulting from the separation of heaven and earth during the emergence of the world from an undifferentiated state; it was interpreted by Aristotle as the pre-philosophic concept of space.

chap-book

small book of sensational tales, in verse or prose, formerly hawked about the streets by chapmen, and designed to gratify popular taste.

character complex

the term for "sense-datum" (q.v.), employed in the movement of Critical Realism.

characteizing

a term used as an adjective or noun without supplying a principle for counting what falls under it. For example, 'thing', 'object', 'place', 'action' etc.

charismata

from the Greek charisma ("gift"). In early Christianity the term applied to the "gifts of the Spirit", especially the gift of "speaking the tongues". Paul carefully broadened the application of the term, insisting that love is the very highest charisma.

charites

the graces, the 3 daughters of Zeus; Euphrosyne, Aglaia, and Thalia. Their characters and qualities were a delight to gods and men alike.

charon

ferryman who transported souls of the dead across the River Styx, his fee being a small coin placed in the mouth of each corpse. He is always represented as aged, bearded, and ragged.

charvaka

Indian philosophical system of Materialism, traceable to the Rig Veda. Its principal development came in 600 B.C. in the no longer extant Brhaspate Sutra. The doctrine of Materialism, called Lokayata, has had many adherents since that time.

(1) the principles of all things are earth, air, fire, and water.

(2) that which cannot be perceived does not exist; to exists is to be perceivable.

(3) intelligence is only body disposed in a certain manner and the soul is only the body as distinguished by intelligence.

(4) the only end of man is the enjoyment of sensual pleasure, and the avoidance of pain. Heaven and hell are the inventions of stupid men.

(5) the practice of religion has its sufficient explanation in providing a good living for the priest, and the authors of the Vedas were "buffoons, knaves, and demons".

(6) even so-called universal ideas and relations are to be understood through perceptual connections, reinforced by memory. And this feature

reduces the power of inference.

(7) the connection of cause and effect must be understood perpetually, also, and when we do so, its basis disappears for we may perceive the two horns of a cow successively and one horn would not seem to be the cause of the other.

(8) finally, neither the existence nor non-existence of anything can be firmly established.

chiliasm

from the Greek term chiliad which means "thousand". The millenarian doctrine that Christ would soon return to initiate a thousand-year region on earth prior to the end of time.

chimaera

triple-bodied monster, at once she-goat, lion and serpent, slain by Bellerophon.

Chinese Logicians the

a 4th century B.C. school of philosophers carrying the traditional Chinese concern with rectification of names in the direction of logical analysis. One of the smallest of the schools, the logicians were without influence after their own-time. Hui Shih and Kung-Lung were the school's most noted thinkers.

chinese philosophy 6th cent B.C. to the present

until recent years the factors related in the philosophical history of this culture have been Confucianism, Taoism, Moism, the Logicians, Legalism, the Y in Yang Schools, and Chinese Buddhism.

chiron

wisest of the Centaurs, he was taught be Apollo and Artemis, becoming extremely proficient in hunting, gymnastics, medicine, music and prophecy. Achilles and Jason were among his pupils.

chloe

title of Demeter as goddess of the young green crops (the name means green).

choice axiom of

an axiom of set theory. Given any set X, the members of which are non-empty disjoint sets (that is, no two member sets of X have any members in common and each member set has at least one member), the axiom of choice states that there exists a (choice) set that consists of exactly one member of each of the members of X. The axiom has been shown to be independent of the other axioms of the set theory.

Chomsky, Avram Noam (1928-)

an American linguist and philosopher whose grammer has revolutionised the scientific study of language. According to Chomsky, the speakers of language have innate ability to create infinite number of sentences that are intelligible. His important works are Cartesian Linguistics, Language and

Mind etc.

Christ, Jesus 4B.C. -29 A.D.
founder of the Christian religion. Born in Bethlehem; childhood in Nazareth. On charges of blasphemy and sedition he was tried and executed on the authority of Rome.

christadelphians
the Brethren of Christ, a religious organization, established in 1833, and claiming to represent the true faith and practice of the apostolic age as revived by John Thomas of Brooklyn. They hold firmly to the verbal inspration of the Bible, and believe that Christ will one day return, assume the throne of David, and rule over the restored tribes of Israel, in whom the saved are incorporated, the damned having to die the second death. The first deth is a state of unconsciousness, but man's resurrection is physical. They reject the Holy Trinity.

christian Science
a denomination which looks to the words and works of Jesus Christ for authority, and emphasizes the practice of spiritual healing. One of the basic teachings of Christian Science is that Man and the Universe are spiritual. Christian Scientists believe that the material, mortal man, who is liable to sickness and sin, is a distorted concept and not the real or actual, spiritual man made in the image and likeness of God. The human body expresses the kind of thinking which governs it. Therefore as the Bible truths concerning spiritual man are embodied in human though, fear, ignorance of God, and sin depart, and regeneration and healing naturally follow.

Mary Baker Eddy founded Christian Science following a spiritual healing she experienced in 1866. Her major written work, Science and health with Key to the Scriptures is used, with the Bible, in all church services and daily study by Christian Scientists.

In 1879 Mrs. Eddy founded the church of Christ, Scientist, in Boston, Massachusetts. Today, it has some 3,300 world-wide branches, over 300 of which are in the British isles.

Christmas
the festival of the Nativity of Jesus Christ, celebrated on 25th December. The observance does not appear to have become general until the latter part of the 4th c. The choice of occasion seems to have been made in opposition to the Pagan Feast of the Sun (Natalis Sol Invicti).

church
interpretation of the nature of the Christian Church, including its relation to the state, varies with the branch or denomination of Christianity under

consideration. Reference should thus be made to Catholicism, Protestantism, Lutheranism etc. for such considerations. Among specific references to the Church, however, we include the following :

(1) John Huss defined the Church as "the body of the predestinate".

(2) Sebastian Franck declared allegiance to the "church universal" rather than to any specific church.

(3) Hooker viewed church and state as aspects of the same government with the power of the state extending over the church.

(4) Pufendorf held that the supreme jurisdiction of religious matters rests in the state, while ecclesiastical power resides in the Church.

(5) Gioberti looked upon the Church as the consumption of the ideal of perfection, and hencε essential to man's well being on earth.

church's theorem

the theorem stated in 1936 by Alonzo Church to the effect that there is no algorithm for the first order functional calculus or any strong theory, such as arithmetic.

cimmerians

a people 'on whom the sun never looks', dwelling according to Homer, in northern or western Europe.

circe

goddess inhabing the island of Aeaea, upon which Odysseus was standed. By her magical arts she could turn men into wild beasts, which she did to Odysseus followers. He, however, with the help of Hermes, who gave him a root (moly) to counteract the spells, was able to secure the restoration of his men. He spent a year with her.

circulus in demonstrando

this non-verbal fallacy is called 'arguing in a circle'. This fallacy occurs when an unproved premise is used to derive a desired conclusion. For example, if a person tends to say that Chinaware is better than earthenware, because it is made of a superior quality of clay, and when asked why the clay is superior, he argues that it is superior because it is used to make Chinaware. This is a circular argument.

circumcision

The Jewish and Moslem rite of cutting off the prepuce in males. The Circumcised. Designation of the Jewish people as a whole.

citta

Sanskrit term which means "mind stuff". A key term in the interpretation of the ego in the Yoga system.

civilization

often regarded as synonymous with 'culture'. Spengler distinguished between the two, finding civilization the final stage in a society's development. Alfred Weber distinguished between the "civilization process" and the "culture process", regarding the former as continous and the latter as sporadic.

class

from the Latin classis. There is no singel all-encompassing term in Greek. Any multiplicity of entities sharing a common characteristic. The idea of classes arose in the development of logic, and is present in all major cultures.

clericalism

a socio-political approach that seeks to strengthen the role of relgion and the Church in different spheres of social life.

clock paradox

a paradox that arises from the special theory of the relativity, which predicts that clocks run more slowly in a frame of reference moving at speeds approaching the velocity of the light when observed from a stationary frame of reference. Thus, if one of a pair of twins embarks on a high-speed space journey, he will, when he returns be younger than his brother who has remained on earth. The resolution to this form of the paradox is that the departure, turn-around, and return of the space not covered by the special theory.

clocks, image of the two

an illustration provided by Geulinex, and later used by Leibniz in presenting his own response to the Cartesian mind body problem. If two clocks are seen to keep perfect time with each other, there are three ways that this could arise :

(1) through mutual influence;
(2) through constant adjustments by the mechanic who cares for them;
(3) through their own inbuilt individual exactitude.

If one substitues mind for one clock and body for the other, the three ways of agreement become three possible responses to the Cartesian problem :

(1) two way interactionism;
(2) occasionalism; and
(3) Leibniz's own preferred solution, harmonious parallel functioning.

Clytemnestra

sister of Helen of Troy and wife of Agamemnon.

the code of manu

an Indian metrical work of 2,685 verses concerned with the development of the orthodox. Brahmanical view in relation to religion, law, custom, and politics.

(1) supporting the four orders (or ashramas) of life—student, householder, hermit and ascetic—the life of the householder, supporting the other three, is declared to be best. But man should pass through all four stages. The third, designed to loosen the bonds of life, requires retirement to the forest for mediation in preparation for the final stage in the attempt

to gain enlightenment.
(2) the duties of the four castes are outlined. Brahmins—teaching, studying, performing sacrifices, accepting gifts from pure men. Kshatriyas—protection of the order of society, including the caste system. Vaisyas—attention to the details of the agriculture and trade. Sudras—servile labour for one of the higher castes; and if this service is given a Brahmin the Sudra is promised birth into a higher caste in his next existence.
(3) women are to be honoured; but kept in dependence by the males of their families—by father, then husband, and finally by sons. A faithful wife will share the fate of her husband beyond this life.
(4) the most virtuous and efficacious act is to recognized the self in all created beings.

cogito ergo sum
it is the fundamental and indubitable foundation of cartesianism. Descartes claims to have constructed a valid philosophical system from this indubitable first principle of philosophy. He reached this 'first principle' of philosophy by employing the 'doubting method'. According to Descartes, the doubting method can demolish any idea that can be doubted, but his 'doubting method' could not but establishe the very existence of this doubting substance which cannot be doubted, i.e. the mind, whose important attribute is consciousness. Thus Descartes arrives at this fundamental axiom of his philosophy, 'I think, therefore I am'.

cognition
from the Latin cognito ('knowledge or 'recognition') the term refers both to the act or process of knowing and to knowledge itself. Competing theories of knowledge are the subject matter of epistemology. Cognition involves perception, memory, institution, and judgment.

cognitive
1. denoting mental process which are connected with understanding, formulation of beliefs, and acquisition of knowledge, and thus distinct from volitional processes, such as wanting or intending.
2. denoting utterances that are both significant and either true or false, in contrast to other utterances, such as commands and exclamations, that are significant and intelligible but cannot be classed as either true or false (sometimes called 'non-cognitive').

cognitive achievement word
a word that, when used correctly in a claim about a proposition (or an object) entails the truth of that proposition (or the existence of the object).

cognitum

the aspects, qualities, properties, attributes, and relations of objects that are given in experience with a definite purpose.

cognoscendum

from the Latin cognoscere ('to know'). Any object of a cognition whether veridical, fictive, abstract, or ideal.

Coherence theory of truth

a theory of the nature of truth which is associated with objective idealism. It states that truth is essentially system, by which is meant that the progress of knowledge is a progress towards a single complete system of thought, and that truth is predicable of this system alone.

coincidential oppositorum

Latin phrase which means "coincidence of opposites", a principle utilized by Nicholas of Cusa.

collective

in von Mises's treatment of probability, an infinite sequence of elements some of which correspond to a certain attribute or result, and which satisfies the conditions of the convergence and randomness.

collective unconscious

in the psychology of C.G. Jung, the inherited unconscious' that contains the "archetypes", the symbolic epitomes of the experience of the whole human species.

collectivism

another name for political holism.

colligation

from the Latin col ("together") and ligare ("to bind").

(1) for Whewell the placing of isolated information under a general conception. The manner in which an elliptical orbit organized separate observations of planetary position was cited by Whewell as an example of colligation.

(2) J. S. Mill pointed out that every instance of induction is colligation, although some instances of colligation, e.g., those involved in immediate or intuitive knowledge, may not be induction.

(3) Peirc held term to its literal meaning and associated the term with deduction rather than induction, holding that in deduction one colligates premises, an then determines what can be derived from them.

combinatorial logic

a branch in mathematical logic that is concerned with the analysis of various concepts that are accepted without further study within the framework of classical mathematical logic. Such concepts are those of variable and function.

common consent argument

arguments from the (almost) universal acceptance of a belief, especially belief in God, to the truth of that belief. Apart from difficulties of determining how nearly universal belief in God has been throughout human history, or what should count as such belief, any argument of the form "(Almost) everyone believes p, therefore p is true" is clearly invalid.

common notions

from the Latin notions communes. This in turn is Cicero's translation of the Greek phrase koinai ennoiai, used by the Stoic philosophers. The concept held that all men possess a common set of the basic ideas serving as the starting point of knowledge (q.v. Stoicism 1).

common sense

1. in general, the kind of opinions about life at large (for example, that the world has existed for a long time or that our minds are incorporeal) that philosophers believe unphiliosophical people take for granted.

2. (in Aristole) the faculty that integrated the data of the five senses into unified apprehensions of objects.

common sense realism

the view that we are able to perceive the external world directly, and that sense-data sense-datum either do not exist or play a subordinate role in perception.

communism

from the Latin communis ('common' 'universal', 'public'). A social structure where all things are held in common. According to Aristotle, communism was first advanced by Phaleas of Chalcedon and Hippodamus of Miletus.

commutation

the logical or mathematical operations whose result remains unchanged although the sequence of operations is changed. Many arithmetical and algebriac operations are commutative. Conjunction, disconjunction, equivalence, and many other operations are commutative in the Propositional Calculus and in the algebra of classes there are comparable operations.

comparative religion

the branch of study which investigates the various religions of mankind, especially in their mutual relations and resemblances. It was largely developed during the 19th c. under the influence of modern evolutionary concepts.

comparision

a kind of juxtaposition of two or more entities or objects to find similarities or differences between them. The method of analogy is basically dependent on comparison.

complete

denoting, very roughly, a formal system in which the rules and axioms of the system allow one to construct enough proofs (axiom; proof). But what counts as 'enough' may be judged relative to different purposes, and there are a variety of the non-equivalent requirements giving rise to non-equivalent notions of the completeness.

completeness

along with dedicability and consistency one of the basic concepts of contemporary metalogic. A calculus or system is complete when:
(1) each of its wellformed formula, or their negates, is a theorem of the calculus; or
(2) when any wellformed formula can either be proved in the system or else introduces inconsistency into it.

composition
it is a verbal fallacy. This fallacy occurs when a particular term is used collectively instead of using it distributively. For example, the sentence, "philosophers are little interested in politics', may be true in the individual cases, but if it is understood in a collective sense, then it is a fallacy because it is not true that all the philosophers are not interested in politics.

composition and division
there are two different ways in which the term 'composition' and 'division' are used, and different fallacies are associated with each. The first is concerned with the reference of terms used in an argument; the second with changes of meaning obtained by different combinations of terms.

compossibility
a Leibnizian principle of coherence defining a possible world, and the possible co-existence of its contents.

comprehension
a term used by John Stuart Mill to signify what is usually called intension.

conatus
from Latin conani meaning to attempt. The term refers to endeavor. In Spinoza's philosphy all things are animated by conatus, the desire to perpetuate their being.

conceit
ingenious fancy, or comparison often witty, sometimes whimsical, of a kind common in 17th c. poets; the term is used contemptuously by those who think such fancies strained or far-fetched.

concept
from the Latin con ('together') and capere ('to seize or tame'). An idea as distinguished from a percept or sensation.

conceptualism
in opposition to realism and nominalism, conceptualism holds that universals are mental concepts. They share the view with the nominalists that the universals cannot exist apart from the particulars. But unlike nominalists, they recognise the existence of general a priori concepts as a special form of knowledge of reality.

conciliar movement
a movement within the Roman Catholic Church asserting the authority of councils in church matters.

concrete universal

a term used in Hegelian philosophy to encapsulate Hegel's view that thinking must be universal (that is, in terms of universal law), but not abstractly universal.

conditional

(1) (adj) describing a statement in which it is claimed that something is, or will be, the case provided that, or on the condition that, some other situation obtains.

(2) a conditional or hypothetical statement. Such statements are characteristically expressed using the word if.

conditional statement

in the Propositional Calculus (q.v. 19) the name given to the binary connection 'if ...then', often symbolized by the horseshoe,'⊃' 'if it rains, then the streets will be wet' would be written it rains ⊃ the streets will be wet'. The general form of the connection is 'p ⊃ q'. The truth table for the conditional statement shows statements of this sort to be true in all save the case where the antecedent is true and the consequent false.

confession

1. acknowledgement or avowal of sin. In Roman Catholic practice, formal acknowledgement of sins to a priest in order to receive absolution or forgiveness. 2. A formulary containing the creed or declared doctrine of a church, as, for example, the Lutheran Confession of Augsburg.

confidant

character in a play or story to whom the hero or heroine unbosom themselves.

configurationism

it is another way of describing Gestalt theory.

confirmation

the relation between propositions when one supports or adds credence to another. Confirmation theory hopes to delimit what kind of proposition or theory is confirmable (that is, capable of gaining support from experience), this being a necessary task of any kind of positivism.

confucianism

one of the famous and the most influential philosophical schools of China founded by Confucius (551-479 B. C.). According to this school of thought, the fate and destiny of man is obtained by the 'Heaven'. Basically all humans are either noble or base. Confucianism teaches that younger must obey the elders, and subordinates to their boses.

congregationalism

a Protestant movement, originating in England in the late 16th and 17th centuries, with the goal of either purifying (the Puritans) or separating from (the separatists) the Established Church.

congruism

the doctrine that grace leads

the elect to yield themselves to God congruently with their own free will.

connotation

from the Latin con ('with') and notare ('to note or mark'). The word thus refers to the group of characteristics or qualities essential to a term. The usual correlate of connotation is 'denotation' the set of things to which the term refers. Intension signification and comprehension are often treated as synonymous with 'connotation'.

conscience

the holding of a conviction that some action is morally obligatory (or wrong) and to be firmly committed to doing (or refraining from doing) it. Those who consider that all moral beliefs provide overriding reasons for acting thereby make them all matters of conscience.

consciousness

a term with two related philosophical uses; first, as for example, for Locke, in the sense of self-knowledge acquired by virtue of the mind's capacity to reflect upon itself in introspective acts analogous with perception, and second, in a broader modern sense, opposed to anaesthesia, designating what is held to be the general property of mental states.

consensus gentium

Latin phrase meaning "the agreement of mankind".

consequence

if S is a set of statements, the statement A is said to be a consequence of S if the truth of A follows from the joint truth of members of S. The force of 'follows form' may be interpreted in various ways, each interpretation giving rise to a different consequence relation.

consequential characteristics

an alternative name for supervenient characteristics.

consequentialism

an umbrella term for any moral theories that state that the rightness or wrongness, goodness or badness of an action is solely dependent on the result the action produces.

consistency

from the Latin con ("with") and sistere ("to stand" or "cause to stand"). The characteristic, then, of being capable of standing together, or in harmony.

consistent and inconsistent

a set of statements is inconsistent if it entails a contradiction or has contradictory consequences, and is consistent otherwise. The bifurcation of the notion of consequence into semantic and syntactic notions creat a corresponding division between notions of consistency.

constant

from the Latin con ("to") and

stare ("stand"). Hence, the quality of standing firm.

constative

a term which was coined by J.L. Austin to refer to an utterance with which one makes a true or false statement. It was initially contrasted with performative.

constructivism

a view, according to which mathematical entities exist in so far as they are constructed by means of intuition or by any other way, and the mathematical propositions are true only when there is a constructive proof in support of them.

consubstantiation

from the Latin con ('with') and substantia ('substance'). The Lutheran doctrine of the Eucharist to the effect that the body and blood of Christ are "in real substantial presence" with the bread and wine.

contemplation

from the Latin con and templum (a space set aside for the observation and interpretation of signs and portents). Although the interpretation of the term has changed, its religious origin has not been entirely lost. The interpretation of theoria, or theory, in Greek philosophy, merely enlarged it with a truth-related aspect.

contextualism

a way of aesthetic interpretation of art that insists on the view that any form of art is to be understood in its cultural context as every form of art is historically conditioned.

contiguity

togetherness in time or place. A basic principle of the Association of Ideas.

contingency

(1) (of entities) the property of not having to exist.

(2) (of events) the property of not having to occur.

(3) (of propositions) the property of not having to be true, or of risking the possibility of being false.

continuity

from the Latin continere, meaning "to hold together". The problem of continuity arises whenever one is concerned with series or fields. It arises, therefore, with respect to numbers, lines, planes, and solids.

continuum

the concept of a reality, or a dimension of reality, without breaks, thus exemplifying continuity.

continuum problem

the problem of how many subsets of natural numbers there are; equivalently, of how many real numbers, that is, points on the continuum, there are.

contradictio in adjecto

from the Latin meaning a "contradiction in what is added". A logical fallacy wherein there is a contradiction between the noun and the adjective of a descriptive phrase, e.g. a dimensionless area.

contradiction

a proposition that involves in asserting something and denial of the same assertion is called a contradiction. In other words, it is a proposition which is both true and false.

contradiction, law of

one of the laws of traditional logic, according to which a proposition cannot be both true and false simultaneously. The first formulation of the law of contradiction was given by Aristotle.

contradiction, principle (or law) of

a logical principle, which in Aristotle's formulation, states that 'The same attributes cannot at the same time belong and not belong to the same subject and in the same respect'.

contradictory

(1) (adj) describing a discourse containing contradictions.

(2) (n) either of two propositions so related that both cannot be true or both cannot be false. Thus the proposition 'It is not the case p' (symbolized as-p, and read 'not p') is the contradictory of the proposition p, and the other way about.

contraposition

refers to a valid form of immediate inference in which a conditional or universal statement appears as premise and its contrapositive as conclusion.

contrapositive

refers to the contrapositive of the conditional statement 'If p, the q' is 'If not -q, then not -p', and of a universal statement 'All As are B' is 'all non-Bs are non -A'.

contrary

either of two propositions so related that both may be false but only one can be true.

convention

any generally accepted literary device or form; often felt to be artificial or excessively formal.

conventionalism

the view that scientific laws are disguished conventions reflecting the decision to adopt one of various possible descriptions.

converse

1. (in Aristotelian logic). The proposition derived by conversion of the original. The converse of 'No S are P is 'No p are S' and of 'Some S are P' is 'Some P are S'. Conversion in both these cases is called simple conversion. The converse of 'All S are P' is 'Some P are S' and the inference in this case is called conversion per accident. 'Some S are not P' has no converse.

2. (in propositional logic). The converse of a conditional statement 'If p then q' is 'if q then p'. In this case the converse is not a logical consequence of the original.

converse fallacy of the

accident

the 'mistake of arguing from a qualified principle, or a particular case (such as, it is never, wrong to kill in order to save your own life), to an unqualified or general principle (such as, it is never wrong to kill). The (rarer) error of arguing from a general rule to a particular case without taking accounts of factors (accidents) that vitiate the rule is known as the fallacy of the accident. Both fallacies are sometimes known by their Latin scholastic tag secundum quid.

conversion

a form of immediate inference in which the order of the terms is reversed. For example, the converse of the statement 'No S are P' is 'No P are S'. Similarly, the converse of 'Some P are S' is 'Some S are P'.

convocation

a representative vince of the Church (as, a proexample, the Convocation of Canterbury).

copts

an ancient Christian Church in Egypt numbering about a million members and still professing the Monophysite doctrine that Christ's human nature was absorbed by his divinity. Their head is a patriarch living at Alexandria whose jurisdiction includes also the Church of Ethiopia. The liturgical language in Egypt liturgical language in Egypt is Coptic, in Ethiopia Gheez, or ancient Ethiopic.

copula

from the Latin co ('together') and apere ('to bind'). In traditioanl logic, a form of the verb 'to be' (plus 'not' in negative proposition) connecting the subject and predicate terms of a proposition.

copyright

exclusive right of an author or his heirs to enjoy for a prescribed term of years the fruit of his labour.

corpuscularian

an obsolete synonym for 'atomic', used particularly in the 17th century in connection with the philosophy of Gassendi, Boyle, and Locke.

corpus hermeticum

a body of Neoplatonic, astrological, and alchemical writings falsely supposed to drive from the Egyptian equivalent of the Greek and Hermes. The position of Hermetism which came from this material was of influence in the late Greek and Roman periods.

correspondence theory of truth

considered, in its widest sense, the claim that truth is agreement with reality—that it consists in a correspondence between (for example) a statement and 'the way things are'.

corroboration

this term is introduced by Karl Popper in his work The Logic of Scientific Discovery in the place of confirmation. According to Popper, a scientific hypothesis is valid if there is sufficient corroboration in support of it. However much corroboration is found in favour of a scientific theory, still it is not conclusively proved.

cosmogony

it is a branch of astronomy that deals with the origin and the development of the heavenly bodies and their systems. Scientific cosmogony goes back to some 200 years when Kant advanced the hypothesis of the development of the planets from nebulae which at one time surrounded the sun. The ancient Greek philosophers based their cosmogony on what they understood to be the qualities and the properties of the four elements (earth, water, air, and fire).

cosmological argument

one of the three standard arguments for God, along with the teleological and ontological arguments.

cosmology

the branch of philosophy, often considered a subdivision of metaphysics, that deals with the Universe as a totality of phenomena, attempting to combine metaphysical speculation and scientific evidence within a coherent framework.

cosmos

the Universe as a whole, including the earth, the solar system, and all other galaxies. According to Pythogoreans, the world is a rational ordered whole.

counter-example

an instance of the kind of thing over which a generalization or universal statement has been made, which lacks the property said to be possessed by all things of that kind.

counterfactual statement

a conditional statement whose antecedent is false and whose consequent is conditionally true.

count noun

a term standing for an item in a countable class. Thus, girls being countable, 'girl' is a count noun.

courage

from the Latin cor ('heart'). One of the four Greek cardinal virtues along with wisdom, temperance, and justice.

covenant

in religious parlance a formal agreement entered into between man and God.

covering law model

refers to the model that represents explanation as a matter of finding a law that covers, in the sense of entailing, the phenomenon to be explained.

Craig's theorem

the proof, provided by William Craig in 1953, that if we axiomatize a scientific theory formally and partition the vocabulary into two parts (one supposedly 'theoretical' and the other 'observational'), then there will be an axiomatization from which all the sentences involving only observational terms are deducible and which itself contains none of the theoretical terms.

creation

the action required both to produce the universe out of nothing and to be its indispensible sustaining cause.

creationism

a view that the world and the nature, the animate and the inanimate, were brought into existence with a single act of creation.

creativity

a process resulting in novelty stressed by some philosophers:

(1) Freud gave an analysis of personal creativity in terms of sublimation and emergence of the sublimated in a novel form.

(2) Whitehead held that creativity is the Category of the Ultimate, and that the universe is involved from moment to moment in a creative advance.

(3) Lossky regarded creativity, as the essential characteristic of both God and man.

credo

Latin for 'I believe'. A creed or confession of faith. A number of Latin phrases beginning with 'credo' have been used as slogans by theologians and by some, philosophers.

credo ut intelligan

a Latin term for 'I believe in order that I may understand'. This term was often used by St. Augustine.

creed

from the Latin credo ('I believe'). A doctrinal formula accepted by a religious group as binding. Creeds have been elaborated in many religions, invariably arising from situations containing disagreement or danger, for the sake of insuring unity among believers.

Creon

king of Corinth, whose daughter Glauce was betrothed to Jason. Medea killed him by her magic.

criterion

from the Greek krinein ('to judge, discern'). The rule or body of rules by which decisions may be reached on the truth or falsity of judgments. Thus, the problem of the criterion usually relates to Epistemology.

critical idealism

another name for Kant's transcendental idealism.

critical realism

the doctrine accepted by some philosophers sympathetic to the view of R.W. Sellars, as published in Critical Realism (1916). Critical realism reatians the belief of commonsense realism in independent physical things, but admits that these are not directly and homogeneously presented to us in perceptual situations. These latter are thought to be very various, and our understanding of them must depend in part on the state and findings of the natural sciences.

criticism

from the Greek krinein ("to judge, discern").

(1) In philosophy the term applies most directly to the critical philosophy of Immanuel Kant as reflected in his Critique of pure Reason, Critique of Practical Reason, and Critique of Judgement. Kant's object was to, investigate the nature and limits of human understanding.

(2) In religion one must distinguish textual criticism (aimed at producing an authentic text) from higher criticism (fitting the text into its historical context). Spinoza is regarded as one of the forerunners of higher criticism (in his Tractatus of Theological-Political Treatise).

culture

from the Latin colere meaning 'to till or cultivate'. The term is sometimes used to include all of the creative expressions of man in all fields of human endeavor. At other times it is confined to creative expression in the areas of the liberal arts. In the second of these senses the term is sometimes extended to personal cultivation.

curia

the Papal court and its functionaries.

Cusa, Nicholas of (1401-1464)

a German philosopher, scientist, and a theologian, who believed that all opposites find their place in God. For example, the opposites such as finite and infinite; the smallest and the greatest; single and multiple, etc.

custom

from the Greek con and probably suere ('to make's own'). Thus, a course of action which has become habitual.

curtain raiser

short dramatic piece performed before the main play of the evening.

Cybele

the great mother goddess of Phrygia.

cybernetics

a branch of science that deals with the common features of processes and control systems in technological devices. The emergence of cybernetics as a science was first noticed by a number of technological and scientific achievements in the theory of automatic control, the radio electronic systems, etc.

cyclops

gigantic being with a single eye in the centre of the forehead. In Hormer, the cyclopes are shepherds.

cyrenaics

adherents of a school of philosophy flourishing in the

4th century BC, purportedly founded by Aristippus of Cyrene, bon viveur, and disciple of Socrates. The Cyrenaics maintained that pleasure is the supreme good, identifying "pleasure" with immediate bodily gratification and denying any positive value to 'mental pleasures' of anticipation and memory or to the cessation of pain. Their grounds were that only our present 'feelings' of pleasure and pain, themselves simply physical motions internal to us, can be truly known to us.

Daedalus

skilful Athenian craftsman. He built the Labyrinth for king Minos of Crete. Later, incurring the king's displeasure, Deadalus made wings for himself and his son Icarus and took winged flight from the island. The father escaped succesfully, but Icarus flew too near the sun, and the heat melted the wax by which his wings were fastened; he fell into the sea and was drowned.

dakshina

sacrificial fee.

dakshinagni

type of fire.

Dalton, John (1766-1844)

a British physicist, who held the view that the atoms are indivisible. His discoveries helped to convert philosophical brand of atomism advocated by ancient Greeks into a scientific one.

Danaus

king of Argos, noted for his 50 daughters, who were pursued by the 50 sons of the king of Egypt, Aegyptus. All the sons except one were murdered on their wedding-night by Danaus's daughters at their father's instigation. The sole survivor, Lynceus, took his revenge by killing Danaus.

Daphne

daughter of the rivergod Ladon. Pursued by Apollo, she was changed at her own entreaty into a laurel.

Daphnis

sicilian shepherd; the reputed inventor of bucolic verse.

darshana

Sanskrit term which means 'knowledge', 'vision', or 'the instrument of vision'. In fact, these meanings coalesce since, in Indian philosophy, an immediate or intutive vision of reality is the goal of every system. Philosophy and religious practice thus tend to become identical. The term is also used to describe each of the six orthdox systems of philosophy which present themselves as interpretations of the Vedic scriptures.

Darwin, Charles Robert (1809-1882)

a very famous British evolutionist whose theories of evolution revolutionised the entire natural science. Darwin explained the nature of evolution by means of natural selection, and survival of the fittest. His magnum opus The

Origin of Species by Means of Natural Selection was published in 1959.

darwinism

in the narrow sense the doctrines; or organic evolution proposed by Charles Darwin. In the broader sense, those doctrines influenced by Darwin's view.

dasa

slave.

dasein

(German for : being there). A term used by Heidegger in the investigation of human existence. Man's particular mode of being-in-the-world is characterized by relatedness to surrounding objects and members of his community, in terms of being concerned with and caring about them. Heidegger distinguishes three constitutive features of Dasein:

1. Faciuality,
2. Existentiality, or the apprehension of his purposive being and potential, and
3. Fallenness, man's tendency to become lost in present preoccupations, forfeiting his unique possibilities and 'authentic' existence.

datum

from the Latin datus, past participle of dare, 'to give', hence, the 'given'. Decision concerning what is immediately given provides one of the critical distinctions among philosophies.

deacon

1. a cleric next below a priest in episcopal churches.
2. one who superintends the secular business of a Presbyterian church.
3. in the early Church an important functionary, entrusted with the care of the sick and the distribution of alms to the poor, as well as taking an active part in the conduct of public worship.

death

in existentialist philosophy death is a very important concept. Man's anxiety and anguish are the outcome of the imagination of the death which cannot be avoided. According to Heidegger "None can die on my death by proxy".

death of God

the 19th-century claim, offered first by Mainlander then by Neitzsche and Sartre, that God is dead. The claim seems an exuberant manner of saying that there is no God and that the belief in God is losing credibility.

decalogue

the ten commandments. The best-known version is to be found in Exodus 20:2-17. A second version is in Deuteronomy 5:6-21. Attributed to Moses, it is more likely that the Decalogue was a product of centuries of deliberation with additions being made even in the 7th century B.C.

decidable

denoting a system or theory

which is expressed in a logically language where there has been an algorithm for determining for any correctly formed sentence of the language, whether that sentence is or is not a theorem of that theory A theorem has been a sentence that is derivable from a theory using rules of logical inference.

decidability

refers to one of the basic concepts of contemporary metalogic, along with 'completeness' and 'consistency'. The decidability or undecidability of a formula or sentence in a given system concerns the presence or absence within that system of a method of proof applicable to the formula or sentence, and completable within a finite number of steps.

decretal

from the Latin decernere ('to decide'). In ecclesiastical history the term referred, intially to papal decrees as distinguished from the decrees of the Council.

decurtate syllogism

from the Latin decurtatus ("curtaïled" or "shortened"). Hence, 'decurtate syllogism' is a synonym for 'enthyememe' a syllogism with a suppressed premise.

deduction

a valid argument in which it is impossible to assert the premises and to deny the conclusion without thereby contradicting oneself. The word is not confined within the restrictions of the traditional syllogisitc form.

defeasible

open to objection. The term is used particularly, in connection with concepts, such as legal responsibility, which are presumed to apply unless one or other of a perhaps indeterminate list of defeating conditions obtains. Every person is thus presumed to be legally responsible for what he did: unless the balance of his mind was disturbed; or he could not have known what he was doing or he acted under intolerable duress; or—etc.

definiendum

a definition consists of two parts—the definiendum and the definiens. The definiendum is the term that is going to be defined.

e.g., A triangle is a three sided closed geometrical figure.

Here 'triangle' is the definiendum.

definiens

the defining feature of the definiendum is called the definiens.

e.g. A triangle is a three sided closed geometrical figure.

Here 'the three sided closed geometrical figure' is the definiens.

definist fallacy

one aspect of the naturalistic fallacy; that of confusing two notions by defining one in terms of the other. Moore thought that if 'good' is defined in terms of some natural property, say 'that which produces pleasure', then the open question argument would show that the two were nevertheless, distinct.

definite description

definite descriptions are important in connection with singular terms, as a singular term without a bearer (or reference) presents problems for the theory of meaning and for logical formalization. For this reason Russell proposed to replace sentences containing definite descriptions by sentences that did not contain them and which, he claimed, were equivalent to the original sentences. In effect, 'The present king of France, is bald' was to be replaced by 'There is something which at present is a king of France and at most one thing at present in a King of France, and that thing is bald'.

definite description, theory of

a theory developed by Russell giving an analysis of descriptive phrases beginning with 'the'.

definite reference

a reference that is made to a definite individual. For example, Gandhi was a prominent leader of Indian freedom movement.

definite description

russell introduced by kind of a singular term called 'definite description' in his theory of descriptions. A definite description like 'The present Prime Minister of India' is not only serves as a denoting phrase, but also picks up an unique individual referent. However, it is an incomplete symbol as it remains meaningless out of the context.

definition

refers to a process or expression that provides the precise meaning of a word or phrase. A definition (definiens), correctly made, will be logically equivalent to the word or phrase being defined (definiendum). Definition may be either of a present established meaning or of a meaning proposed for the future. In the former case the definition is said to be descriptive, in the latter prescriptive or stipulative.

degrees of perfection argument

the fourth of the Five ways, which contends that, since whatever is the most ϕ must be the cause of whatever else is ϕ, all being and goodness in the Universe must be the work of One who is in these respects The Mostest; 'and this we call God'. Any force that this argument possesses derives from Plato's theory of Forms of Ideas.

de inesse

Latin phrase form inesse (being in). A technical term

used by the Schoolmen in two senses:

(1) Propositions were said to be de inesse in the simple eategorical form where are predicate is affirmed (est in), or denied (non est in) of a subject.

(2) Since accidents of substances were held not to exists in their own right (in se), but in something else (in alio), their mode of being with respect to substance was said to be a mode de inesse.

deism

a term that belief in God can commend itself to the human mind by its own inherent reasonableness, without either being supported by apeals to alleged divine revelations or imposed by religious institutions.

delusion

according to J.L. Austin, a delusive experience is one where something is conjured up from nothing. Contrast it with illusion.

demeter

Greek corn-goddess, sister of Zeus and the mother of Persephone. She was identified by the Romans with Ceres.

demiurge

a term which is derived from the Greek for craftsman:

1. In Plato's Timaeus, the maker of the physical world.

2. The maker acknowledged by most gnostic systems, whose cosmogonic myths depict a demonic being either collaborating with God in creation or seeking to destroy the world by introducing evil.

democracy

from the Greek demos ('the people') and kratien ('to rule'). Rule by the people may be exercised either directly, as in pure democracy, or through representatives of the people, as in representative deomocracy.

Democritus (460-370 B. C.)

one of the ancient Greek atomists and a young contemporary of Leucippus. He was nicknamed 'the laughing philosopher'. Democritus was known for his atomic theory. According to him, atoms, being indivisible particles of matter, are immutable, eternal, and continuous in motion.

De Morgan's laws

laws named after Augustus De Morgan (1806-71), one of the pioneers of the algebraic approach to logic.

(1) is formally stated as—(p & q) ≡ - pV - q; that is to deny a conjuction is to assert the negation of at least one of the conjoined statements (and vice versa).

(2) is formally stated as -(p V q) ≡ -p & -q, that is to deny the disjunction of p and q is to assert both the negation of p and the negation of q (and vice versa).

denotation

from the Latin de and notare ('to note' or 'mark'). Correlative to the term 'connotation', the denotation of a term is the thing or set of things to which the term refers. The denotation of 'table' is all the tables that exist, have existed, or will exist.

denote

it is sometimes used as equivalent to 'designate', sometimes used to translate Frege's bedeuten and sometimes used to express the relation between a predicate term and everything to which it applies, that is, its extension.

deontic logic

refers to the formulation of logical principles specific to the concept of obligation, such as the impossibility of something being at once both morally obligatory and forbidden.

deontology

refers to the ethical theory which is taking duty as the basis of morality; the view that some act are morally obligatory regardless of their consequences.

dervish

from the Persian darvish (beggar). A member of a Muslim religious order, resembling Western monasticism, some, times mendicant.

Descartes, Rene (1569-1650)

a French philosopher, mathematician and a physicist, who is regarded as the father of modern western philosophy. According to Descartes, the mind can exist independent of the body, and the body can exist independent of the mind. The most important attribute of the mind is consciousness or thought, while the most important attribute of the body is extension. He also conceived that mind and body are relative substances, whereas the God is the only absolute substance on which these two relative substances are dependent for their existence. Descartes employed methodological scepticism to arrive at the first and fundamental foundation of philosophy called Cogito ergo sum (I think, therefore I am). His important works include: Meditations on First Philosophy, and Discourse on Method.

descending induction

an alternative name for the method of infinite descent.

descriptions, theory of

the theory proposed by Russell in order to reveal the underlying logical form of denoting phrases containing descriptions.

descriptivism

the view that moral judgments have only descriptive, and not prescriptive meaning and can thus be proved by being deduced from statements all straightforwardly factual. Descriptive is thus a form of ethical naturalism.

designatum

from the Latin designo ('to make out or trace'). The

referent of a word, symbol, or expression.

determinism

a view that opposes the freedom of will. In other words, this theory opposes all forms of contingency, and claims that everything that happens is necessarily determined, by a particular pattern or a law. For instance, David Hume advocated the causal indeterminism. According to him, there is no necessary causal connection between one event and the other because such a connection is not given in sense-experience. Kant advocated the causal determinism by holding the view that 'every effect has a cause'. The necessary connection between the cause and the effect, asserts Kant, is not given in sense-experience, but it is known a priori.

deucalion

Greek equivalent of Noah. He and his wife, Pyrrha, repopulated the earth after the flood by throwing over their shoulders stones which came to life.

deus absconditus

a Latin term which means 'the hidden God'. In contrast to a rationalistic and humanistic approach to theology Luther found the divine hiddeness as much as part of religious experience as the divine presence.

deussive natura

(Lating for; God or Nature). The phrase used by Spinoza to denote the one infinite 'substance' to which all attributes must be ascribed.

deva

a Sanskrit term which means 'bright heavenly one'. Originally designating the nature gods of the Vedic religion, sons of the sky father, Dyaus. Later, the designation for God in Hinduism and Buddhism and of the evil spirits in Zoroastrianism. In the latter religion the devas became the deavas or demons, allies of Ahriman, the evil deity in the world struggle between good ad evil.

Dewey, John (1859-1852)

an American pragmatist philosopher, whose pragmatism is a synthesis of the logical and the ethical considerations. His philosophy is popularly known as instrumentalism. His important works include: Reconstruction in Philosophy; and The Quest for Certainty.

dhammapada, the

a Sanskrit term which means 'the path of virtue'. The dhammapada is an early Buddhist document discussing the chief values of life and the path which leads to enlightenment. Moving within the framework of karma and rebirth, the four noble truths of Buddha and eightfold path, the Dhammapada provides meditations concerning the practice of the way to salvation.

dharana

the sixth step in Yogic meditation.

dhyana

a Sanskrit term which means meditation. Central to the practise of Hinduism. Buddhism, and Jainism, Dhyana forms the seventh stage of yogic mediation, leading to the final stage of Samadhi or 'absorption'.

diagonal procedure

refers to the method by which Cantor proved that there are infinite sets that cannot be counted. The real numbers, unlike the rational numbers, are such a non-denumerable set—that is, they cannot be put in a one-to-one correspondence with the natural numbers.

diagonal procedure

refers to the method by which Cantor proved that there is infinite sets that cannot be counted. The real numbers, unlike the rational numbers are such a non-denumerable set—that is, they cannot be put in a one-to-one correspondence with the natural numbers.

dialectical materialism

refers to a metaphysical doctrine held by many Marxists. It asserts that matter is primary or fundamental, and states general laws governing the motion and development of all matter. As such, it is distinguished from historical materialism which is the Marxist theory of history, dealing with the more particular laws governing the development of human society and thought.

dialectics

it was introduced by Socrates for the first time into philosophy. According to him, the dialectics is a method of argumentation. Later it was highlighted by Plato as a science of the first principles. A most incessant analysis of Dialectics was given by Hegel in modern times. According to Hegel, Dialectics operates on the basis of the following laws.

1. law of identity.
2. unity and struggle of opposite forces.
3. the transformation of quantitative changes into qualitative changes.
4. the low of negation of negation.

dialogue

from the same Greek root as 'dialectic' meaning 'discourse'. The term usually refers to the Socratic method of philosophizing through discussion as set forth in Plato's early dialogues featuring the Socratic figure.

Diana

goddess of the moon; identified by the Romans with the Greek Artemis.

dianoetic virtues

from the Greek dianoia ('intellect' or 'mind'). Thus, in

the intellectual virtues in Aristotle a distinction is made between intellectual and moral virtues. The former relate to the reasoning function and the apprehension through intellect of rational principles. The latter concern rational control of man's effective nature.

dichotomy paradox

the alternative name for the stadium paradox of Zeno of Elea.

dictum

Latin term which means 'expression' or 'statement'. Used by the Scholastics in relation to modal propositions.

dictum de omni et nullo

Lattin phrase which means 'principle of everything and nothing. This is the principle of syllogistic inference as formulated by the Scholastics and grounded in Aristotle. What is predicated universally of a subject or class is predicated of everything falling under the subject or belonging to the class. What is denied universally of a subject or class is denied of everything falling under the subject or belonging to the class.

Dido

legendary daughter of Belus, king of Tyre. On the murder of her husband Sychaeus by her own brother Pygmalion, she fled to north Africa and founded there the city of Carthage. Devoted to the memory of her dead spouse she committed suicide rather than submit to a forced marriage with a neighbouring monarch, Iarbas. In the 'Aeneid' Virgil makes her a contemporary of Aeneas, with whom she falls in love. When Aeneas left her for Italy she took her own life.

difference of degree

a difference of degree between A and B can be defined in terms of a spectrum of a actual or possible gradations with no apparently natural delineations between them (vagueness). The differences between age and the youth, poverty and riches, insanity and sanity—all in human terms of the utmost importance—are of this wrongly despised sort.

differentia

refers to that part of the essence of a thing that distinguishes its species from all other species in the same genus.

dilemma

a form of inference that contains two premises, namely, conjunctive affirmation of two hypothetical propositins, and a disjunctive premises containing the grounds for the hypothetical proposition. It also describe a situation involving a choice between equivalent alternatives.

ding an sich

a German phrase which means 'thing-in-itself'. Introduced by Kant the ding an sich is the noumenon lying behind reality.

The question of the Ding an sich, and especially whether the concept is expendable, assumed importance in neo-Kantianism.

Diomedes

Thracian king of the Bistonians. The capture of his man-eating horses was one of the labours of Heracles.

dionysus

from the Greek dios ('god') and Thracian nusos ('son of' or in some interpretations 'tree'). Thus, alternatively 'tree god' or 'son of god' in literal translation.

Dioscuri

joint name of Castor and Polydeuces (Lat. Pollux), the 'lads of Zues'; twin sons of Leda, Castor by her husband, Tyndareus, and Polydeuces by Zeus. According to one story Zeus, on their death, placed them among the stars as the Gemini.

direct and indirect perception

according to Russel, the knowledge by acquanitance is possible through direct perception, whereas the indirect perception of an object in question is possible through the knowledge by discription. For example, the sense data are directly given in sense-experience, while the knowledge of material objects is inferred from the sense-data. Thus the knowledge of material object is possible through indirect perception.

disconfirmation

the term that is opposed to confirmation. In other words, it is called infirmation.

disjunction

from the Latin disjungere ('to disjoin'). In logic, disjunctive propositions are always compound or 'molecular', and feature the connective 'either or'. There are strong and weak disjunctions and in traditional logic weak disjunction is termed 'alteration'.

dissenter

one who dissents from the doctirne and practice of an established church. A nonconformist.

distributed

denoting an assertion that is made of all the member of a class. An undistributed assertion is made of less than all the members of a class. 'All Xs are ϕ is distributed; Some Xs are ϕ and this particular X is ϕ' are not.

distribution

in statistics, the property of a random variable that is identified when a probability is attached to each value of the random variable.

divine right of kings

derived from the medieval doctrine of the two swords, which latter traced all authority to God, the spiritual sword being granted to the Church and the temporal sword to the state, the divine right of kings held that all authority, spiritual no less than temporal, belongs to the monarch and has been granted him by God. This doctrine of the one sword made its appearance with the rise of the national state.

division

this fallacy occurs when a particular term is used distributively instead of using it collectively. For example, the sentence, "Indians are fond of cricket" may be true if it is understood in a collective sense. But if it is understood in a distributive sense, then it is false because every Indian is not fond of cricket.

docetism

a Christological doctrine appearing in early Christianity and apparently influenced by Gnosticism, to the effect that the suffering and death of Jesus was only an appearance. These events occurred with respect to a phantom body or shadow.

docta ignorantia

Latin phrase which means 'learned ignorance' a concept employed by Nicholas of Cusa.

doctor mirabilis

a Latin term for 'miraculous Doctor'. Roger Bacon was known as a Miraculous Doctor. He was a scholastic philosopher and scientist.

doctor universalis

a Latin term for 'Universal Doctor'. Albertus Magnus was knowns as Universal Doctor.

doctrine of the mean (Chung Yung in Chinese).

the most philosophical of the ancient Chinese documents, the Doctrine of the mean existed in the early Han dynasty.

It is man's goal in life to follow the way. This means achieving equilibrium and harmony. Equilibrium is the state before feelings of pleasure, anger, sorrow, and joy are aroused. Harmony is the state in which they are aroused in due measure and degree.

One's conduct should strike the appropriate mean between the deficiency and excess: to serve one's father as one would expect one's son to serve oneself; to serve one's ruler as one expects one's ministers to serve oneself; to serve elder brothers, as one expects one's younger brothers to serve oneself; to be the first to treat friends as one would expect to be treated by them. And in all cases one is to do what is proper to his position, and does not go beyond it.

The three universal virtues are wisdom, humanity, and courage. The five relations they govern are the relations between ruler.

dogma

a Greek term which 'opinion' or 'decree'.

In substantive form the term has had philosophical use, dogmatism naming the position of the Fourth Academy, developed by Philo of Larissa.

dogmatism

the philosophical position of the Fourth Academy.

double aspect theory

in Abbagnano's doctrine of positive existentialism, the theory that every concrete possibility open to man has a positive and a negative aspect.

double effect, principle of

a principle characteristic of, but not confined to, Roman Catholic moral theology. Where some course of action is likely to have two quite different effects, one licit or mandatory and the other illicit, it may be permissible to take that course intending the one but not the other.

double negation

the principle that any proposition implies and is implied by the negation of its negation. Sometimes considered a law of logic, it is the combination of :

(1) the law of non-contradiction (not both p and not-p) and

(2) the law of excluded middle (either p or not-p).

double truth, doctrine of

the doctrine that what is true in religion may not be true in philosophy, and vice versa.

doubt

the state of withholding assent from a proposition, and from its contradictory. Moderate doubt is usually known as Skepticism and its extreme form is known as Pyrrhonism.

druses

moslem political and religious community founded in the 11th c. and living in the Lebanon Mountains. They believe in transmigration of souls.

dualism

a theory concerning the fundamental types into which individual substances are to be divided. It asserts that substances are either material or mental, neither type being reducible to the other.

duhkha (suffering)

it is the first noble truth of Buddhism.

duhkha-nirodha (the cessation of suffering)

it is the third noble truth of Buddhism.

duhka-nirodha-marga (the path of the cessation of suffering)

it is the fourth noble truth of Buddhism.

duhkha-samudaya (the cause of the origin of suffering)

it is the second noble truth of Buddhism. Pratityasamutpada (dependent origination) is expounded from this truth.

duration

from the Latin durare ("to last or endure"). Thus a stretch of time.

Whatever the genesis of the concept, its philosophical use appears to be related to the contrast of time with eternity. St. Augustine analysed the spread of time in psychological terms, finding this concept less clear that of God's eternity, while St. Thomas Aquinas found the term, 'duration', applicable both to time and eternity. Duration and succession apply to time, while eternity is characterised by duration without succession.

duty

from the Latin debere ('to owe'). The sense of 'duty' vies with that of 'good' or 'value' for the honor of serving as the foundation conception of ethics. Ethical systems taking 'duty' as basic are called 'formalistic' or 'decontological', rather than 'teleological' or 'axiological'.

dvapara yuga

era.

dvesa

Sanskrit term signifying the antipathy man develops toward unpleasant things. One of the five kinds of delusive attachment of the Yoga system.

dyadic

according to Russel, a fact is called dyadic when it requires the addition of two singular entities. Thus a dyadic fact is represented by a proposition that consists of two singular terms. For example, Rama is taller than Krishna.

dynamism

from the Greek dynamis ('power'). In a general sense any world view asserting the existence of forces in things not reducible to matter in motion.

dyophysite

one who holds in contrast to Monophysitism the doctrine that two natures, one divine and one human, united in the person of Christ.

dyothelite

one who holds, in contrast to Monothelitism the doctrine that two wills, one divine, and one human, united in the person Christ.

dysteology

this particular doctrine indicates the presence of the factors that defy the adaptation of the good or the desirable ends. In other words, they are called non-teleological factors. For example, agony, disease, death etc.

dyulok

heaven.

easter

the principal Christian festival, commemorating the resurrection of Jesus Christ from the dead. It is observed on the Sunday following the full moon that occurs on or next after 21st march

ebionism

the doctrine of the Ebionites, who were the Jewish Christians in Jerusalem, and later merely a sect among them.

ebiouism

the doctrine of the Ebionites, who were the Jewish Christians in Jerusalem, and later merely a sect among them.

echo

nymph who was deprived by Hera of the power of speech, except to repeat the last words uttered by someone else. She fell in love with the beautiful Narcissus, and when her love was not returned, pined away until only her voice was left. Another form of the story relates how Pan, having been refused by her, caused her to be torn to pieces by frenzied shepherds. Her remains, hidden by Earth, continued to imitate sounds made by others.

economy, principle of

it is another name for 'Ockham's razor'. According to this principle, there is no need to multiply the entities beyond necessity.

ecumenism

a movement, also called the Ecumenical Movement, toward increasing cooperation among the churches and religious orders of the world. Beginning in the West, and still concentrated there, the movement seek to reverse the Western fragmentation of religious witness.

education

a term now rare, once used to designate immediate inference also used to signify the manner in which the substantial forms was drawn from matter in the Aristotelian system.

education, philosophy of

although an attitude toward education is perhaps implicit in most philosophies, only a small minority have made open declaration of its nature.

effective procedure

a procedure (for solving a problem, answering a question, etc.) that consists of a finite number of mechanical steps before reaching the answer (to the problem, question, etc.).

effluxes, theory of

the view which was held by the Greek atomists that the surfaces of objects are constantly emitting thin films of atom (known variously as idola, effluvia, or simulacra) that impinge upon the eye and thus produce the sensation of sight.

egeria, aegeria

Roman nymph, worshipped by pregnant women seeking easy delivery.

egocentric predicament

in a general sense the problem that we wish to know and interpret the world, and must do so from the perspectives available to us, perspectives centred in ourselves or our egos. In a technical sense the term was introduced by R. B. Perry.

eidetic images

mental imagery defined as having the vividness of sense data, but distinguished from hallucinatory sense data as precluding the inclination to believe that there is a genuine perception of a public reality. Eidetic imagery is experienced as projected onto 'the external world'. Those capable of it, usually children, are called eidetikers.

eidola

a Greek term for 'images'. In the accounts of perception given by Democritus and Epicurus 'detached outlines' given off by objects and recived by our senses.

eidos

a Greek term used by Plato to signify 'the Form or the Ideas or the Concepts' that exist in the eternal world (Being).

eiufuhlung

a German term which means 'empathy'.

elatics

a Greek philosophical school that comprises of the philosophies of Parmenides, and his followers like Zeno of Elea, Melissus of Samos, etc. Their approach was monastic, and they vehemently attacked the Heracitus notion of 'flux'.

elder

a senior person exercising official authority in the Jewish synagogue; in the early Christian, and in Presbyterian churches.

electicism

from the Greek ek ('out') and lego ('select'). An attitude which leads to philosophizing by selection, seeking to bring into harmony what is valid from all philosophers while eliminating the mistaken doctrines of the sources.

electra, elektra

the best known figure of this name—there are 3—was the daughter of Agamemnon and Clytemnestra and sister of Orestes whose life she saved.

elenchas

in Socratic dialectic, a form of cross-examination that refutes an opponent's thesis by drawing out contradictory or otherwise intolerable consequences from him. Aristotle uses the word to mean 'refutation'.

emanation

from the Latin e ('from') and mano ('flow'). Emanation is a doctrine of the overflowing superabundance of the divine. An alternative to the doctrine of creation.

emanationism

a theory particularly associated with Neoplatonism, which accounts for the source and structure of reality in terms of a perpetual, spontaneous flowing out (emanation) from a transcendent principle, usually called God or the One.

emergent evolution

the doctrine that novel qualities, not reducible to their antecedents, appear in the course of evolution. The doctrine was held by C. Lloyd Morgan, Boodin (q.v. 3), Smuts, S. Alexander G.H. Lewes, and others.

emotivist theory

the theory that value terms are grounded in emotional attitudes. Applying initially to the field of ethics, the view has been extended to other areas where values are central, such as aesthetics and social philosophy.

empathy

this term refers to a state of partial identification with the art object in such fashion that one's relation to the object combines the senses of both identity and distance.

Empedocles (433 B.C.)

an ancient Greek philosopher who reduced the whole diversity of things in this world to four important elements: earth, water, air and fire. His doctrine of nature was accepted by many ancient and medieval philosophers. The union and the division of elements were explained by him in terms of two opposing forces, namely, attraction and repulsion.

empiricism

usually defined as the thesis that all knowledge or at least all knowledge of matters of fact as distinct from that of purely logical relations between concepts—is based on experience.

empiriocriticism

refers to an empirical, positivist approach to epistemology which was developed by Richard Avenarius and criticized by Lenin in Materialism and Empirio-Critism.

enantiomorphs

a pair of objects related to each other as a right hand is to a left, or as opposite spirals are, or mirror images. Kant, in Prolegomena used them in an argument in favour of the concept of absolute (as opposed to relative) space.

encyclopedists

in philosophy the term is usually reserved by the group of 18th-century French philosophers, known as les philosophies, who, motivated by the view that social evils could be eliminated through the spread of knowledge, collaborated in the project of composing the thirty-five volume French Encyclopedic designed to bring all knowledge into a single compass. Editor of the encyclopedia was Denis Diderot who wrote most of the articles on religion, ancient history and political theory.

endymion

beautiful youth, a shepherd or hunter, beloved by Selene (the moon), who lay with him, each night during his unending sleep, which she herself, it was said, had imposed on him so that she might have him to herself.

energeia

a Greek term which means 'energy', 'action', or 'operation'. As utilized by Aristotle the term signifies both a state of realized potentiality and the activity leading to that state. In both senses the term stands in marked contrast to dynamics ('unrealized potentiality').

Engles, Friedrich (1820-1895)

a German materialist philosopher who collaborated with Karl Marx in writing several important works on politics, history and philosophy. One of his very famous works is The Dialectics of Nature in which Engles tries to explain the role of dialectics in science.

enlightenment (or age of reason)

the era characterized by the emergence, in 18th century France, of progressive and liberal ideas that led to the Revolution and remained influential in western philosophy. Increasing scientific knowledge gave rise to the development of empiricist, naturalist, and materialist doctrines and strong opposition to clericalism. It was the era that saw the publication of the encyclopedic.

ens realissimum

(Latin for; the most real being). God, the absolute possessor of all realities and all the attributes of perfection. The term is used in Kants, discussion of proofs of God's existence.

entelechy

it is a term used by Aristotle to show that the purposefulness or the active principle which converts a possibility into a reality. In other words, it is the realisation of actuality in opposition to mere potentiality. In vitalism, entelechy is considered to be the vital principal that is present in all living beings.

enthymeme

1. a syllogism having a suppressed premise.
2. a conditional holding on formally-reducible material grounds.

entity

from the Latin ens, entis ('thing'). In Scholastic philosophy, initially, any real being. Later, whatever has sufficient separateness of being, whether in reality or thought, to support predications.

enumeration

the term has at least two philosophical connections.

(1) one of the forms of definition is 'definition by emumeration'. This is a definition by listing the individuals or sub-classes making up the denotation of the term.

(2) one of the forms of induction is 'induction by simple enumeration' (also called perfect or complete induction). The form was criticized by Francis Bacon who argued for the 'experimental method'.

episcopacy

government of a church by bishops, as in the Roman, Greek Orthodox, and Anglican communions.

epistle

1. A letter traditionally ascribed to apostolic authorship, ment.
2. a liturgical reading at the Eucharist from such or from

elsewhere in Scripture.

Eos

dawn, daughter of Hyperion and sister of Helios (the sun) and Selene (the moon). The 4 winds were her sons.

epagoge

from the Greek meaning 'a bringing in'. A Greek and Aristotelian term for induction instances of induction are some-times called 'epagogic demonstrations' or 'epagogic syllogisms'.

Epictetus (50-130)

a famous stoic philosopher and a moralist whose teaching have been classified into physics, logic and ethics. He argued that master can be slave of his own passions, whereas a slave can experience freedom in his inner spiritual independence. Good and evil are not inherent in things but they lie in our attitude towards things.

epicureanism

a school of philosophy founded in Athens in 306 B.C. by Epicurus (q.v.). The school, stressing, atomic theory, empiricism, and hedonism, remained an influential factor in the culture life of Greece and Rome from the time of Epicurus in the 4th century B.C. until the 5th century A.D. During this period there is a long record of the polemic between the Epicureans on the one hand and the Stoics, Skeptics, and the Aristotelian or Peripatetic philosophers on the other.

epiphenomenalism

a view that describes consciousness as an epiphenomenon of certain molecular changes that take place in the brain. In opposition to interactionism advocated by Descartes, and psychophysical parallalism advocated by Spinoza, epiphenomenalism maintains that all the mental events are the resultant effects of certain physical events but not vice-versa. This theory was advocated by T.H Huxley.

epiphenomenon

a secondary or added accompaniment to a process, considered as merely incidental and having no part in the further development of the process.

epistemics

a term coined in Edinburgh University in 1969 to label a new school dedicated to the scientific, as opposed to the philosophical, study of knowledge.

epistemology

a branch of philosophy that is concerned with various theories of knowledge. The term epistemology is derived from the Greek term episteme. Epistemologists are chiefly concerned with the aspects such as 'what is knowledge?', the origin and the scope of knowledge, the sowrces of knowledge, and the validity of knowledge. There are two major epistemological theories, namely, Rationalism and Empiricism which are basically responsible for other theories of knowledge. Rationalism maintains that all genuine knowledge is possible through reason alone; while empiricism stichs to the view that all genuine knowlodge is derived from sense-experience. In opposition to these two views, Kant advocated transcendentalism, according to which neither reason for sense-experience in isolation from each other can ever give us the genuine knowledge of reality (phenomenon). Thus he asserts that the pure concepts without the percepts are empty, in as much as the pure percepts without the concepts are sightless.

epistle

1. a letter, traditionally ascribed to apostolic authorship, forming part of the New Testament.
2. A liturgical reading at the Eucharist from such or from elsewhere in Scripture.

episyllogism

a syllogism one or both of whose premises forms the conclusion of a preceding syllogism.

epoche

a Greek term for "suspense of judgment".

(1) the term was used both by Skeptics and members of the Academy, as the appropriate response to the problem of knowledge. 'Suspense of judgment' was regarded as leading to ataraxia, or pleasure in tranquility.

(2) Husserl has adopted the term, insisting upon epoche, or suspense of judgment, as a stage in the phenomenological reduction.

equality

most analyses of the human condition do not find men equal, although the claim in the natural rights doctrine is that all have equal rights Rousseau held equality to be 'unnatural'.

equivalence relation

any transitive, symmetric, and reflexive relation whenever two things a and b are equivalent, or identical in some respect P, the relation expressed by x is the same as y in respect of P will be an equivalence relation. For example, two rods, of whatever material, may or may not have the same length. For some purposes all rods of the same length are equivalent and the relation given by x is the same as y in respect of length is an equivalence relation over the class of rods.

equivalent

1. (material) Two statements are said to be materially equivalent when they have the same truth-value.
2. (formal) two statements A and B are said to be formally equivalent when A may be deduced from B alone by valid argument, and vice versa.

equivocate

to employ equivocal words or expressions, confounding their meanings.

equivocation

from the Latin aeques ("equal") and vocare ("to call"). The sense is that of regarding a word used in two senses as carrying the same meaning when, in fact, the meaning differ.

erastianism

a trend that believes in the authority of secularism rather than in the authority of Church.

Erebus

darkness, son of Chaos and father (by his sister, Nyx) of Aether (the clear air) and Hemera (day).

Erechtheus

fabulous king of Athens, the son of Earth and reared by Athena.

Erigone

daughter of Clytemnestra by her lover Aegisthus. She was saved by Artemis from the vengeance of Artemis from the vengeance of Orestes, Clytemnestra's legitimate son by Agamemnon.

Erinyes, Eumenides

avenging spirits of hideous aspect, punishing especially those who offended against the basic laws of society. They were usually thought of as 3 in number.

Eris

personification of strife, a sister of Ares. She threw the apple of discord among the guests at the wedding of Peleus and Thetis, to which she had not been invited.

eristic

from the Greek eris ('strife'). In Aristotle a mode of argument having as its goal victory in disputation, and thus to be distinguished both from science and from dialectic. The Megarian School of Philosophy is associated with eristic.

eros

a Greek term for 'sexual attraction or physical love'. In Greek myhology, it is believed that Eros is the first God to emerge from Chaos. In contrast to Eros, Agape was used to designate the highest form of love that exists between the God and the humans, or vice-versa.

erotetic

concerning questions, interrogatory. The term is used especially in connection with the logical analysis of questions (also called erotetic logic).

error

originally, a Latin term meaning "a wandering about". Since to fall into error means that one has missed the truth what is said under the latter entry applies here as well. How one falls into error has been the subject of philosophical discussion.

esoterism

from the Greek esoteros ("inner", "interior"). The doctrine that ancient wisdom contains an esoteric part, separate from public writings or lectures available to all (the exoteric part).

esse est percipi

Latin phrase meaning 'To be is to be perceived'. A slogan of Berkeley the statement has had importance for other philosophers as well.

essence

a salient characteristic or a property of a thing that makes what it is. In Aristotle's metaphysics, essence represents an immutable and timeless possibility of existence. Nevertheless, it was Aristotle who classified properties into—essential and accidental. Essential properties are those which constitute the 'thing-in-itself' (Kantian terminology). Accidental features or properties are those whose absence does not change a sharp distinction between the real and the nominal essence. The real essence (nature of substratum), according to Locke, is 'unknown and unknowable', while the nominal essences are produced by the real essence. These nominal essences are none other than the primary qualities (solidity, figure, extention, motion or rest, and number), and the secondary qualities (colours, tastes, smells, etc.). For Kant, essence constitute a 'thing-in-itself'. The apparatus of empirical or phenomenal knowledge (categories of understanding and sense-experience) do not provide us with any knowledge of a 'thing-in-itself'. American pragmatist John Dewey considers that whatever properties happen to interest us are called 'essential'. Hence the essence of a thing varies according to the context.

essentialism

a term which designates three separates philosophical positions:

1. The doctrine, in Plato, of the existence of Forms, that is of really existing abstract entities of which physical objects are imperfect copies.
2. A position holding that something can have an essential property in virtue of a definition, or as described in a certain way.
3. Perhaps, the most important, a metaphysical view dating back to Aristotle, certain aspects of which are currently much discussed. It maintains that some objects—no matter how described—have essences; that is, they have, essentially or necessarily, certain properties, without which they could not exist or be the things they are. This is often seen as equivalent to the claim that there are de re modalities.

eternal

1. everlasting.
2. non-temporal. Plato's Forms or Ideas should surely be

thought of as the latter rather than the former; and, if so, his attempt in Phaedo to base a doctrine of the temporal immortality of the soul upon that theory must have been misconceived.

eternal recurrence

a doctrine, holding that time is cyclical, to be found in both East and West; in Hinduism 'in Greek philosophy' in some medieval thinker and in modern philosophy.

eternity

from the Latin aeternus (from aeviternu, in turn from aevum, 'age'). The problem of time and eternity turns, at least in part, on the ideas of permanence and change. Time is the order of change and eternity is the order of changelessness.

ethical intuitionism

the view that ethical terms are primary and underived. i.e., different in nature from all non-ethical terms and thereby not wholly definable.

ethical naturalism

the view that ethics is a part of the natural world, and that ethical issues can be settled by an appeal to facts.

ethics

a branch of knowledge that is concernted with the study of moral values. Ethical code is the part and parcel of human socities. Its main purpose is to regulate the behaviour of an individual or a group or a society to which he belongs. Moral obligations differ from society to society. Even professional societies such as medical societies, business organisations have their own code of conduct. Ethics has been chiefly, classified into: normative and descriptive ethics. Normative ethics is chiefly concerned with the standardisation of moral principles, whereas descriptive ethics is concerned with the analysis of various ethical concepts and their application to various human situations. Descriptive ethics is a part of meta-ethics.

etiology

from the Greek aitia ('cause') and logos ('theory of'). Thus, the study of causality, usually as restricted to a given class of phenomena.

eucharist

from the earliest times the central act of Christian worship, one both of thanksgiving and, through the consecrated elements of bread and wine, of personal communion with Christ, or whose Body and Blood they are regarded as the symbols or outward signs. It has always been considered to have originated in the last supper of Jesus with his disciples before the crucifixion, and associated, therefore, with his death, interpreted as a sacrifice for human sin. In episcopal churches (as universally in antiquity) its celebration is confined to a bishop or priest.

In the Roman Catholic Church the doctrine of the manner of Christ's presence in the sacrament is known as Transubstantiation. Alternative names for the Eucharist are Mass, Holy Communion, and the Lord's Supper.

eudaemonism

from the Greek eudaimonia ('happines'). The term refers literally to the condition of being blessed by the protection of a benign spirit. Applied to all ethical theories taking happiness as man's chief end, the term is attributed primarily, and most commonly, to the ethics formulated by Aristotle.

eulogon

the doctrine of Arcesilas that probability is the guide to life.

Europa

daughter of the Phoenician king Agenor. Zeus, attracted by her beauty, sent (or came in the form of) a bull which carried her on its back to Crete; there she bore the god 3 sons; Minos, Rhadamanthus and Sarpedon.

eurytus of croton

a follower of Pythagoras, known only for his procedure as associated particular creatures with, and representing them by, particular numbers of pebbles. The most plausible interpretation of this practise is that he considered that the essence of a sort of objects consists in the points required to bound the surfaces of those objects.

euthanasia

etymologically 'euthanasia' means good dying. It is one of the concepts of ethics which has received considerable attention in the field of medical ethics. Euthanasia is administered when a patient is suffering from an incurable disease or a pain that is intolerable.

entychianism

the Christological doctrine that at the incarnation Christ's human nature was absorbed into the divine nature. The doctrine was introduced by Euthychus, head of a monastery outside Constantinople, between 448 and 451 A.D. Since Eutychianism denied that Christ had two distinct natures, and implied that God himself was tempted, suffered, and died, the doctrine was condemned and Eutychus was excommunicated.

evaluative

tending to concern or suggest rules or standards, as opposed to purely descriptive. An evaluative statement implies a value judgement on the part of the person making it.

event

an occurrence (as opposed to a material object), usually thought of as happening at a determinable time and place.

evidence

that which proves or contributes to the proof of a conclusion. The problem of evidence involves the question of the criterion for truth.

evil

from Anglo-Saxon yfel. The opposite and complement of good, and term is almost always defined negatively. Evil has been treated from both religious and philosophical points of view.

evolution

from the Latin ('out') and volvere ('to roll'). The idea of evolution is, in a general sense, a subdivision of the problems of the one and the many, or the problem of permanence and change. If the concept of evolutionary development is taken with sufficient generality it can be shown to have characterized philosophical thought from the beginning, and almost continuously.

excluded middle, law of

one of the traditional laws of logic, according to which a proposition has to be either true or false.

exemplarism

from the Latin exemplum ('model' or 'example'). This term refers to the Platonic-inspired doctrine that finite things are copies of divine ideas. The phrase, exemplary cause, similarly, refers to the causal role of exemplars.

existence

from the Latin ex and sistere ('to step forth, emerge'). Philosophical analyses of the concept of existence are in some respects similar to analyses of the concept of matter. As 'matter' stands in contrast to 'form', so 'existence' stands in contrast to 'essence'. And since mental activity is concerned with the characteristics of things and latter terms, 'form' and 'essence', seem less puzzling than 'matter' and 'existence'. If 'existence' cannot be characterized how is one to discuss it; and if it can be characterized how does it stand in contrast to 'essence'? The puzzle is not far removed from the following analyses.

existential import

a proposition is said to have existential import whenever it entails existence. For example, the statement 'There is a dictionary on the table' has existential import.

existentialism

a philosophical movement challenging essentialism and cencentrating attention on the human situation. Theistic existentialism is usually regarded as beginning with Kierkegaard and atheistic, existentialism with Nietzsche.

existential quantifier

the notation used in Existential Ge eralization and instantiation.

experience

from the Latin experior ('to prove' or 'to put to the test'). The usual use of the term is to refer to information gained from the senses rather that from reason.

explanation
from the Latin ex and planare ('to make level or plain'). The procedure of making a matter clear consists of dividing a complex idea into its simpler parts, or in demonstrating that the idea in question can be deduced from certain premises, or that a state of affairs would have resulted from certain causes, or in a combination of these procedures. That which is to be explained is called the explanandum; that which provides the explanation is called the explanans.

explication
1. in general, explanation.
2. (in logic) a form of analysis by which an imprecise concept is given a precise formal definition in order to make it suitable for formal logical use.

expressive language
according to C.I.Lewis, it is a language through which we express various problems of philosophy.

extension
that which has spatial dimensions. The concept was used by Descartes to distinguish matter, which is extended or has extension, from mind, which he regarded as a thinking substance having no spatial dimensions.

extention and intention
a distinction first introduced by Port Royal logicians like that of denotation and connotation. According to J.S.Mill, extention can replace denotation, whereas intention can replace connotation. In the case of extention, a term can be extended to all the member belonging to a particular class. In the case of intention, a term can be attached to only a specified individual or a particular mainly to separate it from the other individuals or the particulars.

external relation
a relation independent of its terms. The discussion of external relations was of importance in the late 19th and early 20th centuries.

external world
the philosophical problem set by Descartes when, in his 'room with a stove' he argued that his only rock bottom certainty was his immediate present consciousness: 'I think, therefore I am'. The problem was to show whether, starting from there, anyone could know, and how he could know, that there was a universe around him, containing things and other people. It should be remembered that the Cartesian starting point is a subject of consciousness both solitary and incorporeal.

extrasensory perception (or ESP)
the various putative phenomena of acquiring information without any employment of the senses.

extrinsic value

correlate of intrinsic value. The phrase applies to things or states of being valuable not in themselves but in their consequences. 'Instrumental value' is a synonym.

Fa chia

a Chinese term meaning 'legalist school'. One of the ancient Chinese schools of philosophy.

fact

a fact is an event or a phenomenon or a fragment of objective reality that is an object of man's experience. According to Wittgenstein, world consists of facts rather than things.

faculty psychology

from the Latin facere ('to make'). A view of psychology in which mind, psyche, or soul is analyzed into the separate faculties, or powers, of reason, will and sensibility.

faith

a strong belief in something as true or genuine even without sufficient proof. According to Kierkegaad, it is the act of faith that leads one to religious level. Religious faith does not entertain reason at all. Kierkegaard felt that 'faith is the shipwreck of reason'.

fall, the

the lapes, through a whereby, according to Christian theology, Adam and Eve lost their original innocence and happiness and acquired that state of sinfulness, with its unhappy consequences, which has been transmitted to their posterity, and from which man stands in need of deliverance by the redemptive action of God.

fallacies

from the Latin fallacia ('deceit', 'trick', or 'fraud'). The problem of validity in logic sense has its other side in the recognition of types of invalidity. Since fallacies are instances of reasoning which violate the requirement of validity, and since there exists an indefinitely great number of possible ways of reasoning improperly, there can be no comprehensive list of fallacies.

fallacy

an argument involving an invalid, rather than a valid, form of reasoning.

fallibilism

a theory presented by Peirce describing enquiry as an activity generated by a state of unease and aiming to attain a state of rest through finding the right answer to a question. But rest is never assured, since no can know what fresh evidence might present itself to necessitate a change in position.

falsidical

an opposite for the term veridical. Anything that is false is called falsidical.

falsification

showing or demonstrating to be false. In this philosophical sense, as opposed to its ordinary, non-technical sense of 'making false by alteration or deception', this word refers to the precise opposite of verification.

fantacy

an imaginary idea that is often contrasted with something real or objective, e.g., gold-mountain.

fascism

from the Latin fascis, the bundle of rods-including an axe with blade projecting— carried as a symbol of authority before the magistrates of Rome. The name of an Italian political organization founded by Mussolini in 1919, bringing him to power in 1922. Gentile and Ugo Spirito contributed to the theory of the corporate state which Fascists held to be their goal.

fatalism

the doctrine that all things happen according to an inexorable fate. The doctrine is both pre-philosophical and pretheological. The equivalent doctrine in theological thought is pre-destination, and in philosophy its equivalent is determinism.

fate

a superstitious view that all events in one's life are predetermined by some supernatural force. All modern religions consider fate as divine predestination.

father

a priest belonging to a religious order or community, though in the Roman Catholic Church the term is commonly used with reference to priests generally.

fathers (of the Church)

1. authoritative Christian writers of the first 5 centuries (or perhaps as late as the 12th c.). 2. Christian leaders and dignitaries generally, especially when meeting in solemn assembly.

faunus

Roman forest divinity dentified with Pan. Also a god of herdsmen.

feeling

any portion of one's awareness characterized by sensation or emotion.

feitishism

a primitive view that attributed a few magical powers to the objects to influence the life of humans.

Fichte, Johann Gottlieb (1762-1814)

a German philosopher who proclaimed that science of science is the prerequisite for practical philosophy. According to Fichte, religion is a kind of belief in the divine moral law, whereas the practical reason is the foundation of epistemology that satisfies all its subjects.

fictionalism

For Hans Vaihinger the doctrine that fictitious entities, useful but imaginary concepts and principles, lie at the basis of mathematics, science, philosophy, law, and religion.

fideism

the view, recurrent throughout religious history that essential religious doctrines cannot be established by rational means, but only accepted, if at all, by acts of faith. Its extreme form holds that religion requires the acceptance of doctrines actually absurd or contrary to reason (quia impossible).

fides qusereas intellectum

(Latin for faith seeking understanding). A slogan coined by St. Augustine to characterize the Christian intellectual quest.

figure

in logic, one of the four possible arrangements of the terms in a categorical syllogism. Aristotle distinguished only three figures; the isolation of the fourth is traditionally attributed to Galen. Syllogism.

figure, galenian

the fourth figure of the syllogism named after Galen who added it to the three figures of Aristotle.

final cause

that one of Aristotle's four causes which supports the hylozoistic interpretation of matter. Final cause has human purposiveness as its paradigm, and generalizes purpose beyond the human realm. One must suppose, with Aristotle, that the unttained state of the oak can exercise causal power over the acorn.

finite set

refers to a set that is either empty, or is such that there exists a one-to-one correspondence between its members and a subset of the set of natural numbers less than a specified natural number.

finitism

a philosophical standpoint that denies the notion or the category of infinite. According to finitism, there is no infinity in the Universe. Since man's experience is the experience of finite things and their properties, man's thinking is also limited to finite things. put last para of this ten on p. 72 of Dic. of Phil. by Srinivas.

first cause

one of the names of God, derived from the argument—formulated by Aristotle—that every causal chain requires a first, uncaused cause.

first heaven

for Aristotle, the outermost sphere, identified with the region of the fixed stars.

first mover

in aristotle's metaphysics, it represents the origin of motion in the Universe. The 'First Mover or Unmoved Mover' is responsible for all the motion in the Universe. However, the 'First Move' remains unmoved. According to St. Aquinas, there must be some 'First Cause' which is responsible for all the motion in this Universe. This 'First Cause' is none other than God.

first philosophy

in Aristotle's sense the study of being as being. This, along with Theology, is the name Aristotle gave to the book we now call Metaphysics, and to the discipline as well, a study of the concepts existing within and extending beyond specific fields of inquiry.

flash-back

scene in a film, play or novel, that depicts events which have happened earlier.

flatus vocis

Latin phrase meaning 'mere word'. Anselm and Abelard charged that Roscelin held the universal to be a mere word thus opening the issue of nominalism with respect to the problem of universal.

force

from the Latin fortis ('strong'). In physics the cause of the acceleration in the movement of material bodies. As the etymology of the word suggests, the conception had its origin in human effort, and was transferred to the physical world.

Aristotle making locomotion the primary motion, was led to interpret force in mechanical terms, requiring contact between bodies.

In his view there is a direct proportional relation between force, time and distance. The view was immensely influential, and only gradually were other alternatives suggested.

foreknowledge

the doctrine that God has knowledge of the future virtue of his eternity, all events being present to him in totum simul. It is sometimes argued that in this manner the divine Omniscience is compatible with human freedom.

form

from the Latin forma (probably from ferire 'to strike, hew', thus to create a recognizable thing). Forma is a translation of Greek term idea or eidos.

For Plato the individual thing with its class character is explained by the interaction of form and receptacle. The form is received in matter. This constitutes the individual thing and makes it an imitation of the eternal form in which it participates. In this view the eternal forms possess a higher reality than do their temporal imitations.

formalism

the tendency to emphasize form as over against content. In ethics the tendency is most pronounced in Kant and in Deontological Ethics generally.

formal language

an uninterpreted system of signs called formal language. It is conditioned by formation and transformation rules. It is also called logically perfect or ideal language. Wittgenstein developed his earlier view of language by means of logically perfect language.

formally and eminently

scholastic technical term still

used without explanation by Descarts. Thus Meditation VI argues that the power producing what would now be called sense data 'resides in some substance different from me, in which all the reality subjectively in the ideas produced is formally or eminently contained'. The second term means in a pre-eminent manner or degree, the, first specifies a straightforward correspondence with what is found in the effect. Descartes here appeals to that supposed a priori knowledge of causality which Hume was later to deny.

formal mode of speech

refers to the employment of all the various devices for making it unequivocally clear that the true subject of discourse is, where it is, concepts and the logical relations between concepts, rather than objects or events and the supposed contingent facts about those objects or events. The contrast is with material mode of speech. Both expressions were introduced by Rodolf Carnap.

formal system (or theory)

refers to any set of axioms and/or rules of inference written in some specified formal language L. The axioms will be closed wffs (wff) of L, and rules of inference (or transformation rules) are rules according to which proofs can be constructed out of wffs of L.

formation rules

rules defining, often inductively, the notion of a wff (well-formed formula) of a language.

fortuna

Roman goddess, taken as counterpart of the Greek Tyche, 'fortune'.

four elements

according to ancient Greek philosophers, the Universe is composed of four basic elements—earth, air, water and fire. Every element possesses two important qualities. For example, earth (dry and cold), air (wet and hot), water (wet and cold), and fire (dry and hot).

four humours

to maintain proper physical and mental condition, the bodily fluids such as blood, choler (yellow bile), phlegm and melancholy (black bile) must be in a proper proportion. Galen felt that any excess in their quantities may cause some physical or mental illness.

four-term fallacy

refers to a form of defective syllogism that is deficient because the middle term occurs in two distinct senses. Thus 'All kinds cry. That goat is a kid. Therefore that goat cries'.

Frankfurt School

a movement associated with the Institute for Social Research founded within the University of Frankfurt in 1923. It has included Max Horkheimer, Theodor Adorno, and Herbert Marcusa. The uniting idea is the need for a critical Marxism, constructed as involving rejection of positivism, value-freedom, and (crude) materialism, while stressing the actual Hegelian and alleged idealist side of Marx himself.

free Churches

the designation now commonly applied, at least in England, to the dissenting or nonconformist communions.

freedom

from the Middle English freedom ('the state of being free'). The quality of not being constrained by fate, necessity, or circumstances in one's decisions and actions.

freedom of will

a view that is opposed to determinsm. According to this view, an individual acts in certain circumstances as per the dictates of his own will. Thus his actions are neither guided by any other force, nor predetermined.

freewill and determinism

two apparently opposed philosophical concepts; the former postulating that man is able to choose and act according to the dictates of his own will, the latter that all events including human actions, are predetermined. Perplexities arise for both the secularist and still more the theist.

Freud, Sigmund (1856-1939)

a well-known Austrian physician and a founder of psychophysical analysis. He regarded psychic activity as something independent, but existing along with the material process. Freud subjected all the psychic conditions, all the actions of man, and also all the historical events and the social phenomenon to psychoanalysis. He tried to interpret them in terms of unconscious, above all sexual impulses.

friar

a brother or member of certain Christian religious orders founded during the 13 th c. or later, and especially the 4 mendicant orders (that is, those living entirely on alms), Franciscans (Grey Friars), Augustinians, Dominicans (Black Friars), and Carmelites (White Friars).

function

one of the most central concepts in mathematics. It comes to have application in logic as a result of Frege's insistence (in 'Function and Concept') on the analogy between concepts and functions. However, with the increasing use of formal logic in the study of the foundations of mathematics, functions themselves have become objects of study in logic itself.

future

along with past and present, one of the three divisions of time. Determinists generally hold that the future is closed, although not yet occurrent; indeterminists hold that it is open.

futurology

a branch of science that deals with the future of mankind and the prospects of social progress. The term futurology was first introduced by a German Sociologist O. Flechtheim. In other words, it is a science of the future, whose basic aim is to predict the nature and the utility of various scientific disciplines and various steps to be taken in maintaining a bright future of the mankind.

galatea

'milk white'; a seanymph. She turned her beloved Acis, killed by Polyphemus (the Cyclops) with a rock, into a river which thereafter always bore his name.

Galileo Galilel (1564-1642)

Italian mathematician, astronomer, and physicist who founded modern mechanics and cogently argued for the Copernican heliocentric theory of the universe. His views brought him into constant conflict with the religious authorities. In 1633, he was forced to recant and was placed under house arrest for the remainder of his life.

gallicanism

the movement leading to the Gallican articles.

gambler's fallacy

the belief into which a gambler may be tempted, to the effect that a system such as a roulette wheel or a tossed coin has a 'memory', so that after a run of one kind of result another outcome becomes more probable. The fallacy lies in supporting that the so-called law of averages implies this. In fact the theorem applies only where probabilities are constant from repetition to repetition, and so can offer no support to the gambler's belief.

game theory

a mathematical theory dealing with game-like situations in which participants wish to maximize some property (such as utility) in positions of uncertainty, not only with respect to the state of nature but also the actions of other players whose interests may be opposed or parallel to those of the participant.

Gandhi, Mohandas K. (1869-1948)

Indian religious and national leader. Born in Porbandar. Educated in London. Called Mahatma ('great soul'), he combined Hindu, Christian, and philosphic principles in a version of pacifism which include the idea of 'passive resistance'. Thoreau and Tolstoy are specifically credited as having contributed to his thinking.

ganymede

beautiful youth carried off by Zeus to be his cupbearer. The god compensated his father with a gift of marvellous horses, or some say, a golden vine.

garhapatya

type of fire.

Gassendi, Pierre (1592-1655)

a French materialist philosopher who strongly opposed to scholasticism. He questioned Descartes claim that the 'clarity and distinctness' is the criterion of truth.

According to Gassendi, how are we supposed to know that anything is 'clear and distinct' to us. He also attacked the doctrine of innate ideas put forward by Descartes.

gathas

the hymns ascribed to Zoroaster in the Avesta, sacred scriptures of Zoroastrianism.

Gaudepada, 6th or 8th century A.D.

Indian philosopher. The first known systematic exponent of Advaita Vedanta the non-dualistic interpretation of the Vedanta philosophy. Influenced by Nagarjuna, and Vasubandhu, Gaudapada's basic attachment was to the Upanishads. Indeed, one trust of his work lies in showing that both Buddhism and Vedanta, are rooted in the Upanishadic literature.

Gautama or Gotama

a great sage and seer, who founded the Nyaya school. He is also known as Aksapada. He is the author of Nyaya-Sụtra. Nyaya is a combination of pluralistic atomism and logical realism.

ge, gaia

the earth, conceived in vaguely personal terms as a goddess.

gemara

an aramaic term meaning 'completion'. A body of literature amplifying the Mishnah.

generative grammar

the rules that allows speakers to construct (generate) infinite numbers of new sentences in a language.

generation

from the Latin generare ('to beget, create'). One of the Aristotelian types of change. Its opposite is 'curruption'. Generation is a change from non-being to being, while corruption is a change from being to non-being. Relative generation and corruption are types of alteration or change of quality, regarded by Aristotole as one of the three basic types of change. Absolute generation and corruption, although recognized by Aristotle, remain something of a mystery within his system.

genetic

from the Greek genesis ('origin').

(1) As an adjective the term applies to an investigation into origins.

(2) The Genetic Fallacy is committed when the latter stages of a process are evaluated only in terms of its earlier stages.

genetic fallacy
the mistake of arguing that because something is now such and such, therefore it must already have been such and such at an earlier stage; or, becuase it was such and such then, therefore it must be the same now.

genus
in Aristotle's classification, genus involves many classes called species. This classification of contribution is the field of science, especially in the field of natural sciences.

geometry
a science that has its origins practically located in the need of the ancient Egyptians to redraw field boundaries each year as a result of the Nile floods; the laws concerning lines, angles etc. being arrived at by empirical generalization. The Greeks, in particular Euclid (c. 300 B.C.) turned geometry into a deductive theoretical science based on certain postulates, which in recent times has been rigorously axiomatized using only the primitive terms 'point', 'between' and 'congruent'.

gestalt
a German term meaning 'form, shape or 'figure'. The term stands for the principle that perceptual content is a series of configurations of totalities, rather than a series of simple perceptual elements.

gestalt theory
a theory of perception, according to which it is an organised systematic whole that is given in perception; but not the discrete, unconnected parts of any whole. This view is popular in psychology. In opposition to empiricist theory of perception, gestalt theory puts forward the view that 'organised wholes' form the basis for any mental activity rather than transient sensations.

ghost in the machine
a label introduced by Gilbert Ryle in 'The Concept of Mind' (1949) to descibe a thesis of Descartes to the effect that, while the human body may be regarded as an enormously subtle and complicated machine, it only becomes a person when it is joined by an incorporeal soul.

ghrita
clarified butter.

gigantes
the giants. They attacked Olympus, but the gods, helped by Heracles, defeated them and buried them under Mt Aetna.

gilgamesh epic
a work of Assyrian Babylonian literature going back to Sumerian legends 3000 years before Christ. The narrative of the wanderings of Gilgamesh an his friend, Engidu (half-man = half-bull), contains an account of a flood, called the Babylonian Flood Story, of which the Biblical account is a variant.

given, the
an obsolete term for the putative raw data of experience—uncontaminated by theoretical, ordering, or inferential imposition or additions.

Glauce
daughter of Creon, king of Corinth.

glaucus
several figures in Greek mythology bear this name. Best known of them, perhaps, is the son of Sisyphus, and father of Bellerophon. He was killed and devoured by his own mares for having offended Aphrodite.

gnoseology
an obsolete synonym for epistemology.

gnostics
the followers of philosophic-religious school that combines Christian theology with the oriental relgions. The gnostics believe in an unknowable arche which manifests itself in emanation, which is counterposed to the matter.

God
a Anglo-Saxon term of Teutonic origin referring to the object of religious worship. Its meaning therefore, is as varied as human culture itself. The concept has developd in different ways in different settings. A great deal of evidence supports the view that the origin of the conception lies in the numinous feeling linking primitive man to his world, and issuing in animism, mana, and sympathetic magic. It is tempting to say, although arranging cultural stages is hazardous, that the end of this development, given polytheism as an intermediate stage, is monotheism.

Godel, Kurt (1906-1978)
a Czechoslovakian mathematician and logician who is well-known for his first incompleteness theorem. According to his theorem, in any formal system 'S' of arithmetic, there will be a sentence 'P' of the language of 'S' such that if 'S' is consistent, then neither P nor its negation can be proved in 'S'.

Godel's theorem
the proof, published by Kurt Godel in 1931, of the existence of formally undecidable propositions in any formal system of arithmetic. More precisely, his first incompleteness theorem (which is what is usually meant when people talk of Godel's theorem) states that in any formal system S of arithmetic, there will be a sentene P of the language of S such that if S is consistent, neither P nor its negation can be proved in S.
The technique used in proving this result is to translate the syntax of the language of S into arithmetic, thus making S capable of representing its own syntax. This makes it possible to show that there must be a

sentence P of S which can be interpreted (very roughly) as saying 'I am not provable).

God of the gaps

the hostile phrase applied to theories appealing to the concept of God to explain anything science currently finds, inexplicable, for instance, the origins of life or of consciousness. Theologians now generally regard such appeals as creating only the illusion of explanation, and providing no valid basis or support for theism.

golden age

in Greek mythology, a time of paradisal innocence under the rule of Cronus, son of Uranus (Heaven) and Gaea (Earth). The idea of golden age became a potent literary and artistic emblem for a perfect and harmonious relationship between man and Nature and between man and man.

golden mean

moderation in a person's course of life. Aristotle saw the mean as the rational and virtuous course between extremes of excess—for example, temperance shunning both asceticism and profligacy.

golden rule

stated negatively by Confucious 'What you do no want done to yourself, do not do to others', and positively by Jesus 'Do unto others, as you would have others do unto you', the rule is widely held to be the basis of all morality.

good

from Anglo-Saxon god Latin bonum, and Greek agathon. The idea of the good, or of value, plays a role in all philosophical areas but primarily in Ethics Aesthetics, and Axiology.

The distinction between instrumental and intrinsic goodness, or value, begins with the Greeks. Intrinsic goods are those things good in themselves; instrumental goods have their value in making possible another good.

Goodman, Nelson (1906-)

an American philosopher who advocated an extreme form of nominalism. According to Goodman, people objectify similarities since they tend to objectify the properties and the characteristics of various objects in space and time. His important works include: The Structure of Appearance; Fact, Fiction and Forecast.

Goodman's paradox

a linguistic paradox of confirmation or prediction. We predict by projecting regularities beyond our experience (induction). Goodman showed how to define a vocabulary so that hypotheses that look to us as though they predict change have the linguistic form of projecting a regularity Good man introduces a new predicate 'grue', which applies to an object if it has been examined before a certain time t and is green, or has not been examined before t and is blue.

gorgon

according to Hesiod there were 3 of these winged females of terrifying appearance, with enormous teeth and serpents for hair. Medusa, alone of them mortal, was slain by Perseus, who cut off her head. From her blood sprang the winged horse, Pegasus.

gospel

1. the revelation of God's loving and merciful purpose for men revealed in and through Jesus Christ. 2. The proclamation, in the New Testament and by the Church, of the 'good news' of God's purpose for men. 3. One Testament (Matthew, Mark, Luke, John) containing an account of the life, teaching, death, and resurrection of Jesus. These are known as the canonical gospels. (There are some similar books not included in the New Testament and known therefore as non-canonical gosples, such as the 2nd-c. Gospel of Thomas.) 4. a liturgical reading, at the the eucharist or Mass from one of the canonical gospels.

gothic novel

kind of romance, of which Horace Walpole's 'Castle of Otranto' (1764) is the first example. Such novels were thrillers with a medieval setting and with plenty of supernatural machinery. Their purpose, in Jane Austen's phrase, was to be all horrid.

grace

the term entered theology obliquely by way of the three graces, fate fortune, and providence. In theology, grace is the favour, relating to salvation, shown to man by God.

grammatical form

the apparent surface form of an expression, in comparison with the underlying logical structure.

granth

the sacred book of the Sikhs (Sikhism).

greatest happiness principle (or principle of utility)

the basic tenet of utilitarianism, which holds that the supreme good is the greatest happiness of the greatest number of people. Happiness is construed as the maximization of pleasure and minimization of pain; it is contended that only in terms of this programme do concepts like 'good', 'duty', and 'right' have meaning and application.

Greek philosophy

the period of Greek philosophy can be said to run from around 600 B.C. to 600 A.D. In this period of greater than a thousand years not only were all the philosophical alternatives of the Western world sketched out, but many of the scientific theories, which have gained acceptance since that time : among these are the atomic theory, the heliocentric view of the solar system, and organic evolution. The philosophical alternatives occurs usually in schools of philosophy.

grelling's paradox (or paradox of heterologicality)

a semantic paradox presented by K. Grelling (1886-) in 1908. Some words have the same property as that which they name : for example, 'short' is a short word and 'polystllabic' has many syllables. These words are called 'homological' (or 'autological'). In contrast, heterological words such as 'useless' or 'monosyllabic' are not instances of the properties they name. The paradox arises when considering the word 'heterological' itself : if it is heterological then it does not instantiate it merning—but this is what 'heterological' means, therefore the word is homological. Conversely, if 'heterological' is autological, then it must have the charateristic of applying to itself and therefore 'heterological' is heterological.

griffin

fabulous creature, with the body of a lion and the head and wings of an eagle.

guelfs

a term in use in the 13th and 14th century to signify those who favoured the spiritual power in contrast with the Ghibellines who favoured temporal power. The terms were used throughout Italy and Germany referring to the struggles between papacy and beudal nobility, and the emerging urban classes against the feudallords.

guna (quality)

gunas constitute the three aspects: Sattva (light, knowledge, happiness), rajas (mobile, pain, action), and tames (indifference, lazy, dark, dull).

habit

from the Latin habitus ('state or appearance') from habere ('to have, be in a condition'). The Greek term lexis is Aristotle's term for this state or condition of body or mind. Aristotle utilized the concept of habit in his ethics to explain how a disposition to act virtuously is developed from the more capacity to so act. The disposition to act virtously results from virtous habits, and the habit is built upon virtuous activity. The circularity seems not to be vicious. Thomas Aquinas follows Aristotle here.

Hades

Greek god of the Underworld, sometimes called Pluto (the Roman Dis), and son of the Titans, Kronos and Rhea. His wife was Persephone, Demeter's daughter. The realm inhabited by the shades of the dead was also called Hades.

haecceity

from the Latin haecceitas which means 'thisness' or 'specificity'. The principle of individuation of Duns Scotus. Approximations to the view are to be found also in other Schoolmen, especially those of the Oxford school. 'Thisness' is presented as an alternate to matter as the means of understanding the step from infima species (the smallest species) to individual thing.

hallucintaion

a state of experience in which something is always imagined when there is nothing.

Hamilton, Willian (1788-1856)

a Scotish philosopher and a logician who denied objectivity of truth in order to advocate agnosticism. He believed that reality is cognisable through supernatural revelation only. He followed Kantian line by admitting that a priorism and moral postulates as the foundations of religious faith. One of his major works is Metaphysics and Logic.

happiness

from middle English hap, old Norse happ meaning 'good luck'. Also in Greek eudaimonia means 'to be prosperous of well-off' as well as 'to be happy'.

In fulfilment theories of valuation, happiness, as a state of being somehow different from a sum of pleasures, stands as the end of the life. Aristotle's view of happiness sets the pattern in this respect. Epicurus defined happiness, largely at least, in terms of pleasure with prudence an important ancillary value. Aquinas followed Aristotle although adding a theological dimension.

Hare, Richard Mervyn (1919-)

a famous British moral philosopher who attacked ethical naturalism. He claimed that the moral judgements are not mere descriptions of certain actions but imperative or prescriptive. His important works are: The Language of Morals; Freedom and Reason.

Harmonia

daughter of Ares and Aphrodite, and wife of Cadmus.

harmony

from the Greek harmos ('a fitting or joining'). The principle has played a role, modest but continuing, in the philosophy both of the East and of the West.

In the ancient Chinese Doctrine of the Mean the term is defined as a state in which the feeling of pleasure, anger, sorrow, and joy are aroused in 'due measure and degree', and contrasted with 'equilibrium', the state prior to the arousal of such feelings.

harpies

spirits of the winds who carry off (the name means 'snatchers') persons and things. Virgil describes them as monsters with women's faces and bodies, and birds wings and claws.

hasidism

a pietistic mass movement

that began among Jews in early 18th century Russia. Its philosophical roots were in the Kabbalah.

Hatha-Yoga

the term used for the Indian system of mental and physical training, which has been based on certain speculative physiolcgical theories and is intended to give an individual control over his own physical and spriritual well-being. It is commonly known in the West as yoga, but is not to be confused with the Yoga school of philosophy, with which it shares certain techniques of meditation.

heaven

the abode of God and the blessed. Modern Christian theologians prefer to speak of heaven, as also of hell, as conditions rather than places in any literal sense.

Hebe

Greek goddess of youth, daughter of Zeus and Hera. When Heracles was deified she became his wife.

Hecate

according to Hesiod, a daughter of the Titan, Perses. She possessed the power of conferring wealth and other material advantages. Later she appeared as goddess of the magic arts and was associated with the ghost-world. Cross-roads and haunted sports were her favoured places of worship.

Hector

son of Priam, king of Troy, and Hecuba, and husband of Andromache; the bravest of the Trojan champions. He it was who slew Patroclus, to be killed himself by the enraged Achilles. Apollo and Aphrodite saved his body from corruption and it was buried by Priam with great pomp.

Hecuba

daughter of a Phrygian king and wife of Priam. Hector and Paris were among her many children. After the fall of Troy she was carried off as a slave, but for avenging the murder of her son, Polydorus, she was transformed into a bitch, which leaped into the sea and was drowned.

hedonism

an ethical point of view, according to which pleasure is the sole good. Every human action is explained in terms of pleasure. Psychological hedonism is a form of hedonism which holds that every individual seeks his own pleasure or happiness.

hegelianism

the views of those who claim to uphold the doctrines of Hegel have shown considerable differences, not only because of the obscurity of Hegel's writings, but also because there was a fundamental ambivalence in his views. Hegel had argued that history is a process which has a rational end, and soon after his death there was disagreement among his followers about the rationality of the state that history had reached. The so called Old Hegelians argued that contemporary political conditions were rational; the Young Hegelians disagreed, and said that the business of philosophy was to promote a revolution—more specifically, a revolution of ideas.

Heidelberg school

one of the schools of neo-Kantian philosophy active during the last part of the 19th and the first part of the 20th century. Located at the University of Heidelberg, the school took an axiological approach to Kant, holding value to be the key to epistemology.

heilsgeschichte

a German term which means 'holy history' of the 'history of holiness'. A Protestant view of history, arising under this name in the 18th century, which held that the purpose of history is the gradual formation of the Chosen people under the guidance of the Holy Spirit.

Helen

daughter of Zeus and Leda and wife of Menelaus, king of Sparta. Paris seduced her and led her off to Troy, thus causing the Trojan war. Helen later married Paris brother, Deiphobus, but on Troy's fall she returned to Menelaus, with whom she lived in peace for the remainder of her days.

heliocentric theory

the theory, first advanced by Aristarchus of Samos (310-230 B.C.) that the earth and planets revolve round the sun, which remains fixed, and that the earth rotates on its own axis throughout its orbit. Revived by Copernicus in refuting the Ptolemaic system, and upheld by Galileo, the idea of the earth not being at the centre of the universe was opposed as much in times of Aristarchus as in 16th and 17th century Europe, on the ground that it depreciated man's place in the Universe.

Helios

Greek god of the sun. Hyperion was his father. The poets relate that he rose daily from his splendid palace in the east and was drawn in a golden chariot by 4 horses across the arch of the sky to his second palace in the west. He was credited with the power of seeing and hearing all things.

hell

the abode of Satan and the damned.

Hellenistic philosophy

the Hellenistic period in Greek history runs from 323 B.C., the year of Alexander the Great's death, to 30 B.C. when the last major Hellenistic empire was annexed by Rome. Philosophy in this period centred on Athens. Of the four major schools there (Academic, Peripatetic, Epicurean, and Stoic), the Epicureans, with their hedonistic ethics and (denial of providence, were the outsiders). The contrary belief derived ultimately from Socrates in a purposive universe and in the right exercise of reason as the supreme human good found its most forceful advocates in the Stoics. Their principal opponents came from the Academy of Athens with its sceptical rejection of all positive 'dogmatic' belief. Controversy between Stoics and Academics dominated the philosophical scene in the 3rd and 2nd centuries B.C. Later there arose a tendency, variously represented by Panaetius, Posidonius, and Antiochus, to combine Stoicism with the Platonic and Aristotelian doctrines, that ultimately submerged it.

henologinal argument

refers to an alternative name for the degrees of perfection argument for the existence of God.

henotheism

this term was first introduced by Max Muller, according to which each of many gods, when praised, is extolled by the hymn as the supreme God.

Hephaestus

lame Greek god of fire; the Roman Vulcan; he came to be regarded as the divine smith and the patron of the craftsmen.

Hera

pre-hellenic goddess whose Greek name is no more than the title, lady. The daughter of Kronos and Rhea, she figures in Greek mythology as wife and sister of Zeus and patroness of female life in general and of marriage in particular. Her children included Ares, Hebe, and Hephaestus. According to Homer she was jealous and quarrelsome; Zeus himself quailed at her tongue. Argos seems to have been the most ancient place for her worship.

Heracles

the most popular and most widely venerated of Greek heroes. He was a son of Zeus by Alcmene. His strength and prowess were incomparable. Even as a newborn infant he strangled 2 serpents that attacked him in his cradle.

It was especially for certain labours of his adult manhood that he was renowned. These were imposed upon him by Eurystheus, king of Tiryns, to whose service he had to submit himself by command of the Delphic oracle. They were: (1) The killing of the Nemean Lion, the skin of which he afterwards always wore, as well as its head as a helmet. (2) the slaying of the Lernean Hydra, a serpent with 9 heads, the middle one of which was immortal, although for each of the others that was severed 2 more heads grew in its place. Heracles succeeded, however, in burning them and buried the immortal one under a rock. With the creature's bile he prepared his poisoned arrows. (3) the capture of the Arcadian Stag, an animal with golden antlers and brazen feet which it took him a year to catch. (4) the capture of the Erymanthian Boar, which the hero chased into deep snow until it was exhausted. (5) the cleasing of the Augean Stables, which, although the 3,000 oxen of stabled there, had not been cleaned out for 30 years. Heracles, cleansed them in a single day, turning the rivers Alpheus and Peneus through them, (6) the destruction of the voracious Stymphalian Birds, which had brazen claws, wings, and beaks, and ate human flesh. He first startled them with a rattle given him by Athena and then killed them with his poisoned arrows. (7) the capture of the Cretan Bull, which king Minos had omitted to sacrifice, although ordered to do so by Poseidon, Heracles brought it to Eurystheus on his shoulders, but later released it to roam through Greece. (8) the capture of the Horses of Diomedes, which the king always fed on human flesh. The animals killed Heracles friend, Abderus, whose death the hero avenged by slaying Diomedes. Given their master's own body to consume, the horses became tame, but were themselves afterwards destroyed by wild beasts on Mt Olympus. (9) the seizure of the girdle of the Amazon queen, Hippolyte, coverted by Eurystheus daughter, Admete. To gain it Heracles had to murder the queen. (10) The capture of the oxen of the 3-bodied monster Geryon on the fabulous western island of Erythia. On his journey the hero erected 2 pillars on either side of the Straits of Gibraltar. (11) the fetching of the golden apples from the garden of the Hesperides, the whereabouts of which Heracles did not know. He sent the giant Atlas to find them, meanwhile bearing for him the weight of the world. (12) the bringing of the fearsome hound Cerberus up from the underworld without using force of the arms, which the hero did by carrying the monster.

Heracles was famed for many other exploits. When he came to die—on a funeral type of his own making—he was carried off to Olympus on a cloud, receiving there the gift of immortality.

Heraclitus of Ephesus (died after 480 BC)

Greek philosopher known as 'the obscure', 'the riddler' and 'the weeping philosopher'. The most famous doctrine attributed to him had been that all things are in a state of flux; even the unchanging hills change, but more slowly than most other things.

hereditary property

a term used in formal logic. An R-hereditary property (where R is a relation) is any property P such that for any object b and c, if c has the property p and b stands in the relation R to c, then b also has the property, p.

For instance, if R is the relation is greater by three than the property of being exactly divisible by three is R-hereditary among numbers, since, for any numbers b and c if c is exactly divisible by three.

heresy

from the Greek hairesis ('a taking for oneself', 'choice', 'sect'). In the religious tradition of the West the term has come to mean the denial of a revealed truth.

hermeneutics

from the Greek hermeneutikos ('interpretation').

In its classical reference the term refers to the interpretation of texts, especially Biblical, but also philosophical.

In philosophy of the social sciences one view is that the social sciences are more akin in method to hermeneutics than to the iaboratory sciences. Spranger, for example, viewed psychology as a 'hermeneutic of the spirit'.

In philosophy hermeneutics has joined Structuralism in creating a method of interpretation which centers philosophy once again in culture.

Hermes

son of Zeus and Maia. He is familiar in Roman mythology as Mercurius. His best known role was that of messenger of the gods, for which he carried a herald's wand. He also conducted the dead to Hades. He was commonly represented in art as a head supported by a tapering pillar with a phallus affixed to it. Such images were known as Hermae.

hermeticism

the occult tradition based on the late antique treatises known by the collective title of the Corpus Hermeticum.

Hero and Leander

famous lovers; Hero a priestess of Aphrodite at Sestos, Leander a young man from Abydos. Leander used to swim the Hellespont nightly to visit her, until on one occasion a storm blew out the light by which she used to guide him, and he was drowned. In her grief she threw herself into the sea after him.

herodotage

a colloquial name for anthropological literature in which human habits, customs, and beliefs are compared. The reference is to a confrontation, recorded by the Greek historian Herodotus, between rival commitments to burying, burning, or eating dead relations.

Hesperides

daughters—usually 3 in number—of Hesperus, the Evening star, and the guardians of the golden apples given by Ge to Hera on her marriage with Zeus.

heterological

a term that is inapplicable to itself. For example, the term 'Greek' is heterological because it is not a Greek word.

heteronomy

from the Greek heteros and nomos meaning 'the rule of another'. Contrasted with autonomy the term is used by Kant to characterize ethical systems whose principles derive from a source outside the person. In the autonomous system of Kant the self determines itself by means of its own law. Tillich applied the term to a mode of specious reasoning which took its principles from outside itself.

heuristic

serving to indicate or stimulate investigation. In many cases it involves proceeding to a solution by trial and error in the absence of an algorithm. In modern logic, the word describes a process that may solve a particular kind of problem but offers no guarantee of success.

hexameter

line of verse consisting of 6 feet, a measure much used in classical epic poetry.

high Church

one of the 3 main traditions, parties, or schools of thought in Anglicanism, marked by its emphasis on the importance and authority of the Church in its institutional asLect and its assertion of sacerdotal claims. Cf. Anglo-Catholicism, Low Church.

higher order logic

the study of validity in languages of second, or higher, order.

Hinduism 1500 B.C. to the present

the native religious system of India. A religion without a founder, Hinduism reflects in itself the cultural history and social conditions of the Indian people from the time civilisation flowered in the Indus Valley to our day. The various levels of religious insight from magic to ethical idealism coexist in Hindu scriptures and practices. Indeed, it is sometimes said that Hinduism is a Dharma (right action) instead of a religion. Conduct and belief here intermingle. Different modes of conduct and belief coexist in Hinduism; the apparent inconsistencies which result may be moderate by the Hindu insight that the one expresses itself and is expressed in many ways. Accep the point and apparent polytheism of Hinduthought disappear for there are different ways of reaching the Supreme Being, and the gods are merely different names for the one God and different paths leading to the same goal.

The Trimurti, or trinity, or later Hindu mythology, representing three aspects of the Supreme being—Brahma, the creator; Vishnu the preserver; and Shiva the destroyer-is thus also consistent with a strict monotheism; as are the successions of divine incarnations which are said in the Bhagavad-Gita to occur whenever 'the law fails and lawlessness uprises'. In any case, Hinduism is a natural growth characterized by richness but not a doctrine shaped into logical coherence. (1) The scriptures of Hinduism, called Vedas (meaning knowledge) consists of three parts: (a) the Samhitas (meaning collections) include the Rig-veda, a collection of hymns in praise of the gods; the Sama-veda, melodies relating to these hymns; the Yajur-veda sacrificial formulae; and the Atharva-veda, magical formula; (b) the Brahamanas, texts dealing with ritual and sacrifice, their meaning and value; (c) the Upanishads, essentially philosophical discourses, and the primary source for insight into Hindu philosophy.

(2) Comparable to, although more vast in scope than, the position held in Greek culture by the Iliad and Odyssey are the Ramayana (q.v.) and the Mahabharata (q.v.). In process of formation throughout the 1st.

Hindu philosophy

just as it is impossible satisfactory to define Hinduism as a religion, no definition of what is typically Hindu philosophy is possible. It can only be described as those forms of philosophical thought that, regardless of their origins and original motivation, allied themselves with, and were accepted by, the very complex religious superstructure called 'Hinduism', which set itself in opposition to materialism, Jainism, and Buddhism. For most practical purposes, the Vedanta and Mimamsa alone are strictly 'Hindu', by virtue either of their adherence to the fundamental scriptures and rites of Hinduism, or simply because they were accepted as such by the Hindus (thus the advaita Vedanta of Sankara, strictly speaking, trons cends Hindu religion). The four other systems (Samkhya, Yoga, Nyaya, and Vaisesika) which Hinduism includes in its traditional list of six 'orthodox' systems (darsanas), are only nominally Hindu (or religious in the general sense of the word). In particular, the Vaisesika and the Nyaya differ for more from the Vedanta than do the Bundhist Madhyamaka or Vijanavada.

historical explanation

a topic that has been the focus of considerable discussion and argument in the philosophy of history. Recent controversy which echoes earlier disputes concerning the relations between the human studies and the natural sciences, has largely revolved round two opposed claims; the contention that such explanation conforms in its essential structure to explanations of the kind typified in scientific contexts, and the contrary contention that it is sui generis, being susceptible to a quite different pattern of analysis. Proponents of the first position, originally favoured by logical empiricists eager to uphold the unity of scientific method have invoked the deductive nomological (or covering law) model of explanation; an event is explained, in history as elsewhere, in so far as the assertion of its occurrence is derivable from premises comprising descriptions of initial conditions together with 'universal hypotheses' or laws. Proponents of the second, on the other hand, have stressed the crucial role played by notions like meaning and intention in the understanding of human behaviour; it is argued that these set historical accounts within a teleological or rational framework of interpretation that has no counterpart at the level of the scientific thought and enquiry.

historicism

a view that cognizes the things and phenomena in their historical perspective, namely, the process of their origin and development, and the factors responsible for their existence. It is considered to be a major principle of Darwin's theory of evolution.

history philosophy of

two separate branches of enquiry, commonly distinguished as speculative and critical.

1. Speculative philosophy of history. Enquiry characteristically undertaken with the aim of providing an interpretation of the human past considered as a whole. Those who have embarked upon such an enterprise have regarded the course taken by history as conforming to some general orders or design, the task of the philosopher (unlike that of the ordinary practising historian) being one of eliciting a comprehensive pattern in terms of which the historical process in its totality can be seen to have a 'meaning' or to exhibit an overall direction.

2. Critical philosophy of history. Enquiry primarily concerned, not with the human past itself, but with modes of thought and enquiry about that past. Thus it takes as its subject matter the categories in terms of which the historian seeks to comprehend and interpret his material and the presuppositions that underlie his procedures.

As such, it is a second-order

discipline, which in the first instance evolved in response to methodological issues arising from the proliferation of historical studies during the 19th century.

The contention that history had finally taken shape as an autonomous form of thinking, distinguishable from other types of investigation but not for that reason inferior, was central to the work of continental philosophers such as Dilthey and Croce at the turn of the present century, and it was later to be given eloquent expression by the British writer, R.G. Collingwood.

holism

1. The contention that wholes, or some wholes, are more than the sum of their parts. One special version is organicism, urging that some systems that are not literally organisms are nevertheless crucially like organism, whose parts can only be understood in relation to their function in the complete and ongoing whole. 2. (in the social sciences and history). A theory that claims that society may, or should, be studied in terms of social wholes: that is, that the fundamental data of social analysis are not individuals or individual manifestations but rather societal laws, dispositions, and movements.

holy

sacred, set apart for the service of God; hence free from sin, morally pure. The expression 'the Holy is sometimes used as a synonym for God, stressing his otherness.

holy Office

Congregation of the Roman Catholic Church to which all final decisions on questions of faith and morals are referred. Founded in 1542 by Pope Paul III, it was closely associated with the Inquisition.

Holy Spirit, Holy Ghost

the 3rd person of the Trinity in Christian dogma. He is consubstantial and coeternal with the Father and the Son, though proceeding, according to Western theology, from both of them. The doctrine of the Holy Spirit represents in particular the Christian experience of God's inspiring and sanctifying power.

Holy week

the days, in the Christian calendar, from Palm Sunday (the one before Eeaster Sunday) to Easter Saturday in Clusive.

homoiousian

from the Greek homoi ('like') and ousia ('substance'). The doctrine defeated in the Council of Nicaea and later that the Son is of similar, but not identical, essence or substance as the Father.

homological

contrary to heterological, a homological term can be applied to itself. For instance, the word 'English' is homological because it is an English word. Homological is also interpreted as a similarity based on the structure, the origin and the development of any phenomenon.

homo mensura

from Latin meaning 'man the measure'. The phrase applied to the doctrine of the Greek sophist, Protagoras that all standards and judgments are relative to man. The doctrine is sometimes interpreted as an individual and sometimes as a collective relativity.

homonym

a word with the same form or sound as another but different in meaning, as pole (flag) and pole (magnetic) or bear (grizzly) and bear (children).

Horus

Egyptian god of light; son of Isis.

hotri

officiating priest at a sacrifice.

humanism

originally a study of the litteae humaniores or learning of the ancients, the term has now come to mean an attitude of mind based upon human values, in which philosophy and ethics rather than revealed religion are the ultimate sanction.

humanity

from the Latin humanitas ('human nature, feeling, or kindness'). The term is less used in philosophy than is cognates although Stoicism in viewing man as a citizen of the cosmos had clearly arrived at the concept. One of the basic translations of jen in Confucianism is 'humanity'.

(1) in the final development of his point of view Comte called for a religion of humanity. Churches dedicated to this religion were established in a number of countries.

(2) Feuerbach (q.v. 2) regarded humanity as unlimited and capable of achieving any quality, evcn though individual men are finite. Indeed, according to Feuerbach, men—beginning with this unlimited quality of humanity—have mistakenly projected the idea of God.

Hume David (1711-1776)

a Scotish empiricist philosopher who denied the existence of material as well as spiritual substances. According to him, Reality is nothing but a stream of sense impressions. These unconnected, discrete sensory units are neither mental nor material, but neutral entities. Hume's philosophy is also known as pure sensationalism, atomism, neutral monism. Hume conceived that what we suppose cause and effect relation between two entities or events is purely psychological. It is based on 'habit and custom'. He also held the view that there is no continuous self. What is called self is nothing but 'a bundle of sense-impressions'. His important works are: A Treatise of Human Nature; An Enquiry Concerning Human Understanding.

Hume's fork

the increasingly popular nickname for an aggressive employment of Hume's fundamental distinction between propositions stating or purporting to state only 'the relations of the ideas' and propositions stating or purporting to state 'matters of fact and real existence'. (Inquiry concerning Human Understanding (IV (i)). This distinction is substantially the same as that between truths of reason and the truths of fact in Leibniz earlier.

Hume's law

the increasingly popular label for Hume's insistence that the naturalistic fallacy is indeed a fallacy; and hence that conclusions about what ought to be cannot be deduced from premises stating only what was, what is, or what will be and the other way about.

Hyacinthus

beautiful youth, loved by both Apollo and Zephyrus. Apollo accidentally killed him with, a discus, blown aside purposely, some said, by the jealous Zephyrus. In token of the god's mourning, a flower of the same name sprang from the boy's blood.

hygeia

goddess of health and a daughter of Asclepius.

Hylas

son of Theiodamas, king of the Dryopes; Theiodamas was killed by Heracles in a bitter fight, but the boy was spared and became the hero's favourite. One day, when drawing water from a spring at Cius, he was pulled into the water by the nymphs, who were enchanted by his beauty. Heracles, inconsolable, threatened to devastate the land unless its people helped in the search for Hylas. The search was in vain.

hylomorphism

from the Greek hyle ('matter') and morphe ('form'). The doctrine that all physical things have been composed of matter and form. Identified with Aristotle, the doctrine likewise characterizes Thomistic philosophy. Form is the principle of actuality and activity, while matter is the principle of potentiality and passivity.

hylozoism

from the Greek hyle ('matter') and zoe ('life'). A doctrine predicating life of all matter. Held by many early philosophers, among them Thales, suggestions of the view are to be found in most philosophies which find the world to be teleologically ordered. If all living forms are sentient to some degree, Hylozoism becomes a sub-class of Panpsychism.

Hymen
handsome young man whose married life was regarded as a pattern of matrimonial bliss.

hyperboreans
legendary race of Apollo-worshippers dwelling in the far north and much admired by the Greeks.

hypercatalectic
verse having an extra syllable in the last foot.

hyperion
Titan father of Eos, Helios, and Selen.

Hypnos
Greek god of sleep; identified by the Romans with Somnus, son of Nyx (night) and brother of Thanatos (death); he was without a father. According to Hesiod he lived in the Underworld and never saw the light of the day, but unlike his brother he came softly and was welcome to men. He is depicted as winged youth, touching the foreheads of the weary with a branch, or pouring a narcotic liquid into their eyes.

hypostasis
a Greek term that denotes a self-subsistent entity which can act as a basis for other things or objects. For example, a Substratum acts as a base for all the qualities and the attributes. Thus all the qualities and attributes dependent upon a substratum for their existence, but it is not dependent upon them for its existence.

hypothesis
from Newton onwards, a theory or suggestion that still has overtones of the arbitrary or the speculative. Sometimes, even after all reasonable doubt has been dispelled, a theory retains the title of a hypothesis (for example, Avogadro's hypothesis).

hypothetical
describing a valid syllogism consisting of two premises, both conditional in form, and a conditional conclusion.
The three statements forming the argument contain between them just three distinct component propositions each of which appears twice, as for example in 'If the crops fail, the villagers will starve. If there is a drought, the crops will fail. Therefore, if there is a drought, the villagers will starve'.

hypothetico-deductive method
a method of arriving at a scientific theory by formulating an hypothesis from which new scientific predictions are deduced and put to the test of verification. One of the popular advocates of such a theory is Karl Popper.

hypothetico-deductive method
the method of creating scientific theory by making an hypothesis (or set of hypotheses) from which results already obtained could have been deduced, and which also entails now experimental predictins that can be verified

or refuted. There is controversy over the credit that accrues to such hypotheses when a prediction is verified. It is historically unceratin to what extent the method describes actual scientific procedure, where the fit between theory and observation often does not seem as tight as that of strict deducibility.

iambus

poetic foot consisting of a short or unaccented syllable followed by a long or accented one, e.g., 'The way was long, the night was cold'.

icarius

Athenian taught by Dionysus how to cultivate the vine. When some shepherds to whom he gave liquor became drunk they murdered him, thinking he had poisoned them. His daughter, at last finding his buried corpse, hanged herself on a near-by tree.

icon

a sign that has some of the characteristics of that which it signifies, for example, a cloth sample or a portrait.

idea

an object of thinking which is an exclusive property of the mind. Thus ideas are mental. Ideas may represent 'objects, properties, relations, and also imaginary objects'. Epistemologists claim that the ideas constitute the very essence of knowledge; however, they may disagree with each other as regards the sources of such ideas. For instance, Descartes claimed that innate ideas constitute the indubitable foundation of knowledge. For empiricists, the ideas are necessarily obtained through sense experience (of sensation and of reflection). Locke defines an idea as 'whatsoever is the object of understanding when a man thinks'. He claimed that the ideas are the copies of the objects external to us.

ideal

from the Greek idea ('vision' or 'contemplation'). Deriving from the term Plato used to designate the eternal ideas or forms, each of which was perfect of its kind, common usage has retained the valuational aspect of the word while discarding its epistemological or metaphysical aspect.

ideal evidence, paradox of

a paradox which is affecting assignment of probability if a very small probability is assigned to an event, but on slender evidence, then ideal evidence could emerge that further justifies that low valuation. The paradox is that this evidence does not alter the probability assignment, yet it might make the observer more confident than before that the event will not happen.

idealism

a name given to a group of philosophical theories, that

have in common the view that what would normally be called 'the extent world' is somehow created by the mind.

ideatum

the object of, as well as that which is represented in the mind by, an idea.

identity

the relation expressed in logic and mathematics by using the sign. For example, the total obtained by adding two numbers is identical with the addition of those two numbers (2+2=4).

identity, principle of

one of the three laws of thought, the principle-applied variously to statements and to things-holds that a proposition or a thing is identical with itself and implies itself. The principle is useful in logic and can in fact be demonstrated.

identity theory

the view that mental states and brain states are contingently identical. The claim is that this identity is not a matter of definiton but scientific discovery.

identity theory of mind

a materialist theory of consciousness which identifies being in such and such a state of consciousness with being in some corresponding neurophysiological state.

identity theory of predication (or truth)

if predicates, like subjects, are ultimately noun phrases, (the two-term theory) and name objects (the two-name theory), then sentences containing those predicates are true just if subject and predicate are names of the same thing. That is, wahtever are named by subject and predicate are identical.

ideology

a set of ideas or notions, and norms that regulate a particular social and political action. Ideology is a backbone of any social system. However, ideology has become a key term in politics because the struggle between two opposite forces is fought on the ideological grounds.

idols of the mind

the false assumptions and illusions, identified by Francis Bacon in Novum Organum Book I. 39-44, as the four main sources of error besetting the human mind in its pursuit of truth. These are:

(1) The idols of the tribe 'inherent in human nature and the very tribe or race of men, for man's sense is falsely asserted to be the standard of things'.

(2) The idols of the den (or cave), which are peculiar to each individual.

(3) The idols of the market-place, 'formed by the reciprocal intercourse and society of man with man', particularly as a result of 'bad and unapt formation of words', and

(4) The idols of the theatre

attributable to 'false philosophies'.

Idomeneus

king of Crete, who returning from a successful expedition against Troy, encountered a storm and vowed, if delivered, to sacrifice to Poseidon the first living thing he should meet on his arrival home. This was his own son. Idomeneus performed his vow.

iff

it is an abbreviation for 'if and only if'. The presnce of 'iff' makes a statement a biconditional one. For example, 'A statement is meaningful if and only if it is empirically verifiable'.

ignoratio elenchi

a Latin phrase literally meaning 'reasoning from ignorance'. The ignoratio elenchi means 'irrelevant reasoning' and applies to those cases where it is taken to establish some conclusion other than the one, if any, which can be deduced from its premises. It thus applies to the entire list of 'fallacies of relevance'.

illation

the process of inferring a conclusion from a premise or premises, as well as the conclusion thus inferred.

illicit conversion

it is a formal fallacy. This fallacy occurs when a conditional proposition, if p then q is converted into if q then p.

illicit major

a fallacy associated with the categorical syllogism in traditional logic. It is committed when the major term is distributed in the concision but not in the premise.

illicit minor

a fallacy associated with the categorical syllogism in traditional logic. It is committed when the minor term is distributed in the conclusion but not in the premise.

illocution

refers to an utterance in which an illocutionary act (act done in speaking) is performed.

illumination divine

in the history of philosophy both truth and God have often been described in terms of light, and not seldom all three are merged in a single conception.

illusion

form the Latin illudere ('to illude', i.e. 'to deceive, elude, delude'). In philosophy there are many doctrines holding that the world is not as it appears.

illusion, arguments from

the collective name given to all appeals, made for the purpose of casting doubt upon perceptual beliefs, to the possibility and actual occurrence of perceptual error. The term 'illusion' here covers much that would not in non-philosophical context be so called.

Ilus
founder of Ilion, the city of Troy.

imagination
refers to a form of mental activity held to be distinct from cognitive or rational processes; a free, creative ordering of the contents of mind. Imagination in this sense is often confused with the production of mental imagery, which would be better called 'imaging'.

imitation
a translation of the Greek term mimesis. The theory of imitation, treated under cation to aesthetics of the metaphysical theory of participation.

immaculate Conception
the doctrine that the Blessed Virgin Mary was conceived without taint of original sin. Defined by the Roman Catholic Church as a dogma of faith in 1854.

immanence
from the Latin immanerc ('to inhabit'). The term has been used of actions, principles, and in some doctrines of the relation between man and God.

immanent
in-dwelling. The word is often used by pantheists to describe the way in which God dwells in, or is in some sense identified with, the created world.

immaterialism
a term created by Berkeley to characterise his position that there is no material substance.

immediate inference
an inference in which the conclusion follows from one premises alone. There are various types of immediate inference, namely, obversion, conversion, inversion and contraposition.

immediate perception
according to sense-datum philosophers, sense-data are immediately given in sense-experience. Hume envisaged that sense impressions are the immediate objects of perception.

immortalist
refers to a person who believes that somehow people, or some crucial elements in people, survive death and last for ever.

immortality
the phrase 'of the soul' normally follows this term. By 'immortality of the soul' is meant the infinitely prolonged existence of that centre of awarenes to which the term 'I' refers. The concept of immortality is usually viewed as Greek in origin an invention of Socrates or Plato, although it very quickly became an important part of much Christian faith. In Eastern thought the concept is also present, although it is subordinate to a conception of Nirvana in which self-identity is lost.

imperative
the characteristic mood of the main verb in sentences (imperative sentences) with

which conduct-guiding speech acts, such as requests and orders, are standardly performed. Imperatives, that is imperative sentences, are of interest to moral philosophers and logicians. One influential theory states that moral judgments imply imperatives, and hence that, for example, 'if you ought to do X, do it' is a valid inference when the 'ought' is a moral 'ought'.

implication

it is a logical operation that forms a complex proposition from two independent propositions with the help of a logical connective. For example, if today is Tuesday, then tommorow is Wednesday.

imposition first and second

in scholastic logic, terms of first imposition consisted of terms of first and second intention. Terms of second imposition were grammatical terms, e.g., 'noun', 'pronoun', 'verb', etc.

impossibility

in the everyday, colloquial sense, impossibility is always a matter of what—perhaps only in certain circumstances, or by certain people—simply cannot occur or simply cannot be done. In this sense what is naturally impossible, or impossible for men, or impossible for certain men in certain circumstances, would be for God at any time not merely possible but easy.

impression

Hume's term for the material of sensation. He divided impressions into simple and complex, leading to simple and complex ideas.

imputation

in theology the attribution of guilt or merit to one person on the basis of the guilt or merit of another. The concept applies not only to the doctrine of original sin (q.v. 3) but also to that of justification by faith (q.v.).

incarnation

from the Latin in and caro ('flesh'). The term usually refers to the doctrine that God has embodied, or will embody. Himself in human from. The doctrine is held in numerous religions.

incongruent (or incongruous) counterparts

another name for enantiomorphs.

inconsistency

the negation of consistency :

1. in the traditional square of opposition a property of those propositions which cannot be affirmed together, i.e. both contradictories and contraries.
2. in modern logic a set of propositions or propositional functions is said to be inconsistent if one can derive from the set anything whatever.

inconsistent triad

a set of three statements of which at least one must be false because from any two of them the negation of the third may be deduced. Where the deduction is syllogistic, this form of incosistency is sometimes called an antilogism.

incontinence

an alternative term for weakness of will or acrasia.

incorrigible

directly and conclusively verified, not subject to any further tests.

incunabula, incunables

books printed in the infancy printing, that is before the year 1501. [Lat. incunabula, swaddling clothes, (fig.) origin, beginning].

indefinite reference

a reference made to a something or the other. e.g., I met a man.

index

for peirce one of the three major classes or signs.

indexical

an alternative name for token-reflexive.

Indian materialism

a somewhat marginal but long-lived aspect of Indian philosophy, that appears under various labels, such as Carvaka, Lokayata, and Ajivika. None of the original writings of these schools, which flourished as early as c. 600 BC, are extant, and information about their teaching can be gained only from indirect accounts. In most materialist schools man is analysed purely in terms of material components and their inter-action. This analysis is usually connected with a pessimistic attitude; hedonism appears only quite rarely. The influence of this type of thinking was less philosophical (though the Vaisesika may exhibit it) than sociological, for the teaching was used in attacking ritual and mystical religion.

Indian philosophy

although Indian thought developed in an intellectual climate which in many ways was different from and almost-certainly not influenced by, the ancient Greek world, abundant and often striking similarities with Western philosophical thought justify the application of the term 'philosophy' to it. The nature of the world-view taken for granted by the majority of the schools and, in the course of time, an increasingly religious preoccupation nevertheless led Indian philosophy in a somewhat different direction from occidental.

The Vedas have generally been regarded as the ultimate authority in Hinduism, both by those who belong to that religion and by others from the outside. The same is broadly true for Hindu system of philosophy. So much is this the case that nonorthodox systmes cf thought are in large measure defined as those that reject the authority of the Vedas. It is therefore appropriate to begin an examination of the origins of Indian philosophy with the Vedas, while not overlooking the fact that there were other, though less immediately obvious, sources for Indian thought.

The Atharva Veda (AV), despite its more popular character, does in fact contain a greater number of speculative hymns in the Rig Veda. It is interesting to note that it uses the term brahman to denote both its own incantations and the universal principle, or more exactly the term now covers both meaning at the same time, as when Brahman is the origin of the both sat and asat and is also connected with Vac.

The Upanisads are mostly in dialogue form and in some instances record great set debates reminiscent of the debating contests found earlier. Perhaps the best known instance is that where king Janaka of Videha performs a sacrifice and organizes a debating contest with an enormous prize, to which the sage Yajnavalkya stakes his claim even before the start of the contest.

The Katha Upanisad is noteworthy for the mythological framework that it shares with the Taittiriya Brahmana, in which the pious young brahman Naciketas goes voluntarily to the abode of Yama and is then granted three boons by his host in recompense for having been kept waiting three days. Naciketas third boon is to ask about man's destiny after death.

indicative

the characteristic mood of the main verb in ordinary statements and question.

indicator word (or term)

an alternative name for a token-reflexive.

indifference

from the Greek a ('not') and diaphoros ('different'). The term has been applied to a variety of philosophical problems.

Concerning value, for example, Stoics, Cynics, and Skeptics agreed in holding that one could not be indifferent to virtue and vice. Virtue was to be sought and vice avoided. But one should be indifferent with respect to all other attitudes and values.

indifference, principle of

the principle made prominent by Laplace, allowing us to regard events as equally probably if we can see no reason why one should occur rather than the other.

indiscernibility of identicals

the principle that if x and y are identical, then x has every property that y has, and y has every property that x has. The converse of the identity of indiscernibles, it is sometimes called Leibniz's law.

individual

from the Latin individuals

('undivided or indivisible translated from the Greek atomon ('indivisible').

In traditional logic the individual is the logical subject which admits of predicates, and cannot be predicated of anything else; e.g. one says that man, is rational, not that rational is man. From Aristotle through Boethius (who introduced into logic the Latin term individuum) into modern times this usage is current.

individuality

a term which becomes prominent in 19th century Idealism, apparently as a corrective to emphases on absolutness and the organic nature of society.

individuation, principle of

it signifies the principle by which, a philosopher attempts to move in thought from the infima, or smallest, species to the individual member of that species.

Indra

the beneficent storm and fertility god of the Vedic religion. He wields the thunderbolt, brings rain, overcomes his enemies and shares the body with his friends.

indubitable

an epistemological term which denotes the property of being certain, or beyond rational doubt. The indubitability of a proposition is not equivalent to its logical necessity, since some contingent proposition may also be said to be effectively beyond doubt.

induction

from the Latin in and ducere ('to lead in'), first translated into the Latin probably by Cicero from Aristotle's term, epagoge. The widespread distinction between induction as an inference moving from specific facts to general conclusions, and deduction as specific conclusions is no longer respectable philosophically. This distinction disinguishes one kind of induction from one kind of deduction. It is much more satisfactory to think of induction as probable inference and deduction as necessary inference.

indulgence

the remission by the Church of the temporal penalty due for forgiven sin. In modern Roman Catholic practice such remission is either complete (plenary) or else limited (Partial) and is granted in respect of acts of piety and good works.

inevitability

1. logical necessity; if q follows inevitably from p this simply means that it follows necessarily.

2. contingent inescapability; if some occurrence is inevitable, this means that it will happen regardless of all attempts to prevent it.

inference

from the Latin in and ferre ('to

carry or bring'). In logic, the procedure of deriving conclusions from premises. If the conclusion follows from a single premise, the process is said to be one of the immediate inference.

inference, immediate
the type of inference in which the conclusion follows from a single premise.

inference, rule of
a rule for the construction of agruments which says what may be inferred from one or more statements whose logical structure is specified.

infinite
from the Latin in ('not') and finis ('boundary', 'limit', 'end'). Thus that without boundary, limit or end. Etymologically, the term is gained by negation of the term 'finite'. There are those, however, who would claim that the conception of the infinite is prior to that of finite. The conception of the infinite has been associated from the start with series of numbers, magnitudes, times, and spaces. The endlessness of such series provides one conception of infinity, and some hold this to be the basic meaning of the term.

infinite and finite
categories denoting two diametrically opposed views with regard to the aspects of reality. Some philosophers consider the God being Absolute is infinite, while humans being mortals are only finite beings. The categories infinite and finite are also attached to space and time. According to some philosophers, space and time are infinite. But some philosophers regarded space and time to be finite as we are concerned with the finite aspects of space and time.

infinite divisibility
a concept that many philosophers, from Zeno of Elea onwards, have considered to be impossible, since it supposedly leads to paradox. If, they have argued, a (finitesized) existent is infinitely divisible, then it must consist of infinitely many parts. These must either have some size, or lack size and be nothing. If each part has some size or other, however minute, then the aggregate of an infinite number of these parts will be infinitely large. But if each part has no size, then the aggregate would have no size, that is the original existent would be made up of nothing.

infinity
a notion used since the time of the ancient Greeks who applied it to substance. It also occured in the paradox of Zeno of Elea. The concept of the infinite was vague, loosely being taken as 'that which has no beginning or end' or 'that which has no boundary, internal or external.

innate ideas
ideas of knowledge in the mind

prior to and independent of sense experience. For Plato, knowledge of the Forms derives from innate ideas which are accessible to memory (reminiscence, argument from). For Descartes, all principles of science and knowledge are founded on clear and distinct ideas, or incorrigible truths, which are innate in the mind and which may be captured by the method of reason.

innateness
from the Latin in and natus ('born'). In philosophy the doctrine that ideas and principles are present in man from birth.

inquiry
from the Latin in and quaero ('to seek').
Charles Peirce regarded inquiry as self-corrective, and more likely than any other method of having opinion lead to the truth.
For John Dewey inquiry is the heart of philosophic activity and the meaning of the intelligence.

inquisition
from the Latin inquirere ('to inquire'). An institution established within the Roman Catholic Church for the purpose of eliminating heresy, the Inquisition gained its distinctive form over a considerable period of time.

inscription
a linguistic entity, like a sentence. The term figures in some analysts of propositional attitudes, for example, belief.

instinct
in psychological theory, this term refers to an habitual pattern of behaviour that is innate or inherited rather than learned or acquired. The concept of instinct is particularly significant in Freud's psychological theory, where the libido is regarded as the reservoir of instinctual energy which issues in sexual or aggressive behaviour. In behaviourist theory, J.B. Waston distinguished instinctual patterns of responses from those that are conditioned or conditionable.

instrumentalism
a theory developed by American pragmatist John Dewey. This doctrine views that when a person faces any situation or predicament it is the human mind which acts as an instrument to produce ideas, concepts and judgements which in turn help the individual to take a firm decision to overcome a situation or a predicament.

insufficient reason, principle of
an alternative name for the principle of indifference.

intellect
from the Latin intelligere ('to understand). The power or faculty of knowing as compared to will or feeling.

intentionality
from the same root as the term, intension.

interactionism
a dualistic theory of mind-body relation advocated by Descartes. According to him, physical events cause mental events and vice-versa. It is also known as psychophysical interactionism.

inter finitum et infinitum non est proportio
(Latin for : there is no proportion between infinity and finitude). A maximum with an important bearing on Pascall's wager.

interpretation
the assigning of meanings to the expressions of a formal language. Any language can be treated as a system of symbols in which sentences, and other kinds of expressions, are constructed according to the syntactical rules (rules of grammar). To do this is to ignore any meaning that the expressions of the language might have; it is to treat the symbols as constituting an uninterpreted structure or formal language.

intersubjectivity
refers to the property of holding in reference to more than one subject, rather than purely subjectively.

intrinsic value
correlate of extrinsic value. The phrase applies to states of being or experience valuable in themselves without regard to their consequences. 'Final value' is a synonymous expression.

introspection
awareness by an individual of his own state and condition, with particular reference to his mental and emotional activity.

intuitionism
1. (in ethics). The view that (at least some) moral judgments are known to be true by intution.
2. the veiw that there are several distinct moral duties, that cannot be reduced to one basic duty, in contrast, for example, to utilitarianism. While both views can be, and are, held separately, they often go together.

intuitionistic logic
the logic employed and developed by intuitionistic mathematics. It arises out of a view concerning the way in which meaning can be conferred on mathematical statements.

inventio medii
(Latin for: discovery of the middle). The formal name for the logical pons asinorum.

Io
girl loved by Zeus, who turned her into a heifer, hoping thereby to conceal her from his wife. But Hera was not deceived. She set Argus, a monster with a hundred eyes, to keep watch on her until he himself was slain by Hermes at Zeus' command. The goddess, as a gadfly, then tormented the luckless Io, driving her from place to place. At length she found rest on the banks of the

Nile, where she recovered her human forms. The son, Epaphus, whom she bore to Zeus, became king of Egypt and built the city of Memphis. The story of Io's wandering was a favourite tale in antiquity.

Iolaus
son of Iphicles and the constant companion of Heracles.

Ion
son of Apollo and the legendary ancestor of the Ionians.

ionic philosophy
the school of philosophy arising in lonia during the 6th century B.C., originating the development of Greek philosophy.

Iphicles
twin brother of Heracles and father of Iolaus.

Iphigenia
daughter of Agamemnon and Clytemnestra, and sister of Orestes. When the Greek fleet was becalmed by Artemis at Aulis, the seer Calchas declared that only the sacrifice of Iphigenia would satisfy the angry goddess. She was brought to Aulis, therefore, on the pretext that she was to be married to Achilles. But at the last moment Artemis relented and substituted a hind (or some other beast) upon the altar of sacrifice. She then carried off Iphigenia to Tauris to be her priestess, with the duty of sacrificing all strangers shipwrecked on the shore. At length, when Orestes and Pylades arrived at Tauris, she fled with them, carrying with her the sacred image of the goddess. The image is said to have been kept at Brauron in Attica, where Iphigenia herself died. Others say that she died at Megara.

Irene, Eirene
Greek goddess of peace; identified by the Romans with Pax.

iris
personification of the rainbow. Also a divine messenger.

irvingites
a sect following the teaching of a Presbyterian divine. Edward Irving and now known as the Catholic Apostolic Church. It has a fourfold ministry of apostles, prophets, evangelists, and pastors; governance and the expounding of the divine mysteries is the prerogative of the first of these of which none survives now. The organization of the church is based on the features of the Mosaic Tabernacle as a shadow or type of the Christian Church itself. The payment of tithes for the support of the ministry is insisted on.
The theology of the sect is orthodox and strongly sacramentalist, though the doctrine of transubstantiation is rejected. The liturgy, derived from Roman Catholic, Greek Orthodox, and Anglican sources, dates from 1842. The traditional Catholic ceremonial with lights and in cense is

used.

ishtar

Babylonian and Assyrian goddess. Also known as Astarte and Ashtoreth. Goddess of springs, vegetation, the universe of flocks and herds, sexual love, wedlock and maternity, she also bore a negative aspect as the destroyer of life, goddess of storm and war.

Isis

Egyptian goddess, spouse of Osiris and mother of Horus, sometimes identified by the Greeks with Demeter.

Islam

name of the religion founded by Mohammed. 'Messenger of God', what is Islam? The prophet replied, 'Islam is to believe in god and His prophet, to say the prescribed prayers, to give alms, to observe the feast of Ramadan, and to make the pilgrimage to Mecca'.

Islamic philosophy

early Islamic philosophy is characterised by a profound tendency towards syncretism. The theological simplicity of the nascent Islamic religion, which prevailed during the lifetime of its founder, the prophet Muhammad (570-632), later suffered an assault from such diverse elements as Iraqi gnosticism, Christian Hellenism, Persian dualism and Greek thought. The easily understood profession of the Islamic faith, 'There is no god but God and Muhammad is his prophet', was confronted with the concepts and dialectic of Greek philosophy. These last manifested themselves as possible means to the solution of problems that swiftly arose in early Islamic thought. So the study of Islamic philosophy in its early stages is inevitably the study of the influence of Greek philosophy on Islam. Furthermore, philosophy and theology are inextricably mingled.

isolationism

refers to a theory of aesthetic interpretation that holds a work of art may, or should, be understood without reference to its cultural and historical context.

isomorphic

having the same structure, due to resemblance between corresponding parts. The term is applicable in relating material objects, social organization, work of art, and abstract concepts.

isomorphism

the relation that characterises the correspondence between two different structures. Wittegenstein in his logical atomism attempted to show that there is an isomorphic relation between the structure of the world and the structure of language by holding the view that language mirrors the reality.

Ixion

king of Thessaly and father of the Centaurs. He murdered his father-in-law but was cleansed of his blood-guilt and carried off by Zeus to heaven where his attempt to seduce Hera failed; his punishment was to be bound in hell to an everturning fiery wheel.

jacobites

name by which the members of the Syrian National Church are known.

jagati

a metre.

Jaimini

a great sage and seer who was the founder of the Purva Mimamsa school. He is the author of the Mimamsa Sutra. 'Mimamsa' literally means 'revered thought'. The other two prominent exponents of Mimamsa are Prabhakara (650 A.D.) and Kumarila Bhatta (700 A.D.).

jainism

an ancient religion of northern India, so called from the designation of its traditional founders, the Jinas or conquerors, last and most famous of whom was Mahavira, a was Mahavira, a wandering ascetic and teacher. Jain doctrine includes the existence of the soul, rebirth, and karma, but excludes that of a supreme being, although the supreme being, although the existence of other gods is not denied. Unlike Buddhism it emphasizes the soul's reality and permanence. It stresses the importance of right moral conduct. Notable among its teachings is the principle of ahimsa or non-violence, which forbids killing or cruelty. Animal sacrifices are forbidden, as is thee eating of meat. The Jain, who seeks to be a moral conqueror, pursues a simple and ascetic way of life.

jain philosophy

Jainism is an Indian religion founded in the 5th century B.C. by the 'Jina' (conqueror) Mahavira. Its philosophy combines archaic Indian nature-philosophical speculations (compare Vaisesika) with the quest for liberation from the cycle of rebirth. It soon became ossified but it is possible tc point to some creative thinkers, like Kundakunda (4th century A.D.).

The Jain system is presented under seven headings.

(1) Lifeless substances (ajiva), comprising space, the media of movement (dharma) and rest, time, and matter (pudgala), which consists of homogeneous atoms.

(2) An infinte number of souls (jiva). Essentially possessed of unlimited knowledge, power, and bliss, the souls become deprived of these qualities through.

(3) The influx (asrava) of subtle matter on accounts of words, thoughts, and deeds. Weighed down by it, the souls suffer.

(4) Bondage (bandha) in the world of phenomena, in the form of transmigration.

(5) Refusing to allow further matter to enter (samvara), and
(6) Exterminating (nirjara) the already present matter by means of a strict ethical discipline and severepenance, the soul obtains.
(7) Liberation (moksa) and moves upwards to the top of the universe.

Besides its own tradition of a succession of teachers Jainism had some historically proven links to the teachings called Ajivika whose main protagonist, known from Pall Buddhist sources as Makkhali Gosala, is regarded by some as a magadha so that a Vratya connection could be assumed. In its elaborated form, pieced together from fragmentary quotations, the Ajivika philosophy can be described as a kind of fatalistic optimism or salvationist determinism. Fate or destiny governs the world process (saphsdra) as well as individual lives. In the end each individual will reach salvation (moksa) after a very long, though fixed, period of purification in the course of transmigration through all forms of life, of which there is a large, though again fixed, number in samsara.

Jainism perceives itself as an eternal teaching brought to mankind periodically by accomplished teachers called tirthahkaras. There have been twenty-four of them and the name of the first one, Rsabha, is mentioned in the Vedic Kalpasutras in connection with radical teaching on non-violence. Because Jaina sources were codified relatively late, influences from later developments in Buddhist and Hindu teachings were considerable and therefore make a reliable reconstruction of original Jaina views rather difficult and in some respects uncertain.

Jaina ontology is based on the assertion of a plurality of substances. A substance (dravya) is an eternal entity which possesses unchangeable characteristics or qualities (gunas), but on which certain changeable modes, modifications or states (paryayas) can occur. The highest substance is jiva, and there is an infinite number of them. By itself, in its pure form, a jiva, often called also dtman, is perfect, omniscient, eternal, formless and in possession of unlimited energy and infinite bliss. When subject to influences (asravas) from the phenomenal word of modalities (sathsdra), the jiva takes shape, assuming a body born from his or her actions (karmaiarira), loses his or her perfection and becomes a mundane pilgrim (samsari) through innumerable forms of life which are determined by his or her desires and actions. These forms include not only higher and lower celestial beings and inhabitants of invisible worlds, humans, animals, and all forms of organic life, plants and even invisible micro-organisms, but also minerals and elements. The samsaric world process is beginningless and eternal and in its totality unchanging as it comprises the whole of time. In detail, however, for the bound individual consciousness it unfolds in the flow of time in ever-recurring world periods of evolution and devolution reflected in human history as periods of progress and degeneration.

As a salvationist doctrine Jainism aims at providing means for the development of the highest knowledge or omniscience, the natural property of the soul in its pure state. Jaina epistemology is therefore subject to the metaphysical stance which postulates such a state. However, its pragmatic starting point is the everyday samsaris situations of a soul bound by the limitations of a human body. It therefore pays due attention also to the normal epistemological and logical procedures. The two levels of Jaina epistemology are, of course, intermingled, and there is some development of views in evidence without a sufficiently coherent theory being presented. Basiçally, Jaina epistemology accepts two kinds of cognition, direct (pratyaksa) and indirect (paroksa), each being fivefold. Each act of direct cognition is preceded by a kind of indeterminate or general awareness of the existence of the object to be cognized. It is termed 'viewing' (darsana). This can be taken in the context of sensory cognition as sensory perception preceding the clear cognizance of the object, but Jaina epistemology accepts this kind of preliminary viewing or 'dawning' of knowledge as preceding all direct cognitions, including the transcendental kinds.

Indirect cognition includes (1) recollection (smrti) or the capacity to invoke in one's mind objects of past experience; next is (2) recognition (pratyabhijna) which is a kind of combination of perception and memory, as when we see an object and recognize that we saw it yesterday also; then there is (3) inductive reasoning (tarka) and (4) inference (anumana), which deal mainly with syllogistic operations extended to five parts instead to five parts instead of the usual usce, but more sophisticated logic operations were also developed over the centuries; and last there is (5) trustworthy testimony (agama), which comes from a liberated omniscient person and can be verbal if such a person is encountered or written; only Jaina scriptures are recognized as true agama; this channel of cognition provides indirect knowledge of truth to faithful followers who have not yet developed higher direct cognition.

Since transmitting absolute knowledge by an omniscient person on to the level of indirect cognition, verbal or scriptural, cannot be adequately accomplished in conceptual terms, Jaina logic developed for the purpose the doctrine of relative pluralism or multiple modalities (anekanta) and the method of conditioned predication (syadvada).

Basically, anekanta translates the totality of the omniscient knowledge into the notion of the complexity of reality which cannot be expressed in terms of one or other of the possible modalities or standpoints (nayas) and therefore it, in a way, accepts and respects them all, thereby providing a synoptic instead of a one-sided view of reality. This is illustrated by the well-known story of blind men inspecting an elephant.

Because of the salvationist character of Jainism, its metaphysics is closely connected with its ethics. Its main concem is the soul, whose existence needs no proof because it is directly experienced in every process of cognition as the conscious subject. Because the soul in its pure state is omniscient, its consciousness is infinite. In samsara the consciousness is obscured or limited by the soul's actions (karmas), which stick to it like dust particles to the body and burden it so that it sinks to the appropriate position within the universe and takes an incarnation which is determined by the ethical quality of its past actions. Liberation (moksa) is achieved when the soul rises above involvemen in actions and all actions accumulated from the past are exhausted. Good actions promote the soul's temporary well-being in sathsdra, but do not lead to liberation. Of bad actions injury to life is the most detrimenal one. Jaina ascetics take great pains to practise non-injury (ahimsa), to the point of the straining their drinking water to avoid swallowing small organisms, and sweeping the footpath before them to avoid treading on small insects. In the last stages of the path abstention from action may extend to stopping the intake of food and drink to the point of starving to death, at which liberation is reached. But one may reach it during one's lifetime as well, thus becoming a perfect one or a tirthahkara. Jainism developed an elaborate methodical path to liberation which overlaps in many respect with the Buddhist one and with Patanjali's Yoga.

Discarnate siddhas in the state of nirvana enjoy four infinite accomplishments; infinte knowledge, infinite vision, infinite strength and infinite bliss.

James-Lang theory

a theory of emotions advocated by William James in his Principles of Psychology. According to this theory, certain subjective feelings are aroused in the subjects by bodily changes that follow the perception of some exciting fact. This theory is known as James-Lang theory.

Janus

Latin deity of great antiquity, signifying the 'door' or 'opening' and usually depicted with 2 faces, looking in opposite directions. He presided over the beginnings of all enterprises and then was invoked before other gods. His principal festival was on New Year's Day.

Japenesee religion and philosophy

as in India and China, religion and philosophy in Japan have not been sharply differentiated until recent years. The native religion of Japan, Shinto goes back at least 2000 years although it was not named until Buddhism was introduced from China in the 6th century A.D. Confucianism had been introduced in the 5th century A.D. along with the Chinese script.

(1) Confucian influence reached its height in the Tokugawa era (1603-1867). The neo-Confucian philosophers Chu Hsi and Wang Yang-Ming have received special attention and esteem.

(2) All the schools of Buddhism, developed in China, have been imported into Japan. The Ten-T'ai School gave rise to the most powerful Japanese sect, the Nichiren; and the medication school of Ch'an or Zen Buddhism has achieved a development in Japan far beyond anything it had achieved in China.

(3) Following the Meiji restoration of 1868, Japan was opened to Western philosophy with the result that Hegal, Eduard Von Hartmann, Windelband, Rickert, T.H. Green, William James, and John Dewey, exercised influence. From the mid-twenties the power of Marxism has steadily grown; and from the mid-forties the influence of existentialism has been increasing.

Jason

son of Aeson, king of Iolcos and the leader of the Argonauts. When his father's throne was usurped by Pelias and Neleus (Aeson's half-brothers), he was smuggled out of the city and brought up by the Centaur Chiron. Having reached manhood he returned to Iolcos to claim his right. This the usurper Pelias promised him if he would bring back the Golden Fleece, which was fastened to an oak tree in the grove of Ares and guarded by a dragon. He gained the trophy with the help of Medea, daughter of Aeetes, king of Colchis; she had fallen in love with Jason and he carried her off as his wife, taking with them also her young brother Apsyrtus. Aeetes pursued them, but Medea, in order to delay him, killed her brother and scattered the pieces of his dismembered body along the road. Her father stopped to gather them up and the fugitives made good their escape. Meanwhile, Pelias had murdered Jason's father. To avenge the crime, Jason persuaded Medea (the cunning one) to make use of her powers as a witch. Under her influence Pelias own daughters slew him, cut up his body and boiled it believing that they would thus rejuvenate him. His son, Acastus, who succeded him on the throne, drove Jason and Medea from Iolocos. The couple then made their way to Corinth and lived there together for some years until Jason deserted the sorceress for Glauce, daughter of the Corinthian king, Creon. Medea, in a jealous rage, sent the girl a poisoned garment which burnt her to death, killing Creon as well. But Medea's vengeance was still not complete, for she also slew the 2 children she had borne to Jason. She then fled to Athens—it is said in a chariot drawn by winged dragons—and took refuge with Aegeus. Jason committed suicide.

jati (birth, class, part, generality)

according to Buddhism, it is one of the links in the empirical wheel of existence. Nyaya considers jati as one of the sixteen categories.

jehovah's witnesses

a sect founded c 1879 by Charles Taze Russell of Pennsylvania, U.S.A. On his death in 1916 the leadership was assmed by J. F. Rutherford. Describing themselves as 'the Lord's organization', the Witnesses look on all other forms of institutional religion as the work of Satan. They purport to base their teachings on the Bible, but, breaking wholly with traditional Christianity, acknowledge the Chirstianity, acknowledge the authority of Jehovah alone.

jen

(chinese for : humanity and benevolence). The basic principle of Confucius moral and social philosophy.

jesuit

a member of the Roman Catholic religious order known as the Society of Jesus, founded by St. Ignatius Loyola in 1534.

Jewish philosophy
a concern with the ultimate questions of the nature of the Universe and the human condition has been characteristic of Judaism from its beginnings. There has, however, always been a plurality of approaches determined to a large extent by the historical conditions governing Jewish life and the external influences life that have operated on Jewish thought. Like Chrisitanity and Islam, Judaism represents a constructive synthesis of biblical monotheism and Greek philosophy. There has been considerable reciprocal influence between thinkers of the three Mosaic religious traditions.

jivanmukta (liberated while living)
advaita holds that the liberation is possible only when the avidya (ignorance) is completely shattered. Thus the existence of the physical body is not an obstacle to achieve liberation. A person can achieve liberation while he is alive. Such a person is known as Jivanmukta.

jnana
in Hinduism the way of knowledge. Correspondingly, Jnana Yoga is that one of the four types of yoga stressing knowledge as the path to liberation.

jnaṇa-kanda
those parts of Veda that deals with the knowledge of Brahman are known as Jnanakanda. They are aranyakas and Upanisads.

jnanendriya (organs of knowledge)
generally, the five sense-organs are called the organs of knowledge. They are—sight (caksu), touch (tvak), hearing (srotra), taste (rasana) and smell (ghrana). However, Sankhya considers mind (manas) as one of the organs of knowledge.

Jocasta
sister of Creaon, and mother and wife of Oedipus.

judaism
the religion of the Jewish people, parent religion of both Christianity and Mohammedanism. We shall consider Judaism in itself, and in terms of the philosophies developed within its framework.

Religiously, the origin of Judaism is usually traced to a compact between God and Abraham to foster the development of a special people in exchange for their devotion. In fact, this perspective must be associated with the time of the Babylonian exile; at least it was during that period that it was possible to conceive the history of this people as a series of triumphs and defeats, related to their faith and faithlessness in God. And since this view of history is present in the Bible, these are the people of the Book in an unique sense. Be this as it may, the intimate relation of the God to the community accounts for the early history of Judaism as presenting an example of theocracy.

judgment

from the Latin jus ('right') and dicere ('to determine or say'). The current usage of the term is roughly synonymous to 'proposition'.

But an Aristotle used his terms in De Interpretatione, a proposition is a significant assertion, either true, or false, resulting from a judgment. And when he spoke of th relations of opposition among significant assertions it was of contradiction and contrariety among 'propositions', for example.

Jug, Carl Gustuv (1875-1961)

a well-known Swiss psychiatrist and a psychologist, who advocated 'analytical psychology' in the place of Freud's psychoneurosis. Jung recognised four important operations of mental faculty, namely, thinking, feeling, sensation, and intuition.

Juno

one of the principal Roman deities; usually identified with the Greek Hera Long worshipped as queen of heaven, she was patroness of womanhood generally, but especially of marriage, motherhood, and newly born children. She was also recognized as guardian of the finances of the Roman state, with a temple containing the mint on the Capitoine Hill. The month of june, propitious for marriages, is named after her, but her principal festival was the Matronalia, observed on 1st march.

Jupiter

the Roman father of heaven, Diovis pater, identified with the Greek Zeus. His presence was marked by rain, thunder, and lightning. He was Rome's special patron and protector, and his cult was celebrated with great pomp on such outstanding public occasions as the triumph of a victorious general. All things were believed to be subject to his will, so that the future was foreknown to him and indeed made known by him to men by means of signs and omens, in which the Romans believed firmly. As god of justice and virtue, he was also the guardian of the law.

justice

from the Latin jus ('right' or 'law'). In philosophy, the most influential analyses of the term were given by Plato and Aristotle.

(1) the context for Plato's analysis was set by Sophists who contrasted natural and conventional justice, usually preferring the former. Thrasymachus defined justice

as the 'interest of the stronger'.

(2) Plato moved beyond the natural conventional dichotomy, viewing justice in functional terms as the supreme virtue of the state, referring to the condition in which everyone is having and doing what in his own, and not interfering in that which is another's.

(3) Aristotle held justice to be a mean between the injustice of interfering with what belongs to another, and suffering interference one's self. He distinguished between two forms of justice : distributive—one's just share of resources of the state; and retributive—the redress of injury.

(4) Aquins and Locke agree that there is a natural and retional order, identifiable with equity or justice, discernible through the exercise of reason.

justification

theological doctrine according to which man is made, or accounted, righteous by God. In Protestant teaching justification is effected exclusively by divine grace for any man with faith in the merits of Christ's atoning sacrifice, righteousness thus being imputed rather than imparted.

justification by faith

in Christianity, the problem of how one is absolved, or acquitted, of his past actions, or how he acquires his new belong as a Christian.

kabbalah (hebrew for: tradition)

the mystical jewish tradition in general, and in particular the theosophical system whose classical text is the Zohar. Jewish mysticism has its roots in antiquity, and shows strong signs of gnostic influence. Its two main preoccupations were cosmogony (Ma'aseh Bereshith) and the nature of God (Ma'aseh Merkabah); it also had a practical side, aiming at wonder-working and especially the artificial creation of a man.

kaddish

an Aramaic term meaning "holy". A Jewish prayer with the same opening phrases as the Lord's Prayer. Since the Middle Ages the mourner's declaration of faith.

kafir

an Arabic term meaning "infidel". A term applied by Moslems to all unbelievers.

kalam

(Arabic for : speech). In Islamic philosophy the adducing of philosophical proofs to justify religious doctrine. The word is often translated as 'Muslim scholastic theology'; those who practised it were called 'mutakallimun'.

Kali

Hindu goddess. Wife of Shiva. Worshipped as the great and terrible mother, her cult has in the past led at times to human sacrifice. Wearing a necklece of skulls, dead bodies for earrings and a girdle of snakes, she greets her devotees with open mouth and protruding fang-like teeth.

kali yuga

era.

Kanada

he was a great sage and seer, who founded the Vaisesika system. The term Vaisesika is derived from 'visesa', means particularity. Kanada is also known as Kanabhuk, Uluka, and Kashyapa. His system of thought is also called Aluluka darsana. It is believed that the name Kanada was given to him as he used to lead a life of an ascetic by picking up grains form the fields. 'Kana' means particle. He is the author of Vaisesika Sutra.

karaites

Hebrew term meaning "Reader of Scriptures". The term applies to a Jewish sect, contering in Babylon, rising in the 8th century A.D. The group repudiated the Talmud and accepted the Old Testament as sole authority. The movment, flourishing between the 9th and 12th centuries, stimulated defenses of the Talmudic tradition by the Rabbinic group. The sect still continues but with little influence.

Karma

from the Sanskrit kri which means 'deed' or 'action'. The structure of one's life as resulting from one's prior actions in earlier existnce. The view, then, requires reincarnation or metempychosis as its complement.

In Hinduism karma (karma vidhi) is "the way of works". The object of works is to deal with the fact that the soul or self transmigrates, carrying its burden of karma, or effects.

In Jainism karma characterizes reality even down to the atomic level and the concept of "karmic matter" is central.

Karma theory

one of the most important theories in classical Indian philosophy. According to this doctrine, an individual's birth is decided on the basis of his deeds and actions of his earlier birth. Every individual has to reep the fruits of his past deeds and actions. Thus this doctrine substantiates the view that there is rebirth. All the orthodox and some heterodox systems accept this view.

kenosis

from the Greek kenoss which means "empty". The term begins in a Christological dispute centering around Philippians 2.7 where Christ is said to have "emptied himself, taking the form of a servant". According to some this means that Christ derived himself of his divine attributes during his earthly career. According to others the attributes, were retained although hidden from view.

Kepler, Johannes (1571-1630)

a German astronomer and mathematician who substantiated the views of Copernicus as regards the planetary motion. According to Kepler, Planets move in eclipses of which sun is one focus. They do not have uniform motion. Their period of revolution around the sun is the same as the period of their distance from the sun.

ker

in Greek mythology a goddess of death and bringer of evils generally. In the plural, Keres, the word later denoted evil spirits resembling the Harpies.

kerygma

a Greek term which means the "good news", or "gospel". The new testament message of salvation.

Keynes

John Maynard, 1st Baron Keynes (1883-1946). British economist, son of J.N.Keynes. His General Theory of Employment, Interest and Money (1936) was revolutionary, and policies supposedly derived from it guided or misguided many countries until a counte-revolution got under way in the 1970s.

Keynes wrote an important philosophical work A Treatise on Probabiltiy (1921) on probability and induction, in which he argued that probability attaches only to proposition (rather than events), and is objective in that a proposition always has a certain probability, independently of our recognition of it.

khords avesta

one of the five parts of the Avesta, sacred scriptures of Zoroastianism.

king

in the medieval doctrine of the two swords the temporal, in contrast to the spiritual, power. For John Wycliffe the king was God's vicar on earth. The doctrine of the Divine Right of kings in the 17th century regarded the monarch as possessing spiritual, as well as temporal authority.

kingdom of God

a Hebrew concept which looked to the future for the fulfilment of God's rule over mankind. Jesus began his ministry with the announcemnt that the kingdom was at hand, picturing it both as already present and as imminent.

kismet

an Arabic term which means 'fate'.

knowledge

philosophical question about the nature of knowledge belong either to epistemology or to the philosophy of mind (mind, philosophy of). The two groups of questions may be roughly separated by saying that the first group concentrates on the nature of knowledge, whereas the second concentrates on the nature of the knower.

koran

from the Arabic Qur'an from qara'a meaning 'to read'. Hence the meaning is 'the reading' or 'the lesson'. The sacred book of Islam had its origin in 622 A.D. when, after the migration to Medina. Mohammed began to dictate his oracles to a disciple as they were revealed Part of the contents of the Koran derive from the Mecca period (prior to 622); the rest belong to the period from 622 to 632. On Mohammed's death the Koran existed in scattered fragments, even though many Moslems knew large sections by heart. The caliph Abu Bekr assigen to Zaid ibu Thabit the task of collecting all of the parts. The copy made by Zaid had no canonicity and other copies had been made. Othman, a later caliph appointed Zaid and three others to collect all the copies and prepare a text which would be made universally binding. Having done this, all other available copies were destroyed. The result was the Koran. The redactors arranged the chapters, or suras, in an order discriminated only by length. The longer suras were at the beginning, and the shorter toward the end.

Kripke, Saul (1914-)

an American philosopher and logician who has made some worthy advances in the field of modal logic. In his famous work Naming and Necessity, Kripke has argued that only proper names having meaning in virtue of their reference, but not because they have descriptions.

Krishna

along with Rama one of the last two incarnations of Vishnu. Their followers constitude a considerable portion of the Hindu people, and a majority of the Vishnuites. Krishna is acknowledged as the supreme God in the Mahabharata, the Harivamsa and the Puranas, yet his actions reveal a Rajput Cheftain willing to employ questionable means for the sake of personal ends. Supposing that Krishna, the incarnate God, grew from the figure of the chieftain, how did this happen? The path is somewhat complex. In the Vedic period, Krishna, having begun as a tribal head is regarded as a wise man seeking religious truth. Vasudeva, is mentioned quite early as a God mystically, identical with Vishnu. It happend that Krishna became identified with Vasudeva, thus taking over his identification with Vishnu, and thus did a Rajput chieftain become an incarnate God.

Kronos

youngest son of Uranus (Heaven) and Ge (Earth) and leader of the Titan brothers.

Hesiod's account of him is strangely crude. He is thought to be the father of Zeus. It is probable that he represents a pre-Hellenic deity, perhaps of agriculture. It would seem that at a very early date he received human sacrifice.

Kshatriya

the warrior class in Indian tradition.

Kumarjiva 344-413

Chinese Buddhist philosopher. Half-Indian and half-Chinese, Kumarajiva became a monk at the age of seven. He became so influential that kings sent armies to bring him to their courts. The title of 'National Teacher' was conferred on him. More than 1000 monks attended his daily lectures. In ten years he tramslated 72 Buddhist books into chinese. He introduced the Middle Doctrine of Nagarjuna (q.v.) into China. Among these were the really philosophical Buddhist texts. Hence, he made systematic philosophizing about Buddhism possible.

Kusha

sacrifical grass.

kyrie eleison

a Greek phrase which means 'Lord have mercy'. One of the few Greek phrases used in the Roman Mass and the Anglican Communions service, it is of course used in the litanies of the Eastern Church. Its presence in the Western rites may point to a common, vanished litany.

Laertes

king of Ithaca, father of Odysseus. He took part in the expedition of the Argonauts and lived to see his son's return from Troy.

laestrygones

race of cannibal giants encountered by Odysseus in his wanderings.

Laius

the king of Thebes.

lamaism

the system of religious and political doctrine which from the 15th to the 20th centurie ruled Tibet with spiritual influences; also in Mongolia, China, and Siberia. In the middle of the 15th century, to begin the story halfway through, the emperor of China (who also controlled Tibet) named two Buddhist monks to be, one the spiritual ruler and the other, the temporal ruler of Tibet. The spiritual ruler was called the Dalai Lama; the temporal ruler the Pantshen Lama. The reason for the move was that this particular sect of Buddhism, a reform movement, had become astonishingly powerful in numbers and influence. The two Grand Lamas are regarded as incarnations of celestial beings; the Dalai Lama of Avaiokitesvara, the Pantshen Lama of Amitabha. When either Lama died it was the duty of the other to discover the child in whom the bothisattva had become incarnate. The names of all male children born shortly after the death of his counterpart would be laid before him. He would choose three names; a council of holy men after a week of prayer would select by lot one of the three to be the future Grand Lama.

Lamia

queen of the Laestrygones whose children, on account of her illicit love for Zeus, were taken from her by Hera. In revenge Lamia killed every child she could lay hands on. In the plural, Lamiae, her name was given by the Romans to female vampires.

language

a system of communication through which men exchange their ideas, feelings, etc. to other human beings. Language is a product of society. Thus, it is public and intersubjective. Without language men cannot advances in any field of Scientific enquiry. Language consists of words, sentences, statements, and propositions. Words are supposed to be the smallest units of language. They are conventional signs. Sentences are formed out of words. A statement is considered to be the meaing of sentence. If a statement is significantly said to be either true or false then it is considered to be proposition. There are several natural languages. These languages conditioned by the rule of syntax and semantics. Language and thought are closely connected with each other. On the other hand, formal languages are subjected to the rules of formation and transformation.

language game

a key concept in the later work of Wittgenstein. According to his famous analogy between using language and playing games, we have in both various sets of rules or conventions, and these determine what moves are permissible or impermissible, success or failures, each set of rules or conventions, and these determine what moves are permissible or impermissible, success or bailures, each set of rules identifying a distinct game. A given move can be judged only according to the rules of the game to which it belongs. Many time-honoured philosophical problems result from judging moves in the one game by the rules of another, and can be dissolved only by systematic clarification of the relevant differences; hence such clarification should be philosophy's main concern.

Laocoon

Trojan priest who incurred the wrath of Apollo by warning his fellow citizens of the danger of bringing the Greeks wooden horse into the city. The angry god sent 2 enormous snakes to the altar where Laocoon and his 2 sons were sacrificing; the snakes crushed them to death.

Laomedon

king of Troy and Hector's grandfather.

lapithae

legendary people dwelling among the mountains of the Thessaly. Their ruler Peirithous, son of Ixion, was a half-brother of the Centaurs. On his marriage, the Centaurs tried to carry off his bride and other women, but in the fierce struggle which ensued—depicted on the metopes of the Parthenon—they were defeated.

lapouage philosophy of

the phrase covers a variety of activities.

1. philosophers interested in problems, for example, about mind and knowledge, may frame their question in various ways. They may ask directly about mind or knowledge; or they may begin by asking how the words 'mind' and 'knowledge' are used.

2. the procedure of investigating philosophical questions by reflecting on the uses of words generates another meaning of 'philosophy of language'. Here there are two questions. First there is a general question about the justifiability of approaching philosophical questions via a study of how words are used. Second, philosophers who study the use of words use such key terms as 'meaning', 'reference', 'truth', and use.

lares

Roman tuteraly deities, originally gods of the farmland. Their cult came to be observed in private houses, and they themselves were identified with the spirits of the dead. They were represented by statuettes placed in the hearth.

Latinus

king of Latium, whose daughter Lavinia married Aeneas.

law

in a descriptive sense, "law" means "law of nature" an invariatn relationshly found in phenomena by scientific investigation, and thus presumed to hold in the natural world.

law philosophy of

1. the analysis of the nature of law and legal systems; analytic jurisprudence.

2. the critical evaluation of the basis of the legal authority and of the moral rationale behind legal decision making; ethical jurisprudence.

laws of nature

principles that may be either prescriptive or descriptive, but must always be in some sense necessary.

1. The prescriptive law of the nature is conceived as a basic system of moral norms, the necessity of obedience being moral.

2. Descriptive laws of nature are supposed to hold with a (non-logical) necessity, and

cannot be broken; a genuine exception would show only that what had been thought to hold as such as law does not.

laws of thought

in traditional logic one finds stated three principles upon which all logical thinking is held to depend. These are the laws or principles of identity, excluded middle, and contradiction. In modern logic the principles turn out to be tautologies.

lazy sophism

the nickname used by Leibnix and others for the arguments that, since from 'X will be' it follows necessarily tha 'X will be', therefore it must also follow that 'X necessarily and inevitably will be'.

leap

a radical change that takes place in an object or a phenomenon is called a leap. According to Darwin, the transition from one stage to another stage is always explained in terms of a leap.

learning

it is an art of knowing something by means of various methods. For instance, children learn the meaning of words and names of various objects by means of ostentation. According to Socrates, we can learn only those things which are already known to us.

learning paradox

refers to an old problem which was raised in Plato's Socratic dialogues and later found in some writings on education and certain medieval approaches to the knowledge of the nature of God. A person can learn only that which he doesn't know, but if he does not know it, how does he know what he is seeking to learn?

least number principle

the principle that if a property or condition holds for some number then there is a least number that satisfies the condition. This principle is equivalent to the principle of complete induction.

Leda

mother of the Dioscuri and Helen of Troy, Helen and one of the twins, Polydeuces (pollux), being the offspring of Zeus, who visited her in the form of a swan. Her husband, Tyndareus, was the father of Castor.

legalism (Chinese fa chia; the school of law)

a school of thought that flourished in the state of Ch'in. The policies of this school were instrumental in the unification by that state of the central Chinese kingdoms in 221 B.C. The leading theorists, Shang Yang and Han Fei rejected all traditional moral values, making utility to the state the supreme criterion. Through a system of rewards and punishments, set out in a rigid code or law, all human activity was directed towards increasing the power of the state and its ruler, both internally and externally. To this end, the people were set to pursuing only agriculture and warfare, and all alternatives forms of social activity were prohibited.

Leibniz's law

the principle that if one thing is identical with another then anything that is true of the one must also be true of the other. This sounds obviously true.

lemma

something taken for granted or assumed in logic. The most common form of lemma in logic is the dilemma, which implies the need to choose between two alternatives. For example, either do this work or you come with us.

lemures

ghosts of the dead; in Roman belief, sometimes known as Larvae and often regarded as hostile.

Lenin, Viadimir Ilyich 1870-1924

Russian Marxist. Born in Simbirsk (now Ulianov). Studied at Kazan and St. Petersburg. Imprisoned for revolutionary activity in 1895. Exiled to Siberia in 1897. He was in exile most of the time between 1900 and 1917. Headed the Soviet Union from 1917-24.

Principal writings : Materialism and Empirio-criticism (T), 1909; Imperialism (T), 1916; State and Revolution (T), 1917.

Lenin dedicated himself to the Marxist philosophy. In this regard his quest was to discover the strongest version of that philosophy. He began with a Marxism closely oriented to that of Marx himself, abjuring the dialectic, while adhering to materialism. He ended, however, in agreeging with all of the propositions of Engels, while contributing a proposition, or at least a clarification, of his own 4.

lent

the period of 40 week-days extending from Ash Wednesday to Easter Eve; observed by Christians as a time of fasting and penitence in Commemoration of Christ's fasting and temptation in the wilderness.

lethe

river of oblivion, flowing in the underworld. The dead drank of it and forgot life on earth forever.

Leto, Latona

mother, by Zeus, of Apollo and Artemis. She was pursued by the jealous Hera until she reached the floating island of Delos. Here the twins were born.

Leucippus (450-420 B.C.)

one of the ancient Greek atomists who tried to explain the nature of reality in terms of atomic cosmology.

li

Chinese term meaning "property", "good manners". One of the cardinal virtues in Confucianism Li is the outward expression of an inner harmony.

liar paradox

a paradox traditionally attributed to Empimenides the Cretan and supposedly strngthened by Eubulides. The statement, 'I am lying', is true only if it is false, and false if it is true.

libertarianism

1. the view, opposed to determinism, that certain human actions are not (or not entirely) governed by necessitating causal law.

2. whole-hearted political and economic liberalism, opposed to any social and legal constraints on individual freedom.

liberty

from the Latin liberates, from libero ("to set free, liberate"). The term, like freedom has two senses : one is the metaphysical capacity to make decisions freely; the other is the social fact of having a ceratin amount of elbow-room within society.

libitina

early Italian earthdeity, Roman goddess of burials.

life, human

the concept of human life is implicit in all Philosophical and religious discussion.

In Hinduism life is divided into a succession of four stages (ashramas), each with its duties and expectations.

light

the analysis of light through much of the history of the philosophy has been at the same time physical and divine illumination. The Neoplatonic doctrine treated light in dual terms.

likelihood

in connection with a statistical hypothesis on a body of data, the chance of those data occurring if the hypothesis is true.

limited indepedent variety principle of

the name given by J.M.Keynes to the contention that to justify inductive generalizations it has to be assumed "that the objects in the field, over which our generalizations extend, do not have an infinite number or independent qualities".

line, image of the

in Plato's philosophy, the image of the line serves to demarcate the world of Forms from the world of sensible things. According to Plato, the World of Forms is an eternal and immutable world, while the world of sensible things is a replica of the world of Forms.

linguistic philosophy

an approach to Philosophy that holds that a careful study of how language is actually used, taught, and developed in everyday discourse can illuminate and even transform or dissolve, time honoured philosophical problems.

litany

a solemn form of supplicatory

prayer used in public worship, consisting of petitions and responses.

liturgy
generally, the prescribed services of the Church; more particularly the Eucharist. A text containing such services.

locution
any meaningful assertion that abides by the rules of syntax. Contrary to an illocutionary act, locutionary act involves in the use of a locution to express something more clearly.

logic
in its broadest sense logic is the study of the structure and principles of reasoning or of sound argument. Hence it is also a study of those relations in virtue of which one thing may be said to follow from or be a consequence of another.

logical atomism
the philosophy advocated by Russell and early Wittgenstein. According to this doctrine, language mirrors the reality. Unlike physicists, claim logical atomists, they are not interested in physically breaking the atom into its components but they are interested in breaking the atoms into their minute logical structures. Thus they arrive at what are called simples. By doing so, believe logical atomists, certain complicated things can be made intelligible. These logical atoms are supposed to depict the reality in it simplest form possible. However, this doctrine was abadoned by both the writers due to its untenability. Wittgenstein's Tractation Logico-philoscphicus gives a coherent and a systematic account of logical atomism.

logical constants
symbols that represent certain of the devices, independent words, prefixes, suffixes, and inflections in any language that enable one to discern the grammatical structure of a sentence.

logical construction
a term used by philosophers such as Russell and Wisdom, to characterize those things whose status and/or existence we are in doubt about or find problematic.

logical fiction
an object that is only apparently invoked by a sentence.

logical form
the form of an argument which is expressed in a symbolic representation from the structure of which the reasoning procedure adopted is apparent.

logically-black-is-white slide
the abusive nickname for the fallacy of arguing that, because the difference between two extremes is a differnce of degree, therefore those extremes are really the same.

logically perfect language
a language in which grammatical and logical structures correspond with

each other.

logically private language

refers to a language in which all words must be defined in terms of the logically private experience of the individual language user.

logically proper name

a proper name of the kind required by Russell's logical atomism.

logical paradoxes

usually distingushied from the semantic paradoxes in that they can be expressed using only logical or set-theoretic terms.

logical positivism

the point of view of the Vienna Circle of Logical Positivists. The goal of the school, also known as "logical empiricims", was to purify philosophy—sifting out its metaphysical elements, and reconstituting the discipline with logic as its organon. The goal of philosophy in this sense is working out the implications of the logic of science.

logical subject

the subject of a sentence expressed in a logically perfect language, or the object that subject denotes.

logicism

a view advocated by Frege and Russell, according to which mathematics is considered to be the part of the logic. The purpose of lgoicism is to ensure that the knowledge of mathematical truths will have the same status as the knowledge of logical truths.

logistic method

the methof of studying a subject by formalizing it. Lagos, a Greek term meaning "reason, word, speech, discourse, definition, principle, or ratio". The function of the term in philosophy has turned largely on the logos as "reason".

logos

a Greek term meaning "reason, word, speech, discourse, definiton, principle, or ratio". The function of the term in philosophy has turned largely on the logos as "reason".

Loka

region.

lokayata

the Indian philosophical doctrine that holds that this world is the only one that exists and that there is no after-life. The emergence of materialist philosophy in India was preceded by religious and philosophical scepticism. Already some verses in the Rig Veda have been interpreted as expressing doubts about the existence of gods since it was not certain that anybody had ever seen them. The Upanisads testify that some people denied survival after death and the existence of the other world. Buddhist and Jainst sources have preserved a story about King Payasi, who was doubtful about life after death because none of those he had asked before their death to come back and tell him that they were alive elsewhere did so and he could not detect a soul leaving the body by observation or by weighing the body before and after death. The Pali canon gives the names and summaries of teachings of heads of six 'heretical' schools. Philosophical scepticism in the form of radical epist-emological and logical agnosticism is attached there to the name of San-Jaya Belattha, who abstained from making any definite statement about anything because it was not possible to guarantee its truth. Ethical scepticism or relativism, with a touch of naturalist determinism, was advocated by Purana Kassapa, who denied the validity of the concepts of merit in doing good and of guilt in performing evil deeds. Good and evil were not results of ethical causation, but just happened.

Fully fledged materialism is ascribed to Ajita Kesakambali, who denied life after death and the validity of any transcendental knowledge claimed by allegedly perfect teachers. A human being is a product of the four elements, which dissolve after death; the person ceases to exist. The early existence of materialist philosophy as a school of thought advocated on the grounds of logical argument may be further inferred from the Maitri Upanisad which is probably slightly post-Buddhist. It warns against contacts with those who use false logic and confusing arguments to press believers in the Vedas; their doctrine, denying the existence of the self or soul, supported by false proofs, puzzles people, who then cannot distinguish Vedic tore from ordinary human knowledge.

The most extensive and systematic source of Lokayata philosophy is the work Tattvopaplavasimha by Jayarasi which frequently draws on the lost Brhaspatisutras. Some believe that it is the one and only surviving truly Lokayata text, but doubts have recently been expressed about this view. Although Jayarigi proclaims himself to be a follower of Brhaspati, his argumentation often brings him close to the position of a sceptic if not an agnostic. Other systematic expositions of Lokayata philosophy can be found in philosophical manuals which undertaken to summarize the doctrines of several philosophical schools, both orthodox and non-orthodox. A short account of Lokayata philosophy appeared in the m a n u a l Saddarsanasamucchaya by Harlbhadra, which is supplemented by a more extensive and reasonably accurat summary in

Gunaratna's commentary. But the most comprehensive and systematic treatise can be found in the work led Sarvadarsanasahgraha by Madhava under the heading Carvakadarsana. At the end he quotes eleven stanzas from the lost work of Brhaspati.

The name of the school - Lokayata - means 'worldly' or concerned with the world, i.e, the world accessible to the senses, which is regarded as the only real one.

Lokayata ontology is determined by what can be called its radical epistemological empiricism, which recognizes sensory perception as the only valid avenue of our knowledge of reality and, indeed, as the only valid proof of the existence of anything. Whatever cannot be perceived does not exist. Talk of higher invisible worlds, of an afterlife with its rewards and punishments, and of God as the higest ruler of the world, is a product of the fantasy or an invention of deceitful priests in order to gain comfortable livelihoods out of a credulous populace. Loical proof for the existence of the unseen is invalid, because the validity of the general premises is only assumed and cannot be proved unconditionally. This rules out not only what in Europe is known as the ontological proof of God, but also the acceptance of inference as a valid source of view Knowledge, since inference is a process perceived in the mind, which is, however fully dependent on sensory input for its material, a view reminiscent of Locke and Hume. Opponents pointed out that Lokiyatists themselves used inference in refuting other doctrines, but from at least one fragment it transpires that the Lokiyata rejection of inference was not so absolute. Purandara admitted the validity of inference withint the perceptible world if verification by sensory perception was at least conceivable. But he rejected its use and validity wherever the conclusion pointed towards the assumption of some transcendent worlds beyond sensory perception, However, this explanation does not deal with the obvious difficulty that the Lokiyatas themselves derive their dogma of the nonexistence of the unseen transcendent from an inference in which the general premiss itself cannot be proved, but is a metaphysical postulate.

A further problem arises with Lokayata metaphysics when we consider its basic tenet that the world, which is purely material, is composed of a combination of four elements, namely earth, water, air and fire. All things in the world, including man, are the result of different patterns in which the elements combine to produce them. Traces of the doctrine of four elements forming the foundation of the material world can be found as far back as the Rig Veda, but it may be of the older origin as it existed also in ancient Greece, unless we assume a traffic of ideas between India and Greece in antiquity. It is fully spelled in the Uparusads, with a fifth element, ether, added. This doctrine then became accepted by virtually every school of Indian philosophy with various other elements added by different schools to account for mental phenomena. The Lokdyata school, of course, rejected all additional non material elements, but accepted the four 'material' ones while further rejecting ether on the grounds that it cannot be perceived by the senses and therefore it does not exist. The difficulty here is that the four material elements cannot be perceived in their pure form either. This objection was not raised by the opponents of Lokiyata, no doubt because of the universal acceptance of the doctrine of the elements. These elements were, in fact, understood in most systems not as some kind of dead building stones of the world, but as dynamic natural forces or categories of material existence. Thus Buddhism expalins earth as solidity, water as liquidity, air as vibration, and fire as heat/ light. While no detailed explanation of the Lokiyata views of the four elements has been preserved, it could be that they understood them in a similar way to Buddhism and regarded them as perceivable. There is some evidence that Lokiyata accepted the atomic theory, although doubts have been expressed on the matter. Either it regarded atoms as the smallest perceptible particles or concluded that, while atoms were not perceivable, it was enough that their conglomerates were. Lokiyata psychology does not accept the existence of a soul or self separate from the body. The proof is seen in statements in which one clearly identifies oneself with the body, such as 'I am fat' or 'I am thin'. At the same time it is asserted that the expression 'my body' does not prove the existence of a separate, immaterial owner of the body, but is only figurative. The emergence of consciousness is explained by the use of an analogy. When elements combine in a certain configuration to produce person, consciousness emerge, as does the power of intoxication in a mixture of appropriate ingredients through fermentation. When eventually the elements forming the body dissolve at the death of a person, his or her consciousness disappears and he or she is gone for good. The ethics of Lokiyata follow from its basic tenet, which denies any form of individual survival after death. The logical conclusion is that one should live as aggreably as possible. The aim of life is to experience pleasure, which should not be rejected just because it is often associated with hardship or suffering. One ought to enjoy pleasure in the highest measure while thoughtfully avoiding or removing accompanying hard-ships and evils, just as one removes bones when eating fish. There is no reward or punishment beyond death. The highest bliss comes from the embrace of a beautiful woman. Hell is only pain caused by hardship in this world, like swallowing fishbone. Final liberation comes with the death of the body, and it is not necessary to seek it through the acquistion of special knowledge. Performing sacrifices, learning Vedas, asceticism and applying ashes to one's body is the way of life of those who lack intelligence and manliness.

As the preoccupation with refuting Lokiyata philosophy in orthodox and other philosophical writings in India lasted for several centuries, it has to be assumed that it must have had a significant following during that time and that it must have reached a considerable degree of theoretical elaboration, especially in the field of logical argument. The fact that Lokiyata original sources have not been preserved is probably due to the circumstances after Indian creative philosophizing passed its peak and India concentrated under Islamic and other foreign domination on preserving, in the first place, her orthodox religious heritage and those philosophies which were compatible with it.

lottery paradox

refers to a paradox which is arising from the principle that a rational man who believes each of two propositions ought to believe their conjunction. But suppose there is a lottery with one hundred tickets 1, 2, 3, ...10. A rational man may, it is said, believe that 1 will not win, 2 will not win, and so on for each ticket. So he ought, by the principle, to believe the conjunction of all these, which is equivalent to believing that no ticket will win. But one will! So the natural principle of combining rational beliefs has a false consequence.

love

the Latin terms are amnr and caritas, and the principal Greek term are philia, eros, and agape. Philia developed the connotation of the kind of love involved in friendship (jen standing as the Chinese synonym), amor and eros the type of love based on desire, and caritas and agape the sense of a higher or selfless type of love.

low Church

one of the 3 main traditions, parties, or schools of thought in Anglicanism, assigning a reltively low place to the supernatural authority of the clergy, minimizing the divine grace inherent in the scraments, and attaching little importance to ritual and ceremonial. Cf. Anglo Catholicism, High Church.

lowenheim-skolem theorem

the proof, provided by Lowenheim in 1915, that any finite set T of sentences which has a model has a denumerable model, which result Skolem generalized in 1920 to the case where T is a denumerably infinite set of sentences.

loyalty

for Royce the ideal of loyality is a universal, capable of bringing harmony among competing loyalties. The principle of ethics is, from this perspective. "Be loyal to loyalty".

L-truth

for a discussion of L-truth and L-false sentence where 'L' stands for 'logically', and discussion of L-determinate and L-indetermine concepts.

lutheranism

from of Protestant Christianity embodying the teaching of the reformer, Martin Luther. Its main distinctive tenets are that Scripture is the sole rule of faith, and that all other creeds and confessions, though possessing a measure of genuine authority, are subordinate to it, the the will of man is in bondage to sin, and that Justification is by faith alone. The aspect of salvation has always received special emphasis, Lutheranism is practised chiefly in Germany, and is also the established church in Denmark, Norway, and Sweden; it is widely represented in U.S.A.

lyceum

the public garden in Athens that gave its name to the school of philosophy founded by Aristotle in 335 BC.

Lycomedes

king of Scyros to whose court Achilles, disguised as a girl, was sent by his mother so that he would not have to go to the Trojan war—a design frustrated by Odysseus. It was Lycomedes who slew Theseus.

macrocosm

from the Greek makros ('great') and kosmos ('universe'). The term is contrasted with microcosm, from mikros ('small') and kosmos ('universe'). Macrocosm, taken to refer to the universe, is set in contrast to man, the microcosm, a little universe.

Madhava (14th century A.D.)
the chief propagator of Dvaita, according to which world is as real as Brahman. Thus there are two separable realities.

Madhyamika
one of the four chief philosophial schools of Buddhism, the system of the Mean or 'middle way'. Members of the school are called Madhyamikas. Negarjuna is regarded as its founder. The school of Shunyavada was highly influential in shaping Mehayana Buddhism. Chi-Tsang continued the development of the school in China.

magnitudes
a magnitude is intensive if it is possible to order things of a certain type according to it; it is extensive if it is both intensive and different numerical values can be assigned to differing positions in the ordering, such that the ordering by magnitude is preserved when ordered by the relation 'less than'.

Mahabbarata, the
the great Brahman epic poem of the 6th century B.C., which contains the Bhagavad-Gita as one of its parts, the Mahabharata tells the story of two families, both having claims upon the throne, involved in struggle. In addition to the themes of the Bhagavad-Geeta, the poem contains an elaboration of:

1. The four aims of life: righteousness, wealth, worldly, enjoyment and spiritual freedom.
2. The four Ashramas, or the four stations of life and their duties: the student, householder, forest-dweller, and ascetic.
3. The four castes: Brahmin (priest and teacher), Kshatriya (warrior), Vaisya (merchant), Sudra (labourer).

Mahavira (549-477 B.C.)
he is regarded as the twenty-fourth Tirthankara or "founders of the faith of Jainism". According to Jains, Rsabhadeva was the founder of Jaina school of thought.

mahdi
from the Arabic meaning 'the guided, or well-directed, one'. The one who will appear on earth as Allah's represetative to lead the hosts of Islan to world-wide victory. He will be the final Imam.

Maia
daughter of Atlas; she was the eldest and fairest of the Pleiades. Hermes was her son.

maientic
from the Greek maia (midwife). Normally used as an adjective, describing Socrates method of delivering an individual of his ideas.

maitreya
the expected or future Buddha, prophesied by Gautam Buddha, whose incarnation will spread the doetrine, restore the good society, and save all beings.

major premise

in a categorical syllogism, the premise containing the major term.

major term

the predicate term of the conclusion of a categorical syllogism.

man

since philosophy is the work of man, all of its basic divisons, Epistemology, Ethics, Aesthetics, etc., comment upon his nature.

Plato regarded man as essential a tripartite unity of mind, will, and passions.

Hsun Tzu regarded man as naturally evil, and thus requiring the pressure of outward discipline.

manara

spirit.

mandala

book.

mani

jewel or amulet.

manichaeism

it is a relgious movement started by Mani, 'the apostle of God'. It is considered to be a religion independent of Christianity. In other words, it was a revivalism of Buddhism and Zoroastrianism. As a dualistic religion, Manichaeism believed that life is a struggle between two individual principles good and evil.

manifold

a term frequently used by Kant in his Critique of Pure Reason to signify various and discrete elements of sense-experience. The manfold of sense-data is presented to the mind which organises it with the help of concepts.

mantra

a Sanskrit term meaning 'counsel' or 'instrument of thought'. In the Vedas the term refers to hymns and prayers to the gods, as well as to ritualistic or devotional formula.

many questions, fallacy of

a mistake which consists of putting or accepting a question that tacitly takes for granted a false or at least disputations answer to some prior question or questions. It is a common form of intellectual error, though not perhaps in the strict-sense a fallacy.

many-sorted logic

refers to the study of validity in many-sorted languages. A formal language with predicate structure is many-sorted if typographically distinct kinds of names and variables are used with the intention that interpretation of the language will involve assigning to each kind, different categories of objects for their universes of discourse.

many-valued logic

refers to the study of validity and consequence under an interpretation that assigns three or more possible values to the sentences of a formal language.

Marburg school

one of the most important

divisons of Neo Kantianism. Founded by Hermann Cohen (1842-1918) and Paul Natorp (1854-1924), the Marburg school was mainly concerned with philosophy of science.

mariology

the doctrine concerning the Blessed Virgin Mary. It includes the dogmas of the Immaculate Conception and the bodily Assumption.

maronites

a sect of Arabic speaking Christians living mainly in the Lebanon and using Syrise as their liturgical language. They are so called after their founder, Maron, who is believed to have lived in the 4th c. Their head is a patriarch in communion with the See of Rome.

Mars

Roman god of war and one of the tutelary deities of the city; identified with the Greek Ares. Also god of agriculture and the protector of flocks and herds. The wolf was sacred to him.

Marsyas

phrygian satyr who discovered a flute disliked playing the instrument because it distorted her features. Marsyas challenged Apollo to a musical contest, on condition that the loser should place himself entirely in the hands of the winner to do with as he would. The Muses decided in favour of the god, who thereupon tied Marsyas to a tree and flayed him alive. His blood formed a river bearing his name.

Marx, Karl

German social theorist, interested mainly in economics and history. He had little to do with the philosophical doctrines that now, form part of the Marxism. In the first volume of the Das Kapital Marx made use of, and to some extent discussed, a theory of method that owed something to Hegel.

Marx called this a dialectical method, but said that it turned Hegel's dialectic the right way up, in that it was materialistic and not idealistic. But though Marx's dialectic may in a broad sense be called a philosophy of history, it is reallly an account of socio historical development rather than a philosophical theory, and so is the concern of the historian rather than of the philosopher.

Marxism (or classical marxism)

the body of doctrines originally propounded by Marx and Bagels, which involves certain philosophical views. These views (propounded mainly by Engels) rely heavily on the philosophy of Hegel, and in particular on his thesis that change has to be explained in terms of the contradiction.

But whereas Hegel's philosophy is a form of idealism, Marxism declares itself to be a form of materialism. Not, however, 'mechanistic' materialism, but

dialectical materialism, where due weight is given to 'the transformation of quantity into quality'.
This means that mind is not reduced to matter but is seen as coming from matter, though qualitatively different from it.

masa
month.

Masked man fallacy
refers to the mistake of arguing that because someone knows (or does not know) something under one description, they must therefore know it (or they therefore cannot know it) as the same thing when it appears under another description.

mass noun
a term that refers to an uncountable thing or an object. For instance, there are cans of oil in that room. The cans that contain oil can be counted but oil cannot be counted. Here 'oil' is a mass noun.

mass noun
a term which refers to an uncountalbe thing. Glasses of water can be counted, water cannot. Hence water is a mass noun.

materialism
any set of doctrines stressing the primacy of material over spiritual factors in metaphysics, value theory, physiology, epistemology or historical explanation.

mathematics, philosophy of
the study of the concepts of and justification for the principles used in mathematics. Although mathematics is a useful tool in the science, few believe that the subject matter of the mathematics is physical objects or that empirical observation is the ultimate ground for deciding the truth or falsity of the mathematical statements.

matter
refers to that which has traditionally been contrasted either with form or with mind.

maxim
in ordinary language a rule of action, summing up wisdom in an established context. In Kant, a rule providing ethical guidance.

maya
from the Sanskrit maya ('magic'). The term is used in Indian philosophy to refer to the world as an appearance, somehow different from the reality. Indian philosophy contains a range of possible interpretations of the status of the world. On the one extreme of this range, Ramanuja, holds the world to be perfectly real, although finite; at the other extreme Shankara as a representative of the Advaita Vedanta holds the world to be an outright illusion.

Mc Taggart, John McTaggart Ellis (1866-1925)
a British idealist philosopher who held the view that the time is unreal. According to him, reality is essentially spiritual. He denied the

existence of God. His important works include: Studies in Hegelian Dialectic: Studies in Hegelian Cosmology, etc.

mean, dorctrine of the

in the ethics of Aristotle the doctrine that virtue lies between extremes (although closer to excess than to deficiency).

In Chinese philosophy the middle way or Chung Yung in which every feeling is exercised in its proper degree and in harmony with every other.

In Buddhist philosophy, the strategy whereby desire is eliminated and Nirvana gained.

meaning

theories of meaning are formulated through determining a position on the significance and interrelations of sense-data, words and sentences, the use of words and sentences in ordinary language, ideas, and the problem of reference in regard to words, sentences, and ideas.

meaning postulates

devices used by Rudolf Carnap to introduce analytic sentence; into a formal language. Under all interpretations for a formal language L, only logical truths (such as 'no married woman is not married') will remain true invariantly. Analytically true sentences (such as 'all spinsters are not married') will not, however, remain true under all interpretations, since their truth depends on the particular meaning of their non-logical words (such as 'married' and 'spinster').

mechanical explanation

an expression, employed with different and often rather vague connotations, to cover various substantially different areas of denotation.

mechanism

1. a scientific philosophy developed principally by Descartes. In place of the traditional scholastic kind of the scientific explanation, which invoked 'real qualities'. Descartes claimed that his science was 'like mechanics in that it considers merely shapes, sizes, and motions'.

2. the thesis that genuine scientific explanation involves a search for mechanical models. Such models, based are known processes, describe the true mechanisms underlying the phenomenon to be explained.

3. a 'clockwork' universe of the Laplacean type—that is, one governed by strictly deterministic laws.

mediation

the process of connecting two end term by an intermediary. In logic, mediate inference connects the major and minor terms by means of the middle term. In Neoplatonism, God and the world are related by mediation. In theology, Christ is the mediator between God and the world.

meditation

the act of concentrating attention on God or self to increase one's insight about, or relation, to spiritual things.

medusa

one of the Gorgons, slain by Perseus.

Megarian school

a philosophical school active at Megara, near Athens, between the late 5th and early 3rd centuries B.C. No writings of the Megarians have survived and our knowledge of their doctrines and interest is based on references in the works of their contemporaries. They were influenced by Socrates and the Eleatics and were critical of Plato and Aristotle. Some of their contributions to logic are of the lasting interest. Eubulides, the refiner of the liar paradox, was one of their number.

Meinong, Alexius Von (1853-1928)

a German philosopher and a logician who held the view that thinking consists of three important aspects, namely, mental acts, its content and its objects. According to Meinong, objects have two types of existence. Some have objective existence (e.g. chairs, tables, etc.) and some have mere subjective existence (e.g. gold mountains, wingedhorse, etc.). Such objects are called ideal objects. Thus there are two types of existence. The sein of material objects and the sosein of ideal objects.

meliorism

from the Latin melior meaning 'butter'. The doctrine that man, while incapable of perfection, is capable of an indefinitely extending series of improvements. This applies both to the individual man and to the race.

Memnon

son of Eos (Dawn) and Tithonus, king of the Aethopians, and nephew of Priam. He fought against the Greeks in the Trojan war, but was killed by Achilles.

memory

the capacity to bring to mind (a) an event from one's past experience ('I remembermy first day at school') or (b) a previously learnt truth ('I remember the formula for this', I remeber that the book was removed from the shelf'). It is commonly agreed, however, that memory is closely related to knowledge, either as a special case of knowledge, or in so far as it is only possible to remember what was once known.

A central problem about memory concerns how it is possible to acquire present knowledge of that which is no longer present.

Menelaus

king of Sparta, younger brother of Agamemnon and husband of Helen, whose abduction by Paris was the imnmediate cause of the Trojan war, in which Menelaus himself played no very distinguished part. Homer's 'Odyssey' depicts him as at home safe once more with Helen, after a series of adventures which delayed his return for 8 years. He and Helen was eventually translated by Zeus to Elysium.

Menoeceus

son of Creon. In the struggle of the Seven Against Thebes, Tiresias, the blind seer; revealed that only the death of a member of the Sparoti would bring victory to Thebes, whereupon Menoeceus committed suicide.

mentalism

any doctrine insisting upon the exclusive reality of minds and their inner states; the term is also applied to those views of mind which distinguish mental states from brain states.

mentality

the quality of mind is treated under such topics as 'idealism' and 'soul'. But Morgan held mentality to be the emergent of the Psychical correlate. And Whitehead regarded the 'mental pole' as originative of novelty in the universe.

Mentor

old Ithacan to whose charge Odysseus consigned his household. His name has since become a synonym for a well proven adviser.

Mercurius, Mercury

the Roman equivalent of Hermes; he was the god of the traders.

Merleau-Ponty, Maurice (1908-1961)

a French philosopher who tried to establish some relationship between the consciousness and the world in which we live by rejecting the dualistic conception of mind and body. He conceived that the objects of one's own experience are enigmatic. His important work is The Phenomenology of Perception.

Merope

one of the Pleiades and wife of Sisyphus. The faintest star of the cluster (the Pleiades), she hides her face in shame at having married a mortal.

meta

originally a Greek proposition, now employed by English speaking philosophers as a prefix. The usual meaning is 'about as in 'meta-ethics', 'metahistory', and 'metalanguage'.

metahistory

in the broad sense, philosophy of history. The term is often restricted to the discipline's speculative aspect, which attempts to establish a framework of principles that can account for the course of the historical developments.

metalanguage

the language used to talk about an object language and its component words.

metalogic

the term refers simply to the

metalanguage of logic. It is a study of the structure, signs connectives, formulae, theorems, and rules of inference of logic from a syntactic, semantic, and pragmatic point of view. The basic concepts, upon which discussion of metalogic has turned in recent years, are decidability completeness, and consistency.

metamathematics

the study of formal systems, and, especially of the concepts used in mathematics. It is also called proof theory.

metaphilosophy

in terms of subject-matter, Metaphilosophy is the discussion of the nature of philosophy, including of course the nature of its consituent disciplines of Logic, Ethics, Aesthetics, Epistemology, etc.

metaphysics

the term metapysics is derived from the Greek term 'meta-ta-phusica', mean 'beyond physical existence'. This term was first introduced by Aristotle into philosophy. According to Aristotle it is a science of 'first princples'. Thus it is also known as 'First Philosophy'. Its main task is to investigate into the first principles of whatever exists. But in the modern period, metaphysics is treated as a science or a doctrine that deals with the ultimate status of reality. However, some contemporary philosophers have gone a step forward to say that metaphysics deals with supersensible reality. There are two important types of metaphysics, namely, transcendental and immanent. Transcendentalists believe that ultimate reality transcends the limits of all empirical experience, while immanent metaphysician holds that ultimate reality is an all pervading principle. It is omnipresent.

metempsychosis

the idea, tound in Buddhism and other religions originating in the Indian subcontinent that our souls have lived before in the bodies of other men or of non-human animals, and that after death they will in due course be reincarnated into other human or non-human bodies.

methodism

the doctrines and practice of the religious bodies which have emerged from the evangelical movement strted by John Wesley(1703-91), his borther Charles (1707-88), and george Whitefield lived and died a priest of the Church of England, but his movement, which attaches great importance the priesthood of all believers, gradually came to be organized as a separate denomination, at first known as Wesleyanism.Methodism is now world-wide, the Methodist Eepiscopal Church of America being especially influential.

method of concomitant

variation
it is one of the logical methods advocated by J.S. Mill. A phenomenon may vary in any manner whenever another phenomenon varies in a specified manner. Then the phenomenon that varies under a specific manner or a circumstances may be regarded as a cause or an effect, or it is somehow linked up with the phenomenon that varies in any manner through some fact of causation.

methdological holism and methodological individualism
rival banners in an imbroglio in the philosophy of social science. One side presses for explanation in terms of social structures and social wholes, the other insists that everything must be reduced to statements about the component individuals.

methodology
refers to the study of method, usually covering the procedures and aims of a particular discipline, and enquiry into the way in which that discipline is organized.

metis
wise counsel personified in Greek mythology. Wisest among either gods or men, she was Zeus first wife. Afraid that she might give birth to one wiser even than herself, he devoured her at the start of her pregnancy.

Midas
legendary phyrgian king of whom, according to one story, Dionysus, in acknowledgment of his kindly treatment of Silenus, gave the power of turning everything he touched into gold, including, unfortunately, his food. The god saved him from misery by bidding him bathe in the river Pactolus, the sands of which henceforth became gold-bearing. Another version of the tale relates that Midas, for having adjudicated a musical contest against Apollo and in favour of Pan, had his ears changed by Apollo into those of an ass. This monstrous growth he concealed under a cap—but not, of course, from his barber, who was sworn to secrecy. This poor man, so tormented by the knowledge he dared not impart, dug a hole in the ground and whispered the secret into it. A reed sprang up which, in the wind, murmured the words, 'Midas hath ass's ears'.

middle platonism
the developments in Platonism that took place between the establishment of the so-called Middle Academy by Arcesilaus and the advent of Plotinus.

Milesian (or Ionian) school
the group of Presocratics who came from the then Greek cities of the Aegean coast of what is now Turkey. The known figures are Thales, Anaximander, and Anaximenes (all form Miletus),

and Anaxagores of Clazomenae (who spent all his working life in Athens until he was expelled, nominally for godlessness). According to this, 'the earth is full of gods' expresses this conviction that all forces are forces of the universe itself.

millet seed paradox

a paradox highlighted to Zeno of Elea. According to him, when a millet seed does not make any sound when it is fallen on the ground, how come 1000 millet seeds make sound when they are fallen on the ground? Zeno feels that it is highly non-sensical to think that 1000 nothings make sound.

Mill's method

the four 'methods of experimental inquiry' distinguished by J.S. Mill in his Logic (III) (viii). Mill held that all induction involves a search for causes and the methods are thus also contributions to the definition of 'cause'.

mimamsa

one of the systems of Indian philosophy. Originally it concerned itself solely with the hermeneutics of the ancient ritualistic scriptures; this discipline was systemtized by Jaimini in the Karma-mimamsasutras (before the 2nd century AD).

mimesis

a Greek term meaning 'imitation'. When Plato held that 'time is the moving image of the eternity', he was saying that the world is an image or an imitation of the eternal forms of ideas.

mind-body problem

the philosophical problem of how the mind is related to the body, and of what properties, functions, and occurrences, should be regarded as, respectively, mental or physical. This problem is central to both the philosophy of mind and the philosophy of psychology.

mind, philosophy of

the philosophical study of the mind and mental functioning. While the principal task of the philosophy of mind may be regarded as the attempt to provide an account of what mind is, the complexity of the task is such that there is little in philosophical literature that will seem to constitute an integrated theory of the mind perse.

Rather, issues that are central to the philosophy of the mind occur throughout metaphysics, epistemology, logic, aesthetics, and particularly in the contexts of the philosophy of psychology and what is called the mind-body problem.

Minerva

Roman goddess of wisdom and counsel (and originally of the handicrafts). She was identified with the Greek deity, Athena.

minor premises

in a syllogism, in the premise in which the minor term occurs is called a minor premise. For example, the syllogism consists of the following premises.

All men are mortal.
Socrates is a man.
∴ Socrates is mortal.

In this syllogism, 'Socrates' is a minor term. Then the premises 'Socrates is a man' is a minor premise.

minor term
the subject term of the conclusion of a categorical syllogism.

Minos
king of Crete, he was son of Zeus by Europe and brother of Rhadamanthus. Renowned for his wisdom, he was on his death, according to Homer, appointed one of the judges in Hades. His wife was Pasiphae, and Ariadne was one of his 3 children. He pursued Daedalaus from Crete, but on reaching Sicily was drowned in boiling water by the daughter of Cocalus, king of the island.

minotaur
monster offspring of a union between Pasiphae, wife of Minos, king of Crete, and a bull. Half human, half taurine, the creature was kept by Minos in the Labyrinth at Knossos until Theseus killed it.

minyae
legendary Greek people from Thessaly who under their leader Minyas settled in Boeotia.

miracle
a term that is most commonly taken to mean an act that manifests divine power through the suspension or alteration of the normal working of the laws of nature. The idea of laws of nature is thus essential to the idea of the miraculous, but is also, clearly, a major barrier to belief that miracles actually occur.

miraculous doctor
the traditional nickname given to Roger Bacon.

mishnah
in Judaism, the second or oral law forming the basis of the Talmud. the word itself means instruction.

missal
the book containing the service of the mass, including ceremonial directions, for use throughout the liturgical year.

Mithras
ancient persian deity, associated with the sun or light. His cult is said to have been brought to Rome in the middle of the 1st C.B.C. Later it became widely popular, especially in the army. Mithraic sculpture-groups (a young man wearing a cap and slaying a bull, which at the same time is being attacked by a scorpion, a crab, and a dog) are common.

Mnemosyne
personification of memory; mother of the Muses.

modality
refers to the way in which a sentence may characterize another related sentence or proposition as true, that is, the

mode in which it is true.

modal logic

the logic of the necessity and possibility. A modal statement is one in which something is said to be necessarily, or possibly the case.

mode

this term is derived from the Lating term 'modus'. It was John Locke who distinguished simple modes from mixed modes. The simple mode of an idea is a simple way of thinking of an idea. For example, red, hot etc. Mixed modes are those basically required in a moral discourse. They are conglomeration of various simple ideas arranged at the pleasure of the mind. For example, murder, glory etc.

model

1. (of a set of sentences) an interpretation (usually a set theoretic interpretation) of the language in which the sentences are written, which assigns to each sentence of the set the value 'true'.

2. (of a formal system) an interpretation of the set of axioms of that system.

model theory

a branch of mathematical logic devoted to the study of logical relations and of the properties of formal system via their models, that is, set-theoretic interpretations.

modernism

although the term suggest that any one who takes the norms of modern thought and life as decisive in his interpretation of the matter would be a modernist and believe is in modernism, the term in fact has an almost exclusive reference to religious thought.

modus

Latin term meaning 'mode'. Used by the Scholastics in relation to modal propositions.

modus ponens

(Latin for : mood that affirms). In its basic form, an argument that runs 'If p, the q.p. Therefore q affirming the antecedent.

modus tollens

(Latin for: mood that denies). In its basic form, an argument that runs 'if p, then q. But not-q. Therefore not-p'. Affirming the antecendent.

Mohammedanism

the religion founded by Mohammed. The faith is characterised by an exclusive monotheism, the worship of Allah as the one true God, and Mohammed as the greatest of his prophets.

moirae

the Fates 3 in number; Lachesis, who assigned the term of a man's life, Clotho, who move the pattern of his destiny, and Atropos, who finally cut the threads.

moism

Chinese philosophical movement resting on the doctrine of universal love, and providing the chief alternative to Çonfucianism between the 5th and 3rd centuries B.C.

moksa (Snskrit for: liberation)

in most systems of Indian thought, final release from the cycle of the rebirth (samsara) and the sorrows and preplexities of the material world. In this eternal repose the soul recovers its innate integrity; how this is thought to be achieved—whether by merging with Brahman or by eternal existence as a pure spirit—differs from system to system.

Only the heretical materialists denied the doctrine, together with the related doctrines of samsara and karma.

monad

from the Greek term monas meaning 'unit'.

The term's first use was in Pythagorean number theory where it was the name of the first number of the series, and thus the number from which all other numbers are derived. Giordano Bruno used the term as the name of the irreducible onto logical unit of which all else is made up.

monadic

in logic denoting a predicate that requires only the addition of one singular term in order to make a well formed sentence..'...flies' and..'.. is large' are monadic (or oneplace) predicates.

monadology

the title given by one of Leibniz's editors to a metaphysical work written by Leibniz in 1714, and now applied to any metaphysical system such as Leibniz's.

monarchy

from the Greek monos ('alone') and archein ('to be first'). A form of government characterized, by the rule of one person.

monasticism

from the Greek monazein ('to be alone'). A discipline of life characterized by withdrawal from the world, meditation, self-abnegation and some degree of asceticism.

monism

it is a metaphysical theory, according to which there is only one substance. For example, materialists believe that matter is the only reality. Similarly, idealists believe that idea or spirit is the only reality. In this sense, both these systems are monistic in their nature. There is another peculiar system called type monism. For example, in the philosophy of Leibniz, monads are supposed to be the ultimate constituents of reality. Though there are innumerable monads, they all belong to one category in the sense that they share essential features. Thus Leibniz's metaphysics is an example for type monism.

monk

a member of a religious community of men living apart from the world and subject to an ascetic rule. Monasticism has been especially characteristic of Buddhism and Christianity.

monolatry

worship of one God to the exclusion of all others without necessarily denying the existence of the latter. Also called benotheism.

monophysite

one who holds that there is in Christ but a single nature or one composite nature, partly divine and partly human. Cf. Eeutychianism.

monotheism

the idea that there exists one only God, omnipotent over all things.

mood

one of the various ways in which (valid) syllogisms may be constructed within the four figures of the categorical syllogisms. The valid syllogism in each figure are called the moods of that figure.

moral

a term opposed to immoral or amoral. Ethics is a branch of study that deals with moral concepts.

moral argument for the existence of God

an argument best known in the formulation by Kant, which attempts to find sufficient grounds for theism in the specifically moral experience of mankind. According to the Kantian form of the argument, the highest good is a state of affairs in which happiness is distributed in strict proportion to moral virtue.

morality

in many usages, a synonyms of the term, 'ethics' (where most of the issues common to both terms are treated). Shaftesbury held morality to be natural, and independent of supernatural sancetions.

moral sense

a supposed faculty for detecting moral properties. Moral sense theory, a form of intiutionism, popular in the 18th century, holds that the perception of certain actions (or events) arouses distinctive feelings of pleasure or pain in the spectator. These feelings serve both to enable him to distinguish right actions from wrong, and to provide motives to moral behaviour.

moral sense theory

the ethical theory that we are able to distinguish between right and wrong by a distinctive moral sense.

Morpheus

son of Hypnos (Sleep) and god of dreams.

mortalist

refers to a person who believes that when people die that is that, and there is no survival.

Moslem

from the Arabic muslim ('one who submits'). One who professes the faith of Islam, i.e. a follower of Mohammed.

motion

a chief attribute and a mode of existence of all matter. Motion denotes chạnge in reality. The motion of matter is absolute, whereas the rest is relative. In one sense, we are under constant motion as the earth moves round the sun.

music of the spheres

the superb music believed by Pythagoreans to be produced by the regular movements of the heavenly bodies. No earthy ears—except perhaps those of Pythagoras himself—have had the good fortune to hear it.

myrmidons

legendary people dwelling on Aegina, many of whom followed Peleus, Achilles father, to Phthiotis. Homer depicts Achilles as their king and leader in the Trojan war.

mystery religions

the name given to a group of religious cults popular in the Hellenic and Roman periods. The mystery religions were characterized by a body of esoteric knowledge and ceremony which allegedly had the power to purify the initiate and guarantee him union with God and personal immortality. Virtually all of the mysteries centered around dying and rising saviours.

mysticism

what is, claimed to be direct or unmediated experience of the divine in which the human soul momentarily approaches union with God. Many of the great mystics have stressed that this is not primarily or essential a matter of visions or esctasies, as is sometimes supposed, but of total submission of the human will and intellect to God.

myth

from the Greek term mythos meaning 'legend'. Hence, a narrative account taken to be true, but not known to be true. The elaboration of dramatic narratives involving superhuman powers provided the first explanations of the origin and operation of the universe. Myth has some relation to metaphor and can be treated as allegory.

myth of er.

the concluding parable in Plato's Republic (Book X) concerning the fate of the souls after death and the choices available to them before reincarnation. The warrior, Er., apparently slain in battle, returns to the world to narrate his vision of the afterlife, in which the pursuit of wisdom and justice is shown to be the soul's only safeguard against present folly and future degradation. It is noteworthy that Plato, having insisted in the Republic, as elsewhere, that the soul is essentially incorporeal, is quite unable, and makes no attempt, to describe the doings and sufferings of supposedly disembodied souls in any terms other than those appropriate to flesh and blood persons.

mythology

a view of reality that is often characterized as primitive.

Myths were narratives born in the early stages of history when there was not much scientific explanation for certain happenings in this reality. Of late, myth is used as a term that denotes a kind of unwarranted belief in something.

Nagarjuna 100-200

Indian philosopher. A Buddhist and the first systematic expounder of an important school, called Shunyvada holding to the relativity of thought, and the non-duality of the Absolute. The school is also known as the Madhyamika or Doctrine school. There are two aspects to his thought, one negative and the other positive.

Principle writings : Twenty Verses on the Great Vehicle (T); Treatise on the Middle Doctrine (T); Treatise on Relativity (T).

Nagarjuna is the first outstanding figure in the long gallery of Indian Mahayana Buddhists, and the study of his works has many facets of interest. A knowledge not only of the man but also of his thinking is necessary for an understanding of the later developments of Mahayana in India, China and Tibet. Even certain currents in other Indian philosophica systems, especially Vedanta, and occasionally Nyaya and Jaina, are not seen in perspective unless one has Nagarjuna and his pupils in mind.

Our main source for an understanding of Nagarjuna and his cultural background are his own works and the documents belonging to the tradition in which he was active as a creative writer. Nagarjuna wrote in Sanskrit, and while some of his main works are still extant in that language, some are now only available in later Chinese and/or Tibetan translations.

Among the numerous dubious texts ascribed to Nagarjuna may be mentioned in particular: Mahaya-navimsika, Bhavasamkranti, Dasabhumikavibhas, Upayahradaya and Dharmadhatustava. Indispensable for a proper understanding of Nagarjuna's intellectual and religious background are some of the less philosophical of his writings, i.e. SS, an anthology giveing extracts from sixty-eight canonical texts, mainly Mahayana, supplemented by CS, BS, SL and RA, all of which contain copious allusions to or quotations from a large number of holy scriptures, or sutras, belonging to both vehicles.

MK, SS and VV are mostly purely philosophical and abstract in content. The basic idea in these writings is the emptiness (sunyata) of all phenomena, or concepts (dharma), and for this doctrine, which is, properly understood, not a doctrine but rather an attitude, Nagarjuna is largely indebted to the vast teachings of the Prajnaparamita scriptures.

VP is conceived as a criticism of Nyaya philosophy and thus shows Nagarjuna as a patriarch defending Buddhism against the infidel. Most probably we are justified in regarding Nagarjuna as the founder of the Madhyamaka school. Aryadeva is the author of Catuhsataka, the next in importance only to Nagarjuna is himself. His work is largely conceived as a criticism of various non-Buddhist schools left unattacked by Nagarjuna, his teacher. Rahulabhadra and Matrceta also belong to Nagarjuna's school, and their celebrated hymns to the Buddha. In the tradition of Nagarjuna's CS, display the devotional side of early Indian Madhyamaka. Without faith in the Buddha there is no Madhyamaka.

Regarding the date, life and personal circumstances of Nagarjuna little or nothing is known with certainty. From the cocoon of legends surrouding the historical Nagarjuna, the probable truth is that he must have been very active philosophically and also in the practical affairs as an abbot and as court counsellor in south India in the second or third century A.D.

The first solid foundation for Madhyamaka studies was laid with the great La Vallee Poussin's editions of Mutilamadhyamakakarikas de Nagarjuna avec le Prasannapada Commentaire de Candrakirti, Madhyamakavatara par Candrakirti. Traduction tibetaine and Bodhicaryavatarapanjika. Commentary to the Bodhicaryavatara of Santideva. These excellent editions are now in need of minor revision. Literal translations of the ealiest commentary on MK were published by Max Walleser, Die Mittlere Lehre des Nagarjuna. All the English version of MK are unreliable, and one still has to consult MK as found 'in the commentaries of Buddhapilita', Bhavya and Candrakirti, SS, VV, VS, YS, CS, PK, BS and BV have been edited and/or translated in Lindtner. The edition and translation of VV in Bhattacharya, Johnston and Kunst is fairly reliable. RA was edited by Hahn and translated by Hopkins and Lindtner. There are several versions of SL.

An enormous mass of scholarly literature is available in Tibeta, and much of it consists of commentaries and doxographical works in which Madhyamaka plays the most important role. Mostly, the American translators of Tsong Kha-pa seem to have an apologetic rather than a scholarly concern. Quite apart from that, later Tibetan scholarly literature has a very limited value for a proper understanding of the Indian sources, but there is a general, but unhappy, tendency to overestimate its independent merits. Scholars must, of course, go directly ad fontes and leave later Tibetan literature aside. Each tradition should be studied in its own right.

There are undoubtedly several angles from which a systematic presentation of Nagarjuna's religious philosophy may be undertaken. Also, if we use the term 'philosophy' in the sense of love of the result of wisdom, rather than in the sense of love of wisdom, we are justified in speaking of the philosophy of Nagarjuna. What mean to say is that his highest authority is never reason, but faith. In the case of Nagarjuna reason is always ancillary to faith. None the less one may still speak of a system of philosophy. Only by seeing all the pans as a whole can one avoid emphases that would lead to contradictory conclusions about the author's in tentions. The real task, as it is in any systematic research, is to determine the basic patterns that make the mass of the isolated observations immediately comprehensible. Then the important factors can be shifted out, and a judgement made on Nagarjuna's aims and achivement. Basically, Nagarjuna is a yogin.

As a Buddhist Nagarjuna regards ordinary experience as miserable,, or unsatisfactory (dukkha). By 'existence' is meant the five groups (samktra) which taken together from a 'Person' or individual, the physical body (rupa), feelings (vedana), ideas (samjna) the will to live and all its outward expressions (samkara) and, finally, consciousness (vijnana).

A careful observer will be able to confirm that our existence as individuals is characterized by three ineradicable traits: it is (1) conditioned and composite (samskara) and therefore (2) impermanent (anitya), which again implies that existence lacks any immutable constant nucleus, and, as such (3) it is without a self (anatman). These, in a nutshell, are the three aspects of duhkha.

To return to the subject of duhkha, one basic trait, the principle of inconsistancy, unites the three aspects, and that provides the transition to the immediate cause of duhkha. This is karma, literally 'work', a psychological concept corresponding to volition (cetana) and also the deliberate decision to do something (cetayitva). Karma is manifested in the individual's physical, verbal and mental acts of volition. It can be 'neutral' but in most cases it is positively or negatively charged. It is at the same time the functional and the material unique cause for the continuance of the individual's existence in the present and subsequent lives, and has been so since the beginning of time. Karma is the driving force that hustles the individual forward in the circuit of the renewed birth and death (samsara), and even if the individual by exerting his or her own will can guide the course of karma in a favourable or unfavourable direction, it is undoubtedly karma that binds him or her to samsara, according not only to the Buddhists, but many other Indian philosophers also. Only diehard nihilists contest the reality, or efficiency, of karma. One is not even supposed to communicate with such vicious people. There is no sense in investigating the original cause of karma, the basic energy and matter of existence, because it has always been there, and 'Even the buddhas cannot fathom the might of karma'. However, the buddhas have their part to play. They have themselves acknowledged that there is a liberation (moksa) from the bonds of the karma, and they have made a plan (marga) to achieve it. As in other Indian systems liberation occurs with an intuitive realization (jnana) of one or more fundamental facts (tattva). In Nagarjuna's system, Madhyamaka, it occurs, as well shall see, with a full realization (parijnana) of the 'law', or principle of conditioned coorigination (pratityasamutpada) which rules that everything lacks independent existence (nihsvabhavata), is in fact empty (sunyata). This is equivalent to the cessation of samasra; it is exitnction (nirvana, nirodha), where everything transitory comes to rest (santa).

The genesis of the passions is due to the notions of the discursive thought (vikalpa) to evaluations (samkalpa) and abstract constructions (kalpana) of the empirically perceived world (prapanca) that is, existence in all its variety. If karma is due to passion, klesa, and klesa is due to vikalpa (which is accompanied by samkalpa, kalpana and parikalpa, intellectual systematization), then the battle should be joined against vikalpa, and, indeed philosophical activity enters into it here as well. In general, the purpose of yoga is to transcend discursive thought. As soon as vikalpa has differentiated the expansion, the living beings discriminate between the phenomena produced and select them in groups of things (bhava) with specific forms of existence (svabhava). After that, comparisions and evaluations are made, and things are assigned values. This brings about the misconceptions (viparyasa), that something in itself should be attractive (suci), good (sukha), durable (nitya), or anything in and by itself (atman). Out of plain ignorance, one will not admit to oneself that in their true nature they are only abstractions (kevala) and empty hypostases.

That is why philosolphy enters the lists against the activity of vikalpa. Analytical insight (prajna) performs the task of inspecting the differentiated multiplicity and revealing it to be the web (jala) of the vikalpas. The philosophical examination begins by taking the premisses of the ignorant as given. After all, they are in the power of karma and the klesas. Now, let us suppose, as is claimed that there really is a multiplicity of independent entities (svabhava); then that must imply that every single thing (bhava) is cognizable in itself, that it is independent of anything else. It must naturally be unqualified, and as such immutable and a unity. It cannot be composite, for then it would be nothing in itself. As such it really exists nor does not exist, like an image.

Nagel, Ernest (1901-)

a Czech born American philosopher who was chiefly interested in logic and philosophy of science. His important works are: An Introduction to Logic and Scientific Method: The Structure of Science.

naiads myth

fresh-water nymphs.

naive realism

the perfectly gratuitous view that all of the qualities we sense in objects—including sounds, colours, tastes, smells, and tactile sensations, as well as shapes and motions—are in fact characteristics of these objects.

nakshatra

star.

name

a linguistic expression that denotes a particular object or a quality. Proper names are the names given to the objects, qualities, persons, etc. For example, Rama, Ganga etc., are the names of persons.

Nanak

founder of the Sikh religion.

Narcissus

son of the river-god Cephissus. He was, according to legend, a most handsome young man who, for spurning the love of the nymph Echo, was made by Nemesis to be enamoured by the image of himself reflected in the water of a spring. His own love being thus unrequited he pined away and became the flower that now bears his name.

nastika

Sanskrit term which means 'denier'. It applies to any Indian system of thought not accepting the authority of the Vedas. Examples are Charvaka, and Buddhism. To be contrasted with the Astika system which accept the Vedas as authoritative.

natural deduction system

refers to a set of rules for the construction of deductive arguments without any axioms or postulates.

naturalism

this term refers to the philosophical belief that what is studied by the non-human and human sciences is all there is, and the denial of the need for any explanation going beyond or outside the Universe.

naturalistic fallacy

the mistake (which it is not universally agreed always is a mistake) of deducing conclusions about what ought to be from premises that state only what is the case; or the other way about. This was first labelled by G.E. Moore in Principle Ethica (1903).

natural language

the languages such as English, Hindi, Russian etc., are called natural languages. They are different from the artificial languages like Esperanto or Ido.

natural rights

the rights which belong to man by nature, resting not on custom or convention, but on self-evident Principles or fundamental laws of reason.

natural theology

the attempt to prove the existence of God, and sometimes human immortality too, from premises provided by observation of the ordinary course of nature.

natura naturans and natura naturata

Latin phrases meaning 'nature naturing' and 'nature natured', respectively. 'Nature naturing, applies to God as the creative principle of created things, or infinite and eternal Being over against finite, termporal beings. 'Nature natured' applies to the created things which find their principle in God.

nature

from the Latin nature, a translation of the Greek word physis. Both terms derive from roots suggesting production, growth and bringing to birth. Thus the early signification of the term concerned that part of the reality subject to change; and physics was the name of the study charged with the understanding of this aspect of reality.

Nauplius

king of Euboea who, in revenge for the death of his son Palamedes, caused the wreck of many of the Greek ships returning from the Trojan war.

naya

a Sanskrit term which means 'aspect or standpoint'. In Jainism, there are seven nayas from which one can view reality.

necessary and contingent truth

a proposition is said to be necessarily true, or to express a logically necessary truth, if the denial of that proposition would involve a self contradiction; a proposition which happens to be contigently true, or to express a logically contingent truth, is one which could nevertheless be denied, or asserted, without self contradiction.

necessary and sufficient conditions

this is a necessary condition for that if that cannot be without this. This is a sufficient condition for that if this is by itself enough to guarantee that. Necessary and sufficient conditions may both be either logically necessary or logically contingent.

necessitarianism

refers to the doctrine that all events happen by necessity, having either logical or causal determination, and that the will is not free. A synonym for 'determinism'.

necessity

from the Latin ne('not') plus cedere ('to go away'). The Greek term is anagke, and the original concept probably concerned fate or destiny. Necessity may be affirmed of propositions, or things, or of God.

When affirmed of propositions, to say that a proposition is possible to deny that proposition.

necessity and chance

these are two important philosophical categories. These philosophical categories reflect the essence and the manifestations of phenomena. Necessity operates through laws. Whereas chance may or may not occur. It many take any form. In logic, necessity represents univeasality and certainty.

negation

from the Latin term nego, meaning 'deny'. In philosophy the term applies to the denial of a class or property, statement or proposition.

negation of the negation, law of

it is one of the laws of dialectcs, according to which a particular theory or a paradigm is not completely annihilated or negated by a new one, but some of the essential features of an old theory or a paradigm are assimilated into the new.

neleus

he and his brother Pelias were sons of Tyro by Poseidon. He became king of Pylos. All 12 of his sons, excepting only Nestor, were killed by Heracles.

nemesis

Greek and subsequently Roman goddess of retribution, expressing in particular the righteous indignation of the gods at human presumption. She also corrected the balance when fortune obviously favoured any mortal. Her best-known shrine was at Rhamnus in Attica.

neo-confucianism

(Chinese tao hsues : the learning of the Way). A vague term often applied to all developments in Confucianism from the Sung revival in the 11th century onward. This began as a deliberate effort to restore Confucian authority over a society in which, since the 5th century, Buddhism had become entrenched at every level.

neo-hegelianism

neo-hegelianism flourished under the patronage of T.H. Green, F.H. Bradley, J. Royce, and J. McTaggart. Neo-Hegelianism limits its application to the consciousness alone. Its main objective is to defend religion and speculative philosophy.

neo-kantianism

an umbrella term for several philosophical movements in Germany between about 1870 and 1920, often very disparate but all tracing their inspiration back to the spirit, critical method, and works of Kant. They diverged over the emphasis that they place on different parts of the Kant's work, but shared a reaction against speculative metaphysics and a return to the Kantian intention of a synthesis of empiricsm and rationalism. Six different (and often opposing) schools are usually distinguished, perhaps the most influential being the Marburg school.

neoplatonism

according to Neoplatonism, matter is the lowest link in the hierarchy of the Universe. Neoplatonic school was founded by Plotinus. The idealistic doctrines of Plato have been transformed into theosophy. As such, Neoplatonism was against Christianity. It incorporated numerous elements of Oriental magic and mythology. It was also considered to be a link between ancient and medieval thought.

Neoptolemus

son of Achilles by Deidameia, daughter of Lycomedes. He tock part in the Trojan war, making a name for himself as a redoubtable warrior. He slew Priam. He also received Andromache as his captive. Returning safely to Greece he married Hermione, daughter of Menelasu and Helen, and settled in Epirus. He is said to have met with a violent death at Delphi.

neopythagereanism

a movement, originating in the 1st century BC, the main tenet of which were a blend of the teaching of Pythagoras with Platonic, Stoic and Peripatetic material. Mysticism, number symbolism, and astrology were characteristic of Neopythagorean thought, and it was an important precursor of Neoplatonism.

neo-realism

a twentieth century philosophical trend represented by the philosophers like G.E. Moore and Russell. Neo-realist theory of knowledge is based on the view that cognisable thing can directly enter the mind. It recognises the existence of particulars only.

neo-taoism

(Chinese hsueh: mysterious learning). An eclectic form of Taoism that flourished in China. Its exponents used the Lao-tzu, Chuaug-tzu, and I-ching (Book of Changes) as a basis for discussing problems such as the relation between being and non-being and the nature of the absolute knowledge and communication.

neo-thomism

the movement reviving the actual or supposed ideas of St. Thomas Aquinas.

Neptune, Neptunus

Roman god of water; later elevated to god of the sea after his identification with the Greek Poseidon.

Nereus

old sea-god and son of Pontus and Ge. His wife Doris bore him the Nereids or seanymphs.

Nestor

sole surviving son of Neleus. He took part in the battle between the Centaurs and the Lapithae and was also among the Argonauts. He lived to a great age and acquired much wisdom, which he often voiced. He was noted, too, for his love of reminiscene, particularly of his war experiences.

nestorianism

a christological doctrine of the 5th century A.D. advanced by Nestorius, Patriarch of Constantinople. Terming it a 'prosopic-union' of the divine and human (from the Greek term prosopon meaning 'face'), Nestorius held 'the manhood is the face of the God head, and the Godhead is the face of the manhood'. This 'was misinterpreted as the doctrine that the God man is two complete person. It is this misinterpretation that bears the name, Nestorian heresy.

neti netie

Sanskrit phrase which means 'Not this, not this'. Employed in the Upanishad, and by shankara as the only appropriate definition of Brahman.

Neurath, Otto (1882-1945)

one of the leading members of logical positivism who developed the thesis of physicalism. According to physicalism, all empirical statements can ultimately be reducible to physicalistic language. This enables us the intersubjective understanding of language. Neurath held the view that verification consists in comparing one set of statements with another set of statements rather than directly with any form of experience.

neutral monism

the doctrine that the basic entities of the world are neither physical nor mental, but of some neutral 'stuff' which, organized in one manner, yields physical entities, or bodies and when organized in another manner, yields mind. The doctrine was held.

new philosophers, the

a group of French social philosophers, coming into prominence in the 1970's Anti-establishment, anti-Marxist and anti-ideolgical, they are the fruit of the May, 1986, student and worker uprising. Among 1444; Apology for Learned Ignorance, 1449; The Idiot, 1450. The vision of God, 1453; On the Peace of Faith, 1453; as well as mathematical treatises.

Newton, Issac (1642-1727)

British mathematician and physicist who formalized Galilean mechnics, discovered the inverse sqaure law of universal gravitation, and made notable contributions to the theory of light.

nihilism

a philosophical viewpoint that denies every positive ideal or goal. This term was first introduced by Jacobi.

Nike

Greek goddess of victory and identified by the Romans with Victoria; mentioned by Hesiod as daughter of the Titan Pallas and of Styx, and as sister of Zelos (Rivalry), Kratos (Strength) and Bia (Force).

Niobe

daughter of Tantalus and wife of Amphion, to whom she bore 6 sons and 6 daughters (some say 7 of each). For boasting that she was at least equal to Leto, whose 2 children were Apollo and Artemis, her own brood were all killed by Apollo and Artemis. Niobe herself, whose tears were ceaseless, was turned by Zeus into a stone.

nirguna brahman

from the Sanskrit nir ('without') plus guna ('attributes'). Hence, that from of Brahman without attributes or qualities.

nirvana

Sanskrit term which means 'blown out', referring to the extinction of all worldly desires. Referring to the state of release, or salvation, the term is most often associated with Buddhism.

nishada

hunter.

nisus

a Latin term which means 'striving'.

niyama

the second step of Yogic mediation, that of positive ethical preparation.

noetic

1. in general, cognitive.

2. in contrast to empirical and sensuous, pertaining to that

which can be apprehended by reason alone.

nomic

any explanation that is subjected to the laws of nature is called nomic.

nominalism

(in scholastic philosophy) the view that universals have no existence independently of being thought and are mere names, representing nothing that really exists. The nominalist thus denies anything like Plato's theory of Forms or Ideas.

nomothetic

proposing or prescribring a law (of nature).

noncontradiction, principle of

probably the better name for that one of the three laws of thought usually called the Principle of Contradiction. If we accept as its standard statement, 'It is not the case that p is true and not-p is true,' the principle urges upon us the avoidance of contradiction, and hence the appropriateness of the above name.

non-euclidean geometry

the geometry that does not accept the parallel postulate of Euclid. Euclidean Geometry provides certain postulate from which all the theorems can be deducted.

non sequitur

a Latin term for 'it does not follow'. This expression is applicable only for drawing conclusions irrespective of their validity.

no-ownership theory

a metaphysical doctrine of the self, labelled by Strawson. It arises from Cartesian mind-body dualism and maintains that conscious experiences associated with a subject cannot be said to 'belong' to that consciousness : 'Only those things whose ownership is logically transferable can be owned at all'.

normal form

a notion that plays an important role in proof theory. In trying to prove a result about a language L in which proofs can be constructed according to the stipulated rules of inference, it is useful to know that, or whether, all propositions expressible in the language can be expressed in some standard (or normal) form.

normative

tending to establish a standard of correctness by prescription of rules; evalutive rather than descriptive.

normative ethics

the traditional view of Ethics that it is part of the task of the moral philosopher to provide guidance with respect to issues of right and wrong, good and evil. Normative ethics is to be distinguished from Meta. Ethics, the analysis of the logic of ethics and the systems of those who treat of Normative ethics.

nothing

the term is a synonym for the philosophical term, 'non-being', and is thus the formal complement to the term, 'being'. The fact of this complementarity has led even those who wish to grant reality only to various kinds of being, to make reference to non-being, or nothing.

no-true-scotsman move

the term used for a nickname for a manoeuvre that meets the falsification of some cherished generalization by maintaining that the predicate in question, while not perhaps applicable to all run of the mill so-and-sos, is nevertheless essential to true so-and sos.

Notus, Notos

the Greek personification of the south wind.

noumeaon

from the Greek noumenon which means equality 'thing perceived' and 'what is known'. Plato used the term occasionally and always in the latter sense, to refer to the intelligibles or 'thing of thought'.

nous

(Greek for : mind). A term used by the Presocratics to indicate knowledge and reason. For Plato is meant, the rational part of the soul. For Aristotle it was the intellect, in which he distinguished between active and passive reason, the former alone being immortal and eternal.

null (or empty) set

the set with no members. It is usually symbolized as ϕ.

numerical identity

the same is the sense of one and the same thing.

number

beginning with the Pythagorean insight that reality is to be understood in terms of numerical expressions the status of number and the nature of numerical entities have occupied philosophers no less than have the status and nature of ideas. Indeed, the basic positions of Realism. Conceptualism, and Nominalism, which appear in the discussions of universals reappear in the corresponding discussion of number. In these discussions, however, the terms favoured for the respective positions are Platonism, Intutionism and Nominalism.

nyaya

one of the six systems of Indian thought to arise in the period following the Vedic Age, and the formation of the Bhagavad-Gita and many of the sutras. The system was founded by a man named Gautama. It shares with the Vaisesika system a metaphysics which endorses atomistic pluralism and logical realism. But while Vaisesika stresses the metaphysical and ontological side of things, Nyaya is directed toward consideration of logical and epistemological problems.

Nyaya provide the logic, as it were, for the other systems.

Nyctimene

daughter of Èpopeus, king of Sicyon; she took refuge in a forest after having been raped by her father; Athena transformed her into an owl.

Nyx

ancient Greek personification of night; daughter of Chaos; sister of Erebus, Hypnos and Thanatos were her sons.

object

from the Latin ob ('over against') and jacere ('to throw'). The ordinary current meaning of object is that which exists in its own right, as a thing outside the mind. But, intially, that was the meaning of the word 'subject'. When the term came into philosophy use in the Middle Ages the widely held meaning of object (or objectum) was whatever is designated by any intentions reference.

object language

the discussion of a language in metalanguage. For instance, 'Delhi is the capital of India' is the object language.

objectivity

the opposite to subjectivity. Manner of writing in which the author does not comment or take sides but leaves the facts to speak for themselves.

obligation

from the Latin obligare (from ob, 'to', and ligare, 'to bind'). One important tradition in ethics centers on the ideas of obligation and duty. The theory of obligation is called deontology from the Greek deon ('obligation'). Deontic logic studies the types of necessity present in statements of obligation.

observation

a purposive perception of the objective reality that provides us with the primary data for various claims to knowledge. Observation may be simple or complex, or direct or indirect. It is regarded as one of the postulates of scientific investigation.

obverse

refers to the statement which is derived by observation of the original and logically equivalent to it. Obversion of a categorical statement is performed by negating the predicate term and changing the statement from negative to affirmative, or vice versa.

obversion

in scholastic logic, a form of immediate, inference. Aristotle did not regard it as a valid form of inference.

Occam, William of (1283-1349)

a medieval British theologian and scholastic philosopher who advocated nominalism. He introduced a principle of ontological economy that holds that do not multiply entities beyond necessity. Such a principle is popularly known as Occam's razor.

occassion

an external circumstance that provides an impulse for other events. Occassion may give rise to one or other phenomenon.

occasionalism

a doctrine which was put forward by Malebranche. This doctrine attempts to plug a notorious gap in the Cartesian thinking (in the mind body problem. How can mind and body, supposed to be two radically distinct substances, causally interact)? The occasionalists baldly deny and such interaction to be possible: the will of man is incapable of moving the smallest body. How then does my arm go up when I will it?

The true cause, claim the occasionalists, is divine intervention, my willing being merely the occasion for that intervention.

occasional verse

verse written for an occasion or a special event, such as a royal birthday.

occultism

the doctrine that admits the existence of supernatural forces beyond scientific investigation.

Oceanus

son of Uranus and Ge; husband of Tethys and father of the Oceanids (sea-nymphs) and river-gods. He was believed to be the god of the waters encircling the earth.

ockhamism

the term used for the movement of thought initiated by William of Ockham. It consisted in criticism of Scholaasticism, an emphasis on empirical method, and a heightened appreciation of the role of religious faith.

ockham's razor

the principle of ontological economy, usually formulated as 'Entities are not to be multiplied beyond necessity'. These actual words are not in fact to be found in the extant works of William of Ockham.

Odysseus

son and successor of Laertes, king of Ithaca, and father of Telemachus. He is the leading figure in Homer's 'Odyssey' and also appears in the 'Iliad'. He was a man of outstanding bravery, eloquence, and shrewdness.

The 'Odyssey' recounts his adventures over a period of 10 years following the fall of Troy. He first attacked the Cicones at Ismarus, unsuccessfully, and then visited the country of the Lotophagi, or Lotus-eaters, and later that of the Cyclops. Here he fell into the hands of Polyphemus, but contrived to escape by blinding the one-eyed giant, although only after the Cyclops had devoured 6 of the adventurer's companions. He next arrived at Aeolia, the home of Aeolus, who gave him a bag containing all the winds except that needed to bring him home. While Odysseus slept his crew untied the bag and released its contents, which at once blew their ship back to Aeolia, whose inhabitants then declined to help them further. After 6 days sailing Odysseus reached the city of the Laestrygones; he escaped that danger only to land on Aeaea, home of the sorceress Circe, who straight away changed a party of his men, sent out to reconnoitre, into swine.

At her behest, Odysseus journeyed to the land of the Cimmerians, where he entered Hades and met Tiresias, who showed him many other ghosts in the underworld and instructed him to sacrifice to Poseidon in order to appease the god's anger for the injury done to his son Polyphemus. Returning to Aeaea he was sent by Circe on a course which brought him to the island of the Sirens and between Scylla and Charybdis; some of his crew were lost.

Thus he arrived at the island where the cattle of Helios (the sun) were pastured, and his men killed some of the beasts for food, so angering the god, who induced Zeus, when they again put to sea, to destroy their ship with a thunderbolt. Odysseus alone escaped, drifting on a fragment of the vessel to Ogygia, where the nymph Calypso dwelt, whose prisoner he became for 7 years. He was eventually released by order of Zeus (at Athena's intercession) and built a boat by means of which he approached the island of Scheria, home of the Phaeacians, only to be shipwrecked again—this time by Poseidon in sight of land. He swam ashore and fell asleep. Nausicaa and her maidens awoke him. At the court of the her father, king Alcinous, Odysseus related his adventures and misfortunes and was given a ship to take him home at last after his long absence.

On arrival at Ithaca he disguised himself as a beggar, but his faithful old dog Argus recognized him, and with the help of Telemachus, now a grown man, he disposed of the suitors of his wife Penelope by killing them with the bow which he alone could draw. Reconciled with his family 20 years after his departure, he settled down. Odysseus was admired by the Greeks for his determination, cunning, and resourcefulness.

Oedipus

son of Laius, king of Thebes and his wife Jocasta. Unwittingly he married his mother, who, on discovering what had happened, hanged herself. Oedipus blinded himself and went into exile, though accounts of his end vary.

oedipus effect

refers to the impact of the making of a statement, in particular a predictive statement, upon the human situation which that statement refers.

Ogyges

king of Thebes in whose reign a disastrous flood occured in Boeotia and Attica.

oligarchy

from the Greek oligoi ('few') and arche ('rule'). The term literally signifies a form of government characterized by minority rule. For Plato and Aristotle, howevever, it stood for that form of government where the wealthy few rule for their own interests.

Olympus

the higest mountain in Greece, on the border of Macedonia and Thessaly; the legendary home of the gods.

Om

a Sanskrit term connoting assent. Originally, aum, the three letters respectively standing for the absolute, the relative, and the relation between them. Now the mystic and sacred syllable of Hinduism, identified in the Is-a, Mundaka, Mandukya, Taittiriya, and Chandogya Upanishads as standing for the whole world and its parts, including past, present, and future, as well as for Atman, the self of all things. Pronunciation of the syllable in relgious devotion and meditation is a feature of many Indian based systems.

omnipotence

from the Latin omnis ('all') and potens ('powerful'). One of the chief attributes of the absolutistic conception of God. That view should be compared with others in which God is regarded as finite in some respect and infinite in other respects. Nor is the conception of God as a finite bieng negligible in Western thought.

omnipresence

one of the traditional attributes of God. If a thing or being is where it works, then the problem of the divine omnit presence becomes part of the problem of omnipotence and he distinctions important to that concept likwise apply here.

omniscience

from the Latin omnis ('all') and scire ('to know'). Traditionally, one of the chief attributes of God.

In traditional theology the attributes of omniscience includes completely detailed knowledge of the future as well as knowledge of the past and present.

omniscience paradoxes of

problems arising over how God's omniscience can be consistent with his timelessness on his granting freewill to mankind, given that omniscience includes fore-knowledge of future events (including human actions).

one

from the Latin unus and the Greek oine. In Pythagorean number theory the 'one' and the 'Dyad' generate all other numbers.

For Plato the One interpenetrates with Beauty, Truth, and the Good to make something close to a single eternal principle.

one many problem

refers to the problem of how we should account for the fact that we can correctly apply one and the same word to many distinct things.

oncological argument

an argument for God which moves from the definition of His nature as a perfect being to the conclusion that he exists. The argument has several versions.

ontological argument

an argument for God which moves from the definition of His nature as a perfect being to the conclusion that He exists. The argument has several versions.

ontology

refers to the branch of metaphysical enquiry which is concerned with the study of existence itself (considered apart from the nature of any existent object). It differentiates between 'real existence' and 'appearance' and investigates the different ways in which entities belonging to various logical categories (physical objects, numbers, universals, abstractions, etc.) may be said to exist.

open question argument

it is an argument introduced by G.E. Moore to show that 'good' is indefinable. He argues that if 'X' is 'Y' is a definition, then the question 'Is YX?' cannot be substantial. But all the questions of the form 'Is X good?' are open questions.

open society

a society structured to allow its members to advance to whatever level their capacities allow.

open texture

the expression introduced in an influential 1945 article by Fricdrich Waismann as a translation of his original German coinage Porositat der Begriffe. It is not, he explained to be confused with vagueness, being rather the possibility of vagueness. It characterizes most though not all empirical concepts.

operation

a one place operation is a function of one argument whose range is included in its domain.

operationalism

a popular theory in philosophy of science that tries to explain the physical entities, properties and processes in terms of a set of operations and experiments by which they are understood.

operator

refers to the which effects an operation. In logic it is usually expressed as a symbol. Corresponding to each function on objects there is a symbolic operation effected by the symbol for that function.

opinion

parmenides, contrasted opinion with truth, the former relating to sense experience and dealing with appearance, the latter relating to thought and dealing with reality and being.

Ops

Roman goddess of plenty, associated with Saturn.

optimism and pessimism

contrasting attitudes concerning the predominace of good or evil in the world. The former represents general hopefulness regarding the balance of pleasure and pain; the latter the view that hope is unreasonable and that happiness, if attainable, lies beyond the sphere of ordinary experience. The prevailing tone of a particular philosophical system depends mainly upon that system's cosmology and its account of man's role in the universe.

or

a logical connective that can be used in its exclusive or in its inclusive sense. In its exclusive sense, it takes the following form: 'He is either insane or pretending to be insane'. In its inclusive sense, it takes the following form: 'He is either mad or lazy or both'.

oracles, chaldean

a philosophical poem of the 2nd century A.D. describing the descent of the soul into the realm of matter and its possible rise after purification, through the concentric circles of the universe toward its eterm home. Containing Platonic.

order

an arrangement in accordance with intention, principle or rule.

According to Hesig order came out of the chaos through the power of Eros. In addition to eros Greek philosophy has explored many other possible ordering principles including mind and chance variation. Both linear and hierarchical order are implicit in Plato's notion that the world of change has as its pattern a world of ideas. The possibility of graded order is likewise present in medieval thought where the idea of order depends upon a relation of adequation or, commensurability between a thing and its idea in the mind of God.

ordered pair

a pair that basic property of which is that two pairs are identical if the first members of each are identical and the second members of each are identical.

order type

the set of all sets ordinally similar to a given set.

ordinary language

any nontechnical language is called ordinary language. The words of ordinary language will have standard use.

ordination

solemn appointment to an order of ministry in the Church. The book containing the form of such appointment is called the ordinal.

Orestes

son of Agamemnon and Clytemnestra. Saved by his sister Electra from sharing Agamemnon's fate, he avenged his father's death by murdering both his mother and her lover, Aegisthus. But for his own dire crime of matricide he was driven mad and pursued by the Erinyes until (according to the one version) he took refuge, on Apollo's advice, in the temple of Athena at Athens. According to another version he was sent to fetch the statue of Artemis at Chersonesus Taurica, accompanied by his bosom friend Pylades. He eventually inherited his father's kingdom and married Hermione, widow of Neoptolemus.

organismic bilogy

the name of that interpretation of biology which stresses the non-reductionistic nature of the organic level, taking the position that the whole cannot be equated simply with the sum of the activities of the parts.

organon

(Greek for: instrument, tool (Latin Organum),. The name traditionally given to Artistotle's six treatises on logic: Categories; De Interpretation; Prior Analytics; Posterior Analytics Topics; and Sophistical Refutations.

original sin

according to Christian tradition, every human being inherits the sin that he was brought into the world through the disobedience of Adam and Eve. Only by means of Divine grace every human individual can be rescued from such a state.

Orion

Boeotian giant and hunter who at Chios fell in love with Merope. But his ill-treatment of the girls so angered her father that he, with the help of Dionysus, deprived the giant of his sight. Orion, however, was told by an oracle that he would be able to see again if he exposed his eyeballs to the rays of the rising sun. This he did with the assistance of Hephaestus, and his sight was restored. There are many different accounts of his death; some say he was killed (perhaps accidentally) by Artemis, with whom he associated. Afterwards he was placed among the stars.

Orpheus

legendary Greek poet and musician. He was the son of Oeagrus, king of Thrace, and husband of Eurydice. She, having died, it was said, from the bite of a snake, was followed by Orpheus into the Underworld, where he persuaded Hades to permit her to return to earth with him, the condition being that he should not look at her on his upward journey. In its earlier form the tale ended happily. In the later form Orpheus found the condition impossible; glancing at his beloved wife he thus lost her for ever.

orphism

a modern term for two related but different phenomena of ancient Greek religion.

1. a massive tradition of writing, beginning as early as the 7th century BC and supposedly inspired, if not composed, by the mythical singer Orpheus.

2. the way of life expected of those initiated into the Mysteries of Eleusis.

Orthia

spartan name for Artemis. At her altar Spartan boys were ritually flogged.

orthodoxy

from the Greek orthos ('right') and doxa ('opinion'). Correctness of belief as determined by an authoritative standard. To be contrasted with heterodoxy or heresy.

Osiris

Egyptian deity, thought of mainly as god of the Underworld, who with Isis figured in one of the popular Hellenistic mystery-cults.

othering

Plato's concept of negation.

other minds

the problem whether and how anyone knows that any other organism is sentient. For, surely, there is no contradiction in suggesting that the behaviour and talk of others might in every way resembe mine though they were unconscious automata; while someone in a cataleptic trace might be to all appearance dead, yet conscious.

ousia

it is a Greek term for 'substance'. It is one of the ten categories listed by Aristotle. It is also understood as reality.

paganism

heathenism (as viewed by Christians); especially the polytheism of the ancient Graeco-Roman world.

Paine, Thomas (1737-1809)

a British born American political philosopher who held the view that the government and the society are two different things. His attack on Christianity brought him the fame as an atheist. His important works include: The Rights of Man; The Age of Reason.

paksha

fortnight.

Palamedes

son of Nauplius; he took part in the war against Troy. He exposed the deceit of Odysseus who, in order to avoid joining the expedition, feigned madness. Odysseus, however, had his revenge. He planted under Palamedes' bed a letter appearing to implicate him in treacherous dealing with Priam. The ruse was successful and Palamedes was stoned to death. He was remembered in ancient Greece especially for his inventiveness.

Palladium
sacred image of Athena, said to have been given to Troy's founder at Zeus. On it the city's safety depended.

Pan
Greek god of flocks and herds; represented as half goat in shape, having the animal's legs, ears, and horns. In time he came to be regarded as the personification of Nature itself. His sudden appearance—he had a way of darting upon them—used to frighten travellers; hence the word panic. He was the inventor of the syrinx, or Pan-pipes; his favourite sport was to roam the hills and valleys of Arcadia chasing nymphs.

Pandareos
native of Miletus whose daughters were carried off by the Harpies and given to the Erinyes as servants.

Pandarus
Trojan archer favoured by Apollo.

panentheism
from the Greek pan and theos, meaning 'all in God'. The view that all reality is part of the being of God. To be distinguished from Pantheism which identifies God with the total reality.

panis
robbers.

panlogism
a philosophical view that advocates that all the development in nature and society is the realisation of the logical activity of the universal mind. It conceives that the law of logic are the only driving forces of all development. Hegel is considered to be an advocate of panlogism.

panpsychism
the theory that holds that the world is rendered more comprehensible on the assumption that every object is invested with a soul or mind.

pansomatism
the doctrine of Kotarbinski that every sentient entity is a body.

pantheism
refers to the doctrine that the divine is all-inclusive and that man and Nature are not independent of God, but re modes or elements of his Being. Its precise significance—if such indeed there is—depend on the initial conceptions of God (and indepenence).

pantomime
1. representation in dumb show. 2. Elaborate Christmas entertainment for children of all ages.

papa
sin.

papacy
the office of the Roman Pope; the supreme government of the Roman Catholic Church.

parable

short tale that illustrates a moral principle, usually by setting forth the application of the principle to something familiar to the hearer.

paraclete

from the Greek paradaleo ('to call to one'). Hence, a witness, advocate, helper, or comforter. The term is usually applied to the role of the Holy Spirit.

paradigm

in the philosophy of science, a central overall way of regarding phenomena, within which a scientist normally works.

paradigm case argument

refers to the argument that infers from the fact that a word is taught by reference to clear (paradigm) cases, the conclusion that examples of the thing referred to by the word must exist.

paradigm case argument

this argument intends to disprove sceptical contentions by holding that when someone says that this is not certain, then it tantamounts to saying that there is something called certainty.

paradox

a situation when, from a number of premises all generally accepted as true, a conclusion is reached by valid deductive argument, that is either an outright contradiction or conflicts with other generally held beliefs.

parallelism, psychophysical

the doctrine that there is one-to-one correspondence of physical and psychical events throughout the universe.

paralogism

from the Greek para ('beside') and logos ('reason'). Thus, the idea of a conclusion which does not follow reason, i.e., a fallacious syllogism.

paramatman

divine soul, the supreme godhead.

parameshvara

the supreme godhead.

paraphrase

the restaining in other words of the meaning of a piece of writing.

parapsychology

a branch of psychology that is concerned with the forms of senuality which cannot be expalined by means of sense - organs. In other words, it deals with the extra sensory perception.

Paris

second son of Priam and Hecuba, brought up by a shepherd on Mt Ida. He married Oenone, but deserted her for Helen. When Eris threw the golden apple, inscribed 'To the fairest', among the wedding guests at the nuptials of Peleus and Thetis—she herself not having been invited—the honour of possessing it was claimed simultaneously by Hera, Athena, and Aphrodite; Zeus decreed that judgment should lie with Paris. Hera promised him, should he decide in favour of her, the rule of Asia; Athena offered renown in war, and Aphrodite the most beautiful woman in the world for his wife. Aphrodite won, and his reward was the hand of Helen, wife of Menalaus. The result was the Trojan war. Paris fought with Menelaus forces before the city and was defeated, but was saved by Aphrodite. He was said to have killed Achilles, but to have been himself wounded by Philoctetes with one of Heracles' poisoned arrows. He then returned to Oenone, who refused to heal his injury, of which he at last died. She, in her sorrow, took her own life.

parody

imitation of another author's work, where ridicule is the main objective.

Pascal, Blaise (1623-1662)

a French mathematician, philosopher, and a physicist who founded the theory of probability. He weaved between rationalism and scepticism and maintained the superiority of faith over reason.

Pascal's wager

an argument known chiefly from its formulation by Pascal in his posthumous Pensees, but certainly developed earlier.

Pasiphae

daughter of Helios by Perse and wife of Minos, king of Crete. She was so passionately attracted by a magnificent bull sent to her husband by the god Poseidon for sacrifice that she had sexual intercourse with it and so gave birth to a monster, the Minotaur.

pasquinade

lampoon publicly exhibited; from pasquino, the name given to an ancient Roman statue upon which such attacks were affixed.

passion

from the Latin passio, a translation of the Greek pathos ('a passive condition').

One of the categories of Aristotle passion contrasts with action and refers to the condition of a thing as acted upon by other things. The passion of a thing thus refers not to the essence but to the accidents of things, and has a passive sense.

passover

the Jewish feast, observed on the 14th of the month Nisan (Nisan aprox. = April), commemorating the destruction of the first-born of the Egyptians and the passing over of the Israelites by the destroying angel. The term is sometimes applied figuratively to Christ, the Paschal Lamb.

past, the

one of the modes of time, the concept of the past has not received a great deal of attention in terms philosophical analysis.

Bergson presented a doctrine of the past as internal to the present. His analogy is that of a rolling snowball containing its erlier states.

Patanjali

a great seer and sage who was

the founder of Yoga system. He is the author of Yoga Sutra. According to Patanjali, spiritual realisation is the only way to free from all limitations of body, the senses and the mind.

pathetic fallacy

the accepted name for the mistake not strictly a fallacy- of attributing to inanimate objects the feelings, dispositions, and reactions which could only characterise animate creatures, and in particular people.

patristics

from the Latin pater ('father'). The term refers to the Church Fathers and their works in the period between the end of the New Testament, period, and the beginnings of Scholasticism with Erigena in the 9th century.

Patroclus

close friend and personal attendant of Achilles. He was killed by Hector.

pavamana

that which has been purified.

Pax

Roman personification of peace. Identified with the Greek Irene.

peano's postulates

five postulates (or axioms) from which the rest of the arithmetic can be developed. They were presented by Giuseppe Peano, in 1889 (although Richard Dedekind had in fact published them previously in 1888) in order to free the concept of number from dependence upon mere institution. They are:

(1) 0, is a number.

(2) the successor of any number is a number.

(3) no two numbers have the same successor.

(4) 0 is not the successor of any number.

(5) if P is a predicate true of 0, and if whenever P is true of a number n its is also true of the successor of n, then P is the true of every number.

Pearson, Karl (1857-1936)

a British philosopher and mathematician who maintained that the task of science is to classify and describe facts. As a true follower of Mach, he believed that material objects are nothing but a bundle of sensations.

Pegasus

winged horse, the offspring of the dying Gorgon, Medusa, killed by Perseus. Pegasus carried the thunderbolt of Zeus. He was the mount of both Bellerophon when he slew the Chimaera and Persues in his rescue of Andromeda. He was regarded as a symbol of poetic genius. Springs of water gushed forth at the strike of his hoof.

Peirithous

king of the Lapithae and son of Ixion in Greek legend. It was at his marriage-feast that the bride, Hippodameia, was abducted by a Centaur, thus causing the fight between the

Lapithae and the Centaurs. Afterwards he sought to wed Persephone and went down with his friend Theseus to the Underworld to claim her. For this Hades fastened him for ever to a rock to be tomented.

pelagianism

a heresy, propagated by the 5th-century British monk Pelagius. It denied original sin and held that man can, of his own freewill and without the intervention of God's grace, live sinless and attain eternal life.

Peleus

son of Aeacus, king of Myrmidons. He and his brother Telamon murdered their own half-brother Phocus, for which crime their father banished them both. Peleus then went to Phthia, marrying there Antigone, the daughter of its king Eurytion. At the Calydonian boar-hunt he accidentally killed his father-in-law and was again exiled. He took refuge at Iolcos, where Hippolyte (or Astydameia), wife of Acastus, tried to seduce him, accusing him of attempting to dishnour her when he declined her advances. For this Acastus took away Peleus sword while he was asleep during a hunting expedition on Mt Pelion, but he was saved from danger by Hermes and returned to Iolcos, where he slew both Acatus and Hippolyte. His son, by the sea-goddess Thetis, was the great Achilles, whom he outlived.

Pelops

son of Tantalus. In childhood he was killed and cooked by his father, who served his flesh to the gods. They, however, restored him to life. As a youth he was given a present of wonderful horses by his lover, the god Poseidon, and became highly skilled at driving. When therefore Oenomaus, king of Pisa, offered the hand of his daughter Hippodamia to anyone who could beat him in a chariotrace, Plops entered for the contest, although 13 suitors had already been killed by Oenomaus for having lost, death for failure being part of the bargain. But the new competitor bribed the king's charioteer, Myritilus, to remove the linch-pins from his master's vehicle. Thus Oenomaus was thrown and fatally injured. Pelops married his daughter and succeeded to his throne. He took care to get rid of Myrtilus by drowning him in the sea. With his dying breath Myrtilus cursed Pelops, whose descendants suffered accordingly, though Pelops himself seems to have died peacefully.

penance

in Christian practive the Scrament of absolution, administered by a priest, in response to the penitent's contrition and confession.

Penates

Roman spirits of the store-cupboard, who, with the Lares,

were regarded as protectors of the house.

Penelope

wife of Odysseus, to whom she remained faithful during the long years of his absence from home.

pentateuch

the first 5 books of the Old Testament, traditionally ascribed to Moses authorship, but recognized by most biblical scholars to be a composite work of varying dates, its final form being the achievement of the post-Exilic Jewish priests.

pentecost

the Jewish festival of harvest, observed on the 50th day after the and day of Passover.

Penthesilea

daughter of Ares and queen of the Amazons.

Pentheus

grandson of Cadmus, whom he succeeded as king of Thebes. He resisted the importation into his realm of the cult of Dionysus, for which offence the god drove him mad and destroyed his palace. He was later killed by his own mother and other women of Thebes, who took him for a wild beast.

perception

from the Latin, percipio, which covers both the obtaining of knowledge through the senses, and apprehension with the mind.

Perdix

nephew of Daedalus and inventor of the saw, chisel, and compasses. Daedalus became jealous of his skill and threw him from the top of the temple of Athena on the Acropolis. As the fell the goddess changed him into a partridge.

perfection

from the Latin perfectio meaning 'completeness' or 'completion'. The concept has been applied primarily to God, and then in a derivative sense to man.

perfection, principle of

a principle of philosophy of Leibniz which states that God creates the best of all possible worlds that is, a world in which a maximum of perfection is achieved with a minimum of deficiency.

performative utterance

a term introduced by J.L. Austin, according to which an utterance such as 'I promise' is an fact of performance, but not a description of any act.

per genus et differentiam

a Lating term 'by kind and difference'. Aristotle's logic is used on this principle to define various things. Man as 'a rational animal' belongs to a particular species, but this species is a class of the much wider class called genus.

peripatetic

a follower of Aristotle, the word derivating from restless practices in his Lyceum.

perlocution

an utterance with precautionary effects. Effects that may (but need not) be caused by utterances (for example, embarrassment) are called their 'precautionary effects'.

per se notum

a Latin term for 'known through itself'. St. Thomas Aquinas used this term to anything that is self-evident.

Persephone

daughter of Zeus and Demeter; she was obliged to spend 6 months of the year in the Underworld with her husband Hades (Pluto), returning to earth again in the spring.

Perseus

son of Zeus by Danae; he was brought up at the court of king Polydectes, at whose request he slew the Gorgon Medusa. He married Andromeda, and on his return from Aethiopia turned Polydectes and his followers into stone by showing them the Gorgon's head (which he gave afterwards to Athena, who had aided him). He later visited Argos, where he accidentally killed his unwittingly fulfilling a prophecy of the oracle at Delphi. He himself became king of Tiryns and founder of the dynasty of the Perseidae.

person

from the Latin persona, a translation of the Greek prosopon, both words signifying the mask worn by actors on stage. By extension the reference is to the role an individual plays in the drama of life.

personal identity

a philosophical problem concerning the identity of a person. According to this problem what does it mean to say that at this time is the same person as that at that time.

personalism

the theory, largely of 20th-century. American origin, that the person is ontologically fundamental, and that all philosophical enquiry should proceed in reference to the concept of person.

perspectivism

refers to the view that the external world is to be interpreted through different alternative systems of concepts and beliefs and there is no authoritative independent criterion for determining that one system is more valid than another.

Petitio principil

it is a non-verbal fallacy called 'begging the question'. This fallacy occurs when a desired conclusion is drawn from a premises or a general proposition whose validity is in question. For example, it is argued that it is wrong to tax the industrialists as they promote trade in the country. It amounts to saying that "the taxes levied on industrialist is wrong". But this assumption needs adequate justification.

Phaedra

daughter of king Minos of Crete and wife of Theseus.

Phaethon

son of Helios; he was permitted by his father to drive the chariot of the sun for one day, but losing control of the horses he nearly set the earth on fire and was killed by Zeus.

phenomenalism

from the Greek phainomenon ('appearance'). The view that we know only phenomena, and that there are no things behind phenomena causing their appearance. When one separates the phenomena of which one is aware from the objects causing one to have this awareness, the problem arises of determining what these causative objects may be. The difficulties present in the dualism of phenomenon and object have led a number of philosophers to the position of phenomenalism.

phenomenology

a method introduced by Edmund Husserl. It is a study of the essence of intuitive processes. Thus it is an a priori method seeking knowledge by abstracting objects (bracketing out the reality) from their experiential context.

phenomenon

any object or occurrence perceived by the senses.

1. (in Greek philosophy). Sensible appearance, contrasted with the real object apprehended by the intellect.

2. (in Kant). The object interpreted through categories, contrasted with noumenon.

Philemon and Baucis

an old phrygian countryman and his wife. Zeus and Hermes, while on a visit to earth, having been refused hospitality elsewhere, were received by them. Warned by Zeus that the land would be flooded they became priest and priestess of a temple on the mountain where they had taken refuge. In the end they were changed into trees—Philemon into an oak and Baucis a lime.

Philoctetes

famous archer to whom Heracles bequeathed his poisoned arrows. He led a contingent to the Trojan war but was abandoned by the Greeks on Lemnos, suffering from a snake bite. Later, however, he was brought to Troy where he slew Paris with his arrows.

philosopheme

from the Greek philosophema referring to a philosophical proposition or demonstration. Aristotle used the term to distinguish demonstrative reasoning from rhetoric, eristic, and dialectic.

philosopher king

the term coined by Plato and used frequently in his Republic to justify the view that philosophers alone are fit to be the rulers as they possess highest wisdom. According to Plato, those who have the knowledge of the world of Forms are supposed to have endowed with wisdom.

philosopher's stone

the hypothetical substance sought by alchemists (alchemy) for converting base metals into gold. It appears in the alchemical literature under hundreds of different and fanciful names.

philosophes

it is a field of wisdom that is often distinguished from mere fields of learning, and pleasure.

philosophical radicals

followers of Bentham, themselves primarily theoreticians, who aimed at and achieved considerable practical influence.

philosophy

most of what might have appeared here as a general description of what philosophy is about. There are text articles on the various branches of philosophy : aesthetics, ethics, epistemology, logic, and metaphysics. Articles will also be found on the philosophies of education, history, language, law, mind, psychology, religion, science, and space and time, and on political and social philosophy.

philosophy of science

a discipline which attempts to relate philosophy to the fields of scientific inquiry. Depending upon the orientation of the philosopher and the area of the science, the goal of philosophy of science is to discover the nature of science, of the nature of scintific method, or the logic of science, or to explore the interfaces of the fields of science or to axiomatize the sciences—e.g., mathematics, physics—which are axiomatizable. In one sense the philosophy of science extends back to the origins of Western philosophy. From the origin of the philosophy until the period of the Sophists the emphasis of philosophy was on scientific knowledge. Plato and Aristotle devoted attention to science and, its methods. But the development of Philosophy of Science as a discipline required a prior development of the sciences. Hence, it is more appropriate to regard philosophy of science as beginning with the remarkable development of the sciences in the modern period.

Phlegethon

one of the rivers of the Underworld, running not with water but with flames.

phlogiston theory

an 18th-century explanation of combustion which held that every combustible substance contained phlogiston, an inflammable material substance. Phlogiston was thought to be consumed in the process of combustion, leaving the original substance behind. Propounded by J.J. Becher and G.E. Stahl, the theory remained viable for a century until Lavoisier produced his counter theory involving oxygen. Stahl, who defended the theory with great vigor, was influenced in the direction of animism and vitalism by J.B. Van Helmont.

Phoenix

1. fabulous bird of Egypt. When from time to time it destroyed itself on the burning altar of Heliopolis a new bird, fully fledged, sprang from the ashes.
2. Son of Amyntor and Cleobule, Phoenix was accused by his father's concubine of having violated her. Blinded by his father, he fled to Phthia where Chiron restored his slight and Peleus made him king of the neighbouring Dolopians. He then became a guardian of Achilles, whom he accompanied to the Trojan War.

phrastic and neustic

it was R.M.Hare who intrduced this distinction between the phrastic element and neustic element among the sentences. For example, the sentences 'please put on the light' (indicative sentence), 'Put on the light' (imperative sentence), 'Has he put on the light' (interrogative sentence), 'Has he put on the light' (interrogative sentence) have something in common, that is 'put on the light'. The phrastic element refers to this common element, whereas the neustic element refers to the element of difference among the sentences.

physicalism

refers to the doctrine that all proposition asserting 'matter of fact and real existence' can be formulated as statements about publicity observable physical objects and activities (Hume's fork).

physico-theological argument

Kant's teleological argument for the existence of God.

pitris

ancestors.

Plato 428-348 B.C.

Greek philosopher. Born in Athens. Studied under Socrates. Born of a distinguished Athenian family, he early intended to follow a political career, but the trial and death of Socrates turned him toward philosophy. After Socrate's death Plato left Athens, spending some time in travel, including a visit to his friend, Dion brother-in-law of the tyrant, Dionysius. According to the sources, he intended to use Syracuse as a pilot project for an experiment leading toward his perfect state. There is a legend that this visit ended in his being sold into slavery, and rescued by a friend. In any case, on his return to Athens in 388 he founded his famous Academy, the first true university offering a wide range of studies including all of the then extant sciences.

In 367, upon the death of Dionysius I. Dion invited Plato back to supervise the education of Dionysius II. Plato made a brief visit which succeeded at least in establishing a course of royal instruction in mathematics and philosophy. In 361 he visited Syracuse a third time, apparently hoping to gain approval for a federation of Greek city states against Carthage; but this trip, too, ended in failure. He returned to Athens, disappointed by his ventures in practical politics, continuing to spread the influence of the academy until his death.

Principal writings: Apology; Crito; Euthyphro; Ion; Protagoras; Gorgias; Meno; Cratylus; Phaedo; Republic; Symposium; Parmenldes; Sophist; Theaetetus; Phaedrus; Politicus; Philebus; Timaeus; Critias; and Laws.

Plato wrote dialogues for the tile public and lectures for his classes at the academy. The works mentioned above are his dialogues; none of his lectures has survived (the exact opposite is true with respect, to Aristotle). The dialogues are works of art, rich in figurative expression. Indeed, the mixture of metaphor, and analysis, has led some to find metaphor a working part, of his method, both illustrating the analysis and serving as a place-maker for an analysis which for the present eludes the thinker. In both cases he regards metaphor and myth as particularly appropriate to the changing nature of the world of becoming, in contrast to the conceptual nature of the eternal world. There is a good deal of disagreement concerning (a) how we are to separate the work of Plato from that or Socrates, since Socrates appears as potagonist in most of Plato's dialogues; (b) whether Plato had a system of philosophy and if so what is its nature.

Plato's Academy C. 385 B.C. 529 A.D.

the school founded by Plato, in Athens. Named from the gardens in which the school was located, a public place dedicated to the Greek hero, Academus. The school specialized in the study of mathematics, music, astronomy, and dialectic. The history of the school may be divided into four parts, although some scholars prefer a tripartite division: the Ancient or First Academy; the Middle or Second Academy; the New or Third Academy; and the Very New, or Fourth Academy. In the last stage, that of the Fourth Academy, the Academy is sometimes called the School of Athens and is part of the Neoplatonic movement.

platonism

as the philosophy deriving directly or indirectly from the work of Plato, Platonism, can be seen as a commentary on complexities in Plato's own thought.

Plato's philosophy offers almost every obstacle to

simple systematic exposition. He transmitted it to posterity principally through dialogues written over a period of 50 years, during which his thought developed considerably. Modern scholarship distinguishes between :

(1) the inclusive, aporetic dialogues of his early, so-called Socratic period.

(2) the great works of his middle period like the Phaedo and the Republic with their positive metaphysical, psychological, and political doctrines, and

(3) late writings like the Parmenides and the Sophist, in which these doctrines are subjected to redical reappraisal and modification. Even in his middle period, Plato's teachings lead to vary in detail and implications from one-dialogue to another.

The central doctrine in this period, indeed the centre of Plato's whole work as a philosopher, is the theory of Forms or Ideas. These eternal transcendent realities directly apprehended by thought are contrasted with the transient contigent phenomena of our empirical existence. The Forms fulfil a number of barely compatible functions, appearing sometimes in the role of universals (universals and particulars), sometimes as ideal standards, sometimes as the intelligible model or blueprint of the sensible world. Plato's theory of substantive Ideas has to account singlehanded for a variety of facts—ontological, epistemological, and ethical. It shows a variety of philosophical influences, Heraclitean, Pythagorean, Parmenidean, and Socratic; it also reveals like Plato's work as a whole, two contrasting motives; on the one hand, a poetic, religious awareness of an unseen eternal world, dimly reflected in the phenomena around us, and on the other, a mathematical urge to analysis reality into its ultimate units. Doctrines of such complexity do no lend themselves readily to systematic exposition, which Plato anyway distrusted. The dialogue, with its dramatic elements, its ironies, its recourse to mythical figurative language, was his chosen literary vehicle for teachings that he was not propounding as a definitive system.

pleasure

ultimately from the Greek hedone ('delight, enjoyment'). The doctrine that pleasure is the end of life, or that the pursuit of pleasure is built into man's nature, is called Hedonism. Pleasure has been often advanced as man's final value and pain his final disvalue, that we seek the one and shun the other. Aristotle regarded pleasure not as the end of the activity, but as a concomitant of successful functioning.

Pleiades

daughter of the giant, Atlas, and sister of the Hyades, the bringers of rain.

plenitude, principle of

a term coined by Lovejoy to explain the view that we can realize all possibilities in the world. The created Universe does not have any gaps. In other words, it is treated as a continuum.

plenum

space totally filled with matter; the opposite of a vacuum. The concept featured in a number of cosmologies from the Stoics.

pluralism

any system in metaphysics is considered to be pluralistic in which the reality is composed of independent, discrete, unconnected elements that cannot be reduced to one another. In Leibniz's metaphysics, reality consists of many independent, discrete entities called monads. Each monad is a tiny universal by itself. Similarly, for Hume, reality is a stream of impression. Thus Hume's metaphysics is a pluralistic one.

plurality of forms

refers to a doctrine that held that bodies possessed a number of forms—of plants, of elements, etc., the form of light being the highest of these and responsible for generating all the rest.

plurative logic

the little known field of the logic of majorities, also called the pleonoletic logic; if, for instance, 'most as are Bs' and 'Most As are Cs', then necessarily 'Some B is C'. It was Sir William Hamilton who first argued that 'most' is a quantifier on all fours with 'all', 'some', and 'no'.

pluto

'giver of wealth', a euphemistic name for Hades.

pneuma

a Greek term meaning 'air'. The term was used by Stoic philosophers as a principle of animation for the universe, and the term they preferred to psyche or soul, as the principle of animation in man as well.

pneumatology

a branch of metaphysics that deals with the theory and science of spiritual beings such as God, human soul, angels, etc. In the course of 18th century this term was chiefly used to denote the study of the human soul.

poiesis

a Greek term signifying the activity of creating, making, or producing. In Aristotle poiesis defines one of the three types of science, the productive science; and poietic knowledge correspondingly is set in contrast to theoretical and practical knowledge.

polar concepts

the concepts that oppose each other. For example, certainty and uncertainty (doubt), finite and infinite, determinism and indeterminism, etc. According to the polar concept argument, the existence of any concept is derived from its opposite. For instance, unless there is something called certainty the question of uncertainty does not arise.

polarity, principle of

(1) Nicholas of Cusa held that polar opposites apply at the same time to infinite beings. God is the chief example of the principle's applicability.

(2) Fichte, Hegel, and Marx and his followers, believed that such opposites were replaced by a synthesis in the process of dialectic.

political philosophy

centering around the problem of the nature of society and of the state, considering not only how these entities are but now they ought to be ordered.

Plato envisioned a republic in which educational success determine one's role in society, even with respect to those who rule; and the just society has the same structure as the just soul, written large.

Where Plato made the developed individual the basic unit of society, Aristotle regarded the family as that unit. Nor is there a single preferred organisation of the state. Instead, monarchy, aristocracy and polity are the preferred forms of which tyranny, oligrachy and democracy are the deformations.

polity

in Aristotle one of the three desirable forms of government. Polity seemed to have been Aristotle's preference. It has many of the features of constitutional democracy.

polysyllogism

a systematic series of syllogisms leading to a single conclusion.

polytheism

it is a religious doctrine, according to which there are many Gods. For example, Hinduism believes in the existence of many Gods.

polyxena

daughter of Priam and Hecuba; she was put to death as a sacrifice at the demand of Achilles ghost.

pope

from the Greek papas ('father'). Head of the Roman Catholic Church. Bearing the title Pontifex Maximus (meaning 'supreme intermediary between man and God'), the pope is regarded by Roman Catholics as successor to Peter as Bishop of Rome, and bearing in himself all of the powers Christ granted Peter. As of 1870 it was decided that infallibility characterized the pope's utterances when defining doctrines of faith and morals.

port royal

it is a name given to the logic developed by Arnauld, Nicole, and Pascal. According to Port

Royal logic, a careful definition of various terms and concepts is an essential part of logic. What is called modern linguistic analysis has its foundations is Port Royal logic.

Poseidon

Greek god of earthquakes and of water and identified with the Roman Neptune; he is described as son of Kronos and Rhea and a brother of Zeus; living in the depths of the sea. He was also the god of horses; dolphins, too, were sacred to him. Black or white bulls were offered him in sacrifice, and the Isthmian games were held in his honour.

positive philosophy

a phrase introduced by Saint-Simon as a synonyms for positivism, a scientific approach to the world. Schelling meant by the term a positive approach to the universe, an approach which was mythological and spiritualists in tone. With Comte the term Positivism, became standard for the scientific approach.

positivism

a family of philosophies characterised by an extremely positive evaluation of science and scientific method.

The term was introduced by Saint-Simon for whom the implications of the positive philosophy extended beyond philosophy to political, educational, and religious reforms. He found society alternative between critical and organic epochs.

possibility

every probability is a possibility. There are types of possibilities. For instance, there are logical possibilities, empirical possibilities, and technical possibilities. What is logically possible may be empirically impossible and vice-versa.

postulate

from the Latin term postulatum meaning 'demand' 'request', or 'claim'. The term is usually used to indicate those propositions which form the starting point of inquiry which are neither, definitions, nor provisional assumptions nor so certain that they can be taken as axiomatic. They are laid down as ture, and used without demonstration. Thus 'postulate' is one of a family of related terms including 'definition', 'assumption' 'hypothesis' and 'axiom'.

potentially

from the Latin Potentia, derived from potens, meaning 'to be powerful' in a certain respect or 'to have a capacity' of a certain kind. The Latin term is a translation of the Greek dynamics, used, by Aristotle as die name of the factor correlative to actually in the analysis of change.

pragmaticism

a term coined by C.S Peirce in 1905 to denote his own particular variety of pragmatism, after the latter term had been appropriated and its scope widened by other philosophers.

pragmatics

that branch of semiotics concerned with the relations between signs and their users, i.e., with problems of signification.

pragmatism

a label for a doctrine about meaning first made, a philosophical term in 1878 by C.S. Peirce. Consider what effects, which might conceivably have practical bearings, we conceive the object of our conception to have. Then our conception of these effects is the whole of our conception of the object. The term was soon borrowed by William James, F. C.S. Schiller, and John Dewey, who all in their different ways made pragmatism a theory of truth. Thus in his pragmatism James said, "Ideas help us to get into satisfactory relations with other parts of our experience', Peirce reacted by coining the substitute 'pragmaticism', a word too ugly to be purloined. Russell assailed the pragmatist notion of the truth as obscurantist.

prakrti

Sanskrt term which means 'matter' or 'substance'. Along with purusha, which stands for soul or spirituality, one of the two basic concepts of the Sankhya philosophy.

pranayama

Sanskrit term meaning 'breath control'. The fourth step in Yogic meditation.

pratyabara

Sanskrit term meaning 'sense-control'. The fifth step in Yogic meditation.

prayer

supplication or solemn petition of a deity, with or without sacrifice. In Christianity prayer is always offered in the name of Jesus Christ, through whose mediation alone access to God's mercy is believed possible. Prayers to Christ are someetimes, especially by Roman Catholics, offered through a saint.

A distinction is drawn between vocal and mental prayer. The former, to which Protestant Christianity has tended to accord the greater importance, includes praise, adoration, and thanksgiving as well as petition. Mental prayer includes both meditation and contemplation. In Christian theology there has been a consistent tradition whereby the basis of the Church's prayer is to be found in the atoning sacrifice of Christ and his continuing intercession in his risen and glorified state.

preachers, order of

alternate name for the Dominican order.

precept

anything that is given and accepted as a maxim or a rule

that regulates further action or conduct, especially the conduct of an individual in a moral or religious realm.

precognition
knowing something as certain before that is going to take place. Precognition in that sense is a paranormal phenomenon which is obtained from a non-sensory and non-inferential source.

predestination
the doctrine, that man's salvation or damnation was predetermined from eternity by God. When the doctrine holds that not only man's eventual disposition, but every event of his life is predestined, the position is identical to a special kind of determinism.

predicable
from the Latin praedicare ('to proclaim or affirm'). The predicable is that which may be affirmed of something.

predicament
a particular situation which is unpleasant, unfortunate, especially with regard to moral obligations. At times it is important to escape from such situations as there may not be any solution to predicaments. For example, death as a perdicament cannot be overcome.

predicate
in the traditional or subject-predicate logic, that which is affirmed or denied of a subject.

predication
the act of affirming or denying a predicate of a subject. Where modern logic deals with classes, sets and relations, the logic of Aristotle is a logic of predication.

predictability
the capability of being foretold. It means only and exactly what it says, and must therefore be distinguished from both predestination and causal determinism.

prediction
knowledge inferred prior to the occurrence of an event on the basis of past experiences. Inductivists predict that the things that held good in the past may hold good in the future.

prediction paradox
refers to the paradox of propositions that are falsified by the utterance of the prediction they announce.

prejudice
a belief or an opinion or an idea that is held irrespective of its truth or falsity, without proper consideration, or sometimes ignoring the evidence is called a prejudice. A prejudice is always biased. This is an important term for legal science.

prehension span
the maximum number of items that are apprehended by mind at any given moment of attending.

premise (or premiss)
in any argument, one of the statements from which another statement (the

conclusion) is deduced or of which the conclusion is presented as a consequence.

presbyterianism

the form of church government by presbyters, that is, by ministers and elders without the oversight of bishops. It theological tenets and policy rest on Calvinism. The established Church of Scotland is Presbyterian.

prescience

it is a term generally used to denote immediate, non-inferential knowledge. Such a knowledge is about what will happen.

prescriptivism

the view taht the primary function of moral judgement is to prescribe course of action. R.M.Hare, who coined the term, holds that if a statement is prescriptive then :

(a) anyone who sincerely accepts it, and can act upon it does so act, and

(b) it cannot be entalied by a purely descriptive statement.

present

the part of the time lying between the past and the future.

From Aristotle to Newton the present moment was an objective portion of the passage of time.

presocratics

all those ancient Greek speculative philosophers who were chiefly concerned with the nature as a whole prior to Socrates. For instance, Thales is regarded as the father of philosophy. According to him, water is the primordial substance from which everything has come into existence. Apart from Thales, there were Anaxagoras, Anaximander, Democritus, Empedocles, Heraclitus, Pythagoras and so on.

presupposing

(1) Collingwood regarded metaphysics as the study of the absolute presuppositions of a period of time.

(2) Strawson holds that certain difficulties in Russell's theory of definite descriptions can be avoided by keeping in mind that in referring to an entity, one presupposes, without asserting, existence.

presupposition

an assumption that involves either a necessary or a contingent truth. If p is logically presupposed by q and then it is a necessary truth that to deny the assumption p while asserting q would be a contradiction. Presupposition that do not satisfy this requirement involve a contingent truth.

Priam

son of Laomedon; he was king of Troy at the time of the Trojan war, but being an old man took no active part in it. He recovered the body of his son Hector by agreement with Achilles, but on the capture of Troy was slain by Neoptolemus.

priapus
Greek god of fertility, son of Dionysus and Aphrodite; he was looked on as a protector of flocks, bees, grapes, and garden produce, and is represented as an old man with enormous genitals or even by a phallus alone.

pride
the Greek term is hybris. Along with concupiscence, pride is the source of sin in the Christian tradition. Often regarded as a mortal sin, pride implies a lack of dependence on God.

priest
one who officiates in sacred rites, especilly sacrifice. In the Roman Catholic, Eastern Orthodox, and anglican Churches, a minister of the 2nd order, below a bishop and above a deacon. Unlike the latter he has authority to celebrate the Eucharist and pronounce absolution.

prima facie obligations
the label popularized by Sir David Ross for those authentic moral claims that may on occasion be overridden by other and stronger moral claims.

Prima, Henry Habberley (1899-)
a British analytical philosopher who was regarded as the guardian of sense-data. In his book Perception Price tries to present the nature of external world in terms of 'the given' (sense-data). Though he was branded as a phenomenalist, he rejected phenomenalism.

primary and secondary qualities
primary qualities are those which things do actually have, secondary are only powers to produce experiences in us.

principle
it is a source of something. In this sense, it is regarded as innate and inherent. It can also be viewed as a law or a rule that serves as a basis for explanation of various processes.

prithri
the earth.

privacy
the experiences undergone by every individual are private to one's own self. They cannot be shared by others. Such a state of experiences is called privacy.

private language
it is a belief that the language used to describe one's own private experiences is private. According to Wittgenstein, the notion of private language is a myth. Language has to be public in the sense that it is always intersubjective.

privation
the belief that evil is essentially negative—the lack of absence of good (privatio boni).

privileged access
the particular relationship we have to contents of our own consciousness, but that none of us has to the contents of anybody else's.

probabilism
the doctrine that certainty is unattainable, held by the Skeptics including members of the Second Academy.

probability
from the Latin probare ('to prove, to approve'). The Latin is a translation of the 'Greek eulogon (reasonable or sensible'). The term thus refers to the likelihood of the happening of an event, or of the truth of a proposition. Where conclusions follow by necessity in deductive inference, they follow only by probability in induction. Probability theory has been developed into a very sophisticated discipline in modern mathematics.

probability theory
the mathematical theory of probability enables us to calculate the probability of some kind of the event given the probability of others.

problematic
a term in Aristotellian logic used to indicate the mode or modality of a proposition. A problematic proposition is one that asserts that something is possible, for example, 'it is possible that it will rain'.

process philosophy
a term sometimes applied to those philosophies stressing "becoming" rather than "being".

Procrustes
robber who lived near Eleusis. He would tie his victims to a bed, stretching them as on a rack if their limbs were not long enough or cutting off part of them if they were too long. He was killed by Theseus.

progress
in philosophy the conception of progress is to be contrasted with the view that the Golden Age was in the past, and with the view that time is eternal recurrence. Of course, in both West and East, views can be cited where the cycle of time includes periods of progress and of regress or decline.

prolepsis
a Greek term which means 'anticipation' :

(1) in traditional logic the term referred to the anticipation of an objection, and one's response to it.

(2) among the stoics the term was used to refer to any one of the principles or 'common notions' which the soul contains, whether innately or from common experience.

Prometheus
'forethought', the son of the Titan Iapetus and brother of Atlas and Epimetheus. He stole fire from heaven and thus became the earliest teacher and benefactor of the human race. For this Zeus punished him by chaining him to a mountain rock in the Caucasus, where an eagle fed daily upon his liver, which was renewed during the night.

proof theory
the syntactic study of formal

systems that proceeds by examining the structure of the proofs that can be constructed within them.

proper names

proper names may be confined to such terms as 'Socrates', 'Plato', 'Aristotle', and 'Mr. Brown', or extended to all terms which pick out a single individual. In either case, the function of proper names is to refer one to certain objects. They are, then, expected to have denotation.

property

from the Latin probare ('one's own', 'proper'). The term has been used to mark out both what is common to all the members of a class, and that to which a person has a legal title.

prophecy

from the Greek prophetein ('the gift of interpreting the will of the gods'). Interpreting the will of the god sometimes, but by no means always, implied the prediction of future events.

proposition

from the Latin proponere ("to set forth or propose"). A proposition is, hence, an assertion which proposes or denies something, and is capable of being judged true or false.

propositional calculus

that part of logic concerned with the valid inferences and transformations which can be drawn from the relations of proposition to each other :

1. Philo of Megara was the first to work out the definition of material implication. In all other cases it is true. The definition is accepted today. It was worked out independently, however and only later discovered in Philo.

2. Chrysippus had worked out the definitions of Modus Ponens. These definitions likewise became part of the calculus; they had wide currency, and were developed by many different individuals.

propositional function

a technical term due to Russell, used to denote that for which a predicate of predicate logic stands.

proprium (latin for: a possession or characteristic)

a characteristic peculiar to and dependent upon the essence of a species, but not a necessary part of its essence. Aristotle contrasted, in a way that is not entirely clear, proprium with accident.

prosyllogism

a syllogism preliminary to another, its conclusion forming a premise of the syllogism which follows.

protasis

a Greek term meaning "that which is put forward".
In Aristotle's logic, the premise of a syllogism, especially the major premise.
The conditional clause of an "if-then" statement. The second clause is the apodosis.

Proteus
Greek demi-god of the sea who tended Poseidon's seals. He possessed the gift of prophecy, and he had the ability to assume countless different shapes, which made him elusive; those who sought his prophecies had somehow to hold him fast.

protocal sentence
a sentence consisting of an observation report describing directly given experience.

protocol statements
(German: Protokollsatze). According to the Vienna Circle, those, basic statements that are immediately veritiable by 'experience, mutually independent logically, and perhaps also incorrigible.

prudence
from prudentia, the Latin translation of the Greek word, phronesis.
Socrates, viewed the term as the guarantee of virtue in the equation, "virtue is knowledge".

psyche
a Greek term meaning "breath".
In Homer and in Greek life generally the psyche was a subtle, breath-like animating principle which left the body at death and continued to exist as a shade or shadow.

psychokinesis
a term that is popular in parapsychology, according to which a person can move an object without having any physical contact with that object.

psychologism
the theory that psychology is the foundation of philosophy, and that introspection is the primary method of philosophical enquiry.

psychology
from the Greek psyche ('breath') and logos ('knowledge of '). The term psyche was used by Greek philosophers to refer to the vital principle in man.

psychology, philosophy of
refers to the study of the philosophical implications of psychology and psychological research.

psychophysical parallelism
the view that mental (psychical) and bodily (physical) events occur in the separate but parallel sequences.

ptolemaic system
the theory which assumes that the earth is the fixed centre of the universe, surrounded by concentric spherical shells, seven of which are the paths of the moving heavenly bodies, the eighth and outermost accommodating the fixed stars.

punishment
the word in its full and central sense may be defined as the intentional inflication by some authority upon an offender, of some penalty intended to be disagreeable, for some offence against rules authorized by that authority. The references to intention and to an authority are both essential.

punya
good deed.

purana
sacred text.

purgatory
in Roman Catholic teaching, the state after death in which souls are purged or purified from venial sins by suffering.

purism
the emphasis that is laid on purity of things, for example, in the use of language, etc.

putitanism
doctrine or school of English (or Low Country) Protestants of the 16th and 17th c. whose aim was the purification of religious practive from anything not speecifically authorized by Scripture, and who enjoined the strictest purity of conduct.

purusa
(Sanskrit for : self, spirit). In general, the principle of consciousness in man or the Universe. But its exact function is variously conceived in the different systems of Indian philosophy.

purva mimamsa
Sanskrit term meaning 'the early revered thought'. The term refers to a school of Indian thought dealing with the earlier portions of the Vedas, as Uttara Mimamsa or Vedanta dealt with the later part.
(1) Liberation from rebirth leads in this system to life in heaven, and liberation is tied to the doing of one's duty.
(2) Since, the source of information concerning duty is to be found in Vedas, it is necessary that the Vedas be not simply the opinons of men. Accordingly, the Vedas are regarded as eternal. That is to say, there never was a time when they had not been written. The Vedas, hence, are without an author; and apparent refrences to authors are to be understood as references to individuals who explained certain poritons of the Vedas, but did not compose them.
The eternality of the Vedas seems to lead to a theory of language. If the Vedas are eternal, so must be the language of the Vedas. Hence, the relation between word and meaning is held to be non-conventional: there is a natural and inborn relation between the word and its denotation.

putative proposition
a proposition that is supposed to be the case.

pygmalion
king of Cyprus who fell in love with an ivory statue of his own making. Aphrodite, at his prayer, gave it life and he married the maiden thus created.

Pylades
friend of Orestes, whose sister Electra he married.

Pyramus and Thisbe
two young lovers, in a tale of Ovid. Forbidden by their parents to marry, they used to

talk to each other through a chink in the dividing wall of their houses in Babylon. Deciding to elope, they arranged to meet at Ninus tomb. There Thisbe was frightened by a lion with bloody jaws and dropped her veil, which the beast mouthed. Pyramus, finding the garment, thought she was dead and killed himself. She, however, came back, only to discover her lover's body, and in turn took her life. Their blood stained the fruit of a near-by mulberry tree, whose kind has ever since borne blood-coloured berries.

Pyrrho (365-275 B.C.)

an ancient Greek philosopher who advocated scepticism. He is generally regarded as the first systematic sceptic philosopher. According to Pyrrho, one can reach the state of ataraxia (imperturbable state of mind) by suspending all forms of judgement with regard to phenomena.

pythagoreanism

refers to the philosophical teachings and way of life associated with Pythagoras.

Python

female serpent killed by Apollo at Delphi, where the priestess became known as Pythia.

quadrivium

from the Latin quatuor ('four') and viae ('ways'). The four advanced studies—arithmetic, geometry, astronomy, and music—followed the Trivium in the medieval curriculum.

quaestio

it is a Latin term for 'question'. During middle ages a form of philosophical writing has originated from the practice of oral debate in the universities.

qualia

it is a Latin term for 'quality', 'property', 'nature', 'state', 'kind', 'condition'. Quale is the Latin singular for 'of what kind or property' a thing has.

qualification theory

in modern logic the method devised for expressing in symbolic form statements of a general nature.

qualities, primary and secondary

the primary qualities of things are solidity, extension, figure, motion, rest and number. The secondary qualities are colours, sounds, tastes, smells etc.

(1) The distinction between the two types of the qualities was first made by the Greek atomists. Democritus (3; Epicurus 4),

(2) after a long period of neglect the distinction reappeared.

(3) The precise terminology, 'primary qualities', and 'secondary qualities', was introduced by the scientist Robert Boyle and picked up from Boyle by Locke.

(4) Berkeley called the distinction into question in such a way that from the standpoint of Berkeley's system all qualities became secondary. The consequence

was loss of the concept of a material world, and the emergence of Berkeley's philosophy of immaterialism.

quality

(1) one of Aristotle's basic categories, quality is 'that by virtue of which a thing is such and such'. A quality may be a habit, disposition, capacity, or the form and figure of a thing.
(2) in the traditional logic one speaks of the quality of categorical proposition. By this, one means their characteristic of being affirmative or negative (Proposition 1).
(3) Kant followed both Aristotle and the traditional logic by regarding quality as one of the basic categories while deriving from the characteristic mentioned in (2) above the sub-categories of Positive, Negative and Limited.
(4) for Locke's treatment of the term Primary and Secondary qualities.

quantification suppressed

it is an ambiguity that arises in ordinary conversion where we do not know whether the statement refers to all members of a class or only to some members of a class. For example, 'Children like ice-cream'. It is not clear whether 'all children like ice - cream' or 'only some children like ice-cream'.

qualification theory

in modern logic the method devised for expressing in symbolic form statements of a general nature.

quantifier shift fallacy

an argument or a fallacy that involves in the fallacy of confusing universal and particular quantities. For example, 'children like ice-cream'. It is not clear whether 'all children like ice-cream'.

quantity

from the Latin quantitas '(amount)', a translation of the Greek poson.

For Aristotle one of the basic categories. Quantity in his view is either discrete or continuous; if continuous, it is either a magnitude or a temporal span. Quantity is also further divisible into units of the same kind.

quantum

from the Latin quantus ('how much'). Used in philosophy to refer to a finite and determinate quantity, and term has passed into physics where its reference is to the packets of energy, or quanta, or quantum mechanics.

quantum mechanics

a system of mechanics used to explain the behaviour of atoms, molecules, and elementary particles.

quiddity

from the Latin quidditas referring to the 'whatness' of a thing. The term was introduced in the Latin translations of Avicenna to express Aristotle's distinction of second substance, i.e. what a thing is, in contrast to primary substance, i.e. the individual thing itself. Thus the usual sense of the term is as a synonym for form, nature, or essence.

Quine, Willard Van Orman (1908-)

an American logician who followed Carnap and has been most influential empiricist in America. One of his famous papers Two Dogmas of Empiricims is chiefly directed against the 'analyticity and reductionism' practised by empiricists. According to him, these two dogmas of empiricism are logically illfounded. In the same paper Quine attacks the supposed cleavage between 'analytic and synthetic'. His important works include: Mathematical Logic: Word and Object: Philosophy of Logic: The Ways of Paradox, etc.

quintessence

in Aristotelian physics, the pure fifth element (Latin : quinta essentia), believed to be the component of heavenly bodies. It was distinguished throughout the medieval period from earth, air, fire, and water but was believed to be latent in them. Alchemists equating it with the prima material or first matter, from which the rest of the world was made, attempted to distil it from the other elements.

rabbi

Hebrew term which means "my great one". The ordination title for authoritative teachers of Judaism.

Radhakrishna Sarvepalli 1888-1975

Indian philosopher and statesman. Studied at Madras, Taught at Madras, Mysore, Calcutta, Benares, and Oxford. He has served as Ambassador, Vice-president, and President of the Republic of India. Seeking the unity of the world's religion and philosphies, his own Vedantic interpretation—taking Shankara as his point of departure—led to Idealism as his philosophic position.

radical philosophy

refers to a movement started in the 1970 which is centring on a journal of the same name. The journal expresses concern that philosophy should be relevant, not trivial, and that more attention should be given to some continental movements and other relatively neglected areas. "The philosophers have only interpreted the world in various ways". Marx said in 1845, "the point, however, is to change it".

rajas

the quality of passion.

rakshasa

demon.

Rama

Hindu diety. Along with Krishna one of the last two incarnations of Vishnu. Their followers constitute a considerable portion of the Hindu people and a majority of the Vishnuites. Rama is the hero of the great epic work, the Ramayana. In books Two through Six, apparently the original portion of the work, Rama is described simply as the best of men, a dutiful son, loving husband, and possessor of every virtue. But he succeds in apparently superhuman undertakings, and so came to be regarded as more than human. In Books One and Seven, regarded in later addition by the scholarly community, his divinity is acknowledged. Since Vishnu, too, had performed miraculous tasks on behalf of men e.g., destroying demons, there was reason for connecting Rama with Vishnu. The popularity of Rama as an incarnation of Vishnu has continued from the 10th century A.D. to the present.

Ramakrishna (1836-1886)

a public figure and a reformer of Hindu cult, who advocated that there must be only one religion for entire mankind. He tried to reconcile various doctrines of Vedanta by bringing them under one fold. He gave all importance to the wordily activities by rejecting the view that world is illusory.

Ramanuja 11th Cent. A.D.

Indian philosopher. Born in Bautapuri. Originally an adherent of the philosophy of Shankara. Ramanuja fell under the influence of Vaisnavism and finally became head of a school representing this opinion. Dedicating himself to working out the philosophical basis of the hymns of the Attars, Ramanuja became the philosopher for the bhakti, or devotional strand, of Hinduism. Taking Shankara as his opponent, much of his writing was polemical, directed toward refutation of Shankara's philosophy.

Principle writings: Commentaries on the Vedanta Sutras; Vedantatattvasara Vedarthasangraha.

Ramayana

one of the two great epics of Hinduism. Consisting of seven books and 50,000 lines, the Ramayana is both older and shorter than its companion, the Mahabharata. Written between the 6th and 4th centuries B.C., the poem tells the story of the birth, youth, marriage, and exile of Prince Rama; the abduction of his wife by a demon and her return; his reign, final years, and death. As a morality tale, the story depicts the victory of Rama over his enemies, both natural and supernatural, through exemplary behaviour. Interpolations in the 2nd century B.C. transformed the story into one concerning Rama, the incarnation of Vishnu. On this level the poem becomes devotional literature, telling of his love and protection which Rama-Vishnu provides for those who trust him.

ramsey sentence

the sentence generated after the sentences of a scientific theory have been conjoined together, by replacing the theoretical term with variables and existentially quantifying into the result. In plain terms the sentence reproduces the structure of the theory, and its empirical consequences, but removes the impression that we are dealing with understood theoretical items and properties.

random

anything that happens without a definite direction, purpose, order, system, method etc. For example, it is on the basis of random sampling we decide whether the water in a particular area is contaminated or not.

randomness

the situation that arises when, in repetitions of a trial in which there is a known, fixed probability of a particular result, there is a rule for predicting that result that tends towards any different success rate.

rational

1. opposed to irrational.

2. opposed to non-rational or arational. Those who have spoken of man as the rational animal have of course been employing the word in the second sense, meaning capable of either rationality or irrationality, not trying to make it true by definition that everyone in fact achieves the one rather than the other.

rationalism

from the Latin ratio ("reason"). The principle that reason is to be granted, the primary role in explanation.

ratri

night.

Rawls, John (1921-)

an American philosopher who reviewed the social contract theory advocated by Hobbes, Rousseau, and Locke. He argued that no group as a matter of justice, should be better off than any other group. His important work is A Theory of Justice.

real

anything that exists independent of one's perception of it.

realism

1. (in scholasic philosophy). The view that universals (universal and particulars) have a real substantial existence, independently of being thought. Duns Scorus was the most able supporter of this position.

2. (in modern philosophy) Most commonly the view that physical objects exist independently of being perceived. Thus understood, realism obviously reaffirms the standpoint of common sense, and it achieves the status of a philosophy only

because a case against it has been seriously argued.

reality

from the Latin realitas, deriving from res ("thing").

The Indian philosopher, Nagarjuna, looked upon reality as beyond intellect, the non-dual Absolute in which all distinctions merge.

reason

from the Latin ratio ('reckoning').

Applied to a capacity in man to draw logical conclusions, a long tradition has regarded reason as man's most distinctive faculty.

rebellion

man's individual opposition to the state, as contrasted with revolution.

rebirth

the general term, referring to a succession of births, of which Reincarnation is one basic modification. Reincarnation implies the notion of rebirth while denying the existence of soul.

recollection

according to Plato, all knowledge is possible through recollection. He conceived that every individual soul being a part of Universal soul has the knowledge of highest Forms. It is only through recollection that individual soul comes to know it.

recursive

a term in formal logic that refers to a procedure that can go on without any stop unless something is specified to terminate it.

recursive function

any function containing a hereditary property such that when the value of the function has been determined for one number of a series it is determinable for the next member of the series.

redemption

from the Latin redemptio, from redimere ('to buy'). The doctrine that man is ransomed from sin by the divine. It has its most specific form in Christianity.

reductio ad absurdum

a Latin term for 'reduction to absurdity'. It is a way of arguing in which a statement is proved to be true because its falsity leads to absurdity.

reductio ad impossible

Latin phrase meaning "reduction to the impossible". A form of argument which seeks to establish the truth of a proposition by showing that the contradictory of that proposition involves impossible consequences; a form of the reductio ad absurdum.

reduction sentence

a device introduced by Carnap in order to solve the problem of scientific terms that resist explicit definition, such as those denoting dispositional properties.

reference, theory of

an area of contemporary philosophic concern over problems of denotation, or how words and phrases refer.

referent

in logic the first term of a relation whose second term is called the "relatum". If A has the relation R to B, A is the referent and B the relatum.

reflection

according to John Locke, reflection is a form of experiene. In this sense, it is purely internal. The ideas that are produced by reflection are the ideas such as love, hatred, pain, pleasure, etc. Sometimes it is also interpreted as introspection.

reflexivity

the property of those relations in terms of which an entity relates to itself.

reformation

the term is used to describe movements seeking to correct abuses in an established order, often by reverting to the principles and customs of an earlier period.

refute

strictly, not only to deny but also to provide sufficient reason for believing that what is denied is in fact false.

regeneration

from the Latin regeneratus ('to have been born again'). In religion a new, spiritual birth.

reification or reism

a view that regards abstractions as real and prior to their referents. For example, the noun beaty is an abstraction that is attributed to a referent. In this sense, beauty is considered as an actual existent that is prior to the object to which it is attributed to. It is also known as the fallacy of concretism.

reincarnation

the doctrine that the soul becomes incarnate in a succession of bodies until by the necessary purification, or the using up of one's karma final release from the body occurs. A characteristic of Hinduism.

reism

the attempt to preserve an objectivity for all kinds of the philosophies of Brentano and Meinong.

relation

it is one of the categories of understanding postulated by Immanuel Kant. It includes—substance, causality, and community.

relations, internal and external

if an individual X has a property which is such that, by virtue of having that property, X necessarily has a relation R to a certain thing or thigs, then R is an internal relation of X. But if X has a realtion R to a certain thing or things, and there is no property of X such that, by virtue of having that property, X necessarily has this relation, then R is an external realtion of X.

relations, the logic of

the logic of relations is that part of logic concerned with the expression of relational ideas, where e.g., some 'x' has the relation R to 'y'. This may be expressed either as 'xRy' or "R(x,y)'.

relativism

the view that maintains our judgements with regard to any knowledge claim are relative. We cannot have absolute knowledge of any phenomena. Any attempt to arrive at absolute truth, claim relativists, is an absurdity.

relativity

a scientific principle, established in two parts by Albert Einstein. The first part, special relativity, refers to non-accelerated systems and has immense philosophical implications both in respect to the extent to which it upsets the classical notions of time and motion and more specifically because of its impact on the concept of simultaneity.

The second part of Einstein's theory, general relativity, deals with relative motion between accelerated systems. It makes farther extensive modifications to our concepts of space and time, treating time as a non-Euclidean continuum, 'curved' by the presence of matter in such a way that gravitation appears as a consequence of the geometry of the universe.

Space and time are concepts that form part of the models we construct to repreasent the real world. But not all concepts have a counterpart in reality: atoms probably do, phlogiston certainly does not. Relativity has made us modify our concepts of space and time and with it our model of reality: it has also made us reconsider some of the underlying concepts of epistemology itself.

religion

from the Latin religare ('to bind fast]), typically the term refers to an institution with a recognized body of communicants who gather together regularly for worship, and accept a set of doctrines offering some means of relating the individual to what is taken to be the ultimate nature of reality.

religion, philosophy of

it is a branch of philosophy that is concerned with the proofs for the existence of God, the transmigration of soul, the problem of immortality, the nature of good and evil, etc.

reminiscence (or recollection), argument from

Plato's agrument that certain kinds of knowledge could not have been acquired in this life, but involve the recollection (Greek : anamnesis) of a previous acquaintanceship with the Forms or Ideas.

reminiscence, doctrine of

from the Greek term anamnesis. Plato's doctrine of knowledge as recollection.

renaissance

originally a French word

meaning 'rebirth' or 'revival'. Applied to the period of time in Western Europe running from the 14th through the 16th centuries, the term became current after Michelet in 1855 and Burckhard in 1860 used the term in titles of historical works on France and Italy, repectively.

representamen

that which represents, or stands for, another.

representationalism (or representationism)

a generic term that broadly refers to theories of perception wherein the sensing mind is believed not to have direct acquaintance with its objects, but to apprehend them through the medium of ideas that are supposed to represent those objects.

representative theory of ideas

the view, that the mind knows reality only through the mediation of ideas.

representative theory of perception

the view that is also known as representationalism or representationism.

resemblance

one of the basic principles of association. By virtue of resemblance one mental object calls up another. Russell held 'resemblance' to be the one universal indispensable to the life of the mind'.

resistentialism

a fincititious school of fashionable continental philosophy invented by Paul Jennings in 1984. This particular and popular invention is often wrongly included among the many similar contributions of Michael Frayn, consequent upon his undergraduate work in philosophy at Cambridge.

resolution

the final knitting up of the loose ends in a play or a story; it follows the climax.

responsibility

the notion that a person is answerable for his actions and so is a proper subject for praise or blame.

responsibility moral

the view that is one is answerable for his actions in terms of a moral or ethical criterion. The traditional view is that responsibility implies that man has free will.

resurrection

the doctrine that the dead shall rise in bodily form. To be distinguished from the idea of Immortality which supposes an eventual separation of soul from body.

retrodiction

the inverse of prediction, referring to the process by which one makes an inference into the past on the basis of present knowledge.

revelation

the term usually refers to an unveiling of truths which could not be reached by reason alone. The term stands in contrast to reason much as does its corrective term, 'faith'.

Rhea
one of the Titans, the wife of Kronos; the mother of Zeus, Demeter, Hades and Poseidon.

rhetoric
the art of articutalion through which one can impress and persuade others.

Richard's paradox
a paradox presented by Jules Richard in 1905. It involves a diagonal argument concerning denoting phrases; and what they denote and thus considered to be one of the semantic paradoxes.

right
a privilege sanctined to individuals by state. For instance, the Constitution of India has guaranteed certain rights to its citizens.

rigid designator
an expression that designates the same thing in every possible world.

Rig veda
the most important of that divison of the Vedas called the Samhitas. The Samhitas are collections of scripture containing hymns and prayers to the Vedic Gods. The Rig veda, one of four such collection, consists of ten books and was completed before 800 B.C.

rik
incantation.

rin
Japanese, term meaing 'companinoship'.

rishi
seer, sage.

ritu
season.

romanticism
a reaction against the rationalism and empiricism of the period of the Enlightenment, romanticism is best characterized by its idealist celebration of the self, by its respect for the transcendental, and by its conviction of the power of the imagination and of the supreme value of art.

Romulus
legendary founder of Rome; a son of Mars. He and his twin-brother Remus were reared as infants by a she-wolf.

rosicrucianism
a movement for political reform and spiritual regeneration that originated in early 17th century Germany. It centred on a fictitious religious society reputedly founded by a certain Christian Rosenkreuz in 1484. The philosophical content of its teaching is heavily coloured by alchemy, mysticism, and occultism.

Rousseau, Jean-Jacques (1712-1778)
a French political and social philosopher who advocated the social contract theory. According to him, it is the general will which is important than social contract. For the sake of collective general will every individual has to contribute.

rudra
the maleficent storm god of the Vedic religion. Rudra brings the destructive aspects of the strom. He likewise inflicts diseases, but also heals them.

rule of inference
the formula or argument form whereby the conclusion follows from a premise or set of premises.

Russell
Bertrand Arthur William. British philosopher. He subsequently held a variety of university posts in Cambridge and elsewhere, interspersed with other pursuits, literary, educational and political. From his long list of publications the following may be picked out as philosophically the most important : The Philosophy of Leibniz (1900). The Principles of Mathematics (1903), Principia Mathematica (with A.N. Whitehead, 3 volumes, 1910-13). The Problems of Philosophy (1912), Our Knowledge of the External World (1914), The Analysis of mind (1921), The Analysis of Matter (1927), An Enquiry into Meaning and Truth, Human Knowledge : Its Scope and Limits (1948), and Logic and Knowledge (a collection of some of his most important essays) (1956).

Russell's paradox
an important paradox in set theory. Some sets (classes or collection) are members of themselves and some are not. For instance, the set of horses, is not a number of itself since it is a set and not a horse, whereas the set of non-horses is a member of itself.

sabda (verbal testimony)
it is the knowledge obtained by means of verbal testimony. It is one of the valid means of knowledge. Nyaya, Vaisesika, Mimamsa, and Advaita admitted that sabda is a valid means of knowledge.

sabellianism
the doctrine of Sebellius that Father, Son, and Holy Spirits are the same being. The name refers loosely to all interpretations of the Godhead which are more unitarian than trinitarian.

sabha
assembly.

sacerdotalism
from the Latin sacerdos ('a priest'). Any religious system revolving around the priestly order, or the doctrine that ordination confers special powers and rights.

saddueism (or sadduceeism)
the beliefs of the Jewish sect to Sadducees, active around the time of Christ, particularly in so far as they concerned denial of the resurrection of the body and the existence of spirits.

sagehood
the goal of life in neo-Confucian philosophy. Mencius held that everyone has the capacity to become a sage.

saint

holy person; a man or woman eminent for piety and virtue; one canonized by the Church; one of the blessed in heaven whose prayers, according to Roman Catholic and Orthodox teaching, may be invoked by the faithful.

Saint-Simon Claude-Henri de Rouvroy, Comte de (1760-1825)
a French sociologist who emphasized that any political vision must have its base in social and historical conditions. According to him, all the members of working class are industriels.

saksin (the witness-self)
it is the self that witnesses all the human actions. According to Advaita, the saksin is neutral. It is always associated with internal organ (antahkarana)

salvation
from the Latin salvare ('to save'). The Christian term for that state in which man is redeemed, and reconciled to God. The mediator in this event is Jesus Christ, who atones for man's sins.

salva veritate
(Latin for: the truth being preseved). A condition of synonymy, first formulated by Leibniz. Expressions are synonymous (or may be said to have the same meaning) if they are mutually substitutable without altering the truth-value of the statement in which they occur.

sama
sweet song or hymn.

samadhi
Sanskrit term meaning 'concentration'. The eighth and final step in the path of Yogic meditation leading to liberation.

samhita
part of a Veda consisting of incantations.

samiti
assembly.

samsara
(Sanskirt for: transmigration). The doctrine, characteristic of all Indian religions, of an almost endless cycle of death and rebirth.

sanction
anything that serves as an obligation for an individual to act or not to act in accordance with rule or a maxim.

sankhya
one of the six orthodox systems of Indian Philosophy. It was founded by the great sage and seer Kapila. According to sankhya, there are two prime categories—prakroti and purusa. Sankhya and yoga are considered to be the twin systems.

sannyasi
a Sanskrit term meaning 'one who renounces'. The term refers to the fourth or mendicant stage of the Brahman religious life.

Sarpedon
son of Zeus and Europa; he became king of Lycia. He fought in the Trojan war but was killed

by Patroclus.

sat, chit, ananda

Sanskrit phrase meaning 'being, intelligence, and Bliss'. Although Brahman is at times said to be without characteristics, or beyond characterize, these three terms are often taken to characterization the divine consciousness in Hindu philosophy.

satisfaction

a technical term in formal semantics; the condition in which an object, or sequence of objects, 'satisfies' a predicate, that is, the predicate in true of that object, or sequence of objects.

Satkarya-vada (the theory of pre-existent effect)

it is a theory of causation, according to which the effect preexists in its cause prior to its manifestation. This theory is propounded by Sankhya school. According to Sankhya, the world is an emanation of Brahman. It is also known as parinama-vada.

sattva

quality of truth.

Saturn, Saturnus

Roman god of sowing or seed corn, later identified with the Greek Kronos.

satya yuga

era.

satyr

creature, half beast, half man, dwelling in woods and mountains; the satrys attended upon Dionysus and were lazy and lascivious.

sankhya

one of the six orthodox systems of Indian philosophy, arising in response to the Vedas and the heterodox systems. The system is attributed to Kapila, who is said to have lived in the 7th century B.C.

scepticism

in a general sense and with a small s, the philosophical attitude that maintains that sure knowledge of how things really are may be sought, but cannot be found. Scepticism (with a capital S) is the name attached to a particular school of ancient Greek philosophy.

Schelling, Friedrich Wilhelm Joseph Von (1775-1854)

a German idealist philosopher whose transcendental idealism is akin to that of Kant. His transcendental idealism is an attempt to modify the views of Kant with regard to the self and its relation to the world of things. According to Schelling, consciousness is the only immediate object of knowledge.

schema

Greek term meaning 'diagram'. In Kant's philosophy, the term refers to the exercise of the 'Transcendental Imagination', bringing sense and understanding together in particular ways to produce various essential concepts.

scholasticism

the kind of philosophy practised in the schools of the

medieval universities. The roots of the term stretch back to the Greek word for 'leisure', since it was recognized from antiquity that for the contemplation of the ultimate reason for things, leisure is an essential condition. The adjective 'scholastic' is also applied to medieval theology.

school of Athens

the name given to Plato's Academy after its conversion to Neoplatonism.

Schopenhauer, Arthur (1788-1860)

a German idealist philosopher who admitted Kant's classification of the world into phenomenal and noumenal. Accordint to him, will has two important aspects. The phenomenal aspect of the self is that it appears as the object of perception and the self as a Ding-an-Sich (noumenon) is the manifestation of the will.

science

it is a systematic effort to obtain the knowledge of nature, society and thought. In this sense science is nothing but man's systematic understanding of various phenomena. Science is always persuasive and necessarily based on the evidence or proof.

science, philosophy of

organized empirical science provides the most impressive result of human rationality and is one of the best accredited candidates for knowledge. The philosophy of science seeks to show wherein this rationality lies; what is distinctive about its explanations, and theoretical constructions; what makes it off from guesswork and pseudoscience and makes its predictions and technologies worthy of confidence; above all whether its theories can be taken to reveal the truth about a hidden objective reality.

scientism

(1) the belief that the human sciences require no methods other than those of the nutural.

(2) in a more general sense, practices that pretend to be, but are not, science.

scope

of a logical operator, the shortest prepositional function in which it occurs.

scotism

the philosophy of Duns Scotus and his followers.

Scylla and Charybdis

respectively a sea-monster and a whirlpool in the Straits of Messina; of dire peril to mariners.

seafight

the problem set by Aristotle in De Interpretatione IX. Since it is clearly necessary that either there will be a seafight tomorrow or there will not, surely whichever in fact happens must happen necessarily and inevitably.

secondary causes

ordinary, everyday causes 'within the universe' seen in

relation to and in contrast with the first cause.

secularism

from the Latin saecularis ('the times', 'the age', 'the world'). The secular stands in contrast to the sacred, marking an approach to life divorced from the influence of religion, and thus determined by temporal or wordily concerns.

secundum quid

Latin phrase meaning 'according to something'. It is used in Scholastic terminology as a qualifying phrase. An assertion secundum quid is to be taken in a qualified, restrictd, or secondary sense. Failure to take an assertion in its properly restricted sense is sometimes called the fallacy of secundum quid.

Selene

Greek goddess of the moon; later identified with Artemis; Helios (the sun) was her brother. Her latin counterpart was Luna.

self

an obsolescent technical term for a person, but a person thought of as incorporeal and essentially conscious.

self-alienation

it is a condition of the self in which it is aware of its estrangement from itself, and also from other objects or individuals.

self-contradiction

the affirmation by the same person of two propositions that are in contradiction, or contradictory, one to the other. What that person has thus said is self-contradictory.

self-deception

a state resembling but distinguishable from that of ignorance or of false belief, and consising in a motivated blindness to facts that are in some way or for some reason undesirable or unacceptable to the individual concerned.

self-determination

the determination of one's actions by oneself without external compulsion.

self-existence

in Spinoza's philosophy, substance is regarded as self-existent. In that sense, anything that does not depend on any other thing for its existence is self-existent.

self-regarding

a term applied by J. S. Mill to actions that affect only the agent, to be contrasted with not self-regarding (or other regarding) actions.

self realization

the development of the possibilities of the self.

Semantic paradoxes

usually distinguished from the logical paradoxes in that they arise from the use of semantic notions, such as truth and reference.

Semantics (in general)

the study of signs and their relations to what they signify. 'Semiosis' and 'semiotics' are alos used in this sense.

Semele

daughter of Cadmus and mother, by Zeus, of Dionysus; she perished when she beheld her divine lover in all his godly splendour, but eventually joined the immortals on Olympus.

semiotics

the theory of signs; also called semiology. It is traditionally divided into three parts: syntactics, the study of grammar; semantics, the study of meaning, and pragmatics, the study of the actual purposes and effects of meaningful utterances.

sensa

a wide term covering all the locutions used in the perennial attempts to differentiate, from what publicity exists and is actually preceived, that which is merely felt, and the feeling of which does not, of itself, imply that anything either exists or has any specifiable qualities.

sensation

1. ordinarily, having such feeling as cold, pressure, thirst, itches, or pains.
2. technically, mental entities of a kind private to their owner.

sensationalism

a term sometimes used in the history of phylosophy to designate those who hold that all knowledge has its origin in sensation.

sense-data

the term was first introduced by G.E.Moore to denote those objects of sense-experience that are immediately given. Subsequently, the term has been used more freely by H.H. Price, Ayer and other analytical philosophers. According to these philosophers, what is immediately given in sense-experience is called 'sense-datum'.

sense-datum

a term referring to that which is immediately given in awareness. The plural is sense-data.

sense experience

the portion of a living agent's history that is derived from reception of stimuli through the five senses; or, a single identifiable and unified body of such stimuli.

sensible world

the world as we have access to it in sense experience.

sensor

1. an organ of sense in a living things, that receives stimuli.
2. a whole organism that is, among other things, capable of receiving stimuli.

sensorium

the term was put into use by Newton to denote the seat in the brain of sensation and perception.

separation of powers

the separation of power into legislative, executive, and judicial, made concrete in the American Constitution, was recommended by Montaigne.

Serapis

late Egyptian deity who became a cult divinity in the Hellenistic mysteries.

set

a set is a collection of objects that become or form the members of that set.

set theory

the theory of sets was initiated by Cantor and stands at the interface of logic and mathematics. The discipline has moved through many controversies whose locus has centred in the logical paradoxes concerning sets which are and at the same time are not members of themselves. One solution is that of axiomatic set theory.

Seven against Thebes

after the flight of Oedipus, king of Thebes, his 2 sons, Eteocles and Polynices, ruled in his stead as joint sovereigns. This arrangment proving unsuccessful, the brothers agreed to govern the city alternatively, each holding office for 1 year at a time. When, however, Eteocles year of rule ended he refused to allow his brother to succeed him; Polynices appealed to Adrastus, king of Argos, who organized an expedition known as the 'Seven against Thebes'. The outcome was disastrous; the 2 contending brothers killed each other in single combat and 4 of the other chieftains were also slain, though Adrastus himself escaped.

shakha

brach or school.

shastra

sacred text.

shinto

the national religion of Japan, having survived from primitive times long beofe the appearance of either Confucianism or Buddhism. Its history falls into 3 distinct periods: (a) the early period before the influx of Buddhism from Korea in the 6th c. A.D.; (b) the medieval period from the 6 h c. to the 19th c., when the Imperial Throne was restored (1968); and (c) the modern period, in which State Shinto has been a mark of loyalty to the imperial monarchy.

The first of these periods goes back to the primitive Natureworship which resulted from the sense of supernatural power evoked by the objects and forces of the physical environment. Out of this original nature-worship polytheism emerged. The ancient shrines, temples of the naturecult, were simple and austere and contained no image of the deity but only a symbolic or sacramental token of it—in later terminology a shintai or god-body. The veneration of heroes was added later, culminating in devotion to the person of the emperor as a descendant of the sun-goddess, Amaterasu, ruler of the heavens together with her brother, the storm-god, Susanowo. The Shinto myths include a creation-story, according to which, out of the primeval chaos and darkness, came a divine couple, Izanagi (The Male-who-Invites) and Izanami (The Female-who-Invites), who begat in turn the islands of Japan, the spirits of nature, and the 'high gods', Amaterasu, Susanowo, and the moon-god, Tsuki-yomi.

The second period begins with the introduction of the ethical ideals of Confucianism and the religious philosophy of Buddhism. The great historic figure of this age was Prince Shotoku, who, in a turbulent era, taught that the conqueror in battle is not the only hero. The main Shinto scred records date from the 8th c. A.D. and were compiled in order to preserve the ancienttraditions from obliteration by Buddhism and to maintain belief in the divine origin of the ruling family. They do not claim to contain a divine revelation of any kind. For many centuries the Buddhist influence remained powerful and provided a means for interpreting the Shinto scriptures in terms of a consistent religious doctrine. Originally Shinto had no belief in the immortality of the soul and the subsequent growth of the idea, and with it the cult of ancestors, is to be directly attributed to Buddhism.

Eventural reaction against both Buddhism and Confucianism as alien importations led to the rise of Pure Shinto and an increased loyalty to the Throne after the prolonged regime of the feudal nobility. This is the period of Meiji or Enlightened Government, with its adulation of the person of the emperor and the chauvinistic nationalism of State Shinto, reminiscent in some ways of the emperor-worship of imperial Rome in early Christian days. Popular religious belief is met by Sect shinto, a fairly recent development. This consists of a number of separate 'churches'—13 have been officially recognized—each with its own teaching and organization. Of these one of the most interesting is the faith-healing Konkokyo sect, founded in the last century by Bunijiro, a Shinto priest, who believed he was a divine incarnation.

Shiva

Hindu god. Center of worship in the Saiva sect of Hinduism. In the Hindu trinity he is the destroyer, while Brahma creates, and Vishnu preserves. His wife is Kali, a destroyer goddess, who is worshipped as the terrible mother. Shiva's symbol is the linga or phallus; the bull is associated with his worship. He is also the god of mountains and of the overcoming of death. The contrasting ascriptions given to Shiva as destroyer and redeemer may relate to differences of tradition, the former originating in the north and the latter in the south of India.

shraddha

faith, respect, or devotion.

shruti

revelation.

shudra

a serving class.

Shunyavada

Sanskrit term meaning 'criticism'. The core term, shunya, literally means 'negation' or 'void', but is better taken as 'indescribable'. 'Shunyavada is the name of one of the most important of the schools of the Buddhism.

Sibyl

priestess of Apollo, who prophesied by his inspiration. The most famous was the Cumaean Sibyl, who in Virgil directs Aeneas to Hades.

Sidgwick, Henry (1838-1900)

a British moral philosopher who advocated utilitarian ethics. According to Sidgwick, the obligation to promote general happiness is realised only if it is regarded as a moral intution. One of his important works is The Methods of Ethics.

sign

from the Latin signum and the Greek semeion, originally meaning a verbal signal. The theory of signs is usually called Semiotic.

sign and symbol

a satisfactory definition for these terms is not available. For instance, words are supposed to be the conventional signs. Whereas language is considered to be a kind of symbolism. In that sense, language consists of signs. A twister in the sky is said to be a natural sign

signification

most often used as synonymous with 'meaning', 'connotation', or 'intension'.

sikhs

an Indian religious sect, inclining to Hinduism rather than Islam. Its founder was Nanak (1469-1538) whose saying, 'There is no Hindu and no Molem', soon attracted disciples (the word skh means disciple), and he did much to bring Hindus and Moslems toether. As against Hindu poytheism Sikh worship proclaims that there is only one God, the Creator. Its holy book, always open in a Sikh temple (of which the Golden Temple at Amritsar is the most famous), is the Granth, a collection of hymns by Nanak and others. Sikhs wear their hair uncut and carry by tradition a steel comb and bangle. They are noted for their military prowess.

Silenus

son of Hermes, or Pan. He was a woodland deity usually represented as a fat, jovial, and lecherous old man in the train of Dionysus and too drunk to walk. But he was credited with the power of prophecy.

simple enumeration
an inductive method. If this A and that A and the other A are all θ, and these are all the As which you are acquainted with, then it is an induction by simple enumeration to conclude that all As are θ.

simplicity
the contemporary equivalent of Ockham's Razor is the view held by philosophers of science that simplicity is one of the criteria determining the selection of the primitives or undefined predicates at the base of a conceptual system.

sin
strictly, a theological term, mening offence against God. What is a sin, therefore, may or may not violate thisew-worldly moral standards.

Siren
nymph, half woman, half bird, whose enchanting song lured sailors to their doom. Odysseus escaped the sirens only by plugging his men's ears and by having himself tied to his ship's mast.

Sisyphus
legnedary founder and first king of Corinth. For his avarice and fraudulent dealing he was punished in Hades by the vain labour of having for ever to roll a block of marble uphill, whence it always rolled down again.

Smith, Adam (1723-1790)
a Scottish economist and a philosopher who is well-known for his work The Wealth of Nations. His political economy is based on the simple system of natural liberty. He held that the general welfare of humanity is perpetuated only when an individual's own interest is promoted.

social contract
refers to an agreement between individuals, or between individuals and a governing power, in which some personal liberties are freely surrendered in return for the advantages of having a well organized society, or good government.

social contract theory
the doctrine that social organization rests on a contract or compact which the people have made among themselves.

social darwinism
the belief that the development and structure of human societies can be explained in terms of the evolutionary forces that shape non-human bilogy, and particularly in terms of "survival of the fittest".

socialism
from the Latin 'socius' ('comrade'). The term applies to any association, private or public, organized around the principle of group control of property and the production and distribution of wealth.

social philosophy
an expression afflicted with the same vagueness and ambiguity as besets the word 'philosophy'

itself, as well as with other troubles of its own.

society

translation of the Latin societas from socio ('to share or to unite').

Aristotle does make a distinction between state and society since his state is composed of societal units, that is, of families.

sociology

from the Latin socio ('to associate') and logos ('knowledge'). The term is taken to refer to a study of the forms, institutions, functions, and interrelations of human groups.

sociology of knowledge

a misnamed discipline, which is in fact devoted to discovering the social causes of people having whatever beliefs they do have, without prejudice to the quite different question of whatever they have, or there are, sufficient grounds to warrant rating these beleifs as knowledge.

socratic fallacy

the mistake, characteristic of the Socrates of Plato's earlier dialogues, of arguing that no one knows anything about Xs or even that any Xs truly are Xs, unless he can provide a definition of the word 'X'.

Socratic method

the dialectical method supposedly employed by the historical Socrates, and displayed in Plato's earlier dialogues.

Socratic schools

the term is used to refer to schools of philosophy shaped by the influence of Socrates. In this sense Plato's Academy would qualify as one of the Socratic schools; but the mature Platonic thought is, rather, considered as initiaing its own school.

solipsism

the theory that 'I' and my own self alone exists. All others' existence is reduced to my own existence. In fact, every subjective idealist doctrine ultimately boils down to solipsism.

soma

a god of the Vedic religion. Initially an intoxicating beverage of ancient India, Soma by personification became a god.

some

in logic, it is considered as a quantifier. 'Some' denotes at least one. It can also mean everyone except one.

sorites

an argument with any number of premises and term that otherwise satisfy the criteria for syllogisms, and can be set out as a series of syllogisms each of whose conclusions forms one premise of the succeeding syllogism.

sortal universal

a general term that supplies a principle for counting what falls under it.

soul

sometimes it is also used as a

synonym for self. In religion, soul is considered to be an incorporeal, immortal, and immaterial force capable of existing independently of body in other world. According to Plato, soul is an eternal idea; while Hegel regarded it as the lowest sensory manifestation of the spirit in its relation with matter.

sovereignty

from the French souverain referring to the 'chief' or 'supreme' power of the state.

space

along with time, one of the ultimate categories of natural philosophy.

Greek philosophy contrasted the plenum and the void. Where Democritus used the void as his concept of space, that in which atoms move, Parmenides held there could be no empty space, since, as his disciple Zeno of Elea argued, the concept is contradictory; he therefore interpreted space as a plenum; its fullness, indeed, makes motion impossible.

Einstein developed the concept of the relativity of space, and discovered its curvature. The relativity of space-time means that simultaneity can be established only within a given intertial system, and has no validity for observers in systems moving in relation to the given inertial system.

space-time

a four-dimensional order with four coordinates, three of them spatial and one temporal. Specification of the coordinates precisely locates any physical magnitude whatever.

species

a Latin term meaning 'sort' or 'kind'. The Greek is eidos ('form' or 'figure'); the term designates a class standing between the genus and the individuals to which the term refers.

specious present

the least temporal interval such that two modifications of experience, separated by that interval, may nevertheless seem to the subject to be co-present in his consciousness.

speech acts

the acts that are performed while speaking. This term was introduced by J.L. Austin. According to Austin, speech acts can be classified into locutionary, perlocutionary, and illocutionary acts. A locutionary act is one in which a statement is uttered with a definite reference, e.g. This is red. A perlocutionary act is one in which a statement uttered will have some specific effects upon the feelings, thoughts, or behaviour, etc. For e.g. Yor are a wicked person. An illocutionary act is one in which the statement uttered implies the act in question. For example, I promise that I will definitely come. It is not only an utterance but also the performance of an act.

Sphinx
female monster with a human head and the body of a lion. Sent by Hera to Thebes, she devoured all who failed to answer her riddle.

spirit
a word commonly used to translate the Hegelian term Geist (also translated as 'mind'). According to Hegel, spirit differs from nature in that spirit is an 'I', in Hegel's language, spirit has being 'for itself'. Hegel recognizes three types of spirit: subjective, objective and absolute.

spiritualism
a term with both philosophical and religions associations. Philosophically, the term is sometimes used as a synonym of Idealism. In religion the term sometimes refers to the indwelling of the Holy Spirits.

spontaneity
from the Latin sponte meaning 'of free will' or 'voluntarily'.

square of opposition
in medieval texts, a diagram summerizing the logical relations between the four categorical propositions each having the same subject and predicate terms. These propositions are traditionally represented by A.E.I.O.

state
from the Latin status ('standing' or 'position'). A collective entity with territoral boundaries and political organization exercising sovereign power.

state description
in extensional semantics a class comprising, for a given semantical system, every atomic sentence or its negation. A true state description contains all of the true atomic sentences of the system, and the negation of all the false atomic sentences.

state of nature
refers to the condition in which people either did live before, or would live without, making or acceding to a social contract.

statistics
the science of handling information about classes of things, or populations, where each member is associated with one of a set of possible properties or outcomes.

Stentor
Greek herald before Troy, noted for the power of his voice.

stimulus meanings
a concept used by Quine in an attempt to explicate analyticity and synonymy in terms of behavioural dispositions. In addition to the above term he referred to stimulus-analyticity and stimulus-synonymy.

stochastic
denoting a physical process that gives rise to a class of events within which a characteristic has a definite probability; that is, a random variable takes on a defined distribution.

stochastic process
a process whose development is probabilistic, that is whose

stages stages are determined by the values of one or more random variables.

stoicism

from the Greek stoa ('porch'). A Graeco-Roman school of philosophy founded in 108 B.C. in Athens by Zeno of Citium, and developing its greatest influence in the Roman Empire where at one time it was the dominant intellectual influence. The name of the school derives from the location in Athens where the school first met. The doctrines of the school are diverse but they include the development of a logic (divided into rhetoric and dialectic), physics, and an ethic which like-wise involves a theology. Indeed, the Stoics seem to have introduce the division of philosophy into these three disciplines.

stratonion presumption

it is a view according to which whosever wants to postulate the existence of God must give sufficient reason for such a postulation.

straw man

a position, not in fact held by an opponent in an argument, which is invented and assailed in preference to attending to his actual stance.

structuralism

a method of approach, rather than a distinct philosophy, that has application in both linguistics and the social sciences :

1. (in lingustics). The theory that language is best described, in terms of its irreducible structural units in morphology, phonology, etc. Structure, deep and surface.

2. (in the social sciences). The view that the key to the understanding of observed phenomena lies in the underlying structures and systems of social organization.

structure, deep and surface

terms occurring in Chomsky's analysis of grammar. This analysis supposes that speakers possess rules for combining various grammatical elements, such as verbs, tense signs, and nouns, into sequences. These initially unidiomatic strings (the deep, underlying structure) are then converted into vernacular speech by transformation rules. They thus take on the surface structures of everyday speech.

sturm UND drang

a German phrase meaning storm and stress. A movement in Germany opposing the principle of Romanticism to the French ideals of Englightenment.

Styx

river of Greek mythology encircling the Underworld. It was fatal for a mortal to break an oath sworn by it.

subaltern

it is a term that is used in the traditional square of oppositions that is popular in scholastic logic. In this traditional square the universal affirmative proposition (A) and the particular affirmative propositions (I) stand subalten to each other. For example, 'All men are mortal' is a subaltern of 'Some men are mortal'.

subconscious

a mental state or process occurring just below the level of awareness.

subcontraries

in a traditional square of opposites, particular affirmative propositions (I) and particular negative propositions (O) are subcontraries to each other. For example, 'Some crows are black' and 'Some crows are not black' are subcontraries.

subjectivism and objectivism

subjectivism. In its simplest form, the position held by someone who believes that all moral attitudes are merely a matter of personal taste.

Objectivism the relief that there are certain moral truth that would remain true whatever anyone of everyone thought or desired.

subject-predicate logic

Aristotle's logic of predication centering in the theory of the syllogism.

sublime, the

(1) that which is beyond all comaprison great, either mathemtically in terms of limitless magnitude, or dynamically in terms of limitless power.

(2) the term used to designate natural objects that inspire a kind of awed terro through sheer immensity.

subsistence

it is a mode of being that is distinguished from the three-dimentional existence of the objects. According to Meinong and others, subsistence is a monochrome and insubstantial analogue which does not exist in space and time, but is real such as relation, number, universal, spirit, soul etc.

substance

the term refers to the underlying, supporting substratum of change. But 'substance' also contains the idea of the individual subject to change.

substrate (or substratum)

refers to that which bears properties. For example for the subject of any change between a pair of opposites, such as the material withou which heat cannot itself change into cold, is a substrate.

sufficient condition

A is a sufficient condition of B, if whenever there is A, then there is B.

sufficient reason, principle of

in Leibniz the view that nothing takes place without a reason sufficient to determine why it is as it is and not otherwise.

suicide

the act of voluntarily taking

one's own life. The case enters into discussions of freedom and responsibility.

sui generis

(Latin for: of its (or his or her) own kind). Of a thing believed to be unique, and not a member of a class with other fellow members. God is then said to be sui generis.

summum bonum

a Latin term meaning 'the highest good'. The term has been applied to the ultimate ends of man, or to that which is intrinsically good.

sunday

the 1st day of the week, the Christian equivalent of the Sabbath, sometimes known as the Lord's Day and chosen origin-ally as the day of Christ's Resurrection.

suparan

eagle.

supernaturalism

the theological doctrine that the divine is fundamentally different from the temporal order and cannot be approached through its categories, i.e., by means of reason.

supervenient features or characteristics

the qualities of properties that are dependent upon some other qualities or properties.

suppositio

Latin term referring to the specific signfication of a sign.

surplus value

according to Marx the difference between the price paid for a product and the price paid labor in its manufacture.

syllogism

as defined by Aristotle, the founder of the traditional formal logic, a discourse in which, certain things being stated, something other than what is stated follows of necessity from their being so.

symbol

in religious thought and practice, symbols are commonly regarded as sensuous representations of a transcendent reality. In system of logical and scientific thought the term is normally used in the sense of an abstract sign.

symmetry

a property of certain relations and matching geometrical elements. A relation is symmetrical when it is reversible.

symptom

in the work of later Wittgenstein, symptom is contrasted with criterion. According to him, a symptom serves as an evidence rather than a criterion. For example, whenver there is A, it is invariably followed by B. In that sense, A is a symptom of B.

syncategorematic

in traditional logic, denoting a word that cannot stand on its own, but must be joined to a categorematic term in order to enter a categorical proposition, for example, 'all', 'and', and 'some'. In modern logic the sense has been extended to apply to any symbol that has no independent meaning.

synderesis (or synteresis)

in Aquins and other scholastic writers, the innate intellectual quality that enables every man to innate the general and basic principles of practical moral reasoning.

syndicalism

a doctrine that opposed capitalism which is inherently oppressive and inefficient bureaucratic system. It tried to replace capitalism by organized production units called 'syndicats'.

synonymy

the study of identity of meaning, especially as it touches upon the interpretation of analytic statements and the interchangeability of terms.

syntactics

one of the three major aspects of the general theory of signs, along with Semantics and Pragmatics. Syntactics deals with the aspect of the study concerning the relations of the signs of a language to each other.

syntax (of a natural language)

the system of rules governing the grammatical construction of sentences of the language.

synthesis

a process of bringing all the simple elements together to form a complex whole. The method of synthesis is advanced by many philosophers. In Hegel's philosophy, synthesis is nothing but the fusion of two diametrically opposite ideas known as thesis and antithesis.

synthetic a priori judgment, statement, or proposition

a judgment, statement or proposition in which the predicate adds content to the subject, and which yet has the necessity of analytic judgments.

Syrinx

the pipes of Pan.

system

(1) the term is sometimes applied to the characteristic features of the thought of particular individuals and schools, e.g., Plato's system.
(2) in formal terms, by system is meant a set of elements with internal coherence and unity, provided by rules governing their permissible combination and transformation.

system of logic

any set of axioms and/or rules of inference governing some or all of the logical operators. The formal validity of an argument containing those logical operators can be checked by reference to such a system.

tables of induction

the tables of Essence and Presence, Absence in Proximity, and Degrees or Comparison, recommended by Francis Bacon in using inductive method.

tabu

a polynesian term signifying a mysterious potency thought to involve danger to oneself or one's group.

tabula rasa

a Latin term meaning 'blank tablet', the concept that the mind begins without innate knowledge, gaining all knowledge from experience.

tadatmya (identity)

it is a relation of identity between two entities. Sankhya, Bhatta, and Advaita consider this relation as essential internal. It is also known as samsarga.

Tagore, Rabindranath

Indian poet and philosopher born in Calcutta. Educated in London. Founded Visabharati University. His many volumes of poetry were influenced by Bhakti-oriented Bauls of Bengal. His philosophical work was directed toward those central truths which mediate among all positions, or the 'one great principle of unity' in everyone. The following books were written in English.
Selected writings: Sadhana. The Realisation of Life, 1913; Personality, 1917; Creative Unity, 1922; The Religion of Man, 1931; Man, 1937; Towards Universal Man, 1961.

talmud

the body of Jewish civil and religious law not contained in the Pentateuch; it includes the Mishnah and the cludes the Mishnah and the Gemara (comment on the Mishnah).

tamas

quality of darkness.

Tantalus

legendary king in Lydia, father of Pelops and Niobe, who for his offence against the gods was punished, as Homer relates, by being made to stand up to his neck in water; when he attempted to drink it the water receded; above his head hung fruits which the wind blew aside when he reached up to pluck them.

taoism

it is a Chinese philosophical school of thought as old as Confucianism. The two important works of Taoist literature are - Lao-tzu.

tapas

Sanskrit term meaning 'austerity'. One of the means of ethical purification in Yogic meditation.

tarka (reasoning)

it is one of the sixteen categories of Nyaya school. It consists in seeking reason for supporting a statement or argument.

Tartarus

the region below Hades, reserved for the Titans. Later identified with Hades.

taste

one of the five senses. It is also a personal preference.

tattva

Sanskrit term for 'category'. The term we have translated as 'category' in the expositions of, e.g., Jainism and of the Sankhya philosophy.

tat tvam asi

Sanskrit sentence meaning 'that art thou'. The assertion identifying the Atman or inner self, with Brahman, the creater and upholder of all things, is found in the Chandogya Upanishad.

techne

it is a Greek term for 'skill or craft'. In Aristotle's philosophy, the term techne denotes that which is created by humans in contrast to natural things or phenomena. The products of science can be called techne as they are the artefacts of mankind.

Telamon

brother of Peleus; he was the father of Ajax and a companion of Heracles.

Telegonus

Odyssues son by Circe. He arrived one day at Ithaca in search of his father, who unhappily mistook him for a pirate. In the fight Odysseus was killed. Later Telegonus married Penelope, Odysseus widow.

Telemachus

Odysseus son by his wife Penelope; he helped his father slay her unwanted suitors.

teleological argument

from 'teleology' one of the three basic arguments for God, taking the purpose, order, or design of the universe as premise for the conclusion that God exists.

teleological ethics

that family of ethical theories which analyze the right in terms of the ends of action. The emphasis is thus on the consequence likely to flow from decision.

teleology

1. a doctrine that everything in the world has been designed by God to be of service to man.
2. the theory or study of purposiveness in nature: characteristically, certain phenomena seem to be best explained not by means of prior causes, but by ends or aims, intentions or purposes. Teleolgocial explanation seems typical of living or organic things—plants, animals, people. Thus an animal's behaviour is sometimes best described in terms of its goal (food seeking, for example) a chess player's activity can be understood in terms of his purpose—to win. Kant in his Kritik der Urteilskraft (critique of judgment), wrote extensively on teleological judgments. The subject has been much discussed recently in the philosophy of science, especially in connection with biology and psychology and there have been many attempts to show how teleological explanation do not, as they appear to, explain present events by future ones.

telepathy

a form of extra sensory

perception through which one can introspect the minds of others. It is one of the possibility of establishing the knowledge of other minds.

temperament

it represents the bodily, mental and predispositional character of an individual. There are four types of temperament—sanguine, phlegmatic, bilious, and melancholic.

temperance

one of the four Greek cardinal virtues. In Plato the specific virtue of the artisans.

temple

1. a building dedicated to the worship of a god or gods. 2. One of the 3 successive sacred edifices—the Solomnic, the post-Exilic, and the Herodian—of the Jews in Jerusalem, the last being destroyed by the Romans in A.D. 70.

3. occasionally a Christian place of worship, especially a Protestant church in France.

term

(in Aristotelian logic). According to Aristotle, who introduced the device of symbolizing arguments in order to exhibit their forms, a term is that 'into which the proposition is resolved, that is both the predicate and that half of which it is predicated', 'being' or 'not being' being added.

terministic logic

a 13-th century movement of logic in which the nature of language was strongly emphasized. The word was treated first as a physical entity, and only secondly as a significant term.

Terminus

Roman god of boundaries and frontiers.

tertiary quality

it is opposed to primary and secondary qualities. Unlike primary and secondary qualities, tertiary quality is imposed on the object in question by the perceipient. For example, beauty, good, bad, ugly are tertiary qualities.

terza rima

Dante's metre in the 'Divine Comedy', lines of 5 iambic feet with an extra syllable, so rhymed occurs 3 times in alternate lines, except at the beginning and end of the canto. Shelley's 'Ode to the West Wind' is in this metre.

Tethys

daughter 'in Greek mythology' of Uranus and Ge, and wife of Oceanus, her children being the Oceanids.

thanatism

it is a belief that death results in the cessation and annihilation of consciousness.

Thanatos

Greek personification of death. Nyx (night) was his mother and Hypnos (Sleep) his brother.

theism

belief in God, where God is understood to be the single omnipotent and omniscient creator of everything else that exists. He is regarded as a being distinct from his creation though manifesting himself through it, and also essential by personal, caring for and communicationg with mankind, and infinitely worthy of human worship and obedience. Theìsm thus is clearly a 'central element in the whole Judaeo-Christian religion tradition'.

theist

one who believes in the existence of God or in some supernatural power is a theist.

Themis

daughter of Uranus and Ge. In Homer she signifies the order of law and justice.

theodicy

from those ('God') and dike (Justice). A term introduced by Leibniz to characterize the topic of God's government of the world in relation to the nature of man. The problem is the justification of God's goddness and justice in view of the evil in the world.

theology

theologia was originally viewed as concerned with myth. It was Aristotle who first regarded theology as a discipline, identifying it with first philosophy, the highest of the theoretical sciences, a study which was later termed metaphysics.

theorem

anything that is established as a maxim, a rule or a principle. From a theorom one can deduce many valid conclusions.

theoria

it is a Greek term for 'viewing'. According to Plato, theoria means contemplation or the intuitive grasp of the Being 'world of Forms'.

theory-laden

denoting a concept, term, or statement that refers to, and can only be understood in the light of, a particular theory. For example, the phrase 'collective unconscious' makes sense only in the context of Jungian psychology.

theosophy

an esoteric trend in religious thought. Initiates strive towards mystical insight into God's nature.

Thersites

deformed, ill-mannered, and loud-mouthed Greek at the siege of Troy.

Theseus

great Attic hero; son of Aegeus, king of Athens. Sent to Creto to be devoured by the Minotaur. He instead slew the monster with the help of Ariadne, the kings daughter, who had fallen in love with him. Theseus carried her off from Crete, but deserted her at Naxos. He succeeded his father as king, and then made war upon the Amazons, whose captured queen bore him a son, Hippolytus. He was among the Argonauts; during his absence from Athens a revọlt was engineered against him which he failed to quell. He took refuge at Scyros, where he was murdered by Lycomedes.

Thetis

Greek sea-goddess; daughter of Nereus and Doris; Zeus and Poseidon both sought her as wife, but she although unwillingly, married a mortal, Peleus, by whom she bore a son, Achilles.

thinking

the mental activity of (a) theoretical contemplation directed towards some object with a view to reaching a propositional conclusion; or (b) practical deliberation directed towards some object with a view to reaching a decision to act.

thomism

the philosophy emerging from the thought of Thomas Aquinas along with the development of this thought by his followers in later centuries.

thought

the term applies both to the process of mental activity and to its product. The interpretation of either depends upon the position one holds with respect to metaphysics, universals, and epistemology.

time

it is one of the fundamental categories of physical sciences. Philosophers and scientists have interpreted it in several ways. British metaphysician MacTaggart held the view that the time is unreal. According to Kant, time is a form of intuition, and is absolute. Scientists like Newton and Einstein held the view that the time is objective, though absolute, and can exist independent of perceiving subject. All change in space takes place in time. Einstein redically departed from Newton in holding the view that time is a relative concept, and is a fourth dimension of space. Thus space and time are inseparable from each other.

time-lag argument

an argument casting doubt on the reliability of our perception of real physical objects. It was formulated most succinctly by Russell in Human Knowledge.

timocracy

from the Greek time ('honour') and kratos ('rule'). Government based on the criterion of honour. One of Plato's five types of government.

Tiresias

blind soothsayer of Thebes. Even in Hades he still retained his seer's powers.

Titans

the 6 sons and 6 daughters of Uranus and Ge. Kronos and Rhea were the most important. The whole brood revolted against their father. Uranus for having cast his other children by Ge (the Hecatoncheires, or hundred-handed monsters, and the Cyclops) into Tartarus. Kronos in revenge cut off his father's genitals with a sickel given him by Rhea and threw them into the sea. (Aphrodite was born from the waves thus caused). The Titans thereupon deposed Uranus, liberated their brothers from the Underworld and made Kronos their king.

Tithonus

brother of Priam of Troy, loved by Eos (dawn) for his beauty. Unhappily he obtained the gift of immortality without enjoying eternal youth. In disgust at his growing ugliness Eos turned him into a grasshopper.

tmesis

separation of the parts of a compound word by the insertion of another word, as when 'whatsoever things' in written 'what things soever'.

token

any particular specimen of any general class. All these specimens may be descirbed as the several tokens of that single type.

token-reflexive

denoting a word or expression of which it is necessary to know first who is speaking or writing it, and when or where, in order to know to what particulars reference is being made.

topic-neutral

a term describing concepts that are neutral for any particular subject matter.

totemism

from the Ojibwa term ototeman ('brother-sister kinship'). A world-view characteristic of primitive societies in which the group regards itself as having blood realtionship to a given animal (or plant).

traducianism

the doctrine, initiated by Tertullian, that souls are passed along in the process of human generation, souls being produced from souls as bodies are produced from bodies.

tragedy

in the Poetics, Aristotle held tragedy to be an imitation of an action by men better than or like us; the action being serious (passing from happiness to misery by necessity, or at least by probability), complete (i.e, its plot having beginning, middle, and end and in its best form containing a peripety—or reversal of the situation—and recongnition), of a certain magnitude (i.e. usually occurring within the limits of a single day).

transcendence

the doctrine that God is above and independent of his created universe. Its extreme form is Deism. Cf. Immanence.

transcendent

beyond experience. The word is often used by theist to describe the way in which God supposedly exists beyond and independent of the created world.

transcendental argument

an argument that answers the question : of a proposition known to be true, what conditions must be fulfilled for transcendental knowledge to be possible?

transcendentalism

(1) Kant's philosophy of the transcendental, and hence any theory asserting the dependence of the world of experience on the activities of reason.

(2) a mode of thought that emphasizes the intuitive and super-sensuous.

(3) a form of religious mysticism.

(4) the particular doctrine adopted by a movement in New England under the leadership of Emerson and his associates, influenced by Platonism and German idealism and reacting against dogmatic rationalism.

transcendentals

a term used by medieval philosophers to signify predicates that transcend the Aristotelian categories.

transformation rules

the instructions governing the transformation of one with in a formal language into another.

transitivity

a logical and mathematical property of transferability such that the relation x has to y and y to z, x must likewise have to z.

transmigartion

at the time of death the soul or the spirit transmigrates into another body. It is a prevalent view of Hindu religious doctrines.

transubstantiation

a doctrine of the Roman Catholic Church according to which in the Eucharist the whole substance of the bread is changed by divine power, through the act of consecration, into the whole substance of Christ's body, and the whole substance of the wine into the whole substance of his blood, the material qualities (or accidents) of the bread and wine remaining unchanged.

treta yuga

era.

trimurti

a Sanskrit term meaning 'having three shapes'. The Hindu trinity consisting of Brahman, Vishnu and Shiva.

trinity

the doctrine of Christian theology, that the one God exists in 3 persons, Father, Son, and Holy ghost, and one substance. it is held to have been divinely revealed but to remain essentially a mystery. Orthodox exposition of the doctrine seeks to avoid, on theone hand, tritheism, or the idea of 3 independent divine personalities, and on the other, modalism, or the idea that the persons—the personal distinctions within the one Godhead—are but transitory modes of a single divine reality.

triputi (triple form)

in the process of cognition there are three things involved in it. They are the cognizer, the object cognized and the means of cognition. They are called triputi.

Triton
son of Poseidon and Amphitrite represented as half man, half dolphin.

Troy, Ilion
ancient city on the river Scamander in north-west Asia Minor, besieged by the Greeks in the Trojan war. It was believed to have been wholly legendary until in 1873—81 its remains were excavated by Heinrich Schliemann at Hissarlik.

truth
the putative object of knowledge and goal of inquiry, the term stands in contrast sometimes to 'falsity' and at other times to 'opinion'.
The basic theories of truth include the correspondence theory (the true is the coherent system of ideas), the pragmatic theory (the true 'corresponds' to reality), the coherence theory (the truth is the 'workable' or satisfactory solution of a problematic situation), the semantic theory (assertions about truth are in a metalanguage and apply to statements of the base language), the performative theory (the assertion of truth is the performative act of agreeing with a given statement).
Criteria of truth are the marks by which we know the truth. 'Coherence' and 'workability' are examples of such criteria.

truth definition
a formal characterization of the set of true sentences of a language which is already used meaningfully — a characterization which is derived from an interpretation of the language. Any interpretation affords a way of describing the set of true sentences of a language.

truth functional
(of a connective). Describing a connective when the true-value of any statement formed using it is determined in a systmatic way by the truth-values of the connected statements.

truth is always in the middle
a demonstrably false maxim, yet perennially appealing to those who like to see themselves as balanced and moderate judges.

truth-table
a device, sometimes also known as matrix, for exhibiting the conditions under which a truth functional compound is true or false.

truth theory
any account of how, given truth conditions for the semantic elements of a language, the truth-values of the sentences of the language are to be determined.

truth value
a technical term introduced by Frege, who saw a strong analogy between concepts or predicates and mathematical functions. Consequently he

thought of sentences (expressions in which a predicate is applied to an object) as standing for, or denoting, a value in the same way that 3^2 denotes 9, the value of the function x^2 for $x = 3$. When a statement is, or is evaluated as true, it is said to have the truth-value True (indicated by T) and when it is false it is said to have the truth-value. False (indicated by F).

tychism

this term is introduced by Charles Saunders Peirce, the pioneer of pragmatism. According to tychism, the absolute chance is a characteristic feature of the events that take place in this objective world. This theory holds that there are many theories which do not have causees at all. They just take place without any reason. For Peirce believes that all the biological processes are of this nature. In other words, they are tychistic in character.

Tyndareous

son of the Spartan king Oebalus and husband of Leda.

type

the term seems to have been derived from something like the contrast between a seal and its imprint.

For Plato and Aristo le the the term was applid to schematic representation or summary images.

In logic the relation between token and type is roughly that of the meaning of a word to its written or spoken instances.

types, theory of

Russell's attempt to deal with the problem of self-reference. He produced two versions of the theory—the simple and the ramified. The problem itself is famously illustrated by the assertion of Epimenides the Cretan 'All Cretans are always liars'.

Typhon

hundred-headed monster buried by Zeus in Tartarus under Mt Aetna. The creature fathered many other monsters, including Cerberus, the Chimaera, and the Sphinx.

tyranny

a form of government based on the absolute rule, the decision of the ruler serving as law and constitution.

udaharana (illustration)

it is one of the five limbs of a syllogism that is essential for establishing the validity of an argument. For example, wherever there is smoke, there is fire.

udgatri

chorister at a sacrifice.

ultramontanism

the theory that all acclesiastical authority and power belongs of right to the pope. It is opposed to the independent development of ntional churches.

uncaused cause

a cause that does not have any cause to cause it. It is a cause that causes things to happen but it is not caused by anything. The term is generally applied to eternal God.

uncertainty principle

a law of physics, first stated in 1927 by Werner Heisenberg (1901-76), that has profoundly affected quantum theory and the theory of the causation. It states that the position and momentum of a particle cannot both be known without uncertainty because the process of establishing either must effect the other. If Δp is the uncertainty in position and Δq that of momentum, then $\Delta p \Delta q = h/4\pi$, where h is the Planck Constant.

unconscious, the

the doctrine that a portion of man's mental processes or memories exists below the threshold of consciousness.

unction

the anointing with oil or ointment for religious purposes (for example, consecration, confirmation); extreme ~, anointing of the sick in cases of grave illness. In the Roman Catholic, Greek Orthodox, and anglican Churches it ranks as a sacrament.

understanding

understanding is generally considered to be a faculty of mind which has the ability to comprehend, discern, judge, interpret, and explain. In Descartes' philosophy, it is the work of the faculty of understanding to have 'clarity and distinction'. Wittgenstein attacked this view of Descartes. According to him, undestanding is not a mental phenomenon.

undertermined

it is nothing but the inability to judge the correctness or the truth of a given statement or a situation or an event.

undistributed middle, fallacy of the

an argument in which the proposed conclusion is invalidly attained because one of the premises needs to be and is not a distributed assertion.

unextended

in Descartes' philosophy Mind is regarded as an unextended substance. In other words, it does not occupy spacio-temporal relations.

uniats

a term used of the churches of eastern Europe and the Near East whose members adhere to the Roman Catholic faith and acknowledge the papal jurisdiction, but who retain their own organization and liturgies.

uniformity of nature, principle of the

the principle of inductin that similar occurrences follow from similar conditions.

unitarianism

the religious doctrine that God is one, and that Jesus is to regarded as human and not as a supernatural being.

unit class

a class having a single member.

unity
from the Latin unitas ('one'). Thus the character of being one thing, event, idea, society, or whatever.

unity, organic
according to Aristotle, the organic unity represents the fulfilment of a primary activity by the parts as an integral whole. No part of an organic whole can act independently. The parts of an organic whole act in relation to other parts in the same whole. Any change occurring in one part necessarily affects the other parts. For instance, human body is considered to be an organic whole.

universal
an abstract general idea which is apprehended by mind rather than by sense-experience. Mind forms abstract general ideas by abstracting certain essential features from many other features. Thus the reality of universal is independent of any exemplification in space and time. For example, 'chair', 'man', 'tree' etc., are universal concepts.

universalia ante res
it is a Latin term for 'universals independent of things'. According to Plato, Universals have independent existence apart from particular things.

universalia post res
it is a Latin term for 'universals are derived from particulars'. According to nominalists and conceptualists, universals are abstracted from particular existents.

universalizability
the principle that, while individual moral judgments may be particular, they will always imply a universal judgment.

universals and particulars
things are particulars, and their qualities are universals. So a universal is a property predicated of all the individuals of a certain sort or class. Redness is a universal, predicated of all red objects. Universals have been claimed by some philosophers to have an existence distinct from the particular things instantiating the property. For Plato and Platonists, the observed world is only a reflection of the real world, consisting for Plato of the forms, which are something like universals.

universe
'universe' is defined as including everything there is, with the exception of the creator God, if such there be.

universe of discourse
a system of concepts and entities related to a particular topic or area of interest, within which certain terms and expressions acquire their own meaning or significance.

Upanishad, the
the basic philosophical texts of Hinduism.

Uranus
'heaven' in Greek mythology, and husband of Ge (earth) and father of the Titans.

utilitarian calculus
the principle in Utilitarian ethics by which the right act is determined. It is a calculation of the greatest pleasure or least pain to all concerned.

utilitarianism
the doctrine that the principle of greatest utility should be the criterion in ethical matters, and that the criterion is to be applied to the consequences flowing from ethical decisions. The principle is often expressed as the greatest happiness, or the greatest good, for the greatest number.

utility
from the Latin utilis ('useful'). In the philosophic tradition a property of those things which have value not to themselves but as a means of some end.

utility, principle of
it is also known as pleasure principle. According to this doctrine, all the human beings desire pleasure and the absence of pain. Each individual tries to seek his own pleasure.

utopianism
the beliefs of those concerned to establish not just a better but a perfect society.

uttara mimamsa
a Sanskrit term literally meaning 'the later revered thought' and referring to a school of Indian thought dealing with the latter portion of the Vedas. The school is batter known as vedanta, meaning 'end of the vedas'.

vacuous
in logic, describing the status of sentences that are true because their subject terms have no denotation or because their antecedents are false.

vacuous statement
in logic, a vacuous statement is true because its subject term has no denotation or because its antecedent is false. For example, a conditional (if p then q) is true only when its consequent q is true or when its antecedent p is false. So 'if men can fly then arsenic is poisonous' is vacuously true.

vagueness
a word or term is said to be vague, or to have the property, 'vagueness' when there are borderline cases and uncertainty concerning whether or not the term applies to these cases.

Vaibhasika
it is one of the early schools of Buddhism. It represents Hinyana tradition. According to this school of thought, both things and ideas are real and that mind can directly know the objects of perception. The ultimate elements of existence are real, yet they are momentary.

vaiseshika
a Sanskrit term meaning 'particularity'. Vaiseshika is

one of the six systems of Indian thought to arise in the period following the Vedic age. The Vaiseshika Sutra was composed by Kanada, sometimes after 300 B.C. The system and sutra contain the following ideas:

(1) sensible things are composed of invisible atoms, eternal in nature, and bearing one of four characteristics : earth, water, light, and air.

(2) also eternal are the souls which pervade certain bodies for a time. Each individual soul has its individual characteristic, and this is true even after the soul has been freed from the body.

(3) in sum, there are nine substances : earth, water, light, air, ether, time, space, soul and mind.

(4) in the Vaiseshika Sutra God is not mentioned; but commentators borrowed the Nyaya conception of God to complete the system.

(5) the categories of experience are : substance, quality, activity, generality, particularity, inherence, and non-existence.

vaishyas

the commercial class of Indian tradition.

vajra

Indra's weapon.

valid and invalid

terms that may be applied to arguments or to patterns or forms of argument. An argument is valid when it is impossible for its premises to be true and its conclusion false; it is invalid otherwise.

validity

in any system of formal logic, an argument or a proposition is said to be valid in so far as it is deduced or derived from a set of accepted premises. Thus validity is attached to an argument or a proposition that abides by the above said conditions. Validity cannot guarantee truth.

validity and truth

validity in symbolic logic, a term applicable to arguments, is defined by reference to the possible truth-values of the component sentences of arguments. If the argument 'P_1,---P_n, therefore C' is valid, it must be impossible for C to be false when P_1--P_n are all true. This will be the case if the material conditional statement, 'P_1 &...& $\supset$ C is always true. If P_1..P_n, C are all truth, functional compounds, to say that 'P_1 &...&$P_n \supset$ C' is always true is to say that it is a tautology.

value

a theory of value is a theory about what things in the world are good, desirable, and important.

value final

a theory of value is a theory about what things in the world are good, desirable, and important.

value-freedom

the ideal, recommended by Max

Weber, that social scientist should eschew value-judgments about people and institutions within their fields of study.

value theory

the designation, along with Axiology, for the field of philosophy investigating the nature of value and valuation.

vanaspati

tree.

Vardhamana (Mahavira) 599-527 B.C.

Indian philosopher and religious leader. A leader of Jains, Vardhamana systemcatized the doctrines of the movement in terms of his understanding of the traditional founders. Rsabha, Ajitanatha, and Aristanemi. All three of these men are mentioned in the Yajur Veda, a document central to Jainism.

variable

in logic, a variable is a symbol or a sign that is substituted for a statement, or a predicate, or an object or a term or a meaning. For example, the variable p may stand for a statement such as 'Rama is courageous'.

Vasubandhu 4th or 5the cent A.D.

Indian philosopher. Brother of Asanga founder of the Way of Yoga, Vasubandhu was known as the systematizer of the school.

Prinicpal writings : The Treatise in Twenty Stanzas on Representaion-only (T); The Thirty Verses on the Mind-only Doctrine (T).

Vedanta (the end of vedas)

the end portion of Vedas are called upanisads. There are around 108 upanisads. Sankara wrote commentaries on 10 major upanisads.

Vedas

Sanskrit term meaning 'knowledge'. The Vedas are an ancient Indian collection of hymns, rituals, regulations for religious sacrifices, and philosophical essays. The Vedas divide into the following divisons.

(1) there are the Samhitas. These are hymns addressed to gods and goddesses, and were used in the Vedic sacrifices. There are four collections of Samhitas : the Rig Sama, Yajur, and Atharva—one for each of the four main priests of the sacrifice.

(2) the Brahmanas deal with the rules for the sacrifices.

(3) added on to the Brahmanas are the Aranyakas. These interpret the meaning of the Vedic sacrifices. Composed in forest retreats the Aranyakas venture from mysticism into philosophical thought.

(4) the Upanishads form the concluding portions of the Aranykas, and represent the height of Vedic philosophy. The Upanishads are also known as the Vedanta, which means 'the end of the Veda'.

(5) the sutras form a late stage of Vedic literature, expressing

in aphoristic form the essential requirment of the Vedic religion. The sutras deal with priestly matters, domestic rites, social duties, philosophy, magic, astronomy, etc. The Dharma Satras deal with the question of one's social duties. The Laws of Manu is the chief of the Dharma Sutras, and of ancient Hindu codes.

veil of appearance
sense data viewed, as interposing between the experiencer and the external world.

veil diagrams
a more powerful way of representing class relationships than the Euler diagrams (Euler), this type of diagrammatic representation allows one to check the validity of syllogistic inferences by means of three overlapping circles, standing for the terms of the syllogism. The method was developed by John Venn.

Venus
Roman goddess of beauty and sexual love; identified with the Greek Aphrodite. April was the mouth sacred to her.

veridical
in contrast to nonveridical experience such as hallucinations, illusions, delusions, mirages etc., a veridical experience is always characterised by truth.

verifiability
the condition of admitting verification. Verification is any procedure carried out to determine whether a statement is true or false. A statement which might be shown to be true is said to be in principle verifiable.

verification (or verifiability) principle
the criterion of meaning fulness applied by the logical positivists to any proposition.

verity
the quality of being true or genuine is called verity. It is also regarded as the confirmity of a statement with fact or reality.

Vesta
Roman goddess of the hearth and household; a daughter of Saturn. Her temple in Rome was tended by 6 Vestal virgins, dedicated to a life of chastity.

vestments
the distinctive dress worn by the clergy of the Christian Church when conducting its services. It originated in the ordinary secular costume of early Christian times.

vicious circle principle
an explanation of certain logical paradoxes discussed in Russel's theory of types. A vicious circle is generated whenever it is supposed that 'a collection of objects may contain members which can only be defined by means of the collection as a whole'.

Victoria
Roman goddess of victory; identified with the Greek Nike. Her temple was on the Palatine Hill.

vienna circle of logical positivists
a reform movement in philosophy centering in the University of Vienna in the 1920's and 30's. The movement was directed toward the achievement of a scientific philosophy, and the elimination of pseudopropositions, including the propositions of metaphysics.

vijatiya-bheda
it is a difference that exists between two different things. For example, a cow is different from a table.

vijnana (wisdom)
according to Buddhist doctrine of Pratityasamutpa (the dependent origination), vijnana is considered to be one of the links in the causal chain of existence.

vijnanamaya-kosa (the intellectual sheath)
it is located within mental sheath (Manomaya-kosa). The subtle body consists of vijnannamaya-kosa, manomaya-kosa and pranamaya-kosa.

vindication
a justification of induction that seeks to show that, though it may be quite indeterminate as to whether induction will work, or not, it is rational to use it because it will work if any method will. The future Universe may be regular or chaotic. If it is regular, induction will be the best policy. If chaotic, no method will be applicable so the user of induction will be no worse off than anyone else.

virat
female counterpart of purusha.

virgin birth
the doctrine that Jesus Christ had no human father, his mother having conceived by the power of the Holy Spirit. Its scriptural origin is to be found in the gospels of St. Matthew and St. Luke, but in no other part of the New Testament is it alluded to. It should not be confused with the doctrine of the Immaculate Conception.

virtue
although the initial sense of the term included the meanings of "strength" "courage", and "excellence", an ethical signification quickly arose, and has remained central. In recent discussion "virtue", and "vice" have been largely replaced in the singular by "good" and "evil", "right" and "wrong" and in the plural by "values" and "disvales".

visesa (particularity)
it is one of the categories in Vaisesika metaphysics. This is the category that distinguishes one particular from the other. These visesas are eternal, innumberable, and partless. The pluralism of Vaisesaika is the outcome of this category.

Vishnu
Hindu God. Center of worship in the great Vaisnava or

Vishnuite sect of Hinduism. In the Hindu trimurti, or trinity, Vishnu is the preserver where Brahma creates and Shiva destroys.

Vishnuism

Hindu sect.

vitalism

the name given to that interpretation of biological phenomena which assumes the presence of some force or principle within the organism not reducible to the categories of physics and chemistry. In the case of Hans Driesch the vital force is said to be a directing and supporting entelechy.

vivarta-vada (the theory of apparent change)

this theory emphasizes that things appear other than what they are. According to Advaita theory of causation, the world is an illusory appearance superimposed on Brahman by avidya (ignorance).

void

in Pythagorean cosmogony, the factor in the universe by means of which units could be separated and distinguished.

volition

the act of willing that is inherent in human individual. In that sense every physical act is preceded by a volition. This particular theory was bitterly criticised by Gilbert Ryle in his 'The Concept of Mind'. According to Ryle, if volition is a voluntary mental act, then it must originate in some other volition. Then that volition as a mental act must originate in some other volition. Thus it leads to ad infinitum.

Voltaire (1694-1778)

it is a pen name of Francois Marie Arouet. He was a very famous French essayist, historian, and philosopher who is considered to be a major figure of the Enlightenment. He was exiled and imprisoned for his writings.

voluntarism

1. a certain sort of metaphysics (of which Schopenhauer's is typical), that holds that the true nature of reality is will.

2. in controversies about the nature of history, a theory that attaches too much weight to the human will as a factor in history, and too little to 'objective', that is economic, factors. Marxists often accuse other Marxists of 'voluntarism' of this kind.

vortex theory

this theory was advocated by Cartesians and Occassionalists. According to this theory, empty spaces and vacuums do no exist. A subtle matter occupies the entire space. It is also known as 'ether'. There is no unoccupied space. The notion of unoccupied space is an illusion or a false assumption.

voting paradox

a paradox that illustrates a fatal flaw in the attempt to

determine the "collective preference" of a community by means of a simple majority voting system.

vrata

religious rite.

vratya philosophy

with the spread of Vedic orthodoxy, the bulk of the Vratya lore was absorbed into it in a brahmanized form, influencing it in turn and substantially contributing to the blossoming of Upsnisadic philosophy. The sources for Vratya teachings are the Atharva Veda and scattered references in the other three Vedas and in later Vedic and Brahmanic literature.

The mystical philosophy of Vratyas can be classified as metaphysical monism expressed in the imagery of cosmogony, which was reflected in the communal ritual and in salvationist aspirations. The term 'Vratya' reffered originally to a primordial cosmogonic power which manifested itself in the individualized form as Ekavratya, also called Mahadeva, the great god. From him emanated the cosmic Brahmacari, who established the earth, thus producing polarity, and by impregnating her gave rise to multiplicity. This cosmogonic drama produced by the divine trinity was re-enacted in the social context.in fertility rites by a vritya team of three, which ensured the duration of the universe and life in it and the continuity of the community. At the individual level the aspiration of reaching the status of the cosmic Ekavritya, often referred to as the achievement of the immortality, led to the renunciation of worldly life. The aim was the individual reversal of the cosmogonic process and the return to the primeval cosmic transcendence. In practice this meant that one became a celibate brahmacari and, when one became accomplished, one was known as ekavrdtya or arhat, and also as kesin, 'the long-haried one'. The line employing esoteric magic rites with sexual elements continued in obscurity and re-emerged in some varieties of later Tantrism.

vrihati

metre.

Vulcan

Roman god of fire and in particular of furnaces; his festival, the Vulcania, was observed on 23rd August. He was identified with the Greek Hephaestus.

vyavaharika (the relative viewpoint)

it is a standpoint taken in terms of relative viewpoint. According to Advaita, Brahman becomes a saguna Brahman at this level. The plurality of universe consists of many individuals that differ from one another.

weakness of the will

the state of mind. An agent is said to be in it when he performs an intentional action that goes against his better judgment.

Weber-fechner law

a psychophysical law (S = C log R) according to which the intensity of sensation (S) is equal to the logarithm of its stimulus (R) given a constant (C).

weltanschauung

a German term for 'world outlook' or 'world view'. It also denotes a comprehensive account of reality as a whole.

wff

acronym for "well-formed formula". A well-formed formula refers to one which conforms to the requirements of the system of which it is a part.

Whewell, William (1794-1866)

a British philosopher and historian of science who claimed that there cannot be a logic of induction parallel to the logic of deduction, and also insisted that every creative theory of construction in science must be put to the test of falsification. Thus the theory of falsification developed by Karl Popper, strictly speaking is the brain child of Whewell. His important works include: History of the Inductive Sciences: Philosophy of the Inductive Sciences.

whole

a unity or a system as in an organic whole. It also refers to something that has parts.

wholeness

a totality of integral parts of an organism and their interconnections viewed as a whole. Thus a whole is not a mere sum total of its integral parts but more than that.

whole-part, principle of

the nature of whole cannot be apprehended just by analysing its constituent parts. A proper explanation of the nature of a whole is possible only when the interrelationships that exist among its constituent parts are understood.

will

the term refers to a potency, faculty, or force in man involved in decision-making. The view that the will is dominant over the reason is termed 'voluntarism'. The view that reason is determinative over will is termed 'intellectualism' or simply 'rationalism'. In addition there are views providing a balance between reason and will.

will to believe

a concept of William James to the effect that we can believe beyond the evidence in cases where our options are forced, living, and momentous.

Wisdom, Arthur John Terence Dibben (1904-)

a British analytical philosopher who was chiefly influenced by Ludwig Wittgenstein. He supported the views of Russell and Wittgenstein in holding the view that certain entities are no more than 'logical constructions' out of more fundamental entities (for example, sense-impressions). The statement of the 'logical constructs' can be translated into the statements about the latter. His chief works are: Philosophy and Psychoanalysis: Paradox and Discovery.

Wolf, Chritian (1679-1754)

a German rationalist philosopher who was provided a systematic approach to philosophy. As an ideal follower of Leibniz, he felt that philosophy is basically concerned with the study of essence rather than existence. All philosophical maxims can be deduced, claimed Wolf, from Leibniz's principle of sufficient reason and identity.

word, the

Unamuno regarded the world as the intimate expression of the man of flesh and bone; while Heidegger found the Word present in all discourses and capable of reveiatory disclosures of Being.

world soul

it is an analogue of hauman soul. Since world is produced out of life and animation it is regarded as animate. Since it is animate, world as a whole consists of a soul.

wu wei

a Chinese term meaning 'inaction' or 'taking no unnatural action'. A central term in the history of Taoism, the concept is stressed in the Tao-Te-Ching. It is found in Taoist leaders such as Chuang Tzu and Huai-nan Tzu.

Xenophanes (570- 470 B.C.)

Greek philosopher. Born in Colophon. Exiled from his home, probably by a Persian victory'.

Holding that there is no certain knowledge about the gods or any other matter, Xenophanes pointed out that men create gods in their own image, just as animals would make them like themselves had they the ability to draw.

Xenophanes of Colophon (570-475 B.C.)

an ancient Greek philosopher who founded the Elatic school. He is supposed to be a well-known critic of anthropomorphism and mythology. He openly declared that people create Gods only in their own image. In his epistemology, Xenophanes proved that sense-experience cannot give us complete knowledge of reality.

xanophon (430-c 355 B.C.)

Greek writer and moralist. Born in Athens. An active participant in civic life. Xenophon was one of the young Athenians who felt friendship for Socrates. After the latter's death, Xenophon, although not himself a philosopher, answered the charges that

Socrates was guilty of impiety and corrupting the youth. The charges bad been made at the trial and were repeated later by Polycrates.

Xenophon replied to the charges in his Memorabilia by picturing Socrates as a teacher of virtue practical knowledge who exerted a beneficial influence on who knew him.

yahweh

the name of the God of Israel, originally written 'YHWH', without the vowels, as a sign of reverence.

yaj

to sacrifice.

yajna

sacrifice.

Yajur Veda

one of the four Vedas of early Hinduism, the Yanjur Veda is highly ritualistic in character.

yasna

one of the five parts of the Avesta, sacred scriptures of Zoroastrianism.

yin and yang

the two basic concepts in ancient Chinese philosophy. In The Book of Changes these two expressions are used to denote light and darkness, hardness and softness, the male and the females as principle in nature.

Yin Yang philosophy

a Chinese doctrine, not the product of a school of philosophy or of a particular distinguished philosopher, but a natural development which has influenced most Chinese philosophers, and many aspects of Chinese life. Its following ideas are relevant :

1. reality is in constant change, and this change is to be explained by the interaction of two primal elements, forces, or principles : yin, the female principle, negative, passive, weak, yielding: and yang the male principle positive, active, strong assertive. The respective force of these principles in objects and events determine their character.

2. the five cletantnts—mental, wood, water, fire, earth—provide a matrix for the working of yin and yang.

3. the notion of fives, was elaborated into other areas. There are the five activites : apperance, speech, seeing, hearing, thinking. There are five parts of time : year, month, day, zodiacal distinctions, and the calendric calculations. The five blessings : longevity, wealth, health, virtue and an end crowings life. In addition there are five directions, the five musical notes, five sense organs, five metals, five virtues, five feelings, and five social relations.

yoga

a Sanskrit term meaning both 'yoke' and 'union'. Thus, a practical means of discipline leading to union of the individual self and the universal soul. The term may also derive from the root yuj ('to contemplate').

yogaja (extra-sensory perception)

it is one of the forms of extra-sensory perception admitted by Nyaya, such a perception can be cultivated by means of Yoga. The advantage with such a perception is that one is able to perceive things that go beyond the limits of senses.

yupa

sacrificial post.

za-zen

the term for meditation in Zen Buddhism.

zee buddhism

callen zen in Japan, Ch'an in China ('both terms signifying 'meditation'), a form of religion which developed out of, and in reaction to. Hinayana and Mahayana Buddhism.

zen

a Japanese technique of meditation and self-discipline.

Zen Buddhism

called Zen in Japan, Ch'an in China (both terms signifying 'meditation'), a form of religion which developed out of, and in reaction to, Hinyana and Mahayana Buddhism.

zeno's paradoxes

the genius of Zeno of Elea was displayed in developing two sets of arguments designed to discredit opponents of Parmenides of Eelea, in particular the Pythagoreans. First, there were about 40 putative refutations of plurality, of which only two survive. Second, there were the four perennially, fascinating arguments against motion. Either space and time are infintely divisible, in which case motion is continuous and smooth-flowing or else there are indivisible minima, in which case motion is fundamentally cinematographic, proceeding ultimately in tiny jerks.

zetetic

the Greek term for 'an enquiry', 'an investigation', 'a search for something'. It refers to the inquisitiveness of the seeker of the truth.

Zeus

in Greek mythology, the father of gods and men, and most powerful of the immortals. He was pre-Hellenic and was worshipped as the sky-deity, whose presence was marked by lightning, thunder, and rain. He was the son of Kronos and Rhea; Poseidon, Hades, Hestia, Demeter, and Hera were his brothers and sisters, Hera being also his wife. When the world was distributed among them after the overthrow of Kronos, Poseidon obtained the sea, Hades the Underworld, and Zeus the heavens and upper regions, the earth being common to them all.